ADVENTURES IN READING

Adventures in

READING

APPRECIATION

AMERICAN LITERATURE

ENGLISH LITERATURE

MODERN LITERATURE

Adventures for

READERS, BOOK I

READERS, BOOK II

Adventures in READING

MERCURY EDITION

JACOB M. ROSS
PRINCIPAL OF MIDWOOD HIGH SCHOOL,
BROOKLYN, NEW YORK

BLANCHE JENNINGS THOMPSON
INSTRUCTOR, THE UNIVERSITY SCHOOL
OF LIBERAL AND APPLIED STUDIES,
UNIVERSITY OF ROCHESTER

EVAN LODGE
SUPERVISOR OF ENGLISH IN JUNIOR AND
SENIOR HIGH SCHOOLS, CLEVELAND, OHIO

Harcourt, Brace and Company
NEW YORK CHICAGO

[m · 12 · 56]

THE COVER

The cover picture is a scene at Tenaya Lake, in Yosemite National Park, California. It is reproduced here in full color with the permission of Free-Lance Photographers Guild, Inc.

Drawings by John Moment

Acknowledgments for permissions and illustrations are covered by the present copyright for this edition as well as copyrights for the 1936, 1941, 1947, and 1949 editions of *Adventures in Reading.*

CREDITS FOR COLOR PICTURES

1. H. Armstrong Roberts.
2, 3. Air view, Arc de Triomphe, Paris: Ewing Galloway. Connecticut River Valley: Standard Oil Co. (N.J.). Seascape, South America: U.S. Department of Interior. Greenland: Rapho-Guillumette. French Café: Standard Oil Co. (N.J.). Sahara Desert: Philip Gendreau. Jain Temple, Calcutta, India: Black Star.
4, 5. Museum gallery: Museum of Modern Art. Whitman: Culver. Mrs. Roosevelt: Karsh. Burns: Culver. Lincoln: Culver. Dickens: Culver. MacLean: Author's own photo. Churchill: B.I.S. Lagerlöf: Culver. Sandburg: H. G. Hague. Doyle: Culver. Poe: Culver. Shakespeare: N.Y. Public Library. Kipling: Culver. Heine: Culver. Stuart: Dutton. Homer: N.Y. Public Library.
6, 7. Illustration for "Great Expectations": John Moment. Auto workers: Ewing Galloway. Dance: H. Armstrong Roberts. UN General Assembly: Acme. Benchley training dog: from "The Reel Benchley," pub. by A. A. Wyn, N.Y., copyright, Metro-Goldwyn-Mayer Corp.
8. Chartres Cathedral window: James R. Johnson. Albert Schweitzer: Charles R. Joy, by permission from The Beacon Press.

Title-page photograph of Net-thrower, Hawaii, by Fritz Henle.

PRINTED IN THE UNITED STATES OF AMERICA

Preface

TO the editors this new revision of *Adventures in Reading* has quite literally been an " adventure in reading." For more than two years they have searched for new material, interesting to young people, educationally sound, and of genuine literary value. They present the Mercury Edition with the belief that it will offer a rewarding challenge to beginning high school students.

The new *Adventures in Reading,* which is again organized by types to allow as flexible an arrangement as possible, wears a very new look. There is a wide variety of literature ranging from short, easy selections for slow readers to selections of sufficient length and depth to provide rich reading experience for the more competent. There are twelve new short stories; nineteen new titles in the nonfiction sections; three new plays, including a one-hour television script; and a wealth of new poetry, including episodes from Homer's *Odyssey.*

The single greatest addition is *Great Expectations,* in a skillfully condensed but *not* rewritten version. This novel, certainly one of Dickens' finest, is on the way to becoming a standard selection for the beginning high school years. Already published in a separate school edition, it has been thoroughly tested with pupils of various levels of ability. The consensus of both teachers and students is that the story is exciting, tense, dramatic, filled with memorable characters, and rich in ethical values.

A most important new editorial feature of the anthology is its reading-skills program. It is no longer sufficient that young people be exposed to the " best literature," or that they merely learn facts about an author, a literary period, or a form of writing. Today the secondary school English teacher must establish a program developing the many separate skills involved in reading growth. Thus, throughout this book will be found comprehension and reading-recall devices, pre-reading " hints," and constant attention to vocabulary building – all carefully integrated into a program to improve reading skills. Varied and stimulating exercises should strengthen the weak reader, challenge the strong, and, incidentally, save the teacher many hours of planning. The reading-skills program is included in the book itself, where it is most readily available for students and teachers alike, but to supplement the text there is a booklet of Reading Tests to accompany *Adventures in Reading*. A copy of the pamphlet may be obtained on request from the publisher.

As before, *Adventures in Reading* is distinguished for its extensive footnotes and a generous glossary. Pronunciations as well as meanings are given for all difficult words and proper names, both English and foreign. The book lists are now annotated with brief descriptions of each book and include publication data for more recent titles. At the end of the text is an interesting section containing biographical profiles of the authors represented.

The physical attractiveness of this book is clear to anyone who turns its pages. Rich and varied color has been used to enhance the printed word. The full-color opening section makes an admirable start-of-the-term introduction to literature for the young reader. An unusually generous number of photographs, together with the gay colored sketches throughout the text, enrich the student's artistic as well as literary experience.

Altogether, the editors feel that they can present with pride and assurance the Mercury Edition of *Adventures in Reading*.

J. M. R.
B. J. T.
E. L.

Contents

Good Stories Old and New

Stories in Verse

Footprints on the Sands of Time

Lyrics from Many Lands

The Curtain Rises

The Spirit of Adventure

American Songs and Sketches

Great Expectations: A Novel

The Pleasures of Reading

The Color Section

The pages that follow will introduce you to the literature in this book. Here is a colorful preview of the scenes and people you will meet in the selections. When you have met them again in your reading, you can turn back to this section with increased enjoyment.

In books you will discover the pleasures of everyday living

READING IS YOUR PASSPORT

to adventure in faraway places. In books the world lies before you, its paths radiating from great cities to distant lands, to scenes forever new, forever changing. And through books you can explore the ways of men. Reading knows no barrier, neither time nor space nor bounds of prejudice—it admits us all to the community of human experience.

RESTAURAN
CHINA
WORLD DRAMA
OLD HERBACEOUS
Lincoln Treasury
COLLECTED POEMS OF ROBERT FROST
STRODE
SWEDEN

WALT WHITMAN

ROBERT BURNS

FITZROY MACLEAN

ABRAHAM LINCOLN

WINSTON CHURCHILL

ELEANOR ROOSEVELT

CHARLES DICKENS

SELMA LAGERLÖF

READING INVITES YOU

into the gallery of world writers. Within its many halls you will find challenging personalities and share the thoughts of great minds. Literature is a a meeting of individuals; it comes alive when the reader meets the writer.

SANDBURG
EDGAR
ALLAN POE
RUDYARD KIPLING
HEINRICH HEINE
JESSE STUART
WILLIAM
SHAKESPEARE
R ARTHUR
NAN DOYLE
HOMER

BOOKS MIRROR LIFE:

in them you may watch the daily rounds of ordinary people, the charmed scenes of love and laughter, the dramatic events that may change a nation—or a world. Books master time. They allow you with equal ease to live in days gone by or days to come. They can even let you share the great expectations of a boy and girl whose life a century ago was quite different, yet quite like, your own.

Literature finally,
and at its bes
expresses our search
for the good life a
sustains our faith tha
we can achieve it.

ADVENTURES IN READING

Gendreau

Good Stories Old and New

STORYTELLING is probably as old as man himself. When the first cave man came home with a tall tale about the dinosaur that got away, it was the beginning of literature. From that day to our very own, people have been telling stories of travel and adventure, of encounters with dangers, of winning against odds, of love and friendship, or just of everyday experience. A tale may be as short and uncomplicated as an anecdote, or it may be a thousand-page novel, but it is the stuff of storytelling and one of man's most popular diversions.

Surprisingly enough, it has been only in the last two centuries that novels and short stories have been written as such. In the very earliest days, when there was no written language, stories were told by word of mouth; and because the rhythm and rhyme of poetry make both remembering and listening easier, they were told in verse. Even after writing became common, verse was used for storytelling. Prose was left for factual writing like histories or biographies, and verse was used for tales of all kinds. After the printing press was invented, books and magazines became common and a great audience of readers was created. To satisfy the needs of this new audience, writers turned the old tales into a new form – prose narratives or fiction. Thus novels and short stories came to be the most popular reading fare of modern times.

The first printed fiction took the form of long, slow-moving novels. Two or three centuries ago people had plenty of leisure to read and few distractions. They liked their stories long and detailed. But fiction changed with the times, and while more people became educated – and most of them better educated – they also found less time to read. Things were speeded up in most fields of living and no less in literature than in others. The short story was invented. It met the desire of readers for something entertaining and exciting; it had plot and characterization like a novel; and it could be read in one sitting. Today, in America especially (for it was here that short stories were first written), the short story has become the most popular type of fiction. Hundreds of short stories are published every month in magazines and books, and short story readers are numbered in millions.

Just because there *are* so many stories published, the modern reader needs to use judgment and taste in choosing his reading. It is a great waste of time to pick up a magazine and read straight through, one story after another. Many stories, especially "Westerns," the so-called "true stories," and mystery thrillers, are written from a formula; they are turned out as if machine-made. The names of the characters and settings change, but the plots and incidents vary so little that you can read on without using half your mind. A first-rate short story, on the other hand, is a source of enjoyment as well as of lasting value. It is worth your while to find the good stories, old and new, and to use your critical judgment when you read them.

What do you look for in a short story? For one thing, you look for honest and believable characterization. The people in a story should act in accordance with their basic nature as established by the author. They should not become involved in situations or make decisions simply because the plot requires it. In a good story the plot is frequently a series of complications that are the *result* of the natural behavior of the characters.

Besides believable characters, you also want a story to have a plot with excitement and action to hold your attention. Yet an interesting plot is not enough in itself, for you also expect a story to reveal something true and worth while about life. Now this doesn't mean that you read stories to *learn* something. You read them, of course, for enjoyment, but the good story will leave something with you – a thought, a feeling, an idea that makes you better understand life and yourself, and results in your being a richer, more understanding person.

One thing we can all be sure of: we learn to like good stories by reading them. In American literature especially you will find a large number of skillful short story writers. Among the earlier names are those of Washington Irving, Nathaniel Hawthorne, and Edgar Allan Poe. To a later period belong Mark Twain, Bret Harte, O. Henry, Jack London, and Ring Lardner. In the stories old and new that follow, you will also find many excellent short story writers of today: Dorothy Canfield, Mackinlay Kantor, William Saroyan, Walter Edmonds, Morley Callaghan, and others. They should provide you with a yardstick for judging stories that you read elsewhere.

WINNING AGAINST ODDS

MORLEY CALLAGHAN

Luke Baldwin's Vow

In this world there seems always to be conflict between two kinds of people — the practical and the impractical. Impractical people cherish odd, unimportant things of no apparent value to anyone but themselves. Practical people want to have everything in order, everything — and everyone — useful and efficient. They want to " get rid of the rubbish." Impractical people, a bit inclined to be dreamers rather than doers, often have a hard time defending themselves and their useless possessions from the practical people who, in turn, are frequently accused of being hard-hearted. The odds would seem to be against someone like Luke Baldwin, who cherishes a worthless old dog, in defiance of his Uncle Henry. Both Luke and his uncle learn something important about this matter of being practical.

For Better Reading . . . Almost all stories are concerned with human character or human personality (even stories about horses ascribe human qualities to animals!). An alert reader analyzes the characters in a story. He does this by noting what a character says, what he does, and what others in the story say about him. Take note of these clues to character as you read about the uncle and the boy in the following story.

THAT summer when twelve-year-old Luke Baldwin came to live with his Uncle Henry in the house on the stream by the sawmill, he did not forget that he had promised his dying father he would try to learn things from his uncle; so he used to watch him very carefully.

Uncle Henry, who was the manager of the sawmill, was a big, burly man weighing more than two hundred and thirty pounds, and he had a rough-skinned, brick-colored face. He looked like a powerful man, but his health was not good. He had aches and pains in his back and shoulders which puzzled the doctor. The first thing Luke learned about Uncle Henry was that everybody had great respect for him. The four men he employed in the sawmill were always polite and attentive when he spoke to them. His wife, Luke's Aunt Helen, a kindly, plump, straightforward woman, never argued with him. " You should try and be like your Uncle Henry," she would say to Luke. " He's so wonderfully practical. He takes care of everything in a sensible, easy way."

Luke used to trail around the sawmill after Uncle Henry not only because he liked the fresh clean smell of the newly cut wood and the big piles of sawdust, but because he was impressed by his uncle's precise, firm tone when he spoke to the men.

Sometimes Uncle Henry would stop and explain to Luke something about a piece of timber. " Always try and learn the essential facts, son," he would say. " If you've got the facts, you know what's useful and what isn't useful, and no one can fool you."

He showed Luke that nothing of value was ever wasted around the mill. Luke used to listen, and wonder if there was another man in the world who knew so well what was needed and what ought to be thrown away. Uncle Henry had known at once that Luke needed a bicycle to ride to his school, which was two miles away in town, and he bought him a good one. He knew that Luke needed good, serviceable clothes. He also knew exactly how much Aunt Helen needed to run the house, the price of everything, and how much a woman should be paid for doing the family washing. In the evenings Luke used to sit in the living room watching his uncle making notations in a black notebook which he always carried in his vest pocket, and he knew that he was assessing the value of the smallest transaction that had taken place during the day.

Luke promised himself that when he grew up he, too, would be admired for his good, sound judgment. But, of course, he couldn't always be watching and learning from his Uncle Henry, for too often when he watched him he thought of his own father; then he was lonely. So he began to build up another secret life for himself around the sawmill, and his companion was the eleven-year-old collie, Dan, a dog blind in one eye and with a slight limp in his left hind leg. Dan was a fat slow-moving old dog. He was very affectionate and his eye was the color of amber. His fur was amber too. When Luke left for school in the morning, the old dog followed him for half a mile down the road, and when he returned in the afternoon, there was Dan waiting at the gate.

Sometimes they would play around the millpond or by the dam, or go down the stream to the lake. Luke was never lonely when the dog was with him. There was an old rowboat that they used as a pirate ship in the stream, and they would be pirates together, with Luke shouting instructions to Captain Dan and with the dog seeming to understand and wagging his tail enthusiastically. Its amber eye was alert, intelligent, and approving. Then they would plunge into the brush on the other side of the stream, pretending they were hunting tigers. Of course, the old dog was no longer much good for hunting; he was too slow and too lazy. Uncle Henry no longer used him for hunting rabbits or anything else.

When they came out of the brush, they would lie together on the cool, grassy bank being affectionate with each other, with Luke talking earnestly, while the collie, as Luke believed, smiled with the good eye. Lying in the grass, Luke would say things to Dan he could not say to his uncle or his aunt. Not that what he said was important; it was just stuff about himself that he might have told to his own father or mother if they had been alive. Then they would go back

" Luke was never lonely when the dog was with him." (Armstrong Roberts)

to the house for dinner, and after dinner Dan would follow him down the road to Mr. Kemp's house, where they would ask old Mr. Kemp if they could go with him to round up his four cows. The old man was always glad to see them. He seemed to like watching Luke and the collie running around the cows, pretending they were riding on a vast range in the foothills of the Rockies.

Uncle Henry no longer paid much attention to the collie, though once when he tripped over him on the veranda, he shook his head and said thoughtfully, " Poor old fellow, he's through. Can't use him for anything. He just eats and sleeps and gets in the way."

One Sunday during Luke's summer holidays, when they had returned from church and had had their lunch, they had all moved out to the veranda where the collie was sleeping. Luke sat down on the steps, his back against the veranda post, Uncle Henry took the rocking chair, and Aunt Helen stretched herself out in the hammock, sighing contentedly. Then Luke, eying the collie, tapped the step with the palm of his hand, giving three little taps like a signal, and the old collie, lifting his head, got up stiffly with a slow wagging of the tail as an acknowledgment that the signal had been heard, and began to cross the veranda to Luke. But the dog was sleepy; his bad eye was turned to the rocking chair; in passing, his left front paw went under the rocker. With a frantic yelp, the dog went bounding down the steps and hobbled around the corner of the house, where he stopped, hearing Luke coming after him. All he needed was the touch of Luke's hand. Then he began to lick the hand methodically, as if apologizing.

" Luke," Uncle Henry called sharply, " bring that dog here."

When Luke led the collie back to the veranda, Uncle Henry nodded and said, " Thanks, Luke." Then he took out a cigar, lit it, put his big hands on his knees, and began to rock in the chair while he frowned and eyed the dog steadily. Obviously he was making some kind of an important decision about the collie.

" What's the matter, Uncle Henry? " Luke asked nervously.

" That dog can't see any more," Uncle Henry said.

" Oh, yes, he can," Luke said quickly. " His bad eye got turned to the chair, that's all, Uncle Henry."

" And his teeth are gone, too," Uncle Henry went on, paying no attention to what Luke had said. Turning to the hammock, he called, " Helen, sit up a minute, will you? "

When she got up and stood beside him, he went on, " I was thinking about this old dog the other day, Helen. It's not only that he's just about blind, but did you notice that when we drove up after church he didn't even bark? "

" It's a fact he didn't, Henry."

" No, not much good even as a watchdog now."

" Poor old fellow. It's a pity, isn't it? "

" And no good for hunting either. And he eats a lot, I suppose."

" About as much as he ever did, Henry."

" The plain fact is the old dog isn't worth his keep any more. It's time we got rid of him."

" It's always so hard to know how to get rid of a dog, Henry."

" I was thinking about it the other day. Some people think it's best to shoot a dog. I haven't had any shells for that shotgun for over a year. Poisoning is a hard death for a dog. Maybe drowning is the easiest and quickest way. Well,

I'll speak to one of the mill hands and have him look after it."

Crouching on the ground, his arms around the old collie's neck, Luke cried out, "Uncle Henry, Dan's a wonderful dog! You don't know how wonderful he is!"

"He's just a very old dog, son," Uncle Henry said calmly. "The time comes when you have to get rid of any old dog. We've got to be practical about it. I'll get you a pup, son. A smart little dog that'll be worth its keep. A pup that will grow up with you."

"I don't want a pup!" Luke cried, turning his face away. Circling around him, the dog began to bark, then flick his long pink tongue at the back of Luke's neck.

Aunt Helen, catching her husband's eye, put her finger on her lips, warning him not to go on talking in front of the boy. "An old dog like that often wanders off into the brush and sort of picks a place to die when the time comes. Isn't that so, Henry?"

"Oh, sure," he agreed quickly. "In fact, when Dan didn't show up yesterday, I was sure that was what had happened." Then he yawned and seemed to forget about the dog.

But Luke was frightened, for he knew what his uncle was like. He knew that if his uncle had decided that the dog was useless and that it was sane and sensible to get rid of it, he would be ashamed of himself if he were diverted by any sentimental considerations. Luke knew in his heart that he couldn't move his uncle. All he could do, he thought, was keep the dog away from his uncle, keep him out of the house, feed him when Uncle Henry wasn't around.

Next day at noontime Luke saw his uncle walking from the mill toward the house with old Sam Carter, a mill hand. Sam Carter was a dull, stooped, slow-witted man of sixty with an iron-gray beard, who was wearing blue overalls and a blue shirt. He hardly ever spoke to anybody. Watching from the veranda, Luke noticed that his uncle suddenly gave Sam Carter a cigar, which Sam put in his pocket. Luke had never seen his uncle give Sam a cigar or pay much attention to him.

Then, after lunch, Uncle Henry said lazily that he would like Luke to take his bicycle and go into town and get him some cigars.

"I'll take Dan," Luke said.

"Better not, son," Uncle Henry said. "It'll take you all afternoon. I want those cigars. Get going, Luke."

His uncle's tone was so casual that Luke tried to believe they were not merely getting rid of him. Of course he had to do what he was told. He had never dared to refuse to obey an order from his uncle. But when he had taken his bicycle and had ridden down the path that followed the stream to the town road and had got about a quarter of a mile along the road, he found that all he could think of was his uncle handing old Sam Carter the cigar.

Slowing down, sick with worry now, he got off the bike and stood uncertainly on the sunlit road. Sam Carter was a gruff, aloof old man who would have no feeling for a dog. Then suddenly Luke could go no farther without getting some assurance that the collie would not be harmed while he was away. Across the fields he could see the house.

Leaving the bike in the ditch, he started to cross the field, intending to get close enough to the house so Dan could hear him if he whistled softly. He got about fifty yards away from the house and whistled and waited, but there was no sign of the dog, which might be asleep at the front of the house, he knew, or over at the sawmill. With the saws whining, the dog couldn't hear the soft whistle. For a few minutes Luke couldn't make up his mind what to do, then he decided to go back to the road, get on his bike, and go back the way he had come until he got to the place where the river path joined the road. There he could leave his bike, go up the path, then into the tall grass and get close to the front of the house and the sawmill without being seen.

He had followed the river path for about a hundred yards, and when he came to the place where the river began to bend sharply toward the house his heart fluttered and his legs felt paralyzed, for he saw the old rowboat in the one place where the river was deep, and in the rowboat was Sam Carter with the collie.

The bearded man in the blue overalls was smoking the cigar; the dog, with a rope around its neck, sat contentedly beside him, its tongue going out in a friendly lick at the hand holding the rope. It was all like a crazy dream picture to Luke; all wrong because it looked so lazy and friendly, even the curling smoke from Sam Carter's cigar. But as Luke cried out, "Dan, Dan! Come on, boy!" and the dog jumped at the water, he saw that Sam Carter's left hand was hanging deep in the water, holding a foot of rope with a heavy stone at the end. As Luke cried out wildly, "Don't! Please don't!" Carter dropped the stone, for the cry came too late; it was blurred by the screech of the big saws at the mill. But Carter was startled, and he stared stupidly at the riverbank, then he ducked his head and began to row quickly to the bank.

But Luke was watching the collie take what looked like a long, shallow dive, except that the hind legs suddenly kicked up above the surface, then shot down, and while he watched, Luke sobbed and trembled, for it was as if the happy secret part of his life around the sawmill was being torn away from him. But even while he watched, he seemed to be following a plan without knowing it, for he was already fumbling in his pocket for his jackknife, jerking the blade open, pulling off his pants, kicking his shoes off, while he muttered fiercely and prayed that Sam Carter would get out of sight.

It hardly took the mill hand a minute to reach the bank and go slinking furtively around the bend as if he felt that the boy was following him. But Luke hadn't taken his eyes off the exact spot in the water where Dan had disappeared. As soon as the mill hand was out of sight, Luke slid down the bank and took a leap at the water, the sun glistening on his slender body, his eyes wild with eagerness as he ran out to the deep place, then arched his back and dived, swimming under water, his open eyes getting used to the greenish-gray haze of the water, the sandy bottom, and the imbedded rocks.

His lungs began to ache, then he saw the shadow of the collie floating at the end of the taut rope, rock-held in the sand. He slashed at the rope with his knife. He couldn't get much strength in his arm because of the resistance of the water. He grabbed the rope with his left hand, hacking with his knife. The collie suddenly drifted up slowly, like a water-soaked log. Then his own head shot above the surface, and, while he was sucking in the air, he was drawing in the rope, pulling the collie toward him and treading water. In a few strokes he was away from the deep place and his feet touched the bottom.

Hoisting the collie out of the water, he scrambled toward the bank, lurching and stumbling in fright because the collie felt like a dead weight.

He went on up the bank and across the path to the tall grass, where he fell flat, hugging the dog and trying to warm him with his own body. But the collie didn't stir, the good amber eye remained closed. Then suddenly Luke wanted to act like a resourceful, competent man. Getting up on his knees, he stretched the dog out on its belly, drew him between his knees, felt with trembling hands for the soft places on the flanks just above the hipbones, and rocked back and forth, pressing with all his weight, then relaxing the pressure as he straightened up. He hoped that he was working the dog's lungs like a bellows. He had read that men who had been thought drowned had been saved in this way.

"Come on, Dan. Come on, old boy," he pleaded softly. As a little water came from the collie's mouth, Luke's heart jumped, and he muttered over and over, "You can't be dead, Dan! You can't, you can't! I won't let you die, Dan!" He rocked back and forth tirelessly, applying the pressure to the flanks. More water dribbled from the mouth. In the collie's body he felt a faint tremor. "Oh, gee, Dan, you're alive," he whispered. "Come on, boy. Keep it up."

With a cough the collie suddenly jerked his head back, the amber eye opened, and there they were looking at each other. Then the collie, thrusting his legs out stiffly, tried to hoist himself up, staggered, tried again, then stood there in a stupor. Then he shook himself like any other wet dog, turned his head, eyed Luke, and the red tongue came out in a weak flick at Luke's cheek.

"Lie down, Dan," Luke said. As the dog lay down beside him, Luke closed his eyes, buried his head in the wet fur, and wondered why all the muscles of his arms and legs began to jerk in a nervous reaction, now that it was all over. "Stay there, Dan," he said softly, and he went back to the path, got his clothes, and came back beside Dan and put them on. "I think we'd better get away from this spot, Dan," he said. "Keep down, boy. Come on." And he crawled on through the tall grass till they were about seventy-five yards from the place where he had undressed. There they lay down together.

In a little while he heard his aunt's voice calling, "Luke. Oh, Luke! Come here, Luke!"

"Quiet, Dan," Luke whispered. A few minutes passed, and then Uncle Henry called, "Luke, Luke!" and he began to come down the path. They could see him standing there, massive and imposing, his hands on his hips as he looked down the path, then he turned and went back to the house.

As he watched the sunlight shine on the back of his uncle's neck, the exultation Luke had felt at knowing the collie was safe beside him turned to bewildered despair, for he knew that even if he should be forgiven for saving the dog when he saw it drowning, the fact was that his uncle had been thwarted. His mind was made up to get rid of Dan, and in a few days' time, in another way, he would get rid of him, as he got rid of anything around the mill that he believed to be useless or a waste of money.

As he lay back and looked up at the hardly moving clouds, he began to grow frightened. He couldn't go back to the house, nor could he take the collie into the woods and hide him and feed him there unless he tied him up. If he didn't tie him up, Dan would wander back to the house.

"I guess there's just no place to go, Dan," he whispered sadly. "Even if we start off along the road, somebody is sure to see us."

But Dan was watching a butterfly that was circling crazily above them. Raising himself a little, Luke looked through the grass at the corner of the house, then he turned and looked the other way to the wide blue lake. With a sigh he lay down again, and for hours they lay there together, until there was no sound from the saws in the mill and the sun moved low in the western sky.

"Well, we can't stay here any longer, Dan," he said at last. "We'll just have to get as far away as we can. Keep down, old boy," and he began to crawl through the grass, going farther away from the house. When he could no longer be seen, he got up and began to trot across the field toward the gravel road leading to town.

On the road, the collie would turn from time to time as if wondering why Luke shuffled along, dragging his feet wearily, head down. "I'm stumped, that's all, Dan," Luke explained. "I can't seem to think of a place to take you."

When they were passing the Kemp place, they saw the old man sitting on the veranda, and Luke stopped. All he could think of was that Mr. Kemp had liked them both and it had been a pleasure to help him get the cows in the evening. Dan had always been with them. Staring at the figure of the old man on the veranda, he said in a worried tone, "I wish I could be sure of him, Dan. I wish he was a dumb, stupid man who wouldn't know or care whether you were worth anything. . . . Well, come on." He opened the gate bravely, but he felt shy and unimportant.

"Hello, son. What's on your mind?" Mr. Kemp called from the veranda. He was a thin, wiry man in a tan-colored shirt. He had a gray, untidy mustache, his skin was wrinkled and leathery, but his eyes were always friendly and amused.

"Could I speak to you, Mr. Kemp?" Luke asked when they were close to the veranda.

"Sure. Go ahead."

"It's about Dan. He's a great dog, but I guess you know that as well as I do. I was wondering if you could keep him here for me."

"Why should I keep Dan here, son?"

"Well, it's like this," Luke said, fumbling the words awkwardly: "My uncle won't let me keep him any more . . . says he's too old." His mouth began to tremble, then he blurted out the story.

"I see, I see," Mr. Kemp said slowly, and he got up and came over to the steps and sat down and began to stroke the collie's head. "Of course, Dan's an old dog, son," he said quietly. "And sooner or later you've got to get rid of an old dog. Your uncle knows that. Maybe it's true that Dan isn't worth his keep."

"He doesn't eat much, Mr. Kemp. Just one meal a day."

"I wouldn't want you to think your uncle was cruel and unfeeling, Luke," Mr. Kemp went on. "He's a fine man . . . maybe just a little bit too practical and straightforward."

"I guess that's right," Luke agreed, but he was really waiting and trusting the expression in the old man's eyes.

"Maybe you should make him a practical proposition."

"I – I don't know what you mean."

"Well, I sort of like the way you get the cows for me in the evenings," Mr. Kemp said, smiling to himself. "In fact, I don't think you need me to go along with you at all. Now, supposing I gave you seventy-five cents a week. Would you get the cows for me every night?"

"Sure I would, Mr. Kemp. I like doing it, anyway."

"All right, son. It's a deal. Now I'll tell you what to do. You go back to your uncle, and before he has a chance to open up on you, you say right out that you've come to him with a business proposition. Say it like a man, just like that. Offer to pay him the seventy-five cents a week for the dog's keep."

"But my uncle doesn't need seventy-five cents, Mr. Kemp," Luke said uneasily.

"Of course not," Mr. Kemp agreed. "It's the principle of the thing. Be confident. Remember that he's got nothing against the dog. Go to it, son. Let me know how you do," he added, with an amused smile. "If I know your uncle at all, I think it'll work."

"I'll try it, Mr. Kemp," Luke said. "Thanks very much." But he didn't have any confidence, for even though he knew that Mr. Kemp was a wise old man who would not deceive him, he couldn't believe that seventy-five cents a week would stop his uncle, who was an important man. "Come on, Dan," he called, and he went slowly and apprehensively back to the house.

When they were going up the path, his aunt cried from the open window, "Henry, Henry, in heaven's name, it's Luke with the dog!"

Ten paces from the veranda, Luke stopped and waited nervously for his uncle to come out. Uncle Henry came out in a rush, but when he saw the collie and Luke standing there, he stopped stiffly, turned pale, and his mouth hung open loosely.

"Luke," he whispered, "that dog had a stone around his neck."

"I fished him out of the stream," Luke said uneasily.

"Oh. Oh, I see," Uncle Henry said, and gradually the color came back to his face. "You fished him out, eh?" he asked, still looking at the dog uneasily. "Well, you shouldn't have done that. I told Sam Carter to get rid of the dog, you know."

"Just a minute, Uncle Henry," Luke said, trying not to falter. He gained confidence as Aunt Helen came out and stood beside her husband, for her eyes seemed to be gentle, and he went on bravely, "I want to make you a practical proposition, Uncle Henry."

"A what?" Uncle Henry asked, still feeling insecure, and wishing the boy and the dog weren't confronting him.

"A practical proposition," Luke blurted out quickly. "I know Dan isn't worth his keep to you. I guess he isn't worth anything to anybody but me. So I'll pay you seventy-five cents a week for his keep."

"What's this?" Uncle Henry asked, looking bewildered. "Where would you get seventy-five cents a week, Luke?"

"I'm going to get the cows every night for Mr. Kemp."

"Oh, for heaven's sake, Henry," Aunt Helen pleaded, looking distressed, "let him keep the dog!" and she fled into the house.

"None of that kind of talk!" Uncle Henry called after her. "We've got to be sensible about this!" But he was shaken himself, and overwhelmed with a distress that destroyed all his confidence. As he sat down slowly in the rocking chair and stroked the side of his big face, he wanted to say weakly, "All right, keep the dog," but he was ashamed of being so weak and sentimental. He stubbornly refused to yield to this emotion; he was trying desperately to turn his emotion into a bit of good, useful common sense, so he could justify his distress. So he rocked and pondered. At last he smiled, " You're a smart little shaver, Luke," he said slowly. " Imagine you working it out like this. I'm tempted to accept your proposition."

" Gee, thanks, Uncle Henry."

" I'm accepting it because I think you'll learn something out of this," he went on ponderously.

" Yes, Uncle Henry."

" You'll learn that useless luxuries cost the smartest of men hard-earned money."

" I don't mind."

" Well, it's a thing you'll have to learn sometime. I think you'll learn, too, because you certainly seem to have a practical streak in you. It's a streak I like to see in a boy. O.K., son," he said, and he smiled with relief and went into the house.

Turning to Dan, Luke whispered softly, " Well, what do you know about that? "

As he sat down on the step with the collie beside him and listened to Uncle Henry talking to his wife, he began to glow with exultation. Then gradually his exultation began to change to a vast wonder that Mr. Kemp should have had such a perfect understanding of Uncle Henry. He began to dream of someday being as wise as old Mr. Kemp and knowing exactly how to handle people. It was possible, too, that he had already learned some of the things about his uncle that his father had wanted him to learn.

Putting his head down on the dog's neck, he vowed to himself fervently that he would always have some money on hand, no matter what became of him, so that he would be able to protect all that was truly valuable from the practical people in the world.

Analyzing Character in Stories

1. What did you find out about Uncle Henry from the viewpoint of other people in the story? Consider the way the following persons spoke to or about Uncle Henry and acted toward him: Luke's dead father, Aunt Helen, the men at the mill, Mr. Kemp.
2. What is Luke's initial attitude toward Uncle Henry? How does he feel toward him after the dog is condemned? after he has rescued the dog? after talking with Mr. Kemp? after Uncle Henry gives in?
3. What did you learn about Uncle Henry from his actions? Consider the way in which he treats Luke, Old Dan, and the men at the mill. How does Uncle Henry control his own actions and make decisions? What do you think Luke's father wanted him to learn about Uncle Henry?
4. Go back to the beginning and read the first words that Uncle Henry speaks. What do they tell you about his ideas on letting sentiment or emotions decide one's actions? What incidents in the story show that he himself is not completely lacking in sentiment?

Thinking It Over

1. What do you think of Luke's vow? Is money always the answer to a problem such as he faced?
2. It could be said that Uncle Henry's trouble was that he had no experience with younger people, no children of his own. What was it that he did not understand in Luke's point of view?
3. Luke learns something about dealing with overpractical people like Uncle Henry. What is it? In turn, Uncle Henry undergoes an important experience during the story. What does that experience teach him?
4. When you read " The Apprentice " on page 42, you will have a chance to compare the two stories, which are similar in theme and in characterization.

For Your Vocabulary

CONTEXT: A good way to determine the meaning of an unfamiliar word is by context; that is, by noticing the framework of words surrounding that particular word. Near the end of the story, Luke experiences a " glow of *exultation.*" Can you determine the meaning? On page 11 Luke is described as going " slowly and *apprehensively* back to the house." Again, the context offers you a clue to the meaning. When Uncle Henry studies his small notebook at the end of a day, " *assessing* the value " of every business transaction, what is he doing? This phrase gives a clue to defining some related words: *assess, assessor, assessment.* Use these words in sentences.

DESCRIPTIVE WORDS: List as many adjectives or descriptive phrases as you can that show Uncle Henry to be " practical," and make a second list of such words and phrases that show Luke to be " unpractical." Make a list of descriptive verbs, such as *slashed, sobbed,* and *trembled.*

MARY O'HARA

The Blizzard

You have probably read that fine book, *My Friend Flicka,* by Mary O'Hara, and perhaps you have seen movies based on this or other novels that tell of horses in the prairie country. If so, you recall the thrilling sight and sound of a herd of horses in full gallop across the open plain in pursuit of their leader, necks arched, manes and tails flying, hoofbeats pounding in unison. The power, the beauty, the majesty of such a sight is unforgettable. Mary O'Hara is a lover of horses. She has lived with them and observed their behavior in all seasons. When she tells you how the stallion Banner, fleet of foot and mighty of muscle, led his herd to safety in the teeth of a blizzard, and how he took care of the eager little Goblin, Flicka's colt, you know that what she reports is true. You feel as much pride and affection for Banner as if you owned him yourself.

For Better Reading . . . There are several different ways to tell a story. One effective way is from the *inside,* by which the author lets one or more of the characters reveal directly their thoughts and their reactions to the happenings in the story. (In this story, almost all the characters are horses, but they are *characters* nonetheless!) As the story opens, you follow the action through the eyes and reactions of the colt Goblin. Be prepared for shifts in viewpoint that follow and note carefully the places where they occur. That word *viewpoint* is important. It means the particular spot from which you look at life. If you always look through the same window, you always see the same thing. It is good to look out from other people's windows and discover what they see. In this case we see a storm from the point of view of animals.

GOBLIN knew the storm first as intense cold and a prolongation of the night.

Though he had been born in a storm and had been aware of the world as floods of icy rain sluicing upon him before he had been aware of it as anything else, yet then his consciousness had been only faintly awakened and he had received the experience as if through a veil. Now it was different. His awareness had quickened rapidly, sharpened by every hour of living; and his natural independence and tendency to solitary investigation had given him an ability to take life straight without filtration through his dam.[1]

He was nearly three months old.

Intense cold at dawn was a usual thing in late November but in an hour or so would come the sunrise, and mares and colts would turn themselves broadside and stand basking with heads hanging in complete relaxation. Even with zero temperatures and snow on the ground the rays gave warmth and life and penetrated to the vitals.

Today there was the dawn and the falling temperature and a great stillness. It continued. When there should have come the sunrise there came instead a dim twilight. It showed an ocean of cloud hanging low, solid and deep, without shading and without a break. It showed the world crouching beneath it, colorless and withdrawn.

There was something else abroad that could be sensed rather than seen, and Goblin trotted away from the herd to the edge of the rise as if he could find this strange new thing by pursuing it. His muzzle lifted and his nostrils flared till they showed the crimson lining. He was trying to catch the scent of fear.

Now came the snow, moving against them from the east, quiet and hardly noticeable at first, little flakes like tiny cool feathers falling softly on their rough fur coats and melting immediately. As it grew colder the flakes were smaller and harder. The sky sank lower — a fog of snow, surrounding them. The world vanished and the colts looked around in terror and clung close to their dams.

There came a pressure into the storm and a sound, and the mares and colts turned their backs to it and began to move slowly with patient heads and tails blown forward between their legs. The colts whinnied nervously. If it had not been for the stolid resignation of their dams they would have been frantic.

The sound was a wind rising. It came from those caves of disaster far in the northeast, the winds that bring shipwreck on the Atlantic, cyclones in the mid-continent states, and blizzards in the Rockies. Called an "easterner" in the mountain states, it lasts without letup for at least three days, sometimes a week.

As the hours passed, the mares tried to graze, pawing up the snow, and the colts imitated them. They moved in a southwesterly direction, backs to the storm. Banner occasionally climbed a rise and stood there entirely hidden in the white smother. But the mares were oblivious of him, whether he came or went; they had eyes only for their colts.

As the wind rose, the sound of it rose too and a whining note came into it. The snowflakes were needle points of pain. When the colts, whirling about in confusion and fear, felt them for a second on their eyeballs, they whinnied with agony and turned again to their mothers and thrust their heads under their bellies for shelter and a taste of warm milk. For whether or not the mares had food for themselves they never ceased to

[1] dam (dăm): mother.

make milk for their colts. In twenty-four hours of such a storm tens of pounds of weight would be stripped from the mares.

The bodies of all the horses felt different. The snow burrowed into the long fur with which they were prepared for the winter, and the blood heat melted and froze it and they became strange white phantoms moving silently through the white storm. Only their manes and tails, rippling constantly in the wind, were dark.

To themselves, they were heavy and unnatural and the colts asked their mothers, *Are you afraid?* And the dams answered them, No, it is simply something to endure. *All will be well in the end.* And the colts told themselves, *It is nothing to fear. All will be well.* And though they were nervous and panicky yet their faith was complete.

All the fear, all the courage, all the doubt, all the calculation, all the responsibility, all decisions to be made, were Banner's.

An outstanding horse personality is born with one ambition — to be the leader of a great herd. To have the finest mares — a sickling will be driven out or isolated until she regains her health. To raise the finest colts — handsome, strong, swift. To achieve this the stallion will fight and suffer, risk his life, starve, wander in strange lands, steal and plunder, take what punishment comes. Once he has achieved it he is tireless in the care of it. He finds his mares the most luscious pastures — north, south, all over the state; finds them shelter during storms, protection from all enemies. He fights any who would challenge him or steal or hurt his charges, investigates every danger with intrepid bravery and disregard of himself. A stallion always carries scars and fresh wounds, got because of his fearlessness in discharge of duties toward his herd. And because the aim of his master, if he has one, is the same as his own, there is partnership and teamwork between the two.

In this storm Banner was not still a moment. He circled the herd quietly, watchful lest one mare or colt wander away. He climbed every rise. He opened his eyelids against the flaming ice of the storm. His great neck was arched, his mane and tail whipped behind him on the horizontal stream of wind-driven snow. His eyelashes were fringes of tiny icicles. A long one hung from his chin — it was his frozen breath.

How long would it last? Standing on a rise, he peered into the blind smother as if he could find an answer there. Was it just a flurry which would pass with a change of wind?

There was other life abroad in the storm. The jack rabbits were the most at home, warmly hooded in white fur, invisible until they leaped. Then they shot through the air as if propelled by the kick of a mule.

Banner's ears came forward suddenly and he turned his head, straining to hear. The faint yammer of the hunting pack drifted to him through the snow — coyotes,[1] lurking in the neighborhood of his band, of anything living, on the lookout for strays or casualties.

He gave a sudden start. Three coyotes, galloping soundlessly with red tongues lolling out, appeared close before him, passed him, vanished.

Banner turned, picked his way down the hill, and joined his mares. He took them to the water hole. It was in an exposed place, and when they had made the turn of the hill they had to face the storm. They balked and turned away. The stallion forced them. They obeyed

[1] **coyotes** (kī'ōtz): prairie wolves.

Running with the herd is an exhilarating experience – for horses and men. (Toni Frissell)

reluctantly, then scented the water and it drew them and they drank their fill. While they drank, suddenly there were antelope on the other side of the pool, staring at them, bending their slim necks to the water.

Banner guided the mares to a draw[1] between two hills where they had shelter from the wind but no feed. As between days of hunger or days of scourging by the wind he knew they would suffer less from hunger. But still he was questioning. Was it really going to be days? Or only hours?

There was increase in the force of the wind rather than lessening. The craggy peaks of the hills where the rock jutted through the soil were bare; the snow swirled around them and packed the lee side deep.

Drifts were curling down the centers of the draws, piling smoothly up, shaped like waves. The temperature was falling fast. If the wind did not change, it would be thirty below that night. Now, in the daytime, the storm was white. That night it would be a black fury with a bedlam of sustained, screaming sound.

The wind did not change. Night came early. The herd bunched for warmth, and on the outskirts of it the coyotes circled, terrifying the colts with their long, trembling howls.

A few of the mares slept flat on their sides, and all of the colts lay under or close to their mothers. The blizzard screamed over them.

When morning came and Banner again forced them out of the draw to keep them moving and grazing, two of the colts were unwilling to rise. At sight of their dams moving away from them, they struggled and fell back, tried again, got weakly to their feet, shook themselves, and followed slowly.

[1] **draw: a small valley.**

One colt stood, whimpering, over the prostrate body of the old mare which was its dam. Banner and the other mares passed them as if they did not exist. Doom was already written upon them. Before the heat had gone out of the mare's body, the coyotes were at it. The colt screamed and fled, three coyotes racing after. They crowded it and leaped for its throat. The colt reared and struck at the fanged faces, but the teeth of a big gray coyote closed in its jugular vein and the colt went down – its last agonized scream cut sharply in half – The coyotes ripped at the belly of the dead mare.

Banner found shelter for the herd where it was neither swept by the wind nor too deep in drifts. A little grove of aspen in a draw caught the snow. It skipped over the trees, touched earth again, and curled in great combers. Beyond it was a space protected from the worst of the wind and the worst of the drifts. Here the dry snow blew fetlock-deep like a flat, boiling tide.

The colts had the best of it. Hot milk at any moment they wanted it, and the warm bulk of the dam standing between them and the storm. It was the cold that bit into them; and when they slept on the ground the blood in their veins ran thick and slow and they woke shivering.

Many times that second day Banner climbed the peak again. One of his questions was answered. It was not a storm of hours or a single day that any band of healthy mares and colts could weather, it was a blizzard from the east. There was another question – and for this answer he faced the ranch, tail whipped between his legs, mane blown over his eyes. He stood watching, protecting his eyes with his ice-fringed lids, listening for some sound that was not the whine and roar of the storm.

A small figure stood near him, just beneath the peak, looking up at him. Pure white in the storm even without the powdering of snow, he was hardly visible. Banner bent his great head and looked down at him. The Goblin looked back. Neither moved. Then Banner lifted his head again and, without taking notice of the colt, gazed in the direction of the ranch.

Goblin had not been one of the two colts who nearly succumbed during the night. He was filled with interest and curiosity. He was curious about the storm, about the sudden mysterious disappearance of the grass under a deep white blanket. Curious about the white stuff which buffeted his head and blinded his eyes and whined in his ears. He opened his mouth and felt the icy flakes melt on his tongue and mouthed them with astonishment. He did not suffer. He was filled with vigor. In his veins was a hot, swift-running blood, strong to cope with storms. He was at home on the range in any weather.

From the first he had been curious when Banner left the herd. He strained his eyes and his nostrils after him as if it was necessary he should know just what the stallion was doing and why he did it; and at last he followed him to find out. He sniffed, leaned a little closer, then turned his own head here and there in imitation, seeking, listening, noticing, wondering.

At last he moved away. Banner took no notice of him. The white colt vanished in the snow.

Banner was waiting, not for an audible sound nor visible sign, but for the sudden sure knowledge within himself.

It came at about four o'clock in the afternoon.

Rob and Gus had piled the mangers full of hay and fought their way out to the county road and opened the gates. Rob had raised his face toward the saddleback and had given the long cry into the teeth of the wind, useless because it was snatched from his lips even as he gave it so that it seemed like no cry at all.

"Ba-a-anner! Bring 'em in!"

He did it because giving voice to his command brought it to a sharp point within himself. It was the close communion between the two — man and stallion — that would acquaint Banner with the fact that the gates were open, the corrals and mangers ready, and that Rob had called him to come.

The white-shrouded stallion, standing on the crest, felt his own sudden decision. The time had come. He plunged down the slope toward his mares and roused them from their lethargy. They moved out of the shelter into deep snow, sluggish and stiff with the intense cold. Banner nipped and lashed. He drove at Gypsy, who was dry[1] this year, and Banner's favorite and lead mare. She floundered out of the drifts that barred the way and plunged around the shoulder of the hill. The rest followed, gaining speed as they felt the stallion's driving power. They caught his determination. Besides — they knew where they were going. The colts clung close.

Banner took the lead, once they were under way, and the mares followed. They were three miles east of the Goose Bar gates. They ran with the storm behind them. Now and then Banner turned and circled the band, driving them from the rear, his head low, snaking along the snow, his muzzle ruffling it. The hairs of his tail and mane were erect, springing out with a separate life of their own.

The mares began to warm up as their blood ran faster. Excitement spread

[1] **dry: without milk.**

through the herd, and they found strength to squeal and toss their heels and leap the ravines which opened suddenly under their feet.

What Goblin lacked was the long slim legs and the speed of the other colts. But when the command came to go, he galloped at Flicka's side with a fierce eagerness and zest. It was his first run with the herd. The icy air burned in his lungs. His chest expanded. Short-legged as he was, he had to labor to keep up. He did more than scrabble now – he stretched his legs and galloped mightily. A mare sideswiped him, and he went down, and the herd thundered over him, one big body after the other lifting in the air to clear him. He fought to his feet and stood. They were gone. He could neither see nor hear them, only the wind screaming about his head. He stood trembling and cried for his mother. He saw a white shape coming at him. Down-wind from him as she was, he couldn't smell her and hardly recognized her. Close to, he heard her voice and whinnied ecstatically in answer. They plunged forward again, following the herd. Once more he galloped as hard as he could. Suddenly a ravine opened beneath his feet. He leaped bravely – his feet went deep into soft snow – his head went after them. He hit ground and turned a complete somersault and lay stunned, half buried.

Flicka stood over him nickering. She tried to paw the snow off him. The colt struggled, his feet kicking wildly – but he had no purchase.[1] There was a swirling movement behind them. It was the stallion, coming at a gallop, his eyes shining like fire opals through the snow.

He thrust his head into the drift, caught Goblin by the neck as a cat takes a kitten in its mouth, lifted him out, shook him, set him down, and was away again, thundering after the herd – other business to attend to.

Flicka and Goblin galloped on alone. They passed a mare standing motionless in the storm. One foreleg was lifted, the foot dangling loose, broken by a step into a badger hole. Her fine bay colt stood in the lee side of her, still finding his shelter from her crippled body. She tried to follow Flicka and Goblin, hopping on three legs. Then she stopped. They never saw her again.

They passed through the open gates, raced down the stable pasture, and reached the corrals.

The whole herd was feeding at the mangers in the barn and out at the feed racks, those in the east corral under the lee of the cliff. Other horses had come in too. Yearlings. Two-year-olds. Some older horses.

Banner would not go into the stables. He never had. Rob held a bucket of oats to him in the lee of the wall, and the stallion stood before him, his sides heaving, the snow melting off him from the heat of his body and freezing again in icicles here and there. He dipped his mouth in, taking great mouthfuls of the heat-giving grain, lifted his head to chew and look around, to look into Rob's eyes.

Did I do well?

Good work, old boy.

Rob talked to him. The stallion's full dark eyes looked at the man with intelligence and understanding. There was this about humans – this peace and confidence they could give. More than that, the deep, friendly, murmuring voice of his master lifted his load. The stallion laid down his responsibility, his fear, his never-ceasing vigilance, and rested.

His sides expanded and collapsed in a huge sigh.

Before dark, a fine bay colt came

[1] **purchase** (pûr'chĭs): something solid to push against.

whimpering and neighing down the stable pasture, without its dam. It shoved in amongst the other mares. It fed greedily at the feedboxes. Rob, looking at it, saw long, bleeding gouges on haunch and shoulder. Coyotes! Or perhaps timber wolves! Where was its mother? Rob moved around looking for the mare — no sign of it. He left the shelter of the feed racks and went to the fence facing out toward the saddleback, trying to pierce the white smother — the mare might be anywhere out there — dead or alive. No — not alive. Else the colt wouldn't have left her. Wolves.

It was a fine bay colt, well-grown and strong, five months old. Kept in, and sheltered and fed, it would survive. Write off another mare lost.

The band could stay in as long as the storm lasted. There would be a day, perhaps even before it had stopped snowing, when Rob would go to the stables and find them empty, and he would know the stallion had begun to fret for the wind and the wideness of the upland and that as soon as it was safe, he had taken the mares away.

Following the blizzard there was a ground blizzard. Though it had stopped snowing, for forty or fifty feet over the earth the fine powdery snow was lifted and whirled and driven by the wind. Easy for life to be lost in a ground blizzard.

At last the wind stopped and the air was calm and crystal clear, perfumed with so intense a freshness and clearness that it stung the lungs with tiny needles.

Glorious was the sun blazing on the whiteness. Glorious, the deep blue cup of the sky. The whole world glittered and shone. And on the upland the mares moved contentedly on familiar grazing ground and told the colts, *Did we not say so? It is over.*

Goblin kept this knowledge in his heart. And more knowledge of his own finding. *When the cold burns too deep, when there is death in the wind, take the way down the mountain. Gates are open. Mangers are full of hay. There is shelter and food and kindness for all. And the screaming whiteness cannot follow you in.*

Observing from Different Viewpoints

1. This story was told from several viewpoints. You observe the blizzard and its effects through the eyes and reactions of Goblin, of Banner, and of the horses' owner. What was the essential reaction of the stallion to the blizzard? of the colt? How do you account for the difference in their reactions? Was there a certain likeness, too? How do you know that Goblin has leadership qualities? Why do you think Banner went back to rescue Goblin?
2. Compare the reactions of Banner and Goblin to the safety of the ranch corral.
3. What do you learn about the owner when the story shifts to his point of view?

Thinking It Over

1. As you lived through the blizzard with the horses, you were aware that many aspects of their behavior are very like those of human beings. Point out instances in which they showed courage, curiosity, intelligence, pride, terror, and family loyalty. What was the most surprising thing you noticed about them?
2. The author of the story obviously knows a great deal about horses and ranching. Tell some of the things you learned about the problems and hazards of ranch life in winter. Have you read *My Friend Flicka* or *Thunderhead* or John Steinbeck's story " The Red Pony "? If so, recall some of the highlights.
3. Literature, like painting, creates pictures of a scene or an action. But a piece of literature also has *movement,* like a selection of music. This piece of writing is rather like an exciting musical composition that begins quietly, gathers suspense toward a *fortissimo* climax, and then slips down, *di-*

minuendo, toward a peaceful conclusion. See if you can trace this rising-and-falling pattern in the story. Some members of the class will probably know of musical pieces that follow a similar pattern.

For Your Vocabulary

FIGURES OF SPEECH: Putting common words into fresh, arresting arrangements which we call figures of speech – this is one way in which writers create true word magic. The trick of making figures of speech consists of putting together unlike ideas, or in drawing comparisons between unlike things. For example, in this story, you found these phrases: *as if through a veil; an ocean of cloud; like tiny cool feathers; teeth of the wind.* Now, actually, no one was looking through a cloth veil in the story; a cloud cannot be an ocean; and the wind does not have teeth. But you get a picture from these figures of speech that is immediately clear and highly descriptive.

Find the figure of speech near the end of the story that describes the sky. In the paragraph beginning "Banner took the lead," on page 18, find an especially effective figure of speech. Point out others in the story.

Write a paragraph describing a storm you yourself have seen. Make use of several figures of speech in recreating your experience.

WALTER D. EDMONDS

Judge

When his father died, the only legacy that sixteen-year-old John Haskell received was the responsibility for his mother and the eight younger children – and a debt of forty dollars. That sum may not seem like much to us in these days, but to young John in 1830 it was a veritable mountain of money. John wasn't legally responsible for the debt, mind you, but there it was facing him and he could not forget it. To find out how he paid it and what grueling experiences and bitter disappointments he endured, you will have to read this absorbing story of how a boy becomes a man.

For Better Reading . . . Most stories have a *theme.* A good piece of literature usually gives the reader some strong impression about life or about people. Even as we read we are aware that there is something more to the story than just incident and conversation. This " something more " is the theme or main idea behind the story. You can find it if you will ask yourself: how does the story apply generally to my own experience? what does the story suggest as wise or unwise behavior in certain situations? In other words, try to *generalize* from the story.

When Charley Haskell died in the spring, he left a widow with nine children, a four-room house, a rickety barn, and a dollar owing from the Judge for the sale of a calf. The widow was a plain, honest, and fairly easygoing woman. She worked hard enough in the house to keep it and the children's clothes clean, but for outside things she had depended on her husband. For a few weeks after his death she apparently put her trust in God. Then she had a talk with John.

John was the oldest boy. The next oldest was only seven, and in between were girls. She told him, therefore, that it was up to him to take his father's place toward his brothers and sisters. They looked to him for their support, and she depended on him. She kissed him a little tearfully, and took up her existence again exactly where she had left it off when Charley died — as if, by a few words, she had settled it in the accustomed grooves for an indefinite time.

The sight of her unexpected tears, however, had sobered John, so that he hung up his fishing pole and went out to look at the corn patch. He found it full of weeds. It was an unusual thing for him to get the hoe without being told to, but he did, and after he had cleaned the first row, he found that it looked much better when you could see the corn.

When he came in that night to supper, he had a quarter of the field hoed. He called his mother and sisters out to see what he had done and listened with pride as they said that it looked nice. It was while his mother was looking at the corn that she remembered that they had never collected the dollar from the Judge for the calf. She told John that he had better get it that evening.

John was frightened at the idea of going to the Judge's house. In 1830, the settlement at High Falls was a poor place of small houses, which made the Judge's stone house seem like a palace. John, for one, had never seen the inside of it, but he had seen the curtains through the windows, and the oil lamps, when he went by at night, two or even three in the same room. For Judge Doane was the great man of the district. He owned a vast amount of land and held mortgages [1] on most of the rest and had been representative of the county.

John's mother had brushed his coat for him, but even so, it looked very shabby and frayed and outgrown as he knocked on the front door and asked the hired girl if he could see the Judge. He had the feeling that it was an impertinence to ask a person like the Judge to pay a dollar, even when he owed it to you. He thought that probably the Judge would throw him out of the house. But his mother said they needed the dollar for flour, and at least he had to try to get it.

The maid came back for him and led him to the Judge's office, opened the door, and closed it behind him. John stood with his back to the door and his hat in both hands, a lanky, overgrown boy, with a thin, rather pale face, and brown frightened eyes. Compared to the Judge, he looked like someone made of splinters.

"Hello, John," said the Judge. "What do you want with me?"

He sounded not unfriendly, so John managed, after a couple of attempts, to say that he had come for the dollar for the calf.

"Oh, yes," said the Judge. "I'd for-

[1] **held mortgages** (môr′gĭj·ĕz): had documents requiring persons who owed him money to forfeit their land and property should they fail to pay.

gotten about that. I'm sorry."

He got up from his leather armchair and went to his writing desk and took one end of his gold watch chain from the pocket of his well-filled, speckled waistcoat and unlocked a drawer. While his back was turned, John was able to see the room, with the impressive lace on the curtains of the windows, the silver plate hung on the chimney piece, and the fire on the hearth where the Judge burned wood just for the sake of seeing it burn.

The Judge relocked the drawer, replaced the key in his pocket, and handed John a dollar bill. He resumed his seat and told John to sit down for a minute. John did so, on the edge of the nearest chair.

"How are you making out?" asked the Judge.

"All right, I guess," said John. "I wouldn't have bothered you for this, only we had to have flour."

"That's all right," said the Judge slowly. "I should have remembered it. I didn't think of it because your father owed me money anyway."

"I didn't know that," said John. He couldn't think of anything to say. He only looked at the Judge and wondered how his father had had the nerve to borrow money from a man like him.

The Judge made an impressive figure before his fire. He was a massive man with a red face, strong white hair, and uncompromising light blue eyes. He was staring at John, too, rather curiously.

He nodded, after a while, and said, "He owed me forty dollars."

That was what John had wanted to know, but he was shocked at the amount of it. All he could think of to say was, "I didn't know that, sir."

"No," said the Judge, "probably not. He was a kind of cousin of my wife's, but we neither of us said much about it. And after Mrs. Doane died he didn't come around much." His brows drew bushily together and he stared into the fire. "How old are you, son?" he asked.

John replied that he was sixteen.

The Judge went on to ask about the family, the age of each child, and what Charley Haskell had got planted that spring. John answered him everything, and as he did he felt a little more confidence. It seemed odd that anyone living in the High Falls settlement could know so little about anyone else. Why, he knew a lot more about the Judge than the Judge did about him. He told how high the corn stood. He said, "It stands as high as any I've seen around here, excepting yours, Judge. And now I've started looking out for it, maybe it will catch up."

The Judge said, "Hoeing is the best garden fertilizer in the world. And sweat is the next best thing to money."

"Yes, sir," said John. It made him feel proud that he had hoed so much of his corn that day. Tomorrow he'd really get after the piece.

"You can't live on potatoes and corn though," said the Judge. "What are you going to do?"

John was awed to be talking so familiarly to a man half the town was scared of; a man, it was said, who had even talked out in legislature down in Albany. But his face wrinkled and he managed to grin.

"Work, I guess, sir."

The Judge grunted then and stood up and dripped his quid [1] into the sandbox. "You do that and you'll take care of your family all right. Maybe you'll even pay back the forty dollars your father owed me." He held out his hand, which John hardly dared to take. "When do

[1] **quid:** cud of tobacco.

you suppose that'll be?"

John got white. "I don't know, sir."

The Judge smiled.

"I like that a lot better than easy promises, John."

He walked beside John into the hall, his meaty hand on John's shoulder.

"Good luck to you," he said from the front door.

During the summer John managed to get work from time to time, hiring out for as much as forty cents a day, sometimes as often as three days a week. At first he didn't have much luck getting jobs, for though he was a good deal stronger than he appeared to be and worked hard, people remembered his father and preferred getting other help when they could. Besides, in the 30's, there weren't many people in High Falls who could afford to hire help, even at forty cents a day; so, by working in the evenings and on Sundays also, John had ample time to take care of their corn and potatoes and the garden truck he had planted late himself.

He used to wonder how his father had ever been able to take life so easily. He wondered often how it was that he never had time to go fishing that summer. And the one or two times he did have the time, he thought of the forty dollars he owed Judge Doane, and he went out and looked for work. He even found occasional jobs at Greig, five miles up the river, and walked back and forth every morning and evening. Little by little, the forty dollars became an obsession [1] with him, and though at first he had given all his earnings to his mother to spend, he now began to save out a few pennies here and there. When, at the end of August, he had saved out his first complete dollar and held it all at once in his hand, he realized that some day he might pay off the debt; and from there his mind went further, and he began to see that it was even possible that some day he would be able to build a decent house for his mother, perhaps even get married; perhaps, when the settlement became a town, as they said it would, get elected to the town board.

By the middle of October, John had saved up enough money to see the family through the winter, as he calculated it, for besides his secret bit, he had persuaded his mother to lay by some of what he gave her. Further, she had been moved by the sight of a decent garden to preserve some beans and also some berries that the girls had gathered, especially since it was the first time in several years that she had felt able to buy sugar ahead of the immediate demand. The potato piece had yielded forty bushels of potatoes; and the corn, which John had sold, had brought in a few dollars more.

The day before he finished cutting the winter wood supply, John counted up his money and decided he would make the first payment on the forty-dollar debt to the Judge that night. It amounted to five dollars, even, but to John that seemed a great deal.

He went up to the big house when he felt sure that the Judge would have finished his supper; and he had the same business of knocking and waiting in the hall while the maid took his name in. He found the Judge sitting as he had found him the first time, only the fire was about two logs bigger.

"Sit down, John," said the Judge, "and tell me what I can do for you."

John obviously did not know how to begin his business properly, and after watching him under his brows for a moment, the Judge continued in his gruff voice, "I may as well tell you I've kind

[1] **obsession** (ŏb·sĕsh′ŭn): a compelling idea.

of kept my eye on you this summer, John. I like the way you've taken hold. I'm willing to admit, too, that I was kind of surprised. And I'll be glad to help you out."

John flushed right up to his hair.

"I didn't come to ask for anything, Judge." He fished in his pocket and pulled out his coins. His hands were stiffly clumsy. Some of the coins fell to the floor, and one rolled musically all the way under the desk. As he went on his knees to retrieve it, John wished he had had the sense to tie them together instead of jingling them loosely in his pocket all the way up. He couldn't bear to look at the Judge when he handed him the coins. He said, "I wanted to pay something back on that forty dollars, sir. It's only five dollars, even." The Judge had to cup his two hands. "Maybe you'd count it, sir." But it didn't look like so much in the Judge's hands.

The Judge, however, said, "Quite right, John," and counted up the money. Then he went to his desk, put the money in a drawer, and wrote out a receipt which he gave to John.

"Yes, sir," said John, wondering what it was.

The Judge looked grave.

"That's a receipt, John. It says you've paid me back five dollars."

John wondered.

"Why," he said, "it's kind of like money, ain't it?"

"In a way," said the Judge, shaking hands. "What are you going to do this winter, John?"

"I don't know, sir. I tried to get a job from Brown at the hotel, splitting firewood, but he's hired Ance instead. Mr. Freel's got all the help he needs at the tannery."

Those were about the only winter jobs in High Falls a man could hope to find. The Judge nodded and said, "I'd offer you something if it didn't mean getting rid of someone else, John. I couldn't rightly do that."

"No, sir," John said, and started home.

But somehow, he felt so happy all the way home that when he reached the house and found his mother sitting up in the kitchen, he couldn't help telling her the whole business. He blurted it all out — the way he had saved a little now and then until he had actually got five dollars. And then he showed her the receipt.

His mother didn't say a word as she looked at the receipt, but her head gradually bent farther and farther forward, and all at once she started crying. John could not understand at first. Finally she lifted her face to him.

"Oh, John, why did you do that?"

"I wanted to pay off that debt Pa laid up," he said, uneasily. "Ain't that all right?"

"I guess it is, John. But why didn't you tell me first?"

"I kind of wanted to surprise you," he mumbled. "I didn't mean for to make you feel bad, Ma."

"It ain't that, John."

"But ain't I give you enough?"

"Oh, yes. You've done fine, John. But the way you've been working has made me kind of different. I got to thinking people talked to us different now. I never thought about that before."

As he thought it over during the next two or three days, John felt all torn up in his chest. He began to see that by starting to be respectable, he had done more than just work for himself. He had done something to his mother, too. And now, by going through with it, he had put her back where she used to be. It did not seem logical, but that was how it was.

Perhaps he would have fallen back then and there to his old ways of letting the world slide, if he hadn't met Seth one evening at the blacksmith's, where he had gone to get the big cook kettle mended. Seth was there, too, having Jorgen do some work on a few of his beaver traps.

Seth was an Indian. In summer he worked in the sawmills when it occurred to him to do so, but in winter he went into the north woods. People distrusted Seth. They did not like the way he smelled. Even in the forge you could smell him, greasy sweet, through his thick tobacco smoke.

He said he was planning to go north in about two weeks. He was late, but the winter looked slow. He thought the furs would be coming up pretty quick though. Better than last year. Last year he had cleared only two hundred dollars.

" Two hundred dollars," thought John. He wondered how a man like Seth could spend all that. All he knew was that the Indian took it to Utica every spring. He supposed there were places in such a big town that an Indian could go to. Two hundred dollars.

He turned shyly to the Indian.

" How much does a man need to get traps and food for the winter? " he asked.

The Indian turned his brown face. He wasn't amused, or he did not show it if he was.

" Sev'nty-five dollar, maybe. You got a gun? "

John nodded.

" Seventy-five dollars," he thought. He knew only one person who could stake him [1] that much.

The Indian asked, " You going? "

" Maybe," said John.

" You come wit' me. Good range over mine. Plenty room us both. I help you make a cabin."

" I'll see."

It was almost 10:30 at night when he got to the Judge's. He had made up his mind he would ask the Judge, if there was a downstairs light still on when he got there. If not, he wouldn't.

The house was dark on the town side, but when John went round to the office window, his heart contracted to see that the Judge was still up. He tapped on the window. The Judge did not start. He got slowly up and came to the window and opened it to the frosty night. When he saw the boy's white face and large eyes, he said harshly, " What do you want? "

" Please, Judge," said John, " could I talk to you? "

" It's damned late," said the Judge, staring with his cold blue eyes for a while. Then he shut the window, and presently opened the front door. He was looking a little less threatening by then, but he wasn't looking friendly.

" Be as quick as you can," he said, when they were back in the office.

John was as white as a person could be. His tongue stuttered.

" I wanted to ask you something, Judge. But if you don't like it, say so plain. It's about me and getting to trap this winter, on account of that five dollars I paid you." He couldn't think decently straight.

The Judge barked at him.

" Talk plain, boy! Begin at the beginning. What's the five dollars got to do with it? "

John began to talk. He repeated what had happened with his mother, how she felt, how odd it seemed to him, but there it was. The Judge began to sit less stiffly. He even nodded. " Women are the devil," he observed. " You want to take back that money? "

[1] **stake him:** back him financially.

Sunlight sifts through tall hemlocks. In good trapping country like this John learned Indian ways from his friend Seth. (*Armstrong Roberts*)

"No, no, I don't," John said desperately. "But people don't like giving me work yet, and I want Ma to feel respectable. I thought if you could make a stake to go trapping."

"How much?"

"Seth said seventy-five dollars," he almost whispered. "But I guess I could get along with fifty. I'd get the traps and some powder and ball, and I could go light on the food. I don't eat a great lot and I'm a handy shot, Judge."

"Seventy-five dollars," said the Judge. "You're asking me to lend that much to a sixteen-year-old boy, just like that?"

His red face was particularly heavy-looking.

"I'd make it on fifty," said John, "but it was just an idea. If you don't think it's all right, I won't bother you any more."

"Then you want the five back, too, I suppose — makes it eighty. And forty is a hundred and twenty."

"It would be ninety-five, wouldn't it, if you give me fifty?"

"Shut up," barked the Judge. "If I'm going to stake you I'll do it so I'll have a chance of getting my money back. It won't pay me to send you in with so little you'll starve to death before spring, will it?"

John could only gape.[1]

"How about this Seth?" asked the Judge. "He's a drunken brute. Can you trust him?"

"I've met him in the woods," said John. "He's always been nice to me."

The Judge grumbled. He got up and took five dollars from his desk and gave it to John.

"You bring me back that receipt tomorrow night," was all he said.

When John gave the money to his mother, it made her so happy that he felt wicked to feel so miserable himself. It seemed as if all his summer's work had been burned with one spark. And he was frightened to go next night to the Judge's house. But he went.

The Judge only kept him a moment.

He took the receipt and gave John another paper.

"Put a cross in the right-hand bottom corner," he directed; and when John had done so, "That is a receipt for seventy-five dollars. Here's the money. Don't lose it going home."

He walked John to the door and shook hands.

"Good luck. Come here next spring as soon as you get back."

"Thanks," was all John could say.

The Judge made a harsh noise in his throat and fished a chew from his pocket.

"Good-by," he said.

John got Seth to help select his outfit. The Indian enjoyed doing that. And John felt so proud over his new traps, his powder flask and bullet pouch, and his big basket of provisions, and he felt so grateful to the Indian that he offered to buy him a drink out of the two-shilling bit[2] he had left.

"No drink," said the Indian. "Next spring, oh, yes."

He shared his canoe with John up the Moose River, and they spent two weeks getting in to Seth's range. They dumped his stuff in the little log cabin and moved over the range together to the one Seth had selected for John. There they laid up a small cabin just like the Indian's, and built a chimney. They had trouble finding clay to seal the cracks, for by then the frost was hard and snow coming regularly each afternoon.

Then the Indian took John with him while he laid out his own lines, and,

[1] **gape** (gāp): stare wonderingly.

[2] **two-shilling bit:** at that time, fifty cents.

after two days, went with John, showing him what to start on. After that the Indian spent all his spare time making John snowshoes. He finished them just in time for the first heavy snow.

John learned a great deal from Seth that fall. First of all he learned that an Indian in the woods is a much different person from the Indian imitating white men. He had always liked Seth, but he had never suspected his generosity and good humor. Even when the snow got heavy, the Indian paid him a weekly visit and asked him back to his cabin in return.

He learned how to make pens for beaver under water and ice, and sink fresh twigs, and when the younger beaver swam in, to drop the closing pole and let them drown. He never got as good as Seth was, as a still-hunting fisher. But Seth said, either you could do that or you could not; there was no shame in not being able.

But John did well. Early in March his bale of furs had mounted up so well that he had Seth come over and appraise them. The Indian said he had more than two hundred dollars' worth. It would depend on the market. By the end of the month he might have two hundred and fifty dollars' worth.

The snow went down quickly, but the ice held. John began to be eager to leave. He wanted to show his furs. He would be able to pay off the Judge, not only the stake but the share, and also the debt, and he would have a few dollars to start the summer on. Next winter he would make a clear profit. He would put money in the bank.

He went over to Seth's and told him he would start next week. He could not bear to wait, and if he went early he could get across the Moose River on the ice somewhere. The Indian said, "Yes," but he begged John to wait. There was still two weeks for the fur to hold up well, and he had sometimes made some lucky catches in March.

But John's heart was set on going. He couldn't put his mind on trapping any more. He had done so well already. So finally Seth agreed to come over and help him pack his furs and traps. They had a big feed on about the last of John's grub.

In the morning he set out and the Indian walked with him to the end of his own south line, and shook hands.

"You one damn good boy, John," he said unexpectedly. "You come again next year."

"I will sure," said John. "Thanks for all you've done for me, Seth. Without you I wouldn't have done this." He hitched the heavy pack up on his shoulder. "I guess next the Judge, you're about the best friend I ever had."

The Indian's brown face wrinkled all over beneath his battered hat. He made a big gesture with his hand.

"Oh, sure," he said. "Big country. Nice company. Plenty furs us both."

He held John's hand.

He said, "Now listen to Seth. If creeks open, you cut two logs crossing. You mind Seth. You cut two logs. One log roll. Two logs safe crossing water."

"Yes, sure," said John. He wanted to get away. The sun was well up by now.

"'By," said Seth.

John walked hard. He felt strong that morning. He felt like a grown man. The weight of the pack, galling his shoulders, was a pleasure to carry.

Every time he eased it one way or another, he thought about what it was going to mean. He thought about coming home and telling his mother. He would buy her a new dress. He would make a purchase of some calico for his sisters. "Make a purchase," he thought, was quite a mouthful. He'd never even thought of it before.

He would see the Judge. He imagined himself walking into the Judge's office and dropping the pack on the floor, and looking the Judge in the eye. He realized that that meant more to him than doing things for his family.

He remembered the way he had started the winter. He had got Seth to estimate the worth of each first pelt. When they had figured up to forty dollars, he had made a bundle of them. They were still packed together in the bottom of the pack. It seemed to him that getting that first forty dollars' worth was twice as much of a job as all the rest for him to have done.

The snow was a little slushy here and there, but it held up well in the big woods and he made pretty good time. Nights, he set himself up a lean-to of cedar and balsam branches, and sitting before his small fire, he would think ahead a few years. He could see himself some day, pretty near like the Judge. He even figured on teaching himself to read and write — write his own name, anyway. No matter how you looked at it, you couldn't make a cross seem like "John Haskell" wrote out in full, with big and little letters in it.

Mornings, he started with the first gray light, when the mist was like a twilight on the water and the deer moused along the runways and eyed him, curious as chipmunks. He walked south down the slopes of the hills across the shadows of the sunrise, when the snow became full of color and the hills ahead wore a bloody purple shadow on their northern faces.

Now and then he heard the first stirring of a small brook under the snow in a sunny place, and he found breath holes under falls wide open.

He had grown taller during the winter, and he seemed even lankier, but his eyes were still the brown, boy's eyes of a year ago.

He crossed the Moose River on the ice about where McKeever now is, just at dusk. He had not made as good time that day. The snow had been a good deal softer and his legs ached and the pack weighed down a bit harder than usual. But though the ice had been treacherous close to shore, he had found a place easily enough.

That night, however, as he lay in his lean-to, he heard the river ice begin to work. It went out in the morning with a grinding roar and built a jam half a mile below his camp.

He saw it with a gay heart as he set out after breakfast. It seemed to him as if it were the most providential [1] thing he ever had heard of. If he had waited another day before starting, he would have found the river open and he would have had to go back to Seth's cabin and wait till the Indian was ready to come out. But as it was, now, he would have only brooks to cross.

There were a good many of them, and most of them were opening. But he found places to cross them, and he had no trouble till afternoon, when he found some running full. They were high with black snow water, some of them so high that he had to go upstream almost a mile to find a place where he could fell a bridge across.

Each time he dropped two logs and went over easily enough. But each time

[1] **providential** (prŏv′ĭ·dĕn′shăl): fortunate; as if guided by God.

the delay chafed him a little more. By late afternoon, when he was only five miles from High Falls and began to recognize his landmarks, he came to what he knew was the last creek.

It was a strong stream, with a great force of water, and it was boiling full. Where John happened on it, it began a slide down the steep bank for the river, with one bend and then a straight chute.[1] But it was narrow there, and beside where he stood grew a straight hemlock long enough to reach across.

Hardly stopping to unload his pack, John set to work with his ax. The tree fell nicely, just above the water. There was no other tree close by, but John thought about that only for a moment. It was the last creek, he was almost home, and his heart was set on getting there that night. Besides, he had had no trouble on the other crossings. He was sure-footed, and in every case he had run across one log.

He gave the tree a kick, but it lay steady, and suddenly he made up his mind to forget what Seth had said. He could get over easy enough and see the Judge that evening.

With his furs on his back, his ax in one hand and his gun in the other, he stepped out on the log. It felt solid as stone under his feet and he went along at a steady pace. The race of water just under the bark meant nothing to John. His head was quite clear and his eyes were on the other side already, and he thought, in his time, he had crossed a lot of logs more rickety than this one.

It was just when he was halfway over that the log rolled without any warning and pitched John into the creek.

The water took hold of him and lugged him straight down and rolled him over and over like a dead pig. He had no chance even to yell. He dropped his gun and ax at the first roll and instinctively tugged at the traps which weighted him so. As he struggled to the top, he felt the fur pack slip off. He made a desperate grab at them, but they went away. When he finally washed up on the bend and crawled out on the snow, he hadn't a thing left but his life.

That seemed worthless to him, lying on the snow. He could not even cry about it.

He lay there for perhaps half an hour while the dusk came in on the river. Finally he got his feet and searched downstream poking with a stick along the bottom. But he was hopeless. The creek ran like a millrace down the slope for the river and the chances were a hundred to one that the traps as well as the furs had been taken by the strength of water and the slide all the way down to the river.

But he continued his search till nearly dark before he gave up.

By the time he reached High Falls, he had managed to get back just enough of his courage to go straight to the Judge. It was very late, but the office light was still burning, and John knocked and went in. He stood on the hearth, shivering and dripping, but fairly erect, and told the Judge exactly what had happened, even to Seth's parting admonition, in a flat, low voice.

The Judge said never a word till the boy was done. He merely sat studying him from under his bushy white brows. Then he got up and fetched him a glass of whisky.

Though the drink seemed to bring back a little life, it only made John more miserable. He waited like a wavering ghost for the Judge to have his say.

But the Judge only said in his heavy voice, "You'd better go on home. You'd

[1] **chute** (shōōt): a sharp downward descent.

better start hunting work tomorrow." His voice became gruffer: "Everybody has to learn things. It's been bad luck for us both that you had to learn it like this."

John went home. All he could remember was that the Judge had said it was bad luck for them both. It seemed to him that that was a very kind thing for the Judge to say.

John did not see anything of the Judge that summer. He worked hard, planting corn and potatoes and the garden, and later he managed to find work. He seemed to get work more easily that summer. But his family seemed to need more money. Now and then people visited a little, and that meant extra money for food and tea. By working hard, though, John found himself in the fall about where he had been on the preceding year.

He had put in a bid with the tannery for winter work and had had the job promised to him. Two days before he would have started, however, the Judge sent word for him to come to the big house.

The Judge made him sit down.

"John," he said, "you've kept your courage up when it must have been mighty hard. I've been thinking about you and me. I think the best thing for us both, the best way I can get my money back, is to give you another stake, if you're willing to go."

John felt that he was much nearer crying than he had been when he lost his furs. He hardly found the voice to say that he would go.

Seth, for no good reason, had decided to move west in the state, so John had to go into the woods alone. But he had good luck that winter, better even than he had had the year before. He stayed right through to the end of the season, and his pack was so heavy he had to leave his traps behind.

The river was open when he reached it, so he had to ferry himself over on a raft. It took a day to build. And from that point on he took plenty of time when he came to the creeks, and dropped two logs over them, and made a trial trip over and back without his fur pack. It took him three extra days coming out, but he brought his furs with him.

The Judge saw to it that he got good prices; and when the dealer was done with the buying, John was able to pay the Judge for both stakes and for the forty dollars as well. The year after that he made a clear profit.

John did well in the world. He found time to learn to read and write and handle figures. From time to time he visited the Judge, and he found that the Judge was not a person anyone needed to be afraid of. When the Judge died in John's thirtieth year, John was owner of Freel's tannery and one of the leading men of High Falls.

It is a simple story, this of John Haskell's, but it is not quite done. When the Judge died and the will was read, it was found that he had left to John Haskell the big house and a share of his money. There was also a sealed letter for John.

That night in his house, John opened the letter. It was dated the same day as the one on which John had received the money for his first pack of furs. It was just a few lines long and it contained forty dollars in bills.

Dear John: Here is the forty dollars, and I am making you a confession with it. I liked your looks when you came to me that first time. I thought you had stuff in you. It was a dirty thing to do, in a way, but I wanted to make sure of you. I never liked your father and I would never lend him a cent. I invented that debt. Good luck, John.

Finding the Theme

1. What would you say is the theme or the main idea of this story? Is there more than one?

2. John Haskell's education began at the point when he hung up his fishing pole and went out to look at the corn patch. What event followed that opened up an entirely new way of thinking for him?

3. The Judge was the chief factor in John's education. In what way did he attempt to train the boy? Can you defend the Judge's teaching methods? Why were they effective? Why do you think John never resented his apparent harshness?

4. What did Seth the Indian teach the boy besides trapping lore?

5. When did John first begin to think of school and book education? Why did he begin to feel the lack of it? What do you consider to be the most valuable lesson John learned?

Thinking It Over

1. Since this story is about John Haskell, why do you think it is called " Judge "? From the Judge's letter to John, what do you think he had feared would happen to the boy? Did you notice anything in the story to suggest that other people felt the same way? Did your opinion of the Judge change after you read the letter? in what way?

2. What do you think of John's decision to pay the forty dollars? What is a debt of honor? Do you know of any instances in which a person has unknowingly contracted a debt for a dishonest or disabled friend or relative, and has paid it in full, even at considerable sacrifice? Is such a person acting foolishly? Discuss this question.

3. Did you notice the relationship between John and his mother? Why did she cry when he handed her the receipt? What did John do for his family besides providing food and shelter?

4. Do you think people nowadays are careless about small debts? Discuss whether it is fair to buy things for your enjoyment, such as a television set, at a time when you owe money, say, to doctors or dentists (who are so often the last to be paid).

SAMUEL SCOVILLE, JR.

The Reef

A perfect jack-knife dive is a beautiful thing to watch. To the diver, it is beauty, too – the sharp snap from the springboard, the feeling of power and well-being as his body cuts through the air and slips into the cool depths of lake or pool, and as he emerges breathless but triumphant, ready for another try. It's a different matter, however, if you are diving into the shark-infested waters of the Caribbean Sea,[1] where danger lurks behind every coral reef, and a split second means the difference between life and death. Jimmy Tom was a sponge diver. When you read of his courage and self-control in a hair-raising adventure (it will be your hair – Jimmy's was too wet) you will realize why his ancestors, the Carib Indians, once were mighty rulers.

Moon-green and amber, a strip of fading sky glowed across the trail of the vanished sun. Far below, the opal sea paled to mother-of-pearl. Then, over sea and sky, strode the sudden dark of the tropics and in an instant the southern stars flamed and flared through the violet night. A long, tense moment, with sea and sky waiting, and a rim of raw gold thrust itself above the horizon as the full moon of midsummer climbed toward the zenith. Rising, its light made a broad causeway across the sea clear to the dark reef which lurked in the shimmering water.

Suddenly, inked black against the moonpath, showed the lean shape of a canoe. All the way from Carib Island, a day and a night away, Jim Tom, who in his day had been a famous sponge diver, had brought his grandson Jimmy Tom for a first visit to the reef. Both had the cinnamon-red skins of the Red Caribs, who once had ruled mightily the whole Caribbean. Jim Tom's hair was cut to an even edge all the way around his neck; his small, deep-set eyes were like glittering crumbs of black glass, and ever since a day when he dived below the twenty-five-fathom mark both of his legs had been paralyzed.

Swiftly the little craft neared the reef, and only the plash of the paddles broke the stillness. Then in an instant the molten gold of the water was shattered by a figure like a vast bat, with black wings which measured all of thirty feet from tip to tip, a spiked tail, and long antennæ streaming out beyond a huge, hooked mouth. Like a vampire from the pit,[2] it rose into the air, blotting out the moon with its monstrous bulk, and then dropped back with a crash, raising a wave which nearly swamped the canoe. As it disappeared beneath the water, Jimmy Tom turned and looked questioningly at the old man. The latter laughed silently.

"Only a manta ray,"[3] he said at last. "They like to fly around in the moonlight and frighten untried young men," he added slyly.

For answer his grandson stretched out his paddle at full length. It showed in the air rigid and motionless as an iron bar. The old man grunted approvingly.

"You may tremble yet before you are through with the reef," was all that he said, however, as he steered toward the circle of coral which separated the lagoon from the ocean, which beat against the barrier in a crashing surf. Waiting until several of the great rollers had passed, the paddlers caught the crest of a huge wave and in an instant were swept ten feet in air toward the patch of beach which showed beyond the little lagoon. Just as the wave broke, the canoe tilted and rushed down its long slope like a toboggan, clearing the rim of sharp coral and leaping into the still lagoon beyond.

[1] **Caribbean** (kăr′ĭ·bē′ăn) **Sea:** the part of the Atlantic Ocean between the West Indies and Central and South America.

[2] **a vampire from the pit:** a ghost from hell.

[3] **manta ray:** often called a devilfish.

All the rest of that glorious night, as the moon went westering down the sky, the two slept on the rose-red, honey-brown sand, until, without any dawn, the sun suddenly rose above a heliotrope [1] horizon. Then they breakfasted, and Jim Tom became quite talkative — for a Carib.

"We must not waste a moment of this day," he said. "Perhaps before night we may make the hundred of dollars you need for that sloop about which you have been bothering me so long. In my day," he went on severely, "boys were glad enough to have a good canoe."

Jimmy Tom grunted.

"Whoever heard," he said at last, "of making a hundred of dollars in one day?"

"It has been done — and here," returned his grandfather, positively; "but it takes good lungs and — a brave heart."

As they talked, the canoe reached a point where the reef sloped away in a series of terraces to unfathomable depths. There they stopped paddling and stared down through the water which lay before them like a thick sheet of plate glass. The great ledge over which they floated was dotted with thickets of colored corals and purple and gold sea fans,[2] among which schools of brilliant fish sped and lazed and drifted like birds in the air. Molten-silver tarpon shot through shoals of chubby cow pilots, all green and gold and indigo, while turquoise-blue parrot fish raced here and there, and crimson cardinal fish crept in and out of crevices in the rocks. There were angelfish in gorgeous robes of emerald and scarlet, and jet-black butterfly fish with golden fins, orange bills, and vivid blue mouths, while warty purple sea cucumbers showed among clumps of yellow sea anemones.[3]

"This is the treasure ledge of the reef," said Jim Tom, suddenly. "Here too," he went on, "death hides and waits," and he paused for a moment.

Jimmy's answer was to slip out of his unbleached cotton shirt and trousers and stand poised like a red-bronze statue of speed with the long, flat muscles rippling over his lithe body and graceful limbs.

"It was here that your father died," said Jim Tom again. "I was lying watching him search among the sponges," he went on after a pause, "when before my very eyes he was gone. My only son," he went on, his voice rising as he harked back over forgotten years, "in the jaws of one of those accursed sculpins [4] of the deep water, a *tonu* [4] ten feet long."

"And then," asked Jimmy Tom, very softly, as the old man stopped.

"And then," went on the old man, fiercely, "everything went red around me. I gripped my spike and dove and swam, as I never swam before, down to that lurking, ugly demon. In a second I was on him and stabbed him with all my might — once, twice, three times — until, dying, he went off the ledge into the depths below and I followed him beyond, to where no man may dare to swim. There he died. As his hateful mouth gaped, I dragged out your father by the arm and brought him back to the top; but when I climbed with him into the canoe he was dead, and I was as you see me now — dead too from the waist

[1] **heliotrope** (hē′lĭ·ō·trōp): a pale reddish-purple color.

[2] **sea fans:** sea animals without backbones, like coral and jellyfish.

[3] **sea anemones** (ȧ·nĕm′ō·nēz): spineless sea animals.

[4] **sculpins** (skŭl′pĭnz); **tonu** (tō′nōō), words used loosely to describe large, ugly, dangerous fish.

The islands and waters of the Caribbean hold many treasures — moldering pirate hoards, doubloons from long-foundered galleons, and, best of all, the natural wealth of the sea — shells, sponges, corals. (Gendreau)

down. All the rest of that day and all the night beyond and the next day I paddled and paddled until we came home — my dead son and I. No, no," went on the old man, "let us try the safer side of the reef."

For answer, Jimmy Tom quickly fastened in place the outriggers on either side of the canoe, which made it firm and safe to dive from. Around his neck he slipped the "toa,"[1] the wide-mouthed bag with a drawstring into which a sponge diver thrusts his findings. Around his neck, too, he hung the spike, a double-pointed stick two feet long of black palmwood, hard and heavy as iron. Then, standing on the bow seat, he filled his great lungs again and again until every air cell was opened. The old man looked at him proudly.

"You are of my blood," he said softly. "Go with God. I will watch above you and be your guard. Forget not to look up at me, and, if I signal, come back to me fast — for I cannot go to you," he finished sadly.

The young man gave a brief nod and, filling his lungs until his chest stood out like a square box, dived high into the air with that jack-knife dive which was invented by sponge divers and, striking the water clean as the point of a dropped knife, he shot down toward the beautiful depths below. Into his lithe body rushed and pulsed the power and energy of the great swinging sea as he swam through the air-clear water to-

[1] **toa** (tō'ä).

ward a thicket of gorgonias,[1] which waved against the white sand like a bed of poppies. In thirty seconds he was twenty fathoms down, where the pressure of seventy pounds to the square inch would have numbed and crippled an ordinary swimmer, but meant nothing to his steel-strong body, hardened to the depths by years of deep diving. Even as he reached the gleaming thicket he saw, with a great throb of delight, a soft, golden-brown tuft of silk sponge hidden beneath the living branches. The silk sponge is to spongers in the sea what the silver fox is to trappers on the land, and the whole year's output from all seas is only a few score.

With a quick stroke, Jimmy Tom reached the many-colored sea shrub. The moving branches had to be parted carefully with the spike, lest they close and hide, beyond finding, the silky clump growing within their depths. Even as the boy started to slip over his head the cord from which swung the pointed stick, he looked up to see Jim Tom beckoning frantically for him to return. Yet nowhere in the nearby water could he see anything unusual, except a little fish some eight inches long marked with alternate bands of blue and gold, which came close to him and then turned and swam out to sea. Still his grandfather beckoned, his face contorted with earnestness.

The boy hesitated. An arm's length away lay a fortune. It might well be that never again could he find that exact spot if he went back to the surface now. All this passed through his mind in the same second in which he suddenly plunged his bare arm into the center of the gorgonia clump without waiting to use the spike, as all cautious sponge divers do. Following the clue of the waving silken end, he grasped a soft mass. Even as he pulled out a silk sponge, worth more than its weight in gold, something sharp as steel and brittle as ice pierced his hand deep, and he felt a score of spines break and rankle in his flesh like splinters of broken glass. By an ill chance he had thrust his hand against one of those chestnut burs of the ocean, a purple-black sea urchin, whose villainous spines, like those of a porcupine, pierce deep and break off. Setting his teeth against the pain, the boy shifted the silky clump of sponge to his other hand and swam for the canoe with all his might. As he rose he saw his grandfather mouthing the word "Hurry!" every line on his tense face set in an agony of pleading.

Even as the boy shot toward the surface, he caught sight once again of the same brilliant little fish returning from deep water. Close behind it, dim at first, but growing more and more distinct as it came, showed a sinister shape, slate-gray, with yellow-brown stripes, the dreaded tiger shark of deep water, convoyed by that little jackal of the sea, the pilot fish. It was fortunate for Jimmy Tom that the tiger shark is not among the swiftest of its family and that he was halfway to the surface before the cold deadly eyes of that one caught sight of his ascending body. With a rush like a torpedo boat, the thirty-foot shark shot toward the straining, speeding figure, and reached it just as, with a last desperate effort, Jimmy Tom broke water by the canoe. Only the fact that a shark has to be on its back to bring into play effectively its seven rows of triangular, saw-edged teeth saved the boy's life. The tiny tick of time which the fish took in turning enabled the old man, with a tremendous heave of his powerful arms, to drag Jimmy Tom bodily over the gun-

[1] **gorgonia** (gôr·gō′nĭ·*ȧ*): a kind of coral.

wale [1] just as the fatal jaws snapped shut below him.

For a long minute the sea tiger circled the canoe with hungry speed. Then, seeing that his prey had escaped, he swam away, guided, as always, by the strange pilot fish, which feeds on the scraps of the feasts which it finds for its companion.

As the shark turned toward deep water, Jimmy Tom sat up from where he had been lying at the bottom of the canoe and grinned cheerfully after his disappearing foe. Then, without a word, he handed Jim Tom the clump of sponge which, throughout his almost dead heat with death, he had held clutched tightly in his left hand. With the same motion, he stretched out his other hand, filled like a pincushion with keen, glassy spines from the sea urchin.

"Not twice in a long lifetime," said his grandfather, "have I seen a finer silk sponge. Already that sloop is half paid for."

Without further words, he drew from his belt a sharp-pointed knife and began the painful process of removing one by one the embedded spines from the boy's right hand before they should begin to fester. He finished this bit of rough-and-ready surgery by washing out each deep puncture with stinging salt water. When he had entirely finished, Jimmy Tom carefully tucked away the sponge in a pocket fastened to the inside of the canoe and, slipping the wide-mouthed bag again over his neck, stood on the thwart [2] ready for another dive.

"Try to remember with your thick head," said his grandfather, severely, "all that I have told you, and if I signal you to come back, you come."

The boy nodded briefly, took several deep breaths, and again shot down through the water, directing his course toward another part of the reef, where the white sand was dotted with shells, all hyaline [3] or clouded with exquisite colors. As he reached the bottom, the boy's swift, supple fingers searched among crystal-white, purple and rose and gold olivellas, dosinias, and tellinas [4] which, in spite of their beauty, had no special value. Just as he was about to return to the surface empty-handed, his eye caught the gleam of several spires of the rare, sky-white coral showing among the waving waterweed. A hasty look aloft showed no sign of danger from his sentinel, and he still had nearly three minutes before water would exact her toll of oxygen from him. A swift stroke brought him to the edge of the weed bed. Just as he was about to reach for the coral, his trained eye caught sight of a gleaming white, beautifully shaped shell nearly as large as the palm of his hand. With a quick motion, he reached under the wavering leaves and, even as his fingers closed on its corrugated surface, realized that he had found at last a perfect specimen of the royal wentletrap, among the rarest and most beautiful of shells.

In the collections of the world, there are perhaps not six perfect specimens, and sponge divers and shell gatherers along a thousand lonely coasts are ever on the lookout for this treasure of the sea. The pure white rounded whorls [5] of this one were set off with wide, frilled varices,[6] each ending in a point above, the whole forming a perfect crown of snow and crystal indescribably airy and

[1] **gunwale** (gŭn′ĕl): the edge of the boat above the water line.
[2] **thwart** (thôrt): a rower's seat.
[3] **hyaline** (hī′*ȧ*·lĭn): transparent.
[4] **olivellas** (ŏl′ĭ·vĕl′*ȧ*z), **dosinias** (dȯ·sĭn′ĭ·*ȧ*z), **tellinas** (tĕ·lī′n*ȧ*z): all shellfish.
[5] **whorls** (hwûrlz): curves or coils.
[6] **varices** (vâr′ĭ·sēz): uneven, twisted curves.

beautiful. The sight and feeling of this treasure put every thought out of Jimmy Tom's mind save to reach the surface with it as soon as possible. The coral could wait. For that shell any one of the collectors who called at Carib Island would gladly pay him twice the hundred dollars he needed.

Suddenly, even as he turned toward the surface, from a deep crevice in the coral close to his side, shot a fierce and hideous head, like that of some monstrous snake, ridged with a fin which showed like a crest. Before the boy could move, two long jaws filled with curved teeth snapped shut on his right hand and wrist, and he realized with a dreadful pang of fear and pain that he had been gripped by one of the great conger eels which lurk in the crevices of the reef. Eight feet in length and as large around as a man's leg, they are among the most fearsome of all the sea folk which a diver must brave. For a second, Jimmy Tom tugged with all his strength, but with no result except that the greenish-gray body retreated deeper into its cave. Then it was that he remembered what his grandfather had told him was the only way to escape from the deadly jaws of a conger eel. Relaxing every muscle, he allowed his hand to lie limp in the great fish's teeth. Sooner or later, if he kept quiet, the monster would open its jaws for a better grip.

As the cold, deadly eyes stared implacably into his, the beating of his laboring heart sounded in his ears like a drum of doom. If so be that the fierce fish did not relax his grip within the next thirty seconds, the boy knew that his life would go out of him in a long stream of silvery air bubbles. By a tremendous effort of will he strove against the almost irresistible impulse to do something, to pull, to struggle, to slash with his knife at the horrid head. Yet, clinching his teeth grimly, he set himself to that hardest of all tasks — to wait and wait. His eyes, hot and dim with suffused blood, fell on the crowned shell which he held in his free hand, that shell which was to win for him the sloop, and suddenly through the luminous, gleaming water he seemed to see his cabin on faraway Carib Island and his mother's face looking into his.

As the vision faded he felt a slight shifting and loosening of the grim jaws. With a last effort of his will, dimming before the flood of unconsciousness creeping up to his brain, he allowed his body to float limp, and relaxed every straining muscle. Even as he did so, the great jaws gaped apart for an instant and the fierce head thrust itself toward him for a fresh grip. Fighting back the waves of blackness which swept across his eyes, by a quick turn and wrench he freed his imprisoned hand and, with a tremendous scissors kick of his powerful legs, shot away just as the curved teeth struck, empty, together.

Up and up and up he sped, swimming as he had never swum before, yet seeming to himself, under the desperate urge of his tortured lungs, to move slow as the hour hand of a clock. The sunlit surface seemed to move away and away and recede to an immeasurable distance. Just as he felt despairingly that he could no longer resist the uncontrollable desire of his anguished lungs to act, even if they drew in the waters of death, his head shot above the surface. There was a sudden roaring in his ears as the strong arms of Jim Tom pulled him into the canoe. Too weak to speak or move, he lay experiencing the utter happiness there is in breathing, which only the half-drowned may know.

All the rest of that day the boy lay in the shade of the towering coral wall, while old Jim Tom dressed his gashed and pierced hand. As the calm weather still held, the old man decided to spend the night in the canoe just outside the sheer wall of the reef, where the water stretched away to unknown depths. Toward evening the boy's strength came back; and after eating and drinking ravenously, he showed but little effect of the strain to which he had been subjected.

"When the moon rises," said his grandfather at length, "we will start for home."

The boy shook his head obstinately.

"Tomorrow, as soon as it is light," he said, "I dive again to bring up such white coral as has not been seen on Carib Island in my day."

"In your day!" exclaimed old Jim Tom much incensed.[1] "In your minute — for that is all you have lived. Never has any man made a better haul than you. Be satisfied. The reef is not fortunate for the greedy."

"My silk sponge was won from the jaws of a shark and my shell from the conger eel," returned the boy, doggedly. "I ask no favors of the reef."

The old man glanced around apprehensively, while the water seemed to chuckle as it lapped against the coral.

"It is not lucky to talk that way," he said softly. "Sleep now," he went on after a pause. "When morning comes, perhaps there will be a better spirit in you and we will go home."

A little later, while the great moon climbed the sky and the golden sea stretched away unbroken, the two slept. Hours later, Jim Tom awoke with a start. Through his sleep had penetrated the sharp sinister scent of musk, and, even before he opened his eyes, he felt some hostile living presence near him. As he raised his head above the side of the canoe, the still surface of the sea beyond was all a-writhe with what seemed a mass of sea snakes. Suddenly from out of the livid tangle shot toward the boat two thirty-foot tentacles larger around than a man's body, tapering to a point and covered with round, sucking discs armed with claws of black horn, sharp and curved as those of a tiger. The great white squid, the devilfish of unknown depths, which hardly once or twice in a generation comes to the surface, was before him.

For a moment the old man stared in horror at the twisting, fatal tentacles. Then, with a hoarse cry, he roused Jimmy Tom, who started up, grasping the keen machete[2] which always lay in a sheath at the bottom of the canoe. Even as he unsheathed the curved blade, one of the vast, pale streamers reached the canoe, flowed over its side, and licked around the waist of the old man. On the instant, red stains showed through his thin shirt where the armed discs sank deep into his flesh as the horrid arm dragged his helpless body toward the water. Just in time, the boy swung the machete over his head and severed the clutching streamer, and then, with a return stroke, cut through another that licked out toward him across the boat.

As he turned the old man stretched his arm out toward the sea with a gasp of horror. Up through the water came a vast cylindrical shape of livid flesh, many times the size of the canoe, from which long tentacles radiated like a wheel. In the middle of the shapeless mass was set a head of horror, with a

[1] **incensed** (ĭn·sĕnst'): vexed or irritated.

[2] **machete** (mä·chā'tâ): a large, heavy knife.

vast parrotlike beak which gnashed over a mouth like a cavern. On either side of the demon jaws glared two lidless eyes, each larger than a barrel, rimmed around with white. Of an inky, unfathomable black, they stared at the boat with a malignancy which no earthborn creature could equal or endure. Unable to sustain their appalling glare, both of the Caribs thrust their arms before their faces, expecting every second to feel the deadly touch of the armed tentacles.

It was the boy who recovered himself first. Setting his teeth grimly, he suddenly raised his head to face again this demon of the lowest depths. At his exclamation of surprise, the old man forced himself to look up. The water stretched before them empty and unbroken. Only the scent of musk and grisly [1] fragments of the death-pale tentacles in the bottom of the canoe were there to prove that the monster had not been a ghastly dream of the night. Without a word, Jimmy Tom shipped the outriggers [2] and, gripping his paddle, took his place in the bow. All the rest of that night and far into the next day they paddled, until at last Carib Island loomed up on the horizon.

From the sale of the wentletrap and the silk sponge Jimmy Tom bought not only his sloop and a new canoe for Jim Tom, but still had the hundred of dollars which makes a man rich on Carib Island. Yet in spite of the fortune he brought back from the reef, he has never returned to it again. When urged by friends or collectors, he only shakes his head and says oracularly,[3] "Enough is plenty."

[1] **grisly** (grĭz′lĭ): horrible.
[2] **shipped the outriggers:** took in the temporary supports used to balance the boat.
[3] **oracularly** (ô·răk′ū·lẽr·lĭ): solemnly.

Keeping the Setting in Mind

1. Nearly everything that Jimmy Tom does in his quest for the sponges shows skill and endurance that would be noteworthy in any ordinary walk of life, let alone in the setting of this story. What is the geographical setting of the story? In what specific kind of ocean area does the action take place?

2. Point out examples of quick-wittedness, promptness in decision, and courage under pain which are the more remarkable because of the setting. What makes the behavior of Jimmy Tom's *mind* so outstanding? What do you know about the behavior of the human body at low depths under water?

3. How do Jimmy Tom and his grandfather work together in the sea work? What things make the work so dangerous?

4. By what details does the author convey the sense of lurking danger in this setting? Skim through the story to find the descriptions that build up this impression.

Thinking It Over

1. Many stories are concerned with some kind of conflict, some struggle which creates excitement and suspense for the reader. In this story, is the conflict between man and self, between an individual and a group, between man and man, or between man and nature? Is there more than one conflict? What are some of the factors that aided Jimmy Tom in his struggle?

2. What part of the story did you find the most exciting? When did Jimmy Tom show the greatest self-control?

3. No doubt you learned something new about the art of diving or about under-sea life. If the subject interests you, read some of Edward Ellsberg's books which are listed on page 465.

For Your Vocabulary

BUILDING WORD PICTURES: This story is full of word pictures that are poetic, though written in prose. Here, for example, is an arrangement in free verse (unrhymed lines, usually of uneven length) of the first three sentences, with very little change:

" Moon-green
and amber,
A strip of fading sky
Glowed
Across the trail of the vanished sun.
Far
far
below,
The opal sea paled to mother-of-pearl.
Then over sea and sky
Strode the sudden dark of the tropics
And the southern stars
Flamed and flared through the violet night."

Find other vividly worded sentences and read them to the class. Then put them into a free verse arrangement of your own. (Don't end lines with weak words like *and, the,* or *of.* Try to make lines of different lengths.)

Make a free verse poem of your own about the night or the day, a lake, a forest, a mountain, or a plain. Use the most colorful words at your command and don't forget that figures of speech will help you to create word pictures. Roughly, that means using common words in uncommon ways.

GROWING UP

DOROTHY CANFIELD

The Apprentice

Growing up is not an easy process. Have you ever felt that your parents are unjust, that everything is going wrong, that nobody in the world understands you? You may even feel at such times that it would help to pound something hard with your doubled-up fists just to relieve your feelings. What do you do when you get into such a state of mind? Where do you go when it seems to be you against the world? The girl in the following story had a dog. Rollie was her safety valve. On Rollie she concentrated all the pent-up emotions of her heart — but like anything else that we love too much, Rollie was the source of almost paralyzing fear for Peg. You are going to spend an hour with Peg and Rollie and you will see Peg grow up in one frightening and releasing moment.

For Better Reading . . . Outwardly, this is a story of simple and uncomplicated events. It is, in a sense, the record of a young girl's feelings during one hour — and in the changes of her moods you will find plenty of conflict and much excitement. Try to determine the points at which her mood changes, at which she begins to think and act differently.

The day had been one of the unbearable ones, when every sound had set her teeth on edge like chalk creaking on a blackboard, when every word her father or mother said to her or did not say to her seemed an intentional injustice. And of course it would happen, as the fitting end to such a day, that just as the sun went down back of the mountain and the long twilight began, she noticed that Rollie was not around.

Tense with exasperation at what her mother would say, she began to call him in a carefully casual tone – she would simply explode if Mother got going: "Here Rollie! He-ere boy! Want to go for a walk, Rollie?" Whistling to him cheerfully, her heart full of wrath at the way the world treated her, she made the rounds of his haunts: the corner of the woodshed, where he liked to curl up on the wool of Father's discarded old sweater; the hay barn, the cow barn, the sunny spot on the side porch. No Rollie.

Perhaps he had sneaked upstairs to lie on her bed, where he was not supposed to go – not that *she* would have minded! That rule was a part of Mother's fussiness, part, too, of Mother's bossiness. It was *her* bed, wasn't it? But was she allowed the say-so about it? Not on your life. They *said* she could have things the way she wanted in her own room, now she was in her teens, but — Her heart burned at unfairness as she took the stairs stormily, two steps at a time, her pigtails flopping up and down on her back. If Rollie was there, she was just going to let him stay there, and Mother could say what she wanted to.

But he was not there. The bedspread and pillow were crumpled, but that was where she had flung herself down to cry that afternoon. Every nerve in her had been twanging discordantly, but she couldn't cry. She could only lie there, her hands doubled up hard, furious that she had nothing to cry about. Not really. She was too big to cry just over Father's having said to her, severely, "I told you if I let you take the chess set, you were to put it away when you got through with it. One of the pawns was on the floor of our bedroom this morning. I stepped on it. If I'd had my shoes on I'd have broken it."

Well, he *had* told her that. And he hadn't said she mustn't ever take the set again. No, the instant she thought about that, she knew she couldn't cry about it. She could be, and was, in a rage about the way Father kept on talking long after she'd got his point: "It's not that I care so much about the chess set. It's because if you don't learn how to take care of things, you yourself will suffer for it. You'll forget or neglect something that will be really important for *you.* We *have* to try to teach you to be responsible for what you've said you'll take care of. If we – " on and on.

She stood there, dry-eyed, by the bed that Rollie had not crumpled and thought, *I hope Mother sees the spread and says something about Rollie – I just hope she does.*

She heard her mother coming down the hall, and hastily shut her door. She had a right to shut the door to her own room, hadn't she? She had *some* rights, she supposed, even if she was only thirteen and the youngest child. If her mother opened it to say, "What are you doing in here that you don't want me to see?" she'd say – she'd just say –

But her mother did not open the door. Her feet went steadily on along the hall, and then, carefully, slowly, down the stairs. She probably had an armful of winter things she was bringing down from the attic. She was probably thinking that a tall, thirteen-year-old daughter was big enough to help with a chore like that. But she wouldn't *say* anything. She would just get out that insulting look of a grownup silently putting up with a crazy, unreasonable kid. She had worn that expression all day; it was too much to be endured.

Up in her bedroom behind her closed door the thirteen-year-old stamped her foot in a gust of uncontrollable rage, none the less savage and heartshaking because it was mysterious to her.

But she had not located Rollie. She would be cut into little pieces before she would let her father and mother know she had lost sight of him, forgotten about him. They would not scold her, she knew. They would do worse; they would look at her. And in their silence she would hear, droning on reproachfully, what they had said when she had been begging to keep for her own the sweet, woolly collie puppy in her arms.

How warm he had felt! Astonishing how warm and alive a puppy was compared with a doll! She had never liked her dolls much after she had held Rollie, feeling him warm against her breast, warm and wriggling, bursting with life, reaching up to lick her face. He had loved her from that first instant. As he felt her arms around him, his liquid, beautiful eyes had melted in trusting sweetness. And they did now, whenever he looked at her. Her dog was the only creature in the world who *really* loved her, she thought passionately.

And back then, at the very minute when, as a darling baby dog, he was beginning to love her, her father and mother were saying, so cold, so reasonable – gosh, how she *hated* reasonableness! – "Now, Peg, remember that, living where we do, with sheep on the farms around us, it is a serious responsibility to have a collie dog. If you keep him, you've got to be the one to take care of him. You'll have to be the one to train him to stay at home. We're too busy with you children to start bringing up a puppy too."

Rollie, nestling in her arms, let one hind leg drop awkwardly. It must be uncomfortable. She looked down at him tenderly, tucked his leg up under him and gave him a hug. He laughed up in her face – he really did laugh, his mouth stretched wide in a cheerful grin. Now he was snug in a warm little ball.

Her parents were saying, "If you want him, you can have him. But you must be responsible for him. If he gets to running sheep, he'll just have to be shot, you know that."

They had not said, aloud, "Like the Wilsons' collie." They never mentioned that awfulness – her racing unsuspectingly down across the fields just at the horrible moment when Mr. Wilson shot his collie, caught in the very act of killing sheep. They probably thought that if they never spoke about it, she would forget it – *forget* the crack of that rifle, and the collapse of the great beautiful dog! Forget the red, red blood spurting from the hole in his head. She hadn't forgotten. She never would. She knew as well as they did how important it was to train a collie puppy about sheep. They didn't have to rub it in like that. They always rubbed everything in. She had told them, fervently, indignantly, that of *course* she would take care of him, be responsible for him, teach him to stay at home. Of course. Of course. *She* understood!

And now, when he was six months old, tall, rangy, powerful, standing up far above her knee, nearly to her waist, she didn't know where he was. But of course he must be somewhere around. He always was. She composed her face to look natural and went downstairs to search the house. He was probably asleep somewhere. She looked every room over carefully. Her mother was nowhere visible. It was safe to call him again, to give the special piercing whistle which always brought him racing to her, the white-feathered plume of his tail waving in elation that she wanted him.

But he did not answer. She stood still on the front porch to think.

Could he have gone up to their special place in the edge of the field where the three young pines, their branches growing close to the ground, made a triangular, walled-in space, completely hidden from the world? Sometimes he went up there with her, and when she lay down on the dried grass to dream he, too, lay down quietly, his head on his paws, his beautiful eyes fixed adoringly on her. He entered into her every mood. If she wanted to be quiet, all right, he did too. It didn't seem as though he would have gone alone there. Still – She loped up the steep slope of the field rather fast, beginning to be anxious.

No, he was not there. She stood irresolutely in the roofless, green-walled triangular hide-out, wondering what to do next.

Then, before she knew what thought had come into her mind, its emotional impact knocked her down. At least her knees crumpled under her. The Wilsons had, last Wednesday, brought their sheep down from the far upper pasture, to the home farm! They were – she herself had seen them on her way to school, and like an idiot had not thought of Rollie – on the river meadow.

She was off like a racer at the crack of the starting pistol, her long, strong legs stretched in great leaps, her pigtails flying. She took the short cut, regardless of the brambles. Their thorn-spiked, wiry stems tore at her flesh, but she did not care. She welcomed the pain. It was something she was doing for Rollie, for her Rollie.

She was in the pine woods now, rushing down the steep, stony path, tripping over roots, half falling, catching herself just in time, not slackening her speed. She burst out on the open knoll above the river meadow, calling wildly, "Rollie, here, Rollie, here, boy! Here! Here!" She tried to whistle, but she was crying too hard to pucker her lips.

There was nobody to see or hear her. Twilight was falling over the bare, grassy knoll. The sunless evening wind slid down the mountain like an invisible river, engulfing her in cold. Her teeth began to chatter. "Here, Rollie, here, boy, here!" She strained her eyes to look down into the meadow to see if the sheep were there. She could not be sure. She stopped calling him as she would a dog, and called out his name despairingly, as if he were her child, "Rollie! Oh, *Rollie,* where are you?"

The tears ran down her cheeks in streams. She sobbed loudly, terribly; she did not try to control herself, since there was no one to hear. "Hou! Hou! Hou!" she sobbed, her face contorted grotesquely. "Oh, Rollie! Rollie! Rollie!" She had wanted something to cry about. Oh, how terribly now she had something to cry about.

She saw him as clearly as if he were there beside her, his muzzle and gaping mouth all smeared with the betraying blood (like the Wilsons' collie). "But he didn't *know* it was wrong!" she screamed like a wild creature. "Nobody *told* him it was wrong. It was my fault.

I should have taken better care of him. I will now. I will!"

But no matter how she screamed, she could not make herself heard. In the cold gathering darkness, she saw him stand, poor, guiltless victim of his ignorance, who should have been protected from his own nature, his beautiful soft eyes looking at her with love, his splendid plumed tail waving gently. "It was my fault. I promised I would bring him up. I should have *made* him stay at home. I was responsible for him. It was my fault."

But she could not make his executioners hear her. The shot rang out. Rollie sank down, his beautiful liquid eyes glazed, the blood spurting from the hole in his head — like the Wilsons' collie. She gave a wild shriek, long, soul-satisfying, frantic. It was the scream at sudden, unendurable tragedy of a mature, full-blooded woman. It drained dry the girl of thirteen. She came to herself. She was standing on the knoll, trembling and quaking with cold, the darkness closing in on her.

Her breath had given out. For once in her life she had wept all the tears there were in her body. Her hands were so stiff with cold she could scarcely close them. How her nose was running! Simply streaming down her upper lip. And she had no handkerchief. She lifted her skirt, fumbled for her slip, stooped, blew her nose on it, wiped her eyes, drew a long quavering breath — and heard something! Far off in the distance, a faint sound, like a dog's muffled bark.

She whirled on her heels and bent her head to listen. The sound did not come from the meadow below the knoll. It came from back of her, from the Wilsons' maple grove higher up. She held her breath. Yes, it came from there. She began to run again, but now she was not sobbing. She was silent, absorbed in her effort to cover ground. If she could only live to get there, to see if it really were Rollie. She ran steadily till she came to the fence, and went over this in a great plunge. Her skirt caught on a nail. She impatiently pulled at it, not hearing or not heeding the long sibilant[1] tear as it came loose. She was in the dusky maple woods, stumbling over the rocks as she ran. As she tore on up the slope she knew it was Rollie's bark.

She stopped short and leaned weakly against a tree, sick with the breathlessness of her straining lungs, sick in the reaction of relief, sick with anger at Rollie, who had been here having a wonderful time while she had been dying, just dying in terror about him.

For she could now not only hear that it was Rollie's bark; she could hear, in the dog language she knew as well as he, what he was saying in those excited yips; that he had run a woodchuck into a hole in the tumbled stone wall, that he almost had him, that the intoxicating wild-animal smell was as close to him — almost — as if he had his jaws on his quarry. Yip! Woof! Yip! Yip!

The wild, joyful quality of the dog talk enraged the girl. She was trembling in exhaustion, in indignation. So that was where he had been, when she was killing herself trying to take care of him. Plenty near enough to hear her calling and whistling to him, if he had paid attention. Just so set on having his foolish good time, he never thought to listen for her call.

She stooped to pick up a stout stick. She would teach him! It was time he had something to make him remember to listen. She started forward.

But she stopped, stood thinking. One of the things to remember about collies

[1] **sibilant** (sĭb′ĭ·lănt): with a hissing sound.

— everybody knew that — was their sensitiveness. A collie who had been beaten was never "right" again. His spirit was broken. "Anything but a broken-spirited collie," the farmers often said. They were no good after that.

She threw down her stick. Anyhow, she thought, he was too young to know, really, that he had done wrong. He was still only a puppy. Like all puppies, he got perfectly crazy over wild-animal smells. Probably he really and truly hadn't heard her calling and whistling.

All the same, all the same — she stared intently into the twilight — he couldn't be let to grow up just as he wanted to. She would have to make him understand that he mustn't go off this way by himself. He must be trained to know how to do what a good dog does — not because *she* wanted him to, but for his own sake.

She walked on now, steady, purposeful, gathering her inner strength together. Olympian [1] in her understanding of the full meaning of the event.

When he heard his own special young god approaching, he turned delightedly and ran to meet her, panting, his tongue hanging out. His eyes shone. He jumped up on her in an ecstasy of welcome and licked her face.

But she pushed him away. Her face and voice were grave. "No, Rollie, *no!*" she said severely. "You're *bad.* You know you're not to go off in the woods without me! You are — a — *bad* — *dog.*"

He was horrified. Stricken into misery. He stood facing her, frozen, the gladness going out of his eyes, the erect waving plume of his tail slowly lowered to slinking, guilty dejection.

"I know you were all wrapped up in that woodchuck. But that's no excuse. You *could* have heard me, calling you, whistling for you, if you'd paid attention," she went on. "You've got to learn, and I've got to teach you."

With a shudder of misery he lay down, his tail stretched out limp on the ground, his head flat on his paws, his ears drooping — ears ringing with doomsday awfulness of the voice he so loved and revered. He must have been utterly wicked. He trembled, and turned his head away from her august [2] look of blame, groveling in remorse for whatever mysterious sin he had committed.

She sat down by him, as miserable as he. "I don't *want* to scold you. But I have to! I have to bring you up right, or you'll get shot, Rollie. You *mustn't* go away from the house without me, do you hear, *never!*"

Catching, with his sharp ears yearning for her approval, a faint overtone of relenting affection in her voice, he lifted his eyes to her, humbly, soft in imploring fondness.

"Oh, Rollie!" she said, stooping low over him. "I *do* love you. I do. But I *have* to bring you up. I'm responsible for you, don't you see?"

He did not see. Hearing sternness, or something else he did not recognize, in the beloved voice, he shut his eyes tight in sorrow, and made a little whimpering lament in his throat.

She had never heard him cry before. It was too much. She sat down by him and drew his head to her, rocking him in her arms, soothing him with inarticulate [3] small murmurs.

He leaped in her arms and wriggled happily as he had when he was a baby; he reached up to lick her face as he had then. But he was no baby now. He was

[1] **Olympian** (ô·lĭm′pĭ·ăn): godlike.

[2] **august** (ô·gŭst′): majestic; impressive.

[3] **inarticulate** (ĭn′är·tĭk′ū·lât): making sounds which do not represent any definite meaning, as words do.

half as big as she, a great, warm, pulsing, living armful of love. She clasped him closely. Her heart was brimming full, but calmed, quiet. The blood flowed in equable gentleness all over her body. She was deliciously warm. Her nose was still running a little. She sniffed and wiped it on her sleeve.

It was almost dark now. " We'll be late to supper, Rollie," she said responsibly. Pushing him gently off, she stood up. " Home, Rollie, home! "

Here was a command he could understand. At once he trotted along the path toward home. His plumed tail, held high, waved cheerfully. His short dog memory had dropped into oblivion the suffering just back of him.

Her human memory was longer. His prancing gait was as carefree as a young child's. Plodding heavily like a serious adult, she trod behind him. Her very shoulders seemed bowed by what she had lived through. She felt, she thought, like an old, old woman of thirty. But it was all right now. She knew she had made an impression on him.

When they came out into the open pasture, Rollie ran back to get her to play with him. He leaped around her in circles, barking in cheerful yawps, jumping up on her, inviting her to run a race with him, to throw him a stick, to come alive.

His high spirits were ridiculous. But infectious. She gave one little leap to match his. Rollie pretended that this was a threat to him, planted his forepaws low, and barked loudly at her, laughing between yips. He was so funny, she thought, when he grinned that way. She laughed back, and gave another mock-threatening leap at him. Radiant that his sky was once more clear, he sprang high on his spring-steel muscles in an explosion of happiness, and bounded in circles around her.

Following him, not noting in the dusk where she was going, she felt the grassy slope drop steeply. Oh, yes, she knew where she was. They had come to the rolling-down hill just back of the house. All the kids rolled down there, even the little ones, because it was soft grass without a stone. She had rolled down that slope a million times — years and years ago, when she was a kid herself. It was fun. She remembered well the whirling dizziness of the descent, all the world turning over and over crazily. And the delicious giddy staggering when you first stood up, the earth still spinning under your feet.

" All right, Rollie, let's go," she cried, and flung herself down in the rolling position, her arms straight up over her head.

Rollie had never seen this skylarking before. It threw him into almost hysterical amusement. He capered around the rapidly rolling figure, half scared, mystified, enchanted.

His wild frolicsome barking might have come from her own throat, so accurately did it sound the way she felt — crazy, foolish, like a little kid, no more than five years old, the age she had been when she had last rolled down that hill.

At the bottom she sprang up, on muscles as steel-strong as Rollie's. She staggered a little, and laughed aloud.

The living-room windows were just before them. How yellow lighted windows looked when you were in the darkness going home. How nice and yellow. Maybe Mother had waffles for supper. She was a swell cook, Mother was, and she certainly gave her family all the breaks, when it came to meals.

" Home, Rollie, home! " She burst open the door to the living room. " Hi, Mom, what you got for supper? "

From the kitchen her mother announced coolly, "I hate to break the news to you, but it's waffles."

"Oh, *Mom!*" she shouted in ecstasy.

Her mother could not see her. She did not need to. "For goodness sakes, go and wash," she called.

In the long mirror across the room she saw herself, her hair hanging wild, her long bare legs scratched, her broadly smiling face dirt-streaked, her torn skirt dangling, her dog laughing up at her. Gosh, was it a relief to feel your own age, just exactly thirteen years old!

Sensing Change of Mood

The main character's mood, as you first come upon her, is one of dissatisfaction, even bitterness. What developments and changes in mood occur at the following points in the story:

1. When she thinks her father talked on and on after making his point?
2. When she hears her mother in the hallway carrying winter clothes?
3. When she cannot find Rollie around the buildings as usual?
4. When she remembers that the Wilsons' dog was shot for killing sheep?
5. When she first remembers that the Wilsons' sheep have been brought to the home farm?
6. When she imagines that Rollie has attacked the Wilsons' sheep?
7. Immediately after she imagines that Rollie has been shot?
8. When she recognizes Rollie's bark?
9. When she realizes that Rollie has been ignoring her orders?
10. When she remembers the farmers' saying about collies?
11. When Rollie cries?

Thinking It Over

1. What likeness did you discover in the relationship between Rollie and Peg and between Peg and her parents? How are Peg and Rollie alike? Read aloud that high point of the story, the climax, when Peg herself discovers the likeness.
2. In what way does Peg's attitude toward her parents change as a result of her experience? How do you know that the sudden flash of understanding is not going to change Peg's behavior *outwardly* very much?
3. What does the title mean? Do you think that, in training her dog, Peg may train herself too?
4. At one point Peg feels like "an old, old woman of thirty." Then, as she rolls down the hill, she thinks she is acting like a five-year-old. At the very end what does she think about her age? In what way did the roll down the hill make Peg regain her sense of proportion?
5. What do you know about the training of dogs? This is a good topic for discussion and exchange of experiences, as well as for exploration in the library.
6. Dorothy Canfield is perhaps the most understanding of important contemporary writers about young people. Be sure to read others of her stories, such as *Understood Betsy, The Home Maker,* and *The Bent Twig.*

For Your Vocabulary

CONTEXT: There are several places in this story where context gives you the meaning of words whose dictionary definition you may not know. From the context can you define these words which describe the feelings of Peg and her dog: *ecstasy* of welcome (p. 47); guilty *dejection* (p. 47); whimpering *lament* (p. 47); stood *irresolutely* (p. 45); voice he . . . *revered* (p. 47)?

MARGARET
WEYMOUTH JACKSON

The Hero

How about going to a basketball game? There's a good one starting right now between Hilltown High and Stone City. That tall, good-looking fellow is Marvin Whalen, star of the Hilltown team. The cheerleader in the blue satin slacks is his girl Mary. Pretty and peppy, too! See that comfortable-looking woman about halfway up the bleachers? She's looking a bit anxiously at the man next to her. Keep an eye on him. That's Marv's father. He takes his basketball seriously. There's still a little time before the whistle blows, so let's first take a look into the Whalen home at supper time.

For Better Reading . . . Before we look in on the Whalens, however, keep in mind that nearly everything that happens in this story is told from the point of view of Mr. Whalen, the father of Marv Whalen the basketball star. It is important in reading fiction to note which character is chosen by the author to view the events of the story — and why he is chosen. In this instance, the point of view will give you a clue to the meaning of the title of the story.

MR. WHALEN came into the kitchen by the back door and closed it softly behind him. He looked anxiously at his wife.

"Is Marv in?" he asked.

"He's resting," she whispered. Mr. Whalen nodded. He tiptoed through the dining room and went into the front hall as quiet as a mouse, and hung his hat and coat away. But he could not resist peeking into the darkened living room. A fire burned on the hearth, and on the couch lay a boy, or young man, who looked, at first glance, as though he were at least seven feet tall. He had a throw pulled up around his neck, and his stocking feet stuck out from the cuffs of his corduroy trousers over the end of the sofa.

"Dad?" a husky young voice said.

"Yes. Did I waken you? I'm sorry."

"I wasn't sleeping. I'm just resting."

Mr. Whalen went over to the couch and looked down at the long figure with deep concern.

"How do you feel?" he asked tenderly.

"Swell, Dad. I feel fine. I feel as though I'm going to be lucky tonight."

"That's fine! That's wonderful!" said

his father fervently.

"What time is it, Dad?"

"Quarter to six."

"About time for me to get up and have my supper. Is it ready? I ought to stretch a bit."

"You lie still now, Marv. I'll see about your supper."

Mr. Whalen hurried back into the kitchen.

"He's awake," he informed his wife. "Is his supper ready?"

"In a minute, dear. I'm just making his tea."

Mr. Whalen went back into the living room with his anxious, bustling air.

The young man was up from the couch. He had turned on the light in a table lamp. He was putting on his shoes. He looked very young, not more than sixteen. His hair was thick as taffy and about the same color. He was thin, with a nose a little too big, and with clear blue eyes and a pleasant mouth and chin. He was not especially handsome, except to his father, who thought him the finest-looking boy in the whole wide world. The boy looked up a little shyly and smiled, and somehow his father's opinion was justified.

"I couldn't hit a thing in short practice yesterday," Marvin said. "That means I'll be hot tonight. Red-hot!"

"I hope so. I certainly hope so."

"You're going to the game, aren't you, Dad? You and Mother?"

Wild horses couldn't have kept Mr. Whalen away.

Marvin rose from his chair. He went up and up and up. Six feet four in his stocking feet, a hundred and seventy-six pounds, and sixteen years of age. Marvin flexed his muscles, crouched a little, and made a twisting leap into the air, one arm going up over his head in a swinging circle, his hand brushing the ceiling. He landed lightly as a cat. His father watched him, appearing neither astonished nor amused. There was nothing but the most profound respect and admiration in Mr. Whalen's eyes.

"We've been timing that pivot. Mr. Leach had two guards on me yesterday and they couldn't hold me, but I couldn't hit. Well, Dad, let's eat. I ought to be getting up to the gym."

They went into the kitchen, where the supper was laid on a clean cloth at a small round table. There was steak and potatoes and salad and chocolate cake for his parents, toast and tea and coddled eggs for the boy.

"I don't think you ought to put the cake out where Marv can see it, when he can't have any," fussed Mr. Whalen.

Marvin grinned. "It's okay, Dad. I don't mind. I'll eat some when I get home."

"Did you take your shower? Dry yourself good?"

"Sure, Dad. Of course."

"Was the doctor at school today? This was the day he was to check the team, wasn't it?"

"Yes. He was there. I'm okay. The arch supports Mr. Leach sent for came. You know, my left foot's been getting a little flat. Doc thought I ought to have something while I'm still growing."

"It's a good thing. Have you got them here?"

"Yes. I'll get them."

"No. Just tell me where they are. I'll look at them."

"In my room. In my gym shoes."

Mr. Whalen wasn't eating a bite of supper. It just gave him indigestion to eat on game nights. He got too excited. He couldn't stand it. The boy was eating calmly. He ate four coddled eggs. He ate six pieces of toast. He drank four cups of tea with lemon and sugar. In the boy's room Mr. Whalen checked the things in his bag — the white woolen socks, the clean folded towel, the shoes with their arch supports, and so on. The insets looked all right, his father thought. The fine, heavy satin playing suits would be packed in the box in which they came from the dry cleaner's, to keep them from getting wrinkled before the game.

There, alone in Marvin's room, with Marvin's ties hanging on his dresser, with his windbreaker thrown down in a chair and his high school books on the table, Mr. Whalen felt a little ill. He pressed his hand over his heart. He mustn't show his anxiety, he thought. The boy was calm. He felt lucky. Mustn't break that feeling. Mr. Whalen went back into the kitchen with an air of cheer, a plump, middle-aged man with a retreating hairline and kind, anxious, brown eyes. Mr. Whalen was a few inches shorter than his wife. But he had never regretted marrying a tall woman. Look at his boy!

Marv was looking at the funnies in the evening paper. Mr. Whalen resisted the temptation to look at the kitchen clock. The boy would know when to go. He took the front part of the paper and sat down and tried to put his mind on the news. Mrs. Whalen quietly washed the supper dishes. Marvin finished the funnies in the local paper and handed it to his father. Mr. Whalen took it and read the news that Hilltown High was to play Sunset High, of Stone City, at the local gym that evening. The Stone City team hadn't lost a game. They were grooming for the state championship. Mr. Whalen felt weak. He hoped Marvin hadn't read this. Indignation grew in the father, as he read on down the column, that the odds were against the local team. How dare Mr. Minton print such nonsense for the boys to read — to discourage them? It was outrageous. Mr. Whalen would certainly give the editor a piece of his mind. Perhaps Marvin had read it and believed it! Everything was so important — the psychology wasn't good.

Marvin had finished the funnies in the city paper, and he put it down and rose. He said a little ruefully, "I'm still hungry, but I can't eat more now."

"I'll have something ready for you when you get home," his mother said.

Marvin went into his room and came back in his windbreaker, his hair combed smoothly on his head.

"I'll see you at the gym," he said. "Sit where you always do, will you, Dad?"

"Yes. Yes. We'll be there."

"Okay. I'll be seeing you."

"Don't you want me to take you down in the car?"

"No. Thanks, Dad, but no. It'll do me good to run down there. It won't take me but a minute."

A shrill whistle sounded from the street.

"There's Johnny." Marvin left at once.

Mr. Whalen looked at his watch. "Better hurry, Mother. The first game starts at seven. We won't get our regular seats if we're late."

"I'm not going to the gym at half-past six," said Mrs. Whalen definitely. "We'll be there in time and no one will take our seats. If you don't calm down you are going to have a stroke at one of these games."

"I'm perfectly calm," said Mr. Whalen indignantly; "I'm as calm as — as calm as a June day. That's how calm I am. You know I'm not of a nervous temperament. Just because I want to get to the game on time, you say I am excited. You're as up in the air as I am."

"I am not," said Mrs. Whalen. She sat

down at the cleared table and looked at the advertisements in the paper. Mr. Whalen looked at his watch again. He fidgeted.

"You can go ahead, if you like," she said. "I'll come alone."

"No, no," he protested, "I'll wait for you. Do you think we had better take the car? I put it up, but I can get it out again."

"We'll walk," she said. "It will do you good – quiet your nerves."

"I'm not nervous," he almost shouted. Then he subsided again, muttered a little, pretended to read the paper, checked his watch against the kitchen clock to see if it had stopped.

"If we're going to walk . . ." he said in a minute.

Mrs. Whalen looked at him with pity. He couldn't help it, she knew. She folded the papers and put them away, took off her white apron, smoothed her hair, and went to get her wraps. Mr. Whalen was at the front door, his overcoat on, his hat in his hand. She deliberately pottered, getting the cat off the piano and putting him out-of-doors, locking the kitchen door, turning out lights, hunting for her gloves. Mr. Whalen was almost frantic by the time she joined him on the front porch. They went down the walk together, and when they reached the sidewalk they met neighbors also bound for the gym.

"How's Marv?" asked the man next door. "Is he all right?"

"Marv's fine, just fine. He couldn't be better."

"Boy, oh, boy," said the other enthusiastically, "would I like to see the boys whip Stone City! It would be worth a million dollars – a cool million. Stone City thinks no one can beat them. We'd burn the town down."

"Oh, this game doesn't matter so much," said Mr. Whalen deprecatingly. "The team is working toward the tournaments. Be a shame to show all their stuff tonight."

"Well, we'll see. We'll see."

They went ahead. At the next corner they met other friends.

"How's Marv? How's the big boy?"

"He's fine. He's all right." Mr. Whalen's chest expansion increased. Cars were parked all along the sidewalk before the group of township school buildings – the grade school and the high school, with the fine brick gymnasium between them. The walks were crowded now, for the whole town, except those in wheel chairs or just born, went to the games, and this was an important game with Hilltown's hereditary foe. Mr. Whalen grew very anxious about their seats. If Marvin looked around for them and didn't find them . . . He hurried his wife a little. They went into the outer hall of the gymnasium. The school principal was standing there talking to the coach, Mr. Leach. Mr. Whalen's heart plummeted. Had anything gone wrong? Had something happened to Marvin? He looked at them anxiously, but they spoke in normal tones.

"Good evening, Mrs. Whalen. Good evening, Tom."

Several small boys were running up and down the stairs, and the school principal turned and spoke to them severely. The Whalens had to make room for a young married couple, he carrying a small baby, she holding the hand of a little boy. Then they reached the window where the typing teacher was tearing off ticket stubs. Mr. Whalen paid his half dollar and they went inside the iron bar and up the steps to the gym proper.

The gymnasium wasn't half full. The bleachers which rose on either side of the shining, sacred floor with its cabalistic [1] markings were spotted with people. The Hilltown eighth grade was playing the Sugar Ridge eighth grade. The boys scrambled, fell down, got up, and threw the ball, panted and heaved and struggled on the floor. A basketball flew about. A group of smaller children were seated in a tight knot, and two little girls whose only ambition in life was to become high school cheerleaders led a piercing yell:

Hit 'em high,
Hit 'em low;
Come on, eighth grade,
Let's go!

The voices of the junior high were almost piping. Mr. Whalen remembered how he had suffered when Marvin was in the eighth grade and they had to go to the games at six o'clock to watch him play. The junior-high games were very abbreviated, with six-minute quarters, which was all the state athletic association would let them play. Marvin had been five feet ten at thirteen, but too thin. He had put on a little weight in proportion to his height since then, but his father thought he should be heavier. The present eighth-grade team could not compare with Marvin's, Mr. Whalen decided.

But the boys did try hard. They were winning. The gun sounded, the junior high went to pieces with wild cheering, and the teams trotted off the floor, panting, sweating, happy.

Almost at once another group came on in secondhand white wool tops and the old, blue satin trunks from last year. This was the second team. The boys were pretty good. They practiced, throwing the ball from far out, running in under the basket, passing to one another. Mr. and Mrs. Whalen had found their regular seats unoccupied, halfway between the third and fourth uprights which supported the lofty gymnasium ceiling. Mr. Whalen sat down a little weakly and wiped his forehead. Mrs. Whalen began at once to visit with a friend sitting behind her, but Mr. Whalen could not hear what anyone said.

The Stone City reserves came out on the floor to warm up. They looked like first-string men.

Mr. Leach was talking to the timekeeper. He was a good coach — a mighty good coach. They were lucky to keep him here at Hilltown. The luckiest thing that had ever happened to the town was when Mr. Leach had married a Hilltown girl who didn't want to move away. They'd never have been able to hold him otherwise. It meant so much to the boys to have a decent, kindly man to coach them. Some of the high school coaches felt that their teams had to win, no matter how. It would be very bad to have his boy under such an influence, thought Mr. Whalen, who simply could not bear to see the team defeated, and who was always first to yell "Thief!" and "Robber!"

The officials came out in their green shirts, and Mr. Whalen almost had heart failure. There was that tall, thin man who had fouled Marvin every time he had moved in the tournaments last year. He was always against Hilltown. He had been so unfair that Mr. Leach had complained about him to the state association. The only time Mr. Leach had ever done such a thing. Oh, this was awful. Mr. Whalen twisted his hat in his hands. The other official he had seen often. He

[1] **cabalistic** (kăb'ȧ·lĭs'tĭk) **markings:** figures to which a mystic or religious interpretation can be given. Mr. Whalen's feeling about basketball was almost a religious one, so that the markings on the gym floor seemed like the pattern for the performance of a sacred ritual.

was fair — very fair. Sugar Ridge had complained about him for favoring Hilltown, but Mr. Whalen thought him an excellent referee.

The gymnasium was filling fast now. All the high school students — two hundred of them — were packed in the cheering section. The junior high was swallowed up, lost. The cheering section looked as though not one more could get into it, and yet youngsters kept climbing up, squeezing in. The rest of the space was filled with townspeople, from toddlers in snow suits to gray-bearded dodderers. On the opposite side of the gymnasium, the visiting fans were filling their seats. Big crowd from Stone City. Businessmen and quarrymen and stone carvers and their wives and children. They must feel confident of winning, Mr. Whalen thought. Their cheerleaders were out on the floor. Where were Hilltown's? Ah, there they were — Beth and Mary. Hilltown's cheerleaders were extremely pretty adolescents dressed in blue satin slacks with white satin shirts, the word "Yell" in blue letters over their shoulders — a true gilding of the lily. Mary was Marvin's girl. She was the prettiest girl in town. And she had personality, too, and vigor.

Now the two girls leaped into position, spun their hands, spread out their arms, catapulted their bodies into the air in perfect synchronization, and the breathless cheering section came out in a long roll.

Hello, Stone City,
Hello, Stone City,
Hilltown says,
Hello-o-o-o!

Not to be outdone, the Stone City leaders, in crimson-and-gold uniforms, returned the compliment:

Hello, Hilltown . . .

and the sound came nicely across the big gym. Mr. Whalen got a hard knot in his throat, and the bright lights and colors of the gymnasium swam in a mist. He couldn't help it. They were so young. Their voices were so young!

The whistle blew. The reserves were at it.

Mr. Whalen closed his eyes and sat still. It would be so long; the cheering wouldn't really start, the evening wouldn't begin until the team came out. He remembered when Marvin was born. He had been tall then — twenty-two inches. Mr. Whalen prayed, his lips moving a little, that Marvin wouldn't get hurt tonight. Suppose he had a heart attack and fell dead, like that boy at Capital City years ago. Suppose he got knocked against one of the steel uprights and hurt his head — damaged his brain? Suppose he got his knee injured? Mr. Whalen opened his eyes. He must not think of those things. He had promised his wife he would not worry so. He felt her hand, light but firm, on his arm.

"Here are the Lanes," she said.

Mr. Whalen spoke to them. Johnny's parents crowded in behind the Whalens. Johnny's father's hand fell on Mr. Whalen's shoulder.

"How's Marv tonight?"

"Fine, fine. How's Johnny?"

"Couldn't be better. I believe the boys are going to take them."

The two fathers looked at each other and away. Mr. Whalen felt a little better.

"How's business?" asked Johnny's father, and they talked about business a moment or two, but they were not interested.

There was a crisis of some kind on the floor. Several players were down in a pile. Someone was hurt. Mr. Whalen bit the edge of his felt hat. The boy was up now. The Stone City coach was out on the floor, but the boy shook his head. He was all right. The game was resumed.

At last it was over. The reserves had won. Mr. Whalen thought that was a bad omen. The eighth grade had won. The reserves had won. No, it was too much. The big team would lose. If the others had lost, he would have considered that a bad omen too. Every omen was bad to Mr. Whalen at this stage. The floor was empty. The high school band played "Indiana," and "Onward, Hilltown," and everyone stood up and sang.

There was a breathless pause, and then a crashing cheer hit the ceiling of the big gym and bounced back. The Team was out. Out there on the floor in their blue satin suits, with jackets over their white tops, warming up, throwing the ball deftly about. What caused the change? Mr. Whalen never knew, but everything was quick now, almost professional in tone and quality. Self-confidence, authority, had come into the gymnasium. Ten or twelve boys out there warming up. But there was really only one boy on the floor for Mr. Whalen, a tall, thin, fair boy with limber legs still faintly brown from summer swimming. Mr. Whalen did not even attempt to tear his eyes from Marvin.

The Stone City team came out. Mr. Whalen looked away from Marvin for a moment to study them. Two or three of them were as tall as Marvin, maybe taller. He felt indignant. They must be seniors, all of them. Or five year men. He studied the boys. He liked to see if he could pick out the first-string men from the lot. He could almost always do it — not by their skill or their height, but by their faces. That little fellow with the pug nose — he was a first-string man. And the two big ones — the other tall man Mr. Whalen discarded correctly. And the boy with the thick chest. What it was, he wasn't sure — some carelessness, some ease that marked the first-string men. The others were always a little self-conscious, a little too eager.

The referee blew the whistle. The substitutes left the floor, carrying extra jackets. The boy with the pug nose came forward for Stone City. So he was captain? Mr. Whalen felt gratified in his judgment. Marvin came forward for his team. He was captain too. There was a Number 1 in blue on the sleeveless white satin shirt he wore. The referee talked to them. The boys took their positions, the umpire his along the edge of the floor. The cheering section roared:

We may be rough,
We may be tough,
But we're the team
That's got the stuff!
Fight! Fight! Fight!

Mary turned a complete somersault, her lithe young body going over backward, her heels in the air, then hitting the floor to bounce her straight up in a spread eagle. Her pretty mouth was open in a square. The rooting swelled. The substitutes sat down with their coaches. Marvin stood back out of the center ring until the referee, ball in hand, waved him in. The ball went into the air as the whistle blew, and the game was on.

Marvin got the tip-off straight to Johnny. Marv ran down into the corner, where he circled to confuse his guard. Johnny brought the ball down over the line, faked a pass and drew out Marvin's guard, bounced the ball to Perk, who carried it almost to the foul line and passed to Marvin, who threw the ball into the basket. Stone City leaped outside, threw the ball in, a long pass. Perk leaped for it, but missed. The tall Stone

The swift pace and fast-mounting scores of basketball have made it America's most popular sport. More than one hundred million people attend games annually. (Frederic Lewis)

City forward dribbled, dodging skillfully. The guards were smothering him, but he pivoted, flung the ball over his head and into the basket. A basket each in the first minute of play!

Mr. Whalen had stopped breathing. He was in a state of suspended animation. The game was very fast – too fast. Stone City scored a second and a third time. Marvin called time out. Someone threw a wet towel from the bench, and it slid along the floor. The boys wiped their faces with it, threw it back. They whispered together. The referee blew the whistle. Yes, they were going to try the new trick play they had been practicing. It worked. Marvin's pivot was wonderful. The score was four to six.

Marvin played with a happy romping abandon. He was skillful, deft, acute. But he was also gay. The youngsters screamed his name. Mr. Whalen saw Mary's rapt, adoring look. Marvin romped down the floor like a young colt.

At the end of the quarter, the score was fourteen to ten in Stone City's favor. At the end of the half, it was still in Stone City's favor, but only fourteen to thirteen. Stone City didn't score in the second quarter.

Mr. Whalen felt a deep disquietude. He had been watching the tall center on the other team, the pivot man. He had thick, black, curly hair and black eyes. Mr. Whalen thought he looked tough. He had fouled Marvin twice in the first half. That is, he had been called for two fouls, but he had fouled him oftener. Mr. Whalen was sure he had tripped Marvin that time Marvin fell on the floor and cracked his elbow. Marvin had jumped up again at once. The Stone City center was a dirty player and ought to be taken off the floor. The school band was playing, but Mr. Whalen couldn't hear it. He was very upset. If the referees were going to let Stone City foul Hilltown and get away with it . . . He felt hot under the collar. He felt desperate.

"Why don't you go out and smoke?" his wife asked. Mr. Whalen folded his overcoat to mark his place and went out of the gym. He smoked two cigarettes as fast as he could. He would stay out here. The stars were cool and calm above his head. The night air was fresh. He couldn't stand it in the gymnasium. He would wait here until the game was over. If Marvin was hurt, he wouldn't see it. He resolved this firmly. But when the whistle blew and he heard the burst of cheering, he rushed back into the gymnasium like a man going to a fire.

The second half had begun. Again the big center fouled Marvin. Marvin got two free throws and made both good.

Fifteen to fourteen now! The crowd went wild. The game got very fast again. Mr. Whalen watched Marvin and his opponent like a hawk. There! It happened.

Mr. Whalen was on his feet, yelling, "Watch him! Watch him!"

The Stone City center had driven his elbow into Marvin's stomach. Marvin was doubled up. Marvin was down on the floor. A groan went up from the bleachers. Mr. Whalen started out on the floor. Something held him. He looked around blindly. His wife had a firm grip on his coattails. She gave him a smart yank and pulled him unexpectedly down on the bench beside her.

"He doesn't want you on the floor," she said fiercely.

Mr. Whalen was very angry, but he controlled himself. He sat still. Marvin was up again. Mary led a cheer for him. Marvin was all right. He got two more free throws. Now Hilltown was three points ahead. Marvin was fouled again, got two more free throws and missed them both. He was hurt! He never missed free throws — well, hardly ever. What was the matter with the referee? Was he crazy? Was he bribed? Mr. Whalen groaned.

Stone City took time out, and in the last minute of the third quarter they made three quick baskets. It put them ahead again, three points. A foul was called on Marvin — for pushing.

"Why, he never did at all!" yelled Mr. Whalen. "He couldn't stop fast enough — that's not a foul! Just give them the ball, boys! Don't try to touch it!"

"Will you hush?" demanded his wife.

The Stone City forward made one of the two throws allowed. It was the quarter.

The game was tied three times in the last quarter. With five minutes to play, the big center fouled Marvin again. His last personal. He was out of the game. The Hilltown crowd booed him. None so loud as Mr. Whalen, who often talked long and seriously to Marvin about sportsmanship.

Then Marvin got hot. He couldn't miss. Everyone on the team fed him the ball, and he could throw it from anywhere and it went, plop, right into the basket, Marvin pivoted. His height, his spring, carried him away from his guards. Marvin pranced. His long legs carried him where he would. He threw the ball over his head and from impossible angles. Once he was knocked down on the floor, and he threw from there and made the basket. His joy, his perfection, his luck, caused the crowd to burst into continuous wild cheering. Stone City took time out. They ran in substitutes, but they couldn't stop Marvin. Perk would recover the ball; he and Johnny fed it skillfully to Marvin, and Marvin laid it in. The gun went off with Hilltown twelve points ahead.

Mr. Whalen was a wreck. He could hardly stand up. Mrs. Whalen took his arm and half supported him toward the stairs that led down to the school grounds. The Stone City fans were angry. A big, broad-shouldered man with fierce black eyes complained in a loud, quarrelsome voice:

"That skinny kid — that Whalen boy — he foul my boy! Who cares? But when my boy protect himself, what happens? They put him off the floor. They put my Guido [1] out, so Hilltown wins. I get my hands on that tall monkey and I'll fix him."

"Be careful. That's my son you're talking about." The strength had returned to Mr. Whalen. He was strong as a lion. Mrs. Whalen pulled at his arm, but he jerked away. He turned in the crowded stairs. "Before you do anything to Marvin," he said, his voice loud and high, "you'd better do something to me. Your son fouled repeatedly."

"That's a lie!" yelled the other, and Mr. Whalen hit him. He hit him right in the stomach as hard as he could punch him. Instantly there was a melee.[2] Johnny's father was punching somebody, and for a moment the crowd heaved and milled on the stairs. Someone screamed. Something like a bolt of lightning hit Mr. Whalen in the eye, and he struck back.

Friends were pulling him away. The town marshal shouldered good-naturedly between the combatants. The big man was in the grip of others from Stone City, who dragged him back up the stairs. Mr. Whalen struggled with his captors, fellow townsmen, who sympathized with him but had no intention of

[1] **Guido** (gwē'dō).
[2] **melee** (mā·lā'): a confused fight.

" Fifteen to fourteen now! The crowd went wild." (*Reprinted by special permission from* Holiday, *copyright 1951 by the Curtis Publishing Co.*)

letting him fight. Johnny's mother and Marvin's mother hustled their men out into the cold night air.

" Really! " the high school principal was saying anxiously. " Really, we mustn't have any trouble. The boys don't fight. If we could just keep the fathers away from the games! Really, Mrs. Whalen, this won't do."

" I've got a good notion to take a poke at him too," said Mr. Whalen, who was clear above himself.

In the kitchen, Mr. Whalen looked in a small mirror at his reflection. He felt wonderful. He felt marvelous. He was going to have a black eye. He grabbed his wife and kissed her soundly.

" They beat them! " he said. " They beat Stone City! "

" You old fool! " cried Mrs. Whalen. " I declare I'd be ashamed of Marvin if he acted like that. You and Johnny's father – fighting like hoodlums."

" I don't care! " said Mr. Whalen. " I'm glad I hit him. Teach him a lesson. I feel great. I'm hungry. Make some coffee, Mother."

Marvin wouldn't be in for an hour. He would have a date with Mary at the soda parlor, to which the whole high school would repair.[1] They heard the siren blowing; they looked out of the window and saw the reflection of the bonfire on the courthouse lawn. They heard the fire engine. The team was having a ride on the fire engine. Mr. Whalen stood on his front porch and cheered. The town was wild with joy. Not a citizen that wasn't up in the air tonight.

At last Marvin came in. He was cheerful, practical.

[1] **repair** (rê·pâr′): flock; go in a crowd.

"Did you really have a fight, Dad? Someone told me you popped Guido's father. . . . Boy, are you going to have a shiner!" Marvin was greatly amused. He examined his father's eye, recommended an ice pack.

"I want it to get black," said Mr. Whalen stubbornly.

"We sure fixed Guido," said Marvin, and laughed.

"Did you have a fight?" asked his father eagerly.

"Heck, no! I'm going to get him a date with Betty. He noticed her. He's coming up next Sunday. Their team went downtown for sodas because Guido wanted to meet Betty. I wasn't sore at him. I only mean he was easy to handle. I saw right away that I could make him foul me, give me extra shots, get him off the floor. It's very easy to do with a big clumsy guy like that."

Mr. Whalen fingered his swelling eye and watched Marvin eat two hot ham sandwiches and a big slab of chocolate cake and drink a quart of milk. Marvin had already had a soda.

"You must sleep late in the morning," Mr. Whalen said. "Maybe you got too tired tonight. Now, don't eat too much cake."

Mr. Whalen's eye hurt. Mrs. Whalen got him to bed and put a cold compress on it.

"Old ninny," she murmured, and stooped and kissed him. Mr. Whalen sighed. He was exhausted. He was getting too old to play basketball, he thought confusedly.

Noting the Point of View

1. Have you determined who was "the hero" of the story? Was he a real hero?

2. Why was the story told from the point of view of the father? Is the word *hero* used in the usual sense? Did Mr. Whalen really consider himself a bit of a hero until he found out about those fouls? How would the story have been different if told from Marv's viewpoint? from Mrs. Whalen's? Did she consider her husband a hero?

Thinking It Over

1. The things that happen to people usually occur because of the nature of the people themselves. Try to show, from the incident at the end of the game, that what happens to Mr. Whalen occurs because of his character. Can you find other incidents that occur because of someone's character? Point out examples of Mrs. Whalen's calmness and Marv's good balance.

2. Before you judge Mr. Whalen too harshly, consider that he probably doesn't act this way in all his affairs. Find a passage that shows he actually has quite high standards of conduct. What is it, then, that makes his behavior so illogical? Why is there such a difference between his beliefs and his actual behavior?

3. It is very easy to judge events according to one's own prejudice. An unfair thing sometimes strikes us as being perfectly fair – if it happens to benefit us. How is this revealed in the story? Think back to the comments on the Hilltown coach, on the referees, and on the playing of the game.

4. Do you remember Mrs. Whalen's statement: "He doesn't want you on the floor"? What do you think of parents who try to fight all their children's battles? Mention an instance from your own observation in which it would have been better for a child had he been allowed to work out his own problems.

5. Have you had similar experiences with your own parents? Have you ever been annoyed by their fears and anxieties and attempts at advice whenever you take part in a game, a recital, a play, or some other public affair? See if you can analyze their emotions, their point of view. Why do they worry? What is it they want for you?

6. If this were not a story, it would be a good job of sports reporting. Read the article "Ben Hogan" on page 450. Then write a sports article yourself, perhaps an editorial, or a "profile" of a leading sports figure, or maybe an article on a game your school has just played.

ELSIE SINGMASTER

Mr. Brownlee's Roses

In many high schools students are encouraged, during their first or second year, to take exploratory courses to find out where their individual talents lie. Some have a leaning toward science or perhaps languages; some show technical or artistic skill. One shows exceptional musical ability; another, a gift for cooking. This boy will make a fine mechanic, and that girl will be a teacher. But there are always some who seem to have no special gifts at all. They begin to think they are just " dumb " and soon they stop trying to do their best. Don't ever let that happen to you. There is something you can do, probably better than anyone else. Find out what it is. You may discover it just by chance as Jennie Swenson did in the following story. Jennie was the daughter of a Swedish coal miner who was killed in a mine disaster. She wasn't good at Latin or algebra, but she needed a " yob " – and she found it!

As Jennie Swenson closed the outer door of her mother's kitchen, pulling with all her strength against the wind, she heard far up the street a man's loud singing.

I took my girl to a ball one night,
It was a fancy hop;
We danced until the lights went out,
And the music it did stop.

Stanislaus Sobieski, usually called Stan Sobski, night fireman at Mr. Brownlee's greenhouse, was going to his work. His song was old; new songs, he said, did not fit his voice. He was apparently not disturbed by the fact that work began at six o'clock and it was now seven.

To Jennie, Mr. Brownlee's greenhouse was paradise; she did not understand how anyone could be late for work there. All else in the mining town was black and grim; there was no money for paint, and there was no time for cultivating gardens. At each end of Main Street towered a frame structure called a breaker, to whose lofty summit ran cars filled with coal. Beside each breaker rose a mountain of black refuse, separated from the coal as it descended in long chutes.

There had been a third mine along the hillside, and its owner, Mr. Brownlee's father, had built a small greenhouse for his own pleasure. As the mine grew lean, he began to sell flowers. Presently he was shipping a thousand American Beauties each night to New York. The

"Mr. Brownlee's Roses" by Elsie Singmaster. Reprinted by permission of the author.

present Mr. Brownlee was shipping three thousand before he went to war. Now he and his sister were once more sending roses, five thousand in a night — not American Beauties, but newer and more fashionable varieties: Premier and Columbia and Radiance, in various shades of rose and pink; Talisman, a blending of pink and apricot and gold: double white Killarneys and long yellow buds of Souvenir de Claudius Pernet.[1]

Jennie did not know their names or even their distinct and lovely odors; she knew only their colors, seen when she walked slowly by, looking eagerly for panes of glass on which the white paint was worn away. She often watched Mr. Brownlee and his sister. He was tall and a little lame, and his hair was slightly gray; Miss Brownlee was short and broad, but not stout. She had clear blue eyes, wavy hair, and a broad white forehead. Her brother could do no strenuous work; but she worked from morning till night, directing the laborers, inspecting rows of plants, and superintending the packing of roses.

At the same instant that Jennie heard Stan singing, she wound her scarf more tightly around her neck, locked the door, and hung the key behind a shutter. For hours a light snow had been falling, and now an east wind was beginning to blow. Stan had now reached the middle of his song.

And this is what she ate:
A dozen raw, a plate of slaw,
A chicken and a roast,
Some oyster stew and ice cream too,
And several quail on toast.

In the moment while she waited for Stan to pass, Jennie was tempted to turn back to the kitchen and study. There was a good light and perfect quiet — for Mrs. Swenson, a nurse, was on a case, and Jennie's sisters, Anna and Gertrude, lived in Wilkes-Barre.[2]

But what Jennie required for study was not quiet — it was company. There were incomprehensible passages in her Latin lesson; insoluble problems in her algebra. If she did not graduate in June she could not get a position. Better the storm and the long walk to Hilda Yonson's kitchen, where there were no less than eight younger children, than peace and quiet and blankness of mind.

Gertrude and Anna were astonished at her dullness. She could not be a stenographer because she was too slow; she could not teach because she was too dull; she could not be a nurse because she was too timid. The teachers gave aptitude tests, but she showed no aptitude for anything. When she was excited or embarrassed her Swedish tongue refused to say "*j*"; it refused now.

"I must get a yob!" wailed Jennie aloud to the storm.

She stepped from the board walk, already swept bare, into a drift up to her knees. Instantly she laughed and shook the tears out of her eyes. She was a true Swede, tall and broad and strong. She started briskly down the street. The lights in the neighbors' houses were dimmed by whirling snow, but far above them hung a light at the top of the breaker.

She heard a shrill bell which heralded the rising of the elevator from the mine. In a moment a line of tired men would pass the corner. Five years ago there had been an evening when the loud whistle blew and everyone went running and crying to the pit head. Mrs. Swenson had been the first to get there and first

[1] **Souvenir de Claudius Pernet** (sōōv·nēr′ dē klô′dĭ·ŭs pĕr·nā).

[2] **Wilkes-Barre** (wĭlks′-băr′ĕ): a city in Pennsylvania.

to know that she was widowed.

At the third corner Jennie halted. There were two ways to the Yonson house: one down Main Street; the other through side streets, past Mr. Brownlee's greenhouse. Jennie took a step in that direction; then, laughing at herself, ran on down Main Street, then up a sharp hill.

From the Yonson's porch the whole of the Wyoming Valley was visible in daylight — cities and towns and roads, churches and schools and factories; and in every town and village a towering breaker. A part of the valley had a strange and solemn name, "The Shades of Death," a memorial of Colonial war and massacre.

Tim Yonson sat before the stove, in a coal-blackened rocker reserved for his use. His face and hands were clean, but they were not white. He smoked a long pipe and talked to Mrs. Yonson, who was washing dishes. There was a child on each side of the table, each pair of eyes on a book.

"Good efening, Yennie," said Tim.

"Good efening," said Mrs. Yonson.

Hilda looked up. "Hello! Thought you weren't coming."

As Jennie unwound her scarf, Mrs. Yonson set a large plate of Swedish cookies on the table to lighten the evening's labors, and it was not until half-past nine that Jennie rose to leave. Mr. Yonson had gone to bed and so had five or six children.

"I certainly am grateful," sighed Jennie.

Mrs. Yonson had difficulty with many English letters. "Come efery night till you are old, and Hilda will not yet pay what your moder done for us."

Jennie had expected to have the wind in her face, but it blew from every direction in turn. Regardless of the stinging snow, she turned down the dark street which led to Mr. Brownlee's greenhouse. A new section had been added and the low, dimly lighted buildings occupied a solid block.

She walked slowly past. There they were, the pinks, the yellows, the shades of rose! She stood still, though the wind seemed to blow through her. The snow hissed against the glass. How could this thin protection keep the roses safe?

The office was furnished with two broad desks, a half-dozen chairs, a bookcase, and many files. Neither of the Brownlees was in sight; but Mr. Brownlee's gray overcoat hung on a hook, his soft gray hat above it, and a crumpled newspaper lay on the floor beside his chair. At the back of the room a door opened on a stairway leading to the boiler room. The door was ajar; perhaps he was down there with Stan. Probably he would stay in the greenhouse all night. She would, in his place!

In ten minutes she was at home. The house rocked a little in the wind. She shook down the fire, put on fresh coal, and, while it caught, undressed near the stove.

Though she was warm in bed she could not sleep. She shut her eyes, determined not to open them again; then, startled by a sound, she sat up. "Mother?" she called.

There was no answer. The sound came from outside and grew each moment louder.

"I took my girl to a ball one night!" shouted Stan Sobieski at the gate. "To a ball! Fifty cents!"

Jennie was terrified. But Stan was an honest fellow — he would not break into a house! That is, when he was sober! She sprang out of bed and went to the window. She could not see him, but she could hear him. "I took my girl to a social hop!"

He was not going toward the greenhouse; he was going in the opposite direction!

"And this is what she ate! And this is what she ate — " he yelled, from far away. "She ate — "

It was not until Jennie had one knee on her bed and was about to creep back that she was really awake. It was a bitter night, and Mr. Brownlee's roses were in the midst of their most profitable bloom. Suppose the fires should go out? But Mr. Brownlee was there! But suppose Mr. Brownlee had gone home?

Foolish though it seemed, she put on her slippers and went downstairs. In the pale glow from the fire she could see her clothes spread on the chair; they seemed to say, "Put us on! Put us on!"

"How silly!" said Jennie. "I'm going back to bed."

Instantly she had another delusion; she saw thousands of roses standing with drooping heads. No, as plants froze they got stiffer and stiffer and held their heads straight. It was only after the sun came out that they got limp and black.

"I don't care if I am crazy," she said, and began to dress.

As she opened the door the wind seemed to drag her out, rather than drive her back. It blew with a roaring sound, far above her head. She heard a loud crash, as though the roof of a house had been blown off. She could see the breaker light when the clouds of snow blew away, but no other.

She laughed hysterically and ran. Stan had another old song — "I don't know where I'm going, but I'm on my way."

"That's me!" said Jennie.

The great area of dim light was as it had been. She slowed her step; there were the roses, beautiful and unchanged. The office was brightly lighted and still empty of human beings; but Mr. Brownlee's coat hung on its hook, and the door to the boiler room was open.

"It's all right!" thought Jennie.

Above Mr. Brownlee's desk hung a clock with a large face. "Look at me, Jennie!" it seemed to say. It was half-past one! At the same instant she saw that Mr. Brownlee's crumpled newspaper lay exactly where it had been at half-past nine.

Jennie went up the step and opened the door. How warm it was, how sweet, how like paradise!

"Mr. Brownlee!" she called faintly. There was no answer.

"Mr. Brownlee!" Alarm sharpened her voice.

"Who is there?" Undoubtedly it was Mr. Brownlee, speaking from the boiler room.

"Jennie Swenson." She could not help giggling. What did "Jennie Swenson" mean to Mr. Brownlee?

"In the name of mercy, Jennie Swenson, come down here!"

The words were pitiful, yet there was an undertone of amusement. Trembling, Jennie went down the steps. The room was low and paved with brick. At one end was a huge boiler; along one side were coalbins and piles of wood, and along the other shelves filled with cans and bottles of insecticides and sprays. Before the boiler stood an old couch, and on it lay Mr. Brownlee.

"Open that firebox door quick, will you, and pile in wood."

Jennie picked up a chunk as she dashed to the furnace.

"Finer pieces, plenty of them! Pretty low, isn't it?"

"Not so very bad," said Jennie.

"What are you crying for?"

"Will they die?"

"Humph!" said Mr. Brownlee. "Go

Happiness — a purpose in life — began for Jennie in the fragile beauty of a rose. (*Devaney*)

to my desk and take the flashlight you'll find there; then go to the farthest corner of every greenhouse and read the thermometers. And you might pray as you go! "

" Did Stan tie you? " asked Jennie, running up the stairs swiftly.

" Lumbago tied me."

Jennie came running back. The wood in the firebox was burning briskly. Mr. Brownlee's eyes shone like points of fire.

" Forty-eight degrees is the lowest."

Mr. Brownlee threw up his arm. It covered his eyes and mouth. " What did you say your name is? "

" Jennie Swenson."

" Where do you come from? "

" Up the street."

" You come from heaven! " Mr. Brownlee still kept his eyes covered. " Can you put coal on the fire? "

" Sure! "

" Have you no father who may be out looking for you? No mother who is anxious? Are you real? "

" My father was killed in Shaft Eighteen. I guess you remember that time."

" Remember! " exclaimed Mr. Brownlee.

" My mother's a nurse, Mrs. Swenson. She has a case all night. I heard Stan Sobieski going home and I thought of the flowers. He was singing loud."

" Close that lower door," ordered Mr. Brownlee. " Then make the rounds with your flashlight. When you come back, bring yourself a chair."

" The lowest is now above forty-eight," reported Jennie a few minutes later.

"Sit down, Jennie," said Mr. Brownlee. "Now tell me again how you happen to be here."

"I vas" — excited and embarrassed, Jennie spoke rapidly — "I vas studying mine lesson by Hilda Yonson, and I vas coming past so I could see the flowers." Then she recovered her English. "There was no one in the office, but a newspaper was lying all mussed on the floor. When I was in bed I heard Stan going home."

"He wasn't here," said Brownlee. "He never came. I was shoveling coal when this attack of lumbago caught me. It's happened before. All I could do was lie down on Stan's couch. It'll take a stretcher to get me home. My sister is in New York; otherwise she would have been here long ago. Now go on. So you heard Stan going home?"

"Then I came," said Jennie.

"Then you came," repeated Mr. Brownlee. "You got up in the middle of the night in a blizzard and you came."

"I saw the newspaper in the same place," she explained, "and I felt something was wrong."

Again Mr. Brownlee covered his eyes. "Better make another round, Jennie, and you might fetch my overcoat along."

"It's now fifty at the lowest," she reported on her return. "I'll cover you up. I can hear water bubbling in the pipe. I could take a few of those bottles, fill them with hot water, and put them behind you."

"Why, so you could! Open that spigot and you can fill them. Do you go to school?"

"Yes." Jennie sat down in her chair. "But I'm not good at Latin and algebra and geometry. I don't know if I can graduate in June. And I don't know if I can find a" — this time Jennie knew that she had made a slip — "a yob. I'm strong, but I'm not bright."

"No?" said Mr. Brownlee. "Will you kindly take another look at the thermometers?"

"Fifty-two everywhere," she told him jubilantly. "It's three o'clock now, not long till daylight."

"At five-forty my sister's train is due. She'll see the light in the office as they come into the station. Whatever has been our pain and anxiety, Jennie, we shall have the fun of seeing her come down those stairs. While I was at war, you know, the government shut down on luxuries. We couldn't use our own coal to run our own greenhouse, and we lost sixteen thousand plants in one night."

"I have heard of that," Jennie wept.

"You've got to keep the houses fifty-seven at night and fifty-five by day. Below forty-eight there is blight and mildew. Will you please put more coal on, and make another round?"

"Sure!"

At six o'clock that morning the outer door opened, and there was a brisk tap of feet on the linoleum.

"Dick!" called a frightened voice. "Where are you?"

Already Miss Brownlee was on the steps. At the bottom she stood looking from her brother to his guest. Jennie rose, the flashlight in her hand.

"You might take that flash, Alice, and read the thermometers," said Mr. Brownlee in a tired voice.

Like an old woman, Miss Brownlee crept up the steps. Then she ran.

"It's fifty-seven everywhere," she cried, returning. "Have you lumbago? You've been shoveling coal! Where's Stan? What's the matter?"

"Alice, this is Jennie Swenson, Harriet Swenson's daughter," said Mr.

Brownlee. " Last night at one o'clock, lying in her bed, she heard Stan going home, singing as he went. Now Jennie is something of a prowler herself. She comes here — has been coming for a good many years — to peer in at our windows. She looks at the roses; she doesn't handle them, she doesn't even smell them. She has never been in the greenhouse. But, hearing Stan yelling, she dressed and came down, just to look in and see that everything was all right. She says that she's dull, but she observed that my newspaper was lying exactly where she had seen it at nine-thirty."

" I'll put on a little more coal," offered Jennie.

Miss Brownlee looked hard at her. " You certainly have common sense, and you're certainly strong, and you certainly love flowers," she said at last. " Would you come here and work as an assistant? I would teach you all I know."

" When school closes, you mean," put in Mr. Brownlee. " In the meantime we'll help her with her Latin, her Greek, her Hebrew, her calculus, and her what not."

If he thought Jennie would laugh, he was mistaken. She lifted her hand to cover her trembling lips.

" Sure I'd come! " said she.

At half-past six Jennie went up the street. The snow was whirling through the air. Traveling was uncertain because you stepped now on bare, slippery flagstones, now into deep drifts. Jennie had a box on her arm; she carried it as though it were a baby.

Jennie opened the kitchen door of her home. The light was burning and her mother sat before the fire, taking off her shoes. She turned with a start. She had pleasant, tired eyes and a braid of thick light hair.

" Why, Yennie! " she exclaimed. " Where were you out in the night? What have you? "

Jennie sat down, the box in her arms.

" I've got roses in this box," she said. " Red and pink and white and yellow. They have long, long stems. And — moder — oh, moder! I've got a yob! "

Thinking It Over

1. Why did you find such satisfaction in Jennie's good fortune? What are the personal characteristics that make you admire her?

2. Jennie was able to make her own decisions rapidly. What was there in her home life that developed this characteristic?

3. Discuss the problems involved in fitting a person to the job. Have industrial firms or government agencies taken any steps to help people find work at congenial jobs? What are the schools doing? Have you any suggestions yourself?

4. Which of your own skills and accomplishments do you think are marketable? In what ways can you make them known to a prospective employer? What school subjects are you taking to prepare yourself for the future?

5. Plan several job interviews between different types of applicants and employers. Act them out and let the class decide why some are more successful than others. Or write a letter of application for a summer job and have it judged by the class.

For Your Vocabulary

WORD BUILDING: A great many suffixes, such as *-ible, -ble,* and *-less,* always have the same meaning. Jennie found the problems in algebra *insoluble.* She found *incomprehensible* passages in her Latin. These two suffixes (*-ble* and *-ible*) mean " capable of." With this help, work out a definition for the two words. Give the meaning of *unpredictable, excusable, breakable.* The suffix *-less* means " without." What does *regardless* mean? (There is no such word as *irregardless.* Can you see why?) Make six other words with the suffix *-less.*

WILLIAM SAROYAN

The Parsley Garden

Many a time some unhappy teen-ager has had an older person say to him, " Why, what's the matter with you? You haven't anything to worry about. This ought to be the happiest time of your life." Youth is generally considered to be carefree, but it can certainly hold some very unpleasant moments. Growing up is far from simple. There are so many new things to learn, so many strange new desires and impulses to keep under control, so many ways in which one can be hurt. Slowly most young people learn to forge for themselves protective armor, but there are still many sensitive places, still many fears and hopes and plans that older people laugh at or brush aside as unimportant. William Saroyan [1] is an author who is especially good at remembering such things, as you will discover in this story.

Al Condraj was an Armenian-American boy who got into trouble over a hammer. You would hardly believe that a ten-cent hammer could cause one to feel so utterly miserable and angry and humiliated. It wasn't just the hammer, of course. Not even Al knew *exactly* where the trouble lay. Perhaps you can find out.

ONE day in August Al Condraj was wandering through Woolworth's without a penny to spend when he saw a small hammer that was not a toy but a real hammer and he was possessed with a longing to have it. He believed it was just what he needed by which to break the monotony and with which to make something. He had gathered some first-class nails from Foley's Packing House where the boxmakers worked and where they had carelessly dropped at least fifteen cents' worth. He had gladly gone to the trouble of gathering them together because it had seemed to him that a nail, as such, was not something to be wasted. He had the nails, perhaps a half pound of them, at least two hundred of them, in a paper bag in the apple box in which he kept his junk at home.

Now, with the ten-cent hammer he believed he could make something out of box wood and the nails, although he had no idea what. Some sort of a table perhaps, or a small bench.

At any rate he took the hammer and slipped it into the pocket of his overalls, but just as he did so a man took him

[1] **Saroyan** (sä·rō′yän).

firmly by the arm without a word and pushed him to the back of the store into a small office. Another man, an older one, was seated behind a desk in the office, working with papers. The younger man, the one who had captured him, was excited and his forehead was covered with sweat.

"Well," he said, "here's one more of them."

The man behind the desk got to his feet and looked Al Condraj up and down.

"What's *he* swiped?"

"A hammer." The young man looked at Al with hatred. "Hand it over," he said.

The boy brought the hammer out of his pocket and handed it to the young man, who said, "I ought to hit you over the head with it, that's what I ought to do."

He turned to the older man, the boss, the manager of the store, and he said, "What do you want me to do with him?"

"Leave him with me," the older man said.

The younger man stepped out of the office, and the older man sat down and went back to work. Al Condraj stood in the office fifteen minutes before the older man looked at him again.

"Well," he said.

Al didn't know what to say. The man wasn't looking at him, he was looking at the door.

Finally Al said, "I didn't mean to steal it. I just need it and I haven't got any money."

"Just because you haven't got any money doesn't mean you've got a right to steal things," the man said. "Now, does it?"

"No, sir."

"Well, what am I going to do with you? Turn you over to the police?"

Al didn't say anything, but he certainly didn't want to be turned over to the police. He hated the man, but at the same time he realized somebody else could be a lot tougher than he was being.

"If I let you go, will you promise never to steal from this store again?"

"Yes, sir."

"All right," the man said. "Go out this way and don't come back to this store until you've got some money to spend."

He opened a door to the hall that led to the alley, and Al Condraj hurried down the hall and out into the alley.

The first thing he did when he was free was laugh, but he knew he had been humiliated and he was deeply ashamed. It was not in his nature to take things that did not belong to him. He hated the young man who had caught him and he hated the manager of the store who had made him stand in silence in the office so long. He hadn't liked it at all when the young man had said he ought to hit him over the head with the hammer.

He should have had the courage to look him straight in the eye and say, "You and who else?"

Of course he *had* stolen the hammer and he had been caught, but it seemed to him he oughtn't to have been so humiliated.

After he had walked three blocks he decided he didn't want to go home just yet, so he turned around and started walking back to town. He almost believed he meant to go back and say something to the young man who had caught him. And then he wasn't sure he didn't mean to go back and steal the hammer again, and this time *not* get caught. As long as he had been made to feel like a thief anyway, the least he ought to get out of it was the hammer.

Outside the store he lost his nerve, though. He stood in the street, looking in, for at least ten minutes.

Then, crushed and confused and now bitterly ashamed of himself, first for having stolen something, then for having been caught, then for having been humiliated, then for not having guts enough to go back and do the job right, he began walking home again, his mind so troubled that he didn't greet his pal Pete Wawchek when they came face to face outside Graf's Hardware.

When he got home he was too ashamed to go inside and examine his junk, so he had a long drink of water from the faucet in the back yard. The faucet was used by his mother to water the stuff she planted every year: okra, bell peppers, tomatoes, cucumbers, onions, garlic, mint, eggplants, and parsley.

His mother called the whole business the parsley garden, and every night in the summer she would bring chairs out of the house and put them around the table she had had Ondro, the neighborhood handyman, make for her for fifteen cents, and she would sit at the table and enjoy the cool of the garden and the smell of the things she had planted and tended.

Sometimes she would even make a salad and moisten the flat old-country bread and slice some white cheese, and she and he would have supper in the parsley garden. After supper she would attach the water hose to the faucet and water her plants and the place would be cooler than ever and it would smell real good, real fresh and cool and green, all the different growing things making a green-garden smell out of themselves and the air and the water.

After the long drink of water he sat down where the parsley itself was growing and he pulled a handful of it out and slowly ate it. Then he went inside and told his mother what had happened. He even told her what he had *thought* of doing after he had been turned loose: to go back and steal the hammer again.

"I don't want you to steal," his mother said in broken English. "Here is ten cents. You go back to that man and you give him this money and you bring it home, that hammer."

"No," Al Condraj said. "I won't take your money for something I don't really need. I just thought I ought to have a hammer, so I could make something if I felt like it. I've got a lot of nails and some box wood, but I haven't got a hammer."

"Go buy it, that hammer," his mother said.

"No," Al said.

"All right," his mother said. "Shut up."

That's what she always said when she didn't know what else to say.

Al went out and sat on the steps. His humiliation was beginning to really hurt now. He decided to wander off along the railroad tracks to Foley's because he needed to think about it some more. At Foley's he watched Johnny Gale nailing boxes for ten minutes, but Johnny was too busy to notice him or talk to him, although one day at Sunday school, two or three years ago, Johnny had greeted him and said, "How's the boy?" Johnny worked with a boxmaker's hatchet and everybody in Fresno said he was the fastest boxmaker in town. He was the closest thing to a machine any packing house ever saw. Foley himself was proud of Johnny Gale.

Al Condraj finally set out for home because he didn't want to get in the way. He didn't want somebody working hard to notice that he was being watched and maybe say to him, "Go on, beat it." He didn't want Johnny Gale to do something like that. He didn't want to invite another humiliation.

On the way home he looked for money but all he found was the usual pieces of broken glass and rusty nails, the things that were always cutting his bare feet every summer.

When he got home his mother had made a salad and set the table, so he sat down to eat, but when he put the food in his mouth he just didn't care for it. He got up and went into the three-room house and got his apple box out of the corner of his room and went through his junk. It was all there, the same as yesterday.

He wandered off back to town and stood in front of the closed store, hating the young man who had caught him, and then he went along to the Hippodrome and looked at the display photographs from the two movies that were being shown that day.

Then he went along to the public library to have a look at all the books again, but he didn't like any of them, so he wandered around town some more, and then around half-past eight he went home and went to bed.

His mother had already gone to bed because she had to be up at five to go to work at Inderrieden's, packing figs. Some days there would be work all day, some days there would be only half a day of it, but whatever his mother earned during the summer had to keep them the whole year.

He didn't sleep much that night because he couldn't get over what had happened, and he went over six or seven ways by which to adjust the matter. He went so far as to believe it would be necessary to kill the young man who had caught him. He also believed it would be necessary for him to steal systematically and successfully the rest of his life. It was a hot night and he couldn't sleep.

Finally, his mother got up and walked barefooted to the kitchen for a drink of water and on the way back she said to him softly, "Shut up."

When she got up at five in the morning he was out of the house, but that had happened many times before. He was a restless boy, and he kept moving all the time every summer. He was making mistakes and paying for them, and he had just tried stealing and had been caught at it and he was troubled. She fixed her breakfast, packed her lunch, and hurried off to work, hoping it would be a full day.

It was a full day, and then there was overtime, and although she had no more lunch she decided to work on for the extra money, anyway. Almost all the other packers were staying on, too, and her neighbor across the alley, Leeza Ahboot, who worked beside her, said, "Let us work until the work stops, then we'll go home and fix a supper between us and eat it in your parsley garden where it's so cool. It's a hot day and there's no sense not making an extra fifty or sixty cents."

When the two women reached the garden it was almost nine o'clock, but still daylight, and she saw her son nailing pieces of box wood together, making something with a hammer. It looked like a bench. He had already watered the garden and tidied up the rest of the yard, and the place seemed very nice, and her son seemed very serious and busy. She and Leeza went straight to work for their supper, picking bell peppers and tomatoes and cucumbers and a great deal of parsley for the salad.

Then Leeza went to her house for

some bread which she had baked the night before, and some white cheese, and in a few minutes they were having supper together and talking pleasantly about the successful day they had had. After supper, they made Turkish coffee over an open fire in the yard. They drank the coffee and smoked a cigarette apiece, and told one another stories about their experiences in the old country and here in Fresno, and then they looked into their cups at the grounds to see if any good fortune was indicated, and there was: health and work and supper out of doors in the summer and enough money for the rest of the year.

Al Condraj worked and overheard some of the things they said, and then Leeza went home to go to bed, and his mother said, "Where you get it, that hammer, Al?"

"I got it at the store."

"How you get it? You steal it?"

Al Condraj finished the bench and sat on it. "No," he said. "I didn't steal it."

"How you get it?"

"I worked at the store for it," Al said.

"The store where you steal it yesterday?"

"Yes."

"Who give you job?"

"The boss."

"What you do?"

"I carried different stuff to the different counters."

"Well, that's good," the woman said. "How long you work for that little hammer?"

"I worked all day," Al said. "Mr. Clemmer gave me the hammer after I'd worked one hour, but I went right on working. The fellow who caught me yesterday showed me what to do, and we worked together. We didn't talk, but at the end of the day he took me to Mr. Clemmer's office and he told Mr. Clemmer that I'd worked hard all day and ought to be paid at least a dollar."

"That's good," the woman said.

"So Mr. Clemmer put a silver dollar on his desk for me, and then the fellow who caught me yesterday told him the store needed a boy like me every day, for a dollar a day, and Mr. Clemmer said I could have the job."

"That's good," the woman said. "You can make it a little money for yourself."

"I left the dollar on Mr. Clemmer's desk," Al Condraj said, "and I told them both I didn't want the job."

"Why you say that?" the woman said. "Dollar a day for eleven-year-old boy good money. Why you not take job?"

"Because I hate the both of them," the boy said. "I would never work for people like that. I just looked at them and picked up my hammer and walked out. I came home and I made this bench."

"All right," his mother said. "Shut up."

His mother went inside and went to bed, but Al Condraj sat on the bench he had made and smelled the parsley garden and didn't feel humiliated any more.

But nothing could stop him from hating the two men, even though he knew they hadn't done anything they shouldn't have done.

Thinking It Over

1. Al stole that hammer all right. But why? Could you determine some of the things that were the matter with Al? What do you think that he needed most on that August day when he wandered into Woolworth's?

2. What was the strongest emotion Al felt after he was released by the store manager? Why wasn't he more relieved? How do you know that he was not really a thief? Why did he choose the particular means he

took to relieve his humiliation?

3. Why wasn't Al's mother of more help to him? Did she understand him at all? Find a passage indicating that she knew more about him than appears on the surface. Why didn't she mention the hammer as soon as she came home with Leeza and saw him making the bench? What do you learn about Al and his mother from their home life?

4. After Al had figured out a solution to his problem, he still was not completely satisfied. What were the complicated emotions that made him hate the men who were actually being fair with him? He learned at least part of a hard lesson from the hammer incident. What did he still have to learn?

5. What significance do you see in the title of the story? What did the parsley garden mean to Al's mother? Did it mean anything to Al?

6. If you have not yet read "Mama and Big Business" (p. 290), this might be a good time to do so. There are many points of similarity in the two stories and there are basic differences, too. Compare the experiences of Al and Katrin, the causes and the results of their actions. Which of them seemed to you the more fortunate? Why?

7. Did you notice the rather unusual quality of Mr. Saroyan's style? He uses very simple words, and when Al is anxiously thinking out his problem, the sentences follow his thought in the same disjointed way that we actually do think in such circumstances. Does the style suit the story?

MEETING THE UNUSUAL

PEDRO A. ALARCÓN

The Stub Book

"The Stub Book" is an amusing little story by the Spanish writer, Pedro Alarcón.[1] In spite of its brevity, it works up quite a bit of suspense and provides an amusing character study. If you like to see justice done and the villain get what's coming to him, you will enjoy reading how a seemingly simple-minded old peasant outwitted a thief.

For Better Reading . . . Despite its simplicity, this story is full of subtle touches of humor and character study. These are largely contributed by the special style of writing – a genial, easygoing style like that of a folk tale. To enjoy these qualities in the story, read attentively, noticing particular phrases and passages.

[1] **Pedro Alarcón** (pä'thrō ȧ'lär·kōn').

"The Stub Book" by Pedro A. Alarcón, translated by Armando Zegri, printed by arrangement with Maxim Lieber.

UNCLE Buscabeatas's [1] back began to curve during the period of which I am going to relate, and the reason was that he was sixty years old, forty of which had been spent working a piece of ground that bordered the banks of the Costilla.[2]

That year he had cultivated on his farm a crop of prodigious pumpkins, as large as those decorative balls on the railings of monumental bridges; and these pumpkins had attained an orange color, both inside and outside, which fact signified that it was now the month of June. Uncle Buscabeatas knew each one of them most perfectly by its form, its state of ripeness, and even by its name, especially the forty specimens that were fattest and richest in color and which seemed to be saying, "Cook us!" And he spent all his days gazing on them tenderly, and sadly exclaiming:

"Soon we shall have to part!"

In the end he decided, one fine afternoon, on the sacrifice, and pointing to the ripest among his beloved pumpkins, which had cost him so much effort, he pronounced the terrible sentence:

"Tomorrow," he said, "I will cut this forty and take them to the Cadiz [3] market. Happy that man who will eat them!"

And he walked back into his house with slow steps and spent the night with the anguish of a father who is going to marry off his daughter on the following day.

"My poor dear pumpkins!" he sighed time and time again, unable to fall asleep. But he then reflected and came to a decision with these words:

"What else can I do but sell them? I cultivated them with that end in view. At least I will realize fifteen *duros* [4] on them."

Imagine, then, his extreme astonishment, his unmitigated fury, and his desperation when, going the following morning to the farm, he discovered that he had been robbed during the night of his forty pumpkins. To save further explanation, I will merely say that he attained the most sublimely tragic fury, frantically repeating in a terrible voice:

"Oh, if I catch you, if I catch you!"

Then he began to reflect coldly and decided that his beloved objects could not yet be in Rota, his native village, where it would be impossible to put them on sale without risking their being recognized, and where, in addition, pumpkins fetch a very low price.

"They are in Cadiz, as sure as I live!" he deduced after pondering. "The infamous rogue, the robber, robbed me last night at nine or ten o'clock and escaped with them at midnight in the cargo boat. I will leave this very morning for Cadiz in the hour boat, and I shall be very much surprised if I do not catch the robber and recover the daughters of my labor."

So saying, he yet remained about twenty minutes in the vicinity of the scene of the catastrophe, as though caressing the mutilated plants, or counting the missing pumpkins, or planning a species of dire punishment on the culprit, until it was eight o'clock, and he left in the direction of the pier.

The hour boat was almost ready to sail. This humble boat leaves every morning for Cadiz promptly at nine o'clock, carrying passengers, just as the cargo boat leaves every night at midnight with a cargo of fruit and vegetables.

It is called the first hour boat because

[1] **Buscabeatas** (bo͞os′kȧ·bā·ä′tȧs).
[2] **Costilla** (kōs·tē′[l]·yä): a small river.
[3] **Cadiz** (kȧ·dĭz′): a city in Spain.
[4] **duros** (do͞o′rōz): Spanish dollars.

in this space of time and sometimes even in forty minutes, when the wind is at the stern, it makes the three leagues that separate the ancient town of Duque de Arcos [1] and the old town of Hercules.

That morning at ten-thirty Uncle Buscabeatas paused in front of a vegetable counter in the Cadiz market place and said to a bored policeman who was standing by:

"Those are my pumpkins. Arrest that man!"

And he pointed to the merchant.

"Arrest me!" exclaimed the merchant, utterly surprised and enraged. "Those pumpkins are mine. I bought them. . . ."

"You'll be able to tell that to the *alcalde*," [2] answered Uncle Buscabeatas.

"I won't."

"You will."

"You are a thief."

"You're a rascal."

"You should speak with more politeness, less indecency. Men should not talk to each other in this fashion," the policeman said with extreme calm, punching each of the contestants on the chest.

Meanwhile a crowd had collected, and it was not long before there appeared the police inspector of the public market, the judge of provisions.

The policeman resigned his charges to his superior and informed the latter of the matter at issue. With a pompous expression the judge questioned the merchant.

"Where did you get these pumpkins?"

"From Uncle Fulano,[3] the old man from Rota," the merchant answered.

"That would be the man!" cried Uncle Buscabeatas. "That's the fellow I suspected! When his farm, which is poor, produces little, he begins to rob his neighbors."

"But admitting the theory that you have been robbed last night of forty pumpkins," pursued the judge, turning to the old farmer, "how could you prove that these and no others are yours?"

"Why?" replied Uncle Buscabeatus. "Because I know them as well as you know your daughters, if you have any. Don't you see that I have raised them? Look here! this one is called 'the round one,' and that one, 'the fat fellow,' and this one, 'the red one,' that one, 'Manuela' . . . because she resembles my youngest daughter."

And the poor old man began to cry bitterly.

"All this is very good," answered the judge. "But the law does not rest satisfied with the fact that you recognize your pumpkins. It is necessary that authority should be convinced at the same time of the pre-existence of the thing in question and that you should identify it with indisputable proofs. . . . *Señores*,[4] you needn't smile. I'm a lawyer."

"Well, you will soon see the proofs, without leaving this place, that these pumpkins were raised on my farm!" said Uncle Buscabeatas, to the great astonishment of the spectators.

And dropping on the ground a package which he had been carrying in his hand, he knelt till he was able to sit on his feet and then tranquilly began to untie the knots of the handkerchief that had held the package.

The astonishment of the judge, the merchant, and the bystanders reached its climax.

"What is he going to take out?" everybody asked.

At the same time, the crowd was aug-

[1] **Duque de Arcos** (dōō′kê dā är′kōs).
[2] **alcalde** (äl·käl′då): mayor.
[3] **Fulano** (fōō·lä′nō).
[4] **Senores** (så·nyō′rås): Gentlemen.

mented by a new curiosity seeker. Seeing him the merchant exclaimed:

"I am glad you are here, Uncle Fulano! This man says that the pumpkins which you sold me last night, and which are on this very spot, were stolen. You can explain. . . ."

The newcomer turned more yellow than wax and tried to escape; but circumstances materially prevented him, and in addition the judge suggested that he remain.

Meanwhile, Uncle Buscabeatas confronted the supposed thief and said:

"You will now see what is good!"

Uncle Fulano recovered his composure and explained:

"We will see which of us can prove what he is trying to prove. For if you cannot prove, and you will not be able to prove, your charge, I will have you sent to prison for libel. These pumpkins were mine. I raised them on my *ejido* [1] farm as I did all the rest I brought this year to Cadiz, and no one can prove the contrary."

"Now you will see!" repeated Uncle Buscabeatas, finishing the untying of the handkerchief and opening it.

Then the old farmer scattered on the floor a quantity of pumpkin stalks, still green and exuding sap, the while seated on his feet and half dead with laughter, he addressed the following speech to the judge and the spectators:

"Gentlemen, have you ever paid taxes? If you have, have you seen that green book that the tax collector carried, from which receipts are cut, leaving a stub by which it can be proved if such and such a receipt is counterfeit or not?"

"What you are talking about is the stub book," gravely observed the judge.

"That is what I am carrying with me. The stub book of my garden, that is, the stalks that were attached to these pumpkins before they were stolen from me. And if you do not believe me, look at them. This stalk belonged to this pumpkin. Nobody can doubt it. This other one, as you can easily see, belonged to this one. This one, which is wider, must belong to this other one. Exactly! And this one. . . . And that one. . . . And that one!"

And as he said these words, he fitted a stalk to the hollow remaining in the pumpkin when it was plucked, and with astonishment the spectators perceived that the irregular base of the stem exactly fitted the white and small form of the concavity, which represented what we might call the scars of the pumpkins.

Then all the spectators, including the policeman and the judge himself, crouched low and began to assist Uncle Buscabeatas in this singular verification, all saying at one and the same time, with childish glee:

"Yes, yes! It is certainly so! Don't you see? This one belongs here? This one here. That one there! That one there!"

And the laughter of the men blent with the whistling of the street gamins, with the imprecations of the women, with the tears of triumph and happiness of the old farmer, and the shoves given the robber by the policemen anxious to lead him off to jail.

It is unnecessary to say that this pleasure was granted them; that Uncle Fulano was obliged to return to the merchant the fifteen *duros* he had received; that Uncle Buscabeatas returned to Rota with deep satisfaction, though he kept saying all the way:

"How beautiful they looked in the market place! I should have brought back Manuela, so that I might eat her tonight and keep the seeds."

[1] **ejido** (ē·hē′thō): public or community.

Reading Attentively

A careful reading shows you that this story is more than a simple little detective tale.

1. The very first sentence in the story gives you a clue to the author's tone, his attitude toward his characters. How would you characterize that attitude? Is it sympathetic, mocking, condescending, or what?
2. Explain how the title fits the story.
3. With whom did the bystanders seem to sympathize? Why?
4. Which character seems to you most amusing? Which part of the story?
5. Read aloud sentences that show skillful touches of humor and character revelation. Find little word pictures of Uncle Buscabeatas, Uncle Fulano, the judge, and the policeman.
6. Why would an ending that told of Uncle Fulano's imprisonment be inappropriate for this story?

For Your Vocabulary

WORD BUILDING: Anything that is *prodigious* is of the nature of a prodigy, something marvelous or vast or huge. The suffixes *-ous, -eus, -os,* and *-us* mean " full of " or " in the nature of." If something is *bulbous,* it is in the nature of a bulb. What are the adjectives formed from *danger, poison, riot, space, humor, courtesy?* Can you make others by using the suffixes given here?

Something that is *indisputable* — the accent is on the *dis,* by the way — is not open to dispute or argument. The *in-* prefix means " not," and the *-able* suffix means " capable of "; therefore, it is not capable of dispute.

Verification came to English from the Latin through several steps. It is from *verus* (true) + *ficare* (to make). Literally, *verify* means " to make true." Today it means " to prove or confirm." Can you suggest a good definition for *verification?*

SELMA LAGERLÖF

The Silver Mine

The truest wealth of a country is its people. Vast dominions, rich natural resources, treasuries filled with gold are nothing if the citizens are not honest, loyal, and free to make their own destinies. No country is greater than its leadership, however. In a kingdom the king should be worthy to lead. In a democracy the people rule; therefore the people must be worthy to rule. The president, the governor, the mayor, the teacher, the pastor, the parent, even the student still in school, each in his own sphere of influence, must measure up to his responsibility. Now, all this is clear enough when you think about it, but sometimes it requires an unusual event or circumstance to make us think. In Selma Lagerlöf's [1] story a king makes an unexpected visit — and comes away a wiser man.

[1] **Lagerlöf** (lä′gẽr·lûf).

For Better Reading . . . Some stories are constructed like "wheels within wheels." There is an outer story around an inner story. Most parables and legends are of this sort. The inner story tells a moral or a lesson that affects the characters in the outer story. You will notice this in the following tale. Try to determine which story is more important.

KING Gustav[1] III was traveling through Dalecarlia.[2] He was pressed for time, and all the way he wanted to drive like lightning. Although they drove with such speed that the horses were extended like stretched rubber bands and the coach cleared the turns on two wheels, the King poked his head out of the window and shouted to the postilion,[3] "Why don't you go ahead? Do you think you are driving over eggs?"

Since they had to drive over poor country roads at such a mad pace, it would have been almost a miracle had the harness and wagon held together! And they didn't, either; for at the foot of a steep hill the pole broke — and there the King sat! The courtiers sprang from the coach and scolded the driver, but this did not lessen the damage done. There was no possibility of continuing until the coach was mended.

When the courtiers looked around to try to find something with which the King could amuse himself while he waited, they noticed a church spire looming high above the trees in a grove a short distance ahead. They intimated to the King that he might step into one of the coaches in which the attendants were riding and drive up to the church. It was a Sunday, and the King might attend services to pass the time until the royal coach was ready.

The King accepted the proposal and drove toward the church. He had been traveling for hours through dark forest regions; but here it looked more cheerful, with fairly large meadows and villages, and with the Dal River gliding on light and pretty, between thick rows of alder bushes.

But the King had ill luck to this extent: the bell ringer took up the recessional chant just as the King was stepping from the coach on the church knoll and the people were coming out from the service. But when they came walking past him, the King remained standing, with one foot in the wagon and the other on the footstep. He did not move from the spot — only stared at them. They were the finest lot of folk he had ever seen. All the men were above the average height, with intelligent and earnest faces, and the women were dignified and stately, with an air of Sabbath peace about them.

The whole of the preceding day the King had talked only of the desolate tracts he was passing through, and had said to his courtiers again and again, "Now I am certainly driving through the very poorest part of my kingdom!" But now, when he saw the people, garbed in the picturesque dress of this section of the country, he forgot to think of their poverty; instead his heart warmed, and he remarked to himself, "The King of Sweden is not so badly off as his enemies think. So long as my subjects look like this, I shall probably be able to defend both my faith and my country."

He commanded the courtiers to make

[1] **Gustaf** (gŭs′täv).
[2] **Dalecarlia** (dăl′ĕ·kär′lĭ·*ȧ*): a region in west central Sweden.
[3] **postilion** (pōs·tĭl′y*ŭ*n): rider on one of the leading horses of a coach team.

known to the people that the stranger who was standing among them was their King and that they should gather around him, so he could talk to them.

And then the King made a speech to the people. He spoke from the high steps outside the vestry, and the narrow step upon which he stood is there even today.

The King gave an account of the sad plight in which the kingdom was placed. He said that the Swedes were threatened with war by both Russians and Danes. Under ordinary circumstances it would not be such a serious matter; but now the army was filled with traitors, and he did not dare depend upon it. Therefore there was no other course for him to take than to go himself into the country settlements and ask his subjects if they would be loyal to their King and help him with men and money, so he could save the Fatherland.

The peasants stood quietly while the King was speaking to them, and when he had finished they gave no sign either of approval or disapproval.

The King himself thought that he had spoken well. The tears had sprung to his eyes several times while he was speaking. But when the peasants stood there all the while, troubled and undecided, and could not make up their minds to answer him, the King frowned and looked displeased.

The peasants understood that it was becoming monotonous for the King to wait, and finally one of them stepped out from the crowd.

"Now, you must know, King Gustaf, that we were not expecting a royal visit in the parish today," said the peasant, "and therefore we are not prepared to answer you at once. I advise you to go into the vestry and speak with our pastor, while we discuss among ourselves this matter which you have laid before us."

The King apprehended that a more satisfactory response was not to be had immediately, so he felt that it would be best for him to follow the peasant's advice.

When he came into the vestry, he found no one there but a man who looked like a peasant. He was tall and rugged, with big hands, toughened by labor, and he wore neither cassock nor collar, but leather breeches and a long white homespun coat, like all the other men.

He rose and bowed to the King when the latter entered.

"I thought I should find the parson in here," said the King.

The man grew somewhat red in the face. He thought it annoying to mention the fact that he was the parson of this parish, when he saw that the King had mistaken him for a peasant. "Yes," said he, "the parson is usually on hand in here."

The King dropped into a large armchair which stood in the vestry at that time and which stands there today, looking exactly like itself, with this difference: the congregation has had a gilded crown attached to the back of it.

"Have you a good parson in this parish?" asked the King, who wanted to appear interested in the welfare of the peasants.

When the King questioned him in this manner, the parson felt that he couldn't possibly tell who he was. "It's better to let him go on believing that I'm only a peasant," thought he, and replied that the parson was good enough. He preached a pure and clear gospel and tried to live as he taught.

The King thought that this was a good commendation, but he had a sharp ear and marked a certain doubt in the tone.

Swedish villagers leaving church on Sunday morning. Many of them are wearing the traditional costumes which were everyday dress in King Gustav's time.

"You sound as if you were not quite satisfied with the parson," said the King.

"He's a bit arbitrary," said the man, thinking that, if the King should find out later who he was, he would not think that the parson had been standing here and blowing his own horn; therefore he wished to come out with a little fault-finding also. "There are some, no doubt, who say the parson wants to be the only one to counsel and rule in this parish," he continued.

"Then, at all events, he has led and managed in the best possible way," said the King. He didn't like it that the peasant complained of one who was placed above him. "To me it appears as though good habits and old-time simplicity were the rule here."

"The people are good enough," said the curate, "but then they live in poverty and isolation. Human beings here would certainly be no better than others if this world's temptations came closer to them."

"But there's no fear of anything of the sort happening," said the King, with a shrug.

He said nothing further, but began thrumming on the table with his fingers. He thought he had exchanged a sufficient number of gracious words with this peasant and wondered when the others would be ready with their answer.

"These peasants are not very eager to help their King," thought he. "If I only had my coach, I would drive away from them and their palaver!" [1]

The pastor sat there troubled, debating with himself as to how he should decide an important matter which he must settle. He was beginning to feel happy because he had not told the King who he was. Now he felt that he could speak with him about matters which otherwise he could not have placed before him.

After a while the parson broke the silence and asked the King if it was an actual fact that enemies were upon them and that the kingdom was in danger.

The King thought this man ought to have sense enough not to trouble him further. He simply glared at him and said nothing.

"I ask because I was standing in here and could not hear very well," said the parson. "But if this is really the case, I want to say to you that the pastor of this congregation might perhaps be able to procure for the King as much money as he will need."

"I thought that you said just now that everyone here was poor," said the King, thinking that the man did not know what he was talking about.

"Yes, that's true," replied the rector, "and the parson has no more than any of the others. But if the King would condescend to listen to me for a moment, I will explain how the pastor happens to have the power to help him."

"You may speak," said the King. "You seem to find it easier to get the words past your lips than your friends and neighbors out there, who never will be ready with what they have to tell me."

"It is not so easy to reply to the King! I'm afraid that, in the end, it will be the parson who must undertake this on behalf of the others."

The King crossed his legs, folded his arms, and let his head sink down upon his breast. "You may begin now," he said in the tone of one already asleep.

"Once upon a time there were five men from this parish who were out on a moose hunt," began the clergyman. "One of them was the parson of whom

[1] **palaver** (pȧ·lăv′ẽr): foolish talk.

we are speaking. Two of the others were soldiers, named Olaf and Eric Svärd; [1] the fourth man was the innkeeper in this settlement, and the fifth was a peasant named Israel Per Persson." [2]

"Don't go to the trouble of mentioning so many names," muttered the King, letting his head droop to one side.

"Those men were good hunters," continued the parson, "who usually had luck with them, but that day they had wandered long and far without getting anything. Finally they gave up the hunt altogether and sat down on the ground to talk. They said there was not a spot in the whole forest fit for cultivation; all of it was only mountain and swampland. 'Our Lord has not done right by us in giving us such a poor land to live in,' said one. 'In other localities people can get riches for themselves in abundance, but here, with all our toil and drudgery we can scarcely get our daily bread.'"

The pastor paused a moment, as if uncertain that the King heard him, but the latter moved his little finger to show that he was awake.

"Just as the hunters were discussing this matter, the parson saw something that glittered at the base of the mountain, where he had kicked away a moss tuft. 'This is a queer mountain,' he thought, as he kicked off another moss tuft. He picked up a sliver of stone that came with the moss and which shone exactly like the other. 'It can't be possible that this stuff is lead,' said he.

"Then the others sprang up and scraped away the turf with the butt end of their rifles. When they did this, they saw plainly that a broad vein of ore followed the mountain.

"'What do you think this might be?' asked the parson.

"The men chipped off bits of stone and bit into them. 'It must be lead, or zinc at least,' said they.

"'And the whole mountain is full of it,' added the innkeeper."

When the parson had got thus far in his narrative, the King's head was seen to straighten up a little and one eye opened. "Do you know if any of these persons knew anything about ore and minerals?" he asked.

"They did not," replied the parson.

Then the King's head sank and both eyes closed.

"The clergyman and his companions were very happy," continued the speaker, without letting himself be disturbed by the King's indifference; "they fancied that now they had found that which would give them and their descendants wealth. 'I'll never have to do any more work,' said one. 'Now I can afford to do nothing at all the whole week through, and on Sundays I shall drive to church in a golden chariot!' They were otherwise sensible men, but the great find had gone to their heads and they talked like children. Still they had enough presence of mind to put back the moss tufts and conceal the vein of ore. Then they carefully noted the place where it was, and went home. Before they parted company, they agreed that the parson should travel to Falun [3] and ask the mining expert what kind of ore this was. He was to return as soon as possible, and until then they promised one another on oath not to reveal to a soul where the ore was to be found."

The King's head was raised again a trifle, but he did not interrupt the speaker with a word. It appeared as though he was beginning to believe that the man actually had something of importance he wished to say to him, since

[1] **Olaf . . . Svärd** (ō'läv svârd).

[2] **Israel Per Persson** (ĭz'râ·ĕl pĕr pĕr'sŏn).

[3] **Falun** (fä'lŭn').

he didn't allow himself to be disturbed by his indifference.

"Then the parson departed with a few samples of ore in his pocket. He was just as happy in the thought of becoming rich as were the others. He was thinking of rebuilding the parsonage, which at present was no better than a peasant's cottage, and then he would marry a dean's daughter whom he liked. He had thought that he might have to wait for her many years. He was poor and obscure and knew that it would be a long while before he should get any post that would enable him to marry.

"The parson drove over to Falun in two days, and there he had to wait another whole day because the mining expert was away. Finally he ran across him and showed him the bits of ore. The mining expert took them in his hand. He looked at them first, then at the parson. The parson related how he had found them in a mountain at home in his parish, and wondered if it might not be lead.

"'No, it's not lead,' said the mining expert.

"'Perhaps it is zinc, then?' asked the parson.

"'Nor is it zinc,' said the mineralogist.

"The parson thought that all the hope within him sank. He had not been so depressed in many a long day.

"'Have you many stones like this in your parish?' asked the mineralogist.

"'We have a whole mountainful,' said the parson.

"Then the mineralogist came up closer, slapped the parson on the shoulder, and said, 'Let us see that you make such good use of this that it will prove a blessing both to yourselves and to the country, for this is silver.'

"'Indeed?' said the parson, feeling his way. 'So it is silver!'

"The mineralogist began telling him how he should go to work to get legal rights to the mine and gave him many valuable suggestions, but the parson stood there dazed and did not listen to what the mineralogist was saying. He was thinking how wonderful it was that at home in his poor parish stood a whole mountain of silver ore, waiting for him."

The King raised his head so suddenly that the parson stopped short in his narrative. "It turned out, of course, that, when he got home and began working the mine, he saw that the mineralogist had only been fooling him," said the King.

"Oh, no, the mineralogist had not fooled him," said the parson.

"You may continue," said the King as he settled himself more comfortably in the chair to listen.

"When the parson was at home again and was driving through the parish," continued the clergyman, "he thought that first of all he should inform his partners of the value of their find. And as he drove alongside the innkeeper Sten Stensson's place, he intended to drive up to the house to tell him they had found silver. But when he stopped outside the gate, he noticed that a broad path of evergreen was strewn all the way up to the doorstep.

"'Who has died in this place?' asked the parson of a boy who stood leaning against the fence.

"'The innkeeper himself,' answered the boy. Then he let the clergyman know that the innkeeper had drunk himself full every day for a week. 'Oh, so much brandy, so much brandy, has been drunk here!'

"'How can that be?' asked the parson. 'The innkeeper used never to drink himself full.'

"'Oh,' said the boy, 'he drank because he said he had found a mine. He was very rich. He should never have to do anything now but drink, he said. Last night he drove off, full as he was, and the wagon turned over and he was killed.'

"When the parson heard this he drove homeward, distressed over what he had heard. He had come back so happy, rejoicing because he could tell the great news.

"When the parson had driven a few paces, he saw Israel Per Persson walking along. He looked about as usual, and the parson thought it was well that fortune had not gone to his head too. Him he would cheer at once with the good news that he was a rich man.

"'Good day!' said Per Persson. 'Do you come from Falun now?'

"'I do,' said the parson. 'And now I must tell you that it has turned out even better than we had imagined. The mineralogist said it was silver ore that we had found.'

"That instant Per Persson looked as though the ground had opened under him. 'What are you saying, what are you saying? Is it silver?'

"'Yes,' answered the parson. 'We'll all be rich men now, all of us, and can live like gentlemen.'

"'Oh, is it silver?' said Per Persson, looking more and more mournful.

"'Why, of course it is silver,' replied the parson. 'You mustn't think that I want to deceive you. You mustn't be afraid to be happy.'

"'Happy!' said Per Persson. 'Should I be happy? I believed it was only glitter that we had found, so I thought it would be better to take the certain for the uncertain; I have sold my share in the mine to Olaf Svärd for a hundred dollars.' He was desperate and, when the parson drove away from him, he stood on the highway and wept.

"When the clergyman got back to his home, he sent a servant to Olaf Svärd and his brother to tell them that it was silver they had found. He thought that he had had quite enough of driving around and spreading the good news.

"But in the evening, when the parson sat alone, his joy asserted itself again. He went out in the darkness and stood on a hillock upon which he contemplated building the new parsonage. It should be imposing, of course, as fine as a bishop's palace. He stood there long that night, nor did he content himself with rebuilding the parsonage! It occurred to him that, since there were such riches to be found in the parish, throngs of people would pour in and, finally, a whole city would be built around the mine. And then he would have to erect a new church in place of the old one. Toward this object a large portion of his wealth would probably go. And he was not content with this, either, but fancied that, when his church was ready, the King and many bishops would come to the dedication. Then the King would be pleased with the church; but he would remark that there was no place where a king might put up, and then he would have to erect a castle in the new city."

Just then one of the King's courtiers opened the door of the vestry and announced that the big royal coach was mended.

At the first moment the King was ready to withdraw, but on second thought he changed his mind. "You may tell your story to the end," he said to the parson. "But you can hurry it a bit. We know all about how the man thought and dreamed. We want to know about how he acted."

"But while the parson was still lost in

his dreams," continued the clergyman, "word came to him that Israel Per Persson had made away with himself. He had not been able to bear the disappointment of having sold his share in the mine. He had thought, no doubt, that he could not endure to go about every day seeing another enjoying the wealth that might have been his."

The King straightened up a little. He kept both eyes open. "Upon my word," he said, "if I had been that parson, I should have had enough of the mine!"

"The King is a rich man," said the parson. "He has quite enough at all events. It is not the same thing with a poor curate who possesses nothing. The unhappy wretch thought instead, when he saw that God's blessing was not with his enterprise, 'I will dream no more of bringing glory and profit to myself with these riches, but I can't let the silver lie buried in the earth! I must take it out, for the benefit of the poor and needy. I will work the mine, to put the whole parish on its feet.'

"So one day the parson went out to see Olaf Svärd, to ask him and his brother as to what should be done immediately with the silver mountain. When he came in the vicinity of the barracks he met a cart surrounded by armed peasants, and in the cart sat a man with his hands tied behind him and a rope around his ankles.

"When the parson passed by, the cart stopped and he had time to regard the prisoner, whose head was tied up so it was not easy to see who he was. But the parson thought he recognized Olaf Svärd. He heard the prisoner beg those who guarded him to let him speak a few words with the parson.

"The parson drew nearer, and the prisoner turned toward him. 'You will soon be the only one who knows where the silver mine is,' said Olaf.

"'What are you saying, Olaf?' asked the parson.

"'Well, you see, parson, since we have learned that it was a silver mine we had found, my brother and I could no longer be as good friends as before. We were continually quarreling. Last night we got into a controversy over which one of us five it was who first discovered the mine. It ended in strife between us, and we came to blows. I have killed my brother and he has left me with a souvenir across the forehead to remember him by. I must hang now, and then you will be the only one who knows about the mine; therefore I wish to ask something of you.'

"'Speak out!' said the parson. 'I'll do what I can for you.'

"'You know that I am leaving several little children behind me,' began the soldier, but the parson interrupted him.

"'As regards this, you can rest easy. That which comes to your share in the mine they shall have, exactly as if you yourself were living.'

"'No,' said Olaf Svärd, 'it was another thing I wanted to ask of you. Don't let them have any portion of that which comes from the mine!'

"The parson staggered back a step. He stood there dumb and could not answer.

"'If you do not promise me this, I cannot die in peace,' said the prisoner.

"'Yes,' said the parson slowly and painfully. 'I promise you what you ask of me.'

"Thereupon the murderer was taken away, and the parson stood on the highway thinking how he should keep the promise he had given him. On the way home he thought of the wealth which he had been so happy over. What if it really were true that the people in this community could not stand riches? Already four were ruined who hitherto had been dignified and excellent men. He seemed to see the whole community before him, and he pictured to himself how this silver mine would destroy one after another. Was it befitting that he, who had been appointed to watch over these poor human beings' souls, should let loose upon them that which would be their destruction? "

All of a sudden the King sat bolt upright in his chair. " I declare! " said he, " you'll make me understand that a parson in this isolated settlement must be every inch a man."

" Nor was it enough with what had already happened," continued the parson, " for as soon as the news about the mine spread among the parishioners they stopped working and went about in idleness, waiting for the time when great riches should pour in on them. All the ne'er-do-wells there were in this section streamed in, and drunkenness and fighting were what the parson heard talked of continually. A lot of people did nothing but tramp round in the forest searching for the mine, and the parson marked that as soon as he left the house people followed him stealthily to find out if he wasn't going to the silver mountain and to steal the secret from him.

" When matters were come to this pass, the parson called the peasants together to vote. To start with he reminded them of all the misfortunes which the discovery of the mountain had brought upon them, and he asked them if they were going to let themselves be ruined or if they would save themselves. Then he told them that they must not expect him, who was their spiritual adviser, to help on their destruction. Now he had declared not to reveal to anyone where the silver mine was, and never would he himself take riches from it. And then he asked the peasants how they would have it henceforth. If they wished to continue their search for the mine and wait upon riches, then he would go so far away that no word of their misery could reach him; but if they would give up thinking about the silver mine and be as heretofore, he would remain with them. 'Whichever way you may choose,' said the parson, 'remember this, that from me no one shall ever know anything about the silver mountain.' "

" Well," said the King, " how did they decide? "

" They did as their pastor wished," said the parson. " They understood that he meant well by them when he wanted to remain poor for their sakes. And they commissioned him to go to the forest and conceal the vein of ore with evergreen and stone, so that no one would be able to find it – neither they nor their posterity."

" And ever since the parson has been living here just as poor as the rest? "

" Yes," answered the curate, " he has lived here just as poor as the rest."

" He has married, of course, and built a new parsonage? " said the King.

" No, he couldn't afford to marry and he lives in the old cabin."

" It's a pretty story that you have told me," said the King. After a few seconds he resumed, " Was it of the silver mountain that you were thinking when you said that the parson here would be able to procure for me as much money as I need? "

" Yes," said the other.

" But I can't put the thumbscrews on him," said the King. " Or how would you advise that I get such a man to show me the mountain – a man who has renounced his sweetheart and the allurements of life? "

"Oh, that's a different matter," said the parson. "But if it's the Fatherland that is in need of the fortune, he will probably give in."

"Will you answer for that? " asked the King.

"Yes, that I will answer for," said the clergyman.

"Doesn't he care, then, what becomes of his parishioners? "

"That can rest in God's hands."

The King rose from the chair and walked over to the window. He stood for a moment and looked upon the group of people outside. The longer he looked, the clearer his large eyes shone; and his figure seemed to grow. "You may greet the pastor of this congregation, and say that for Sweden's King there is no sight more beautiful than to see a people such as this! "

Then the King turned from the window and looked at the clergyman. He began to smile. "Is it true that the pastor of this parish is so poor that he removes his black clothes as soon as the service is over and dresses himself like a peasant? " asked the King.

"Yes, so poor is he," said the curate, and a crimson flush leaped into his roughhewn face.

The King went back to the window. One could see that he was in his best mood. All that was noble and great within him had been quickened into life. "You must let that mine lie in peace," said the King. "Inasmuch as you have labored and starved a lifetime to make this people such as you would have it, you may keep it as it is."

"But if the kingdom is in danger? " said the parson.

"The kingdom is better served with men than with money," remarked the King. When he had said this, he bade the clergyman farewell and went out from the vestry.

Without stood the group of people, as quiet and taciturn as they were when he went in. As the King came down the steps, a peasant stepped up to him.

"Have you had a talk with our pastor? " said the peasant.

"Yes," said the King. "I have."

"Then of course you have our answer? " said the peasant. "We asked you to go in and talk with our parson, that he might give you an answer from us."

"I have the answer," said the King.

Noting Interplay of Character

1. How does the King treat his attendants? How does he treat the villagers? How do they react to him and why?

2. Note the change that comes over the King as he and the pastor talk. What is your opinion of the King in the beginning? during the early part of the conversation? at the end?

3. How does the King discover that the "peasant" is really the pastor? Find sentences which show that the King is beginning to suspect the truth and other sentences that show he is sure of it.

4. What, by the way, is the pastor's final answer to the King?

Thinking It Over

1. A person is not really good until he has been tempted *not* to be and still succeeds in remaining good. The pastor tells the King that the people in his village are good but that they would be no better than any others if they were subjected to temptation. How does the story he tells the King prove this? How was the parson himself tempted?

2. How do you know that the mineralogist who tested the ore was a wise man? What evidence is there that the pastor, too, is a wise man? When did wisdom come to Olaf Svard?

3. Which actually shows greater qualities of leadership — the King or the pastor?

4. In what does the wealth of a country consist? Is wealth always money? What else can it be? What is meant by the phrase *natural resources?* Make a list of the most important natural resources of your own country. Discuss the question of citizens' responsibilities in conserving resources.

5. How would you like to plan a Scandinavian program? Perhaps someone in your class has relatives who live in one of the northern countries. The fathers and mothers or grandparents of some of your classmates may have been born there. Find out about Scandinavian music, literature, folklore, art, cooking, weaving, embroidery, metalwork. Have an exhibit and perhaps a recital. Scandinavian folk dances would make an interesting specialty. Appoint your committees and get to work.

For Your Vocabulary

WORD BUILDING: The Greek form *-logy* means " a speaking or saying," " a science," or " a theory." *Biology* is the study or science of life; *zoology* is that branch of *biology* devoted to animal life. On page 84 you find the word *mineralogist.* The suffix *-ist* means " one who." What, then, is a *mineralogist?* What other words can you form with *-logy* as a part?

CONTEXT: How can you tell what the word *controversy* means (page 86)? what other word gives you the clue? Find the word *arbitrary* on page 82. Read the sentence in that paragraph that explains *arbitrary.* The word *imposing* occurs on page 85. What other word in the same sentence means the same thing?

SAKI (H. H. MUNRO)

The Interlopers

Ever since Cain in anger and jealousy killed his brother Abel, men have continued to quarrel and sometimes to destroy each other. Why do men fight? There are many answers, none of them satisfactory. Fear is a basic motive, of course. When food is scarce, men destroy those with whom they might have to share; they attack when they are threatened with physical harm; they kill to protect their young. But these are all primitive instincts. Too often it is a different reason that causes men to fight — jealousy perhaps, envy, misunderstanding, or unwillingness to share the world's goods. Still, the picture is not wholly dark. There are always men of peace, men of good will. Sometimes, however, they wait too long to show their better side, as you will see in the story that follows. Saki [1] is the pen name of the well-known English writer, H. H. Munro, who chose the name, meaning " cupbearer " or " bearer of joy," from a character mentioned in the famous FitzGerald translation of the *Rubáiyát of Omar Khayyám.*

[1] **Saki** (sä'kĭ).

In a forest of mixed growth somewhere on the eastern spurs of the Carpathians,[1] a man stood one winter night watching and listening, as though he waited for some beast of the woods to come within the range of his vision, and later, of his rifle. But the game for whose presence he kept so keen an outlook was none that figured in the sportsman's calendar as lawful and proper for the chase; Ulrich von Gradwitz [2] patrolled the dark forest in quest of a human enemy.

The forest lands of Gradwitz were of wide extent and well stocked with game; the narrow strip of precipitous woodland that lay on its outskirt was not remarkable for the game it harbored or the shooting it afforded, but it was the most jealously guarded of all its owner's territorial possessions. A famous lawsuit, in the days of his grandfather, had wrested it from the illegal possession of a neighboring family of petty landowners; the dispossessed party had never acquiesced in the judgment of the courts, and a long series of poaching forays [3] and similar scandals had embittered the relationships between the families for three generations. The neighbor feud had grown into a personal one since Ulrich had come to be head of his family; if there was a man in the world whom he detested and wished ill to it was Georg Znaeym,[4] the inheritor of the quarrel and the tireless game-snatcher and raider of the disputed border-forest. The feud might, perhaps, have died down or been compromised if the personal ill will of the two men had not stood in the way; as boys they had thirsted for one another's blood, as men each prayed that misfortune might fall on the other, and this wind-scourged winter night Ulrich had banded together his foresters to watch the dark forest, not in quest of four-footed quarry, but to keep a lookout for the prowling thieves whom he suspected of being afoot from across the land boundary. The roebuck,[5] which usually kept in the sheltered hollows during a storm wind, were running like driven things tonight, and there was movement and unrest among the creatures that were wont to sleep through the dark hours. Assuredly there was a disturbing element in the forest, and Ulrich could guess the quarter from whence it came.

He strayed away by himself from the watchers whom he had placed in ambush on the crest of the hills, and wandered far down the steep slopes amid the wild tangle of undergrowth, peering through the tree trunks and listening through the whistling and skirling [6] of the wind and the restless beating of the branches for sight or sound of the marauders. If only on this wild night, in this dark, lone spot, he might come across Georg Znaeym, man to man, with none to witness — that was the wish that was uppermost in his thoughts. And as he stepped around the trunk of a huge beech he came face to face with the man he sought.

The two enemies stood glaring at one another for a long silent moment. Each had a rifle in his hand, each had hate in his heart and murder uppermost in his mind. The chance had come to give full play to the passions of a lifetime. But a man who has been brought up under the code of a restraining civilization cannot easily nerve himself to shoot down his neighbor in cold blood and without

[1] **Carpathians** (kär·pā′thĭ·ănz): mountains between Poland and Czechoslovakia.
[2] **Ulrich von Gradwitz** (o͝ol′rĭk fôn grăd′vĭtz).
[3] **poaching forays** (fŏr′āz): raids on other people's property to steal game.
[4] **Georg Znaeym** (gā·ôrk′ znām).
[5] **roebuck** (rō′bŭk′): males of a small, graceful species of deer.
[6] **skirling** (skûrl′ĭng): shrill screaming.

word spoken, except for an offense against his hearth and honor. And before the moment of hesitation had given way to action a deed of Nature's own violence overwhelmed them both. A fierce shriek of the storm had been answered by a splitting crash over their heads, and ere they could leap aside a mass of falling beech tree had thundered down on them. Ulrich von Gradwitz found himself stretched on the ground, one arm numb beneath him and the other held almost as helplessly in a tight tangle of forked branches, while both legs were pinned beneath the fallen mass. His heavy shooting boots had saved his feet from being crushed to pieces, but if his fractures were not as serious as they might have been, at least it was evident that he could not move from his present position till someone came to release him. The descending twigs had slashed the skin of his face, and he had to wink away some drops of blood from his eyelashes before he could take in a general view of the disaster. At his side, so near that under ordinary circumstances he could almost have touched him, lay Georg Znaeym, alive and struggling, but obviously as helplessly pinioned down as himself. All round them lay a thick-strewn wreckage of splintered branches and broken twigs.

Relief at being alive and exasperation at his captive plight brought a strange medley of pious thank offerings and sharp curses to Ulrich's lips. Georg, who was nearly blinded with the blood which trickled across his eyes, stopped his struggling for a moment to listen, and then gave a short, snarling laugh.

"So you're not killed, as you ought to be, but you're caught anyway," he cried, "caught fast. Ho, what a jest — Ulrich von Gradwitz snared in his stolen forest. There's a real justice for you!"

And he laughed again, mockingly and savagely.

"I'm caught in my own forest land," retorted Ulrich. "When my men come to release us you will wish, perhaps, that you were in a better plight than caught poaching on a neighbor's land, shame on you."

Georg was silent for a moment; then he answered quietly: "Are you sure that your men will find much to release? I have men, too, in the forest tonight, close behind me, and *they* will be here first and do the releasing. When they drag me out from under these branches it won't need much clumsiness on their part to roll this mass of trunk right over on the top of you. Your men will find you dead under a fallen beech tree. For form's sake I shall send my condolences [1] to your family."

"It is a useful hint," said Ulrich fiercely. "My men have orders to follow in ten minutes' time, seven of which must have gone by already, and when they get me out — I will remember the hint. Only as you will have met your death poaching on my lands I don't think I can decently send any message of condolence to your family."

"Good," snarled Georg, "good. We fight this quarrel out to the death, you and I and our foresters, with no cursed interlopers [2] to come between us. Death and damnation to you, Ulrich von Gradwitz."

"The same to you, Georg Znaeym, forest-thief, game-snatcher."

Both men spoke with the bitterness of possible defeat before them, for each knew that it might be long before his men would seek him out or find him; it

[1] **condolences** (kŏn·dō′lĕn·sĕz): expressions of sympathy.
[2] **interlopers** (ĭn′tĕr·lōp′ẽrz): meddlers; intruders.

was a bare matter of chance which party would arrive first on the scene.

Both had now given up the useless struggle to free themselves from the mass of wood that held them down; Ulrich limited his endeavors to an effort to bring his one partially free arm near enough to his outer coat pocket to draw out his wine flask. Even when he had accomplished that operation it was long before he could manage the unscrewing of the stopper or get any of the liquid down his throat. But what a Heaven-sent draught it seemed! It was an open winter, and little snow had fallen as yet, hence the captives suffered less from the cold than might have been the case at that season of the year; nevertheless, the wine was warming and reviving to the wounded man, and he looked across with something like a throb of pity to where his enemy lay, just keeping the groans of pain and weariness from crossing his lips.

"Could you reach this flask if I threw it over to you?" asked Ulrich suddenly. "There is good wine in it, and one may as well be as comfortable as one can. Let us drink, even if tonight one of us dies."

"No, I can scarcely see anything; there is so much blood caked round my eyes," said Georg, "and in any case I don't drink wine with an enemy."

Ulrich was silent for a few minutes, and lay listening to the weary screeching of the wind. An idea was slowly forming and growing in his brain, an idea that gained strength every time that he looked across at the man who was fighting so grimly against pain and exhaustion. In the pain and languor[1] that Ulrich himself was feeling the old fierce hatred seemed to be dying down.

"Neighbor," he said presently, "do as you please if your men come first. It was a fair compact. But as for me, I've changed my mind. If my men are the first to come you shall be the first to be helped, as though you were my guest. We have quarreled like devils all our lives over this stupid strip of forest, where the trees can't even stand upright in a breath of wind. Lying here tonight, thinking, I've come to think we've been rather fools; there are better things in life than getting the better of a boundary dispute. Neighbor, if you will help me to bury the old quarrel I — I will ask you to be my friend."

Georg Znaeym was silent for so long that Ulrich thought, perhaps, he had fainted with the pain of his injuries. Then he spoke slowly and in jerks.

"How the whole region would stare and gabble if we rode into the market square together. No one living can remember seeing a Znaeym and a von Gradwitz talking to one another in friendship. And what peace there would be among the forester folk if we ended our feud tonight. And if we choose to make peace among our people there is none other to interfere, no interlopers from outside. . . . You would come and keep the Sylvester night[2] beneath my roof, and I would come and feast on some high day at your castle. . . . I would never fire a shot on your land, save when you invited me as a guest; and you should come and shoot with me down in the marshes where the wildfowl are. In all the countryside there are none that could hinder if we willed to make peace. I never thought to have wanted to do other than hate you all my life, but I think I have changed my mind about things too, this last half-hour. And you offered me your wine flask . . . Ulrich von Gradwitz, I will be your friend."

[1] **languor** (lăng'gẽr): weakness.

[2] **Sylvester** (sĭl·vĕs'tẽr) **night**: a folk holiday.

For a space both men were silent, turning over in their minds the wonderful changes that this dramatic reconciliation would bring out. In the cold, gloomy forest, with the wind tearing in fitful gusts through the naked branches and whistling round the tree trunks, they lay and waited for the help that would now bring release and succor to both parties. And each prayed a private prayer that his men might be the first to arrive, so that he might be the first to show honorable attention to the enemy that had become a friend.

Presently, as the wind dropped for a moment, Ulrich broke silence.

"Let's shout for help," he said. "In this lull our voices may carry a little way."

"They won't carry far through the trees and undergrowth," said Georg, "but we can try. Together, then."

The two raised their voices in a prolonged hunting call.

"Together again," said Ulrich a few minutes later, after listening in vain for an answering halloo.

"I heard something that time, I think," said Ulrich.

"I heard nothing but the pestilential wind," said Georg hoarsely.

There was silence again for some minutes, and then Ulrich gave a joyful cry.

"I can see figures coming through the wood. They are following in the way I came down the hillside."

Both men raised their voices in as loud a shout as they could muster.

"They hear us! They've stopped. Now they see us. They're running down the hill toward us," cried Ulrich.

"How many of them are there?" asked Georg.

"I can't see distinctly," said Ulrich. "Nine or ten."

"Then they are yours," said Georg. "I had only seven out with me."

"They are making all the speed they can, brave lads," said Ulrich gladly.

"Are they your men?" asked Georg. "Are they your men?" he repeated impatiently as Ulrich did not answer.

"No," said Ulrich with a laugh, the idiotic chattering laugh of a man unstrung with hideous fear.

"Who are they?" asked Georg quickly, straining his eyes to see what the other would gladly not have seen.

"*Wolves.*"

Tracing the Story Line

1. How much of the beginning of the story can be considered as background? Find the sentence which shows that the explanatory background is completed and the actual incidents of a specific night are about to begin.

2. From the conversation of the two men *before* the tree falls on them, what action do you expect to happen?

3. The falling tree ends Ulrich's struggle to kill Georg Znaeym or to throw him off his land. What new course does he decide upon? (Where is the action taking place now?) Point out the paragraphs through which this struggle continues. Find the one in which Ulrich seems to have won the argument.

4. Now that the men are united in a common struggle against the tree and nature, they are still trying to outdo each other. How? What sentences hint at the startling conclusion?

5. Summarize the story line in six or seven statements. Use the two below and add others:

a. On stormy night, landowner goes into forest to hunt and kill poacher.

b. Enemy meets enemy, but . . . (continue).

For Your Vocabulary

CONTEXT: If you don't already know the meaning of the word *wrested* on page 90, examine the words near by and make a synonym for it. In the same sentence is the phrase *acquiesced in.* Can you suggest another phrase that might be used instead? Check this with your dictionary. Two sentences later you come across the word *compromised,* which has several meanings. The sentence makes clear the meaning that is intended here. What word could you substitute for it? What synonym would you suggest for *pinioned* near the end of paragraph four?

SIR ARTHUR CONAN DOYLE

The Redheaded League

Everybody loves a mystery story. "Whodunits," as some humorist has called them, roll from the press in vast quantities every month. Mystery thrillers form a large part of the movie output, the air waves are nightly thick with unsolved radio detective yarns, and unnamed horrors lurk in the shadows of the television screen. Edgar Allan Poe, the first great short story writer, invented the detective story and no writer has done more to popularize it than Sir Arthur Conan Doyle, who created the most famous of all detectives, Sherlock Holmes. Together with his helpful friend, Dr. Watson, you will find him meeting the unusual, with his customary cleverness, in "The Case of the Redheaded League."

For Better Reading . . . In general, an author may follow one of several "detective story patterns." His detective may be a "lone wolf" amateur, scorned by the legal authorities, or an official police detective, or a private investigator to whom troubled persons (even the police sometimes!) come for help. A variation on these three patterns is that which provides a friend of the detective – a "helper" who sees all the evidence but has to have it explained to him. In the following story it is easy to determine which pattern is used. Try to be alert, however, to each clue. Note the questions asked by the detective and the significance attached to some of the answers. You may prove to be a bit quicker at clues than Dr. Watson.

I HAD called upon my friend Mr. Sherlock Holmes one day in the summer of last year, and found him in deep conversation with a very stout, florid-faced elderly gentleman with fiery red hair. With an apology for my intrusion I was about to withdraw when Holmes pulled me abruptly into the room and closed the door behind me.

"You could not possibly have come at

a better time, my dear Watson," he said cordially.

"I was afraid that you were engaged."

"So I am. Very much so."

"Then I can wait in the next room."

"Not at all. This gentleman, Mr. Wilson, has been my partner and helper in many of my most successful cases, and I have no doubt that he will be of the utmost use to me in yours also."

The stout gentleman half rose from his chair and gave a bob of greeting, with a quick little questioning glance from his small fat-encircled eyes.

"Try the settee," said Holmes, relapsing into his armchair and putting his fingertips together as was his custom when in judicial moods. "I know, my dear Watson, that you share my love of all that is bizarre and outside the conventions and humdrum routine of everyday life. You have shown your relish for it by the enthusiasm which has prompted you to chronicle and, if you will excuse my saying so, somewhat to embellish so many of my own little adventures."

"Your cases have indeed been of the greatest interest to me," I observed.

"You will remember that I remarked the other day, just before we went into the very simple problem presented by Miss Mary Sutherland,[1] that for strange effects and extraordinary combinations we must go to life itself, which is always far more daring than any effort of the imagination."

"A proposition which I took the liberty of doubting."

"You did, Doctor; but nonetheless you must come round to my view, for otherwise I shall keep on piling fact upon fact on you until your reason breaks down under them and acknowledges me to be right. Now Mr. Jabez[2] Wilson here has been good enough to call upon me this morning, and to begin a narrative which promises to be one of the most singular which I have listened to for some time. You have heard me remark that the strangest and most unique things are very often connected not with the larger but with the smaller crimes, and occasionally occur where there is room for doubt whether any positive crime has been committed. As far as I have heard, it is impossible for me to say whether the present case is an instance of crime or not; but the course of events is certainly among the most singular that I have ever listened to. Perhaps, Mr. Wilson, you would have the kindness to recommence your story."

The portly client puffed out his chest with an appearance of some little pride, and pulled a dirty and wrinkled newspaper from the inside pocket of his greatcoat. As he glanced down the advertisement column, with his head thrust forward and the paper flattened out upon his knee, I took a good look at the man and endeavored, after the fashion of my companion, to read the indications which might be presented by his dress or appearance.

I did not gain very much, however, by my inspection. Our visitor bore every mark of being an average commonplace British tradesman, obese,[3] pompous, and slow. He wore rather baggy gray shepherd's-check trousers; a not overclean black frock coat, unbuttoned in front; and a drab waistcoat with a heavy brassy chain, and a square pierced bit of metal dangling down as an ornament. A frayed top hat and a faded brown overcoat with a wrinkled velvet collar lay upon a chair beside him. Altogether,

[1] **Miss Mary Sutherland**: a character in "A Case of Identity," another Sherlock Holmes story.

[2] **Jabez** (jā′bĕz).

[3] **obese** (ō·bēs′): very fat.

look as I would, there was nothing remarkable about the man save his blazing red head and the expression of extreme chagrin[1] and discontent upon his features.

Sherlock Holmes's quick eye took in my occupation, and he shook his head with a smile as he noticed my questioning glances. "Beyond the obvious facts that he has at some time done manual labor, that he takes snuff, that he is a Freemason,[2] that he has been in China, and that he has done a considerable amount of writing lately, I can deduce nothing."

Mr. Jabez Wilson started up in his chair, with his forefinger upon the paper but his eyes upon my companion. "How, in the name of good fortune, did you know all that, Mr. Holmes?" he asked. "How did you know, for example, that I did manual labor? It's as true as gospel, for I began as a ship's carpenter."

"Your hands, my dear sir. Your right hand is quite a size larger than your left. You have worked with it and the muscles are more developed."

"Well, the snuff, then, and the Freemasonry?"

"I won't insult your intelligence by telling you how I read that, especially as, rather against the strict rules of your order, you use an arc and compass breastpin."

"Ah, of course, I forgot that. But the writing?"

"What else can be indicated by that right cuff so very shiny for five inches, and the left one with the smooth patch near the elbow where you rest it upon the desk?"

"Well, but China?"

[1] **chagrin** (shȧ·grĭn′): mental distress caused by wounded pride, failure, or disappointment.
[2] **Freemason:** a member of a well-known secret society, now usually called the Masonic Lodge.

"The fish which you have tattooed immediately above your wrist could only have been done in China. I have made a small study of tattoo marks, and have even contributed to the literature of the subject. That trick of staining the fishes' scales a delicate pink tint is quite peculiar to China. When, in addition, I see a Chinese coin hanging from your watch chain, the matter becomes even more simple."

Mr. Jabez Wilson laughed heavily. "Well, I never!" said he, handing me the paper. "I thought at first that you had done something clever, but I see that there was nothing in it after all."

I took the paper from him and read as follows:

To the Redheaded League: On account of the bequest of the late Ezekiah[3] Hopkins, of Lebanon,[4] Pa., U.S.A., there is now another vacancy open which entitles a member of the league to a salary of four pounds a week for purely nominal services. All redheaded men who are sound in body and mind and above the age of twenty-one years are eligible. Apply in person on Monday, at eleven o'clock, to Duncan Ross, at the offices of the league, 7 Pope's Court, Fleet Street.

"What on earth does this mean?" I ejaculated after I had twice read over the extraordinary announcement.

Holmes chuckled and wriggled in his chair as was his habit when in high spirits. "It is a little off the beaten track, isn't it?" said he. "And now, Mr. Wilson, tell us all about yourself, your household, and the effect which this advertisement had upon your fortunes. You will first make a note, Doctor, of the paper and the date."

"It is the *Morning Chronicle* of April 27, 1890. Just two months ago."

[3] **Ezekiah** (ĕz′ē·kī′ȧ).
[4] **Lebanon** (lĕb′ȧ·nŭn).

"Very good. Now, Mr. Wilson."

"Well, it is just as I have been telling you, Mr. Sherlock Holmes," said Jabez Wilson, mopping his forehead. "I have a small pawnbroker's business at Coburg Square, near the City.[1] It's not a very large affair, and of late years it has not done more than just give me a living. I used to be able to keep two assistants, but now I only keep one; and I would have a job to pay him but that he is willing to come for half wages, so as to learn the business."

"What is the name of this obliging youth?" asked Sherlock Holmes.

"His name is Vincent Spaulding, and he's not such a youth either. It's hard to say his age. I should not wish a smarter assistant, Mr. Holmes; and I know very well that he could better himself, and earn twice what I am able to give him. But, after all, if he is satisfied why should I put ideas in his head?"

"Why, indeed? You seem most fortunate in having an employee who comes under the full market price. It is not a common experience among employers in this age. I don't know that your assistant is not as remarkable as your advertisement."

"Oh, he has his faults too," said Mr. Wilson. "Never was such a fellow for photography. Snapping away with a camera when he ought to be improving his mind, and then diving down into the cellar like a rabbit into its hole to develop his pictures. That is his main fault; but, on the whole, he's a good worker. There's no vice in him."

"He is still with you, I presume?"

"Yes, sir. He and a girl of fourteen, who does a bit of simple cooking and keeps the place clean — that's all I have in the house, for I am a widower and never had any family. We live very quietly, sir, the three of us, and we keep a roof over our heads, and pay our debts, if we do nothing more.

"The first thing that put us out was that advertisement. Spaulding came down into the office just this day eight weeks, with this very paper in his hand, and he says, 'I wish to the Lord, Mr. Wilson, that I was a redheaded man.'

"'Why that?' I asked.

"'Why,' says he, 'here's another vacancy in the League of the Redheaded Men. It's worth a little fortune to any man who gets it; and I understand that there are more vacancies than there are men, so that the trustees are at their wits' end what to do with the money. If my hair would only change color, here's a nice little berth all ready for me to step into.'

"'Why, what is it, then?' I asked. You see, Mr. Holmes, I am a very stay-at-home man and, as my business came to me instead of my having to go to it, I was often weeks on end without putting my foot over the door mat. In that way I didn't know much of what was going on outside, and I was always glad of a bit of news.

"'Have you never heard of the League of the Redheaded Men?' he asked, with his eyes open.

"'Never.'

"'Why, I wonder at that; for you are eligible yourself for one of the vacancies.'

"'And what are they worth?' I asked.

"'Oh, merely a couple of hundred a year; but the work is slight and it need not interfere very much with one's other occupations.'

"Well, you can easily think that that made me raise my ears; for the business has not been overgood for some years, and an extra couple of hundred would have been very handy.

[1] **the City**: the commercial district of London.

"'Tell me all about it,' said I.

"'Well,' said he, showing me the advertisement, 'you can see for yourself that the league has a vacancy, and there is the address where you should apply for particulars. As far as I can make out, the league was founded by an American millionaire, Ezekiah Hopkins, who was very peculiar in his ways. He was himself redheaded, and he had a great sympathy for all redheaded men; so, when he died, it was found that he had left his enormous fortune in the hands of trustees, with instructions to apply the interest to the providing of easy berths to men whose hair is of that color.'

"'But,' said I, 'there would be millions of redheaded men who would apply.'

"'Not so many as you might think,' he answered. 'You see it is really confined to Londoners, and to grown men. This American had started from London when he was young, and he wanted to do the old town a good turn. Then, again, I have heard it is no use to apply if your hair is light red, or dark red, or anything but real, bright, blazing, fiery red. Now, if you cared to apply, Mr. Wilson, you would just walk in; but perhaps it would hardly be worth your while to put yourself out of the way for the sake of a few hundred pounds.'

"Now it is a fact, gentlemen, as you may see for yourselves, that my hair is of a very full and rich tint, so that it seemed to me that, if there was to be any competition in the matter, I stood as good a chance as any man. Vincent Spaulding seemed to know so much about it that I thought he might prove useful, so I just ordered him to put up the shutters for the day and to come right away with me. He was very willing to have a holiday, so we shut the business up and started off for the address that was given us in the advertisement.

"I never hope to see such a sight as that again, Mr. Holmes. From north, south, east, and west every man who had a shade of red in his hair had tramped into the City to answer the advertisement. I should not have thought there were so many in the whole country as were brought together by that single advertisement. Every shade of color they were — straw, lemon, orange, brick, Irish-setter, liver, clay — but, as Spaulding said, there were not many who had the real, vivid, flame-colored tint. When I saw how many were waiting, I would have given it up in despair; but Spaulding would not hear of it. How he did it I could not imagine, but he pushed and pulled and butted until he got me through the crowd and right up to the steps which led to the office. We wedged in as well as we could, and soon found ourselves in the office."

"Your experience has been a most entertaining one," remarked Holmes as his client paused and refreshed his memory with a huge pinch of snuff. "Pray continue your very interesting statement."

"There was nothing in the office but a couple of wooden chairs and a deal table,[1] behind which sat a small man with a head that was even redder than mine. He said a few words to each candidate as he came up, and then he always managed to find some fault in them which would disqualify them. Getting a vacancy did not seem to be such a very easy matter after all. However, when our turn came, the little man was much more favorable to me than to any of the others, and he closed the door as we entered so that he might have a private word with us.

"'This is Mr. Jabez Wilson,' said my

[1] **deal table:** a table made of plain, unfinished wood.

assistant, 'and he is willing to fill a vacancy in the league.'

"'And he is admirably suited for it,' the other answered. 'He has every requirement. I cannot recall when I have seen anything so fine.' He took a step backward, cocked his head on one side, and gazed at my hair until I felt quite bashful. Then suddenly he plunged forward, wrung my hand, and congratulated me warmly on my success.

"'It would be injustice to hesitate,' said he. 'You will, however, I am sure, excuse me for taking an obvious precaution.' With that he seized my hair in both his hands and tugged until I yelled with the pain. 'There is water in your eyes,' said he as he released me. 'I perceive that all is as it should be. But we have to be careful, for we have twice been deceived by wigs and once by paint.' He stepped over to the window and shouted through it at the top of his voice that the vacancy was filled. A groan of disappointment came up from below, and the folk all trooped away in different directions until there was not a red head to be seen except my own and that of the manager.

"'My name,' said he, 'is Mr. Duncan Ross, and I am myself one of the pensioners upon the fund left by our noble benefactor. When shall you be able to enter upon your new duties?'

"'Well, it is a little awkward; for I have a business already,' said I.

"'Oh, never mind about that, Mr. Wilson!' said Vincent Spaulding. 'I shall be able to look after that.'

"'What would be the hours?' I asked.

"'Ten to two.'

"Now a pawnbroker's business is mostly done of an evening, Mr. Holmes, especially Thursday and Friday evenings, which is just before payday; so it would suit me very well to earn a little in the mornings. Besides, I knew that my assistant was a good man and that he would see to anything that turned up.

"'That would suit me very well,' said I. 'And the pay?'

"'Is four pounds a week,' he answered.

"'And the work?'

"'Is purely nominal.'

"'What do you call purely nominal?'

"'Well, you have to be in the office, or at least in the building, the whole time. If you leave, you forfeit your whole position forever. The will is very clear upon that point. You don't comply with the conditions if you budge from the office during that time.'

"'It's only four hours a day, and I should not think of leaving,' said I.

"'No excuse will avail,' said Mr. Duncan Ross, 'neither sickness, nor business, nor anything else. There you must stay, or you lose your billet.'

"'And the work?'

"'Is to copy out the *Encyclopædia Britannica.* There is the first volume of it in that press. You must find your own ink, pens, and blotting paper, but we provide this table and chair. Will you be ready tomorrow?'

"'Certainly,' I answered.

"'Then good-by, Mr. Jabez Wilson, and let me congratulate you once more on the important position which you have been fortunate enough to gain.' He bowed me out of the room, and I went home with my assistant, hardly knowing what to say or do — I was so pleased at my own good fortune.

"Well, I thought over the matter all day, and by evening I was in low spirits again; for I had quite persuaded myself that the whole affair must be some great hoax or fraud, though what its object might be I could not imagine. It seemed altogether past belief that anyone could make such a will, or that they would pay such a sum for doing anything so simple as copying out the *Encyclopædia Britannica.* Vincent Spaulding did what he could to cheer me up, but by bedtime I had reasoned myself out of the whole thing. However, in the morning I determined to have a look at it anyhow; so I bought a penny bottle of ink, and with a quill pen and seven sheets of foolscap [1] paper I started off for Pope's Court.

"Well, to my surprise and delight everything was as right as possible. The table was set out ready for me, and Mr. Duncan Ross was there to see that I got fairly to work. He started me off upon the letter A and then left me, but he would drop in from time to time to see that all was right with me. At two o'clock he bade me good day, complimented me upon the amount that I had written, and locked the door of the office after me.

"This went on day after day, Mr. Holmes, and on Saturday the manager came in and planked down four golden sovereigns for my week's work. It was the same next week, and the same the week after. Every morning I was there at ten, and every afternoon I left at two. By degrees Mr. Duncan Ross took to coming in only once of a morning, and then, after a time, he did not come in at all. Still, of course, I never dared leave the room for an instant; for I was not sure when he might come, and the billet was such a good one, and suited me so well, that I would not risk the loss of it.

"Eight weeks passed away like this, and I had written about Abbots, and Archery, and Armor, and Architecture, and Attica, and hoped with diligence that I might get on to the B's before very long. It cost me something in foolscap, and I had pretty nearly filled a shelf with my writings. And then suddenly the whole business came to an end."

"To an end?"

"Yes, sir. And no later than this morning. I went to my work as usual at ten o'clock; but the door was shut and locked, with a little square of cardboard hammered on the middle of the panel with a tack. Here it is, and you may read for yourself."

He held up a piece of white cardboard, about the size of a sheet of note paper. It read in this fashion:

THE REDHEADED LEAGUE IS DISSOLVED
July 9, 1890

Sherlock Holmes and I surveyed this curt announcement and the rueful face behind it, until the comical side of the affair so completely overtopped every consideration that we both burst out into a roar of laughter.

"I cannot see that there is anything very funny," cried our client, flushing up to the roots of his flaming head. "If you can do nothing better than laugh at me, I can go elsewhere."

"No, no," cried Holmes, shoving him back into the chair from which he had half risen. "I really wouldn't miss your case for the world. It is most refreshingly unusual. But there is, if you will excuse my saying so, something just a little funny about it. Pray what steps did you take when you found the card upon the door?"

"I was staggered, sir; I did not know what to do. I called at the offices round, but none of them seemed to know anything about it. Finally I went to the landlord, who is an accountant living on the ground floor, and I asked him if he could tell me what had become of the Red-headed League. He said that he had never heard of any such body. Then I

[1] **foolscap:** large sheets of paper, measuring about 13 x 16 inches.

asked him who Mr. Duncan Ross was. He answered that the name was new to him.

"'Well,' said I, 'the gentleman at No. 4.'

"'What, the redheaded man?'

"'Yes.'

"'Oh,' said he, 'his name is William Morris. He is a solicitor, and was using my room as a temporary convenience until his new premises were ready. He moved out yesterday.'

"'Where could I find him?'

"'Oh, at his new offices. He did tell me the address. Yes, 17 King Edward Street, near St. Paul's.'

"I started off, Mr. Holmes; but when I got to that address it was a manufactory of artificial kneecaps, and no one in it had ever heard of either Mr. William Morris or Mr. Duncan Ross."

"And what did you do then?" asked Holmes.

"I went home to Saxe-Coburg Square, and I took the advice of my assistant. But he could not help me in any way. He could only say that if I waited I should hear by post. But that was not quite good enough, Mr. Holmes. I did not wish to lose such a place without a struggle and, as I had heard that you were good enough to give advice to poor folk who were in need of it, I came right away to you."

"And you did very wisely," said Holmes. "Your case is an exceedingly remarkable one, and I shall be happy to look into it. From what you have told me I think that it is possible that graver issues hang from it than might at first sight appear."

"Grave enough!" said Mr. Jabez Wilson. "Why, I have lost four pounds a week."

"As far as you are personally concerned," remarked Holmes, "I do not see that you have any grievance against this extraordinary league. On the contrary you are, as I understand, richer by some thirty pounds, to say nothing of the minute knowledge which you have gained on every subject which comes under the letter A. You have lost nothing by them."

"No, sir. But I want to find out about them, and who they are, and what their object was in playing this prank – if it was a prank – upon me. It was a pretty expensive joke, for it cost them two and thirty pounds."

"We shall endeavor to clear up these points for you. And, first, one or two questions, Mr. Wilson. This assistant of yours who first called your attention to the advertisement – how long had he been with you?"

"About a month then."

"How did he come?"

"In answer to an advertisement."

"Was he the only applicant?"

"No, I had a dozen."

"Why did you pick him?"

"Because he was handy and would come cheap."

"At half wages, in fact?"

"Yes."

"What is he like, this Vincent Spaulding?"

"Small, stout-built, very quick in his ways, no hair on his face, though he's not short of thirty. Has a white splash of acid upon his forehead."

Holmes sat up in his chair in considerable excitement. "I thought as much," said he. "Have you ever observed that his ears are pierced for earrings?"

"Yes, sir. He told me that a gypsy had done it for him when he was a lad."

"Hum!" said Holmes, sinking back in deep thought. "He is still with you?"

"Oh, yes, sir; I have only just left him."

"And has your business been attended to in your absence?"

"Nothing to complain of, sir. There's never very much to do of a morning."

"That will do, Mr. Wilson. I shall be happy to give you an opinion upon the subject in the course of a day or two. Today is Saturday, and I hope that by Monday we may come to a conclusion.

"Well, Watson," said Holmes when our visitor had left us, "what do you make of it all?"

"I make nothing of it," I answered frankly. "It is a most mysterious business."

"As a rule," said Holmes, "the more bizarre a thing is the less mysterious it proves to be. It is your commonplace, featureless crimes which are really puzzling, just as a commonplace face is the most difficult to identify. But I must be prompt over this matter."

"What are you going to do, then?" I asked.

"To smoke," he answered. "It is quite a three-pipe problem, and I beg that you won't speak to me for fifty minutes."

He curled himself up in his chair, with his thin knees drawn up to his hawklike nose, and there he sat with his eyes closed and his black clay pipe thrusting out like the bill of some strange bird. I had come to the conclusion that he had dropped asleep, and indeed was nodding myself, when he suddenly sprang out of his chair with the gesture of a man who has made up his mind, and put his pipe down upon the mantelpiece.

"Sarasate[1] plays at St. James's Hall this afternoon," he remarked. "What do you think, Watson? Could your patients spare you for a few hours?"

"I have nothing to do today."

"Then put on your hat and come. I am going through the City first, and we can have some lunch on the way."

We traveled by the underground[2] as far as Aldersgate; and a short walk took us to Saxe-Coburg Square, the scene of the singular story which we had listened to in the morning. It was a poky, little, shabby-genteel place – four lines of dingy two-storied brick houses looking out into a small railed-in inclosure, where a lawn of weedy grass and a few clumps of faded laurel bushes made a hard fight against a smoke-laden and uncongenial atmosphere. Three gilt balls and a brown board with "Jabez Wilson" in white letters, upon a corner house, announced the place where our redheaded client carried on his business. Sherlock Holmes stopped in front of it, with his head on one side, and looked it all over, with his eyes shining brightly between puckered lids. Then he walked slowly up the street and then down again to the corner, still looking keenly at the houses. Finally he returned to the pawnbroker's and, having thumped vigorously upon the pavement with his stick two or three times, he went up to the door and knocked. It was instantly opened by a bright-looking, clean-shaven young fellow, who asked him to step in.

"Thank you," said Holmes. "I only wished to ask you how you would go from here to the Strand."

"Third right, fourth left," answered the assistant promptly, closing the door.

"Smart fellow, that," observed Holmes as we walked away. "He is, in my judgment, the fourth smartest man in London, and for daring I am not sure that he has not a claim to be third. I know something of him."

"Evidently," said I, "Mr. Wilson's assistant counts for a good deal in this

[1] **Sarasate** (sä'rä·sä'tā): a Spanish violinist and composer.

[2] **underground:** subway train.

Sherlock Holmes (Basil Rathbone) makes an observation to his admiring friend, Dr. Watson (Nigel Bruce). This is a scene from " The Hound of the Baskervilles," another exciting Sherlock Holmes mystery. (Culver)

mystery of the Redheaded League. I am sure that you inquired your way merely in order that you might see him."

"Not him."

"What then?"

"The knees of his trousers."

"And what did you see?"

"What I expected to see."

"Why did you beat the pavement?"

"My dear Doctor, this is a time for observation — not for talk. We are spies in an enemy's country. We know something of Saxe-Coburg Square. Let us now explore the parts which lie behind it."

The road in which we found ourselves as we turned round the corner from the retired Saxe-Coburg Square presented as great a contrast to it as the front of a picture does to the back. It was one of the main arteries which convey the traffic of the City to the north and west. The roadway was blocked with the immense stream of commerce flowing in a double tide inward and outward, while the footpaths were black with the hurrying swarm of pedestrians. It was difficult to realize, as we looked at the line of fine shops and stately business premises, that they really abutted on the other side upon the faded and stagnant square which we had quitted a moment before.

"Let me see," said Holmes, standing at the corner and glancing along the line. "I should like just to remember the order of the houses here. It is a hobby of mine to have an exact knowledge of London. There is Mortimer's, the tobacconist; the little newspaper shop, the Coburg branch of the City and Suburban Bank, the Vegetarian Restaurant, and McFarlane's carriage-building depot. That carries us right on to the other block. And now, Doctor, we've done our work; so it's time we had some play. A sandwich and a cup of coffee; and then off to violinland, where all is sweetness and there are no redheaded clients to vex us with their conundrums."

"You want to go home, no doubt, Doctor," he remarked as we emerged.

"Yes, it would be as well," I answered.

"And I have some business to do which will take some hours. This business at Coburg Square is serious."

"Why serious?"

"A considerable crime is in contemplation. I have every reason to believe that we shall be in time to stop it. But today being Saturday rather complicates matters. I shall want your help tonight."

"At what time?"

"Ten will be early enough."

"I shall be at Baker Street at ten."

"Very well. And, I say, Doctor! There may be some little danger, so kindly put your army revolver in your pocket." He waved his hand, turned on his heel, and disappeared in an instant among the crowd.

I trust that I am not more dense than my neighbors, but I was always oppressed with a sense of my own stupidity in my dealings with Sherlock Holmes. Here I had heard what he had heard; I had seen what he had seen; and yet from his words it was evident that he saw clearly not only what had happened but what was about to happen, while to me the whole business was still confused and grotesque. What was this nocturnal expedition, and why should I go armed? Where were we going, and what were we to do? I had the hint from Holmes that this smooth-faced pawnbroker's assistant was a formidable man — a man who might play a deep game. I tried to puzzle it out, but gave it up in despair and set the matter aside until night should bring an explanation.

It was a quarter past nine when I

started from home and made my way across the Park, and so through Oxford Street to Baker Street. Two hansoms were standing at the door and, as I entered the passage, I heard the sound of voices from above. On entering his room I found Holmes in animated conversation with two men, one of whom I recognized as Peter Jones, the official police agent, while the other was a long, thin, sad-faced man with a very shiny hat and oppressively respectable frock coat.

"Ha! Our party is complete," said Holmes, buttoning up his pea jacket and taking his heavy hunting crop from the rack. "Watson, I think you know Mr. Jones of Scotland Yard? Let me introduce you to Mr. Merryweather, who is to be our companion in tonight's adventure."

"We're hunting in couples again, Doctor, you see," said Jones in his consequential [1] way. "Our friend here is a wonderful man for starting a chase. All he wants is an old dog to help him do the running down."

"I hope a wild goose may not prove to be the end of our chase," observed Mr. Merryweather gloomily.

"Not likely; we know the man and there's nothing he won't try. John Clay, the murderer, thief, smasher, and forger. He's a young man, Mr. Merryweather; but he is at the head of his profession, and I would rather have my handcuffs on him than on any criminal in London. He's a remarkable man, is young John Clay. His grandfather was a duke, and he himself has been to Eton and Oxford. His brain is as cunning as his fingers and, though we meet signs of him at every turn, we never know where to find the man himself. He'll crack a safe in Scotland one week and be raising money to build an orphanage in Cornwall the next. I've been on his track for years, and have never set eyes on him yet."

"I hope that I may have the pleasure of introducing you tonight," said Holmes. "I've had one or two little turns also with Mr. John Clay, and I agree with you that he is at the head of his profession. It is past ten, however, and time that we started. If you two will take the first hansom, Watson and I will follow in the second."

Sherlock Holmes was not very communicative during the long drive, and lay back in the cab humming the tunes which he had heard in the afternoon. We rattled through an endless labyrinth of gaslit streets until we emerged into Farringdon Street.

"We are close there now," my friend remarked. "This fellow Merryweather is a bank director and personally interested in the matter. I thought it as well to have Jones with us also. He is as brave as a bulldog, and as tenacious as a lobster if he gets his claws upon anyone. Here we are, and they are waiting for us."

We had reached the same crowded thoroughfare in which we had found ourselves in the morning. Our cabs were dismissed and, following the guidance of Mr. Merryweather, we passed down a narrow passage and through a side door which he opened for us. Within there was a small corridor which ended in a very massive iron gate. This also was opened and led down a flight of winding stone steps which terminated at another formidable gate. Mr. Merryweather stopped to light a lantern, and then conducted us down a dark, earth-smelling passage and so, after opening a third door, into a huge vault or cellar which was piled all round with crates and massive boxes.

"You are not very vulnerable from

[1] **consequential** (kŏn′sē·kwĕn′shăl): assuming or showing self-importance.

above," Holmes remarked as he held up the lantern and gazed about him.

"Nor from below," said Mr. Merryweather, striking his stick upon the flags which lined the floor. "Why, dear me, it sounds quite hollow!" he remarked, looking up in surprise.

"I must really ask you to be a little more quiet," said Holmes severely. "You have already imperiled the whole success of our expedition. Might I beg that you would have the goodness to sit down upon one of those boxes, and not to interfere?"

The solemn Mr. Merryweather perched himself upon a crate, with a very injured expression on his face, while Holmes fell upon his knees on the floor and, with the lantern and a magnifying lens, began to examine minutely the cracks between the stones. A few seconds sufficed to satisfy him, for he sprang to his feet again and put his glass in his pocket.

"We have at least an hour before us," he remarked, "for they can hardly take any steps until the good pawnbroker is safely in bed. Then they will not lose a minute, for the sooner they do their work the longer time they will have for their escape. We are at present, Doctor — as no doubt you have divined — in the cellar of the City branch of one of the principal London banks. Mr. Merryweather is the chairman of directors, and he will explain to you that there are reasons why the more daring criminals of London should take a considerable interest in this cellar at present."

"It is our French gold," whispered the director. "We have had several warnings that an attempt might be made upon it."

"Your French gold?"

"Yes. We had occasion to strengthen our resources and borrowed, for that purpose, thirty thousand napoleons [1] from the Bank of France. The crate upon which I sit contains two thousand napoleons packed between layers of lead foil. Our reserve of bullion is much larger at present than is usually kept in a single branch office, and the directors have had misgivings upon the subject."

"Which were very well justified," observed Holmes. "And now it is time that we arranged our little plans. I expect that within an hour matters will come to a head. In the meantime, Mr. Merryweather, we must put the screen over that dark lantern."

"And sit in the dark?"

"I am afraid so. I see that the enemy's preparations have gone so far that we cannot risk the presence of a light. And, first of all, we must choose our positions. These are daring men and, though we shall take them at a disadvantage, they may do us some harm unless we are careful. I shall stand behind this crate, and do you conceal yourselves behind those. Then, when I flash a light upon them, close in swiftly. If they fire, Watson, have no compunction about shooting them down."

I placed my revolver, cocked, upon the top of the wooden case behind which I crouched. Holmes shot the slide across the front of his lantern, and left us in pitch darkness — such an absolute darkness as I have never before experienced. The smell of hot metal remained to assure us that the light was still there, ready to flash out at a moment's notice. To me, with my nerves worked up to a pitch of expectancy, there was something depressing and subduing in the sudden gloom and in the cold, dank air of the vault.

[1] **napoleons** (nȧ·pō′lē·ŭnz): French gold coins, no longer used. They were worth nearly four dollars apiece.

"They have but one retreat," whispered Holmes. "That is back through the house into Saxe-Coburg Square. I hope that you have done what I asked you, Jones?"

"I have an inspector and two officers waiting at the front door."

"Then we have stopped all the holes. And now we must be silent and wait."

What a time it seemed! From comparing notes afterward it was but an hour and a quarter, yet it appeared to me that the night must have almost gone and the dawn be breaking above us. My limbs were weary and stiff, for I feared to change my position; yet my nerves were worked up to the highest pitch of tension, and my hearing was so acute that I could not only hear the gentle breathing of my companions but I could distinguish the deeper, heavier inbreath of the bulky Jones from the thin, sighing note of the bank director. From my position I could look over the case in the direction of the floor. Suddenly my eyes caught the glint of a light.

At first it was but a lurid spark upon the stone pavement. Then it lengthened out until it became a yellow line, and then, without any warning or sound, a gash seemed to open and a hand appeared — a white, almost womanly hand, which felt about in the center of the little area of light. For a minute or more the hand, with its writhing fingers, protruded out of the floor. Then it was withdrawn as suddenly as it appeared, and all was dark again save the single lurid spark which marked a chink between the stones.

Its disappearance, however, was but momentary. With a rending, tearing sound one of the broad white stones turned over upon its side, and left a square, gaping hole through which streamed the light of a lantern. Over the edge there peeped a clean-cut, boyish face, which looked keenly about; and then, with a hand on either side of the aperture,[1] the man drew himself shoulder-high and waist-high until one knee rested upon the edge. In another instant he stood at the side of the hole and was hauling after him a companion, lithe and small like himself, with a pale face and a shock of very red hair.

"It's all clear," he whispered. "Have you the chisel and the bags? Hello! Jump, Archie, jump, and I'll swing for it!"

Sherlock Holmes had sprung out and seized the intruder by the collar. The other dived down the hole, and I heard the sound of rending cloth as Jones clutched at his skirts. The light flashed upon the barrel of a revolver; but Holmes's hunting crop came down on the man's wrist, and the pistol clinked upon the stone floor.

"It's no use, John Clay," said Holmes blandly. "You have no chance at all."

"So I see," the other answered, with the utmost coolness. "I fancy that my partner is all right, though I see you have got his coattails."

"There are three men waiting for him at the door," said Holmes.

"Oh, indeed. You seem to have done the thing very completely. I must compliment you."

"And I you," Holmes answered. "Your redheaded idea was very new and effective."

"You'll see your friend again presently," said Jones. "He's quicker at climbing down holes than I am. Just hold out while I fix the handcuffs."

"I beg that you will not touch me with your filthy hands," remarked our prisoner as the handcuffs clattered upon his wrists. "You may not be aware

[1] **aperture** (ăp′ẽr·t͡ûr): opening.

that I have noble blood in my veins. Have the goodness, also, when you address me, always to say 'sir' and 'please.'"

"All right," said Jones, with a stare and a snigger. "Well, would you please, sir, march upstairs where we can get a cab to carry your highness to the police station?"

"That is better," said John Clay serenely. He made a sweeping bow to the three of us and walked quietly off in the custody of the detective.

"Really, Mr. Holmes," said Mr. Merryweather as we followed them from the cellar, "I do not know how the bank can thank you or repay you. There is no doubt that you have detected and defeated in the most complete manner one of the most determined attempts at bank robbery that has ever come within my experience."

"I have had one or two little scores of my own to settle with Mr. John Clay," said Holmes. "I have been at some small expense over this matter, which I shall expect the bank to refund; but beyond that I am amply repaid by having had an experience which is in many ways unique, and by hearing the very remarkable narrative of the Redheaded League."

"You see, Watson," he explained, in the early hours of the morning, as we sat together in Baker Street, "it was perfectly obvious from the first that the only possible object of this rather fantastic business of the advertisement of the league, and the copying of the *Encyclopædia,* must be to get this not overbright pawnbroker out of the way for a number of hours every day. It was a curious way of managing it, but really it would be difficult to suggest a better. The method was no doubt suggested to Clay's ingenious mind by the color of his accomplice's hair. The four pounds a week was a lure which must draw him. And what was it to them, who were playing for thousands? They put in the advertisement, one rogue has the temporary office, the other rogue incites the man to apply for it, and together they manage to secure his absence every morning in the week. From the time that I heard of the assistant having come for half wages, it was obvious to me that he had some strong motive for securing the situation."

"But how could you guess what the motive was?"

"Had there been women in the house, I should have suspected a love affair. That, however, was out of the question. The man's business was a small one, and there was nothing in his house which could account for such elaborate preparations and such an expenditure as they were at. It must, then, be something out of the house. What could it be? I thought of the assistant's fondness for photography and his trick of vanishing into the cellar. The cellar! There was the end of this tangled clue. Then I made inquiries as to this mysterious assistant, and found that I had to deal with one of the coolest and most daring criminals in London. He was doing something in the cellar — something which took many hours a day for months on end. Once more, what could it be? I could think of nothing save that he was running a tunnel to some other building.

"I had got so far when we went to visit the scene of action. I surprised you by beating upon the pavement with my stick. I was ascertaining whether the cellar stretched out in front or behind. It was not in front. Then I rang the bell and, as I hoped, the assistant answered it. We have had some skirmishes, but we had never set eyes upon each other before. I hardly looked at his face. His knees were what I wished to see. You must yourself have remarked how worn, wrinkled, and stained they were; they spoke of those hours of burrowing. The only remaining point was what they were burrowing for. I walked round the corner, saw that the City and Surburban Bank abutted on our friend's premises, and felt that I had solved my problem. When you drove home after the concert I called upon Scotland Yard, and upon the chairman of the bank directors, with the result that you have seen."

"And how could you tell that they would make their attempt tonight?" I asked.

"Well, when they closed their league offices that was a sign that they cared no longer about Mr. Jabez Wilson's presence; in other words, that they had completed their tunnel. But it was essential that they should use it soon, as it might be discovered or the bullion might be removed. Saturday would suit them better than any other day, as it would give them two days for their escape. For all these reasons I expected them to come tonight."

"You reasoned it out beautifully," I exclaimed, in unfeigned admiration. "It is so long a chain, and yet every link rings true."

"It saved me from ennui,[1]" he answered, yawning. "Alas! I already feel it closing in upon me. My life is spent in one long effort to escape from the commonplaces of existence. These little problems help me to do so."

"And you are a benefactor of the race," said I.

He shrugged his shoulders. "Well, perhaps, after all, it is of some little use," he remarked. "*L'homme c'est rien — l'œuvre c'est tout,*[2] as Gustave Flaubert[3] wrote to Georges Sand."[4]

[1] **ennui** (än′wē): boredom.

Watching for Clues

1. Why does the author mention the shop helper so often at the beginning of the story?

2. Assuming right off that some kind of skullduggery is at hand, how do you know that Mr. Wilson is not involved in it?

3. Why should Holmes want to tap the pavement outside the pawnshop? Did you guess his intent when you got this far in the story?

4. Holmes reels off the lists of shops and buildings on the street off the pawnbroker's square. What clue was given here that a robbery attempt was under way?

5. If you were watching closely for clues, perhaps you also noticed some flaws in the tight-knit circumstances and events of the mystery. For example, it is not explained how the two criminals knew that the gold was stored simply in crates in the bank vault and that they would need only a chisel. The disposal of dirt from the tunnel offers another problem. Also, the removal of the gold in its weighty form by two small men is a puzzle. See if you can defend the author by explaining away these details!

Thinking It Over

1. If you were producing this story as a television play or as a movie, you would have to decide how many scenes (continuous action in one setting is a *scene*) are required. Can you identify four major scenes in the story? Can you think of radio or movie actors who might well fill the roles of Sherlock Holmes, Dr. Watson, and Clay?

2. Mr. Wilson, after hearing Holmes' deduction of personal facts about him, decided it was not really clever, after all. What are some of the rather unusual branches of knowledge or information possessed by a detective? What personal characteristics

[2] **L'homme c'est rien — l'œuvre c'est tout** (lôm sĕ ryăɴ′ — lûvr′ sĕ to͞o′): The man is nothing — the work is everything.

[3] **Gustave Flaubert** (gü·stäv′ flō·bâr′): French writer.

[4] **Georges Sand** (zhôrzh säɴ′): French novelist.

make Holmes able to use the information he gets?

3. What is the purpose of Dr. Watson in the story? He certainly isn't much of a detective. Can you compare him with other characters in detective stories, or movies or plays, you have read or seen?

4. Scotland Yard is a famous institution. It will make an interesting subject for reading and research; look it up.

For Your Vocabulary

WORD BUILDING: The word *manual* comes from the Latin *manus,* or hand. When you learn that Jabez Wilson had once done manual labor, what does it mean to you? What other terms or situations in which the word *manual* is used can you name? Another word with a Latin origin is *nominal,* which means "in name only." The work Wilson was to do for the League, therefore, was not serious or hard work, just work in name only. From its base — *nom-,* meaning "name" — can you define *nominate?* or *nominee?* or *nomenclature?* A *labyrinth* is a place with many complicated and puzzling pathways. Amusement parks sometimes have entertainment devices called labyrinths. Look up the word and discover the story behind its origin — it's a fascinating story.

FACING PROBLEMS

MacKINLAY KANTOR

That Greek Dog

When you think of Greece you are probably reminded of mythology or art. Perhaps you remember Ceres, the goddess of the Earth, or Mars, the god of war, or Apollo, the god of light and healing. You recall pictures you have seen of the great sculpture and beautiful temples that were created in ancient Greece. It is a land remote from you in time and space — a kind of storybook country. Greece is a living country, however. It is a land that has suffered much from famine, poverty, and the ravages of war, but its citizens are still proud, courageous, and freedom-loving as in the olden days. Many Greeks have come to this country in the course of the years to become Americans, useful and worthy citizens of a land that is made up of peoples from many lands.

The story which follows is about a dog, but it is much more than a dog story. If there isn't a lump in your throat as you finish, maybe you haven't yet grasped what it takes to make an American.

He received . . . praise that will never die, and with it the grandest of all sepulchers, not that in which his mortal bones are laid, but a home in the minds of men.

— THUCYDIDES [1]

In those first years after the first World War, Bill Barbilis [2] could still get into his uniform; he was ornate and handsome when he wore it. Bill's left sleeve, reading down from the shoulder, had patches and patterns of color to catch any eye. At the top there was an arc — bent stripes of scarlet, yellow, and purple; next came a single red chevron with the apex pointing up; and at the cuff were three gold chevrons pointing the other way.

On his right cuff was another gold chevron, only slightly corroded. And we must not forget those triple chevrons on an olive-drab field which grew halfway up the sleeve.

People militarily sophisticated, there in Mahaska Falls, could recognize immediately that Mr. Basilio [3] Barbilis had been a sergeant, that he had served with the Forty-Second Division, that he had been once wounded, that he had sojourned overseas for at least eighteen months, and that he had been discharged with honor.

His khaki blouse, however, was worn only on days of patriotic importance. The coat he donned at other times was white — white, that is, until cherry sirup and caramel speckled it. Mr. Barbilis was owner, manager, and staff of the Sugar Bowl.

He had a soda fountain with the most glittering spigots in town. He had a bank of candy cases, a machine for toasting sandwiches, ten small tables complete with steel-backed chairs, and a ceiling festooned with leaves of gilt and bronze paper.

Beginning in 1920, he had also a peculiar dog. Bill's living quarters were in the rear of the Sugar Bowl, and the dog came bleating and shivering to the Barbilis door one March night. The dog was no larger than a quart of ice cream and, Bill said, just as cold.

My medical office and apartment were directly over the Sugar Bowl. I made the foundling's acquaintance the next day, when I stopped in for a cup of chocolate. Bill had the dog bedded in a candy carton behind the fountain; he was heating milk when I came in, and wouldn't fix my chocolate until his new pet was fed.

Bill swore that it was a puppy. I wasn't so certain. It looked something like a mud turtle wearing furs.

"I think he is hunting dog," said Bill with pride. "He was cold last night, but not so cold now. Look, I make him nice warm bed. I got my old pajamas for him to lie on."

He waited upon the sniffling little beast with more tender consideration than ever he showed to any customer. Some people say that Greeks are mercenary. I don't know. That puppy wasn't paying board.

The dog grew up, burly and quizzical. Bill named him Duboko.[4] It sounded like that; I don't know how to spell the name correctly, nor did anyone else in Mahaska Falls.

The word, Bill said, was slang. It meant tough or hard-boiled. This animal had the face of a clown and the body of a hyena. Growing up, his downy coat changing to wire and bristles, Duboko resembled a fat Hamburg steak with onions which had been

[1] **Thucydides** (thů·sĭd′ĭ·dēz): a Greek historian of ancient times.

[2] **Barbilis** (bär·bē′lĭs).

[3] **Basilio** (bä·sē′lē·ō).

[4] **Duboko** (dōō·bō′kō).

left too long on the griddle.

At an early age Duboko began to manifest a violent interest in community assemblage of any kind or color. This trait may have been fostered by his master, who was proud to be a Moose, an Odd Fellow, a Woodman, and an upstanding member of the Mahaska Falls Commercial League.

When we needed the services of a bugler in our newly formed American Legion post and no bona fide [1] bugler would volunteer, Bill Barbilis agreed to purchase the best brass instrument available and to practice in the bleak and cindery space behind his store. Since my office was upstairs, I found no great satisfaction in Bill's musical enterprise. It happened that Duboko also lent his voice in support — a Greek chorus, so to speak, complete with strophe [2] and antistrophe.[3]

Nevertheless I could register no complaint, since with other members of the Legion I had voted to retain Bill as our bugler. I could not even kick Duboko downstairs with my one good leg when I discovered him in my reception room lunching off my mail.

Indeed, most people found it hard to punish Duboko. He had the ingratiating, hopeful confidence of an immigrant just off the boat and assured that he had found the Promised Land. He boasted beady eyes, lubberly crooked paws, an immense mouth formed of black rubber, and pearly and enormous fangs which he was fond of exhibiting in a kind of senseless leer. He smelled, too. This characteristic I called sharply to the attention of his master, with the result that Duboko was laundered weekly in Bill's uncertain little bathtub, the process being marked by vocal lament which might have arisen from the gloomiest passage of the *Antigone*.[4]

Mahaska Falls soon became aware of the creature, in a general municipal sense, and learned that it had him to reckon with. Duboko attended every gathering at which six or more people were in congregation. No fire, picnic, memorial service, Rotary conclave, or public chicken-pie supper went ungraced by his presence.

If, as sometimes happened on a crowded Saturday night, a pedestrian was brushed by a car, Duboko was on the scene with a speed to put the insurance-company representatives to shame. If there was a lodge meeting which he did not visit and from which he was not noisily ejected, I never heard of it. At Commercial League dinners he lay pensive with his head beneath the chair of Bill Barbilis. But, suffering fewer inhibitions than his master, he also visited funerals, and even the marriage of Miss Gladys Stumpf.

Old Charles P. Stumpf owned the sieve factory. He was the richest man in town; the nuptials of his daughter exuded an especial aura of social magnificence. It is a matter of historical record that Duboko sampled the creamed chicken before any of the guests did; he was banished only after the striped and rented trousers of two ushers had undergone renting in quite another sense of the word. Grieved, Duboko forswore the Stumpfs after that; he refused to attend a reception for the bride and bridegroom when they returned from the Wisconsin Dells two weeks later.

There was one other place in town where Duboko was decidedly *persona*

[1] **bona fide** (bō′nȧ fī′dē): true, real, actual.
[2] **strophe** (strō′fē): part of a song sung by the Greek chorus while performing a choral dance.
[3] **antistrophe** (ăn·tĭs′trô·fē): the part of the song answering the strophe.
[4] **Antigone** (ăn·tĭg′ô·nē): a famous Greek tragedy.

non grata.[1] This was a business house, a rival establishment of the Sugar Bowl, owned and operated by Earl and John Klugge.[2] The All-American Kandy Kitchen, they called it.

The Brothers Klugge held forth at a corner location a block distant from the Sugar Bowl. Here lounged and tittered ill-favored representatives of the town's citizenry; dice rattled on a soiled mat at the cigar counter; it was whispered that refreshment other than soda could be purchased by the chosen.

The business career of Earl and John Klugge did not flourish, no matter what inducement they offered their customers. Loudly they declared that their failure to enrich themselves was due solely to the presence in our community of a Greek — a black-haired, dark-skinned Mediterranean who thought nothing of resorting to the most unfair business practices, such as serving good fudge sundaes, for instance, to anyone who would buy them.

One fine afternoon people along the main street were troubled at observing Duboko limp rapidly westward, fairly wreathed in howls. Bill called me down to examine the dog. Duboko was only bruised, although at first I feared that his ribs were mashed on one side. Possibly someone had thrown a heavy chair at him. Bill journeyed to the Clive Street corner with fire in his eye. But no one could be found who would admit to seeing an attack on Duboko; no one would even say for a certainty that Duboko had issued from the doorway of the All-American Kandy Kitchen, although circumstantial evidence seemed to suggest it.

Friends dissuaded Bill Barbilis from invading the precinct of his enemies, and at length he was placated by pleasant fiction about a kicking horse in the market square.

We all observed, however, that Duboko did not call at the Kandy Kitchen again, not even on rare nights when the dice rattled loudly and when the whoops and catcalls of customers caused girls to pass by, like pretty Levites,[3] on the other side.

There might have been a different tale to tell if this assault had come later, when Duboko was fully grown. His frame stretched and extended steadily for a year; it became almost as mighty as the earnest Americanism of his master. He was never vicious. He was never known to bite a child. But frequently his defensive attitude was that of a mother cat who fancies her kitten in danger. Duboko's hypothetical kitten was his right to be present when good fellows — or bad — got together.

Pool halls knew him; so did the Epworth League. At football games an extra linesman was appointed for the sole purpose of discouraging Duboko's athletic ardor. Through some occult sense, he could become aware of an approaching festivity before even the vanguard assembled. Musicians of our brass band never lugged their instruments to the old bandstand in Courthouse Park without finding Duboko there before them, lounging in an attitude of expectancy. It was Wednesday night; it was eight o'clock; it was July — the veriest dullard might know at what hour and place the band would begin its attack on the "Light Cavalry Overture."

Duboko's taste in music was catholic

[1] **persona non grata** (pẽr·sō′nȧ nŏn grā′tȧ): an unacceptable person.

[2] **Klugge** (klo͞o′gė).

[3] **Levite** (lē′vīt): the Bible character who "passed by on the other side" when he saw the man who had been set upon by thieves.

and extensive. He made a fortuitous appearance at a spring musicale, presented by the high school orchestra and glee clubs, before an audience which sat in the righteous hush of people grimly determined to serve the arts, if only for a night.

The boys' glee club was rendering selections from *Carmen* — in English, of course — and dramatically they announced the appearance of the bull. The line goes, "Now the beast enters, wild and enraged," or something like that; Duboko chose this moment to lope grandly down the center aisle on castanetting toenails. He sprang to the platform. . . . Mahaska Falls wiped away more tears than did Mérimée's [1] heroine.

In his adult stage Duboko weighed forty pounds. His color suggested peanut brittle drenched with chocolate; I have heard people swear that his ears were four feet long, but that is an exaggeration. Often those ears hung like limp brown drawers dangling from a clothesline; again they were braced rigidly atop his skull.

Mastiff he was, and also German shepherd, with a noticeable influence of English bull, bloodhound, and great Dane. Far and wide he was known as "that Greek dog," and not alone because he operated out of the Sugar Bowl and under the aegis [2] of Bill Barbilis. Duboko looked like a Greek.

He had Greek eyes, Greek eyebrows, and a grinning Greek mouth. Old Mayor Wingate proclaimed in his cups that, in fact, he had heard Duboko bark in Greek; he was willing to demonstrate, if anyone would only catch Duboko by sprinkling a little Attic [3] salt on his tail.

That Greek dog seldom slept at night; he preferred to accompany the town's watchman on his rounds, or to sit in the window of the Sugar Bowl along with cardboard ladies who brandished aloft their cardboard sodas. Sometimes, when I had been called out in the middle of the night and came back from seeing a patient, I would stop and peer through the window and exchange a few signals with Duboko.

"Yes," he seemed to say, "I'm here. Bill forgot and locked me in. I don't mind, unless, of course, there's a fire. See you at Legion meeting tomorrow night, if not at the County Medical Association luncheon tomorrow noon."

At this time there was a new arrival in the Sugar Bowl household — Bill's own father, recruited all the way from Greece, now that Bill's mother was dead.

Spiros [4] Barbilis was slight, silver-headed, round-shouldered, with drooping mustachios which always seemed oozing with black dye. Bill put up another cot in the back room and bought another chiffonier from the secondhand store. He and Duboko escorted the old man up and down Main Street throughout the better part of one forenoon.

"I want you to meet friend of mine," Bill said. "He is my father, but he don't speak no English. I want him meet all my good friends here in Mahaska Falls, because he will live here always."

Old Mr. Barbilis grew deft at helping Bill with the Sugar Bowl. He carried trays and managed tables, grinning inveterately, wearing an apron stiff with starch. But he failed to learn much English except "hello" and "good-by" and

[1] **Mérimée** (mā′rē′mā′): Prosper Mérimée, a French writer, author of the novel on which the opera *Carmen* is based.

[2] **aegis** (ē′jĭs): literally, a shield; figuratively, protection.

[3] **Attic:** pertaining to the city of Athens in Greece. "Attic salt" is a figure of speech meaning "wit."

[4] **Spiros** (spē′rōs).

a few cuss words; I think that he was lonely for the land he had left, which certainly Bill was not.

One night – it was two o'clock in the morning – I came back to climb my stairs, stepping carefully from my car to the icy sidewalk in front of the Sugar Bowl. I moved gingerly, because I had left one foot in the Toul sector[1] when a dressing station was shelled; I did not like icy sidewalks.

This night I put my face close to the show window to greet Duboko, to meet those sly and mournful eyes which, on a bitter night, would certainly be waiting there instead of shining in a drifted alley where the watchman prowled.

Two pairs of solemn eyes confronted me when I looked in. Old Mr. Barbilis sat there, too – in his night clothes, but blanketed with an overcoat – he and Duboko, wrapped together among the jars of colored candy and the tinted cardboard girls. They stared out, aloof and dignified in the darkness, musing on a thousand lives that slept nearby. I enjoy imagining that they both loved the street, even in its midnight desertion, though doubtless Duboko loved it the more.

In 1923 we were treated to a mystifying phenomenon. There had never been a riot in Mahaska Falls, nor any conflict between racial and religious groups. Actually we had no racial or religious groups; we were all Americans, or thought we were. But, suddenly and amazingly, fiery crosses flared in the darkness of our pasturelands.

I was invited to attend a meeting and did so eagerly, wondering if I might explore this outlandish nonsense in a single evening. When my car stopped at a cornfield gate and ghostly figures came to admit me, I heard voice after voice whispering bashfully, "Hello, Doc" . . . "Evening, Doc. Glad you came." I was shocked at recognizing the voices. I had known the fathers and grandfathers of these youths – hard-working farmers they were, who found a long-sought freedom on the American prairies and never fumed about the presence of the hard-working Catholics, Jews, and Negroes who were also members of that pioneer community.

There was one public meeting in the town itself. They never tried to hold another; there was too much objection; the voice of Bill Barbilis rang beneath the stars.

A speaker with a pimply face stood illuminated by the flare of gasoline torches on a makeshift rostrum, and dramatically he spread a dollar bill between his hands. "Here," he cried, "is the flag of the Jews!"

Bill Barbilis spoke sharply from the crowd. "Be careful, mister. There is United States seal on that bill."

In discomfiture the speaker put away his bank note. He ignored Bill as long as he could. He set his own private eagles to screaming, and he talked of battles won, and he wept for the mothers of American boys who lay in France. He said that patriotic 100 per cent Americans must honor and protect those mothers.

Bill Barbilis climbed to the fender of a car. "Sure," he agreed clearly, "we got to take care of those mothers! Also, other mothers we got to take care of – Catholic mothers, Greek mothers, Jew mothers. We got the mothers of Company C, One Hundred Sixty-eighth Infantry. We got to take care of them. How about Jimmy Clancy? He was Catholic. He got killed in the Lorraine sector. Hyman Levinsky,

[1] **Toul** (tōōl) **sector:** a battleground of World War I.

he got killed the same day. Mr. Speaker, you don't know him because you do not come from Mahaska Falls. We had Buzz Griffin, colored boy used to shine shoes. He go to Chicago and enlist, and he is wounded in the Ninety-second Division!"

It was asking too much for any public speaker to contend against opposition of that sort, and the crowd thought so, too, and Duboko made a joyful noise. The out-of-town organizers withdrew. Fiery crosses blazed less frequently, and the flash of white robes frightened fewer cattle week by week.

Seeds had been sown, however, and now a kind of poison ivy grew within our midst. Bill Barbilis and Duboko came up to my office one morning, the latter looking annoyed, the former holding a soiled sheet of paper in his hand. "Look what I got, Doc."

The message was printed crudely in red ink:

We don't want you here any more. This town is only for 100 per cent law-abiding white Americans. Get out of town! Anti-Greek League.

It had been shoved under the front door of the Sugar Bowl sometime during the previous night.

"Bill," I told him, "don't worry about it. You know the source, probably; at least you can guess."

"Nobody is going to run me out of town," said Bill. "This is my town, and I am American citizen, and I am bugler in American Legion. I bring my old father here from Greece to be American, too, and now he has first papers." His voice trembled slightly.

"Here. Throw it in the wastepaper basket and forget about it."

There was sweat on his forehead. He wiped his face, and then he was able to laugh. "Doc, I guess you are right. Doc, I guess I am a fool."

He threw the paper away and squared his shoulders and went downstairs. I rescued a rubber glove from Duboko and threw Duboko into the hall, where he licked disinfectant from his jaws and leered at me through the screen.

A second threatening letter was shoved under Bill's door; but after that old Mr. Spiros Barbilis and Duboko did sentry duty, and pedestrians could see them entrenched behind the window. So the third warning came by mail; it told Bill that he was being given twenty-four hours to get out of town for good.

I was a little perturbed when I found Bill loading an Army .45 behind his soda fountain.

"They come around here," he said, "and I blow hell out of them."

He laughed when he said it; but I didn't like the brightness of his eyes, nor the steady, thrice-assured activity of his big clean fingers.

On Friday morning Bill came up to my office again; his face was distressed. But my fears, so far as the Anti-Greeks were concerned, were groundless.

"Do you die," he asked, "when you catch a crisis of pneumonia?"

It was one of his numerous cousins, in Sioux Falls. There had been a long-distance telephone call; the cousin was very ill, and the family wanted Bill to come. Bill left promptly in his battered, rakish roadster.

Late that night I was awakened by a clatter of cream cans under my window. I glanced at the illuminated dial of my watch, and lay wondering why the milkman had appeared some two hours before his habit. I was about to drop off to sleep when sounds of a scuffle in the alley and a roar from Duboko in the

Barbilis quarters took me to the window in one leap.

There were four figures down there in the alley yard; they dragged a fifth man — nightshirted, gagged, struggling — along with them. I yelled, and pawed around for my glasses, spurred to action by the reverberating hysterics of Duboko. I got the glasses on just before those men dragged old Mr. Barbilis into their car. The car's license plates were plastered thick with mud; at once I knew what had happened.

It was customary for the milkman to clank his bottles and cans on approaching the rear door of the Sugar Bowl; Bill or his father would get out of bed and fetch the milk to the refrigerator, for there were numerous cream-hungry cats along that alley. It was a clinking summons of this sort which had lured the lonely Mr. Barbilis from his bed.

He had gone out sleepily, probably wondering, as I had wondered, why the milkman had come so early. The sound of milk bottles lulled Duboko for a moment.

Then the muffled agony of that struggle, when the visitors clapped a pillow over the old man's face, had been enough to set Duboko bellowing.

But he was shut in: all that he could do was to threaten and curse and hurl himself against the screen. I grabbed for my foot — not the one that God gave me, but the one bought by Uncle Sam — and of course I kicked it under the bed far out of reach.

My car was parked at the opposite end of the building, out in front. I paused only to tear the telephone receiver from its hook and cry to a surprised Central that she must turn on the red light which summoned the night watchman; that someone was kidnapping old Mr. Barbilis.

The kidnappers' car roared eastward down the alley while I was bawling to the operator. And then another sound — the wrench of a heavy body sundering the metal screening. There was only empty silence as I stumbled down the stairway in my pajamas, bouncing on one foot and holding to the stair rails.

I fell into my car and turned on the headlights. The eastern block before me stretched deserted in the pale glow of single bulbs on each electric-light post. But as my car rushed into that deserted block, a small brown shape sped bulletlike across the next intersection. It was Duboko.

I swung right at the corner, and Duboko was not far ahead of me now. Down the dark, empty tunnel of Clive Street the red tail-light of another car diminished rapidly. I hitched away to the left; that would mean that Mr. Barbilis was being carried along the road that crossed the city dump.

Slowing down, I howled at Duboko when I came abreast of him. It seemed that he was a Barbilis, an Americanized Greek, like them, and that he must be outraged at this occurrence and eager to effect a rescue.

But he only slobbered up at me and labored along on his four driving legs, with spume flying behind. I stepped on the gas again and almost struck the dog, for he would not turn out of the road. I skidded through heavy dust on the dump lane, with filmier dust still billowing back from the kidnappers' car.

For their purpose the selection of the dump had a strategic excuse as well as a symbolic one. At the nearest boundary of the area there was a big steel gate and barbed-wire fence; you had to get out and open that gate to go through. But if you wished to vanish into the region of river timber and country roads beyond,

Mr. Barbilis "had a soda fountain with the most glittering spigots in town." (*Ewing Galloway*)

you could drive across the wasteland without opening the gate again. I suppose that the kidnappers guessed who their pursuer was; they knew of my physical incapacity. They had shut the gate carefully behind them, and I could not go through it without getting out of my car.

But I could see them in the glare of my headlights – four white figures, sheeted and hooded.

Already they had tied Spiros Barbilis to the middle of a fence panel. They had straps, and a whip, and everything else they needed. One man was tying the feet of old Spiros to restrain his kicks, two stood ready to proceed with the flogging, and the fourth blank, hideous, white-hooded creature moved toward the gate to restrain me from interfering. That was the situation when Duboko arrived.

I ponder now the various wickednesses Duboko committed throughout his notorious career. Then for comfort I turn to the words of a Greek – him who preached the most famous funeral oration chanted among the ancients – the words of a man who was Greek in his blood and his pride, and yet who might have honored Duboko eagerly when the dog came seeking, as it were, a kind of sentimental Attican naturalization.

"For even when life's previous record showed faults and failures," said Pericles,[1] with the voice of Thucydides, to the citizens of the fifth century, "it is just to weigh the last brave hour of devotion against them all."

Though it was not an hour by any means. No more than ten minutes had elapsed since old Mr. Barbilis was dragged from his back yard. The militant action of Duboko, now beginning, did not occupy more than a few minutes

[1] **Pericles** (pĕr′ĭ·klēz): an Athenian statesman.

more, at the most. It makes me wonder how long men fought at Marathon,[1] since Pheidippides[2] died before he could tell.

And not even a heavy screen might long contain Duboko; it is no wonder that a barbed-wire fence was as reeds before his charge.

He struck the first white figure somewhere above the knees. There was a snarl and a shriek, and then Duboko was springing toward the next man.

I didn't see what happened then. I was getting out of the car and hopping toward the gate. My bare foot came down on broken glass, and that halted me for a moment. The noise of the encounter, too, seemed to build an actual, visible barrier before my eyes.

Our little world was one turmoil of flapping, torn white robes — a whirling insanity of sheets and flesh and outcry, with Duboko revolving at the hub. One of the men dodged out of the melee, and stumbled back, brandishing a club which he had snatched from the rubble close at hand. I threw a bottle, and I like to think that that discouraged him; I remember how he pranced and swore.

Mr. Barbilis managed to get the swathing off his head and the gag out of his mouth. His frail voice sang minor encouragement, and he struggled to unfasten his strapped hands from the fence.

The conflict was moving now — moving toward the kidnappers' car. First one man staggered away, fleeing; then another who limped badly. It was an unequal struggle at best. No four members of the Anti-Greek League, however young and brawny, could justly be matched against a four-footed warrior who used his jaws as the original Lacedaemonians[3] must have used their daggers and who fought with the right on his side, which Lacedaemonians did not always do.

Four of the combatants were scrambling into their car; the fifth was still afoot and reluctant to abandon the contest. By that time I had been able to get through the gate, and both Mr. Barbilis and I pleaded with Duboko to give up a war he had won. But this he would not do; he challenged still, and tried to fight the car; and so, as they drove away, they ran him down.

It was ten A.M. before Bill Barbilis returned from Sioux Falls. I had ample opportunity to impound Bill's .45 automatic before he came.

His father broke the news to him. I found Bill sobbing with his head on the fountain. I tried to soothe him, in English, and so did Spiros Barbilis, in Greek; but the trouble was that Duboko could no longer speak his own brand of language from the little bier where he rested.

Then Bill went wild, hunting for his pistol and not being able to find it; all the time, his father eagerly and shrilly informed Bill of the identifications he had made when his assailants' gowns were ripped away. Of course, too, there was the evidence of bites and abrasions.

Earl Klugge was limping as he moved about his All-American Kandy Kitchen, and John Klugge smelled of arnica and iodine. A day or two passed before the identity of the other kidnappers leaked out. They were hangers-on at the All-American; they didn't hang on there any longer.

I should have enjoyed seeing what took place, down there at the Clive

[1] **Marathon** (măr′ȧ·thŏn): scene of a famous battle in Greece.

[2] **Pheidippides** (fī·dĭp′ĭ·dēz): famous runner who carried news of the battle of Marathon.

[3] **Lacedaemonians** (lăs′ē·dē·mō′nĭ·ănz): Spartans.

Street corner. I was only halfway down the block when Bill threw Earl and John Klugge through their own plate-glass window.

A little crowd of men gathered, with our Mayor Wingate among them. There was no talk of damages or of punitive measures to be meted out to Bill Barbilis. I don't know just what train the Klugge brothers left on. But their restaurant was locked by noon, and the windows boarded up.

A military funeral and interment took place that afternoon behind the Sugar Bowl. There was no flag, though I think Bill would have liked to display one. But the crowd of mourners would have done credit to Athens in the age when her dead heroes were burned; all the time that Bill was blowing taps on his bugle, I had a queer feeling that the ghosts of Pericles and Thucydides were somewhere around.

Restating in Other Words

What situation in the story is suggested, or what is meant, by the following lines:

1. " At an early age Duboko began to manifest a violent interest in community assemblage of any kind."
2. " Friends dissuaded Bill Barbilis from invading the precinct of his enemies, and at length he was placated by pleasant fiction about a kicking horse in the market square."
3. " Duboko's taste in music was catholic and extensive."
4. " Mahaska Falls wiped away more tears than Mérimée's heroine."
5. " Fiery crosses burned less frequently, and the flash of white robes frightened fewer cattle week by week."
6. " Seeds had been sown, however, and now a kind of poison ivy grew within our midst."

Understanding Allusions

Allusions are nothing more than references to some historical or literary event (or person or saying) that are used by an author to make a point in his writing. " The ninth-graders converged on the school gymnasium like a task force on Saipan " would be an allusion to World War II. Try to find the meaning of the following allusions in this story, applying the meaning in each instance to the story itself.

1. Greek chorus
2. Antigone (Tell her story.)
3. Pericles (Tell something about him.)
4. Thucydides (What did he write?)
5. Pheidippides (How did he die?)
6. Lacedaemonians (For what were they noted?)

Thinking It Over

1. According to the title this is a dog story. Is it really? What is the author trying to tell us through the story of Duboko?

2. No true American will stand for intolerance of any kind. How is this shown in the story? In what way did Bill show that he was a better American than his enemies?

3. The doctor was shocked at the voices he recognized at the secret meeting. The fathers and grandfathers of these young men would never have joined such an organization. How were these young fellows persuaded to do so? What was their real reason for disliking the Greek?

4. Write an editorial that might appear in a local paper after an incident of this kind, or write a letter to the editor protesting such un-American organizations as " the Anti-Greek League."

For Your Vocabulary

WORD ORIGINS: Have you ever used the word *sophisticated* in an admiring way? There is a danger in the background of this word! The old Greek philosophers, the *Sophists,* were skilled in making twisted arguments. *Sophistry* is deceptive or subtle reasoning. *Sophisticated* means, in one sense, " artificial, lacking in naturalness." Look up the origin of *sophomore.* When Bill Barbilis had *sojourned* overseas, how long did he stay? The French created the form from two Latin words, *sub* (under or about) + *diurnis* (of the day). What definition can you give for *diurnal, per diem,* and *journeyman?*

MANUEL KOMROFF

The Thousand-Dollar Bill

Do you remember reading as a child all those old tales about people who find charms, or lucky pieces, or great wealth? There was Aladdin and his magic lamp; the poor fisherman and the flounder that was a magician; the old couple and the three wishes; and many others. There must be something about finding riches that appeals to the imagination, for such stories occur in all languages, old and new. Manuel Komroff gives us one in a modern setting. Henry Armstrong finds a thousand-dollar bill on a certain Friday morning and sets in motion a strange chain of events.

For Better Reading . . . Have you learned to read beneath the surface? Some stories and poems and plays have two levels of meaning. There is the surface story — the straightforward telling of what happens to the characters. But there is also a beneath-the-surface story which is concerned with larger issues or more important clues. The story of Henry Armstrong is really an *allegory,* which means that the main character is a symbol of certain human traits or qualities. The thousand-dollar bill in the story is a symbol too; it stands for something other than money. As you read, try to extend the meaning of the story, try to get beneath the surface at the more important ideas that are suggested.

I WISH it were within my power to arrange for every man and woman in this world to find a thousand-dollar bill. To discover a thousand-dollar bill suddenly, when you least expect it, is a sensation that each should experience for himself at least once in his brief lifetime.

And if this should happen to a young fellow in the morning of his life, to a fellow uncertain about his position and about what he wanted to do — in fact, if it should happen to anyone who needed it — it would touch off a spring that would release a whole world of hidden things. And most lively things, too. But it is not often that a thousand-dollar bill is ever lost or found, and the only time I know it happened was quite recently, in a little town called Fairview.

Fairview is clean, orderly, well managed, and quite pleased with itself. It is everything a model town should be, but it was fast asleep until last week. Now it is awake, buzzing with activity and destined to become a more important place — all because a young fellow by the name of Henry Armstrong found a thousand-dollar bill in the middle of the street last Friday morning at nine o'clock.

Very few people in Fairview outside of those who work for the bank had ever seen a thousand-dollar bill. In fact, when Henry Armstrong stooped down to pick it up, it looked to him like a ten-dollar bill. When he unfolded it, it looked like a hundred-dollar bill, but then he blinked his eyes and fixed them hard on the number in the corners of the note, and it rolled up to one thousand. There was no denying it. It was printed in full round numbers — not a dollar more or less. For a moment it seemed fantastic.

Henry walked along the street slowly, holding the bill in his hand. It was nine o'clock in the morning and he was on his way to the office. But it was Friday, and his step was slightly hesitant, for while Friday was the day the French & Jones Insurance Company made up the pay envelopes, still . . .

Business had not been very active and the boss, Mr. French, had not been over-agreeable of late. He had made a lot of noise about overhead and expenses and taxes and new regulations that cut profits and commissions and all those little details that bookkeepers mark down in bright red figures. During the past month, several men had been laid off, and it was on Friday that they always got the bad news.

Henry had received several small and encouraging raises during his first couple of years in the business, but during the past year he had felt his position was not oversecure. That is why his steps were hesitant and he dreaded the sight of his Friday envelope.

When the catalogue of the new diseases of man is tabulated, I am sure that they will find a certain corrosion of the mind caused by uncertainty. Uncertainty brings on fear and loss of confidence in yourself and in your relations to others. It is an acid that eats into the core of man's nature and changes him without reason into something he should not be. But if you ever found a thousand-dollar bill, you might discover something unexpected in yourself. This is what happened to Henry.

Anyone in Fairview would have told you that Henry Armstrong was a good boy. Some would even have told you that he was timid, afraid of his own shadow, modest, retiring, and apprehensive. All these things were evident in Henry, at least on the surface. But such a conclusion would have been very wrong. With the thousand-dollar bill folded in his pocket he straightened up; he took a deep breath; his step became firm, his stride almost aggressive.

He sailed into the office and called out as loudly as he could, "Is the boss in yet?" And when he was told that the boss was not in, he turned about and ordered, "You tell Mr. French I will be back shortly; I want to talk to him." His words had the air of aggression. This would not have happened if the thousand-dollar bill had not been in his pocket.

Henry walked down the street rapidly until he came to the office of the Fairview *Chronicle*. Here he wrote out an advertisement to say that he had found a thousand-dollar bill; "Owner please communicate with Henry Armstrong." The clerk said it would cost $1.60 to run this advertisement, and Henry asked him if he might not come in after lunch and bring him the money, as he did not have $1.60 in change. He had only the thousand-dollar bill.

This could not be decided by a mere clerk, and so the business manager was consulted, and he of course wanted the advice of Mr. Young, the editor.

Mr. Young was a man who enjoyed the ironies [1] of life, and his remark was, "A fellow finds a thousand-dollar bill and he hasn't got the dollar-sixty to advertise. . . . Well, hang it," he said, "why should he advertise? Let me talk to him. No one has ever found a thousand-dollar bill in this town before. I think that ought to be good for some news."

Mr. Young went out to the advertising office and spoke to Henry. "Look here, young fellow, if you'll give us the facts, we'll write a piece about this for the front page, and you won't have to advertise at all. That will save you a dollar-sixty and give us a lively little story. Was the money in a billfold?"

"No."

"Were there any papers with it by which it might be identified?"

"No."

"Well, then, I don't see how anyone can claim it unless he happened to know the number of the bank note."

Henry reached in his pocket and said, "I'll show you the bill."

"No, no," said the editor excitedly, "I don't want to see it because there is no other way of identification. And I'd advise you, young fellow, not to show it to anyone, for anyone could make a mental note of the number and then send someone to claim possession. . . . Where did you find the bill?"

"On Main Street, on my way to the office. It was in the roadway and it might have blown out of a passing car."

The editor made note of these facts and also of Henry's full name, his address, and the insurance company where he worked. Then he said, "In the event the money is not claimed, have you any idea what you are going to do with it? I think many of our readers would be interested to know."

The renewed confidence that Henry got from the bill led him to say, "I know exactly what I'm going to do with this thousand dollars, and I'd like all Fairview to know. I'm going to marry Miss Dolly Summers. We have waited a long time and kept putting it off just because things weren't so good. Five dollars of this money will go to the parson."

"That's fine," said Mr. Young. "That makes a good story. It'll be on the front page tomorrow morning. I'm very glad you didn't have the dollar-sixty for the classified advertisement. This story is worth a good deal to Fairview, and it leads me to conclude that if you have a lot of money you do not need a little. Only the poor are required to pay in full. You see, there is a philosophy here." Then, changing the subject, he asked, "Were you born in Fairview?"

"Yes, I was born here, but I do not want to spend my whole life here."

"What's wrong with Fairview?"

"Well, the first thing is, it's an old man's town. It is run by a council of old men who have control of everything and feel as though everything they do is just all right. Well, it may be according to the way they think, but not according to how the younger people feel. I talk to young people about it every day, and none of us is going to stay in Fairview long if we have a chance to get out and try a more enterprising place."

"What do you mean by enterprising?"

"If I told you that you had no right to run your newspaper trucks up and down the streets of Fairview without having them fully insured, because it's

[1] **ironies** (ī′rō·nĭz): inconsistencies.

only a matter of time before you kill someone, you would say I am only trying to sell you something, and you would draw into your shell in the typical Fairview way. This illustrates my point. But you are wrong to run those trucks as you do without having them fully covered."

"How do you know our trucks carry no insurance?"

"Our office has been trying to sell you some business and your answer has always been that you know how to avoid trouble and that a newspaper that has the power of the printed word does not need to pay for something it already owns. You can influence opinion in your favor. You can soft-pedal any news you do not like. And that is either downright dishonest or it is wholly lacking in enterprise."

"Is that so, young man?" said the editor.

"I knew you wouldn't like what I said, but you asked for it. Perhaps yesterday I might not have been so bold, but today I feel differently." And with that Henry walked out of the office.

It was now half-past nine and he should have been back at his desk in the office, but he thought he might run in to break the news to Dolly. And he did. He ran in and told the whole story so rapidly that she could not understand anything at all, and could only exclaim, "What has got into you!"

"Nothing except this," and Henry drew the bill from his pocket and waved it in her face. He pointed to the corner of the note and said, "Count them for yourself. Three zeros — one, two, three — that makes one grand exactly."

"What's wrong with you, Henry? I never saw you like this before!"

"You don't know anything yet. And Mr. Young, the editor of the Fairview *Chronicle* — well, I just told him what I thought of him, and that's one thing that won't appear in the paper tomorrow!"

"Why, Henry, what's got into you?"

"And before I left the office, I told them I wanted to see Mr. French as soon as I got back. My talk with him will be brief and to the point. I think it is time for him to know what's what, and he's going to know it right away."

"Why, Henry, I never saw you like this. You'd better cool down. You're going to lose your job if you talk like that to Mr. French."

"Lose my job!" shouted Henry. "That job isn't worth losing."

When Henry got to the office, a great hush fell over the place. Mr. French had evidently been given the message and had asked the telephone operator to let him know the moment "the young fellow returns." She had just told him when Henry came into the private office unannounced.

"I came to tell you that I am no longer working for you," he said. "I thought it would be much better to tell you than to wait and have you tell me. I want you to know, Mr. French, I have nothing against you or the firm personally. I just think the whole scheme is wrong, and you and your management are in error. Coming to work this morning I found a thousand-dollar bill, and I'm going to look around and see if there isn't something else I'd rather do. The one thing I can't stand is the uncertainty, and I'd like to explain to you why fellows like me feel as they do — if you'd like to hear it."

"Yes, go on. I think it would amuse me to hear what a thousand-dollar bill can say."

"That's just the point, Mr. French. If I hadn't found this bill, you might never have known the truth. But you're wrong in assuming that the thousand-dollar bill is doing the talking. Anybody in your office would tell you the same thing if he only felt free to do so, but no one wants to lose his job. And so all of us live from week to week wondering who will be next, and this is a state of insecurity, and insecurity causes fear and timidity that is bad for business.

" It's an oppressive atmosphere to work in and your staff is ill at ease, and if you think your clients and customers do not sense this you're greatly mistaken. You're not getting the best out of your employees unless you can take them a little more into your confidence and let them feel that they are just as secure as your business warrants. But you yourself have become timid and you go around fuming about overhead and other expenses. That's all true, but it throws a fog over the whole place. The overhead wouldn't matter at all if we only had more business. And we'd have a lot more business if everyone connected with this firm was not afraid of his shadow.

" That's my whole story, Mr. French, and you will pardon me for speaking so plainly. I want to thank you very much for everything, and I hope you'll bear me no grudge. Good-by." He offered Mr. French his hand.

" Sit down," ordered Mr. French.

" I'd be glad to, on the understanding that I'm not working for you."

" Very well. I cannot yet make up my mind whether I am listening to the crackle of a thousand-dollar bill or to Henry Armstrong."

" I think you are listening to something that you should have heard a long time ago. The thousand-dollar bill has only loosened my tongue and given me the courage to say frankly what is in my mind. It has given me a freedom which you should have encouraged in everyone around you because it means more business and more happiness for those who are working for you."

" This seems an interesting theory, but I wonder." The word " wonder " was no sooner spoken than the phone rang.

" Excuse me, Mr. French," said the operator, " but the editor of the *Chronicle* is on the phone and would like to speak with Mr. Armstrong."

" Just a minute, please." Mr. French handed the telephone to Henry.

" This is Mr. Young, of the *Chronicle.* I want to apologize for cutting our conversation so short. I didn't exactly like what you said, but I'd like to talk to you again. And I'd like your permission to write an editorial on the subject, ' Fairview, an Old Man's Town.' I would not mention your name, of course. Are you free for lunch? "

" Yes, I am free for lunch. Yes, twelve-thirty is all right. I'll call for you at the office."

Then Mr. Young said something more, and Henry replied, " Yes, that would include full liability. I'll speak to Mr. French about it. He'll be glad to give you copies of the quotations rendered some time ago. Not at all. Yes. Thank you. Twelve-thirty. Good-by, Mr. Young."

Then he turned to Mr. French and said, " That was the editor of the *Chronicle.* I ran over this morning to put in a small announcement in the Lost and Found Column in case someone wanted to claim the thousand-dollar bill, and I had a few words with Young. I was bold enough to tell him what I thought. He would like you to send him the quotations on insuring the company trucks — full liability."

" He's had these quotations many times. Who is handling this account? "

" Why, everyone in the office tried to

handle it. And the reason there was nothing doing, Mr. French, was just plain timidity. This only proves what I've been saying."

"Well, how would it be if you took him the figures this noon?"

"You understand, I'm not working for you, Mr. French, but I'd be very glad to do that for you."

Mr. French said, "You got here at nine this morning, and you announced boldly, 'Tell Mr. French I want to talk to him,' and with that you sailed out of the office. I understand that you went to the office of the *Chronicle*, and then, returning here, you walked into this room and you said . . . Would you mind going over the whole thing again? I want to get it all straight."

"There is a little point you do not know about, Mr. French. From the office of the *Chronicle* I ran over to tell Dolly Summers the news. She warned me that if I spoke to you as I meant to, I'd lose my job, little realizing that I didn't want the job.

"You see, it is hard for people in Fairview to conceive of anyone throwing up a job. You are born here, you go to school here, you find yourself a job when you get out, and you are supposed to work at it for the rest of your life. And you live all your life in fear that something might happen that will cause you to lose your job. And fear makes you no good to yourself, and little good to your boss. You think of everything but the one thing that you should think of, and that is that the price you pay for the job may be more than the job is worth. A thousand-dollar bill might not mean much to you now, Mr. French, but if you had found a thousand-dollar bill when you were my age, what would you have done?"

"Well, I don't know exactly. When I was your age, I was working for the general store in Fairview. A thousand-dollar bill would have bought the whole store, and I'd have bought it, not because I wanted to engage in that kind of business but solely for the personal satisfaction I would have had in ordering that old miser Joseph Green out of the place. I suppose you feel the same way about me. Well, there was a time when you might have had the whole place for a thousand dollars." He laughed.

Henry smiled and said, "How much do you want for it now, Mr. French?" And this turned the whole thing into a joke. And while they were both laughing at it, the telephone rang. It was Dolly Summers, calling Henry.

"Hello, Henry! I'm glad I got you. I was so excited I didn't know what I was saying, but I think you're right. You tell Mr. French exactly what you think of him. That girl reporter who runs the society page for the *Chronicle* was around here. She wanted to know when we were going to be married."

"Well, what did you tell her?"

"I told her you were resigning your position, and as soon as everything was straightened out, we would call her up."

"Call her up at once, darling, and tell her that everything is going through as per schedule and that we're going to take that house on Maple Street within the coming week."

"I'll call her up at once. Darling, you're wonderful."

He hung up the receiver, and Mr. French remarked, "You seem to be sailing ahead with all burners on. Have you made any definite plans yet?"

"Yes, Mr. French, my plans are very definite. The first thing I decided was that indecision should be avoided, and that even if I haven't anything definite

I'm going to be definite. And the second thing is that from now on I'm going to say what is in my mind."

"How long do you think the thousand dollars will last you?"

"It mightn't last me ten minutes, but it's going to start me."

"In a business of your own?"

"I don't know. I mightn't need it at all. You know, if you have cash put away, your credit is good."

"Well, there's something in that. Still, until you find something you might remain on here. Would you listen to a proposition?"

"Yes, I would."

"Well, Henry, all you've got to do is go ahead with the confidence you've displayed in yourself this morning, and I'll let you write your own ticket."

"What would that ticket look like?"

"Well, an offer that is not generous is no offer at all. Let me propose three things – a contract for three years; full commission on all business that comes to the firm through you; and a twenty-five dollar raise, starting at once, with an increase the second year and another the third."

Henry called Dolly at once to tell her that he had not resigned.

Dolly said, "Gee, there's been more excitement here in the last hour than there's been in ten years. The telephone's been ringing every minute. The whole town's asking what you're going to do with the thousand-dollar bill."

"We might frame it, just for luck. See you later. Good-by."

The luncheon with Mr. Young lasted until almost three o'clock. Henry returned to the office and casually ordered a clerk to write up the policies for the Fairview *Chronicle* "as per terms quoted!" And then he said, "Mr. French wants to look them over before they are sent out. I'll be back in an hour."

He hurried over to see Dolly and told her about the terms of the new contract with French & Jones. He also told her how the editor was going to write an editorial about "Fairview, an Old Man's Town."

"But one point was left open," Henry said. "Mr. Young said he could quote the remarks in his editorial as coming from 'one of the younger set.' But it would be better if he could name the person. I said I needed a little time to give him my answer."

"Well," said Dolly thoughtfully, "I suppose if it comes out bad, you don't want your name attached to it, and if it comes out good, you'll want the credit for it."

"That's the whole thing in a nutshell."

"Well, that doesn't seem right to me. If you believe in what you say, I think you should be willing to stand by it."

That afternoon, when Henry got back to the office, he had another interview with Mr. French.

"Before I sign that contract with you, Mr. French, there is something I want to tell you. It is possible I may be tarred and feathered or ridden out of town on a rail, so you ought to put in a clause to protect yourself. This editorial that the *Chronicle* is printing tomorrow . . ."

He went on to explain what it was all about, and when he was through Mr. French remarked. "Well, it's about time something happened in this town. You're certain to have more support than you imagine, mark my words. And as for the contract, we'll take a chance on that."

The next day, Saturday, the story of the thousand-dollar bill was on the front page, and there was also a little box saying: "What is wrong with Fairview? An open attack that demands an answer! See page 5 editorial."

That night the old men of the town council held a meeting, in which they framed a long reply to be printed in the *Chronicle,* but they could not agree on the facts or on the language, and twice during the meeting they telephoned Henry. The first time their spokesman said, "We are taking up this matter with our legal advisers. We feel that your remarks are libelous. What we should like to know from you is: Are we right in assuming that the remarks attributed to you in this morning's paper are correct? In other words, have you been quoted correctly?"

Henry replied, "Yes, every word of it is correct. And there's a lot more that hasn't been said that you can expect to come later."

An hour later the telephone rang again. This time the old men said nothing about libel, but they felt that the criticism against them was unjust. "If the younger people of the town of Fairview had any criticism, they might have come before the council at any public meeting and aired their grievances. The council was always ready to listen, they would like to know what other matters Henry referred to, so they could reply to them too."

"You have enough to do to reply to the statements in this morning's paper. I'm not willing to place my cards in your hands, but I am willing to put them down on the table and let the public decide. The *Chronicle* has promised to give me a chance to reply to your answer. And that is all I have to say."

The council had never faced an open broadside like this before and they were unable to deal with it. The typewritten statement they gave to the *Chronicle* said that if the younger people of Fairview wanted a representation in the city council they had only to elect someone who was over twenty-one years of age and could qualify. And that was all — except that a full reply to the charges would come later.

Fairview seemed to take on a new lease of life. The telephone company had to put on two extra girls. On Sunday the old men held another meeting in the afternoon and they decided to invite Henry to speak to them on what the younger people in Fairview expected.

At first Henry refused, saying that he had no authority to speak for the younger set. The council called up Mr. Young; Mr. Young went over to see Mr. French, and they both drove to Henry's house. But Henry was around the corner looking over the house on Maple Street with Dolly.

The landlord was saying, "Well, Mr. Armstrong, you've certainly got things stirred up in this quiet little town. And if you want to sign a lease on this place I can give you an attractive figure, for I'd rather have someone in this house who's more responsible than a fly-by-night." [1]

The Monday morning *Chronicle* carried an account of the special meeting of the councilmen at which they heard criticisms and charges from young Henry Armstrong. There was also an editorial commending the action of the city council in appointing Armstrong to fill the vacancy caused by the death of one of the members some months before. And it also commended Mr. Armstrong's willingness to work with the council in the face of his minority handicap, for the old men could outvote him.

This all meant more business for French & Jones. People whom Henry had not seen for over a year wanted to make appointments.

[1] **fly-by-night:** a person who leaves town by night in order to avoid paying his bills.

But on Friday, exactly one week after Henry had found the thousand-dollar bill, he and Dolly were making out a list of things they meant to buy, and Henry drew the bill from his pocket. " Well, I guess we'll have to change our lucky bill," he said. " It would have been nice to put it away." Then he examined it closely, and even scratched it with his fingernail.

" Look, Dolly. There is something funny about this. See here. There are no silk threads in the paper. The little red marks are only printed on and there are no blue ones. Even a dollar bill has red and blue threads that are buried deep in the paper."

He drew a dollar bill from his pocket and compared it with the lucky thousand-dollar note. It was evident that the found note was counterfeit.

Henry did not know what to say. But after a brief silence he smiled and said: " Well, I guess that cooks our goose. We might as well tear up the list of things for the house. It's a good thing, Dolly, we didn't try to cash this. We'd have been the laugh of the town."

Dolly laughed. " Yes, it is funny! " she said, and she laughed some more.

" I don't see the joke," said Henry.

" Well, instead of tearing up the list of things for the house, we'll make it bigger and better and longer. And I'm glad that the bill is a counterfeit. Now nobody will claim it, and we can keep it for luck."

" I suppose you'd like to frame it? "

" Yes. What difference does it make if it's real or not real? This bit of paper released things that were in you all the time. It made you believe in yourself. And this confidence would not have broken out if you'd known the bill was a counterfeit."

" I guess that's right," said Henry.

" And what's more, it's shaken up the whole of Fairview. You've had a raise in salary; you've done more business for your firm than anyone has ever done in a single week; you've had at least ten thousand dollars' worth of publicity; and you've secured a seat on the city council — the youngest member in the history of Fairview. What more would you like? The bill has accomplished its purpose just as well as if it had been genuine. How much do you expect to get for a thousand dollars? "

" Don't forget," said Henry — " add a dollar to the list for framing the thousand-dollar bill." And they both laughed so hard that tears came to their eyes.

Reading Beneath the Surface

1. At the beginning of the story, Henry Armstrong worked for someone else and lived in constant fear of losing his job. What word describes the state of mind in which he and thousands of workers like him live out their lives? Of what is he a symbol?

2. What does the thousand-dollar bill symbolize? How did the discovery of the bill change Henry? How did he himself analyze the change in his outlook on life?

3. What is the symbolic meaning of the city council? of the younger people of Fairview? of the sudden offers that came to the " new " Henry?

4. Did it make any difference that the thousand-dollar bill was counterfeit? Does the story make its point in spite of this fact? How would the deeper meaning of the story be weakened if the bill had actually been valid?

Thinking It Over

1. There are two interesting statements in the story. One is " If you have cash put away, your credit is good." The other is " Only the poor are required to pay in full." How are these two statements related? Do you recall any other folk sayings about money?

2. What accusation did Henry level at his own boss and the firm for which he

worked? What criticisms did he make of the newspaper? Do they seem to you to have been justified? Discuss whether such criticisms can be made of other organizations.

3. How did Dolly show her native honesty?

4. What do you think about Henry's theory of greater participation by employees in the affairs of the business for which they work? Do you know of any examples in real life?

5. From the point of view of the storyteller's art, why did the author keep anyone from seeing the bill but Henry? What reason for this fact is given in the story itself? What do you know about counterfeit money? See what you can find out.

GUY DE MAUPASSANT

The Necklace

"Neither a borrower nor a lender be," says Shakespeare in one of his plays. The wisdom of his advice is well exemplified in "The Necklace," by the famous French short story writer, Guy de Maupassant.[1]

What would you do if you had foolishly borrowed some expensive bit of jewelry from a friend to wear to a dance or a party and lost it? Would you confess immediately? Would you make a tentative offer to replace the article, thus forcing your friend to say that it didn't matter and you mustn't think anything more about it? Or would you try to replace it without confessing that you had lost it? Mme Loisel, in the story that follows, had such a choice to make, and the results of that decision add up to a story you will not soon forget.

SHE was one of those pretty and charming girls who are sometimes, as if by a mistake of destiny, born in a family of clerks. She had no dowry, no expectations, no means of being known, understood, loved, wedded, by any rich and distinguished man; and she let herself be married to a little clerk at the Ministry of Public Instruction.

She dressed plainly because she could not dress well; but she was as unhappy as though she had really fallen from her proper station, since with women there is neither caste nor rank, and beauty, grace, and charm act instead of family and birth. Natural fineness, instinct for what is elegant, suppleness of wit, are the sole hierarchy, and make from women of the people the equals of

[1] **Guy de Maupassant** (gē dẽ mō·pȧ·säɴ′).

the very greatest ladies.

She suffered ceaselessly, feeling herself born for all the delicacies and all the luxuries. She suffered from the poverty of her dwelling, from the wretched look of the walls, from the worn-out chairs, from the ugliness of the curtains. All those things, of which another woman of her rank would never even have been conscious, tortured her and made her angry. The sight of the little Breton [1] peasant who did her humble housework aroused in her regrets, which were despairing, and distracted dreams. She thought of the silent antechambers hung with Oriental tapestry, lit by tall bronze candelabra, and of the two great footmen in knee breeches who sleep in the big armchairs, made drowsy by the heavy warmth of the hot-air stove. She thought of the long *salons* [2] fitted up with ancient silk, of the delicate furniture carrying priceless curiosities, and of the coquettish perfumed boudoirs made for talks at five o'clock with intimate friends, with men famous and sought after, whom all women envy and whose attention they all desire.

When she sat down to dinner, before the round table covered with a tablecloth three days old, opposite her husband, who uncovered the soup tureen and declared with an enchanted air, "Ah, the good *pot-au-feu!* [3] I don't know anything better than that," she thought of dainty dinners, of shining silverware, of tapestry which peopled the walls with ancient personages and with strange birds flying in the midst of a fairy forest; and she thought of delicious dishes served on marvelous plates, and of the whispered gallantries which you listen to with a sphinxlike smile while you are eating the pink flesh of a trout or the wings of a quail.

She had no dresses, no jewels, nothing. And she loved nothing but that; she felt made for that. She would so have liked to please, to be envied, to be charming, to be sought after.

She had a friend, a former schoolmate at the convent, who was rich and whom she did not like to go and see any more, because she suffered so much when she came back.

But one evening her husband returned home with a triumphant air, and holding a large envelope in his hand.

"There," said he. "Here is something for you."

She tore the paper sharply, and drew out a printed card which bore these words:

THE MINISTER OF PUBLIC INSTRUCTION AND MME GEORGES RAMPONNEAU [4] REQUEST THE HONOR OF M. AND MME LOISEL'S [5] COMPANY AT THE PALACE OF THE MINISTRY ON MONDAY EVENING, JANUARY 18TH.

Instead of being delighted, as her husband hoped, she threw the invitation on the table with disdain, murmuring, "What do you want me to do with that?"

"But, my dear, I thought you would be glad. You never go out, and this is such a fine opportunity. I had awful trouble to get it. Everyone wants to go; it is very select, and they are not giving many invitations to clerks. The whole of-

[1] **Breton** (brĕt′ŭn): from Brittany.
[2] **salons** (sȧ·lôɴ′): formal reception rooms.
[3] **pot-au-feu** (pô·tō·fû′): broth of meat and vegetables.
[4] **Mme Georges Ramponneau** (mȧ·dȧm′ zhôrzh räɴ·pô·nō′).
[5] **M. . . . Mme Loisel's** (mẽ·syû′ . . . mȧ·dȧm′ lwȧ·zĕlz′).

ficial world will be there."

She looked at him with an irritated eye, and she said, impatiently, "And what do you want me to put on my back?"

He had not thought of that; he stammered, "Why, the dress you go to the theater in. It looks very well to me."

He stopped, distracted, seeing that his wife was crying. Two great tears descended slowly from the corners of her eyes toward the corners of her mouth. He stuttered, "What's the matter? What's the matter?"

But, by a violent effort, she had conquered her grief, and she replied, with a calm voice, while she wiped her wet cheeks, "Nothing. Only I have no dress, and therefore I can't go to this ball. Give your card to some colleague whose wife is better equipped than I."

He was in despair. He resumed, "Come, let us see, Mathilde.[1] How much would it cost, a suitable dress, which you could use on other occasions, something very simple?"

She reflected several seconds, making her calculations and wondering also what sum she could ask without drawing on herself an immediate refusal and a frightened exclamation from the economical clerk.

Finally she replied, hesitatingly, "I don't know exactly, but I think I could manage it with four hundred francs."

He had grown a little pale, because he was laying aside just that amount to buy a gun and treat himself to a little shooting next summer on the plain of Nanterre,[2] with several friends who went to shoot larks down there of a Sunday.

But he said, "All right. I will give you four hundred francs. And try to have a pretty dress."

The day of the ball drew near, and Mme Loisel seemed sad, uneasy, anxious. Her dress was ready, however.

Her husband said to her one evening, "What is the matter? Come, you've been so queer these last three days."

And she answered, "It annoys me not to have a single jewel, not a single stone, nothing to put on. I shall look like a pauper. I should almost rather not go at all."

He resumed, "You might wear natural flowers. It's very stylish at this time of the year. For ten francs you can get two or three magnificent roses."

She was not convinced. "No; there's nothing more humiliating than to look poor among other women who are rich."

But her husband cried, "How stupid you are! Go look up your friend Mme Forestier,[3] and ask her to lend you some jewels. You're quite thick enough with her to do that."

She uttered a cry of joy. "It's true. I never thought of it."

The next day she went to her friend and told of her distress.

Mme Forestier went to a wardrobe with a glass door, took out a large jewel box, brought it back, opened it, and said to Mme Loisel, "Choose, my dear."

She saw first of all some bracelets, then a pearl necklace, then a Venetian cross, gold, and precious stones of admirable workmanship. She tried on the ornaments before the glass; hesitated; could not make up her mind to part with them, to give them back. She kept asking, "Haven't you any more?"

"Why, yes. Look. I don't know what you like."

All of a sudden she discovered, in a black satin box, a superb necklace of diamonds, and her heart began to beat with an immoderate desire. Her hands

[1] **Mathilde** (må·tēld′).
[2] **Nanterre** (näɴ·târ′).
[3] **Forestier** (fô·rĕ·styā′).

trembled as she took it. She fastened it around her throat, outside her high-necked dress, and remained lost in ecstasy at the sight of herself.

Then she asked, hesitating, filled with anguish, "Can you lend me that, only that?"

"Why, yes, certainly."

She sprang upon the neck of her friend, kissed her passionately, then fled with her treasure.

The day of the ball arrived. Mme Loisel made a great success. She was prettier than them all, elegant, gracious, smiling, and crazy with joy. All the men looked at her, asked her name, endeavored to be introduced. All the attachés [1] of the cabinet wanted to waltz with her. She was remarked by the minister himself.

She danced with intoxication, with passion, made drunk by pleasure, forgetting all in the triumph of her beauty, in the glory of her success, in a sort of cloud of happiness composed of all this homage, of all this admiration, of all these awakened desires, and of that sense of complete victory which is so sweet to woman's heart.

She went away about four o'clock in the morning. Her husband had been sleeping since midnight in a little deserted anteroom with three other gentlemen whose wives were having a very good time.

He threw over her shoulders the wraps which he had brought, modest wraps of common life, whose poverty contrasted with the elegance of the ball dress. She felt this and wanted to escape so as not to be remarked by the other women, who were enveloping themselves in costly furs.

[1] **attachés** (ăt′ȧ·shāz′): persons attached to an embassy staff.

Loisel held her back. "Wait a bit. You will catch cold outside. I will go and call a cab."

But she did not listen to him, and rapidly descended the stairs. When they were in the street they did not find a carriage; and they began to look for one, shouting after the cabmen whom they saw passing by at a distance.

They went down toward the Seine [2] in despair, shivering with cold. At last they found on the quay [3] one of those ancient noctambulant coupés [4] which, exactly as if they were ashamed to show their misery during the day, are never seen round Paris until after nightfall.

It took them to their door in the Rue des Martyrs,[5] and once more, sadly, they climbed up homeward. All was ended for her. And as for him, he reflected that he must be at the ministry at ten o'clock.

She removed the wraps, which covered her shoulders, before the glass, so as once more to see herself in all her glory. But suddenly she uttered a cry. She had no longer the necklace around her neck!

Her husband, already half undressed, demanded, "What is the matter with you?"

She turned madly toward him, "I have — I have — I've lost Mme Forestier's necklace."

He stood up, distracted. "What! . . . How? . . . Impossible!"

And they looked in the folds of her dress, in the folds of her cloak, in her pockets, everywhere. They did not find it.

He asked, "You're sure you had it on when you left the ball?"

[2] **Seine** (sān): French river which runs through Paris.
[3] **quay** (kē): a stretch of paved river bank.
[4] **coupés** (ko͞o′pāz′): cabs.
[5] **Rue des Martyrs** (rü dā mȧr·tēr′): Street of the Martyrs.

A quiet corner in the Montmartre section of Paris — the charm of its old houses and cobbled streets has made this district a favorite dwelling of artists. (French Embassy — Information Bureau)

"Yes, I felt it in the vestibule of the palace."

"But if you had lost it in the street we should have heard it fall. It must be in the cab."

"Yes. Probably. Did you take his number?"

"No. And you, didn't you notice it?"

"No."

They looked, thunderstruck, at one another. At last Loisel put on his clothes. "I shall go back on foot," said he, "over the whole route which we have taken, to see if I can't find it."

And he went out. She sat waiting on a chair in her ball dress, without strength to go to bed, overwhelmed, without fire, without a thought.

Her husband came back about seven o'clock. He had found nothing.

He went to police headquarters, to the newspaper offices, to offer a reward; he went to the cab companies — everywhere, in fact, whither he was urged by the least suspicion of hope.

She waited all day, in the same condition of mad fear before this terrible calamity.

Loisel returned at night with a hollow, pale face; he had discovered nothing.

"You must write to your friend," said he, "that you have broken the clasp of her necklace and that you are having it mended. That will give us time to turn round."

She wrote at his dictation.

At the end of a week they had lost all hope.

And Loisel, who had aged five years, declared, "We must consider how to replace that ornament."

The next day they took the box which had contained it, and they went to the jeweler whose name was found within. He consulted his books.

"It was not I, Madame, who sold that necklace; I must simply have furnished the case."

Then they went from jeweler to jeweler, searching for a necklace like the other, consulting their memories, sick both of them with chagrin and with anguish.

They found, in a shop at the Palais Royal,[1] a string of diamonds which seemed to them exactly like the one they looked for. It was worth forty thousand francs.[2] They could have it for thirty-six.

So they begged the jeweler not to sell it for three days yet. And they made a bargain that he should buy it back for thirty-four thousand francs in case they found the other one before the end of February.

Loisel possessed eighteen thousand francs which his father had left him. He would borrow the rest.

He did borrow, asking a thousand francs of one, five hundred of another, five louis [3] here, three louis there. He gave notes, took up ruinous obligations, dealt with usurers and all the race of lenders. He compromised all the rest of his life, risked his signature without even knowing if he could meet it; and, frightened by the pains yet to come, by the black misery which was about to fall upon him, by the prospect of all the physical privations and of all the moral tortures which he was to suffer, he went to get the new necklace, putting down upon the merchant's counter thirty-six thousand francs.

When Mme Loisel took back the necklace, Mme Forestier said to her with a chilly manner, "You should have re-

[1] **Palais Royal** (pȧ·lā′ rwȧ·ăl′): a shopping neighborhood in Paris.

[2] **franc:** French coin, at that time worth about twenty cents.

[3] **louis** (lo͞o′ĭ): a French gold coin worth twenty francs, nearly four dollars in those days.

turned it sooner. I might have needed it."

She did not open the case, as her friend had so much feared. If she had detected the substitution, what would she have thought, what would she have said? Would she not have taken Mme Loisel for a thief?

Mme Loisel now knew the horrible existence of the needy. She took her part, moreover, all of a sudden, with heroism. That dreadful debt must be paid. She would pay it. They dismissed their servant; they changed their lodgings; they rented a garret under the roof.

She came to know what heavy housework meant, and the odious cares of the kitchen. She washed the dishes, using her rosy nails on the greasy pots and pans. She washed the dirty linen, the shirts, and the dishcloths, which she dried upon a line; she carried the slops down to the street every morning, and carried up the water, stopping for breath at every landing. And, dressed like a woman of the people, she went to the fruiterer, the grocer, the butcher, her basket on her arm, bargaining, insulted, defending her miserable money sou [1] by sou.

Each month they had to meet some notes, renew others, obtain more time.

Her husband worked in the evening making a fair copy of some tradesman's accounts, and late at night he often copied manuscript for five sous a page.

And this life lasted ten years.

At the end of ten years they had paid everything – everything, with the rates of usury and the accumulations of the compound interest.

Mme Loisel looked old now. She had become the woman of impoverished households – strong and hard and rough. With frowsy hair, skirts askew, and red hands she talked loud while washing the floor with great swishes of water. But sometimes, when her husband was at the office, she sat down near the window and she thought of that gay evening of long ago, of that ball where she had been so beautiful and so feted.[2]

What would have happened if she had not lost that necklace? Who knows? Who knows? How strange life is, and how changeful! How little a thing is needed for us to be lost or to be saved!

But one Sunday, having gone to take a walk in the Champs-Elysées [3] to refresh herself from the labors of the week, she suddenly perceived a woman who was leading a child. It was Mme Forestier, still young, still beautiful, still charming.

Mme Loisel felt moved. Was she going to speak to her? Yes, certainly. And, now that she had paid, she was going to tell her all about it. Why not?

She went up.

"Good day, Jeanne."

The other, astonished to be familiarly addressed by this plain goodwife, did not recognize her at all, and stammered, "But – Madame! I do not know – You must be mistaken."

"No. I am Mathilde Loisel."

Her friend uttered a cry. "Oh, my poor Mathilde! How changed you are!"

"Yes, I have had days hard enough, since I have seen you, days wretched enough – and that because of you!"

"Of me! How so?"

"Do you remember that diamond necklace which you lent me to wear at the ministerial ball?"

"Yes. Well?"

"Well, I lost it."

[1] **sou** (sōō): a French coin worth about a cent.

[2] **feted** (fā'tĕd): entertained and admired.

[3] **Champs-Elysées** (shäɴ zā·lē·zā'): an avenue in Paris.

"What do you mean? You brought it back."

"I brought you back another just like it. And for this we have been ten years paying. You can understand that it was not easy for us — us who had nothing. At last it is ended, and I am very glad."

Mme Forestier had stopped. "You say that you bought a necklace of diamonds to replace mine?"

"Yes. You never noticed it, then! They were very like."

And she smiled with a joy which was proud and naïve at once.

Mme Forestier, strongly moved, took her two hands.

"Oh, my poor Mathilde! Why, my necklace was paste! It was worth at most five hundred francs!"

Reconstructing the Story

Try answering these questions about the steps in the plot in this story. When you have finished, you will have a good idea of how a piece of fiction is constructed. "The Necklace" has often been called an almost perfect short story in form.

1. Main character is introduced in opening situation. (Who? What? When? Where?)
2. Incident occurs which causes problem. (What? Why?)
3. In solving problem, main character or characters take a course of action which leads to other difficulties. (What? Why?)
4. A major catastrophe occurs. (What? Why? When? Where?)
5. Main character or characters work their way out of the difficulty. (How? When?)
6. Solution. (What? Where does it occur? Does it satisfy?)
7. Keep this plot analysis in mind and see if you can find other stories in this book that follow the same pattern.

Thinking It Over

1. Who was the weaker character, M. or Mme Loisel? What kind of person was Mme Loisel? What is your feeling toward her? Why did she marry her husband? For what reasons do you consider her a good or a bad wife? What about M. Loisel as a husband?
2. Mme Loisel was discontented and envious. What did she seem to expect of life? How did she fail in her own contribution to life? At what point in the story do you begin to feel a grudging admiration for her? Why?
3. Do you think our movies and radio have a tendency to make American women discontented? Have you ever felt dissatisfied because you wanted clothes, or homes, or "good times" such as are depicted in the movies? Discuss this point.
4. Try writing a sequel to this story. What did Mme Forestier do about the valuable necklace which she had supposed to be imitation? What happened to M. and Mme Loisel?

For Your Vocabulary

COMMON AND UNCOMMON WORDS: When Mme Loisel danced with *intoxication*, you know that she was sober enough but that she was simply carried away by the good time she was having. The medieval Latin *intoxicatus* meant "drugged" or "poisoned." An even earlier Greek word, *toxikon* — from which *toxic* is taken — meant "arrow poison." What are the meanings for the present-day English words *toxic, antitoxin, toxicology*? How do you suppose *intoxication* came to be a word describing a drunken condition?

A more unusual word is *noctambulant*, which translated literally would mean "night-walking." It comes from the Latin *nox, noctis* (night) + *ambulare* (to walk). Can you think of other words made up from one or the other of these base words?

The common word *paste* means here a brilliant lead-glass composition used in making artificial jewelry.

ENJOYING HUMOR

JESSE STUART

The Champion

The story of what happened to Sam Whiteapple, the champion eater of Raccoon Creek, is a good example of folk humor. It is a tall tale, an exaggerated yarn such as can be heard in the hills or back country of America, wherever folks still live simply, close to the soil, matching their wits against nature and coming together now and then to swap tales about their triumphs or defeats. Tall tales are told over and over again, often in a bolder form with each telling, until they become favorite legends typical of the community where they grow. Some of them eventually find their way into print, dressed up a bit by a literary artist, but retaining much of their original flavor.

The hills of eastern Kentucky are the soil in which "The Champion" grew. (You will become better acquainted with this region when you read the autobiographical selection by Jesse Stuart on page 208.) "On any Saturday in the year," says its author, "I can stand on the street corner of Greenup, Kentucky, and see characters come in from the hills, characters I have used in short stories, poems, novels. . . . Many of these people know they are characters in my writings, and if I have used them in a way they think is favorable, they are very proud." Whether the original Sam Whiteapple was proud to appear as champion in this tale is not disclosed, but the contest he waged is an amusing piece of folklore. This is a homespun story, exaggerated, but in a way realistic. It's the kind of story that anyone who likes to swap yarns will enjoy.

"Now, Lester, you know that I can outeat you," Sam Whiteapple said as he followed me down the path from our house to the barn. "I ain't seen anybody yet that I can't outeat."

Sam stood in the path and looked me over. He slapped his big stummick with his big pitchfork hands. He had walked six miles to get me to try to outeat him. "Right here's where I put the grub," he said. "This old nail keg will hold it."

Sam laughed a big horse laugh and showed two rows of yaller teeth. His beady, black eyes squinted when he looked into my eyes. Sam looked tough as a shelled-bark hickory too. His face was covered with black beard—so black that it made his yaller teeth look like two white rows of corn between his beardy lips. Sam was a hardworkin' man, too, fer his overall knees were threadbare and the seat of his overalls was good as new. His overall suspenders had faded on his blue workshirt. His gray-checked cap bill stood over his face like a front porch.

"I've heard you was a great eater," Sam said. "I've just come over to put you under the table. I want to show you who is the champion eater in these parts."

"It's in crop time, Sam," I said. "Any other time but now."

"Why not now?" Sam ast.

"It knocks me out," I said. "I don't want to be knocked out. I've got too much work to do."

"You know which side of your bread is buttered," Sam laughed. He bent over until he nearly touched the ground; he slapped his ragged overall knees, and laughed. "Old Beanpole Lester Pratt can't take it. You got a mouth big enough to shovel in grub, but you can't take it. The eatin' championship goes to Raccoon Creek. There's where I winned it from Gnat Hornbuckle when I et a hog's head."

"That ain't no eatin'," I said. "I could eat that much and still be hungry."

"What about five stewed hens and all the trimmings?" Sam said. "I winned the chicken-eatin' contest over on Uling Branch. I was full to the neck. Didn't think I could get the last bite down my gullet but I did."

"You didn't eat that many hens."

"Ast Porky Sturgill," Sam said. "He et the least – just a couple of hens. He had to pay for all the hens six men et. I'll tell you it's fun to get a real square meal and let the other feller pay fer it. I've never paid for a meal yet. I've winned every eatin' contest. I've got the nail keg to put it in and you've just got a hollow beanpole there."

Sam hit me on the stummick and laughed as I started to open the barn-lot gate.

"Wonder if Sam could outeat a cow," I thought. "No, he couldn't eat corn nubbins,[1] fodder, or hay. Wonder if he could outeat a mule. No, a mule et more roughness than anything else. Sam couldn't eat hay or fodder." Then it flashed through my mind if Sam could outeat a hog. But Sam couldn't eat the things a hog et. Sam wouldn't get down and drink slop from a trough and gnaw corn from the cob on the ground. What could he eat with?

Just then my black game rooster run across the barn lot. He could always put away more corn than any chicken I'd ever seen. He'd eat so much corn I often wondered where he put it. He was tall with a long neck and a big craw. His face was red as a sliced beet. He didn't have any comb, for it was cut off so other roosters couldn't peck it when I took him to fight.

"Sam, you're braggin' about your big nail-keg stummick," I said. "You can't eat as much shelled corn as that rooster."

"You wouldn't try to be funny, would you?" Sam ast.

"No, I mean it."

"Huh, never et with a rooster but I'd just like to show you," Sam said. "If I could eat the same grub, I'd eat with a mule, horse, cow, or hog. It wouldn't make no difference to me. I've fed livestock around the barn and I know how much they eat. I know how much I can eat. I'll tell you I've got a big capacity. When I drink water in the cornfield it takes a gallon bucket full of cold water to make me a swig. You talk about that

[1] **corn nubbins:** ears of corn used as fodder.

little chicken! You make me laugh."

The rooster stopped in the barn lot. He held his head up to one side and cackled. He looked at us with the glassy-lookin' eye that was turned toward us. His red face beamed. It wasn't as large as the side of a big watch. I looked at the rooster and then I looked at Sam. He stood head and shoulders above me. I didn't know he was so tall. He looked short, for his shoulders were so broad and his stummick bulged out so in front. His sleeveless arms looked like fence posts folded across the bib of his overalls. Sam was bigger than a lot of fattenin' hogs I'd seen. Maybe he could outeat my tall slim game rooster; I didn't know. But if he did, he would have to put a lot of corn in his craw!

"Can old Sam outeat you, boy?" I ast my rooster.

My black game rooster cackled. He cocked his head to one side and looked at Sam. He cackled louder.

"He says that you can't outeat him, Sam," I told Sam. "Said he was ready to take you on!"

"That rooster can't understand what you say," Sam laughed. He looked at me as if he believed though that the rooster could understand what I said.

"Can he outeat you, boy?" I ast my rooster.

He cackled louder than ever. He cackled like he was skeered.

"W'y, that silly chicken," Sam chuckled. "You shell the corn and I'll show you who's the champion of this barn lot in just a few minutes. I won't haf to swaller enough corn to spile my dinner to beat him."

We walked from the gate down to the corncrib. The chickens followed me to the crib, for I allus shelled 'em corn in front of the crib. The rooster walked toward us, cacklin' like he was tryin' to say somethin'.

"What's your rooster sayin' now?" Sam ast.

"He's cussin' you," I said. "He says that you can't eat corn with a chicken."

"Tell him in chicken talk that I got a good gullet," Sam said. "Tell him I got a place to put shelled corn that's bigger than his craw."

I opened the crib door and got an ear of corn. I shooed the rest of the chickens back from the crib. My rooster stood there. He wouldn't shoo. He wasn't a chicken that you could shoo easily. If you shooed him too much he was liable to fly at your face and try to spur you. He never had as much as he could eat, for I left 'im in fightin' trim. Now I would give him all that he could eat. He stood with his neck feathers ruffled up like he was goin' to fight. His feathers were black and shiny as a crow's wing. His spurs were straight as sourwood sprouts and sharp as locust thorns. He acted like he owned the barn lot and that he would as soon spur Sam as to outeat him.

"Now, Sam, I'll give him a grain of corn every time I give you one," I said.

"Any old way suits me," Sam said. "This eatin' contest ain't going to last long nohow. I'm just doin' this fer fun to say that I outet Lester Pratt's black game rooster since old Beanpole Lester was afraid to eat with me."

Sam ketched the grain of corn in his big mouth when I pitched it to him. It was fun fer Sam. He laughed and swallered the corn. Then I pitched my rooster a grain. He picked it up in his hooked bill and swallered it. He quirked [1] and wanted more.

"He laughed at you, Sam," I said.

[1] **quirked:** Say this word aloud and think of the sound roosters and hens make. This sound will give you the meaning of this word.

"Throw us the corn," Sam said. "We'll see who laughs last."

Sam stood there a big giant in our barn lot. I'd throw a grain of corn first to Sam and then one to my rooster. The hens stood back. They were wantin' the corn I was throwin' to Sam and to my rooster but Sam thought they were lookin' on and hopin' that their hero would win.

That ear of corn didn't last as long as frost on a hot plate. I kept shellin' corn and pitchin' to Sam and my rooster until my arm got tired. Every time a hen quirked or made a funny noise in her throat Sam thought she was makin' fun of him. He would screw up his big beardy face and look sour at something little as a hen. Sam stood by the corncrib. He never moved out of his tracks. He would stand there and crane his big bull neck and swallow.

"Ain't your throat gettin' awful dry?" I ast.

"Nope, it ain't," Sam said. "A little grain of corn just draps down my gullet. You'd better ast your rooster and see if his throat is gettin' dry."

Just then I pitched my rooster a grain of corn and he sneezed.

"My rooster says his throat is okay," I said.

Sam looked a little funny when the rooster sneezed. I could tell he didn't have the confidence that he did have when we started the contest. Sam was lookin' a little worried. Maybe it was because of all the noises the chickens made.

"Am I 'lowed to chew my corn?" Sam ast.

"Nope, you're not," I said. "The rooster ain't got no teeth and you're supposed to swaller your corn like he does. What's a little grain of corn nohow?"

"Nothin' to look at it," Sam groaned, "but a lot of swallered corn gets heavy. I can feel a heavy lump right down at the end of my gullet."

"I guess my rooster feels it too," I said. "Watch him stretch his neck when he swallers a grain."

I looked down at my feet, and there was a pile of corncobs big enough to start a fire in the fireplace. There was a pile of cobs big enough to cook a big dinner in our cookstove. I'll tell you it was a horse and cat between Sam and my rooster. At first I thought Sam would swallow more corn than my game rooster. Now I doubted that he would. I wondered where my rooster was puttin' so much corn. His craw had begun to swell. When he reached down to get a grain he nearly toppled over from the weight of his craw. But he reached down and picked up a grain, stood up as straight as Sam, and swallowed it.

"I'd like to have a sip of water," Sam said. "I'd like to dampen my gullet. It's gettin' a little dry."

"My rooster ain't ast fer water yet," I said. "You've got to abide by the same rule he does. See, he's never made a sound. He just stands up straight and swallers his corn."

"It's gettin' hard to get down," Sam said as he craned his neck and twisted his head from first one side to the other.

I could see now that Sam was worried. His eyes showed it. He didn't have any confidence at all. My rooster looked cheerful. He acted that way when he picked up a grain of corn in his fightin' beak. His eyes looked bright. He was confident and in fine spirits.

"Where's that chicken puttin' all that corn?" Sam ast.

"I don't know," I said. "You will haf to ast the chicken."

But Sam Whiteapple didn't ast the

chicken. Old Sam kept strugglin' with a grain of corn. He was tryin' to get it down. His eyes begin to look watery. And Sam didn't have his natural color. There was a place on Sam's cheek where the beard didn't reach and that was allus rosy red. Now it was turning pale. Sam moved out of his tracks when he tried to get another grain down. He run a little circle like a dog followin' his tail when he lays down. I kept my eye on Sam to see that he didn't spit the grain of corn out. Finally Sam got it down. My rooster swallowed his but he acted like he was gettin' plum full up to his ears. His craw was swellin' all the time. But 'peared like he knowed what was up. And he was goin' to beat Sam.

I pitched Sam another grain of corn. He ketched it in his big mouth. I never saw a big man wrestle with a little grain of corn like Sam did. He worked and worked and finally he got it down by screwin' up his face, gruntin' and groanin' and runnin' a little circle. Tears come to his eyes and flowed down his beardy cheeks.

"'Pears like I got a bushel of shelled corn in my gullet," Sam said. "It's lodgin' now in my windpipe. I'm gettin' short of breath."

I had just pitched my rooster another grain of corn and he had had time to grab it when Sam fell like a tree. If my rooster hadn't been a quick one, he wouldn't 've got out of Sam's way. Sam sprawled like a sawed-down oak on the barn lot. His arms fell limp as two rags. It skeered me nearly to death. I shook Sam. He wouldn't talk. He didn't move or anything. His mouth was open and I saw three grains of corn on his tongue. I felt to see if his ticker was still goin'. I thanked my God that it was. My rooster walked away with his flock of hens. He was crawheavy, for he almost toppled over on his face. But he flew up on a fence post and crowed. He'd et more corn than Sam. I wanted to break the news to the boys on Raccoon Creek that my rooster had outet their champion eater. But I had to get on a mule and get a doctor.

"A man's a fool that will do a thing like this," Doc Hornbuckle said. "A big fine-lookin' man like Sam Whiteapple ought to have more sense than to eat corn with the chickens. Swallowin' corn grains that have never been chewed. Get him home!"

I harnessed the mules and hitched them to the spring wagon. Doc helped me load Sam on the wagon. Doc strained his back liftin' on Sam. Finally we got him on the spring wagon, and I hauled him to Raccoon Creek. I left him with his people. His pa was awful mad at me about it. But I didn't have nothin' to do with my rooster eatin' more corn than Sam. I told his pa that too. He said his crop was in the weeds and he needed Sam's help.

It was a funny thing the way people talked when Sam was so bad off the next two weeks. We'd go there and sit up all night. We'd talk about the corn Sam swallered. Some thought that Sam would have to swallow pieces of broken dishes, eggshells, and white gravels from the creek just like a chicken did to work on the corn in Sam's craw. I told them Sam didn't have a craw and that Doc Hornbuckle would bring him out of it if anybody could, if they'd just listen to Doc's orders.

The last night I was over to the settin-up, Doc Hornbuckle said, "Don't you ever try to outeat another chicken, Sam. You have ruint your stummick. You'll haf to go easy fer a year. You can't do much work. You'll just have to putter about the place. I'm goin' to haf to put you on a cornflake diet. You'll haf to eat cornflakes and warm sweet milk mornin', noon, and night."

Sam's eyes got awful big when Doc Hornbuckle said "cornflakes."

Appreciating Humor

1. Humor is a personal thing to a large extent. You can easily discover a few common reasons for laughter, but when you compare your ideas of what is comic with the ideas of others, you're likely to find a great variance. A class discussion on humor might bring this out. In this story notice that Sam suffers acutely (and almost dies), yet the whole episode seems funny. Why is it that we sometimes find personal misfortunes amusing (for example, when watching a man run after a hat in a high wind, or seeing someone slip on a banana peel)? What is the humor in a "practical joke," such as you have seen played on people? Perhaps you don't consider such jokes humorous. Why? Absurd contrast also makes us laugh, as, for instance, when we hear a dignified gentleman try to use slang or "jive talk." What examples of absurd contrast do you find in "The Champion"?

2. Much of the fun of this story would be lost if "Old Beanpole" Lester Pratt didn't take his own story so seriously. Can you find passages that reveal he is telling his story in a serious tone? In what way is this an example of absurd contrast, as mentioned above?

3. At what point in the story do you feel that Lester can hardly resist Sam's wager? How does Sam taunt him? With what amusing speculations does Lester spar for time?

4. What all-too-human folly lies behind Sam's desire to bet Lester that he can out-eat him? Do you know of any other ridiculous contests, from your own experience or from reading, that you can compare to this one?

5. How does Lester view Sam's defeat? How do Sam's father and the doctor and the folks who went to "the settin-up" each view it? What about Sam?

6. If you enjoyed this folk yarn, here are some other stories in similar vein that the class might enjoy hearing:

"The Celebrated Jumping Frog of Calaveras County" by Mark Twain

"Baker's Blue Jay Yarn" by Mark Twain

"Windwagon Smith" by Wilbur L. Schramm in *Windwagon Smith and Other Yarns* (Harcourt, Brace, 1947)

Several stories from *Paul Bunyan* by Esther Shepherd (Harcourt, Brace, 1941), and *Tall Tale America* by Walter Blair (Coward-McCann, 1944).

For Your Vocabulary

COLLOQUIAL LANGUAGE: In this story Sam and Lester speak *colloquially*, that is, in the informal language that people use among themselves in everyday affairs and in familiar surroundings. But notice also that their speech is more than just colloquial. It also reveals a *dialect,* which is made up of certain expressions and ways of pronunciation found only in a particular locality. (There is, for example, a New York City dialect, a Vermont dialect, an East Texas dialect, etc.) All of us use colloquial speech constantly, and some of us may use dialect occasionally. Yet both of these uses of language are different, still, from *illiterate* speech. Illiterate speech disregards the accepted usages of educated people ("he *et*" and "he *winned*" and "you *was* a great eater" are examples from this story), and tends to be found among uneducated or educated but careless people.

1. Find examples in the story of the three types of language mentioned here: *colloquial, dialectal, and illiterate.* What examples of native language struck you as picturesque and, moreover, showed that Lester is a keen observer?

2. Try to become aware of dialectal speech in your own community or part of the country. Compare your local speech with the east Kentucky, hill-country expressions in "The Champion."

3. Colloquial, or informal, speech is appropriate for certain social situations but not for others. For example, Sam may well speak of "shoveling in grub," but he would hesitate to use this expression at a banquet – if he ever got to one. Is *illiterate* speech ever really appropriate? Do you think people who use it know they are doing so?

O. HENRY

The Ransom of Red Chief

It is no exaggeration to say that this story is one of the funniest tales in American literature. O. Henry was a master of the short story, but besides his art he also had a fine sense of humor and an understanding of what Americans like to laugh about. Certainly they have been laughing over " The Ransom of Red Chief " for years, with its story of a strange kidnapping. If your family includes a five-to-ten-year-old cowpuncher who wears a ten-gallon hat and a pair of chaps, who lurks in ambush behind the garden shrubbery, and shoots from the hip with a cap pistol — you'll know what the kidnappers were up against. It was plenty!

For Better Reading . . . Part of the fun of this story — and, it must be recognized, part of whatever reading difficulty it presents — lies in the style of writing, particularly the vocabulary. The characters use a mixture of slang and bad grammar as well as important-sounding words which gives the story its very special style. Do not worry about understanding the exact meaning of every word. You will get the sense all right.

IT looked like a good thing: but wait till I tell you. We were down South, in Alabama — Bill Driscoll and myself — when this kidnapping idea struck us. It was, as Bill afterward expressed it, " during a moment of temporary mental apparition "; [1] but we didn't find that out till later.

There was a town down there, as flat as a flannel cake, and called Summit, of course. It contained inhabitants of as undeleterious [2] and self-satisfied a class of peasantry as ever clustered around a Maypole.

Bill and me had a joint capital of about six hundred dollars, and we needed just two thousand dollars more to pull off a fraudulent town-lot scheme in western Illinois with. We talked it over on the front steps of the hotel. Philoprogenitiveness,[3] says we, is strong in semi-rural communities; therefore, and for other reasons, a kidnapping project ought to do better there than in the radius of newspapers that send reporters out in plain clothes to stir up talk about

[1] **apparition** (ăp′ȧ·rĭsh′ŭn): misused for *aberration* (ăb′ēr·ā′shŭn), a lapse or departure from the normal.

[2] **undeleterious** (ŭn′dĕl·ē·tēr′ĭ·ŭs): incapable of doing harm.

[3] **Philoprogenitiveness** (fĭl′ō·prō·jĕn′ĭ·tĭv·nĕs): love of children.

such things. We knew that Summit couldn't get after us with anything stronger than constables and, maybe, some lackadaisical bloodhounds and a diatribe [1] or two in the *Weekly Farmers' Budget*. So, it looked good.

We selected for our victim the only child of a prominent citizen named Ebenezer Dorset. The father was respectable and tight, a mortgage fancier and a stern, upright collection-plate passer and forecloser. The kid was a boy of ten, with bas-relief [2] freckles, and hair the color of the cover of the magazine you buy at the newsstand when you want to catch a train. Bill and me figured that Ebenezer would melt down for a ransom of two thousand dollars to a cent. But wait till I tell you.

About two miles from Summit was a little mountain, covered with a dense cedar brake. On the rear elevation of this mountain was a cave. There we stored provisions.

One evening after sundown, we drove in a buggy past old Dorset's house. The kid was in the street, throwing rocks at a kitten on the opposite fence.

"Hey, little boy!" says Bill, "would you like to have a bag of candy and a nice ride?"

The boy catches Bill neatly in the eye with a piece of brick.

"That will cost the old man an extra five hundred dollars," says Bill, climbing over the wheel.

That boy put up a fight like a welterweight cinnamon bear; but, at last, we got him down in the bottom of the buggy and drove away. We took him up to the cave, and I hitched the horse in the cedar brake. After dark I drove the buggy to the little village, three miles away, where we had hired it, and walked back to the mountain.

Bill was pasting court plaster over the scratches and bruises on his features. There was a fire burning behind the big rock at the entrance of the cave, and the boy was watching a pot of boiling coffee, with two buzzard tail feathers stuck in his red hair. He points a stick at me when I come up, and says:

"Ha! cursèd paleface, do you dare to enter the camp of Red Chief, the terror of the plains?"

"He's all right now," says Bill, rolling up his trousers and examining some bruises on his shins. "We're playing Indian. We're making Buffalo Bill's show look like magic-lantern views of Palestine in the town hall. I'm Old Hank, the Trapper, Red Chief's captive, and I'm to be scalped at daybreak. By Geronimo! [3] that kid can kick hard."

Yes, sir, that boy seemed to be having the time of his life. The fun of camping out in a cave had made him forget that he was a captive himself. He immediately christened me Snake-eye, the Spy, and announced that, when his braves returned from the warpath, I was to be broiled at the stake at the rising of the sun.

Then we had supper; and he filled his mouth full of bacon and bread and gravy, and began to talk. He made a during-dinner speech something like this:

"I like this fine. I never camped out before; but I had a pet 'possum once, and I was nine last birthday. I hate to go to school. Rats ate up sixteen of Jimmy Talbot's aunt's speckled hen's eggs. Are there any real Indians in these woods? I want some more gravy. Does the trees moving make the wind blow? We had

[1] **diatribe** (dī'ȧ·trīb): an abusive article or speech.

[2] **bas-relief** (bä'rē·lēf'): low relief; raised slightly from a background, like certain sculptures.

[3] **Geronimo** (jĕ·rŏn'ĭ·mō): an Indian chieftain.

five puppies. What makes your nose so red, Hank? My father has lots of money. Are the stars hot? I whipped Ed Walker twice, Saturday. I don't like girls. You dassent catch toads unless with a string. Do oxen make any noise? Why are oranges round? Have you got beds to sleep on in this cave? Amos Murray has got six toes. A parrot can talk, but a monkey or a fish can't. How many does it take to make twelve?"

Every few minutes he would remember that he was a pesky redskin, and pick up his stick rifle and tiptoe to the mouth of the cave to rubber for the scouts of the hated paleface. Now and then he would let out a war whoop that made Old Hank the Trapper shiver. That boy had Bill terrorized from the start.

"Red Chief," says I to the kid, "would you like to go home?"

"Aw, what for?" says he. "I don't have any fun at home. I hate to go to school. I like to camp out. You won't take me back home again, Snake-eye, will you?"

"Not right away," says I. "We'll stay here in the cave a while."

"All right!" says he. "That'll be fine. I never had such fun in all my life."

We went to bed about eleven o'clock. We spread down some wide blankets and quilts and put Red Chief between us. We weren't afraid he'd run away. He kept us awake for three hours, jumping up and reaching for his rifle and screeching: "Hist! pard," in mine and Bill's ears, as the fancied crackle of a twig or the rustle of a leaf revealed to his young imagination the stealthy approach of the outlaw band. At last, I fell into a troubled sleep, and dreamed that I had been kidnapped and chained to a tree by a ferocious pirate with red hair.

Just at daybreak, I was awakened by a series of awful screams from Bill. They weren't yells, or howls, or shouts, or whoops, or yawps, such as you'd expect from a manly set of vocal organs – they were simply indecent, terrifying, humiliating screams, such as women emit when they see ghosts or caterpillars. It's an awful thing to hear a strong, desperate, fat man scream incontinently [1] in a cave at daybreak.

I jumped up to see what the matter was. Red Chief was sitting on Bill's chest, with one hand twined in Bill's hair. In the other he had the sharp case knife we used for slicing bacon; and he was industriously and realistically trying to take Bill's scalp, according to the sentence that had been pronounced upon him the evening before.

I got the knife away from the kid and made him lie down again. But, from that moment, Bill's spirit was broken. He laid down on his side of the bed, but he never closed an eye again in sleep as long as that boy was with us. I dozed off for a while, but along toward sunup I remembered that Red Chief had said I was to be burned at the stake at the rising of the sun. I wasn't nervous or afraid; but I sat up and lit my pipe and leaned against a rock.

"What you getting up so soon for, Sam?" asked Bill.

"Me?" says I. "Oh, I got a kind of a pain in my shoulder. I thought sitting up would rest it."

"You're a liar!" says Bill. "You're afraid. You was to be burned at sunrise, and you was afraid he'd do it. And he would, too, if he could find a match. Ain't it awful, Sam? Do you think anybody will pay out money to get a little imp like that back home?"

"Sure," said I. "A rowdy kid like that

[1] **incontinently** (ĭn·kŏn′tĭ·nĕnt·lĭ): without restraint.

is just the kind that parents dote on. Now, you and the Chief get up and cook breakfast, while I go up on the top of this mountain and reconnoiter." [1]

I went up on the peak of the little mountain and ran my eye over the contiguous vicinity. Over toward Summit I expected to see the sturdy yeomanry of the village armed with scythes and pitchforks beating the countryside for the dastardly kidnappers. But what I saw was a peaceful landscape dotted with one man plowing with a dun mule. Nobody was dragging the creek; no couriers dashed hither and yon, bringing tidings of no news to the distracted parents. There was a sylvan attitude of somnolent sleepiness pervading that section of the external outward surface of Alabama that lay exposed to my view. "Perhaps," says I to myself, "it has not yet been discovered that the wolves have borne away the tender lambkin from the fold. Heaven help the wolves!" says I and I went down the mountain to breakfast.

When I got to the cave I found Bill backed up against the side of it, breathing hard, and the boy threatening to smash him with a rock half as big as a coconut.

"He put a red-hot boiled potato down my back," explained Bill, "and then mashed it with his foot; and I boxed his ears. Have you got a gun about you, Sam?"

I took the rock away from the boy and kind of patched up the argument. "I'll fix you," says the kid to Bill. "No man ever yet struck the Red Chief but what he got paid for it. You better beware!"

After breakfast the kid takes a piece of leather with strings wrapped around it out of his pocket and goes outside the cave unwinding it.

"What's he up to now?" says Bill, anxiously. "You don't think he'll run away, do you, Sam?"

"No fear of it," says I. "He don't seem to be much of a home body. But we've got to fix up some plan about the ransom. There don't seem to be much excitement around Summit on account of his disappearance; but maybe they haven't realized yet that he's gone. His folks may think he's spending the night with Aunt Jane or one of the neighbors. Anyhow, he'll be missed today. Tonight we must get a message to his father demanding the two thousand dollars for his return."

Just then we heard a kind of war whoop, such as David might have emitted when he knocked out the champion Goliath.[2] It was a sling that Red Chief had pulled out of his pocket, and he was whirling it around his head.

I dodged, and heard a heavy thud and a kind of a sigh from Bill, like a horse gives out when you take his saddle off. A rock the size of an egg had caught Bill just behind his left ear. He loosened himself all over and fell in the fire across the frying pan of hot water for washing the dishes. I dragged him out and poured cold water on his head for half an hour.

By and by, Bill sits up and feels behind his ear and says: "Sam, do you know who my favorite Biblical character is?"

"Take it easy," says I. "You'll come to your senses presently."

"King Herod," says he. "You won't go away and leave me here alone, will you, Sam?"

I went out and caught that boy and shook him until his freckles rattled.

[1] **reconnoiter** (rĕk′ŏ·noi′tēr): explore; investigate.

[2] **Goliath** (gō·lī′ăth): the Biblical giant whom David killed with a sling.

"If you don't behave," says I, "I'll take you straight home. Now, are you going to be good, or not?"

"I was only funning," says he sullenly. "I didn't mean to hurt Old Hank. But what did he hit me for? I'll behave, Snake-eye, if you won't send me home, and if you'll let me play the Black Scout today."

"I don't know the game," says I. "That's for you and Mr. Bill to decide. He's your playmate for the day. I'm going away for a while, on business. Now, you come in and make friends with him and say you are sorry for hurting him, or home you go, at once."

I made him and Bill shake hands, and then I took Bill aside and told him I was going to Poplar Cove, a little village three miles from the cave, and find out what I could about how the kidnapping had been regarded in Summit. Also, I thought it best to send a peremptory letter to old man Dorset that day, demanding the ransom and dictating how it should be paid.

"You know, Sam," says Bill, "I've stood by you without batting an eye in earthquakes, fire, and flood — in poker games, dynamite outrages, police raids, train robberies, and cyclones. I never lost my nerve yet till we kidnapped that two-legged skyrocket of a kid. He's got me going. You won't leave me long with him, will you, Sam?"

"I'll be back some time this afternoon," says I. "You must keep the boy amused and quiet till I return. And now we'll write the letter to old Dorset."

Bill and I got paper and pencil and worked on the letter while Red Chief, with a blanket wrapped around him, strutted up and down, guarding the mouth of the cave. Bill begged me tearfully to make the ransom fifteen hundred dollars instead of two thousand. "I ain't attempting," says he, "to decry the celebrated moral aspect of parental affection, but we're dealing with humans, and it ain't human for anybody to give up two thousand dollars for that forty-pound chunk of freckled wildcat. I'm willing to take a chance at fifteen hundred dollars. You can charge the difference up to me."

So, to relieve Bill, I acceded, and we collaborated a letter that ran this way:

EBENEZER DORSET, ESQ.:

We have your boy concealed in a place far from Summit. It is useless for you or the most skillful detectives to attempt to find him. Absolutely, the only terms on which you can have him restored to you are these: We demand fifteen hundred dollars in large bills for his return; the money to be left at midnight tonight at the same spot and in the same box as your reply — as hereinafter described. If you agree to these terms, send your answer in writing by a solitary messenger tonight at half-past eight o'clock. After crossing Owl Creek, on the road to Poplar Cove, there are three large trees about a hundred yards apart, close to the fence of the wheat field on the right-hand side. At the bottom of the fence post, opposite the third tree, will be found a small pasteboard box.

The messenger will place the answer in this box and return immediately to Summit.

If you attempt any treachery or fail to comply with our demand as stated, you will never see your boy again.

If you pay the money as demanded, he will be returned to you safe and well within three hours. These terms are final, and if you do not accede to them no further communication will be attempted.

TWO DESPERATE MEN.

I addressed this letter to Dorset, and put it in my pocket. As I was about to start, the kid comes up to me and says:

"Aw, Snake-eye, you said I could play the Black Scout while you was gone."

"Play it, of course," says I. "Mr. Bill will play with you. What kind of a game is it?"

"I'm the Black Scout," says Red Chief, "and I have to ride to the stockade to warn the settlers that the Indians are coming. I'm tired of playing Indian myself. I want to be the Black Scout."

"All right," says I. "It sounds harmless to me. I guess Mr. Bill will help you foil the pesky savages."

"What am I to do?" asks Bill, looking at the kid suspiciously.

"You are the hoss," says Black Scout. "Get down on your hands and knees. How can I ride to the stockade without a hoss?"

"You'd better keep him interested," said I, "till we get the scheme going. Loosen up."

Bill gets down on his all fours, and a look comes in his eye like a rabbit's when you catch it in a trap.

"How far is it to the stockade, kid?" he asks, in a husky manner of voice.

"Ninety miles," says the Black Scout. "And you have to hump yourself to get there on time. Whoa, now!" The Black Scout jumps on Bill's back and digs his heels in his side.

"For heaven's sake," says Bill, "hurry back, Sam, as soon as you can. I wish we hadn't made the ransom more than a thousand. Say, you quit kicking me or I'll get up and warm you good."

I walked over to Poplar Cove and sat around the post office and store, talking with the chaw-bacons that came in to trade. One whiskerando says that he hears Summit is all upset on account of Elder Ebenezer Dorset's boy having been lost or stolen. That was all I wanted to know. I bought some smoking tobacco, referred casually to the price of black-eyed peas, posted my letter surreptitiously, and came away. The postmaster said the mail carrier would come by in an hour to take the mail on to Summit.

When I got back to the cave, Bill and the boy were not to be found. I explored the vicinity of the cave, and risked a yodel or two, but there was no response.

So I lighted my pipe and sat down on a mossy bank to await developments.

In about half an hour I heard the bushes rustle, and Bill wabbled out into the little glade in front of the cave. Behind him was the kid, stepping softly like a scout, with a broad grin on his face. Bill stopped, took off his hat, and wiped his face with a red handkerchief. The kid stopped about eight feet behind him.

"Sam," says Bill, "I suppose you'll think I'm a renegade,[1] but I couldn't help it. I'm a grown person with masculine proclivities and habits of self-defense, but there is a time when all systems of egotism and predominance fail. The boy is gone. I have sent him home. All is off. There was martyrs in old times," goes on Bill, "that suffered death rather than give up the particular graft they enjoyed. None of 'em ever was subjugated to such supernatural tortures as I have been. I tried to be faithful to our articles of depredation; but there came a limit."

"What's the trouble, Bill?" I asks him.

"I was rode," says Bill, "the ninety miles to the stockade, not barring an inch. Then, when the settlers was rescued, I was given oats. Sand ain't a palatable substitute. And then, for an hour I had to try to explain to him why there was nothin' in holes, how a road can run both ways, and what makes the grass green. I tell you, Sam, a human can only stand so much. I takes him by the

[1] **renegade** (rĕn′ē·gād): a traitor; a deserter.

neck of his clothes and drags him down the mountain. On the way he kicks my legs black-and-blue from the knees down; and I've got to have two or three bites on my thumb and hand cauterized.

"But he's gone" — continues Bill — "gone home. I showed him the road to Summit and kicked him about eight feet nearer there at one kick. I'm sorry we lose the ransom; but it was either that or Bill Driscoll to the madhouse."

Bill is puffing and blowing, but there is a look of ineffable peace and growing content on his rose-pink features.

"Bill," says I, "there isn't any heart disease in your family, is there?"

"No," says Bill, "nothing chronic except malaria and accidents. Why?"

"Then you might turn around," says I, "and have a look behind you."

Bill turns and sees the boy, and loses his complexion and sits down plump on the ground and begins to pluck aimlessly at grass and little sticks. For an hour I was afraid for his mind. And then I told him that my scheme was to put the whole job through immediately and that we would get the ransom and be off with it by midnight if old Dorset fell in with our proposition. So Bill braced up enough to give the kid a weak sort of a smile and a promise to play the Russian in a Japanese war with him as soon as he felt a little better.

I had a scheme for collecting that ransom without danger of being caught by counterplots that ought to commend itself to professional kidnappers. The tree under which the answer was to be left — and the money later on — was close to the road fence with big, bare fields on all sides. If a gang of constables should be watching for anyone to come for the note, they could see him a long way off crossing the fields or in the road. But no, sirree! At half-past eight I was up in that tree as well hidden as a tree toad, waiting for the messenger to arrive.

Exactly on time, a half-grown boy rides up the road on a bicycle, locates the pasteboard box at the foot of the fence post, slips a folded piece of paper into it, and pedals away again back toward Summit.

I waited an hour and then concluded the thing was square. I slid down the tree, got the note, slipped along the fence till I struck the woods, and was back at the cave in another half an hour. I opened the note, got near the lantern, and read it to Bill. It was written with a pen in a crabbed hand, and the sum and substance of it was this:

TWO DESPERATE MEN.

Gentlemen: I received your letter today by post, in regard to the ransom you ask for the return of my son. I think you are a little high in your demands, and I hereby make you a counterproposition, which I am inclined to believe you will accept. You bring Johnny home and pay me two hundred and fifty dollars in cash, and I agree to take him off your hands. You had better come at night, for the neighbors believe he is lost, and I couldn't be responsible for what they would do to anybody they saw bringing him back.

Very respectfully,

EBENEZER DORSET.

"Great pirates of Penzance!" says I; "of all the impudent ——"

But I glanced at Bill, and hesitated. He had the most appealing look in his eyes I ever saw on the face of a dumb or a talking brute.

"Sam," says he, "what's two hundred and fifty dollars, after all? We've got the money. One more night of this kid will send me to a bed in Bedlam.[1] Besides being a thorough gentleman, I think Mr. Dorset is a spendthrift for making us

[1] **Bedlam** (bĕd'lăm): an asylum for the insane.

such a liberal offer. You ain't going to let the chance go, are you? "

"Tell you the truth, Bill," says I, "this little he ewe lamb has somewhat got on my nerves too. We'll take him home, pay the ransom, and make our getaway."

We took him home that night. We got him to go by telling him that his father had bought a silver-mounted rifle and a pair of moccasins for him, and we were going to hunt bears the next day.

It was just twelve o'clock when we knocked at Ebenezer's front door. Just at the moment when I should have been abstracting the fifteen hundred dollars from the box under the tree, according to the original proposition, Bill was counting out two hundred and fifty dollars into Dorset's hand.

When the kid found out we were going to leave him at home, he started up a howl like a calliope [1] and fastened himself as tight as a leech to Bill's leg. His father peeled him away gradually, like a porous plaster.

"How long can you hold him?" asks Bill.

"I'm not as strong as I used to be," says old Dorset, "but I think I can promise you ten minutes."

"Enough," says Bill. "In ten minutes I shall cross the Central, Southern, and Middle Western States, and be legging it trippingly for the Canadian border."

And, as dark as it was, and as fat as Bill was, and as good a runner as I am, he was a good mile and a half out of Summit before I could catch up with him.

[1] **calliope** (kă·lī'ō·pē): a mechanical organ with a sharp whistling sound. Sam probably called it kăl'ĭ·ōp.

Becoming Aware of the Writer's Style

1. Instead of writing "everything was peaceful as far as I could see," O. Henry uses these words: "There was a sylvan attitude of somnolent sleepiness pervading that section of the external outward surface of Alabama which lay exposed to my view." Here is language that is humorous because it is exaggerated and unnecessarily high-flown. Can you find other examples, particularly on pages 144 and 149?
2. Compare the style of this story with that of other stories you have read in this book. Make specific references.
3. What are some of the names that O. Henry calls the townspeople, in an attempt to show a city man's attitude toward them (see pp. 144 and 149)?

Thinking It Over

1. Hank and Bill are obviously crooks, but somehow the author contrives to make them seem quite likable — as if they were a couple of cowhands just playing at the kidnapping project that backfired on them. How does he do it? Why do we not take the kidnapping seriously?
2. Most humor depends on incongruity or inconsistency of some kind. It is the unreasonable and pathetic helplessness of the two kidnappers in the hands of one small boy that makes the story so funny and adds to its particular style or flavor. Which part amused you the most?
3. O. Henry's real name was William Sidney Porter. The *O* in his pen name doesn't stand for anything. It is just an initial that he picked out by chance (note the *period* after the *O*). He lived in the South and the West and, most fruitfully of all for his short story writing, in New York City. Look up some of his books.
4. This is a good story to read aloud. Could you manage a cowboy drawl? Perhaps you would rather just read some of the conversations between Bill and Hank. The whole story can be dramatized. Why not try your hand at it?

JAMES THURBER

The Night the Ghost Got In

If you don't recognize James Thurber's name, maybe you will recall seeing some of his remarkable cartoons, with their queer-looking people and melancholy dogs with drooping ears. His drawings, like almost everything he writes, are original, funny, and sometimes startling. The following narrative is an account of something that could happen in almost any American family – if James Thurber were on hand to turn the whole thing into a hilarious farce. In spite of the title, you will discover that this is not precisely a ghost story.

THE ghost that got into our house on the night of November 17, 1915, raised such a hullabaloo of misunderstanding that I am sorry I didn't just let it keep on walking, and go to bed. Its advent caused my mother to throw a shoe through a window of the house next door and ended up with my grandfather shooting a patrolman. I am sorry, therefore, as I have said, that I ever paid any attention to the footsteps.

They began about a quarter past one o'clock in the morning, a rhythmic, quick-cadenced walking around the dining-room table. My mother was asleep in one room upstairs, my brother Herman in another; Grandfather was in the attic, in the old walnut bed which once fell on my father. I had just stepped out of the bathtub and was busily rubbing myself with a towel when I heard the steps. They were the steps of a man walking rapidly around the dining-room table downstairs. The light from the bathroom shone down the back steps, which dropped directly into the dining room; I could see the faint shine of plates on the plate rail; I couldn't see the table. The steps kept going round and round the table; at regular intervals a board creaked, when it was trod upon. I supposed at first that it was my father or my brother Roy, who had gone to Indianapolis but were expected home at any time. I suspected next that it was a burglar. It did not enter my mind until later that it was a ghost.

After the walking had gone on for perhaps three minutes, I tiptoed to Herman's room. "Psst!" I hissed, in the dark, shaking him. "Awp," he said, in the low, hopeless tone of a despondent beagle – he always half suspected that something would "get him" in the night. I told him who I was. "There's something downstairs!" I said. He got up and followed

"The Night the Ghost Got In" from *My Life and Hard Times* by James Thurber. Reprinted by permission of the author.

me to the head of the back staircase. We listened together. There was no sound. The steps had ceased. Herman looked at me in some alarm — I had only the bath towel around my waist. He wanted to go back to bed, but I gripped his arm. " There's something down there! " I said. Instantly the steps began again, circled the dining-room table like a man running, and started up the stairs toward us, heavily, two at a time. The light still shone palely down the stairs; we saw nothing coming; we only heard the steps. Herman rushed to his room and slammed the door. I slammed shut the door at the stairs top and held my knee against it. After a long minute I slowly opened it again. There was nothing there. There was no sound. None of us ever heard the ghost again.

The slamming of the doors had aroused Mother; she peered out of her room. " What on earth are you boys doing? " she demanded. Herman ventured out of his room. " Nothing," he said gruffly, but he was, in color, a light green. " What was all that running around downstairs? " said Mother. So she had heard the steps, too! We just looked at her. " Burglars! " she shouted intuitively. I tried to quiet her by starting lightly downstairs.

" Come on, Herman," I said.

" I'll stay with Mother," he said. " She's all excited."

I stepped back onto the landing.

" Don't either of you go a step," said Mother. " We'll call the police." Since the phone was downstairs, I didn't see how we were going to call the police — nor did I want the police — but Mother made one of her quick, incomparable decisions. She flung up a window of her bedroom which faced the bedroom windows of the house of a neighbor, picked up a shoe and whammed it through a pane of glass across the narrow space that separated the two houses. Glass tinkled into the bedroom occupied by a retired engraver named Bodwell and his wife. Bodwell had been for some years in rather a bad way and was subject to mild " attacks." Most everybody we knew or lived near had *some* kind of attacks.

It was now about two o'clock of a moonless night; clouds hung black and low. Bodwell was at the window in a minute, shouting, frothing a little, shaking his fist. " We'll sell the house and go back to Peoria," we could hear Mrs. Bodwell saying. It was some time before Mother " got through " to Bodwell. " Burglars! " she shouted. " Burglars in the house! " Herman and I hadn't dared to tell her that it was not burglars but ghosts, for she was even more afraid of ghosts than of burglars. Bodwell at first thought that she meant there were burglars in his house, but finally he quieted down and called the police for us over an extension phone by his bed. After he had disappeared from the window, Mother suddenly made as if to throw another shoe, not because there was further need of it but, as she later explained, because the thrill of heaving a shoe through a window glass had enormously taken her fancy. I prevented her.

The police were on hand in a commendably short time — a Ford sedan full of them, two on motorcycles, and a patrol wagon with about eight in it and a few reporters. They began banging at our front door. Flashlights shot streaks of gleam up and down the walls, across the yard, down the walk between our house and Bodwell's. " Open up! " cried a hoarse voice. " We're men from headquarters! " I wanted to go down and let them in, since there they were; but Mother wouldn't hear of it. " You haven't

Police were all over the place. (*James Thurber*)

a stitch on," she pointed out. "You'd catch your death." I wound the towel around me again. Finally the cops put their shoulders to our big heavy front door with its thick beveled glass and broke it in; I could hear a rending of wood and a splash of glass on the floor of the hall. Their lights played all over the living room and crisscrossed nervously in the dining room, stabbed into hallways, shot up the front stairs and finally up the back. They caught me standing in my towel at the top. A heavy policeman bounded up the steps. "Who are you?" he demanded. "I live here," I said. "Well, whattsa matta, ya hot?" he asked. It was, as a matter of fact, cold; I went to my room and pulled on some trousers. On my way out, a cop stuck a gun into my ribs. "Whatta you doin' here?" he demanded. "I live here," I said.

The officer in charge reported to Mother. "No sign of nobody, lady," he said. "Musta got away. Whatt'd he look like?"

"There were two or three of them," Mother said, "whooping and carrying on and slamming doors."

"Funny," said the cop. "All ya windows and doors was locked on the inside tight as a tick."

Downstairs we could hear the tromping of the other police. Police were all over the place — doors were yanked open; drawers were yanked open; windows were shot up and pulled down; furniture fell with dull thumps. A half-dozen policemen emerged out of the darkness of the front hallway upstairs. They began to ransack the floor — pulled beds away from walls, tore clothes off hooks in the closets, pulled suitcases and boxes off shelves. One of them found an old zither that Roy had won in a pool tournament. "Looky here,

Joe," he said, strumming it with a big paw. The cop named Joe took it and turned it over. "What is it?" he asked me. "It's an old zither our guinea pig used to sleep on," I said. It was true that a pet guinea pig we once had would never sleep anywhere except on the zither, but I should never have said so. Joe and the other cop looked at me a long time. They put the zither back on a shelf.

"No sign o' nuthin'," said the cop who had first spoken to Mother. "This guy," he explained to the others, jerking a thumb at me, "was nekked. The lady seems historical."[1] They all nodded, but said nothing — just looked at me. In the small silence we all heard a creaking in the attic. Grandfather was turning over in bed. "What's 'at?" snapped Joe. Five or six cops sprang for the attic door before I could intervene or explain. I realized that it would be bad if they burst in on Grandfather unannounced, or even announced. He was going through a phase in which he believed that General Meade's men, under steady hammering by Stonewall Jackson, were beginning to retreat and even desert.

When I got to the attic, things were pretty confused. Grandfather had evidently jumped to the conclusion that the police were deserters from Meade's army, trying to hide away in his attic. He bounded out of bed wearing a long flannel nightgown over long woolen underwear, a nightcap, and a leather jacket around his chest. The cops must have realized at once that the indignant white-haired old man belonged in the house, but they had no chance to say so. "Back, ye cowardly dogs!" roared Grandfather. "Back t' the lines, ye lily-livered cattle!" With that he fetched the officer who found the zither a flat-handed smack alongside his head that sent him sprawling. The others beat a retreat, but not fast enough; Grandfather grabbed Zither's gun from its holster and let fly. The report seemed to crack the rafters; smoke filled the attic. A cop cursed and shot his hand to his shoulder. Somehow we all finally got downstairs again and locked the door against the old gentleman. He fired once or twice more in the darkness and then went back to bed.

"That was Grandfather," I explained to Joe, out of breath. "He thinks you're deserters."

"I'll say he does," said Joe.

The cops were reluctant to leave without getting their hands on somebody besides Grandfather; the night had been distinctly a defeat for them. Furthermore they obviously didn't like the "layout"; something looked — and I can see their viewpoint — phony. They began to poke into things again. A reporter, a thin-faced, wispy man, came up to me. I had put on one of Mother's blouses, not being able to find anything else. The reporter looked at me with mingled suspicion and interest. "Just what is the real lowdown here, Bud?" he asked. I decided to be frank with him. "We had ghosts," I said. He gazed at me a long time as if I were a slot machine into which he had, without results, dropped a nickel. Then he walked away. The cops followed him, the one Grandfather shot holding his now-bandaged arm, cursing and blaspheming. "I'm gonna get my gun back from that old bird," said the zither-cop. "Yeh," said Joe. "You — and who else?" I told them I would bring it to the station house the next day.

"What was the matter with that one

[1] **historical:** the policeman means *hysterical* (hĭs·tĕr′ĭ·kăl), that is, wildly emotional and excitable.

policeman?" Mother asked after they had gone. "Grandfather shot him," I said. "What for?" she demanded. I told her he was a deserter. "Of all things!" said Mother. "He was such a nice-looking young man."

Grandfather was fresh as a daisy and full of jokes at breakfast next morning. We thought at first he had forgotten all about what had happened, but he hadn't. Over his third cup of coffee he glared at Herman and me. "What was the idee of all them cops tarryhootin' round the house last night?" he demanded. He had us there.

Finding Added Meanings

Sometimes a sentence or statement means more than appears on the surface. The added meaning can be humorous, as in this story. What, for example, might be a hidden meaning for the sentence, "Most everybody we know or lived near had *some* kind of attacks"? And what (p. 155) was passing through the men's minds in the passage: "Joe and the other cop looked at me a long time"? What do you make of the passage (p. 155) beginning "'What was the matter with that one policeman?' Mother asked after they were gone." Find other passages that seem to mean more than the words actually say.

Thinking It Over

1. Nobody ever explained the ghost, come to think of it. What is your explanation? What effect do you get from Grandfather's comment at the end?

2. As we have already seen, a good deal of humor depends on incongruity. The word means "inconsistency" or "unsuitableness." If you saw a man wearing running shorts and a top hat, you would laugh because his costume would be out of place. Point out passages in the story that depend upon incongruity for their humor.

3. Policemen and detectives are frequently made the victims of the humorists. Why are such officials so often the butt of humorists' stories and jokes?

4. You might take time to exchange a few anecdotes about times in your own household when everyone became excited over nothing.

GOOD STORIES OLD AND NEW

Suggestions for Free Reading

Atkinson, E. S., *Greyfriar's Bobby*
A favorite dog story that never grows old.

Becker, May Lamberton (ed.), *Golden Tales of Our America* (Dodd, 1929); *Golden Tales of the Far West* (Dodd, 1935); *Golden Tales of New England* (Dodd, 1931); *Golden Tales of the Prairie States* (Dodd, 1932)

Benét, Stephen Vincent, *Thirteen O'Clock* (Farrar, 1937)
Stories and legends of American life.

Björnson, Björnstjerne, *A Happy Boy* (Macmillan, 1931)
Call him byûrn′styâr′nĕ byûrn′sŏn. School life in Norway long ago.

Canfield, Dorothy, *Something Old, Something New* (W. R. Scott, 1949)
Nine true stories of "the people who are America." Read *Raw Material* (Harcourt, 1923), too, to learn about "the stuff of which stories are made."

Chesterton, Gilbert Keith, *The Father Brown Omnibus* (Dodd, 1945)
The best of Chesterton's popular detective stories.

Commager, Henry Steele, *St. Nicholas Anthology* (Random House, 1948)
Best loved stories, verse, and illustrations from the old *St. Nicholas Magazine.*

Daly, Maureen, *My Favorite Stories* (Dodd, 1948)
Author of *Seventeenth Summer* collects her favorites.

Davis, Richard Harding, *Gallagher and Others* (Scribner, 1927)
Gathering the news before the age of the teletype and the candid camera.

Dickens, Charles, *Christmas Stories* (World, 1946)
Contains the famous "Christmas Carol."

Doyle, Sir A. Conan, *Complete Sherlock Holmes* (Doubleday, 1936)
Stories by a master teller of detective stories.

Ferris, Josephine Helen (ed.), *Love Comes Riding* (Harcourt, 1929); *Adventure Waits* (Harcourt, 1928)
Romantic tales for girls.

Finger, Charles, *Tales from Silver Lands* (Doubleday, 1924)
Stories from South America.

Fon Eisen, Anthony, *Storm, Dog of Newfoundland* (Scribner, 1948)
Raging seas, mighty whales, icebergs, romance – and a dog, right in the middle of a good story.

Harte, Bret, *The Luck of Roaring Camp and Other Stories*
Good western yarns by a master storyteller.

Hawthorne, Nathaniel, *Twice-Told Tales*
Old favorites by a famous American author.

Heydrick, A., and Thompson, B. J., *Americans All* (Harcourt, 1942)
A cross section of America in story.

Irving, Washington, *Sketch Book*
Contains Rip Van Winkle and the story of Ichabod Crane and the Headless Horseman.

Kipling, Rudyard, *The Day's Work* (Macmillan, 1939)
Ships, bridges, engineers, and builders. Browse through other collections of short stories by Kipling. You will be sure to find something interesting.

Kjelgaard, Jim, *Snow Dog* (Holiday, 1948)
A man and a dog against the elements. Read also *A Nose for Trouble* (poachers, game wardens, mountaineers, and a smoke-colored dog). (Holiday, 1949)

Lieber and Williams, *Great Stories of All Nations* (Tudor, 1927)

Mirrielees, Edith (ed.), *Twenty-Two Short Stories of America* (Heath, 1937)
Easy and interesting.

O'Brien, Jack, *Silver Chief* (Winston, 1933)
Wolves and thieves and a trapper's dog.

Ollivant, Alfred, *Bob, Son of Battle*
The story of a gallant Scotch sheep dog.

O'Rourke, Frank, *Bonus Rookie* (Barnes, 1950)
How the big leagues hunt for future baseball stars.

Poe, Edgar Allan, *The Gold Bug and Other Tales and Poems; Complete Short Stories*
Strange, mysterious, and highly interesting.

Rounds, Glen, *Stolen Pony* (Holiday, 1948)
Cowpunchers, horse thieves, a blind pony, and a mighty smart dog.

Scholz, Jackson, *Goal to Go* (Morrow, 1945)
Football at the U.S. Naval Academy.

Steinbeck, John, *The Long Valley* (Viking, 1938)
Contains "The Red Pony."

Terhune, Alfred Payson, *Lad: a Dog* (Dutton, 1926)
Good dog story.

Van Dyke, Henry, *The Blue Flower*
Imaginative stories with deep spiritual background. Volume contains "The Blue Flower."

Watson, Helen Orr, *Trooper: U.S. Army Dog* (Houghton, 1943)
An American G.I. and his dog from back home. Read also *Topkick: U.S. Army Horse* and *White Boots.*

Williams, Blanche Colton, *The Mystery and the Detective* (Appleton-Century 1938); *New Narratives; Book of Short Stories* (Appleton-Century, 1918)
Good short stories in all these collections.

Wright, Willard, *The World's Great Detective Stories* (Scribner, 1927)
Jam-packed with whodunits.

Henle from Monkmeyer

Stories in Verse

POETRY has been treasured by the people in all countries from earliest times until the present, and poems that tell a story are some of the brightest gems in their treasuries.

In the faraway, dim past, the minstrel or reciter of long stories in verse had a ready and eager audience. Kings and servants, generals and camp followers, all gathered to welcome him. The minstrel brought entertainment and drama into the frequently dull lives of his listeners at a time when there was but little written literature and when only a few persons could read what there was. He did more than entertain, too. He gave his listeners a common tradition, a sense of belonging together. Long poems, or epics, like the *Odyssey*, episodes of which you will read in this book, told the history of the race, recounting the deeds of noble warriors who had won great renown.

In a later time, but still before the days of printing, shorter story-poems became popular. There were the folk ballads, which were sung in accompaniment to music and handed down by word of mouth for generations. Still later, as printing became widely known and as education made for not only more readers but also more writers, the tradition of telling stories in verse was carried on by many individual writers, including some of the greatest poets.

The variety of narrative poetry we now have available to us for our reading enjoyment is immense. There are many kinds of narrative poems – poems to suit every taste. If you like rugged, he-man stories, for example, you will enjoy the picturesque tales of the Yukon told by Robert W. Service in poems like "The Shooting of Dan McGrew." If you like stories of action and adventure you will want to read Sir Walter Scott's *Lady of the Lake* and Rudyard Kipling's popular "Gunga Din," which can be found in this book. Certainly one of the most famous poems in the English language is the strange and mysterious *Rime of the Ancient Mariner* by Samuel Taylor Coleridge, which you will find in any library. A more recent narrative as powerful in its own way is Robert Nathan's "Dunkirk," a quiet story of a British boy and his sister in their rescue of troops during World War II.

All of us like stories, but there is something especially appealing about those in verse, for poetry is the most intense, the most beautiful, and often the most memorable way of telling a story. There is a treasure for you in poetry, as for our ancestors centuries ago, if you know how to find it.

The Reading of Poetry

ONE thing about poetry is perfectly clear: it is meant to be read aloud. The meter, or beat, in poetry is like the measure in a piece of music; and its repetition of sounds, which we call rhyme, has a distinctly musical quality. Like music, then, poetry should be heard. But the reading of poetry is not as difficult as the mastery of a musical instrument; nearly everyone can learn to read poetry skillfully with a little knowledge and practice. Stories in verse — narrative poems — are especially effective when read aloud. Thus the selections that follow will give you an opportunity for increasing your skill in reading and your enjoyment of poetry.

Perhaps your teacher can arrange to have each of you read a stanza before the class, and better yet, let you hear yourselves on a wire or tape recorder so that you can improve your reading. If you have this opportunity, you will want to avoid some of the mistakes that many persons make in reading poetry aloud.

One of the most serious mistakes is that of forcing the voice into unnatural rhythms or of overemphasizing the meter. Because poetry has a somewhat different appearance from prose, we tend to forget that the lines can be read naturally and easily, almost in a conversational tone of voice. As a first pointer, then, keep in mind the *sense* of what you are reading. Don't pause at the end of a line if the *sense* doesn't pause there. Similarly, don't try to "help" the poet by stressing the meter in a singsong, or by an exaggerated rise and fall of your voice. Just read the lines as you would read a play or a story, making the pauses that the punctuation or sense or your own breath span requires.

Remember too that poetry must mean something. You will want to read the lines so that your listeners will get the true meaning — and to do this, you too must understand what the lines mean. Understanding a poet's meaning is not so difficult as many persons believe. Chiefly the poet does two simple things. Besides giving us the pleasure of hearing beautifully measured sounds, he also conveys certain thoughts and emotions to us by his writing. It's as simple as that!

One thing that sometimes hinders our understanding of a line or a poem is the poet's use of *figurative language*. Figurative language means merely that one thing is compared with another or that one thing stands for another. We say that a football fullback is a " battering ram," or a " pile driver," or a " galloping ghost." When we say that a quarterback is " foxy," we mean that he has the qualities of a fox, that he is crafty and cunning and elusive. These examples are metaphors. If we say a person is " crafty *as* or *like* a fox," then we are using a simile (sĭm'ĭ·lē). Metaphors and similes are the two most common figures of speech, and they give much added color and meaning to both prose and poetry.

Another difficulty in understanding poetry is *inverted word order;* that is, words not arranged in the usual manner (" tired he is," for example, rather than " he is tired "). Finally, we may also have trouble occasionally with the *unusual words* that poets use.

Let's examine these difficulties – and perhaps we can discover how they can be overcome with just a little thought – by close reading of a stanza from William Rose Benét's poem, " The Skater of Ghost Lake," which appears on page 178. (Before you begin, however, read the entire poem.)

> Black as if lacquered the wide lake lies;
> Breath is a frost-fume, eyes seek eyes;
> Souls are a sword-edge tasting the cold.
> Ghost lake's a deep lake, a dark lake and old!

The very first line, you notice, contains an inversion, but its meaning is plain enough:

> The wide lake lies black, as if lacquered.

But at once you see that this word order does not have the rhythm and the immediate colorfulness of the original statement. Compare the two word orders closely in order to prove this to yourself.

> Black as if lacquered the wide lake lies.
> The wide lake lies black, as if lacquered.

Do you notice the difference? The inverted order of " wide lake lies " forces an almost equal accent or stress onto each word, so that the long vowel sounds at the end of the line are emphasized and the whole effect becomes musical. The other word order? Well, it sounds just like prose, doesn't it!

Now look at the second line of the stanza, which presents some figurative language. Here is a metaphor, because " breath " is called a " frost-fume." You yourself have probably spoken of " fumes " from an automobile exhaust. Now think of fumes being made by the breath of the two skaters, and you will know that the night is cold even before you read it in the next line.

This third line is the most challenging in the entire stanza:

Souls are a sword-edge, tasting the cold.

" How can souls be a sword-edge," you may well ask, " and how can a sword-edge ' taste ' the cold? " Here is a typical instance where some poetry readers run into trouble. The meaning is simple, really, and the line doesn't mean much more than it says on the surface. In this brilliant metaphor Benét is simply saying: *These two persons, in love with each other, and out skating in the moonlight, swerve and cut across the ice in such close unison that they might be a single flashing blade exploring the mystery of the lake on a very cold night.* At least, you might give this interpretation to the stanza after reading more of the poem.

The last line of the stanza is a refrain, or a line that is repeated several times throughout the poem. Its meaning you will know if you have read the entire selection.

Not all poetic stanzas have so many special qualities as this one, fortunately for the beginning reader. We have examined here a rather difficult piece of verse so that you will know what to look for in reading other poems. In most poems a simple, direct story is told, or a fairly clear thought or feeling is expressed. Very often you will be able to sum up in a few words the idea or story in a poem.

Keep in mind, as you search for meanings, that you may not find a great moral or lesson in every poem. Poets are persons who feel the events of life more intensely than the rest of us, and so they occasionally express nothing more direct than pure joy or sadness. A poet may say only that standing on a mountaintop brings a mood of elation, that autumn makes him sad, or that waves lapping against a shore somehow bring peace to him. At any rate, you should try to feel the mood or the emotion which dominates a poem, even if you cannot always sum up the so-called " meaning " of it. In music it is enough for most persons to feel that a selection is happy or sad or vigorous; it is not necessary that one must imagine a whole story in order to enjoy a piece of music. Poetry is somewhat different, in that the story is there – in words! But a great part of the enjoyment, as with music, comes from the sympathetic appreciation of moods and emotions.

You are your own pilot on the sea of poetry. Anchors aweigh! May you stop at many happy islands!

BALLADS OLD AND NEW

In some sections of the United States it is still possible to find folk ballads that can be traced back over five hundred years to England and Scotland. Perhaps you have heard the story of hard-hearted Barbara Allen, one of the old ballads that is now popular on the radio and recordings. We have our modern ballads too, though they are usually composed by individual writers and not by the people, or "folk." Most of the old ballads are sad in mood. They tell of cruelty, misunderstandings, murder, revenge, or disaster of some kind. The hard life of people in primitive times is thus reflected in song.

THE CRUEL BROTHER

In this story of long ago there is romance and tragedy. There are three sisters who attend a gay ball, and a gallant knight who woos and wins one of them. Try to decide why the brother in the story acted as he did.

There was three ladies played at the ba',°
With a hey ho and a lily gay.

There came a knight and played o'er them a',
As the primrose spreads so sweetly.

The eldest was baith° tall and fair, 5
But the youngest looked like beauty's queen.

1. **ba'**: ball. (Notice the small circle after the word **ba'**. This sign is used in the poetry sections of this book to call your attention to each word or phrase which has a footnote.) 5. **baith**: both.

The midmost had a graceful mien,
But the youngest looked like beauty's queen.

The knight bowed low to a' the three,
But to the youngest he bent his knee. 10

The lady turned her head aside,
The knight he wooed her to be his bride.

The lady blushed a rosy red,
And said, "Sir knight, I'm o'er young to wed."

"O lady fair, give me your hand, 15
And I'll make you lady of a' my land."

"Sir knight, ere ye my favor win,
You maun° get consent frae a' my kin."

He's got consent frae her parents dear,
And likewise frae her sisters fair. 20

18. **maun**: must.

He's got consent frae her kin each one,
But forgot to spier at° her brother John.

Now, when the wedding day was come,
The knight would take his bonny bride home.

And many a lord and many a knight 25
Came to behold that lady bright.

And there was nae man that did her see,
But wished himself bridegroom to be.

Her father dear led her down the stair,
And her sisters twain they kissed her there. 30

Her mother dear led her through the close,°
And her brother John set her on her horse.

She leaned her o'er the saddlebow,
To give him a kiss ere she did go.

He has ta'en a knife, baith lang and sharp, 35
And stabbed the bonny bride to the heart.

She hadna ridden half through the town,
Until her heart's blude stained her gown.

"Ride softly on," said the best young man,
"For I think our bonny bride looks pale and wan." 40

"O lead me gently up yon hill,
And I'll there sit down, and make my will."

"O what will you leave to your father dear?"
"The silver-shod steed that brought me here."

22. **spier** (spēr) **at**: ask. 31. **close**: yard.

"And what will you leave to your mother dear?" 45
"My velvet pall° and my silken gear."

"What will you leave to your sister Anne?"
"My silken scarf and my gowden° fan."

"What will you leave to your sister Grace?" 49
"My bloody clothes to wash and dress."

"What will you leave to your brother John?"
"The gallows tree to hang him on."

"What will you leave to your brother John's wife?"
"The wilderness to end her life."

This fair lady in her grave was laid, 55
And a mass was o'er her said.

But it would have made your heart right sair,
To see the bridegroom rive° his hair.

46. **pall**: cloak. 48. **gowden** (goud'ĕn): golden. 58. **rive**: tear.

How Well Did You Read?

1. Why did the brother in this poem kill his sister? Line 18 sheds a little light here. Possibly you can suggest some adjectives which would describe him better than *cruel.*

2. Who are the speakers in lines 15 and 17? Who in lines 41 and 43?

3. What is a knife "baith lang and sharp"? What is the meaning of *sair,* line 58? How would you accent *lady,* line 55, and how would you pronounce *said,* line 56?

4. What is the meaning of the particular things the dying bride leaves to each member of her family? Is there a good reason why she does not mention the bridegroom at the end?

BINNORIE

Here is another tale of two sisters and a lover who chooses the younger. But in this poem it is not a brother who causes the tragedy. Note the refrain lines in italics. In many of the old ballads the refrains are repeated in every stanza. Perhaps you would like to experiment with this arrangement if the class reads the poem aloud.

There were two sisters sat in a bower;
Binnorie, O Binnorie!
There came a knight to be their wooer,
By the bonnie milldams o' Binnorie.

He courted the eldest with glove and ring, 5
But he loved the youngest above everything.

The eldest she was vexèd sair
And greatly envied her sister fair.

Upon a morning fair and clear,
She cried upon her sister dear: 10

" O sister, sister, take my hand,
And we'll see our father's ships to land."

She's taken her by the lily hand,
And led her down to the river-strand.

The youngest stood upon a stone, 15
The eldest came and pushed her in.

" O sister, sister, reach your hand!
And you shall be heir of half my land."

" O sister, I'll not reach my hand,
And I'll be heir of all your land." 20

" O sister, reach me but your glove!
And sweet William shall be your love."

" Sink on, nor hope for hand or glove!
And sweet William shall be my love! "

Sometimes she sank, sometimes she swam, 25
Until she came to the miller's dam.

Out then came the miller's son,
And saw the fair maid floating in.

" O father, father, draw your dam!
There's either a mermaid or a swan." 30

The miller hastened and drew his dam,
And there he found a drowned woman.

You could not see her waist so small,
Her girdle with gold was broidered all.

You could not see her lily feet, 35
Her golden fringes were so deep.

You could not see her yellow hair
For the strings of pearls that were twisted there.

You could not see her fingers small,
With diamond rings they were covered all. 40

And by there came a harper fine,
To harp to the king when he should dine.

And when he looked that lady on,
He sighed and made a heavy moan.

He's made a harp of her breast-bone, 45
Whose sound would melt a heart of stone.

He's taken three locks of her yellow hair,
And with them strung his harp so rare.

He went into her father's hall, 49
And there was the court assembled all.

He laid his harp upon a stone,
And straight it began to play alone.

" O yonder sits my father, the King,
And yonder sits my mother, the Queen;

" And yonder stands my brother Hugh,
And by him my William, sweet and
true." 56

But the last tune that the harp played
then —
Binnorie, O Binnorie!
Was, " Woe to my sister, false Helen! "
By the bonnie milldams o' Binnorie.

How Well Did You Read?

1. What clue is there in the first few lines to show that the sisters are from a highborn family? What later clues do you find?
2. Did the young man propose to the older daughter, or did he merely give presents to the older, while giving his heart to the younger? Try to support your answer by referring to specific lines in the poem.
3. Was there any question in your mind as to the real meaning of *swam,* line 25? Look closely at this line.
4. There are a number of poetic inversions, or words in reversed order, in lines 33 to 43. Can you point them out?
5. Did you pronounce the word *vexèd,* in line 7, with two syllables?

SOUTHERN SHIPS AND SETTLERS

ROSEMARY AND STEPHEN VINCENT BENÉT

Like his older brother, Stephen Vincent Benét was a writer who liked to explore the folk history of America and turn it into stories and ballads. With his wife Rosemary he wrote a series of memorable ballads in *A Book for Americans,* from which " Southern Ships and Settlers " is taken. Here is a poem which will make you proud of being an American, no matter what part of this country your ancestors settled in or what countries in the Old World they came from.

O, where are you going, " Goodspeed " and " Discovery "?
With meek " Susan Constant " to make up the three?
We're going to settle the wilds of Virginia,
For gold and adventure we're crossing the sea.

And what will you find there? Starvation and fever. 5
We'll eat of the adder° and quarrel and rail.
All but sixty shall die of the first seven hundred,
But a nation begins with the voyage we sail.

O, what are you doing, my handsome Lord Baltimore?
Where are you sending your " Ark " and your " Dove "? 10
I'm sending them over the ocean to Maryland
To build up a refuge for people I love.

Both Catholic and Protestant there may find harbor,
Though I am a Catholic by creed and by prayer.

6. adder: literally, a poisonous snake; here, dissension and gall, or hate.

The South is Virginia, the North is New England. 15
I'll go in the middle and plant my folk there.

O, what do you seek, "Carolina" and "Albemarle,"
Now the Stuarts are up and the Roundheads° are down?
We'll seek and we'll find, to the South of Virginia,
A site by two rivers and name it Charles Town. 20

And, in South Carolina, the cockfighting planters
Will dance with their belles by a tropical star.
And, in North Carolina, the sturdy Scotch-Irish
Will prove at King's Mountain the metal they are.

O, what are you dreaming, cock-hatted James Oglethorpe? 25
And who are the people you take in the "Anne"?
They're poor English debtors whom hard laws imprison,
And poor, distressed Protestants, fleeing a ban.

I'll settle them pleasantly on the Savannah,
With Germans and Highlanders, thrifty and strong. 30
They shall eat Georgia peaches in huts of palmetto,
And their land shall be fertile, their days shall be long.

All:
We're the barques and the sailors, the bread on the waters,
The seed that was planted and grew to be tall,
And the South was first won by our toils and our dangers, 35
So remember our journeys. Remember us all.

18. **Stuarts . . . Roundheads:** Royalist and Puritan parties; the Roundheads wore their hair cut short, straight around.

For Your Vocabulary

NAMES: Did you look up *Savannah* in line 29? Of course you know that there is a large city in Georgia by this name. Here it refers to the Savannah River in Georgia. What is the geographical meaning of the word? What names of rivers or cities near you carry a geographical meaning? What is the common meaning, for example, of *Butte*, Montana? Also, did you notice that "Carolina" and "Albemarle" and several other names have quotation marks around them? This isn't done for such names as Lord Baltimore and James Oglethorpe. What is the reason for the difference in punctuation? If you like the sounds and curious histories of unusual names, be sure to look up Stephen Vincent Benét's famous poem "American Names."

THE DICK JOHNSON REEL

HERMAN FETZER
(Jake Falstaff)

Don't look now, but all of the towns mentioned in this rollicking ballad can actually be found on an Ohio road map. If you can't hear fiddles playing, hands clapping, and feet tapping a barn floor in this poem, then your imagination needs a spring tonic!

(The old men say their grandfathers heard Dick Johnson sing the chorus of this song in the timberlands of northern Summit County, Ohio.)

Old Dick Johnson, gentleman, adventurer,
Braggart, minstrel, lover of a brawl,
Walked in the timber from Northfield to Hudson.
(Backward, forward and sashay all!) 4
Old Dick Johnson, joker and wanderer,
Poet, vagabond, and beater of the track,°
Sang a song of his bravery and prowess:
(Ladies go forward and gents go back!)

6. **track:** trail; a beater of the track was just a follower of the trail.

Chorus: Ripsi, rantsi,
Humpsy, dumpsy; 10
I, Dick Johnson,
Killed Tecumseh!

Old Dick Johnson, fighter of the Indians,
Sang from Boston to the hills of Bath;
Sang the song of his muscle and his musket. 15
(Swing your partners and leave a path!)
The redskin sleeps where the wheat is growing,
But Old Dick Johnson's ghost is free,
And it sings all night from Richfield to Twinsburg: 19
(All hands 'round with a one-two-three!)

Chorus: Ripsi, rantsi,
Humpsy, dumpsy;
I, Dick Johnson,
Killed Tecumseh!

THE RHYME OF THE CHIVALROUS SHARK

WALLACE IRWIN

Life would be dull indeed if it weren't for a little nonsense now and then. It is relished, we are told, by the wisest men. This poem is based on the idea that a *man*-eating shark won't eat —— but that would be telling!

Most chivalrous fish of the ocean —
To ladies forbearing and mild,
Though his record be dark, is the man-eating shark,
Who will eat neither woman nor child.

He dines upon seamen and skippers, 5
And tourists his hunger assuage,
And a fresh cabin boy will inspire him with joy
If he's past the maturity age.

A doctor, a lawyer, a preacher,
He'll gobble one any fine day, 10
But the ladies, God bless 'em, he'll only address 'em
Politely and go on his way.

Square dancing today is just as much fun as it was in pioneer times. (Gendreau)

I can readily cite you an instance
  Where a lovely young lady of Breem,
Who was tender and sweet and delicious to eat, 15
  Fell into the bay with a scream.

She struggled and flounced in the water,
  And signaled in vain for her bark,
And she'd surely been drowned if she hadn't been found
  By the chivalrous man-eating shark. 20

He bowed in a manner most polished,
  Thus soothing her impulses wild;
" Don't be frightened," he said, " I've been properly bred –
  And will eat neither woman nor child."

Then he proffered his fin and she took it – 25
  Such a gallantry none can dispute –
While the passengers cheered as the vessel they neared,
  And a broadside was fired in salute.

And they soon stood° alongside the vessel,
  When a life-saving dinghy° was lowered 30
With the pick of the crew, and her relatives too,
  And the mate and the skipper aboard.

So they took her aboard in a jiffy,
  And the shark stood attention the while,
Then he raised on his flipper and ate up the skipper 35
  And went on his way with a smile.

And this shows that the prince of the ocean,
  To ladies forbearing and mild,
Though his record be dark, is the man-eating shark
  Who will eat neither woman nor child. 40

29. stood: came. 30. **dinghy** (dĭng′gĭ): a small boat.

Thinking Over Ballads Old and New

1. There are ten different versions of " The Cruel Brother " and probably a number of " Binnorie " and other ballads of this type. Why do you suppose so many versions of a single poem have come into being?

2. Some of Sir Walter Scott's " Border Ballads " are easier to read but have the same characteristics as the original old ballads. If you don't know " Lochinvar " and " Lord Ullin's Daughter," look them up now. *The Lady of the Lake* is Scott's famous long story-poem, which you will want to read if you're ambitious.

3. There are four distinct parts to " The Cruel Brother " – the wooing, the wedding, the tragedy, and the making of the will. How would you label the parts to " Binnorie "?

4. " Southern Ships and Settlers " tells

just a part of the story of the settling of America. What groups settled in the Hudson Valley region, at Plymouth, and at Philadelphia? Name some parts of this country that today have large populations descended from either recent or former immigrants from other countries. What nationality groups do you find in your city or community or state? Name some of the contributions to America of a nationality group that is *not* your own.

5. A very small bit of local folklore is the basis for " The Dick Johnson Reel." By the way, you might look up the great Indian chief Tecumseh. Possibly you can find out how he actually died.

6. Right now might be a good time for you to try your hand at a bit of ballad writing. A humorous or dramatic local happening or a picturesque person who once played an important part in the story of your community might serve as a ballad subject. If you want a simple, easy model to follow, you might imitate the following stanza:

That níght the víllage jaíl burned dówn
The tówn had lóng been fást asléep;
Old Jím the társhall ín his béd
Was coúnting cárefullý some shéep.

Note that all lines have four beats or stresses, that only the second and fourth lines rhyme. Sometimes a good effect can be achieved by shortening lines two and four to only three beats: (2) *The town was fast asleep;* (4) *Was slowly counting sheep.* Whatever model you use in the first stanza, be sure to follow it exactly throughout the poem.

OTHER TALES IN RHYME

There are many tales in rhyme besides those told in ballad form. These tales range from short poems to long " books " like Homer's *Iliad* or his *Odyssey*. No matter what the length of the poem, you will see that each is the story of a dramatic incident or series of incidents, or is at least written in a dramatic manner. What is a dramatic incident? It's a happening in which there is action, suspense, and character revelation. These features make for good stories both in prose and poetry, as you have discovered from reading fiction.

Heroism, mystery, romance, and even incidents of everyday life have furnished poets with the subject matter of narrative verse, one of the most pleasing kinds of poetry, admirably designed as it is for reading to friends on a quiet evening, when our fancy will take us to far places and strange times.

GUNGA DIN

RUDYARD KIPLING

" Gunga Din " isn't so much a story as it is a biographical profile in verse. It is written in dramatic form in the rough language of a British soldier in India, and the hero is no knight in armor, no regimental officer, not even a private. He is a humble native water carrier, ordered around and abused by everyone, but a hero nevertheless.

You may talk o' gin and beer
When you're quartered safe out 'ere,
An' you're sent to penny-fights an' Aldershot° it;
But when it comes to slaughter
You will do your work on water, 5
An' you'll lick the bloomin' boots of 'im that's got it.
Now in Injia's sunny clime,
Where I used to spend my time
A-servin' of 'Er Majesty the Queen,°
Of all them black-faced crew 10
The finest man I knew
Was our regimental bhisti,° Gunga Din.
He was " Din! Din! Din!
You limpin' lump o' brick dust, Gunga Din!
Hi! Slippey *hitherao!* 15
Water, get it! *Panee lao,*°
You squidgy-nosed old idol, Gunga Din."

The uniform 'e wore
Was nothin' much before,
An' rather less than 'arf o' that be'ind, 20
For a piece o' twisty rag
An' a goatskin water bag
Was all the field equipment 'e could find.
When the sweatin' troop train lay
In a sidin' through the day, 25
Where the 'eat would make your bloomin' eyebrows crawl,
We shouted " Harry By! "°
Till our throats were bricky-dry,
Then we wopped 'im 'cause 'e couldn't serve us all.
It was " Din! Din! Din! 30
You 'eathen, where the mischief 'ave you been?
You put some *juldee*° in it
Or I'll marrow you° this minute
If you don't fill up my helmet, Gunga Din! "

3. **Aldershot:** the largest permanent military camp in England at that time. 9. **Queen:** Queen Victoria (1819–1901). 12. **bhisti** (bē′stē): water carrier. 16. **Panee lao** (pä′nā lä′ō): bring water quickly. 27. **Harry By:** O brother. 32. **juldee:** speed. 33. **marrow you:** cut the marrow out of you.

'E would dot an' carry one° 35
Till the longest day was done;
An' he didn't seem to know the use o' fear.
If we charged or broke or cut,
You could bet your bloomin' nut,
'E'd be waitin' fifty paces right flank rear. 40
With 'is mussick° on 'is back,
'E would skip with our attack,
'An watch us till the bugles made " Retire."
An' for all 'is dirty 'ide
'E was white, clear white, inside 45
When 'e went to tend the wounded under fire!
It was " Din! Din! Din! "
With the bullets kickin' dust spots on the green;
When the cartridges ran out,
You could hear the front ranks shout, 50
" Hi! ammunition mules an' Gunga Din! "

I shan't forgit the night
When I dropped be'ind the fight
With a bullet where my belt plate should 'a' been.
I was chokin' mad with thirst 55
An' the man that spied me first
Was our good old grinnin' gruntin' Gunga Din.
'E lifted up my 'ead,
An' he plugged me where I bled,
An' 'e guv me 'arf a pint o' water – green. 60
It was crawlin' and it stunk,
But of all the drinks I've drunk,
I'm gratefulest to one from Gunga Din.
It was " Din! Din! Din!
'Ere's a beggar with a bullet through 'is spleen; 65
'E's chawin' up the ground,
An' 'e's kickin' all around:
For Gawd's sake git the water, Gunga Din! "

'E carried me away
To where a dooli° lay, 70
An' a bullet come an' drilled the beggar clean.
'E put me safe inside,
An' just before 'e died,
" I 'ope you liked your drink," sez Gunga Din.
So I'll meet 'im later on 75
At the place where 'e is gone –
Where it's always double drill and no canteen.

35. **dot . . . one:** work methodically. 41. **mussick** (mo͞o′sĭk): waterskin. 70. **dooli** (do͞o′lē): a kind of stretcher.

'E'll be squattin' on the coals
Givin' drink to poor damned souls,
An' I'll get a swig in hell from Gunga Din! 80
Yes, Din! Din! Din!
You Lazarushian-leather Gunga Din!
Though I've belted you and flayed you,
By the livin' Gawd that made you,
You're a better man than I am, Gunga Din! 85

How Well Did You Read?

1. As you probably guessed from your reading, " Gunga Din " is a wonderful poem to put to music. Like Kipling's " Mandalay," it has been sung by many famous modern singers. Try to find a recording of either for playing in class.

2. What is the meaning of *penny-fights,* line 3? And what does line 5 mean to you? Try to explain *wopped,* line 29, and *cut* in line 38.

3. What clues tell you that the action in this poem took place some time ago? Who do you think the speaker is? Give a reason for your answer.

IT WAS A FAMOUS VICTORY

FRANKLIN PIERCE ADAMS

The well-known F. P. A. of newspaper, radio, and television renown is also a writer of clever light verse. In this poem he writes a parody of a famous story-poem, " The Battle of Blenheim " by Robert Southey. Someone should read Southey's poem to the class, so that all can appreciate the satire in *both* the original and the parody.

It was a summer evening;
Old Kaspar was at home,
Sitting before his cottage door —
Like in the Southey pome —
And near him, with a magazine, 5
Idled his grandchild, Geraldine.

" Why don't you ask me," Kaspar said
To the child upon the floor,
" Why don't you ask me what I did
When I was in the war? 10
They told me that each little kid
Would surely ask me what I did.

" I've had my story ready
For thirty years or more."
" Don't bother, Grandpa," said the child;
" I find such things a bore. 16
Pray leave me to my magazine,"
Asserted little Geraldine.

Then entered little Peterkin,
To whom his gaffer said: 20
" You'd like to hear about the war?
How I was left for dead? "
" No. And, besides," declared the youth,
" How do I know you speak the truth? "

Arose that wan, embittered man, 25
The hero of this pome,
And walked, with not unspritely step,
Down to the Soldiers' Home,
Where he, with seven other men,
Sat swapping lies till half-past ten. 30

How Well Did You Read?

1. Determining the *tone* of a piece of writing, or an author's attitude toward his material, is important. What line in the first

stanza tells you, suddenly and specifically, that the tone is satirical, which means holding something up to ridicule? Two words give you the clue. What single word in the second stanza emphasizes this impression? What rather common failing of old people is the author satirizing, or making fun of?

2. Look up the word *gaffer*. Does it really mean " grandfather "? What humorous misspellings can you find?

DUNKIRK ROBERT NATHAN

" Dunkirk " is one of the great poems to come out of World War II. The heroes of this poem are a sixteen-year-old boy and his younger sister, who play a part in one of the most dramatic and gigantic rescues in history. In all, 338,226 men were transferred from the beaches of Dunkirk to England, with a total of 900 vessels engaged in an operation that lasted from May 26 to June 4, 1940. This was, as Winston Churchill said, England's darkest and yet finest hour. Of the 693 small boats, 266 were sunk, besides 6 out of the 39 destroyers and 17 out of the 113 trawlers. Overhead, small groups of British fighters attacked German squadrons that numbered as high as 40 and 50. The chances that Will and Bess would come out safely were not good. But they had a little sailboat, the *Sarah,* and their army needed rescuing. . . .

Will came back from school that day
And he had little to say,
But he stood a long time looking down
To where the gray-green Channel water
Slapped at the foot of the little town, 5
And to where his boat, the *Sarah P,*
Bobbed at the tide on an even keel,
With her one old sail, patched at the leech,°
Furled like a slattern down at heel.

He stood for a while above the beach; 10
He saw how the wind and current caught her.
He looked a long time out to sea.
There was steady wind and the sky was pale,
And a haze in the east that looked like smoke.

Will went back to the house to dress. 15
He was halfway through when his sister Bess,
Who was near fourteen and younger than he
By just two years, came home from play.
She asked him, " Where are you going, Will? "
He said, " For a good long sail." 20
" Can I come along? "
" No, Bess," he spoke.
" I may be gone for a night and a day."

8. **leech:** edge.

Through the mists to " the wet men waiting on the sands " came hundreds of craft — fishing trawlers, small pleasure boats, naval vessels — to complete one of the greatest evacuations in history. (*Combine Photos*)

Bess looked at him. She kept very still.
She had heard the news of the Flanders rout,
How the English were trapped above Dunkirk, 25
And the fleet had gone to get them out —
But everyone thought that it wouldn't work.
There was too much fear, there was too much doubt.

She looked at him and he looked at her.
They were English children, born and bred. 30
He frowned her down, but she wouldn't stir.
She shook her proud young head.
" You'll need a crew," she said.
They raised the sail on the *Sarah P*,
Like a pennoncel° on a young knight's lance, 35
And headed *Sarah* out to sea,
To bring their soldiers home from France.

There was no command, there was no set plan,
But six hundred boats went out with them
On the gray-green waters, sailing fast, 40
River excursion and fisherman,
Tug and schooner and racing M,
And the little boats came following last.

35. **pennoncel** (pĕn′ŭn·sĕl): a small pennant.

From every harbor and town they went
Who had sailed their craft in the sun and rain, 45
From the South Downs, from the cliffs of Kent,
From the village street, from the country lane.
There are twenty miles of rolling sea
From coast to coast, by the sea gull's flight,
But the tides were fair and the wind was free, 50
And they raised° Dunkirk by the fall of night.
They raised Dunkirk with its harbor torn
By the blasted stern and the sunken prow;
They had raced for fun on an English tide,
They were English children bred and born, 55
And whether they lived or whether they died,
They raced for England now.

Bess was as white as the *Sarah's* sail,
She set her teeth and smiled at Will.
He held his course for the smoky veil 60
Where the harbor narrowed thin and long.
The British ships were firing strong.

He took the *Sarah* into his hands,
He drove her in through fire and death
To the wet men waiting on the sands. 65
He got his load and he got his breath,
And she came about, and the wind fought her.

He shut his eyes and he tried to pray.
He saw his England where she lay,
The wind's green home, the sea's proud daughter, 70
Still in the moonlight, dreaming deep,
The English cliffs and the English loam –
He had fourteen men to get away,
And the moon was clear and the night like day
For planes to see where the white sails creep 75
Over the black water.
He closed his eyes and he prayed for her;
He prayed to the men who had made her great,
Who had built her land of forest and park,
Who had made the seas an English lake; 80
He prayed for a fog to bring the dark;
He prayed to get home for England's sake.
And the fog came down on the rolling sea,
And covered the ships with English mist.
The diving planes were baffled and blind. 85

51. **raised:** sighted.

For Nelson was there in the *Victory,*
With his one good eye, and his sullen twist,
And guns were out on *The Golden Hind,*°
Their shot flashed over the *Sarah P;*
He could hear them cheer as he came about. 90

By burning wharves, by battered slips,
Galleon, frigate, and brigantine,
The old dead captains fought their ships,
And the great dead admirals led the line.
It was England's night, it was England's sea. 95

The fog rolled over the harbor key.°
Bess held to the stays and conned° him out.
And all through the dark, while the *Sarah's* wake
Hissed behind him, and vanished in foam,
There at his side sat Francis Drake, 100
And held him true and steered him home.

88. **Golden Hind:** Sir Francis Drake's flagship. 96. **key:** a low reef-like island. 97. **conned:** directed.

How Well Did You Read?

1. Read the first stanza and tell how it differs in tone from such poems as "Gunga Din" and "The Dick Johnson Reel." Would you say that this tone is characteristic of the whole poem?

2. What is the picture of Dunkirk's harbor in lines 52 and 53? Why is there a *smoky veil* over part of the harbor?

3. Who is meant by *her* in line 77? By *them* in line 90? Does *fought their ships* in line 93 mean that the dead sea captains fought the enemy ships or that they directed their ships? Specifically, how were the rescuers being attacked?

THE SKATER OF GHOST LAKE

WILLIAM ROSE BENÉT

There is a romance in this story-poem, but it is the haunting mystery that will remain indelibly in your mind. What really happened in this story? You will have to believe just what you choose to believe after reading. If you read the introduction on page 161, you are already familiar with some of the qualities of this verse, and if you really appreciate it, you will know that William Rose Benét is a word-wizard.

Ghost Lake's a dark lake, a deep lake and cold:
Ice black as ebony, frostily scrolled;
Far in its shadows a faint sound whirrs;
Steep stand the sentineled deep, dark firs.

A brisk sound, a swift sound, a ring-tinkle-ring; 5
Flit-flit — a shadow, with a stoop and a swing,
Flies from a shadow through the crackling cold.
Ghost Lake's a deep lake, a dark lake and old!

Leaning and leaning, with a stride and a stride,
Hands locked behind him, scarf blowing wide, 10
Jeremy° Randall skates, skates late,
Star for a candle, moon for a mate.

Black is the clear glass now that he glides,
Crisp is the whisper of long lean strides,
Swift is his swaying — but pricked ears hark. 15
None comes to Ghost Lake late after dark!

Cecily° only — yes, it is she!
Stealing to Ghost Lake, tree after tree,
Kneeling in snow by the still lakeside,
Rising with feet winged, gleaming, to glide. 20

Dust of the ice swirls. Here is his hand.
Brilliant his eyes burn. Now, as was planned,
Arm across arm twined, laced to his side,
Out on the dark lake lightly they glide.

Dance of the dim moon, a rhythmical reel, 25
A swaying, a swift tune — skurr of the steel;
Moon for a candle, maid for a mate,
Jeremy Randall skates, skates late.

Black as if lacquered the wide lake lies;
Breath is a frost-fume, eyes seek eyes; 30
Souls are a sword-edge tasting the cold.
Ghost Lake's a deep lake, a dark lake and old!

Far in the shadows hear faintly begin
Like a string pluck-plucked of a violin,
Muffled in mist on the lake's far bound, 35
Swifter and swifter, a low singing sound!

Far in the shadows and faint on the verge
Of blue cloudy moonlight, see it emerge,
Flit-flit — a phantom, with a stoop and a swing . . .
Ah, it's a night bird, burdened of wing! 40

11. Jeremy (jĕr'ĕ·mĭ). **17. Cecily** (sĕs'ĭ·lĭ).

Pressed close to Jeremy, laced to his side,
Cecily Culver, dizzy you glide.
Jeremy Randall sweepingly veers
Out on the dark ice far from the piers.

" Jeremy! " " Sweetheart? " " What do you fear? " 45
" Nothing, my darling — nothing is here! "
" Jeremy?" " Sweetheart? " " What do you flee? "
" Something — I know not; something I see! "

Swayed to a swift stride, brisker of pace,
Leaning and leaning, they race and they race; 50
Ever that whirring, that crisp sound thin
Like a string pluck-plucked of a violin;

Ever that swifter and low singing sound
Sweeping behind them, winding them round;
Gasp of their breath now that chill flakes fret; 55
Ice black as ebony — blacker — like jet!

Ice shooting fangs forth — sudden — like spears;
Crackling of lightning — a roar in their ears!
Shadowy, a phantom swerves off from its prey . . .
No, it's a night bird flit-flits away! 60

Low-winging moth owl, home to your sleep!
Ghost Lake's a still lake, a cold lake and deep.
Faint in its shadows a far sound whirrs.
Black stand the ranks of its sentinel firs.

How Well Did You Read?

1. Look first for the colors described in the poem. What patterns of color do you see?

2. Now listen for the sounds conveyed by the poem. What do you hear?

3. Finally, look for movement. Pick out words and phrases that describe the movements of the skaters and the night bird.

4. List the words that contribute to the eerie, ghostly effect.

5. What do you think Jeremy saw? Do you think it had anything to do with the name of the lake? What do you think happened to Jeremy and Cecily? The story of the two skaters is so lightly etched in that you may almost believe what you wish about the outcome of the story.

For Your Vocabulary

POETIC DEVICES: A poet uses many devices, or tricks, to make his language more musical and colorful. One of these devices is *alliteration,* which consists of repeating the same consonant at the beginning of two or more words in a line or sentence. For example, " Steep *s*tand the *s*entineled *d*eep, *d*ark firs "; " *M*uffled in *m*ist." Find other examples in the poem. Still another device is called *onomatopoeia* (ŏn′ȯ-măt′ȯ·pē′yȧ), in which the sound of a word suggests its meaning (the bee *buzzes,* the rocket *whizzes*). Notice the phrase " *skurr* of the steel " in this poem. Can you find other examples of these combined sound-and-sense words? Which ones do you consider the most effective?

THE RAVEN

EDGAR ALLAN POE

" The Raven " is another mystery story-poem, and a very famous one. There are probably hundreds of people who say, " Quoth the Raven, ' Nevermore,' " without having the slightest idea where the line comes from. " The Skater of Ghost Lake " has a wild, fantastic sort of beauty. " The Raven " has a more somber quality throughout, yet with as great beauty in the sound of the lines. Poe was an artist with words, both in his great short stories and in his poetry. Note how smoothly the lines lend themselves to oral reading. Try to enjoy the poem for sound as much as for story. Be on the lookout for alliteration in this poem, too.

Once upon a midnight dreary, while I pondered, weak and weary,
Over many a quaint and curious volume of forgotten lore —
While I nodded, nearly napping, suddenly there came a tapping,
As of someone gently rapping, rapping at my chamber door.
" 'Tis some visitor," I muttered, " tapping at my chamber door — 5
Only this and nothing more."

Ah, distinctly I remember it was in the bleak December,
And each separate dying ember wrought its ghost upon the floor.
Eagerly I wished the morrow; vainly I had sought to borrow
From my books surcease° of sorrow — sorrow for the lost Lenore. 10
For the rare and radiant maiden whom the angels name Lenore —
Nameless *here* forevermore.

And the silken, sad, uncertain rustling of each purple curtain
Thrilled me — filled me with fantastic terrors never felt before;
So that now, to still the beating of my heart, I stood repeating, 15
" 'Tis some visitor entreating entrance at my chamber door,
Some late visitor entreating entrance at my chamber door —
This it is and nothing more."

Presently my soul grew stronger; hesitating then no longer,
" Sir," said I, " or Madam, truly your forgiveness I implore; 20
But the fact is I was napping, and so gently you came rapping,
And so faintly you came tapping, tapping at my chamber door,
That I scarce was sure I heard you " — here I opened wide the door —
Darkness there and nothing more.

Deep into that darkness peering, long I stood there wondering, fearing, 25
Doubting, dreaming dreams no mortal ever dared to dream before;
But the silence was unbroken, and the stillness gave no token,
And the only word there spoken was the whispered word, " Lenore! "
This I whispered, and an echo murmured back the word " Lenore " —
Merely this and nothing more. 30

10. **surcease** (sûr·sēs′): end.

Back into the chamber turning, all my soul within me burning,
Soon again I heard a tapping somewhat louder than before.
"Surely," said I, "surely that is something at my window lattice;
Let me see, then, what thereat is, and this mystery explore;
Let my heart be still a moment and this mystery explore — 35
'Tis the wind and nothing more."

Open here I flung the shutter, when, with many a flirt and flutter,
In there stepped a stately Raven of the saintly days of yore.
Not the least obeisance made he; not a minute stopped or stayed he;
But with mien of lord or lady perched above my chamber door, 40
Perched upon a bust of Pallas° just above my chamber door —
Perched, and sat, and nothing more.

Then this ebony bird beguiling my sad fancy into smiling
By the grave and stern decorum of the countenance it wore,
"Though thy crest be shorn and shaven, thou," I said, "art sure no craven, 45
Ghastly grim and ancient Raven wandering from the nightly shore:
Tell me what thy lordly name is on the Night's Plutonian° shore!"
Quoth the Raven, "Nevermore."

Much I marveled this ungainly fowl to hear discourse so plainly,
Though its answer little meaning — little relevancy bore; 50
For we cannot help agreeing that no living human being
Ever yet was blessed with seeing bird above his chamber door,
Bird or beast upon the sculptured bust above his chamber door,
With such name as "Nevermore."

But the Raven, sitting lonely on the placid bust, spoke only 55
That one word, as if his soul in that one word he did outpour,
Nothing further then he uttered, not a feather then he fluttered,
Till I scarcely more than muttered, "Other friends have flown before;
On the morrow *he* will leave me, as my hopes have flown before."
Then the bird said, "Nevermore." 60

Startled at the stillness broken by reply so aptly spoken,
"Doubtless," said I, "what it utters is its only stock and store,
Caught from some unhappy master whom unmerciful Disaster
Followed fast and followed faster till his songs one burden bore,
Till the dirges of his Hope that melancholy burden bore 65
Of 'Never — nevermore.'"

But the Raven still beguiling all my fancy into smiling,
Straight I wheeled a cushioned seat in front of bird and bust and door;
Then, upon the velvet sinking, I betook myself to linking

41. **Pallas** (păl′ȧs): Pallas Athene (ȧ·thē′nē), Greek goddess of wisdom. 47. **Plutonian** (plōō·tō′nĭ·ăn): In Greek and Roman mythology, Pluto ruled the kingdom of the dead.

Fancy unto fancy, thinking what this ominous bird of yore, 70
What this grim, ungainly, ghastly, gaunt, and ominous bird of yore
Meant in croaking "Nevermore."

This I sat engaged in guessing, but no syllable expressing
To the fowl, whose fiery eyes now burned into my bosom's core;
This and more I sat divining, with my head at ease reclining 75
On the cushion's velvet lining that the lamplight gloated o'er,
But whose velvet violet lining with the lamplight gloating o'er
She shall press, ah, nevermore!

Then, methought, the air grew denser, perfumed from an unseen censer
Swung by seraphim whose footfalls tinkled on the tufted floor. 80
"Wretch," I cried, "thy God hath lent thee – by these angels he hath sent thee
Respite – respite and nepenthe° from thy memories of Lenore!
Quaff, oh, quaff this kind nepenthe, and forget this lost Lenore!"
Quoth the Raven, "Nevermore."

"Prophet!" said I, "thing of evil! prophet still, if bird or devil! 85
Whether Tempter sent, or whether tempest tossed thee here ashore,
Desolate yet all undaunted, on this desert land enchanted –
On this home by Horror haunted – tell me truly, I implore:
Is there – *is* there balm in Gilead?° – tell me – tell me, I implore!"
Quoth the Raven, "Nevermore." 90

"Prophet!" said I, "thing of evil – prophet still, if bird or devil!
By that Heaven that bends above us, by that God we both adore,
Tell this soul with sorrow laden if, within the distant Aidenn,°
It shall clasp a sainted maiden whom the angels name Lenore:
Clasp a rare and radiant maiden whom the angels name Lenore!" 95
Quoth the Raven, "Nevermore."

"Be that word our sign of parting, bird or fiend!" I shrieked, upstarting.
"Get thee back into the tempest and the Night's Plutonian shore!
Leave no black plume as a token of that lie thy soul hath spoken!
Leave my loneliness unbroken! quit the bust above my door! 100
Take thy beak from out my heart, and take thy form from off my door!"
Quoth the Raven, "Nevermore."

And the Raven, never flitting, still is sitting, still is sitting
On the pallid bust of Pallas just above my chamber door;
And his eyes have all the seeming of a demon's that is dreaming, 105
And the lamplight o'er him streaming throws his shadow on the floor:
And my soul from out that shadow that lies floating on the floor
Shall be lifted – nevermore!

82. respite (rĕs′pĭt) **and nepenthe** (nē·pĕn′thē): a short period of rest and forgetfulness. **89. balm** (bäm) **in Gilead** (gĭl′ē·ăd): a reference to the Bible; Gilead was a part of ancient Palestine, and balm is a healing lotion. **93. Aidenn** (ā′dĕn): from the Arabic for Eden.

How Well Did You Read?

1. What had the author been doing, and why, when he was first aroused by the tapping on the door? What mood does this establish for the reading of the poem? Pick out words which help to convey that mood.

2. What examples of *alliteration* (see p. 180) do you find in stanzas two and three? in stanza five? Point out others.

3. What might have been in the author's mind as he whispered "Lenore!" in line 28? Where, later, did he decide the Raven had come from? What explanation have you for the Raven?

4. Explain the meaning of *burden,* line 65, and *divining,* line 75.

5. Line 80 is often criticized as being mistaken in sense, or illogical. Can you see how this might be true?

6. Does the author address lines 81 to 83 to the Raven or to himself? What do you make of "these angels," line 81?

For Your Vocabulary

RHYME: There are some interesting rhyming patterns in this poem. You know that the usual kind of rhyme goes like this: *child-wild, lie-I, almost-ghost.* The words in each set have a closeness of sound to each other. But in this poem there is a special kind of rhyme called *identical rhyme,* in which the words in a set are almost exactly the same and sometimes actually the same. Notice the following rhyme from "The Raven": *shore-shore-more.* What other identical rhymes can you find? Still another special kind of rhyme is called *internal rhyme.* Most often the poet will rhyme words at the end of his lines, but with internal rhyme he rhymes a word in the middle of the line with the word at the end. Notice in line 13 of the poem: "And the silken sad un*certain* rustling of each purple *curtain.*" What other instances of internal rhyme can you find?

THE GLOVE AND THE LIONS

LEIGH HUNT

What makes a poem last for over a hundred years? Sometimes the story that is told makes it last; sometimes it is the poetic art of the writer that keeps it alive; and sometimes it is a truth which the poet has uttered that gives a poem a permanent place in literature. Here is a poem with a dramatic story – and an important truth.

King Francis was a hearty king, and loved a royal sport,
And one day, as his lions fought, sat looking on the court;
The nobles filled the benches, with the ladies in their pride,
And 'mongst them sat the Count de Lorge, with one for whom he sighed.
And truly 'twas a gallant thing to see that crowning show, 5
Valor and love, and a king above, and the royal beasts below.

Ramped and roared the lions, with horrid laughing jaws;
They bit, they glared, gave blows like beams, a wind went with their paws;
With wallowing might and stifled roar they rolled on one another,
Till all the pit with sand and mane was in a thunderous smother; 10
The bloody foam above the bars came whizzing through the air;
Said Francis then, "Faith, gentlemen, we're better here than there."

De Lorge's love o'erheard the King, a beauteous lively dame,
With smiling lips and sharp bright eyes, which always seemed the same;
She thought, "The Count, my lover, is brave as brave can be; 15

He surely would do wondrous things to show his love of me;
King, ladies, lovers, all look on; the occasion is divine;
I'll drop my glove, to prove his love; great glory will be mine."

She dropped her glove, to prove his love, then looked at him and smiled;
He bowed, and in a moment leaped among the lions wild. 20
The leap was quick, return was quick, he has regained his place,
Then threw the glove, but not with love, right in the lady's face.
" By heaven! " said Francis. " Rightly done! " and he rose from where he sat;
" No love," quoth he, " but vanity, sets love a task like that."

Thinking Over Other Tales in Rhyme

1. " Dunkirk " is a remarkable story. What does the poet mean by saying, at the end of the poem, that Sir Francis Drake is the one who " steers " Will home? Why Drake rather than some other great English admiral? A footnote on his ship the *Golden Hind* gives you a clue. Write a prose account of the expedition as though you were Will or Bess doing an eyewitness story for a newspaper.

2. What kind of person is the soldier who tells the story of " Gunga Din "? Lines 75 to 80, pages 173–74, give you his opinion of himself — at least, of his chances in the hereafter. The Indian regiments of the British army led a dangerous and strange existence. You will like Kipling's short stories about the British " Tommies," as well as the poems like " Danny Deever " in *Barrack Room Ballads.*

3. " It Was a Famous Victory " is a humorous poem, and yet it has its serious side too. To whom, at least, is the story of the poem serious? Little Geraldine and Peterkin are exaggerated, of course, but don't you suppose that children often unconsciously hurt their elders by being rude? How can one keep from being rude even though bored?

4. William Rose Benét's " The Skater of Ghost Lake " is different from " Southern Ships and Settlers." Can you discuss some of these differences? Consider such items as subject matter, mood, tone, and type of poem.

5. If you have never read any of Poe's short stories, perhaps his poem " The Raven " will make you curious enough to investigate. Start with " The Pit and the Pendulum " if you want a real spine thriller. You will find others of his poems very suitable for reading aloud. Try " The Bells " and " Annabel Lee." " The Bells " is particularly good for sound effects.

6. Do you agree with King Francis in " The Glove and the Lions "? Look at the last two lines of the poem. If you do agree, then what do you think of De Lorge's leaping into the arena in the first place?

For Your Vocabulary

WORD BUILDING: An interesting word oddity occurs in " The Cruel Brother." Here the middle sister is described as having a graceful *mien,* or bearing. The word probably comes from *demeanor,* with an influence from the French and from the Breton *min,* meaning " beak." Perhaps the way in which a bird held its beak gave it a certain air or bearing. Does the dictionary make a distinction between *mien* and *demeanor? Assuage* as used in " The Rhyme of the Chivalrous Shark " means " to satisfy an appetite." It can also mean " to lessen pain or grief " and " to soothe or calm passion." Its Latin origin is *ad* (to) + *suavis* (sweeten). *Spleen* comes from the Greek *splen* and means either " an organ of the body " or " spite." Which meaning has it in " Gunga Din "? The bird in " The Raven " showed a grave and stern *decorum.* What distinction exists between this word and *mien* and *demeanor?* The adjective form is *decorous.* Do you know its meaning and pronunciation? In the same poem, line 50, the raven's answer bore little *relevancy* — little relation or connection — to the questions asked. Responses which lack this relation or connection are said to be irrelevant.

AN EPIC TALE

HOMER

The Odyssey

A TALL TALE OUT OF THE PAST

When 'Omer smote 'is bloomin' lyre,
He'd 'eard men sing by land and sea;
And what 'e thought 'e might require,
'E went an' took — the same as me!

The market girls an' fishermen,
The shepherds an' the sailors, too,
They 'eard old songs turn up again,
But kep' it quiet — same as you!

They knowed 'e stole; 'e knowed they knowed.
They didn't tell, nor make a fuss,
But winked at 'Omer down the road,
An' 'e winked back — the same as us!

— RUDYARD KIPLING

Much as the modern storyteller Kipling has put it, the famous tale makers of the past like Homer often simply wove together the old, familiar stories. Sometimes they provided new heroes or new incidents, and frequently the tales grew taller and taller. Finally some tales became great literature.

As you read about Odysseus [1] (also called Ulysses [1] by the Romans), the hero celebrated by the blind Greek minstrel, Homer, you may be struck by the odd notion that the stories have a modern cartoon-strip quality. For the hero is a man of great shrewdness and tremendous physical power who arouses either the love or the wrath of the fates and gods, and who no sooner survives one catastrophe than he is threatened by another. Of course, the *Odyssey* is hardly a comic strip. It is an epic poem that has survived thousands of years to become part of our tradition in great literature.

The epic opens after Odysseus has taken part with other Greek leaders in the long siege and final conquest of Troy. He and his men are on their way home to Ithaca, their native land, with their ships loaded with booty taken from Troy. Odysseus is anxious to return to his beautiful wife Penelope and his son, but the gods would have it otherwise. The ships are driven by storms to strange places where dangers threaten.

Adventures and calamities quickly follow one another. Once a scouting party approached the island palace of the goddess Circe,[2] a strangely magical place where charmed wolves and lions fawned on Odysseus' men like friendly dogs. The goddess herself served the men a feast — but the food was drugged! Then she turned them into swine. Odysseus went alone to the rescue, even as a cartoon-strip hero might do, and he was preserved from a like fate only because he had been given a charm by the gods. When Circe's magic failed, she realized that other gods were involved in this man's fate, and that he must indeed be the great Odysseus, whose coming had been foretold. So she obligingly turned the men of the scouting party back into their human forms and then entertained the entire com-

[1] **Odysseus, Ulysses** (ō·dĭs'ūs, ū·lĭs'ēs).

[2] **Circe** (sûr'sē).

pany for a whole year! She even tried to keep Odysseus for her husband.

In such manner the adventurers wandered slowly homeward. But gods, giants, monsters, and other instruments of fate took such a violent hand in their affairs that only Odysseus survived — and then only through the aid of Athena,[1] the goddess of wisdom.

Four of the best episodes in this long story-poem (or epic) are those which tell of the encounters with the Lotus-eaters, the Cyclops,[2] the Sirens, and with Scylla[2] and Charybdis.[2] The first of these were men who ate a sort of flower-fruit that had drug-like powers. The Cyclops were one-eyed giants, and the Sirens were creatures shaped partly like women and partly like birds, whose songs lured passing seamen to their deaths. Scylla and Charybdis were a pair of neighbor monsters who also preyed upon seamen; if you escaped one, the other was sure to get you! Actually, Scylla was a huge rock on the Italian coast, and Charybdis was a whirlpool off the nearby Sicilian coast. The storytellers, of course, turned these natural wonders into demons.

[1] **Athena** (*ȧ*·thē′n*ȧ*).
[2] **Cyclops, Scylla, Charybdis** (sī′klŏps, sĭl′*ȧ*, k*ȧ*-rĭb′dĭs).

Remembering all this, perhaps you can wink with Kipling "at 'Omer down the road." The famous blind minstrel knew that many of his tales were old — and that all of them were very, very tall.

For Better Reading . . . As you read try to put your imagination to work so that you can see the deep blue of the Mediterranean Sea as color film might show it. Try to visualize the rocky crags and the mountains running up from the seashore, the wooded islands, the many-oared ships with their bright sails, the rich palace settings, the muscular brown bodies of the men, the glinting armor, and the fearsome creatures. Also, since you are living in the second half of the twentieth century, you might imagine what Hollywood could do with the songs, the feasts, the battles, and the storms.

Finally, remember that in Homer's day the known world was very, very small. These heroes of an even earlier period sailed little wooden ships on seas inhabited by monsters and surrounded by mystery.

THE ODYSSEY

[Odysseus is in the banquet hall of a generous king who helps him on his way after all his comrades have been killed and his last vessel destroyed. Odysseus tells the story of his adventures thus far.]

I am
Odysseus, great Laertes'° son,
For cunning plans of every kind
Known among men; and even to heaven
Has spread my fame. My native land 5
Is Ithaca,° a sun-bright island
Low of shore which lies far out
To sea and toward the west. Rugged
It is, this land of mine, yet breeds
A sturdy youth, and I can find 10
No land more sweet to me than this,
My native Ithaca. But come,

2. **Laertes** (lā·ûr′tēz).

6. **Ithaca** (ĭth′*ȧ*·k*ȧ*): an island off the west coast of Greece.

For I will tell the many sorrows
Zeus° sent upon me as I traveled
Homeward from hapless Troy. 15

THE LAND OF THE LOTUS-EATERS

Great Zeus, who guides the clouds, sent forth
Against our ships a wild north wind,
A raging tempest, and enshrouded
In dark clouds land and sea. Deep night
Came rolling from on high. Our ships 20
Drove headlong, while their sails were riven
Asunder by that gale; but these
We stored beneath the decks, still toiling
In dread of death, and striving ever,
Rowed on and reached the land 25
Where dwell the Lotus-eaters, men
Whose food is flowers. And we all
Here went ashore and drew us water,
And by the sides of their swift ships
My men prepared their meal. And now
When we at last had had our fill 31
Of meat and drink, I sent forth men
To learn what manner of mankind
That live by bread might dwell here. Two
I chose to go and sent with them 35
A third, a herald. And these quickly
Went forth into that land and mingled
Among the Lotus-eaters. Never
Did these men, eaters of the lotus,
Plan evil to my men, and yet 40
They gave them of the lotus flower
And bade them eat of it, and lo,
Whatever man of them but tasted
That blossom strange and honey-sweet,
Naught cared he then to hasten back 45
With tidings to the ships, or ever
Turn homeward any more, but longed
To dwell there with the Lotus-eaters,
And pluck and eat the lotus blossoms 49
And think no more of home. But these
I brought back to the ships by force,
Though they lamented, and I dragged them
Aboard the hollow ships and bound them
Beneath the benches. Then I bade
The rest, my true companions, hasten
Aboard the ships, lest one of them 56
Taste of the lotus, too, and lose
All memory of home. So straightway
They came aboard and sat them down
In order on the thwarts and smote 60
The foaming sea with oars.

THE CYCLOPS

So thence
We sailed upon our way sad-hearted.
And now we came unto the land
Where dwell the Cyclops – arrogant 65
And lawless beings, who, with trust
In the undying gods, plow not
Nor plant with hands a single plant.
Yet crops spring up for them unsown 69
On fields untended – wheat and barley
And vines that bear full-clustered grapes
To make them wine. The rain of Zeus
Still brings increase in all. These men
Have neither meeting place for council
Nor settled laws. They live apart 75
On lofty mountain ridges, dwelling
In hollow caverns. Each makes laws
For wife and child, and gives no heed
To any save himself.
Thither we sailed 80
Seeking the land. Surely it was
Some god that gave us guidance thither
Through the dense night, for we could see
Nothing before our eyes: the mist
Shut close about the ships; no moon 85
Showed forth in heaven, for clouds enclosed it.
So no man with his eyes beheld
That isle or saw the long seas rolling
Against the land till we had beached
Our well-benched ships. 90
Now we looked

14. **Zeus** (zūs): chief of the gods, ruler of the elements; the thunderbolt is his sign.

And saw not far away the mainland
Where dwelt the Cyclops. And we saw
Smoke rise, and heard the speech of men
And bleat of sheep and goats. Then came 95
The setting of the sun and darkness;
And there we slept beside the breakers.
But when the earliest dawn appeared
Rose-fingered, then I called together
My men and spoke to all: 100

"Rest here,
Dear comrades, while with my own ship
And my own men I go to learn
What men these are — if wild and cruel
And ignorant of right, or kind 105
To every stranger and with hearts
That fear the gods."

Now when we reached
That land that lay hard by, we saw
Upon its utmost point a cave 110
Close to the sea: high-roofed it was,
With laurel overhung, and many
The flocks of sheep and goats that there
Found shelter in the night. Around it
A courtyard lay, high-walled with stones
Set deep in earth, with lofty pines 116
And high-leaved oaks. Within this lair
A man was wont to sleep, a monster
Who grazed his sheep far off, alone,
Nor ever mingled with his kind, 120
But lonely dwelt — lawless and evil.
And marvelously was he shapen —
This monstrous being, not like mortals
That live by bread, but like a peak
That rising rough with woods stands forth 125
Apart from other hills.

And I
Now bade my trusty men to bide
Close by the ship and guard the ship,
But twelve I chose, the best of all, 130
And we set forth. I bore with me
A goatskin filled with dark sweet wine,
Sweet and unmixed, a drink for gods.
Who drank that red wine, honey-sweet,
He took one cup, no more, and served it
Mingled with water twenty times 136
The measure of the wine; and yet
Up from the mixing bowl there rose
Rare scent and sweetness, till no man
Could find it easy to refrain 140
From drinking of that wine. I filled
A great skin with this, and I bore it
As I set forth, and bore besides
Food in a leathern sack. For now
My fearless heart foresaw a meeting
With a strange man of monstrous might — 146
A savage, scornful of the gods
And of man's law.

Straightway we reached
His cave and entered, but we found not
The man within. For far away 151
He herded, while they grazed at pasture,
His goodly flock. So on we passed
Far into that great cave and marveled
At all we saw within. Here stood 155
Crates heaped with cheese and here were pens
Crowded with lambs and kids. My men
Besought me eagerly to carry
The cheeses thence, and come again
And loose the kids and lambs and drive them 160
In haste to our swift ship, then sail
Away o'er the salt sea. But this
I would not grant, though better far
Had I but done so! For I hoped
To look upon this man — he might 165
Give gifts of friendship. But, alas,
When he appeared, he was to bring
My poor men little joy!

So there
We kindled fire and of that cheese 170
We made an offering, and ate
Ourselves thereof, and sat and waited
Until at last he entered, driving
His flock before him. He bore in
Dry wood to cook his meal, a load 175
Of wondrous weight, and down he flung it

Within the cave, with such a crash
We cowered back with fear and crouched
In the cave's corner. Then he drove
Into that spacious cave the sheep 180
That he must milk, and left the others —
The rams and goats — without, to roam
The high-walled court. Then in its place
He set the massive rock that closed
The doorway of the cave: he raised it
Lightly aloft, a weight so vast 186
That never two and twenty wagons,
Four-wheeled and firmly built, might stir it
From where it lay on earth — so great
That towering crag was that he set 190
To close his door.

Now sat he down
And milked his sheep and bleating goats
That he might sup thereon. And now,
When he had labored busily 195
And finished every task, he stayed
And kindled up the fire and saw us
And asked us:

"Strangers, who are you, 199
And whence do you come sailing hither
Over the sea's wet ways? What errand
Can bring you hither? Or perchance
You wander purposeless, like robbers
Who rove the seas and venture life
To bring to strangers in far lands 205
An evil fortune."

So he spoke,
And at his words our hearts within us
Were crushed and broken, for we feared
The man's deep voice and monstrous body. 210
Yet I spoke up and answered, saying:
"We are Achæans° come from Troy;
We wander blown by every wind
Over the sea's great gulf, still striving
To reach our homes, yet ever go 215
On alien ways, by paths we never
Have willed to travel — so it pleases
Zeus to decree. Now we come
Hither before your knees to pray you
Give welcome to your guests and grant us 220
Such gifts as guests should have. Respect,
O mighty one, the gods, for we
Are suppliants, and Zeus avenges
The suppliant and stranger: he
Is god of strangers, watching over 225
Each worthy wanderer."

So I spoke,
And pitiless of heart, he answered:
"Stranger, you either are a fool
Or come from a far land, to bid me 230
Fear or beware the gods! We Cyclops
Fear not your ægis-wielding° Zeus
Nor any god above. For we
Are mightier far than they. I would not
Show mercy to your men or you 235
To shun the wrath of Zeus, nay, never
Unless my own heart bade. But come,
Tell me, where left you your good ship
When you came hither? Was it near
Or at the land's far end? Nay, tell me,
For I would know." So asked he, striving 241
To trap the truth from me, but caught not
My tried mind unaware. So thus
With crafty words I spoke:

"The god 245
Who shakes the earth, Poseidon,° broke
My ship asunder, for he drove her
Upon the cliffs that line your land
And dashed her on the rocks. A tempest
Had blown us in from sea and I 250
And these my comrades here but barely
Escaped sheer death."

So I replied.
He, cruel-hearted, made no answer,
But springing up, reached forth his hands 255
And seized my comrades. Two at once

212. Achæans (ȧ·kē′ănz): term used for nearly all Greeks.

232. ægis-wielding (ē′jĭs-wēld′ĭng): shield-bearing. **246. Poseidon** (pŏ·sī′dŏn): god of the sea.

He snatched up in his grasp and dashed them
To earth like helpless puppies. Forth
The brains flowed, moistening the ground. 259
Then limb from limb he tore their bodies
And made his meal, devouring them
Savagely as a lion bred
Among the mountains. Naught of them
He left uneaten — flesh or entrails 264
Or marrowy bones. And we cried out
In lamentation and uplifted
Our hands to Zeus, to see a deed
So horrible. Numb terror laid
Hold on our hearts. And now the Cyclops, 269
When he had filled that monstrous belly
With flesh of men, and followed this
With draughts of unmixed milk, lay stretched
Full length upon the cavern floor
Among his flock.
And now I formed 275
This plan within my daring heart —
To venture nearer and to draw
My keen sword from my thigh and thrust it
Deep in his breast, straight to the spot
Where lay his liver, feeling first 280
To seek the place; and yet a thought
Withheld me, for we all, each man,
Must then have met sheer death; for never
Could our strength stir from that high door
The massive stone he set there. So 285
Lamenting there we sat and waited
The sacred dawn.
And when the dawn
Came, rosy-fingered, then once more
He kindled fire and milked his flock
Of wondrous sheep, in order due, 291
Setting her young by each; and now
When he had labored busily
And finished every task, he seized
Once more upon two men and made
His morning meal. And after this, 296
His breakfast done, he drove away
His goodly flock, moving with ease
The mighty door-stone thence, then set it
In place as lightly as a man 300
Would set the lid upon a quiver.
And now I pondered how I best
Might find revenge, if but Athene°
Would hear my prayer. And this plan seemed
Best to my mind at last: 305
There lay
Close by the pens, a mighty staff
Cut by the Cyclops. Olive wood
It was, still green, for he had cut it
To use when it had dried: it seemed,
As we stood gazing, the great mast 311
Of some broad ship of twenty oars,
Laden with cargo, a black ship
That sails the great gulf of the sea,
So long and thick it seemed. So there
I took my stand by it and cut 316
A fathom's length away, and this
I gave my men and bade them shape it.
They made it smooth, while I stood by
And brought it to a point and charred it
In glowing fire; and then I took it 321
And hid it in the dung that lay
In heaps about the cave. I bade then
My company cast lots to see
Which men of them would dare to join me 325
And lift that stake and bore it deep
Into his eye when gentle slumber
Should come upon him. And the lot
Fell on the four I should have chosen,
And I myself became the fifth 330
To share the venture.
And now came
The Cyclops home at evening, herding
His well-fleeced flocks. Straightway he drove
Into that cavern, one and all, 335
His goodly flocks, nor left he any

303. Athene (ȧ·thē′nē): also **Athena.**

In the wide court without. He felt,
Perhaps, some sense of coming evil;
Perhaps some god had warned
him. Next 339
He set in place the massive door-stone,
Lifting it lightly, then once again
He seized on two of my companions
And made his evening meal.
And now
I stood before him, and thus spoke, 345
The while I held forth in my hands
An ivy bowl, filled with dark wine:
" Here, Cyclops, take this wine, and
drink
After your feast of human flesh, 349
And learn how good a drink we kept
Hidden within our ship. I brought it
An offering to you, in hope
You might have pity on my sorrows
And help me home. But you, alas, 354
In rage exceed all patience! Madman!
How shall there ever come hereafter
Another stranger here to seek you
From any land on earth, if you
Thus scorn all human laws! "
So said I. 360
He took the wine and drank it. Vastly
That sweet drink pleased him. And
again
He begged of me:
"In goodness give me
Yet more, I pray. And tell me now 365
Your name, and quickly! I will give you
A gift to make your heart rejoice."
So thrice I bore that glowing wine
And gave it him, and thrice in folly
He drained it off. Then when the wine
Had stolen round his wits, I spoke 371
And said in honeyed words:
" O Cyclops,
You ask my far-famed name, and this
I now will tell. My name is Noman."
And he with cruel heart replied: 376
" Noman, of all his company,
I shall eat last. This shall be
My gift to you – my guest."
Then down he sank and on his back
Lay flat, his thick neck bent aside, 381
And from his throat there poured forth
wine
And fragments of men's flesh.
And now 384
Deep under heaped-up coals I thrust
That stake till it grew hot, and stirred
The courage of my men with speech
Lest one of them should shrink with fear
And fail my need.
And now that stake 390
Of olive wood, green as it was,
Was ready to burst forth in flame,
All glowing with fierce heat. I drew it
Forth from the fire, while round about
me 394
My men stood ready. Then – for surely
Some god had breathed into our hearts
High courage – they laid hold upon
That sharpened olive stake and thrust it
Deep in his eye, the while above them
I leaned upon its top and turned it 400
As one who with an auger bores
A great ship timber. Those below him
Twist it by thongs on either side,
And still it ever turns unceasing.
So holding that huge stake of wood 405
Deep in his eye, we kept it turning.
Round that hot brand, forth poured the
blood;
And round it all his brows and lashes
Were singed off by the blast that came
Out of that burning eye. Its roots 410
Seethed in the fire. As when a smith
Dips a great ax or adze in water
To temper it, and loud it hisses –
For so steel gets its strength – even so
His eye hissed round that olive stake.
And loud his cry and terrible 416
Till the rocks echoed and we fled
Away in fear. Then from his eye
He wrenched away that stake, thick
clotted 419
With his own blood and raging hurled it
Out of his hands. Then loud he shouted

To all the Cyclops who dwelt round him
In caves upon the windy heights.
They heard his shout and straggling gathered,
One here, one there, from every side,
And standing all about his cave 426
They asked what grieved him.
"What can ail you,
O Polyphemus,° that so loudly
You cry out in the heavenly night 430
And keep us sleepless? Is some man,
Some mortal, driving off your flocks
Against your will; or is some man
Now slaying you by force or cunning?"
And thus in answer from his cave 435
Spoke mighty Polyphemus:
"Friends,
Noman is slaying me by cunning,
Nor uses force at all!"
And they 440
With wing'd words thus replied:
"Since no man
Now does you violence, while you
Are there alone, this illness sent
By mighty Zeus, no man may shun 445
In any way. But pray you now
To your great father, Lord Poseidon."
So said they and then went their way.
And in my heart I laughed to think
How with that name and my shrewd plan 450
I had deceived them.
But the Cyclops,
Groaning in agony and anguish,
Went groping with his hands, and lifted
The great rock from the door and there 455
He sat athwart the doorway, stretching
His hands, to catch, if it might be,
Any who sought to pass the door
Among the sheep; for in his heart
He hoped that I might prove so foolish
As thus to venture. But I still 461
Sat planning how to bring this peril
To a good end and win us all —
My men and me — escape. Full many
The plan and trick I fashioned, striving
For life itself, for great the peril 466
And close at hand. And at the last
This, as I deemed, was of them all
The wisest plan.
There in the cave 470
Were well-grown rams of thickest wool,
Fair beasts and great, and dark of fleece.
These silently I bound together
With twisted willow withes, whereon
The Cyclops slept, that savage monster
Who knew no law nor right. I bound them 476
By threes together and the midmost
Bore under him a man; the others,
One on each side, were to conceal
And save my comrades: so there went
A man to each three sheep. And I, 481
Myself, now seized upon a ram,
The best of all that flock, and grasped
His back from underneath, and lay
Beneath his shaggy belly; there 485
Twisting my fingers deep within
That wondrous fleece, I hung, face upward,
With steadfast heart. And so, lamenting,
We waited sacred dawn.
And now, 490
When earliest dawn came rosy-fingered,
Then forth the rams went to the pasture,
But all the unmilked ewes went bleating
About their pens with swollen udders.
Their lord, though torn by cruel pain,
Yet, ere each ram passed, made him stand 496
And felt along his back. He guessed not
In his dull mind, that there beneath
Those fleecy breasts, were bound my men.
Now to the door, last of them all, 500
The great ram slowly came, weighed down
With heavy fleece and with the burden

429. **Polyphemus** (pŏl′ĭ·fē′mŭs): the name of the Cyclops who has imprisoned Odysseus.

The blinded Cyclops in fury throws rocks after the departing ship. (Illustration by N. C. Wyeth in The Odyssey, *G. H. Palmer trans., published by Houghton Mifflin Co.)*

Of me and my shrewd plans. Upon him
The mighty Polyphemus then
Laid searching hands, and said: 505
" Dear ram,
Why do you cross the cave so slowly,
Last of the flock? Till now, you never
Lagged thus, but ever first of all 509
Sped forth with mighty strides to crop
The soft bloom of the grass, and ever
Were first to reach the running waters,
And first, when evening came, to long
To turn back home. And yet you now
Come last of all. Surely you sorrow 515
Over your lord's lost eye! A villain
Has quenched its sight – he and his crew
Of wretched fellows, mastering
My wits with wine, this fellow Noman!
Not yet, I say, has he escaped 520
The death that waits him. Would but you
Could know my thought and had the power
To speak in words and let me know
Where he is skulking from my wrath!
For I should smite him down and dash 525
His brains about the cave – here, there,
Aye, on the ground! By such a deed
My heart might find some ease from all
The evils that this worthless Noman
Has brought upon me." So he spoke,
And sent the ram forth through the doorway. 531

And now, when we were safe outside
That cavern and its yard, I loosed
My grip upon the great ram's fleece
And then unbound my men in turn, 535
Setting them free. And then in haste
We drove that flock before us – sheep
Most rich in fat, most long of stride –
And yet we often turned our heads
To glance behind us ere we came 540
Safe to our ship. Welcome indeed
We were to our dear comrades, snatched
From death itself; and yet they wept
Lamenting those we lost. But this
I would not suffer, but forbade, 545
With lifted brows, all lamentation,
And bade them quickly bear aboard
Into the ship those many sheep
So fine of fleece, and sail away
Across the salt sea waves. And they 550
Went then aboard and took their seats
Each in his place, and smote with oars
The whitening sea.

[And so the men escaped, although their ship was nearly swamped by huge rocks hurled by the blind Cyclops, whom Odysseus could not resist taunting when the vessel was still within shouting distance.

Following this adventure is one rather like the story of Pandora, whose curiosity made her open a box which released all sorts of afflictions and illnesses into the world. As Homer told the tale, Odysseus and his men next visited Aeolus,[1] god of the winds, who gave Odysseus a sack bound with a silver cord. Aeolus also gave him a favoring west wind, which carried the fleet swiftly homeward to Ithaca. During the voyage Odysseus guarded the bag night and day. But on the last night, with land already in sight, he decided he could safely relax his vigilance. As soon as he was asleep, some of his men, thinking the bag contained a treasure which their leader selfishly intended to keep for himself, opened it. Stormy blasts were released, driving the ships away from the homeland they had just sighted. Odysseus returned to Aeolus to seek his help, but this time they were sent on their way at once without further gifts.

After this they lost more men and ships to some savage giants, and then came the year-long visit with the goddess Circe. Following their adventure here, Odysseus made a journey into the Land of the Dead to find out, from the spirit of a famous soothsayer, just what things he must do in order to reach his native land. Before going

[1] **Aeolus** (ē′ō·lŭs).

onward the men returned briefly to Circe's island, and here the goddess gave Odysseus some good advice.]

CIRCE'S WARNINGS

Then mighty Circe
Spoke thus, and said: "Now all these things
Are past and ended. Listen well
To what I have to tell. May heaven
Help you to heed it. You will first 5
Come to the Sirens, to those women
Who weave a magic spell that masters
All men who hear their song. For he
Who turns him from his way in folly
To hear the Sirens' song — no more 10
Shall he behold his wife and children
Coming to greet him, glad of heart
That he is home again. They sit,
These Sirens, in a grassy meadow,
And here they sing their clear, sweet song 15
And weave their spell. And all about them
Lie heaps of gleaming bones; and bodies
Shriveled, with shreds of skin.

Row swiftly
And drive your ship till safely past. 20
But first mold honeyed wax and stop
Your comrades' ears, that none of them
May hear that song. Yet if you long
With your own ears to hear it, bid them
First bind you hand and foot and lash you 25
Upright in your swift ship, your back
Against the mast, with ropes cast round you.
So you may listen with delight
And hear the Sirens' song. Yet first
Command your men that if you beg them 30
To set you free, they then must bind you
In faster lashings.

When your men
Have urged your ship past these — what road 34
You next must take, I shall not tell you.
Take counsel with your heart, and choose.
I will make both ways plain. On one
Great rocks o'erhang the sea: against them
Roll in and break the mighty waves
Of dark-eyed Amphitrite.° Thence 40
No ship of man escapes, if once
She turn her thither. There together
Forevermore the planks of ships
And bodies of slain men go tossing
At will of rolling waves, and swept 45
By tempests of dread fire.

There rise
Beside the other way two crags,
And one of these soars high to heaven
With pointed peak. About the summit
A cloud hangs ever, dark and sullen, 51
Nor ever passes thence. Nor ever
Does the clear light of heaven touch
That peak, in summer or in harvest. 54
No mortal man might climb it — nay,
Nor find him foothold, though he had
A score of hands and feet, that rock
Rises so smooth, like polished stone
On every side. Midmost the front 59
Of this great crag, and deep in shadow
There lies a cave. Westward it looks
And toward the land of Death. And thither,
You must, illustrious Odysseus,
Steer with your ship.

Within this cave 65
Dwells Scylla, ever uttering
Her dreadful yelping cry, her voice
Shrill as a new-born whelp's. There dwells she,
A monstrous shape of evil. No one
Can see that sight unshaken, nay, 70
Not though a god should face her. Twelve
Her hanging feet are, and six necks
She stretches forth, on each a head

40. **Amphitrite** (ăm'fĭ·trī'tē): wife of Poseidon and goddess of the sea.

Hideous to see, and in each head
Teeth in three rows, close-set and bristling, 75
Filled with black death. And there she sits,
Sunk to her middle in that cave,
And stretches forth from that dread gulf
Her fearful heads, and fishes, groping
About the crag, for sharks or dolphins,
Or whatso greater beast her fortune 81
May make her prey — for many such
The deep-voiced sea-nymph Amphitrite
Has in her pastures. Not one seaman
Can boast his ship has passed her by 85
Without some hurt. From each dark ship
She ever snatches, with each head,
One man away to death.

And now,
Odysseus, you shall see, close by, 90
The second crag. Lower it lies
Yet near the other: one could shoot
A shaft across to it. Upon it
There stands a fig tree, great and tall
And all in leaf. And under this 95
The dread Charybdis swallows in
The dark sea-water. Thrice each day
She sends it up and thrice again
She sucks it down, and terrible
That sight to see. I pray that you 100
May not be there when she is sucking
The water in, for no one then
Could save you from that evil — nay,
Not he that shakes the earth. So turn
Your ship to Scylla's crag and drive her
Swiftly upon her way. Far better 106
Lose six men from your ship than all
Should die together."

So she spoke,
And answering her I said: "Nay, goddess, 110
Tell but this, and truly: may not
I find me out some way to shun
This dire Charybdis and yet fight
That other from my ship when she
Would make my men her prey?" 115

So spoke I,
And thus at once the goddess answered,
"Rash you are ever, with a heart
Set upon war and deeds of danger. 119
Can you not yield, when this must be,
To the immortal gods! This monster
Is not a mortal, but a thing
Of living evil none may slay,
Dread, fierce, unconquerable: no man
May fight against it. Courage here 125
Avails you nothing. This alone
Is best — to flee from her! What though
You linger by her rock and arm you,
I fear lest then she once again
Stretch forth those fearful heads and snatch 130
As many more. Nay, rather drive
Upon your way.

And now you reach
The island of Thrinacia.° Here
Are pastured all the Sungod's cattle 135
And his fat flocks. For seven herds
Of cattle graze here, seven flocks
Of goodly sheep, and there are fifty
In every flock. They bear no young
Nor do they ever die. If these 140
You leave unharmed and fix your hearts
Upon the homeward way, you yet
May come, though suffering sore perils,
To Ithaca. But if you harm them,
Then naught can I foresee but ruin 145
For you and ship and men. Nay, though
Yourself, you yet escape, then late,
In evil plight you shall come home,
With loss of all your men."

So said she, 150
And straightway came the dawn, rose-fingered,
And thence the goddess passed away
Up through the island. Then I turned
Back to the ship, and bade my men
Embark and loose the cables. 155

THE SONG OF THE SIRENS

Quickly
They went aboard and took their seats,

134. **Thrinacia** (thrĭn·ā′shĭ·ȧ).

Each man in his own place, and smote
The whitened sea with oars. And now
There came, behind our dark-prowed ship, 160
A favoring wind to fill our sail,
A welcome comrade, sent by Circe,
That fair-tressed goddess of dread power,
Who speaks with mortals. So we trimmed
Our good ship's tackle right, and then
Sat at our ease, while wind and helmsman 166
Held her course true. And now I said,
Sad-hearted, to my men:
"Unfitting
It is, friends, that but one or two 170
Should hear the sacred prophecies
Of that dread goddess, Circe. These
I now shall tell you, for then either
We die foreknowing what shall fall,
Or we escape and shun the death 175
And doom that wait us.
This she first
Bids us: — to shun the wondrous Sirens,
With their sweet voices and their meadows
Abloom with flowers. For she bade 180
That I alone should hear their song.
So bind me fast in bonds — aye, lash me
Upright against the mast, that thence
I may not stir, and cast strong ropes
About me, too. If I entreat you 185
And bid you set me free, then bind me
Yet tighter than before."
And so
I told them all she said. And ever
Our good ship sailed on swiftly, nearing
The Sirens' island, for the wind 191
Blew fair and drove her on. And now
The wind ceased suddenly; there came
A calm without a breath: some god
Laid all the sea to sleep. So now 195
My men rose, furled the sail, and stowed it
Within the hollow ship, and sitting
In order on the thwarts, they smote
With polished oars the whitening sea.
But I, with my keen blade, now cut 200
A great round lump of wax, and kneaded
The fragments with my hands, till swiftly
The wax was softened. With this, I stopped
The ears of all my crew, in turn;
Then fast they bound me, hand and foot 205
Upright in my swift ship, my back
Against the mast, with ropes cast round me.
Then once again they sat and smote
The foaming sea with oars.
And now 210
When we were but so far away
As a man's cry may reach, and lightly
Went driving on — our ship's swift flight,
As close to land she sped, escaped not
The Sirens' sight, and they upraised 215
At once their clear, sweet song:
"Come hither,
O famed Odysseus, mighty glory
Of the Achæans. Turn your ship
But hither to the shore and hearken 220
The song we sing, for no man ever
Has steered his black ship hence till he
Has heard the honey-sweet delight
Of music from our lips; then forth
He went upon his way with joy 225
And fuller wisdom. For we know
All that the Argives° and the Trojans°
Endured on Troy's wide plains; we know
All that befalls mankind on earth,
The nourisher of all." 230
So sang they,
Uttering their sweet song. My heart
Yearned to hear further, and I bade
My men to loose me, and I frowned

227. **Argives** (är'jīvz): as used by Homer, almost any Greeks; **Trojans** (trō'jănz): men of Troy.

The sirens tempt Odysseus with their sweet song. (Illustration by N. C. Wyeth in The Odyssey, *G. H. Palmer trans., published by Houghton Mifflin Co.)*

My bidding with my brows, but they
Bent busier to their oars, and two, 236
Eurylochus and Perimedes,°
Arose and bound me ever faster
With double lashings. But at last,
When we had passed them and no more 240
Might hear the song those Sirens sang
And their sweet voices, then my men
Took quickly from their ears the wax
Wherewith I stopped them, and they loosed
The bonds that bound me. 245

SCYLLA AND CHARYBDIS

And we now
Had left that isle behind, but soon
I saw the smoke of flying spray,
And huge seas rolling, and I heard
The boom of breakers. From the hands
Of my affrighted men the oars 251
Fell and trailed idle, roaring through
The running sea beside us. Quickly
The ship lost way and stopped, for now
My men no longer toiled, with hands
Upon the tapered oars. Now swiftly 256
I passed through all the ship and paused
By each in passing, cheering him
With gentle words:

"We are not, friends, 260
Untried in danger. This new peril
That lies before us is no greater
Than when the Cyclops caught and held us
Fast in his hollow cave. Yet thence 264
We found escape — all through my valor
And wit and shrewdness; and I think
That we shall live to tell the tale
Of this day too. But rouse you now.
Do as I bid you. Steer boldly forth
Out of these smoking seas and head her
Straight for yon crag, and take good heed 271
Lest she swing wide and sweep us all
Into sore peril!"

So I spoke,
And they obeyed my order quickly, 275
And yet I did not speak of Scylla,
That monster none may face, in fear
Lest they from terror drop their oars
And hide within the hold. Slight heed
I gave to Circe's hard command 280
I should not arm me. I put on
My glorious armor and I grasped
Two spears in hand and took my station
On the decked prow, for there I thought
I first should see appear this Scylla 285
That dwelt within the rock, to bring
My men destruction. And yet nowhere
Could I behold her, and my eyes
Wearied with wandering up and down
That shadowy wall of stone. 290

So onward
Into that strait we sailed lamenting —
On one side Scylla, on the other
Dreadful Charybdis. Terribly 294
She swallowed down the salt sea-water
Then vomited it forth till all
Was tossed and whirling like a caldron
Above a raging fire; and spray
Flew high and fell upon the tops 299
Of the tall crags. But when once more
She sucked the salt sea down, we saw
The whirl's wild depths laid bare; the waters
Roared loud about the rocks; far down
We saw the bottom of the deep 304
Blackened with sand. Pale terror then
Laid hold on us: we saw the monster
And feared death near.

And on that instant
Scylla reached forth and snatched my men
Out of my hollow ship — six men, 310
My best in strength and courage. Lo,
Even as I looked along the ship
To seek them, there I saw, above me,
Their hands and feet as up she swung them
Aloft in air. And loud they cried, 315

237. **Eurylochus** (ū·rĭl′ō·kŭs); **Perimedes** (pĕr′ĭ-mē′dēz).

Calling, for the last time, my name.
There she devoured them, one and all,
Before her doorway, while they shrieked
And still stretched out their hands to me
In dying agony. That sight 320
Was saddest of all sights my eyes
Have ever seen, while through sore trials
I wandered the sea's ways.

THE ISLE OF THE SUN

So now 324
We had escaped the Clashing Rocks,
And Scylla and the dread Charybdis,
And quickly came to the fair isle
Of the great Sun. And here were cattle
Goodly and broad of brow, and here
Full many fat flocks of the god 330
Who rides on high in heaven. I heard
While yet in my black ship at sea
The low of cattle in the stalls
And bleat of sheep. Then to my mind
There came the words that I should shun 335
This island of the Sun who gladdens
The heart of man. And thus I spoke
With heavy heart, to my companions:
"Now hear my words, my comrades, you 339
Who have endured such trials. Hearken
While I speak forth the warning words
Foretold that here the worst of evils
Should come upon us. Let us therefore
Drive swiftly our black ship till we
Have left this isle behind." 345

[But Odysseus' men were exhausted by the many dangers they had escaped, and they insisted on landing so they could rest and prepare fresh food. To avoid trouble, Odysseus permitted them to go ashore after they solemnly vowed not to harm the cattle of the Sun. But strong winds held them to the island throughout the month, and eventually their food ran out. Odysseus prayed to the gods, but fell asleep. When he returned to the camp, he was horrified to find his men feasting on the sacred cattle.]

Now came
To the great Sun who rides on high,
His shining shepherdess, in haste,
To tell him we had slain his cattle. 349
Then thus with angry heart he spoke
To all the gods:

"O Father Zeus,
And all ye other gods that dwell
In bliss forever – grant me now
Vengeance upon these men that follow
Laertes' son, Odysseus. They, 356
In insolence, have slain the cattle
That ever were my heart's delight,
Whether I mounted starry heaven
Or turned me down from heaven's summit 360
To earth again. Nay, if they make
No fit atonement for my cattle,
I will go down to Death's dark land
And shine among the dead."

Then answered 365
Zeus, he who guides the clouds, and said:
"O Sun, still shine upon the gods
And on the mortal men that dwell
On fruitful earth. For my bright bolt
Shall smite their swift ship into fragments 370
Out on the wine-dark deep." All this
Calypso° of fair tresses told me,
Who heard it, so she said, from Hermes,°
The messenger.

Now when I came 375
Back to the ship and shore, I spoke
To this man and to that and blamed
Each in his turn. But we could find
No remedy: the kine were dead.
And now the gods showed fearful portents: 380

372. Calypso (kă·lĭp′sō): a sea nymph. **373. Hermes** (hûr′mēz): messenger of the gods, known to the Romans as Mercury.

The stripped hides crawled, and the dead flesh —
Both raw and roasted — lowed aloud
Like living cattle. So six days
My trusty comrades ate their fill,
For they had driven forth and slain 385
The Sun's best cattle. But when Zeus,
The son of Cronus,° brought around
The seventh day, the wind that blew
So fierce a tempest, ceased. Then quickly 389
We went aboard and launched the ship
To the wide sea and raised her mast
And hoisted her white sail.

THE DESTRUCTION OF THE SHIP

And now,
When we had left the isle behind us,
And yet no other land appeared — 395
Nothing but sea and sky, then Zeus,
The son of Cronus, set in heaven
Over our hollow ship, a cloud
Of sullen blue which darkened all
The deep below. And now our ship 400
Sped on, yet not for long; for swiftly
Out of the west there burst a gale
Shrieking in raging blasts. A gust
Snapped the two forestays° of the mast.
Back fell the mast upon the stern, 405
And all its tackle lay entangled
In the ship's hold. And as it fell,
Striking the stern, it struck the helmsman
Upon the head and broke and shattered
Each bone within. Down he fell headlong, 410
As falls a diver, from the deck:
His proud soul left his body. Zeus
Now thundered from on high and hurled
His bolt upon the ship. She quivered
Through all her length, struck by the bolt 415
Of Zeus: a smoke of sulphur filled her;
And straightway from the ship my men
Fell to the sea, and breakers swept them
On past the black ship's side, like sea-birds.
And so now God forever ended 420
Their hopes of home.

Still to and fro
I hastened through the ship. At last
A great wave tore her keel away 424
Out of her frame, and on the billows
It floated bare. The mast had broken
Clear from the keel, but still the backstay
Kept it close by. And with this stay,
Twisted of oxhide, I made fast
The two together, mast and keel. 430
And seated on them both, I drifted
Before that deadly storm.

At last
The west wind that had blown in tempest,
Ceased, but the south wind now arose
And brought my heart new grief, for now 436
I must remeasure all the way
To where lay waiting that dread peril,
Charybdis. All that night I drifted
And with the rising sun I came 440
To Scylla's cliff and dread Charybdis.
She, even then, was sucking down
The salt sea-water. I was borne
Aloft, far up to that tall fig tree,
And there I clung fast, like a bat; 445
Yet never might I find me foothold
To set my foot on, nor yet climb
Into that tree; for far below
Its roots lay, and its branches spread
Great-limbed and long, and stretched out wide, 450
Shading Charybdis.

Steadfastly
I clung there till she vomit forth
The mast and keel again. Yet these,
For all my eager watch, came late; 455
For even when a man arises

387. **Cronus** (krō′nŭs): father of Zeus, dethroned by Zeus. 404. **forestays** (fōr′stāz): ropes from the top of the mast to the deck at the front of the ship.

To seek his supper, who all day
Has sat in the assembly, hearing
And judging many a bitter quarrel
Of men at strife — even at that hour 460
There shot in sight, out of Charybdis,
The beams I sought. I loosed my hold
With hands and feet, and fell; and dropped
There in the midst and just beyond
Those massive beams. On these I mounted, 465
And seated on them, rowed my way
With empty hands.

[Much, much more, happened after Odysseus was left rowing with his hands from the whirlpool. After floating for some time, he came to the island of the goddess Calypso, who detained him for a little matter of seven years and who would have married him, had not Zeus sent orders to release him. Then he made a great raft which was stocked with supplies by Calypso, but the raft was wrecked by Poseidon, father of the blinded Cyclops. When Odysseus again floated to land, he found he was on the island of a generous king, Alcinoüs,[1] who entertained him royally. It was at a banquet given by Alcinoüs that Odysseus told that part of the story which you have just read. Following this, Alcinoüs gave him rich presents and oarsmen to take him home to Ithaca.

Odysseus had now been gone for twenty years, and in his absence powerful suitors had come to seek the hand of his wife Penelope[2] and had feasted daily in his halls at his expense. They even plotted to get rid of his son Telemachus,[3] just then reaching manhood. In order to meet this final danger posed by the suitors, Odysseus arrived at his home disguised as a beggar. With the aid of the goddess Athena, Telemachus, and a few faithful servants, Odysseus then slew all the suitors in a bloody battle.]

[1] **Alcinoüs** (ăl·sĭn′ô·*ŭ*s).
[2] **Penelope** (pê·nĕl′ô·pê).
[3] **Telemachus** (tê·lĕm′*ȧ*·k*ŭ*s).

How Well Did You Read?

THE CYCLOPS

1. Lines 73 to 79 contain a criticism of the government maintained by the Cyclops. What insight does this give you into the government of the Greeks?
2. Find illustrations in the Cyclops story that give a foreshadowing of disaster. Read the lines.
3. What is the meaning of " venture life " in line 204?
4. Without looking up the answer, tell why Odysseus did not stab the Cyclops to death as he first thought of doing. What does this tell you about Odysseus?
5. Odysseus calls the Cyclops dull. What acts of the latter might bear this out?
6. At the end of the section on the Cyclops, why did Odysseus forbid his men to lament the dead?
7. From your reading of this part of the story, what did you learn about the Greek gods? What was their relationship to mortals? to each other?

CIRCE'S WARNINGS

1. Explain " she turn her thither," line 42.
2. Scylla's teeth, line 76, are described as being " filled with black death." Does this mean that her teeth are black? If not, what does it mean?
3. What are the *pastures* referred to in line 84?
4. In line 189 Odysseus says he tells his shipmates " all " that Circe has told him. In what sense is he being truthful? What course of action would you have taken at this point?
5. What is the meaning of " smoking seas " in line 270?
6. Judging from the various things that happen, and perhaps looking again at the advice given by Circe, what do you think was the Greeks' outlook on fate? Do you agree with this viewpoint?

Thinking It Over

1. Odysseus, besides being a classical hero, is an interesting person. Point out actions or incidents which show his leadership, his fairness to his men, his courage, and his cunning. Can you point out inci-

dents which show his heartlessness and pride and self-conceit? Has he other weaknesses?

2. Reports on Zeus, Athena, Hermes, Poseidon, and other Greek gods will be of special value to the class. A committee might divide the work of making reports and of bringing to the class (or drawing on the board) pictures of these deities. If lantern slides are available, they will be of special interest.

3. A large map of the Mediterranean will be helpful, especially if it shows classical names and places. Perhaps your librarian can help you with this problem, or your history teacher.

4. Write some diary excerpts, pretending that you are a member of the party; better yet, send a letter home to Ithaca by Hermes.

5. A number of common terms or sayings have come down to us from the Greek and Roman myths. Manufactured articles, too, have frequently taken their names from mythology. The Ajax, Diana, and Phoenix automobiles have long since disappeared, but there is still one that takes its name from a mythical figure. Do you know which it is? Can you name any other commercial products with names taken from mythology? Why is a collection of maps called an atlas? What is meant when a girl athlete is called an amazon? Possibly you may have heard someone jokingly use the phrase, " Beware of Greeks bearing gifts." If you don't know the meaning of this, you might look up the wooden-horse episode of the Trojan War. What is meant when a person says he is " between Scylla and Charybdis "?

6. What do you think of the attitude of the travelers in the poem toward their hosts? What about their attitude toward the property of others? Defend or criticize them. In addition, comment on the attitude of Odysseus toward his men; of his men toward him.

7. This version of the *Odyssey* is greatly shortened, of course, and the class may be interested in more complete reports on various parts of the tale, such as Odysseus' visit to the Land of the Dead or his final return to Ithaca.

8. Many supernatural occurrences happen in this tale. Recount some of the most unusual. Why would the ancient Greeks be likely to believe in monsters and other supernatural beings?

9. At various points in the story the men – and Odysseus – weep for their wives and long to be home. Yet they never go directly toward Ithaca. If this seemed odd to you, perhaps you might hunt for reasons why they were " detoured."

10. *The Iliad* is another poem by Homer you may want to look up in translation. It tells the events of the last year of the Trojan War — the war that began because of the beautiful Helen of Troy. It was from this war that Odysseus and his men were returning homeward when they encountered the adventures described in the *Odyssey.*

For Your Vocabulary

COMMON WORDS: At one place the rowers are mentioned as being seated at the *thwarts,* and at another the Cyclops placed himself *athwart* the door of his cave. Look up the meanings and compare with our common verb, *to thwart.* Incidentally, you might find from what country this seafaring term has come. Odysseus and his men came to the Cyclops as *suppliants* or petitioners, praying for a welcome and for the gifts commonly given to strangers. Look up the words *supplant, supple, supplement, supplicant,* and *supply.* Find out what they mean, what other words they came from, and use them in sentences. When Odysseus visited the Land of the Dead, he talked with the spirit of a famous *soothsayer. Sooth* is an Anglo-Saxon term meaning truth. Therefore, what would the whole term mean? What is a more common *modern* synonym?

METAPHORS AND SIMILES: This selection has many figures of speech, some of which are used over and over. One of these is used to describe the dawn. Another term which is used frequently is *honey* or *honeyed.* Find examples of these two.

STORIES IN VERSE

Suggestions for Free Reading

Adams, Franklin Pierce, *Innocent Merriment* (McGraw-Hill, 1942)

Himself a very able humorist in verse, F. P. A. here chooses some poetry of the same kind from other writers.

Adshead, Gladys L., and Duff, Anis, *An Inheritance of Poetry* (Houghton, 1948)
Pages 108 to 179 have a good ballad section, and you'll like the other poems too.

Arnold, Matthew, *Sohrab and Rustum, and Other Poems*
" Sohrab and Rustum " is a *don't miss* classic.

Benét, William Rose, *Fifty Poets* (Duffield and Green, 1933)
This is a fine group of short modern poems selected by their authors — who also give their reasons for choosing them.

Benét, William Rose, *With Wings as Eagles* (Dodd, 1940)
These are Mr. Benét's work — lively, humorous ballad-type poems about the pioneers of flying.

Campbell, O., and Sharp, C. J., *English Folk Songs from the Southern Appalachians* (Putnam, 1917)
If you like folk songs and their long history, this book is for you. It has 122 pages.

Clark, Thomas Curtis, *300 Favorite Poems* (Willett, Clark, 1945)
An excellent collection of the old, the new, and the humorous.

Coffin, Robert P. T., *Ballads of Square-Toed Americans* (Macmillan, 1933)
Yankee seafaring men wore square-toed shoes, in case you're wondering.

Ferris, Helen Josephine, *Love's Enchantment, Story Poems and Ballads* (Doubleday, Doran, 1944)
Here is a slender collection of old favorites together with some of the newer romance narratives.

Field, Rachel, *Points East* (Brewer and Warren 1930)
New England of some years ago comes to life in these well-told narrative poems.

Finger, J. C., *Frontier Ballads* (Doubleday, Page, 1927)
These ballads and folk songs have woodcut illustrations and music.

Gillis, Adolph, and Benét, William Rose, *Poems for Modern Youth* (Houghton, 1938)
Accent is on modern writers in this collection of English and American writers.

Guiterman, Arthur, *Ballads of Old New York* (Harper, 1920)
The early settlers are portrayed entertainingly in Mr. Guiterman's nimble verse.

Hay, John, *Pike County Ballads, and Other Poems* (Houghton, 1912)
Did you know that Lincoln's secretary was a well-known writer? The ballads are dialect stories of frontier days, and later.

Hufford, Laura Mae, *My Poetry Book* (Winston, 1934)
Story poems and ballads in this collection are on pages 407 to 434. There's some good modern verse, too.

Jerrold, Walter, *Book of Story Poems* (Stokes, 1924)
Both boys and girls will like this collection.

Korson, George, *Coal Dust on the Fiddle* (U. of Penn. Press, 1943)
The Pennsylvania coal country is the setting for these ballads. There is excellent background material on the songs.

Malloch, Douglas, *Tote Road and Trail* (Bobbs-Merrill, 1917)
Boys ought to like these ballads of the lumberjacks.

Malone, Ted, *Yankee Doodles* (McGraw-Hill, 1943)
A definite Yankee flavor seeps through these song and story poems.

Masefield, John, *Poems* (Macmillan, 1935)
If you are interested in shorter narratives, try the " Salt Water Ballads " first. Longer ones worth reading are " Dauber," " Reynard the Fox," and " Right Royal." Read also *Saltwater Poems and Ballads* (Macmillan, 1942)

Service, Robert W., *Spell of the Yukon* (Dodd, 1916)
This small book is especially for boys!

Snow, Wilbert, *Down East* (Gotham House, 1932) and *Main Coast* (Harcourt, 1923)
These little books bring into sharp focus the rugged Maine coast and its rugged people.

Whittier, John Greenleaf, *Complete Poetical Works*
Look for the ballads titled " The Tent on the Beach."

Ewing Galloway

Footprints on the Sands of Time

THE poet Longfellow once called the record of man's upward climb "footprints on the sands of time." Biography is the written record of those footprints, and it is one of the most rewarding types of reading. A biography tells the story of a person's life. When a person writes his own story, we call it an autobiography. Other than answering our natural questions about the subject, the most important thing that a biography does is to show us the gradual development of a person's character. Although there must inevitably be other persons in the story, we are interested in them chiefly as they affect the nature and career of the main character.

One reading pleasure to be gained from a successful biography is the number of fascinating details that are told about the subject. We like to read homely and amusing family or school anecdotes, reports of childish quarrels, even records of embarrassing moments – because they tend to increase our feeling of intimacy with the subject of the biography. As he grows into adult life and takes his place in the world, we become alert to the society he lives in, to the causes of his actions and their effects, and to his relationship with his community, his country, and the world at large. When we finish a fine biography, we feel that we have entered into another person's mind, and perhaps made a new friend.

In our own times, the fences of the world are down. We realize with increasing force that all men must co-operate with each other if they are to survive. The more we know about our fellow men, of every creed and color, the greater is our hope and chance of peace. In every country of the world there are people just like us. They differ in racial heritage, perhaps, or in their social customs or religion, but they are all human beings. They are brave or cowardly, wise or foolish, selfish or heroically self-sacrificing, just like the people we know; but the ones who challenge our interest and emulation are the brave, the wise, and the generous – the ones who make the deeper footprints on the sands of time.

When you read a good biography, you are bound to learn something that will help you to make decisions of your own, for to learn about another person is, in a sense, to learn about yourself. Biography gives us insight into human actions and desires.

As you read more and more in this interesting field, you will become more critical of the way a biographer handles his subject. Is he too flattering? Is he making an obvious effort to belittle his subject? Or is he making an honest attempt to draw a complete picture? Does the writer of an autobiography manage to record his achievements (and his failures) with modesty and good humor? Keep these questions in mind as you read.

In the biographies that follow, you will read about outstanding persons in such fields as literature, science, and world leadership. They will almost certainly excite your interest and inspire you toward an honest effort to do your part in creating a better world. You will also read about ordinary people who, whether they achieved fame or not, are of interest to us because we have a human curiosity in life itself. We want to know how they, too, found their way across the sands of time.

JESSE STUART

The Thread That Runs So True

A great source of pride in our country is the fact so many prominent Americans in all walks of life rise to recognition out of poverty and obscurity. Such a man is Jesse Stuart, one of our best-known young novelists and short story writers. Like Abraham Lincoln, he received his early education in a one-room country school in Kentucky. There wasn't much in the room but benches, a stove, a water pail, the teacher's desk, some charts, and a few ragged books. But Jesse Stuart decided that he wanted to become a writer; it took him many a long heartbreaking year, but he made it.

When you read the following excerpts from his recent autobiographical book, *The Thread That Runs So True,* you will admire his courage and respect his honesty, and you will probably wish that you could have him for a teacher. Since that is impossible, Mr. Stuart has very kindly sent the readers of this book the following personal message. Mrs. Roosevelt, elsewhere in this book, urges you to study languages and to learn about other nations. Mr. Stuart adds another kind of advice:

> " If I were teaching you now, as I have taught hundreds of others, I would tell you that you will not take any subject in high school that will not be im portant to you later. I would say take care of your bodies since you will have only one. Keep fit. Go out for some form of athletics. Know at least one game and play it well. Learn a trade or, at any rate, learn to work with your hands. I learned to be a blacksmith myself, and my brother, a shoe repairman. Work is good for you and it's fun to learn. It is wonderful to be young and in high school. These are the great days of your life.
>
> " One of the most important things is your character. I would rather have a B pupil with an A character than an A pupil with a B character. Learn about the great country you live in. Be good citizens. Be somebody. You are young now, but the responsibility of running the country will soon be yours. Be ready to do a good job. Have fun and play, but work, work, work . . . live, live, live . . . and good luck to you! "
>
> Sincerely,
>
> Jesse Stuart

For Better Reading . . . Biography and autobiography offer us a chance to study character and to discover why people act as they do. Watch for the small details that build up your impressions of Mr. Stuart and the other mountain folk. They are real and vital and the things they do seem stranger than fiction. Apply the skills you use in reading stories here: pay attention to motives as well as to actions.

[When he was not quite seventeen, and not yet graduated from Landsburgh High School, Jesse Stuart went to teach at Lonesome Valley in a grammar school where his sister had taught for a time. As the new schoolmaster, he lived with the family of John Conway. Besides getting settled on his first day of teaching, he had a larger problem – Guy Hawkins, the school bully.]

MONDAY morning when I started on my way to school, I had with me Don Conway, a pupil twenty years of age, who had never planned to enter school again. I was the new teacher here at Lonesome Valley and I didn't know what kind of brains he had. He had left school when he was in the fourth grade. But I did know that he had two good fists and that he would be on my side. All day Sunday while I had worked at the schoolhouse, I was trying to think of a plan so I could stay at Lonesome Valley School. I knew I had to stay. I knew if one had to go it would be Guy Hawkins. I might have to use my head a little but that was why I had it.

It had taken a lot of persuasion to get Don Conway to return to school. He had planned to get married after his tobacco crop was sold. But I explained the value of an education to him in dollars and cents. I told him I would teach him how to measure a field and figure the number of acres, how to figure the number of bushels in a wagon bed or cornbin, and how many cubic yards of dirt one would have to remove to dig a cellar or a well. Don Conway was interested in this type of knowledge. I told him no man should be married and live on a farm unless he knew these simple things, for he could easily be cheated the rest of his days. I was interested in his learning these things all right, but I was interested in something else.

Don, his two small brothers, his sister Vaida, and I went to school together. I congratulated John Conway for sending all his children but one. I told him he should set the example for other farmers on the creek. It would have been hard on John to try to worm and sucker [1] his ten acres of tobacco and care for his other crops if Flossie, his older daughter, had not volunteered to help him. And Bertha, his wife, assured him she would divide her time between the housework and work in the field.

Flossie, eighteen years old, who had left school six years ago, would gladly have started back to school if I had insisted. But I knew John and Bertha had to have someone left to help them. I insisted and almost begged Don to return to school when he and I were sitting on the porch late one Sunday afternoon and Ova Salyers and Guy Hawkins rode past on their horses. They glanced toward the porch for their first look at the new teacher, never spoke but rode silently down the road.

Don Conway looked at Guy Hawkins and Ova Salyers and then he looked at me. He didn't ask me how old I was. I didn't tell him in eighteen more days I would be seventeen. One had to be eighteen before he was old enough to teach school. Don Conway knew the fate of my sister when she was employed to teach the Lonesome Valley School. He knew how Guy Hawkins had blacked her eyes with his fists, had whipped her before the Lonesome Valley pupils. She was a fair-haired, beautiful blue-eyed girl of nineteen when she had come to Lonesome Valley. She went home a nervous wreck, long before her school was finished. After I'd seen the way my sister was beaten up, I begged to go to Lonesome Valley. My parents would have none of it. They thought if I went hunting trouble I would get more than my share. . . . Then I had John Hampton, a rural teacher and friend, contact John Conway and get the school for me. Superintendent Staggers didn't want me to go to Lonesome Valley. But there wasn't anything he could do about it after John Conway, Lonesome Valley District School trustee, recommended me. That was why I was here to teach school.

When Don and I reached the schoolhouse, at least thirty-five pupils were there waiting outside. Guy Hawkins and Ova Salyers were standing together near the coal house with their torn and tattered first-grade books. They looked out of place with the other pupils. They were larger than either Don or me. They were older too. They looked at me when I said " Good morning " to them. Many of the pupils turned shyly away and did not speak. They were waiting for the schoolhouse to be unlocked so they could rush in and select their seats. Each had his dinner basket or bucket in his hand. The majority of them carried tattered-edged and backless books.

The girls wore pigtails down their backs tied with all colors of ribbons. They wore clean print dresses and they were barefooted. Not one pupil in my school, large or small, boy or girl, wore a pair of shoes. I'd never seen in my life so many barefooted people, young, middle-aged, and old, as I had seen in Lonesome Valley. Wearing gloves on their hands in summer was the same to them

[1] **to worm and sucker:** to free from worms and cut off shoots, or suckers.

as wearing shoes on their feet. They just didn't do it.

" Well, I'm opening the door," I said, to break the silence of my pupils.

When I opened the door, they laughed, screamed, and raced for the schoolhouse. Their shyness was gone now. There was a mad scramble to get inside the schoolhouse for seats. Then there was some discussion among them as to who would sit by whom. Girls had selected their seatmates. There were a few controversies and a few hurt feelings. Often two pupils wanted to sit by the same person. No trouble with Guy and Ova. They walked inside reluctantly and sat down in a seat on the boys' side farthest from my desk.

" Now let me make an announcement to you before school starts," I said, after walking up to my desk. " There will not any longer be a girls' side and a boys' side. Sit any place you want to."

They looked strangely at one another. Not one boy would cross to the girls' side. Not one girl would cross to the boys' side. In Lonesome Valley it was hard to break a teaching tradition more than a century old. But after I had been to high school, where there were no such things as a girls' side and a boys' side in a schoolroom, I didn't see why it wouldn't work in Lonesome Valley. Little did I dream that what I had said here would make news in Lonesome Valley, that it would be talked about by everybody, and that many would criticize me and call my school " a courting school." Boys and girls sitting together? Who had ever heard tell of it?

When I walked down the broad center aisle and pulled on the bell rope, the soft tones sounded over the tobacco, corn, and cane fields and the lush green valley; with the ringing of this bell, my school had begun. I knew that not half the pupils in the school census were here. There were one hundred and four in the school census, of school age, for whom the state sent per capita money to pay for their schooling. I had thirty-five pupils. I thought the soft tones of this school bell through the rising mists and over warm cultivated fields where parents and their children were trying to eke out a bare subsistence from the soil might bring back warm memories of happy school days. For I remembered the tones of the Plum Grove school bell, and how I had longed to be back in school after I had quit at the age of nine to work for twenty-five cents a day to help support my family. If I could have, I would have returned to school when I heard the Plum Grove bell. So I rang the bell and called the Lonesome Valley pupils back to school – back to books and play. For going to school had never been work to me. It had been recreation. And I hoped it would be the same for my pupils in Lonesome Valley.

When I dismissed my pupils for the first recess, a fifteen-minute period between the beginning of the school day and the noon hour, I was amazed to see them all jump up from their seats at the same time and try to be the first out of the house. Big pupils pushed past the little ones, and there was so much confusion and disorder I knew they would never leave the room like this again. Why were they running? I wondered. I had a few minutes' work to do before I could join them on the playground. Before I had finished this work, I heard the tenor of their uneven voices singing these familiar words:

> The needle's eye that does supply,
> The thread that runs so true,
> Many a beau have I let go,
> Because I wanted you.

Many a dark and stormy night,
When I went home with you,
I stumped my toe and down I go,
Because I wanted you.

I walked to the door and watched them. They had formed a circle, hand in hand, and around and around they walked and sang these words while two pupils held their locked hands high for the circle to pass under. Suddenly the two standing — one inside the circle and one outside — let their arms drop down to take a pupil from the line. Then the circle continued to march and sing while the two took the pupil aside and asked him whether he would rather be a train or an automobile. If the pupil said he'd rather be an automobile, he stood on one side; if a train, he stood on the other of the two that held hands. And when they had finished taking everybody from the circle, the two groups faced each other, lined up behind their captains. Each put his arms around the pupil in front of him and locked his hands. The first line to break apart or to be pulled forward lost the game.

Fifteen minutes were all too short for them to play "the needle's eye." I let recess extend five minutes so they could finish their second game. It had been a long time since I had played this game at Plum Grove. These words brought back pleasant memories. They fascinated me. And my Lonesome Valley pupils played this game with all the enthusiasm and spirit they had! They put themselves into it — every pupil in school. Not one stood by to watch. Because they were having the time of their lives, I hated to ring the bell for "books." I lined them up, smaller pupils in front and larger ones behind, and had them march back into the schoolroom.

Guy Hawkins and Ova Salyers were the last on the line. When they came inside the door, Guy asked permission to go with Ova after a bucket of water. We didn't have a well or a cistern at the schoolhouse. We had to get water from some home in the district. I told them they could go but not to be gone too long, for the pupils, after running and playing, were thirsty. The July sun beat down on the galvanized tin roof. This made the pine boards so hot inside they oozed resin.[1] We raised all the windows, but still the place was hot as the room in which I slept at Conways'. My little room upstairs with a high unscreened window of only one sash didn't cool off until about midnight. Then I could go to sleep.

The first bucket of water Guy and Ova brought didn't last five minutes. The majority of the pupils were still thirsty. I sent Guy and Ova back for more, telling them to borrow another bucket. I sent them in a hurry. And I knew I had to do something about the dipper problem. At Plum Grove, too, we had all drunk from the same dipper, but when I went to Landsburgh High School I was taught something different.

So I made "an important announcement" to my pupils. I told them each had to bring his own drinking cup the next day. It could be a glass, teacup, gourd, dipper, just so it was his own and no one else drank from it. My pupils looked at one another and laughed as if my announcement was funny. But I had seen sweat run from their faces into the dipper, and the next in line put his mouth where the sweat had run or where the other pupil had put his lips. I noticed, too, several pupils had put the rim up near the handle to their mouths, so I knew they didn't like to drink after the others.

[1] **resin** (rĕz'ĭn): a brownish, sticky substance found in pine wood.

Jesse Stuart (second from left) watches a group of students play "The Thread That Runs So True" outside a one-room school like the one where he started his teaching career. (*Louisville* Courier-Journal)

On Tuesday they brought their dippers, tin cups, and glasses. Only a few had forgotten, and I stopped with my busy schedule of classwork long enough to teach them how to make paper drinking cups. I showed them how to take a clean sheet of paper from a tablet and fold it to hold water. I gave them a lecture about drinking water. I told them never to drink from a stream. I told them how I had gotten typhoid fever twice: once from drinking cool water from a little stream, and once from drinking in a river. I had my pupils use the dipper to dip water from the bucket into their cups. They accepted my suggestion gladly. I also borrowed another water bucket from Bertha Conway and brought it to school. The one bucket allowed me for thirty-five pupils (and there would be more as soon as the farmers were through with their summer plowing and worming and suckering tobacco, stripping their cane and boiling the juice to sirup) was not enough. They played hard at recess and noon and in the "time of books" sat in a schoolroom almost as hot as a stove oven.

Tuesday when I stood beside Guy Hawkins and showed him how to hold his book when he read, my pupils laughed until I had to stop them. I was trying to teach Guy to read as he stumbled over the simple words in the *First Grade Reader*. My pupils laughed because Guy was taller by two inches than I was and heavier. He had a bullneck almost as large as his head, and a prominent jaw. His beard was so heavy that he had to shave every day.

Wouldn't Coach Wilson like to have him! I thought. He would make the best tackle Landsburgh High School ever had.

Guy had big hands. His right hand covered the back of his *First Reader.* And he had powerful arms. The muscles rippled under his clean blue-faded shirt. I measured him as I stood beside him. I knew that if I ever had to fight him, it would be a fight. And I knew that I wasn't going to fight him unless he forced me to fight. He was more powerful physically than I was. And the outcome of our fight might depend on the one who successfully landed the first haymaker to the other's jaw.

Then I looked down at Ova Salyers sitting on the recitation seat beside me. Another tackle for Coach Wilson, I thought. This pair would be a coach's dream. Pity some coach doesn't have 'em instead of me.

If it were not for these two young men, I wouldn't have had any trouble disciplining my school. All the other pupils played hard and they were obedient. They would have been good in their class work if they had had the proper training. I had ten-year-old pupils just starting to school. Nineteen-year-olds in the first grade. Fourteen-year-olds in the second grade. I had one twelve-year-old girl in the eighth grade. They had not been promoted because they had never attended a full school term. They had taken the same grade over and over until they could stand and recite some of the beginning lessons from memory.

"Guy, how long have you been in the first grade?" I asked.

"Oh, about eight years," he laughed.

"You're not going to be in it any longer," I said.

"Why?" he asked.

"Because I'm going to promote you," I said. "Tomorrow you start in the second grade."

Then I had Ova Salyers read. He had also been in the first grade eight years. I promoted him.

When these young men sat down again I saw them look at each other and laugh as if they thought my promoting them was funny. I knew they accepted school as a joke, a place to come and see people. A place where they could join a circle of smaller children and play "the needle's eye." And I knew there wasn't much chance of reasoning with either one. But I had a feeling that time would come. I didn't believe they were coming to school for any good. I felt that Guy was waiting his chance for me. I was not going to take any chances; I was going to give him the full benefit of the doubt.

The following Monday I had stayed at the schoolhouse to do some work on my school records, and Don Conway had gone home with his sister and brothers. This was the first afternoon I had stayed at school after all my pupils had gone. The room was very silent, and I was busy working when I heard soft footsteps walking around the building. I looked through the window on my left and I saw Guy Hawkins' head. His uncombed, tousled hair was ruffled by the Lonesome Valley wind.

I wondered why he was coming back. I wondered if he had forgotten something.

Then I realized this was the first time he had been able to catch me by myself. And I remembered a few other incidents in Greenwood County's rural schools where a pupil had come back to the school when the teacher was there alone, and had beaten the tar out of him. I could recall three or four such incidents. But I didn't have time to think about them. Not now. Guy came in the door with his cap in his hand. I didn't want him to see me looking up at him, but I did see him coming down the broad middle aisle, taking long steps and swinging his big arms. He looked madder than any man or animal I had ever seen. He walked up to my desk and stood silently before me.

"Did you forget something, Guy?" I asked.

"Naw, I've never forgot nothin'," he reminded me.

"Then what do you want?" I asked.

"Whip you," he said.

"Why do you want to whip me?" I asked him.

"I didn't like your sister," he said. "You know what I done to her."

"Yes, I know what you did to her," I said.

"I'm a-goin' to do the same thing to you," he threatened.

"Why do you want to fight me?" I asked him. I dropped my pencil and stood up facing him.

"I don't like you," he said. "I don't like teachers. I said never another person with your name would teach this school. Not as long as I'm here."

"It's too bad you don't like me or my name," I said, my temper rising.

"I won't be satisfied until I've whipped you," he said.

"Can you go to another school?" I asked him. "The Valley School is not too far from where you live."

"Naw, naw," he shouted, "if anybody leaves, you'll leave. I was in Lonesome Valley first. And I ain't a-goin' to no other school because of you!"

"Then there's nothing left for us to do but fight," I said. "I've come to teach this school and I'm going to teach it!"

"Maybe you will," he snarled. "I have you penned in this schoolhouse. I have you where I want you. You can't get away! You can't run! I aim to whip you right where you stand! It's the same place where I whipped your sister!"

I looked at his face. It was red as a sliced beet. Fire danced in his pale blue, elongated eyes. I knew Guy Hawkins meant every word he said. I knew I had to face him and to fight. There was no other way around. I had to think quickly. How would I fight him?

"Will you let me take my necktie off?" I said, remembering I'd been choked by a fellow pulling my necktie once in a fight.

"Yep, take off that purty tie," he said. "You might get it dirty by the time I'm through with you."

I slowly took off my tie.

"Roll up the sleeves of your white shirt too," he said. "But they'll be dirty by the time I sweep this floor up with you."

"Sweep the floor up with me," I said.

He shot out his long arm but I ducked. I felt the wind from his thrust against my ear.

I mustn't let him clinch me, I thought.

Then he came back with another right and I ducked his second lick. I came around with my first lick—a right—and planted it on his jaw, not a good lick but just enough to jar him and make him madder. When he rushed at me, I sidestepped. He missed. By the time he had turned around, I caught him a haymaker on the chin that reeled him. Then I followed up with another lick as hard as I had ever hit a man. Yet I didn't bring him down. He came back for more. But he didn't reach me this time. He was right. I did get my shirt dirty. I dove through the air with a flying tackle. I hit him beneath the knees. I'd tackled like this in football. I'd tackled hard. And I never tackled anybody harder than Guy. His feet went from under him, and I scooted past on the pine floor. I'd tackled him so quickly when he had expected me to come back at him with my fists, that he went down so fast he couldn't catch with his hands. His face hit flat against the floor and his nose was flattened. The blood spurted as he started to get up.

I let him get to his feet. I wondered if I should. For I knew it was either him or me. One of us had to whip. When he did get to his feet after that terrible fall, I waded into him. I hit fast and I hit hard. He swung wild. His fingernail took a streak of hide from my neck and left a red mark that smarted and the blood oozed through. I pounded his chin. I caught him on the beardy jaw. I reeled him back and followed up. I gave him a left to the short ribs while my right in a split second caught his mouth. Blood spurted again. Yet he was not through. But I knew I had him.

"Had enough?" I panted.

He didn't answer. I didn't ask him a second time. I hit him hard enough to knock two men down. I reeled him back against a seat. I followed up. I caught him with a haymaker under the chin and laid him across the desk. Then he rolled to the floor. He lay there with blood running from his nose and mouth. His eyes were rolled back. I was nearly out of breath. My hands ached. My heart pounded. If this is teaching school! I thought. If this goes with it! Then I remembered vaguely I had asked for it. I'd asked for this school. I would take no other.

Guy Hawkins lay there sprawled on the unswept floor. His blood was mingled with the yellow dirt carried into the schoolroom by seventy bare feet. I went back and got the water bucket. With a clean handkerchief, I washed blood from his mouth and nose. I couldn't wash it from his shirt. I put cool water to his forehead.

I worked over a pupil — trying to bring him back to his senses — whom only a few hours before I had stood beside and tried to teach how to pronounce words when he read. "Don't stumble over them like a horse stumbles over frozen ground," I told him, putting it in a language he would understand. I had promoted him. I'd sent Guy and Ova after water when other pupils had wanted to go. On their way to get water, I knew they chewed tobacco and thought they were putting something over on me. I had known I couldn't allow them to use tobacco at school. I had known the time would eventually come. But I wanted to put it off as long as I could. Now I had whipped him and I wondered as I looked at him stretched on the floor how I'd done it. He was really knocked out for the count. I knew the place where we had fought would always be marked. It was difficult to remove bloodstain from pine wood. It would always be there, this reminder, as long as I taught school at Lonesome Valley.

When Guy Hawkins came to his senses, he looked up at me. I was applying the wet cool handkerchief to his head. When he started to get up, I helped him to his feet.

"Mr. Stuart, I really got it poured on me," he admitted. "You're some fighter."

This was the first time he had ever called me "Mr. Stuart." I had heard, but had pretended not to hear, him call me "Old Jess" every time my back was turned. He had never before, when he had spoken directly to me, called me anything.

"I'm not much of a fighter until I

have to fight, Guy," I said. "You asked for it. There was no way around. I had to fight you."

"I know it," he said. "I've had in mind to whip you ever since I heard you's a-goin' to teach this school. But you win. You winned fair, too," he honestly admitted. "I didn't think you could hit like that."

Guy was still weak. His nose and mouth kept bleeding. He didn't have a handkerchief and I gave him a clean one.

"Think you can make it home all right, Guy?"

"I think so," he said.

He walked slower from the schoolhouse than he had walked in. I was too upset to do any more work on my record book. I stood by the window and watched him walk across the schoolyard, then across the foot log and down the Lonesome Creek Road until he went around the bend and was out of sight. Something told me to watch for Ova Salyers. He might return to attack me. I waited several minutes and Ova didn't come. Guy had come to do the job alone.

I felt better now that the fight was over, and I got the broom and swept the floor. I had quickly learned that the rural teacher was janitor as well, and that his janitor work was one of the important things in his school. I believed, after my brief experience, that the schoolhouse should be made a place of beauty, prettier and cleaner than any of the homes the pupils came from so they would love the house and the surroundings, and would think of it as a place of beauty and would want to keep it that way.

The floor was easy to sweep. But it was difficult to clean blood from the floor. I carried a coal bucket of sand and poured it on the blood and then shoveled up the sand and carried it out. I had the blood from the floor. Then I scrubbed the place, but the stain was there. I could not get it from the oily, soft pine wood. I knew this was one day in my teaching career I would never forget.

I didn't expect Guy Hawkins to return to Lonesome Valley School. I thought his schooling was ended. But when he left the schoolhouse he didn't take his books. I wondered if he would come back to get them, and, if he came, would he bring his father or one of his married brothers with him? Would he start another fight? The same thoughts must have troubled John Conway. When I went to school on Tuesday morning, John went with me.

This was John Conway's first visit to the school, for his farm work had piled up on him since all of his children but Flossie were going to school. When we got there, big Guy Hawkins with his black eyes and swollen lips was in a circle with the other pupils, going around, and singing "The Needle's Eye." Guy greeted me: "Good morning, Mr. Stuart."

Then John Conway smiled and turned to go. I watched him cross the foot log and go into the little store. I joined in the game, "the needle's eye," with my pupils. Guy Hawkins and I were captains. I was the hard-boiled egg and he was the soft-boiled egg. When we took pupils from the line and asked them whether they would rather be a soft-boiled or a hard-boiled egg, the majority chose the soft-boiled egg. Guy Hawkins got three-fourths of the pupils. And when we formed our tug of war to pull against each other, his side toppled my side. They pulled us all over the yard, and everybody laughed, especially Guy Hawkins. It was great fun. And never did Guy Hawkins or a pupil ask me about the fight. If they talked about it, I didn't know. I did notice them observing the bloodstain on the floor. If Guy Hawkins ever said anything against me to a fellow pupil again, I never heard of it. He had, for the first time, become a pupil like the rest. He had, for the first time, acted as if he was a part of our school.

[After his first year of teaching, Jesse Stuart finished high school himself. Later he completed his college work in three years and took a teaching job at another small rural school, Winston High School, where he had fourteen pupils and where he himself comprised the entire faculty. As at Lonesome Valley, Jesse lived with a neighborhood family, the Baylors, but as this part of his account begins, he prepares for a visit to his home at Landsburgh, to see the county superintendent.]

Nobody could keep me from starting home. I was determined to go. I needed more novels, books of short stories, books of poems and essays for my pupils to read. I wanted to see Superintendent Larry Anderson. When Lucretia Baylor learned I was determined to go, she prepared a quick hot lunch for me. She did this while I packed my clothes and got ready. For my teaching day ended at 3:30 P.M., and I had walked the three-fourths mile from the school to Baylors' in a hurry. It was early in the afternoon, but the dark December skies hung low over the valley, and there were six inches of snow on the ground. I had seventeen miles ahead of me. The only way I could get to my destination was to walk.

"If you were a boy of mine," Ottis Baylor said, "I wouldn't let you go. Not on a seventeen-mile journey on a night like this! I advise you against going. I know the road to Landsburgh better than you do. I've walked it enough to know. It's a treacherous road when you leave the Tiber Valley Road and try the short cut around Laurel Ridge."

I knew that I wasn't listening to Ottis Baylor. I was going, anyway. I knew that I was fast on foot. I had walked thirty-five miles in a day. That hadn't even made my legs or feet sore. If I could walk this far on a short day, then I was as positive as death, by steady walking, I could cover a mile every twelve minutes. I thought: If I had luck, I could make the journey in three and a half hours. I allowed myself four hours and that was plenty of time. And I was leaving Baylors' at four.

The massive black cloud rested on the east and west walls of the valley like a roof. The east wall was the one I had to climb. When I reached the top I would be on Laurel Ridge. By going this way, I could cut three miles from my walking distance. I knew the path to Laurel Ridge. I'd been over it many times before. Whether the snow was broken over this path or not, I did not know. I did not care. I said good-by to the Baylors, and I was on my way.

The December wind whistled in the barren shoe-make [1] tops, where the red birds hopped from limb to limb and chirruped plaintive notes. Snowbirds stood by the clumps of dead ragweed the snow hadn't covered. They were searching for a scanty supper of the frozen seeds. Though time was early on this short winter day, I thought darkness might come soon. Going up the mountain, I made excellent time. I followed the path all right. I had to break the snow, for no one had traveled this path. I knew how to follow the path by the

[1] **shoe-make:** sumac (sho͞o′măk), a small tree or shrub.

clumps of trees, rock cliffs, and fences. These were the landmarks to follow.

Before I reached a small opening near Laurel Ridge, I lost my path. I walked into a forest of tough-butted white oaks. They grew close together shutting out the diminishing winter light. I had never seen these trees before. I turned quickly, retracing my steps until I found the path. I knew I had been in too much of a hurry. I'd have to be more careful. But why should I worry now? I had at least reached Laurel Ridge, for there was a five-strand, rusty barbed-wire fence nailed to the trees. I knew this fence. It followed Laurel Ridge some distance before it turned back down the mountain. When I held my arm up to look at my watch, I couldn't see the figures on the dial. I didn't know what time it was, but I knew it was early. I knew I was in the snow cloud. For the big snowflakes were falling around me. I could see them dimly, these white flakes about the size of dimes, falling just in front of my eyes. I could feel them hitting my overcoat.

All I had to do was turn to my left after I reached Laurel Ridge. That was the right direction. I could follow the wire fence even if I had to follow it with my hand as I walked. I had one free hand. I carried my suitcase with my right hand. My left hand was free. But I didn't touch the fence. Not yet. I was following Laurel Ridge Road. I was following it with my feet. I had hunted much at night in my lifetime. Darkness had never bothered me too much. But now I couldn't see the woods and I knew it couldn't possibly be six o'clock. I was in a snowstorm. I could hear the snowflakes falling through the barren oak tops whose branches interlocked above the road.

Then I heard voices, and the sound was sweet to hear. I had barely time to side-step for two mule teams. I almost walked into a mule before I saw him. Yet there was a lighted lantern on the joltwagon the mules were pulling. When I recognized Eif Potters, he stopped his mule team in great surprise. He asked me where I was going on a night like this. Then I knew what he was talking about.

The fury of the storm almost blotted out the lantern light. It didn't give light more than six feet away. The snowflakes were larger than nickels. They were almost as large as quarters. I was in the cloud I'd seen before I left Baylors'.

I told Eif Potters and his son Zeke, who was sitting on the wagon beside him, I was on my way home. That snow wasn't falling down in Tiber Valley when I left, not more than two hours ago. He told me they hadn't been in the snowstorm until they reached the top of Raccoon Hill. Then he invited me to get on the wagon and go home with them, but I refused. When I refused he said he would loan me his lantern, but that they couldn't get around Laurel Ridge without it. Said he had five more miles to go, that he had taken a load of tobacco to Landsburgh and was getting back the same day, that he and his mules were very tired to push through five more miles of darkness and storm.

On this lonely ridge, high up in a snow cloud, I said good night to Eif and Zeke and was on my way, for I had lost about five minutes talking to them. I hadn't walked but a few steps when I looked back. The mule teams, wagon, riders, and lantern had disappeared in the storm. Yet I heard the jingling of the mules' harness, and I heard the men's voices as they talked to each other. Then I plunged on, alone, taking in both sides of the road. I hunted for the fence with an outstretched hand in the darkness, but I couldn't find it.

Eif had warned me about one place. He told me if I bore too far to my left I would go into a vast tract of timber that lay on the east wall of Tiber Valley. And for this reason, I bore to my right, feeling with my feet while the snow came down as I had never felt it fall before. One thing I had forgotten to ask Eif for was matches. He was a pipe smoker too. He had smoked his pipe all the time he sat on his wagon and talked to me. If only I had a match! I was stumbling over the road. Once I went in water to my knee. Then I knew I must be on the Laurel Ridge Road. This was a deep wagon-wheel rut, and Eif had driven over it and had broken the thin ice down to the water. My foot was wet. Water squashed in my shoe. One of my galoshes was filled with water.

Then I stepped into a hole of water with my dry foot. I went in to my knee. Both pant legs were wet to my knees. Again and again I stepped into water, but my feet were already wet and it didn't make any difference if I did get them wet again. I kept moving. I followed the road the best I could. I knew I was on the Laurel Ridge Road. That was the main thing. I would soon reach the turnpike at the top of Raccoon Hill. That was where the Laurel Ridge Road ended. And this distance was approximately three miles from where my path from Baylors' had gone through the barbed-wire fence onto the Laurel Ridge. If I could only see my watch! I had surely walked three more miles!

Time in the night, I thought, when one was walking alone, might seem longer than it actually was. I kept on going. I waded water, and I waded snow. The snow was almost as deep as my galoshes were high. I walked on and on and on. Then I knew I'd gone far enough to reach the turnpike on Raccoon Hill . . . the turnpike that would take me straight to Landsburgh. While I thought about the fast time I would be able to make on the turnpike when I reached it, I suddenly walked into a cornfield. I thought it was a cornfield. I thought I was standing beside a fodder shock. It stood like a white wigwam before me. I pushed my hand through the snow and felt the dry fodder stalks. I knew now that I was lost.

I couldn't even retrace my steps. I couldn't see them. If it had been light enough for me to see them, I couldn't have followed them far because they would have been snowed under. I was lost, that was all. I was in this cornfield and I would have to make the best of it. I stood beside the fodder shock — this tiny thing of security — while I screamed at the top of my voice. I knew that in this part of Greenwood County there was much wasteland. There were miles and miles where there wasn't a house. But I screamed, anyway. I thought somebody might hear me and come to my rescue. The only answer I got was the faraway barking of a fox. When I screamed he mocked me with his barking.

When I had reached this fodder shock, my feet were still warm and my face was wet with perspiration. But in this open space where corn had grown on the mountaintop there was an incessant sweep of wind. The wind carried the snow directly at me. I could measure the speed of the wind by the way the soft flakes hit my face. The soft flakes felt like grains of corn. I had to start walking to keep warm. I had to do something in a hurry. Then a thought came to me. If there was one fodder shock here, there were others. The cornfield must be fairly large to give the wind such great velocity. I was almost afraid to leave the fodder shock I had already found. Even when I did, I held to my suitcase. I walked a few paces and found another fodder shock. I put my arm around the top of the shock and dragged it back to the first one. I carried eight fodder shocks to one place. The fodder shocks were not large. The shocks were not as tall as I was. I used one hand to carry them; I held to my suitcase with the other. I was afraid I'd lose it and that it would soon be snowed under. Besides, I had other ideas.

After I'd pulled these fodder shocks together, I laid the heavy ends of the fodder to the windward side of the mountain. I bedded three shocks down on the snow. Then I put a shock on each side of the floor I'd made. I stood two shocks up on the windward side, to pull down on me as soon as I was ready to lie down. The last shock I stood up, to use where the fodder would be thinnest above me. Then I stood on the fodder and pulled off my shoes. The wind-driven snow was cold to my wet feet and legs. I pulled off my overcoat and wet pants. I took a dry soiled shirt from my suitcase and dried the water from my feet and legs. I tied dry dirty shirts around my feet. I put on a pair of soiled trousers I was taking to have dry-cleaned. I bundled myself with all the clothes I had in my suitcase. I lay down and spread my overcoat over me. Now I reached up and pulled the fodder shocks down upon me. The fodder quilt was thick but not too heavy. I lay there and listened to the mice in the fodder around me and the ticking of my watch while over me the wind moaned and the snow fell.

I knew that I should not go to sleep. For if I did the wind might blow the fodder from over me. I would freeze to death and I would not be found in this cornfield until the farmer came to haul his fodder home. I must have been half asleep when I heard the hoot owls start calling to one another from the timber all around this cornfield. I didn't know exactly where they were. But I knew they frequented the less populated places. From their calls, coming from all directions, I knew this must be their meeting place. I no longer heard the wind nor felt it seeping through the fodder. I parted the fodder stalks to see what had happened. There were a million bright stars high in the clear blue sky, and in a short distance all around me — for there was not more than two acres of this cornfield — I could see the dark outlines of trees. Among these trees were the hoot owls. They were on every side. They cried jubilantly to each other, asking always the same: "Who, who are you?"

I pulled the fodder quilt back over me and lay there listening to the hoots of the owls, to the mice over me, around me and through the fodder, and to the ticking of my watch. I thought that I could stay awake until morning. Since the skies had cleared, I knew the weather before morning would be sub-zero on this mountaintop. I went to sleep dreaming that I would not go to sleep.

When I awoke there were fewer stars in the sky. Daylight didn't come on these short December days until nearly eight. I tried to see what time it was, but I couldn't see the hands of my watch. The owls had flown away, and all was silent save for the ticking of my watch and the mice that had never slept the whole night through. I had slept warm on this cold night. I had warmed the fodder for the mice. The place was comfortable for all of us. But now I sat up and placed the fodder around me like a wigwam. I wanted the day to break so I could put on my clothes and be on my way. I had never been so hungry in my life.

Just as soon as it was light enough to see what I was doing, I started dressing. The legs of the pants I'd pulled off were frozen stiff and hard. My shoes had frozen so that I couldn't get them on. I didn't have a match to build a fire to thaw them. It was impossible to put them on. I wrapped a soiled shirt around each foot. I put my feet into my frozen galoshes. I put my frozen shoes and pants into my suitcase. It was light enough for me to see dim footprints in the snow. I could retrace myself. I wanted to see where I had made my mistake.

I followed my tracks, dim little prints in the crusted snow, for more than a mile. Then I came to Laurel Ridge. Far, far, down below, I could see Hinton Valley, now a great white silence except for the dark, leafless, sleeping trees. And to my right, if I had gone just fifty feet to my left, I would have found the turnpike on Raccoon Hill. I had borne too far to my right after Eif Potters had warned me about turning left. I had gone somewhere on the mountain between the headwaters of North Fork and Raccoon, where I had found the cornfield and slept in the fodder.

Though it was Saturday morning, when farmers would be on their way to Landsburgh, I was the first person on the turnpike. The white silence of snow that was even with the tops of my galoshes remained unbroken until I made a path. I walked down Raccoon Hill, and in the distance, somewhere far down the road, I heard voices. They were coming toward me. I was going toward them. Their shouts at their teams grew louder. I saw three teams hitched to a snowplow and the county roadworkers were breaking the road. I walked past them, and they looked at me. I hadn't noticed the fodder blades still hanging to my overcoat, and I brushed them off before I stopped at Gullet's gristmill.

I knew Ephraim Gullet. When I went inside the gristmill, he asked me if I wasn't traveling early. I told him I had been lost and had slept on the mountain. He put more coal in the potbellied stove. He made a pot of coffee. I thawed my shoes and my pant legs while I drank hot coffee and warmed myself in front of the red-hot stove. Ephraim told me that his thermometer was twelve below at six that morning. He couldn't understand how I had stripped my clothes and dried the water from my legs and feet there on the mountaintop facing the great sweeps of snow-laden wind. He couldn't understand how I had managed to survive the rigor of the raw elements on the mountaintop when it was twelve below in the valley.

When Superintendent Larry Anderson unlocked his office door at nine that Saturday morning, I was there waiting for him. I had caught a ride in on a coal truck from Gullet's gristmill to Landsburgh.

"Well, well, how did you get here so early?" Superintendent Anderson asked. "You didn't come all the way from Winston this morning?"

"Just part of the way," I said.

He didn't ask me where I stayed. And I didn't tell him. I had something else I wanted to talk to him about.

"How are you getting along with your school out there?" he asked me.

"I think I'm getting along all right," I said. "What reports have you heard?"

"Good reports," he said.

"I'm glad to hear the reports about my teaching have been favorable," I said. "I am learning myself. My pupils are working me as hard as I am working them!"

My superintendent thought I was joking. He started laughing. He laughed until he couldn't talk.

"I'm telling you the truth," I said. "I'm not telling you a joke. I've worked harder than I did in high school or in college!"

Superintendent Larry Anderson laughed harder than before. He laughed so loud anybody in the corridors of the courthouse could have heard him.

"You know there's not anything as good for a man as a good laugh early in the morning," he said.

I knew that he still thought I was joking.

"Superintendent Anderson," I said seriously, "I'm up against teaching those fourteen pupils. I've not got a slow one among them. I've got a couple of average pupils, and they can do every bit of work I give them. And," I explained, with a gesture of my hand for emphasis, "I've got one pupil that's a genius. He knows more facts than I do. He's only a freshman in high school. I tell you, Budge Waters is a genius! If he isn't, I'm terribly dumb. I've got six or seven A pupils and he's above them!"

Superintendent Larry Anderson sat silently looking at me for a minute. We were in his office alone. Then he spoke thoughtfully: "Well, what is your problem?"

"I haven't any," I said. "I've not had to discipline a pupil. They work hard. They play hard."

I knew he was wondering why I had come to his office.

"But there is one thing I'd like to do," I said. "That's why I've called on you this morning. I'd like to test my own judgment to see if I am wrong or right in my opinion of my pupils. I'd like to know how to go about entering them in the state scholastic contest. The contest is held each spring, isn't it?"

"Oh, yes," he said, "but there is an elimination process. Your pupils will have to take an examination against the pupils in Landsburgh High School! Then, if you are successful there," he explained, "they'll go to Auckland to enter the district contest. If they are successful there, they'll go on to the state contests!"

I knew that to get past Landsburgh, now a joint city-and-county high school, we'd have to compete with the best from nearly four hundred pupils. To get past the regional, we'd have to compete with the best, selected from thousands. Yet, it took only one brain to win a contest. I knew Budge Waters had that brain if it was properly trained. I thought he was capable of competing state-wide. I thought Billie Leonard could take the district in algebra. And I was willing to challenge big Landsburgh High School in all the five subjects I was teaching my pupils.

"If it's all right with you, Superintendent," I said, "you make arrangements and set a date for us to meet Landsburgh High School in algebra, Latin, English, plane geometry, and history!"

"I'll do it," he smiled. "Would sometime in January suit you?"

"Any time's all right with me," I said. "Make it convenient for the Landsburgh High School!"

"That's fair enough," he said.

"This is all I wanted to see you about," I said.

With these words, I left him alone in his office.

When I told my pupils about a scholastic contest with Landsburgh High School, I watched their expressions. They were willing and ready for the challenge. The competitive spirit was in them.

"We must review everything we have covered in our textbooks," I told them. "We must cover more territory in our textbooks too. Hold up your right hands if you are willing!"

Every pupil raised his hand.

Right then we started to work. In addition to regular assignments, my pupils began reviewing all of the old assignments we had covered.

Despite the challenge ahead and all the reviewing and study we planned to do, we never stopped play. The Tiber River was frozen over. The ring of skates and merry laughter broke the stillness of the winter nights. We skated on the white winding ribbon of ice beneath the high, cold winter moon. Often we'd skate until midnight. We'd hear the wind blow mournfully over the great white silence that surrounded us and sing lonesome songs without words in the barren branches of the bankside trees. And we'd hear the foxes' barking, high upon the walls of sheltering cliffs, mocking the music of our ringing skates.

On winter days when the snow had melted, leaving the dark earth a sea of sloppy mud, we designed floor games for our little one-room school. They were simple games such as throwing bolts in small boxes. And we played darts. We also played a game called "fox and goose." We made our fox-and-goose boards and we played with white, yellow, and red grains of corn. We had to make our own recreation. I never saw a distracted look on a pupil's face. I never heard one complain that the short, dark winter days were boresome because there wasn't anything to do. I think each pupil silently prayed for the days to be longer. We were a united little group. We were small but we were powerful. We played hard, and we studied hard. We studied and played while the December days passed.

One day in early January, we dismissed school. This was the first time we had dismissed for anything. We had never lost an hour. I had actually taught more hours than was required. This was the big day for us. It was too bad that another blizzard had swept our rugged land and that a stinging wind was smiting the valleys and the hills. But this didn't stop the boys and me from going. Leona Maddox, my best Latin pupil, couldn't go along. Her father, Alex Maddox, wouldn't let her ride a mule seventeen miles to Landsburgh to compete in a contest on a day like this. I couldn't persuade him to let her go.

On that cold blizzardy morning, Budge Waters rode his mule to school very early and built a fire in the potbellied stove. When the rest of us arrived on our mules at approximately seven o'clock, Budge had the schoolroom warm. We tied our mules to the fence, stood before the fire, and warmed ourselves before we started on our journey. Then we unhitched our mules from the fence and climbed into the saddles. Little clouds of frozen snow in powdery puffs arose from the mules' hoofs as six pupils and their teacher rode down the road.

Though the force of wind in the Tiber Valley was powerful, it was at our backs. The wind was strong enough to give our mules more momentum. We made good time until we left the valley and climbed the big hill. Here, we faced the wind. It was a whipping wind — stinging, biting wind on this mountain

Jesse Stuart surveys his native hills. (*Louisville* Courier-Journal)

– that made the water run from our eyes and our mules' eyes, but for us there was no turning back. We were going to Landsburgh High School. That was that. We were determined to meet this big school; big to us, for they outnumbered us twenty-six to one. Soon we were down in Hinton Valley. Then we rode to the top of the Raccoon Hill, where we faced the stinging wind again.

"Mr. Stuart, I have been thinking," Budge Waters said, as we rode along together, "if you can sleep in a fodder shock when it's twelve degrees below zero, we can take this contest from Landsburgh High School! I've not forgotten how you walked seventeen miles to carry us books. All of your pupils remember. We'll never let you down!"

Budge Waters thought of this because we were riding down the mountain where I had slept that night. Then we rode down into the Raccoon Valley, and Billie Leonard, only thirteen years old, complained of numbness in his hands, feet, and lips. He said he felt as if he was going to sleep. I knew what he was talking about. I had had the same feeling the day Ottis Baylor had put my hands and feet in cold water. We stopped at a home, tied our mules to the fence, and went in and asked to warm. Bert Patton, a stranger to us, piled more wood on the open fire until we were as warm as when we had left the schoolhouse. We told him who we were and where we were going.

"On a day like this!" he said, shaking his head sadly.

We climbed into the saddles again. We were over halfway now. The second hitch would put us at Landsburgh High School. We had valley all the way to Landsburgh, with walls of rugged hills on each side for windbreaks.

At eleven o'clock we rode across the

Landsburgh High School yard, and hitched our mules to the fence around the athletic field. There were faces against the windowpanes watching us. Then we walked inside the high school, where Principal Ernest Charters met and welcomed us. He told us that he was surprised we had come on a day like this and that we had been able to arrive so soon.

In the principal's office my pupils and I huddled around the gas stove while we heard much laughter in the high-school corridors. The Landsburgh High School pupils thought we were a strange-looking lot. Many came inside their principal's office to take a look at us. We were regarded with curiosity, strangeness, and wonder. Never before had these pupils seen seven mules hitched to their schoolyard fence. Never before had they competed scholastically with so few in number — competitors who had reached them by muleback. The Landsburgh High School principal didn't feel about the contest the way we felt. To him, this was just a "setup" to test his pupils for the district contest which would soon be held. He told me this when he went after the sealed envelopes that held the questions. We warmed before the gas stove while he made arrangements for the contest.

"These questions were made out by the state department of education," he said when he returned. "I don't know how hard they are."

My pupils stood silently by the stove and looked at each other. We were asked to go to one of the largest classrooms. A Landsburgh High School teacher had charge of giving the tests. When the Landsburgh High School pupils came through the door to compete against my pupils, we knew why Principal Charters had selected this large classroom. My pupils looked at each other, then at their competitors.

I entered redheaded Jesse Jarvis to compete with ten of their plane-geometry pupils. I entered Billie Leonard against twenty-one of their selected algebra pupils.

"Budge, you'll have to represent us in grammar, English literature, and history," I said. "And I believe I'll put you in civil government. Is that all right?"

"Yes," he agreed. Budge had never had a course in civil government. All he knew about it was what he had read in connection with history.

"Robert Batson, you enter in history and grammar.

"Robin Baylor, you enter in algebra.

"Snookie Baylor, you enter in algebra and plane geometry.

"Sorry, Mr. Charters," I said, "we don't have anyone to enter in Latin. My best Latin pupil, Leona Maddox, couldn't make this trip."

After the contest had begun, I left the room. Miss Bertha Madden was in charge. I took our mules to Walter Scott's barn on the east end of Landsburgh, where I fed and watered them.

With the exception of an interval when the contestants ate a quick lunch, the contest lasted until 2:30 P.M. I had one pupil, Budge Waters, in four contests. I had planned to enter him in two. Just as soon as Budge had finished with civil government, we started grading the papers. All the pupils were requested to leave the room.

We graded the papers with keys. Mr. Charters, Miss Madden, and two other teachers, and I did the grading. Mr. Charters read the answers on the keys, and we checked the answers. Once or twice we stopped long enough to discuss what stiff questions these were. We wondered how far we would have gotten if we — all of us, college graduates — had taken the same test. One of the teachers asked me, while we graded these papers, if Budge Waters had ever seen these questions before.

When we were through grading the papers, Mr. Charters called the contestants into the classroom.

" I want to read you the scores of this contest," Principal Charters said. His voice was nervous.

" Budge Waters, winner in English literature.

" Budge Waters, winner in grammar.

" Budge Waters, winner in history with almost a perfect score.

" Budge Waters, winner in civil government.

" Why didn't you bring just this one boy? " Principal Charters asked me.

" Because I've got other good pupils," I quickly retorted.

" Billie Leonard, winner in algebra, with plenty of points to spare.

" Jesse Jarvis, second in plane geometry, lost by one point.

" Snookie Baylor and Robin Baylor tied for second place in algebra.

" Congratulations," said Principal Charters, " to your pupils and to you, on your success. It looks as though Winston High will represent this county in the district scholastic contest. I've never heard of such a remarkable thing."

When we left the Landsburgh High School we heard defeated pupils crying because " a little mudhole in the road like Winston beat us."

In a few minutes our mule cavalcade passed the Landsburgh High School. Faces were against the windowpanes and many pupils waved jubilantly to us as we rode by, our coat tails riding the wind behind our saddles, and the ends of our scarfs bright banners on the wind. We rode victoriously down the main street of Landsburgh on our way home.

Drawing Conclusions about People

1. List personal characteristics exhibited by the author in this selection. Quote an incident to illustrate each characteristic.

2. Did you conclude that the author was brave, foolish, or revengeful in taking the Lonesome Valley job? Defend your answer.

3. Probably you were amused by the idea of nineteen-year-olds joining enthusiastically in a game with much smaller pupils. Can you come to any conclusions about *why* they should do so?

4. What conclusion do you draw about Guy Hawkins? Was he entirely bad?

Thinking It Over

1. On the frontispiece to Jesse Stuart's book is this quotation from Daniel Webster:

" If we work upon marble, it will perish; if we work upon brass, time will efface it; if we rear temples, they will crumble into dust; but if we work upon immortal minds, if we imbue them with principles, with just fear of God and love of our fellow men, we engrave on those tablets something which will brighten to all eternity."

Why do you think Mr. Stuart used this quotation? What does it mean? What has it to do with teaching? Mr. Stuart believes that education is the " thread that runs so true " and that the teacher is the " needle's eye " through which it passes. How does he himself measure up as a teacher against Webster's statement?

2. How do we know that Stuart is telling the truth without exaggeration? How does he measure up as a writer of autobiography according to the introduction to this section of your book?

3. After two tough battles, one with a bully and one with a blizzard, you were probably not surprised to find Mr. Stuart winning a battle of wits. Winston High was about as small in size as a high school can be. In what ways was it great? What drove Stuart and his pupils to amass knowledge as they did? Of what use was it to them? By the way, how do you think you would fare against those mule-riding pupils from the " little mudhole in the road "?

JOSEPH GOLLOMB

Albert Schweitzer: Genius in the Jungle

In the summer of 1949, there came to this country on his first visit one of the most remarkable men of our time – a man who is widely hailed as a scholar in philosophy, theology, music, languages, and medicine. Newspapers and magazines were full of the story of Dr. Albert Schweitzer.[1] A half-century before, at the age of thirty, Schweitzer held doctor's degrees in three fields; he was an accomplished organist and already a dean at Strasbourg University. Yet he had given up his position to begin the grueling seven-year course in medicine so that he might go as a medical missionary to help the natives of a lonely forest in French Equatorial Africa. Against the wishes and advice of friends he carried out his purpose, and for more than thirty years he has maintained a hospital in the African jungle, only occasionally returning to Europe to give lectures or organ recitals in order to raise funds for his work. With him into the jungle went his wife, a brilliant woman who studied nursing in order that she might work with him.

The following account of Schweitzer's life in Equatorial Africa, from Joseph Gollomb's [2] biography, begins just after he had made his momentous decision.

For Better Reading . . . As you may have noted from your study of other selections, your judgment of a character, real or fictional, is formed by what others say about him, as well as by what he himself says and does. As you observe Dr. Schweitzer's behavior and as you see him through the eyes of others, try to form a judgment of your own about him.

A FEW days after he made his decision, Schweitzer thrust a batch of letters into a mailbox. Some of them broke the news of his decision to family and friends. Others were withdrawals from a host of activities, and included his resignation as Principal of the Theological College of St. Thomas,[3] with its lifelong security of income and its stately residence. As a medical student, he wrote, he would have no time to do anything else.

[1] **Schweitzer** (shvī'tsẽr).
[2] **Gollomb** (gŏl'ôm).
[3] **Theological College of St. Thomas:** a part of the University of Strasbourg in France.

He had expected protests, but not the storm that broke.

Friends who had confided intimately in him reproached him for keeping them ignorant of so drastic a change in his own life.

Others even had unflattering theories as to why he was doing this: he was disappointed with his slow progress in the world. He did not bother answering this until much later in one of his books. "There was not the least ground for saying this, since even as a young man I was fortunate enough to get such recognition as others get only after long years of struggle." He laughed at himself and agreed heartily with those who called him a crackpot.

There were those who quoted the Bible at him, about the man to whom God had given a talent to use but who buried it instead.

Others asked him why he should waste years in studying medicine. "You're an ordained preacher already. Why not go there and simply preach?"

"Because I want to help with more than words."

He had a difficult time with a brilliant French woman. "You want to help medically?" she said. "Splendid! Stay in Europe, give lectures and recitals, write books that will bring you royalties, and you will make enough money to send twenty doctors out there, instead of just yourself."

He tried to argue that he had to be on the scene himself.

"Nonsense!" she retorted. "With enough money you can hire just as competent executives, no matter how good you are."

She had the best of the argument, but she changed nothing.

His friend and teacher, Widor,[1] scolded him. "You're like some general whose brains are needed more than his body, but who takes a rifle and exposes himself needlessly on the firing line."

The other members of the Paris Bach[2] Society were even more impatient with Schweitzer. They were men of music, and to them giving up a great gift for music was as criminal as if a painter were to sacrifice his eyesight.

"At least take along an organ with you," they insisted. "We'll gladly give you one."

He pointed out that the last lap of his voyage would be in native canoes of hollowed tree trunks that were not designed to transport organs.

"Then we'll get you a small piano."

He told them that the climate and insects would rot its insides in no time.

But they paid no attention and went ahead with plans of their own.

His university colleagues objected also. "Service? Of course. But you teach. Isn't that service, too?"

He pointed out that there were others who could take his place in Europe but that there was not a doctor for hundreds of miles around in the Gabon.[3]

He found that hardest of all was to dispel the worries of his family. His parents knew all about the Gabon country, and he could offer them no assurance that their fears for him were groundless.

He was glad when his medical course began.

First-year students at the Strasbourg University were amazed to see the recent head of one of its colleges sitting

[1] **Widor** (vē·dôr′), **Charles Marie:** French organist and composer.

[2] **Bach** (bäĸ): eighteenth-century German organist and composer.

[3] **Gabon** (gȧ·bôɴ′): a territory in French Equatorial Africa.

among them, a beginner like themselves.

He threw himself into his studies and found himself "intoxicated with delight" in dealing at last with a world of concrete facts, anatomy, chemistry, physiology, physics, and other sciences, after so many years of philosophical abstractions.[1]

A medical course anywhere is a full-time program, and Schweitzer's was no exception.

But calls still came to him to come and save this or that old organ from destruction.[2] After the many years he had put in trying to save them, he found he could not refuse these appeals for help. So he took time off, studying on trains and giving up sleep to make up for the time lost in classes.

He still had his book on Bach to finish. He worked at that, too.

He was also preaching at the Church of St. Nicholas. "Preaching was a necessity of my being." That meant time out for sermons and their preparation, and he gave them all the care he had devoted to them when they were his chief preoccupation.

He still had concerts to give. So he traveled to Paris, Barcelona, and to other cities, often spending whole nights, as before, in rehearsing on the organ he was to play the next day.

It was inevitable, therefore, that by the end of the third year at the medical school he found himself in "the worst crisis of exhaustion that I can recall at any time in my whole life."

By that time a little sleep was even worse than none at all, as so often happens when one has overdrawn on one's reserves. He had to have something that would rest him more than sleep. At such times, when it would seem that he could not take any more, and if the Church of St. Nicholas were deserted, he would climb to the organ loft and play.

Helene Bresslau would be listening somewhere below. Or she would sit by his side at the console [3] and pull out the stops he indicated, so that in effect they would be playing as one.

And somehow he got through with his course by October 1911, though there was still a state medical examination to take. There was a fee to pay, and he had to earn the money for it by performing at a musical festival in Paris. Those who heard him did not in the least suspect that he was in a fog of utter exhaustion.

On the morning of December seventeenth, after his last examination, he rose stiffly, and almost literally staggered out into a dark winter night. "I could not grasp the fact that the terrible strain of my medical course was behind me. Again and again I had to assure myself that I was really awake, and not dreaming. The voice of a friend who was walking with me seemed to come from some distant sphere. . . ."

He had a year to put in as a hospital intern.[4]

He put in full time there, too, but also busied himself with the thousand and one details of preparation for Africa.

He had resigned his post at St. Nicholas Church.

"I avoided as far as possible going past either St. Nicholas or the university. The sight of the places where I had carried on my work, and which I could

[1] **philosophical abstractions** (fĭl′ô·sŏf′ĭ·kăl ăb·străk′shŭnz): ideas about religion and morals, general theories rather than facts.

[2] As an organist Schweitzer had developed an interest and talent in the restoration of old organs. He was called to several European cities to direct the repair and retuning of these massive instruments.

[3] **console** (kŏn′sōl): the keyboard of the organ.

[4] **intern** (ĭn′tûrn): a student doctor attached to a hospital staff to get practical training.

never resume, was too painful for me."

After his year at the hospital he spent several months in Paris studying tropical medicine.

Then followed rounds of soliciting funds to build and run a hospital in the Gabon. Some friends gave gladly. In others he saw a change of manner when they learned that for the first time in their experience Albert Schweitzer was asking for help instead of giving it. On the other hand, he was touched by the readiness with which a group of German professors contributed to what, after all, was to be of benefit in a French colony. For at this time there was saber-rattling in Berlin and a cry for war against the French, and in France there was angry talk of revenge against their old foes, the Germans.

To the contributions he received he added whatever he could make at several recitals and concerts, until he had the equivalent of $5,000, enough to assure his work in Africa for two years.

He married Helene Bresslau on June 18, 1912.

Many changes followed. "Until then I had been engaged only in intellectual work. But now I had to make lists of things to do, to go shopping for days on end, to check accounts and deliveries, prepare lists for customhouse examinations, and other endless details." The man to whom "time was a precious gift" had to devote it now to countless items such as drugs, bandages, surgical instruments, and even the kitchenware the Schweitzers would need in their housekeeping.

At last, however, seventy packing cases of supplies were boxed and sent to Bordeaux,[1] the Schweitzers' port of departure.

But he kept one heavy case to take along with them, two thousand francs in gold coin.

His wife asked him why, since paper money was so much easier to carry.

Gravely he told her.

In towering mountains on whose slopes snow and ice have been piling there comes a time when so much as a man's shout and its echo can let loose an avalanche. For years Russia, France, and Great Britain, on the one hand, and Germany and Austro-Hungary, on the other, had been piling up armament and racing to build up armies and navies. It would take very little to let loose such a war as the world had never known.

Schweitzer prayed that it would not happen, but if war did come he was determined nevertheless to build his hospital. And since paper money would be almost worthless in the event of war, he was taking gold instead.

So that, while along with the rest of the world he hoped for the best, he was prepared for the worst.

[Arriving at Lambaréné[2] in French Equatorial Africa, the Schweitzers found practically no provisions and absolutely no buildings for a hospital and clinic. Beginning with rude huts, which Schweitzer himself built with the help of his trusted native helper, Joseph, the doctor made plans to build a hospital. Meanwhile he struggled to provide for his patients in a hen house converted into a "surgery."]

Lambaréné, a village of several hundred houses, mostly native huts, lies across the river from the Paris Mission post and gave the place name to the mission and the grounds on which the "hospital" was located. The main house of the mission and the boys' school were

[1] **Bordeaux** (bôr·dō'): seaport city in southwestern France.

[2] **Lambaréné** (lâɴ·bȧ·rā·nā').

on the hill farthest upstream; the Schweitzer home and the "surgery" were on the middle hill; and the girls' school and another building occupied the third.

The jungle wall was only sixty feet away and was a hundred feet high, a barrier to any breeze that might have come, and in itself was the source of heat that seemed to come from a vast furnace.

No one dreamed of using the jungle paths for a stroll or for cooling shadow. There was no other place for a walk but the rectangle of cleared land on which the mission stood, a third of a mile long and only a third of that as wide. Everyone in the settlement knew the dimensions almost to a foot, much as a prisoner knows his cell.

"If we could only cut down a corner of the jungle which shuts in the lower end of the mission," Schweitzer wrote. "We might then get a bit of breeze from the river. But we have neither the money nor the men for such a project."

He had neither the money nor the men for projects he needed more vitally.

"My work is rendered all the harder by the fact that I can keep so few drugs in the hen house. For almost every patient I have to cross to my home, there to weigh out or to prepare the needed medicine, which is very fatiguing and wastes much time. When will the work on the iron building for the hospital be seriously begun? Will it be ready before the rainy season comes? What shall I do if it is not ready then? It is so hot in the hen house that it is impossible to work there, and the sun pours in through the roof. . . . More and more patients keep coming, but my supplies are giving out. Quinine, antipyrine, bromide of potassium, salol, and dermatol, they are almost gone. . . . It may be three, four months before I get any more from Europe. . . ."

His estimate of the time was a bit of evasion. If war did come, it would not be merely a matter of months before the supplies would come. . . .

That was his mood one day. The next day, refreshed perhaps by Bach or a night of sleep less broken than usual by calls from the "surgery," he wrote:

"Yet what are all these disagreeable things compared to the joy of being here, working, helping? However limited one's means, how much one can do! Just to see the relief and joy of those who have been treated, bandaged, and given rest after they had dragged their poor bleeding feet through the jungle, that in itself makes work here worth while. . . ."

Nevertheless, trifles that would not have troubled even a laboratory assistant in Europe became almost major problems for the head of the hospital in Lambaréné.

He had to give medicines, for instance, to discharged patients to take along. In Europe there would have been containers, paper envelopes, cardboard boxes. In the steaming climate of Lambaréné paper containers simply fell apart, and only bottles and cans would do. Schweitzer had only a limited number of them, and he would beg his patients to return them to him. But they remained in the native villages as prized possessions and ornaments. Every mail from Schweitzer to friends in Europe were begging letters, for bottles big and little and other durable containers. ". . . and please don't forget the corks for the bottles, and do send some test tubes and tin cans! How I look forward to the day when I can have enough of them!"

But they were trifles, after all, in comparison with his growing imperative need for more hospital space, grounds, and buildings. For that he would have to apply to the regional heads of the missionary organization that was about to have a conference at Samkita at the end of July.

He had no choice but to go there.

One misty morning before daybreak Schweitzer and two missionaries set out in a canoe manned by twelve natives. The canoe was also loaded with pineapples, to quench the thirst of passengers and crew, and with bunches of bananas for the crew's food supply. Schweitzer wished they had more substantial food for the hard paddling they would have to do, but the natives themselves seemed to worry little about it and were singing as they started out.

But their singing stopped abruptly when the first rays of the sun showed several dark shapes swimming in the river ahead of them, and the natives gave them wide berth. They were a herd of hippopotamuses, whose moods are unpredictable, and Schweitzer approved wholeheartedly of the detours they had to make even though it meant a delay in arriving at Samkita.

Sunrise brought out the tsetse [1] flies, whose bite goes through the thickest cloth, but they shy away from bright colors, and Schweitzer and the others wore such colors for protection.

They reached Samkita by late afternoon, and at the sight of new faces, white missionaries and their Negro colleagues, Schweitzer felt an almost forgotten pleasure.

The conference lasted a week.

"I felt it inspiring to be working with men who for years had renounced so much in order to devote themselves to the services of those who had so little," Schweitzer wrote.

[1] **tsetse** (tsĕt′sē): a disease-carrying **fly.**

He was among the speakers at the conference, and he had to touch on religion. A young missionary, fresh from school and full of zeal, disagreed with some of his statements. He knew Schweitzer only as the doctor from Lambaréné, and was quite tolerant with him. "I disagree with Dr. Schweitzer," he said, "but then he can't know everything. After all, he is not a theologian."

The former head of the theological school of the Strasbourg University did not contradict him.

The conference not only approved of Schweitzer's request for more ground and a new building but also contributed some of the cost of putting it up.

On his return to Lambaréné, Schweitzer managed to round up several laborers, "after a world of trouble," and the work of clearing the site for the new building began. But the laborers proved to be "magnificently lazy," and Schweitzer had to join the work gang, while the native foreman "lay in the shade and occasionally threw us an encouraging word."

Fortunately a lumber merchant came along and lent Schweitzer eight of his workers, at the high rate of pay they demanded. In two days the site was leveled, and Schweitzer took hope. But payday dashed it, for the laborers went to Lambaréné, spent the money on a roaring drunk, and Schweitzer and Joseph had to finish the clearing in their spare time and without help.

Then a hurry call came from a woman missionary who was desperately ill at a post far up the river, and Schweitzer had to go. The trip there and back took several days.

When his canoe neared the landing Schweitzer was startled by a change in the skyline on the middle hill.

The corrugated iron building was up.

Two of the mission workers, together with Joseph and several of the natives who had come to the hospital with their sick, had combined to spring a surprise on the doctor.

Schweitzer rejoiced over it as though a palace had been presented him. There were two rooms, each thirteen feet square, and two smaller rooms under the projecting roof of thatch. The floors were cement. Along the walls were shelves of mahogany and rosewood, which along the Ogooué [1] were cheaper than the cheapest lumber elsewhere.

The addition to the hospital set off a veritable outbreak of more feverish building. Schweitzer himself did the work of several men. Joseph performed heroic labors. Two of the missionaries, M. Kast, a Swiss, and Señor Ottoman, an Argentine, who had already done much of the work on the corrugated iron building, now helped with the others.

A small new building served as a waiting room.

The corrugated iron building became the surgery.

A neatly constructed hut became Joseph's private residence. Temporary shelters went up for the families and friends of the sick.

Finally one morning the walls and the roof of the sick ward itself went up.

In the morning Schweitzer summoned sixteen patients into the building that was as yet only a shell. With a pointed stick he marked out sixteen rectangles on the earthen floor with passages between them. Each patient lay down in a rectangle. Their families and friends were sent off with axes to bring in the makings of the beds.

Canoes scurried up and down the river and were back in a few hours with cut poles, masses of jungle vines strong as rope, and piles of dried grass.

At each corner of a rectangle short, stout posts were driven into the ground, every one of them with a forked top. They supported six-foot poles for the sides of the beds and shorter ones for the ends. The tough vines were strung tightly across and were so close together that they made a resilient [2] spring for mattresses of dried grass.

Now the patients lay down on comfortable beds, with space under each for food and cooking utensils. By nightfall the problem was to keep the healthy from ousting the sick from the beds that proved so enticing.

But every improvement of the hospital became so publicized in the jungle that it brought all the more patients.

With their increase a new and vital problem arose.

The understanding had been that patients and their friends and families would bring their own food. That was the theory. What actually happened was that they seldom brought enough, especially when the patient had to stay longer than was expected.

The result was that quarrels arose among them when food shortages developed. Schweitzer was now called upon to act as judge and peacemaker, as well as doctor.

One day, for instance, a native helped himself to another's canoe at night, and went fishing. When he came back the next morning the owner of the canoe raised a commotion and demanded the fish as his. Schweitzer had to intervene.

He heard both sides, then decided.

"You are both in the right and also in the wrong," he said. "You, as owner of the canoe, are in the right because he should have asked permission to use it.

[1] **Ogooué** (ō'gô·wā'): the river on which Lambaréné is situated.

[2] **resilient** (rê·zĭl'ĭ·ĕnt): elastic.

Albert Schweitzer: theologian, philosopher, physician, organist — humanitarian. (Combine)

Therefore, you are entitled to a third of his catch. But you are also in the wrong on two counts. You should have fastened your canoe with a padlock, as you have been shown. And you are guilty of laziness. There was good moonlight for fishing and you stayed in bed."

He turned to the other. "You were wrong in taking the canoe without permission, so you owe the owner a third of the fish. But you were right in making use of the moonlight to go fishing. Therefore, you are entitled to a third of what you caught. And the hospital is entitled to a third because it took place on our grounds, and you have taken some of the doctor's time in adjusting this dispute."

However just the verdict may have been, with its profit to the hospital, it did nothing to solve the growing and basic problem of food for all.

"Paradox[1] though it may seem," Schweitzer wrote, "nowhere is it easier to starve than amidst the luxurious vegetation of the game-haunted forests of Equatorial Africa."

For, lavish though the region was with jungle growth, it was not generous with food for human beings. Practically all the citrus fruits, bananas, yams, potatoes, and other fruits and vegetables had been introduced along the Ogooué by whites. The natives had learned to grow bananas, plantains, and other foods, but cultivation had been crude and beset with difficulties. The banana rapidly exhausts the soil, and the natives have to clear the jungle for new plantations every few years. Elephant herds often raid them, and whatever they don't eat they destroy.

Rains often fail the natives, and drought brings famine.

[1] **paradox** (păr′ȧ·dŏks): a statement which seems to contradict itself.

Fishing is a fairly dependable source of supply, but in spite of the wealth of wild life in the jungles the hunting is not so good. Notwithstanding the fabled skill with bow and arrow that the primitive savage is supposed to have, it is sometimes more fable than fact; and, though many have learned to use guns in hunting, the weapons are often as poor as the natives' marksmanship. Then, too, after you have shot something high in the jungle growth you may find it almost impossible to get at it through the tangle.

All of which made it imperative for Schweitzer to develop an unfailing source of food for his hospital. He rounded up a work gang of natives and set them to clearing land for a plantation.

Just then another hurried call for him came from a distant post, and he had to take a canoe and a crew along to go there. He left word that the tract must be cleared, or nearly so, by the time he got back.

His crew and he took guns along, and the natives were looking forward to some good hunting.

But they complained throughout the trip.

"Nothing ever happens when we go with you," said their spokesman. "If we were with Mr. Calder [one of the missionaries], he would have shot some monkeys and birds. But you pass them by and never a shot!"

He pointed above their heads, at beautifully crested cranes, green and gold tree birds, and other gorgeously plumaged food.

It was a cruel dilemma for the man who had since childhood harbored a great dislike of killing living things, and whose philosophy was that all living beings must be treated with like reverence. Yet he was letting personal feelings stand in the way of food for his men.

He compromised. He shot no birds. But when a monkey showed high in the thick tangle of greenery, he fired. The body dropped through the branches but caught where it would be hard to get at. The natives tried but took so long that Schweitzer joined them.

They came back without the animal Schweitzer had shot, but in his arms was an infant monkey that had been left motherless.

Instead of adding to the food supply he had brought back one more mouth to feed.

When he got out of the canoe at Lambaréné, Schweitzer was still pondering his dilemma and the problem set up by his unwillingness to destroy any living thing.

Just then he caught sight of a movement in the grass, a pair of beautifully colored but deadly coral snakes, with their newly hatched brood. Snakes along the Ogooué are everywhere — underfoot, in the greenery, and they even drop into canoes from trees overhead. They range from the smallest of the species to the giant pythons and boa constrictors, and practically all are deadly.

Roaming in the grass near the coral snakes were several naked native children.

For some moments the artist in Schweitzer reveled in the sinister beauty of the parent snakes, and the instinctive, already exquisite grace of their young. Then he raised his gun and blasted parents and younglings into so much flying pulp.

He hurried to see what progress had been made on clearing the plantation.

Not a stroke of work had been done in his absence.

Every white at the mission was as overworked as Schweitzer, and the help they had given him in the past was at the expense of their own work. This time they had not been able to help him.

Nor had Joseph done anything about the plantation. He had taken Schweitzer's place to a remarkable extent, even performing complicated treatment of emergency patients. Though he could not read, he had memorized the looks of scores of labels on medicine bottles and had used their contents without a mistake.

Mrs. Schweitzer had not helped with the orchard. Her housework included not only her home but also the whole hospital. The laundry alone was a full-time job. In addition, she was everything from nurse to cook and surgical assistant, for Joseph had long been promoted out of the kitchen. With her husband away, in addition to all her other work, she had had to take on many of his tasks with the sick as well as with the others, from babies to the aged, with their many disputes and other personal problems.

But there in the shade, by the side of the work they were supposed to have done, lay the laborers and their foreman, taking their ease. Schweitzer came over and glared at them for a time, then the whole mission could hear his anger.

But the foreman rose and said quietly, "Do not shout at us so, Doctor; it is all your own fault. Stay here and we will work, but when you are at the hospital or away somewhere else, we are alone and do nothing."

He was faced by a condition that was as hard to change as the climate, since it was partly due to the climate.

That meant one more demand on him.

But how much more could he do? Could he even keep up what he had been doing? For he and his wife had been in Lambaréné over a year now, in a climate that was hard even on easygoing whites, and the Schweitzers had been anything but easygoing.

Schweitzer knew now that tropical anemia [1] was developing in both his wife and himself, and in addition he had caught some infection that had better be seen to by a skilled surgeon before long.

Finally Schweitzer was forced to make a painful decision. He reduced the number of his patients to a minimum, sent the others away, left Joseph in charge, and set out for Cape Lopez [2] with his wife, where they could get medical attention and some recuperation.[3]

The Schweitzers were sitting in the cabin of the river steamer, limp with heat and exhaustion, their eyes closed.

The boat had reached the mouth of the Ogooué, then made a sharp turn. Suddenly the Schweitzers were startled. They had forgotten the feel of ocean air. They opened their eyes in the breeze that came in, stared incredulously at each other, smiled like children who had been inexpressibly surprised by some marvelous gift, closed their eyes again, and let the heavenly freshness flow through their famished veins. Then they sank into the sweetest sleep, it seemed to them, that they had ever known. When they awoke, the hollows about their eyes were lighter, their eyes themselves had lost their lackluster look, and their cheeks were tinged with the faint promise of returning health.

[1] **anemia** (ȧ·nē′mĭ·ȧ): a condition in which the blood lacks its normal number of red corpuscles.

[2] **Cape Lopez:** a cape marking the southern border of the Gulf of Guinea, on the west coast of Africa.

[3] **recuperation** (rē·kū′pĕr·ā′shŭn): regaining of health and strength.

Schweitzer's infection got well of its own accord.

Meanwhile a Frenchman, whose wife had been cured at the Schweitzers' hospital, invited them to stay at his house at Cape Lopez. It was on a hill overlooking the ocean, and the Schweitzers spent whole days in armchairs on the porch, just looking at the Atlantic Ocean.

Then they went back to Lambaréné.

[During World War I, Schweitzer was forced, for a brief time, to close down the hospital when he was interned by the French authorities as a German-born alien. However, he continued his work for thirty-five years, returning to Europe only rarely to give concerts and lectures. In 1949, at the age of seventy-four, he visited America. As always before, he returned to Lambaréné, where he still remains.]

For years Schweitzer's friends in America had been urging him to come for a visit. Harvard University had invited him to deliver the Lowell Lectures and be an honored guest at the Tercentenary [4] Celebration of its founding. Dr. Albert Einstein, at that time head of the Institute for Advanced Studies at Princeton, had invited him to come there and use its facilities to finish his third volume on the philosophy of civilization. "There, in this sorry world of ours," he said of Schweitzer, "is a great man."

But Schweitzer had been afraid to come here. Gandhi, the spiritual leader and martyr of India, had also been asked to visit America but had refused. He had felt that the richest land in the world was too materialistic to understand his emphasis on the spiritual. Schweitzer had the same misgivings.

But in the summer of 1949 the two-

[4] **Tercentenary** (tûr·sĕn′tē·nĕr′ĭ): three-hundredth anniversary.

hundredth anniversary of the birth of Goethe[1] was to be celebrated, among other places, at Aspen, Colorado, under the auspices of some of the most celebrated educators, artists, and humanitarians. Schweitzer was invited to deliver an address on Goethe.

His wife and his daughter had already visited America, and their reports must have been a factor in his acceptance.

American reporters and cameramen are no respecters of persons apart from their intrinsic worth. When the queen of a European country, for instance, arrived here some years ago, a ship-news cameraman called, "Hey, Queen, park the body a little to the left, will ya?" His words caused amusement in America but no particular shock, partly because the woman expected everybody to kneel before her.

When Schweitzer arrived there was more than the usual turnout of ship-news reporters, photographers, and newsreel men. They swarmed about him, to the astonishment of many of his fellow passengers, who had not known he was on board or had never heard of him. Hardened newsmen reported that almost never before had a visiting celebrity been treated by reporters and photographers with the respect, verging on awe, they accorded Schweitzer.

And the press all over America treated him the same way. One reporter wrote of America's chance to "touch the hem of the man's garment."

Even "the man on the street" began to hear of him.

Schweitzer found that America understood him very well indeed.

He in turn was touched, for instance, when someone told him of the heavy winter storms of 1948–49 that would have killed hundreds of thousands of cattle more than it did in our West had it not been for the food that had been dropped to them from planes. "Ah," Schweitzer said with tears in his eyes, "what a magnificent achievement! *Vive L'Amérique!*"[2]

And Americans have responded, with more than words, by *their* wish for long life to Albert Schweitzer and his works.

Long ago someone asked him why he never took in the sights in the cities and countries where he gave lectures and concerts. He smiled. "I'll begin sightseeing when I am seventy-five."

He did not stop for sightseeing in America. Within a few months of his seventy-fifth birthday, he was hurrying back to the Gabon, heartened by the material and other aid he had received for the big colony of lepers he had established there.

"How wonderful have been the experiences vouchsafed me all these years!" he has written. "When I first went to Africa I prepared to make three sacrifices. To abandon the organ, to renounce the academic teaching activities to which I had given my heart, and to lose my financial independence, relying for the rest of life on the help of friends.

"These three sacrifices I had begun to make, and only my intimate friends knew what they cost me.

"But now there has happened to me what happened to Abraham when he was prepared to sacrifice his son. I, like him, have been spared the sacrifice."

Evaluating Character

1. What were the first reactions of Dr. Schweitzer's friends when they learned of his decision to become a medical missionary? What did you think of the friends? Why did they oppose his plans so much?

[1] **Goethe** (gû'tĕ): German poet and dramatist.

[2] **Vive L'Amérique** (vēv·là·mā·rēk'): Long live America!

2. What did you learn about Dr. Schweitzer from the way his friends contributed to the expedition? Why was he especially touched by one contribution? Pick out other incidents that tell you something about Schweitzer through what others say or do.

3. Was Schweitzer a " dreamer " or a practical person? Support your answer by citing specific incidents.

4. Why was Dr. Schweitzer reluctant to shoot birds and animals? Why did he compromise his belief in the two instances described here?

5. Go back to the passages quoted from Schweitzer's own writings and find sentences that reveal his character.

6. Write a half-page sketch of Dr. Schweitzer based on what you have just read.

Thinking It Over

1. Look among late 1949 magazines and in the clipping file in the library for more material on Dr. Schweitzer. You will want to read also the complete book from which this selection was taken.

2. You learned that Dr. Schweitzer has established a large leper colony in the Gabon. If you don't know the story of Father Damien, the famous " Man of Molokai," look him up, too, especially in the book *Father Damien,* by Robert Louis Stevenson.

3. We are frequently reminded in these days that the world is beset by materialism. Many people have too great a love of material objects and conveniences like automobiles, television sets, electrical appliances, and the like. Dr. Schweitzer, on the other hand, heroically gave up all comfort in order to serve humanity. Do you think that the two different ways of life can be reconciled? Must all of us choose one or the other? Discuss.

For Your Vocabulary

CONTEXT CLUES: See whether you can determine the meaning of *colleagues* (p. 233) from the nearby words. Does *saber-rattling* (p. 231) actually mean a rattling of swords in their scabbards? From the rest of the sentence, determine the meaning of *imperative need* (p. 232). What is the meaning of *dilemma* (p. 236)? of *durable* (p. 233)?

RACKHAM HOLT

Son of the South

George Washington Carver was one of this country's great men of science. He discovered many ways of using productively plants like the peanut and the sweet potato that had hitherto been wasted, with the result that he contributed to the better living of all of us. Honors of every kind were heaped upon him. Schools were named for him; medals and honorary degrees were bestowed upon him. Yet this distinguished scientist was the son of a slave.

The mother of George Washington Carver was owned by a Missouri farmer, " Uncle Mose " Carver, a man who did not believe in slavery and quickly accepted its abolition. When Carver was a baby, he and his mother were carried off by a cruel mob one day. His mother never recovered, but a neighbor brought back to Uncle Mose a tiny bundle, saying doubtfully, " I guess it's alive yet." It was. That was in 1860. The frail little boy had in him a divine spark. Against great odds he managed to get an education. He taught at the famous Tuskegee Institute, founded by Booker T. Washington, and he spent every spare moment in endless research for the benefit of others until his death in 1943. In the following selection you see George Washington Carver as a boy, already showing a desire to know things.

For Better Reading . . . It is the character-revealing incident that gives biography one of its strongest appeals. As you read this description of Carver's boyhood, keep in mind that he became one of our outstanding American scientists. What qualities are needed by a scientist? Note those qualities in the small boy that would be likely to serve him in the field of science.

THE first bright day of spring a little boy was in the woods gently scraping at the earth. He came to a piece of bark, and when he had raised it he peered into the hollowed space beneath. One by one, handling each with anxious care, he lifted from the snug hole the cans and gourds from which sprouted young shoots. He lined them up on the ground and then sat back on his thin haunches and raptly watched the twinkle of yellow sun on the brave green leaves and fronds of his ferns and his particular treasure, a begonia. The temperature in the foothills of the Ozarks sometimes fell to fifteen below zero and the ground was frozen for a foot. George had protected his plants from this winter cold, bringing them out for sun and then covering them over again. Now it was spring, and they were ready to live once more.

The neighbors knew the child had a magic way with growing things. They called him the Plant Doctor, and he made house-to-house calls in Diamond Grove to prescribe for ailing plants; sometimes cuttings wouldn't root, some were wilting, some drying, and he would recommend more or less water, more or less sun. If they were seriously ill he carried them away to his secret garden. It was far enough off and hidden by bushes and nobody knew about it but himself. There he would prune or knock out the soil and shift [1] until he had nursed them back to health and bloom. He never lost a plant in his sanatorium.

George did not know how it happened that he had a green thumb. There were a good many things he did not know. The first thing he inquired about was rain. What was rain? What made it? Then what were hail and snow? Why, for instance, was a flower? Out of one box of rose moss came different-colored flowers — yellow, white, rose, pink, striped, spotted — all from the same piece of earth. " Why? " he whispered to himself. " I wish I knew."

It was in the nature of this boy to cherish his plants in solitude and, besides, Aunt Sue Carver would not allow him to bring his trash into the house. Sometimes he smuggled in a fistful of

[1] **knock out the soil and shift:** shake off the poor soil surrounding the roots and replace it with a better type of soil.

flowers or grass or even a few heads of oats, going to bed with them gripped in his hands and waking in the morning still clutching the withered remains. Usually she would exclaim as he appeared in the doorway, "George, what have you got there?" and out would come toads or frogs, grasshoppers that leaped among the hot wheatstalks, or dragonflies that zoomed above the little stream rippling down below the cabin. Or it might be some pretty feathers or interesting-looking rocks — very much the same sort of litter he was to pick up on his rambles and bring into his laboratory all the days of his life.

As he walked back from his garden through the tall trees of walnut, oak, and hickory — people preserved their timber then — taking short steps because he was undersized, or as he hopped across the rutted fields sniffing the wet smell of damp earth freshly turned up to the sun, he piped in a high, childish falsetto. He had an impediment in his speech, the result of the whooping cough in infancy, and violent attacks of croup which he had over and over again. He stammered, and half the time no one could understand what he was trying to say; but he was forever singing. He sang, too, about his duties, which were never-ending.

The Carvers had two houses a few feet apart, one room each, the roofs of hand-split boards, and the cracks between the logs chinked with mud. But the "big" house was just for company, and when it was occupied George trotted across to it carrying the meals. In the little house lived George and his brother Jim, Aunt Sue and Uncle Mose Carver. Most of the country people called each other after this fashion; the older folk were "Uncle" or "Aunt," and the younger ones were "Cousin" this or that, though lacking any blood relationship.

No plants bloomed in the Carver home; it had no decoration of any sort. The furnishings were merely two wide wooden beds, a small spinning wheel with a treadle for fine linen and a big one for heavy wool, some stools, and a cross-legged table on which were ranged the pewter, blue- and pink-flowered dishes, and stubby, bone-handled knives and two-pronged forks — very elegant for their time. When the rains came or the autumn chill, the door and the window shutter, usually swinging wide on wooden hinges, had to be closed, and the family ate and worked by the light of tallow dips. At all seasons they went to bed with the chickens and rose at four in the morning.

Work was the order of each day. George liked some of it. He would walk down the rows in the cornfield very fast with Martha Jane Williams, Uncle Mose's niece, carrying a little bucket of corn, dropping kernels in perfect rhythm — two steps, three grains, two steps, three grains.

He could not keep up with Jim, who was not merely two years older but big and strong and very active — a handsome fellow. Being so much more healthy, Jim did the heavier work and was not around the house very much as George was. The frail and rather pathetic little boy was sick a good deal. Nevertheless, he had to do his work whether he felt well or not; there could be no lagging on a farm. The garden had to be planted and weeded and the fruit picked; the cows had to be milked, the sheep sheared, the horses fed and groomed. George often carried water to a favorite colt of Uncle Mose — a pretty animal.

Uncle Mose was more than a trader in fine horses. He bred and trained his racers and trotters so carefully that they brought high prices; three hundred dollars in Missouri in Reconstruction days [1] was the equivalent of three thousand a few years later. Men came from far distances to buy them.

His bloodhounds, too, which he kept for fox hunting, were well bred, and there were seldom less than twenty. Twenty hounds can make considerable commotion, with a mess of little puppies yelping in soprano and the big fellows baying in bass. When this sort of din arose, more often than not it was because George had stirred them up by chasing or being chased by them; they would run a man as quickly as they would a fox, once they got the habit, and Uncle Mose would soon appear and put a stop to it.

He was a strict disciplinarian in some ways. The stick-and-mud chimney of the house had cracks and niches in it, and in a certain convenient hollow a certain hen was determined to nest. One of the hounds made this joyful discovery and neglected to destroy the evidence of broken shells lying about. A sucking-egg dog was unpardonable to Uncle Mose. He switched it until it was broken of the evil habit.

Though he was a stern man, he would not tolerate cruelty. He did not swear as a rule, but anyone who wanted to hear what he could do in this respect had only to abuse stock. He learned that one of his neighbors, who had recently moved into the countryside, did not feed his horse properly. One day the fellow came driving up behind the poor rickety animal, its ears poked through a big straw bonnet on its head. George thought the hat was intended more as a decoration than as a protection against the sun and looked apprehensively at the scowl already spreading over Uncle Mose's face; even his beard appeared to bristle.

The man didn't know him very well and greeted him affably, "Mornin', Uncle Mose."

Silence was the only answer.

The man tried again, "Mornin', Uncle Mose."

Silence.

He tried to lighten the atmosphere with conversation, "What d'ya think o' my horse's bonnet?"

"Well, now, Ben, since you asked me I'll tell you. I think if the horse had less millinery and more oats it'd appreciate it more." Then he stomped away to the barn, growling in his deep voice, "A man that'd be mean to his horse'd be mean to his wife."

The Carver farm of one hundred and forty acres was almost self-contained. When someone was sick they didn't send for a doctor; they gathered roots, herbs, and barks, and prepared their own medicines. It was George's job to peel the bark from the north side of the tree; the bark was then boiled and sweetened with honey to make a drench for horses with botts.[2] He also had to collect sassafras bark and spicebushes to put in the lard and make it smell good. Ashes were saved in a hopper, and at fall hog-killing time stacks and stacks of soap, both hard and soft, were made.

Fields of flax stretched away, and hemp grew in the fence corners. Now that George's mother was gone, Aunt Sue did all the spinning on what had been Mary's wheels. She wove the cloth of flax, hemp, and wool, making heavy working garments for Uncle Mose and Jim, George's little short dresses, and her own long, billowing skirts for wear-

[1] **Reconstruction** (rē′kŏn·strŭk′shŭn) **days:** the years following the War Between the States.

[2] **botts** (bŏts): a disease of horses.

ing about the house and hoop skirts for visiting — no lady ever went out without her hoops. To dye the clothing, oak bark was used for black, hickory for yellow, and chestnut for browns. They tanned their own leather and made shoes to wear in the winter from the hides of deer, which were as plentiful as rabbits.

George learned little of what sort of person his mother had been. He could not ask Aunt Sue, because she always cried when Mary's name was mentioned. He did know that she had been honest in speech and upright in all her ways. Once Aunt Sue commented on George's remarkable co-ordination between hand and eye, saying he was like Mary that way. Mary had not been able to read — she could not tell one letter from another; but if she had ever seen a certain almanac before, she could find any page in it more quickly than Aunt Sue.

George's hands seemingly were intended for making things. He had often seen Aunt Sue knitting with her four shining needles. Then of a sudden he thought, "I can do that!" So he stood for a while, watching just how her fingers moved, and went outside and picked up turkey feathers. He stripped the barbs until just a little tuft was left at the end. Then he took the top of a mitten and the top of a stocking, raveled them out, and started knitting long strips of the different colors with his improvised needles. Occasionally thereafter he knitted something practical, but chiefly he knitted just because he wanted to know how.

The boys were allowed to do pretty much as they pleased during the intervals between tasks. The split-puncheon [1] floor had to be scrubbed every Saturday morning. George followed the prescribed routine faithfully and then settled down out of doors to the churning. That had to be finished before they could go fishing. He and Jim took turns beating and beating the old dasher,[2] but one time it simply would not get warm enough to make the butter come.

In order to hasten the processes of nature, George scooped up a dipperful of hot water from the big iron pot in which the clothes were washed and dyed and stealthily poured it in. He had tried this before and in his impatience had poured in so much the butter was spongy. Consequently he knew that if he and Jim were caught Uncle Mose would lint their jackets and they would be made to stay at home. But the fish were waiting down in the spring branch.

This time he was more careful, and finally the butter came. He presented it to Aunt Sue. She looked at it suspiciously. "Why is it so white?"

Did George reply, "It has been scalded"? He did not. He remembered the answer of the little girl whose father asked her if she knew what a lie was: "An abomination unto the Lord and an ever present help in time of trouble." A boy who wants to go fishing is not always responsible. He had recourse to this form of help and stuttered innocently, "I d-d-don't know."

Since there was the butter to prove he had worked, and it was not too white, no further reprimand [3] was forthcoming. He grabbed his miscellaneous assortment of worms, crickets, crawfish scales, and pieces of meat, and dodged down to the branch.

When George fished, often the flapping object on the end of his string was only a sucker; and nobody cared to eat it, because it was so full of bones. But

[1] **split-puncheon** (pŭn′chŭn): made of logs split and smoothed.

[2] **dasher:** the movable part of a butter churn.

[3] **reprimand** (rĕp′rĭ·mănd): a severe scolding.

he never went fishing without catching something, and his perch or catfish or sunfish or occasional eel Aunt Sue cooked in the ashes of the fireplace.

It was years before a "parlor cook" stove was brought in — a great wonder, and neighbors came from miles around to admire it. Before that, all of the cooking was done in the fireplace. Aunt Sue beat the batter and shaped it in a skillet. Then she fitted the skillet with a tight lid, set it on the coals, and piled more coals in the hollowed place on top. Out would come a savory loaf of fatty corn bread four inches deep.

As a little boy George used to make sandwiches, though he had never heard of such things. Often for dinner the family had dodgers — corn meal wet with water, patted with the hands into an ellipse,[1] and baked brown. George would take one of these dodgers which had been left on the plate, split it, lay strips of home-cured fat meat between, and start for the woods. On the way he would pull a wild onion and add it to his sandwich. Thus fortified, and with no inclination to work, he could stay out all day until suppertime, and then meander home.

Once, way back in infancy's dim, distorted memory, there was a time when no food was to be had except corn, and not much of that. It must have been sometime after the raiders had returned to the farm and tipped over the beehives one by one until they had found the money. But the hard days and hungry nights had passed, Uncle Mose's industry had made him prosperous again, and now corn — corn was everywhere. It hung yellow and drying from the smoke-blackened rafters; they ground it for gruel; they boiled it like rice; they parched it to eat as children do popcorn. They had hazelnuts, butternuts, pecans, and walnuts from the woods. Uncle Mose had plowed the fence rows, dropped in walnuts, and stepped on them. Now he had great walnut hedges around the farm.

He would have no timber cut and no holes dug on the place. A company drilled once and found a heavy vein of lead, but he would not allow them to go further. They offered a good sum to open it up, but he said no. And he made them cover the shaft and go away.

Nothing was bought save coffee and sugar. And these were bartered for farm products. The Carvers were good livers, though no waste was permitted. On Sundays they had the usual chicken dinner, and if it was not all eaten it appeared on the table for Monday breakfast; then it came on again for dinner and for supper. Uncle Mose would say as he reached for the neck, "Got to eat it sometime. Might as well do it now."

Nothing was thrown out; nothing was burned up that an animal could eat. Extra supplies were put away for use during the winter. The huge smokehouse was full of meat, butter, and lard. Apples, peaches, pears, and blackberries were laid out in the sun to dry before storing. Vegetables were banked. Cabbage plants by the hundred were turned down in trenches in the fields where they had grown, covered with six inches of dirt, and only their roots left sticking up. George would dig these as needed, slough[2] off the outer leaves, and there would be nice white cabbageheads.

Home canning was in its infancy and none too easy. But Aunt Sue had three cans she kept year after year and opened only for most unusual company. The lid of the can had a groove which she filled

[1] **ellipse** (ĕ·lĭps′): a kind of flattened sphere or football shape.

[2] **slough** (slŭf): to cast off or discard.

with a half-spun roll of cotton and covered with sealing wax.

But first you had to make the sealing wax out of beeswax. Uncle Mose, an expert bee hunter, had fifty or sixty hives. He would go out with a pan of bait of honey and beebread and burn it on live coals. The bees smelled it four or five miles away and came to sip. Then he watched which way they went, followed, and located their tree. After nightfall he and Jim smoked them out with a fire of rags and tobacco and cut the tree down. Sometimes they got a washtub full of honey. Then they cut off a section of the log, and put a top on it, and that would be the hive.

George did not participate in this operation; he watched from a distance because the bees would run for him. As it was, he was swelled up most of the time with stings. Uncle Mose did not even wear a net. Often the bees took a notion to pick out another tree for themselves, and he scraped around with his hand until he found the queen. Then he clipped her wings to keep her from wandering off in search of a new home and taking the whole swarm with her.

Wild turkeys and wild geese abounded; and once Uncle Mose killed a bear, which the family ate for a long time.

On a farm now owned by the Baynhams, there was a big cave from which a spring continually gushed forth, and it was full of bears. George would not venture too near it on this account, but he did commit a daring act of another sort one day. The Baynham place was one of the finest farms in that section, and the brick-and-frame house one of the most imposing. George was tolerated by some of the neighbors as a comical little chap; he could make them die laughing just looking at him. Others thought his prankishness pathetic and gave him special liberties. Nevertheless, he knew he had no business going beyond the kitchen. In some way, however, he got into the parlor, where the family portraits were hanging on the wall – the first paintings he had ever seen.

The lines and colors appeared very beautiful to him, and through an involved system of questioning he discovered that they had been made by someone called an "artist." He thought to himself, "He made them with his hands; he made them with his hands. I want to do that."

All the way home he said it over and over and finally, as though the thought took complete possession of him, he stammered the words aloud: "He made them with his hands; he made them with his hands. I want to do that." And the refrain sang through his head for days.

After that he was always drawing. He had nothing to draw with, but wherever he found a blank space on a stone or board or even on the ground he scratched something or other. He made colors out of pokeberries, roots, and bark, and painted on cans, wooden pails, pieces of glass, anything. This occupation was as secret as his little greenhouse in the woods; he would not dare bring any such foolishness into the house.

Uncle Mose was no more severe with Jim and George than he would have been with his own sons; boys were brought up that way. He did not teach them by the negative method – don't do this and don't do that. Once a year each would be given the privilege of going to the town of Neosho,[1] the county seat, eight miles away. But they could not go together, lest the older influence the younger. Furthermore, it was rightly judged that two children together could

[1] **Neosho** (nē·ō′shō).

concoct mischief one would not think of alone.

About a week before it was time for Jim or George to embark upon this great adventure, Uncle Mose would call them to him and pronounce a parable: "Once upon a time there were two boys in the same family. One was a spendthrift. He threw away all his money on gewgaws,[1] jewelry, and prize boxes. The other saved his money and bought a setting of eggs. He raised chickens and sold them until he had enough to buy a pig. He raised piglets and sold them until he had enough to buy a heifer. He raised a couple of calves and sold them and bought a colt. It grew into a horse, and by that time he had enough money for a saddle and bridle. Finally he was able to buy a suit of clothes."

At that point Moses Carver would stop. There was no need of his going further, because that was the highest peak to which anyone could climb.

When the time came for Jim or George, whichever was having his turn, to start for town he emptied the blacking box he used as a bank, free to spend its contents as his fancy led him. But when he returned Uncle Mose would say, "Let's see what you bought." If the old gentleman was pleased with George's straw hat or five cents' worth of fishhooks, he exclaimed with much gusto, "That's good!" He did not quite understand when the boy brought home a steel-and-bone crochet hook, so he said nothing. But he would look at Jim's big glass heart or jew's-harp and merely remark, "A fool and his money are soon parted." And that was the end of that. No scolding was necessary to drive the lesson home.

George never explained the reason for his early return from one of these trips. At first it had been exciting. He had encountered the big ornamental wagon of a medicine man and slipped through the crowd collected to hear the banjo pickers and listen to a spiel about wizard oil, which would cure anything. To hear the medicine man talk you could cut off a pup's tail, sprinkle a few drops of oil on it, and the tail would grow again in five minutes.

When this palled, George had gone walking along — his eyes delighted with such items of interest as the brick courthouse in the public square, which had two stories, one on top of the other. With so many new scenes pulling his attention this way and that, he could not be expected to watch where he was going. Suddenly, as he turned a corner, he bumped into the legs of a Negro, big and powerful. George had never seen a black face before, except his brother's; he was completely terrified and turned and ran for home without any purchase at all.

Any inclination toward gambling George may have had was nipped at his first venture. Uncle Mose's nephew Dick was full of pranks and jokes. He came over one Saturday afternoon and exclaimed, "Jim and George, come here! I'll betcha each fifteen cents ya kin put on your shoes an' tie 'em any way ya want — hard's ya kin — an' run aroun' the house three times an' they'll be ontied."

Both Jim and George promptly put on their shoes and tied the rawhide laces in hard knots. Gaily they ran around the house — this was easy money — three times. They came back panting but triumphant.

"Jest like I said," shrieked Dick. "Yur shoes is on an' tied!"

Jim declared it was a swindle and wouldn't pay. But George offered no ar-

[1] **gewgaws** (gū′gôz): showy trifles.

gument. He went to his box and fished out ten cents in paper money and five big copper coins, which he silently handed over. Gone was his little hoard, but he was cured of betting.

George did not have much time for play, but he did sometimes join the other boys at shinny. He always bore a nick in his shin where a tin can swiped him. There was no such thing as a ball. Balls made of rags were used for throwing purposes, but one of these would not have lasted long under the furious assaults of shinny. Instead, a tin can was knocked back and forth between the two teams with sticks of hickory or anything else that had a knob on it. You had to keep it going; and if you managed to knock it through the other boys' line, you won.

When George did play, he had so much fun that, like any other boy, he was likely to keep shoving off the fact that it was growing later and later and he still had to get the stock in. One particular time Uncle Mose was making one of his rare trips to Neosho and probably wouldn't be back for quite a while yet.

Finally it was unmistakably twilight, and George had to stop. But by this time the barn was so dim he couldn't see to fork the hay down. He slipped into the house, abstracted the tin lantern, and lit the candle. It was strictly forbidden to have a light in the barn with all that hay about. He was working as fast as he could by the feeble light that flickered through the holes punched through the tin when he became aware that Uncle Mose had arrived and was standing there watching him. He hurried even faster; one word of back talk and he would have been in for it. But Uncle Mose let him finish and put the lantern back, apparently counting on fear to take the place of a switching.

Parties then were for young and old together. More often than not they consisted of husking bees, apple parings, logrollings, wool pickings, or quilting parties. Uncle Mose was the best fiddler thereabouts. A really first-class party could not be held without Uncle Mose playing his fiddle. He tried taking George to one of these gatherings, but the youngster was alarmed by the crowd and the noise; he slipped out and walked home.

Little boys made cornstalk fiddles the same way little girls made rag dolls. "Cornstalk fiddle and rausum [1] bow makes best old music you ever did know." Young stalks had a better resonance than old, dried ones, and with a bow strung from a wisp of a horse's tail George could produce a sort of rhythm to jig to. He did not know anything to speak of about music; but he knew more than anybody else except Uncle Mose, and willingly showed some of the women in the neighborhood how he made music come out of an organ or guitar.

He had a wonderful memory and, at what they called their "literaries," was good at singing or debating on some such subject as "Was the mother of a chicken the hen that laid the egg or the one that hatched it?"

Shooting matches were the big thing for grownups. The men would chip in and buy a sheep or an ox and then shoot for the parts — hindquarter, foreside, and so on. If anyone hit a bull's-eye, he had another shot. Uncle Mose was so good that if he got the first try he was sure to drive the animal home. Jim practiced until he reached the same point; he, too, was ruled out, to give the others a chance.

George, on the other hand, was com-

[1] **rausum:** probably rosin (rŏz'ĭn), used on violin bows.

pletely helpless with a gun. His long suit was to bring down game with rocks. He was a center shot with a rock, and no rabbit could get out of his way. Whatever he threw at he hit. He used to throw at snowbirds, little birds that came to pick up bits of grain and seed scattered in the course of feeding the stock. He took pleasure in doing that. Then one morning he threw a sharp pellet and knocked off the top of a bird's head – scalped it. He ran and picked it up and the blood trickled over his hand. He stood and looked at it for a while until the tears started. He cried and cried and couldn't seem to stop. That was the last of the murder of the innocents.

George himself was very much like a young bird, all head and mouth. And he looked like one as he sat way out on a limb, where the huskier youths did not dare to follow, and laughed at them. His body was so slight it could go anywhere his head could go. When he was the one to be chased, he was always far ahead; muscular farm lads could climb a fence pretty fast, but George could go through any crack in it. Then he would dodge out of sight in some small hiding place and rest until he had strength to light out again. He could have kept this up all day and they could never have caught him, because they would be all worn out with steady running.

Once he came back from a chase crying. The old folks asked why he wept, but he wouldn't answer. He wouldn't tell them he had poked his head through a crack and stuck there; he couldn't wiggle through. His frame had begun to grow a little, as it ought; but this was a distinct calamity to George.

With one of Uncle Mose's hunting knives George contrived to fashion some crutches for a crippled boy, so that he might play with the others; but you couldn't just manufacture a knife. For George, a knife of his own was an impossible wish. Then one night he had a dream. He dreamed he saw a watermelon lying in a cornfield. It had been cut and partially eaten and the rind was lying at the foot of three cornstalks. Also lying at the foot of the three cornstalks was a tiny lady's knife, not much larger than a pencil, with a black handle and two blades.

George could hardly swallow his breakfast, he was in such a hurry, and it was just growing light when he made a direct line over fences and across furrows to the place of his dream. There were the three cornstalks, there were the remnants of the watermelon, and there was the knife – his to polish in the earth, his to use for whatever purpose he wished, his to keep by him always until he was a man.

This vision did not seem strange to him then, nor did he thereafter consider his special gift of sight at all odd. He merely said, "It is easy for me to foresee things." He did not speak of it as a child because it tied up somehow with faith and religion and the proverb: "Those that seek me early shall find me." But Uncle Mose did not believe in the Bible.

The Locust Grove schoolhouse, started during Reconstruction, was less than a mile from the Carver home. Here church was held each Sunday morning, a Methodist or Baptist or Presbyterian coming out from Neosho on horseback to conduct the services.

Though practically all the community life in those days centered around the church, and the Carvers were considered infidels because they did not attend, Uncle Mose was of sufficient quality and substance to be respected in spite of his unbelief.

George Washington Carver in his laboratory — a childhood curiosity about growing things and a " green thumb " started him on a long and distinguished career. (*Acme*)

If a neighbor had malaria just when the grain had ripened, Uncle Mose joined the other neighbors who came to help with the harvest. When death carried some away, he gave a piece of his land not far from the house to be used as a graveyard. Though he himself did not attend the buryings, George did. The little group of mourners stood on fence rails laid about the fresh grave to keep their feet dry, but he had been born to stand apart. A little way off from the others and alone, his feet in the mud, he watched with solemn eyes the earth reclaim its own.

The new Constitution of Missouri provided for free school instruction for all between the ages of five and twenty. But that, somehow, did not seem to include George. Though he could not go to school with white children, he was permitted to attend the Sabbath-school class which was held before the church services; and afterward he could sit on the steps and listen to the singing. Even as a very little boy he had a studious nature. He was quiet and a good listener and accepted the Word in a serious manner, wandering about afterward and holding a solitary communion with nature.

Sundays as well as weekdays he made a faithful pilgrimage to his three-by-six garden plot, occasionally digging up his plants to see if they were growing. He brooded over questions he could not answer: how roses became double, why the leaves on the same tree were different, why clover and oxalis [1] folded at night and on dark days, what insects were doing in the flowers. He longed to be able to " mix " flowers, as he called it, and planted them close together, hoping they would mix.

From the time he was virtually a baby in the woods he wanted to know the name of every stone, insect, and flower he saw. He had a book given him by Aunt Sue — Webster's old blueback speller — that had a picture of a man climbing a high cliff on the top of which stood a temple of learning. Few people thereabouts could even write, but George had studied the speller until he knew every word. However, it did not reveal the names of the birds, so he made up names to suit himself. Having once tasted of the fruit of knowledge and caught a glimpse of the mysteries hidden in words, he could not rest content.

He had not made knowledge a part of himself until he had done something with it; abstractions had to be made concrete. When stray copies of *Little Women* and *Little Men* found their way out to those parts, he said, " I can do that. I can write a book." And straightway he wrote a long, long story after what he considered was the general manner of Miss Alcott.

George looked with longing at the doors of the schoolhouse closed to him and announced grandly that someday he was going to have a school of his own where boys could learn to do cooking and housework the same as girls. He was going to teach the things he himself could do with his hands. This was childish prattle and laughed at as such. He was told he didn't know what he was talking about, which was quite true; but he stubbornly continued to cherish the notion in secret, and never entirely relinquished it.

[1] **oxalis** (ŏk'sȧ·lĭs): sorrel, a common field plant, somewhat like clover in appearance.

George had had no contact with the rest of the four million lately emancipated who were stirring with a vast racial longing for education, which would free their minds as well as their bodies. It is probable that the yearning within him was an individual thing and would have driven him on regardless of his color.

When he finally stammered out his consuming desire, the Carvers did not seek to hold him back. Accordingly this frail boy, smaller than his theoretical ten years, placed his bare black feet on the road to knowledge. Abandoning the security of home and the safety that lies in familiar things, George set out willingly to school.

Noting Incidents That Reveal Character

1. How is George revealed to have been a remarkably gifted child? Which of his characteristics shown here indicate that he had the temperament and interests necessary for someone who wishes to become a research scientist? What information or incidents support your opinion?

2. What examples of the young boy's intense curiosity can you find? What made him so anxious to obtain formal education? Do you think it was fortunate or unfortunate that he had no formal schooling until he was ten years old? Why?

Thinking It Over

1. In what ways were the early years of George Carver like those of Abraham Lincoln? What other similarities do you note between the two men?

2. When you read the description of George Carver as a small boy, how did it make you realize that it is unfair to judge people by their appearances? With all his handicaps George might have been a very lonely and miserable little boy. What saved him?

3. See if you can find *Up from Slavery*, the story of that other great American Negro, Booker T. Washington. Compare the lives and achievements of the two men. Also find out something about Tuskegee Institute.

4. What other accomplished Negroes do you know about in the fields of literature, music, sports, or the theater?

For Your Vocabulary

WORD BUILDING: To *apprehend* means to seize, in the original Latin form *apprehendere*, and even today we say that police *apprehend* a criminal. But it also means to seize an idea, or grasp a meaning, or to look forward to an approaching event with anxiety. George looked *apprehensively* at Uncle Mose's scowl (p. 243). What is the meaning here?

When the author writes "*abstractions* had to be made concrete" (p. 251), she means that George was not satisfied with a general idea until he had done something about it. How is this illustrated in the account of George's boyhood activities? However, the word *abstracted* on page 248 has a different meaning. When George *abstracted* the tin lantern, he simply took it secretly.

CONTEXT: On page 241 you read that even as a little boy George "had a green thumb." Can you give a working definition of this term from reading the paragraph in which it occurs? From the context of the rest of the sentence on page 244, what do you think "lint their jackets" means? George had "an *impediment* in his speech" (p. 242). What word a little farther on explains this term? The Carver farm was "almost self-contained" (p. 243). How does the whole paragraph following explain that phrase?

TOWARD GREATER FREEDOM

SALLY KNAPP

First Lady of the U.N.

"You are coming of age in a time when world affairs will touch your lives so closely that you will need to take a greater interest in everything that goes on in the world than did your immediate forebears. Try to learn all you can about the other people in the world. If you can learn languages easily, learn as many as possible because this nation is going to be one of the deciding factors in the world of the future."

Eleanor Roosevelt

These words are addressed personally by Mrs. Roosevelt to the young people reading this book.

Mrs. Roosevelt is not only the widow of Franklin Delano Roosevelt, our late President; she is also a very great lady in her own right. "The plain fact is," says Clare Boothe Luce, former Congresswoman from Connecticut, "that Mrs. Roosevelt has done more good deeds, on a bigger scale, for a longer time, than any other woman who ever appeared on our public scene. No woman has ever so comforted the distressed – or distressed the comfortable."

In order to get a full insight into Mrs. Roosevelt's contributions to world peace and understanding, you will want to read her autobiography, *This I Remember*. The following sketch describes her present activities, particularly as a delegate from the United States to the United Nations.

ELEANOR ROOSEVELT now lives in a conveniently located apartment in New York, but she is there very little of the time. Her base of operations is a triangular area with one apex at Hyde Park, another at Lake Success, and the third in New York. And, of course, she makes many trips away from home base, to California, Paris, or London.

Her apartment in New York is a homey place. Family portraits, ship models, and other treasures crowd her living room. Books of all kinds fill the bookshelves, and a few special favorites stand between book ends on the table. Very few books in this large library are first editions; no volume was chosen for its fine binding. It is a well-read collection, reflecting the tastes of a person interested in just about everything. The lady of the house has the same lack of formality as her apartment. Her ideas are modern, yet she remains simple and somewhat old-fashioned, in the best sense of the word.

When Eleanor Roosevelt craves a little peace and quiet, she drives up to Hyde Park, with the intention of resting there for a few days. But she rarely has time to hang up her hat before some job calls her back again. So, breathing one last lungful of fresh country air, she heads for New York again. She likes Manhattan, though. "I enjoy the hurry and bustle, the mixture of people, and the great variety of things they are doing. It stimulates me to get out and do something." As if she needed such stimulation!

Every morning she sits at the desk in the Washington Square apartment, dictating her daily column to her secretary and answering her multitudinous mail. Despite frequent interruptions by the telephone, she doesn't take long to get this work done. The words flow easily from her lips; she hesitates only now and then, for emphasis.

Eleanor Roosevelt has certainly upset the tradition that Presidents' widows should be seldom seen and never heard. After President Roosevelt's death, she announced that she intended to lead a "private and inconspicuous existence." She hasn't yet had time to get around to it. She still puts in the bustling kind of day a woman thirty years younger would find exhausting. She is more active now than she ever was as First Lady.

Certainly today, as a representative to the United Nations, she is more of a public figure than when Franklin Roosevelt was alive. When the United Nations was first being formed, our State Department was very anxious to have a woman on the team. She seemed the ideal choice. Everyone was happy when President Truman gave Eleanor Roosevelt the appointment. She took the job gladly, and dedicated herself to the United Nations and the cause of peace with the same wisdom and determination she shows in everything she does.

"I consider it an honor to work with the United Nations," she said, when she accepted the appointment. "I hope I can deserve the confidence of those who appointed me and the good will and respect of those who work with me."

The new appointee got along well with the State Department, until that body did a reverse end run on the Palestine question.[1] That offended Eleanor's sense of fairness, and her criticism became quite sharp. She did not hesitate to speak her mind on what she didn't like about this country's foreign policy.

The State Department has had a rather rude awakening. Eleanor Roosevelt does not always behave like the idealistic but impractical woman they expected her to be. There are times when she even gets "real tough" about an issue and speaks out at a United Nations meeting, and at other times she changes many "no's" to "yes's," or "maybe's," by her sensible, humble suggestions.

When she first began work with the United Nations, Eleanor Roosevelt had had little experience in dealing with public affairs at the diplomatic level. She was first to admit that her knowledge was limited. But she started with a strong desire to learn and understand, and with a real feeling of good will for all people.

With her appointment to the Human Rights Commission of the United Nations, she began a new chapter in her wide expanse of activities. She sits with the social, humanitarian, and cultural committees dealing with such world problems as refugees, world health, and equality of women. These are, in new garb, the same principles she has been fighting for on the home front for years.

The other members of the commission elected her to be their chairman. They didn't realize what an unorthodox chairman she would be. Why, she actually read the texts of what had gone on in previous meetings, word for word, instead of just skimming. And she remarked, while in Geneva for a United Nations meeting, that her hotel accommodations "seemed unnecessarily elegant." She even attended every session she was supposed to attend. When she was invited to a luncheon by the King and Queen of England, she replied: "I'd be delighted to come, but I'll have to leave early to attend a subcommittee meeting."

Her chairmanship of the Human Rights Commission is dispatched with the same efficiency with which she runs her private life. One year the commission convened in early December. The delegates groaned. "That means none of us will get home for Christmas. You know how these conferences drag on and on," they said. But they reckoned without their chairman. She has seventeen grandchildren, and feels very strongly about spending Christmas with her family.

On December 3 she announced: "I expect delegates to attend to all matters on the agenda[2] within two weeks." On December 17, the commission wound up

[1] **Palestine question:** In 1948 there was a dispute and later armed warfare between the newly formed State of Israel and the Arab nations neighboring it.

[2] **agenda** (*ȧ*·jĕn′d*ȧ*): list of things to be done.

its last piece of business. Eleanor Roosevelt's comment on this modern miracle was simply: "I just made them work from the beginning, the way delegates usually work the last few days of a conference."

Some time later, Eleanor Roosevelt presided at a meeting which climaxed her first three years of work in the United Nations. The Commission of Human Rights, after more than one hundred meetings, had finally ratified the preamble and twenty-eight articles of a document known as the Universal Declaration of Human Rights. This charter set standards for the fifty-eight member nations in regard to such rights as freedom from arbitrary arrest, the right of the individual to have an education, and the right of every person to work for a living. These are the privileges that we take for granted in the United States, but they do not exist in many other countries.

It was a long hard struggle to get fifty-eight different races, nationalities, and governments to agree to these principles, but they finally did. Once passed by the Economic and Social Council, the Declaration would have the weight of a treaty, and every nation ratifying it would agree to make its laws conform to these principles. The next step will be to devise a means of enforcing the Declaration, and of providing specific penalties for nations violating it.

Eleanor Roosevelt knows that it is not just foolish optimism to hope that, in the future, all nations may be brought together in peaceful, lasting unity. The first great step – the ratification of the Declaration – has been taken and, as she says: "These articles will be the cornerstone in the building of a peaceful world."

At meetings of the United Nations she expresses her beliefs frankly and forcibly. She has a broad, tolerant viewpoint. Even her adversaries call her one of the greatest women in America. Her fellow delegates admire her keen grasp of world affairs. At times, when she enters the Assembly, all other representatives spontaneously rise to their feet. They accord this honor only to her.

It is more than her honesty and straightforward ability that earns Eleanor Roosevelt such homage. In a world where nearly everyone has some ax to grind, she is a noble exception. She is a tower of unselfishness in an organization where individuals and nations are looking out primarily for their own interests. To many, she is the American conscience – what we might all do in the interest of world peace if we had the ability, opportunity, and the necessary "push."

Eleanor seldom allows herself the luxury of losing her patience. But she has temporarily misplaced it several times at United Nations meetings, when some politician has held forth on the perfection of our country, and the lowliness of all others. She said on one such occasion: "We cannot always be sure our government is right. We shall do our best to make it so, but we cannot believe in the rightness of some things that we know exist here. We know human nature is not perfect – in the United States as well as elsewhere. I would like to feel sure that some way was found to watch us as well as other nations."

Nothing could show more clearly that she is a thoughtful, truth-seeking person – not a blind patriot.

Eleanor Roosevelt is the kind of person who will continue to grow as long as she lives; she can't stand still; she must keep developing. Her enthusiasm is as strong as ever. At United Nations meetings, as she listens to a speech by another delegate, her enthusiasm often gets the better of her, and she grasps the triangular sign in front of her and waves it frantically, as a signal that she wants to say something.

She is now more at ease as a speaker than when she first faced an audience years ago. She also feels more free to speak, knowing that her ideas will be credited only to her, not to the President or the Administration.

Although she had been called everything, from a pacifist to a warmonger,[1] her views on world peace are very simple. It is just a matter of co-operation, she believes, and an ability to see the other fellow's point of view. World peace must be built upon confidence in one another. To those who accuse her of being too idealistic, she answers: "Remember that every step forward is the product of someone who dreamed dreams."

She is not dogmatic; she wishes only that the nations will do something to promote world peace — not necessarily in her way.

She ended one speech about peace for the future by saying, "Let's do something. If we don't do what I have suggested, let's do something else — but for heaven's sake, let's do something." Then she added: "The United States could assume leadership in the United Nations if we only knew what we wanted and felt strongly about it."

Someone once asked her what she thought of the Russian delegates with whom she came in contact at the United Nations meetings. She answered, "As individuals, I like them very much. As representatives of their government, I find them at times irritating, and at times difficult to work with. They are tied by instructions given them by their government and are allowed very little, if any, individual flexibility, which makes compromise and co-operation very difficult."

Not even the importance of being an official delegate to the United Nations can keep Eleanor Roosevelt from being herself. She puts in the same hard day of work she always has. Only an exceptionally well-disciplined person could carry out her program. When her United Nations committees are in session, she is there at nine in the morning and often doesn't get home until seven-thirty at night. When, for the thousandth time, someone marveled at all she accomplishes, she merely said, "I manage to do a lot because I'm interested in my work, and because I am blessed with good health and don't worry about things that have already happened."

Representing the United States at the United Nations is only the first of Eleanor's many post-White House activities. She has still a colossal daily schedule of talk, conferences, and personal appearances. She frequently lectures on such favorite topics of her own as international government, education, Negro problems, and labor unions for domestic workers.

Time is so precious to her that she has learned to make the most of spare moments of rest. She can fall asleep at will and has perfected the art of taking brief naps at public gatherings. Her cat-nap technique is so accomplished that only those within a few feet of her can tell she's asleep.

She can still manage a day in which she attends a breakfast conference at Bryn Mawr College, in Pennsylvania, speaks at a fund-raising luncheon for a boys' school in New York, drives to

[1] **warmonger** (wôr′mŭng′gẽr): one who attempts to stir up war.

Eleanor Roosevelt: first lady of the U.N. — her boundless enthusiasm and untiring energies have been freely dedicated to the cause of world peace. (Acme)

Poughkeepsie [1] for a Girl Scout powwow in the evening — and keeps her daily column, monthly magazine page, and multitudinous correspondence up to date.

Someone once asked her what she looked forward to most in her life out of the White House. She answered simply: "Freedom from public notice." But she will never have it, she just can't keep out of things. Her enthusiasm for a good cause is as great today as it ever was.

Eleanor is very happy in her United Nations work and considers it the climax of her career, but she could have had a dozen other posts, such as Senator from New York, or Cabinet member, or high office in any one of several government agencies. She has always said she was not interested in holding public office, probably because she thinks her freedom would be limited in the multitude of tasks she feels should be done. Pressed for an exact reason she once said: "I certainly could not run for political office while my husband was so active in politics. I am too old now. I think this is a time when young people should be encouraged to go into politics — not old ladies."

She has been an ardent feminist and a strong champion for woman's rights, but she has consistently refused all offers of high public office for herself. When asked if she felt it would have been nice to have been born a man, she answered, "No. I've often wished to be more effective as a woman — but I never felt that trousers could do the trick."

People who know her only through newspapers and magazines think of her as a homely woman, but those who have met her face to face say that pictures fail to show the queenliness and kindliness which give her face real beauty. She is not homely — merely unphotogenic.[2] She herself has said, "One has to be philosophical about pictures."

Eleanor claims that her appearance was somewhat improved by the acquisition of "two lovely new porcelain teeth." These replaced the two front teeth she had knocked out in an auto accident. It is like her to have felt so badly about falling asleep at the wheel that she penalized herself beyond the temporary suspension of her license. She confined her driving, for a long time, to the immediate vicinity of Hyde Park, though this must frequently have been very inconvenient.

When one considers how much praise and admiration have been heaped upon her, her modesty is unbelievable. She couldn't understand why, when she went abroad by plane during the war, such elaborate precautions were taken for her safety. What a target for the *Luftwaffe* [3] she would have been! She remarked that the aircraft crew seemed surprised to have a woman aboard. Evidently it never occurred to her that their surprise might have something to do with who that woman was.

She remarked to a friend that she must be getting old, when a young lady, riding with her in a bus, had risen and offered Eleanor her seat. Again it never occurred to her that this courtesy was a personal tribute.

She wishes always to do as much for herself as possible and be the least possible trouble to others. One morning at Hyde Park, she awoke to discover that nearly two feet of snow had fallen dur-

[1] **Poughkeepsie** (pô·kĭp′sĭ): a city in New York, sixty-five miles north of New York City, on the Hudson River.

[2] **unphotogenic** (ŭn·fō′tô·jĕn′ĭk): having features or facial expressions that do not photograph well.

[3] **Luftwaffe** (lo͝oft′väf′ĕ): the German air force in World War II.

ing the night. She was scheduled to broadcast that morning from Poughkeepsie, five miles away. Only main roads, at best, would be plowed by then, and it looked as though the broadcast would have to be canceled.

The telephone rang in Eleanor's study. It was the studio executive. "I really don't know what to do. I can send a sleigh to pick you up at the main road but I doubt that a horse could get through the road leading into your place," he said. "Don't worry," she answered, "I'll get to the highway all right."

An hour before broadcast time she set out. She plowed her way through, on foot, for two miles. Sometimes she had to make her way through shoulder-high drifts, piled up at the sides of the road by the wind, but she reached the highway. After the broadcast she was driven back to her jumping-off place, and she calmly hiked the two miles back to her home. "It was easy returning," she said, "because I could step in the tracks I had made on the way out."

When she went to Geneva to attend a meeting of the United Nations Commission on Human Rights, she was received with great ceremony and honor. The Swiss people waited eagerly for a glimpse of her, although one might think that, accustomed as they were to foreign dignitaries, they'd have been very bored with important people by then. Eleanor Roosevelt, however, was more to them than a statesman, more than the head of a government – she was unique. They crowded around the hotel where the meeting was to be held.

European heads of government urged her to visit them and talk to their people during her United Nations trips. "It would do more for morale than anything we can think of," kings, queens, and presidents would say. Even Stalin was no exception. His first words of greeting to Elliott Roosevelt, on his visit to Russia, were, "When is your mother coming?"

When she visited London to unveil a statue of her late husband, a London newspaper said: "She is welcome not only for her great name, but for her own endearing qualities of heart and mind." Winston Churchill added, "We must ascribe to her the marvelous feat that a crippled man, victim of a cruel affliction, was able for more than ten years to ride the storms of peace and war at the helm of the United States. The debt we owe to President Roosevelt we also owe to her."

As she entered her London hotel, all the men in the crowd outside respectfully removed their hats. That evening, as she entered the royal box at Covent Garden, the hall shook with a thundering ovation.

The position she holds in the world today far surpasses that which she held when she was First Lady, although it is unofficial. A recent poll conducted by the *Woman's Home Companion* indicates that in the minds of thousands of readers she is the most popular living American of either sex. The New York *Times* once said:

"She could be elected 'Mrs. America' by a landslide of votes." There are a great many who would elect her "First Lady of the World."

As long as she lives, Eleanor Roosevelt will have a hand in shaping her country's destinies – and the destinies of the world.

Thinking It Over

1. What impression do you get of Mrs. Roosevelt as a personality? In what ways do you suppose she has, in her career,

" comforted the distressed — or distressed the comfortable "? Find examples in the text.

2. Name several of Mrs. Roosevelt's qualities as a person. Read aloud passages in illustration of each.

3. Have you ever read Mrs. Roosevelt's syndicated newspaper column, " My Day "? What do you think of it?

4. The author says Mrs. Roosevelt is not a " blind patriot " and gives an illustrative incident. What is meant by this?

5. On page 256, in the paragraph beginning " Not even the importance . . ." there are several important secrets to personal happiness. What are they? How would you apply them to the careers of other figures in this book?

For Your Vocabulary

WORD ORIGINS: *Multus,* from the Latin, means " much " or " many." A *multitude* is a large group of persons; the adjective *multitudinous* means " many things " — or simply " many," or " in great quantities." What meaning can you give to these words: *multiply, multicolored, multiform, multimillionaire, multisyllabic?*

The terms *orthodox* and *unorthodox* are exact opposites. If a person's actions are *orthodox,* they are conventional or approved or generally acceptable. This is a word of Greek origin meaning " right in opinion." What would *unorthodox* mean when used to describe a baseball pitcher? a religious belief or group of worshippers? a procedure undertaken by a business concern? What is your own most unorthodox habit?

SYNONYMS: Choose the term in each series that most nearly matches the italicized one:

1. *inconspicuous* — helpless, unexplainable, unplanned, not noticeable.
2. *convened* — withdrew, disbanded, deliberated, assembled.
3. *ratified* — approved, disapproved, outlawed, discussed.
4. *arbitrary* — disagreeable, without reason, generous, vigorous.
5. *adversaries* — beliefs, desires, advertisements, opponents.
6. *dogmatic* — opinionated, automatic, sullen, orderly.

CARL SANDBURG

Abe Lincoln Grows Up

In all the long line of America's great men, there is no more beloved figure than that of Abraham Lincoln, who was born in poverty, rose to the highest office in the land, and died a martyr to his belief in the equal rights of all men. Many writers have told his story; in fact, more books have been written about Lincoln than about any other person in history. One of the most appealing biographies is Carl Sandburg's *Abe Lincoln Grows Up.*

In an earlier part of the book, Sandburg tells what is known of the Lincoln family from Revolutionary days down to the time a son is born to Nancy Hanks. They were hardy, active, typical American frontiersmen, playing their part in the Revolution, in fighting the Indians, in pushing back the wilderness.

Thomas Lincoln, Abe's father, lived in various places in Kentucky, hiring out to farmers, learning the carpenter's trade, finally buying a farm of his own near Elizabethtown in Hardin County. The region was still wilderness, with only a few farms and settlements. Life was a constant struggle with nature and against the Indians. The manners of the frontiersmen were understandably crude. Grudges were settled by fist fights, and the stocks and the whipping post were still accepted methods of punishment.

In this rough country Tom Lincoln courted and married Nancy Hanks and took her to live in a cabin close to the courthouse in Elizabethtown. Tom worked hard and became known as a reliable man whose word could be depended upon. Nancy Hanks believed in God and her Bible. She worked hard and suffered much, but she kept her eyes fixed on the promise of eternal glory.

The first child of Tom and Nancy was a daughter, Sarah. In 1808 they "moved out from Elizabethtown to the farm of George Brownfield, where Tom did carpenter work and helped farm." Here the Lincolns occupied a cabin of their own among the wild crab-apple trees. They didn't stay long, however — pioneers were always on the move. Their next home was destined to become famous in history, for it was here that Abe was born and spent his earliest years.

For Better Reading . . . In reading a newspaper article, or a biography or essay, it is important to pay attention to the detailed information presented. Keep the facts in mind as you read along so that later references to them will be clear. This is just like keeping the plot of a story straight. Secondly, be ready to go behind the facts. Not every idea or statement is presented directly by the writer. You are expected to draw conclusions from the facts you find.

On the Knob Creek farm the child Abraham Lincoln learned to talk, to form words with the tongue and the roof of the mouth and the force of the breath from lungs and throat. "Pappy" and "Mammy," the words of the people meaning "father" and "mother," were among the first syllables. He learned what the word *name* meant; his name was Abraham, the same as Abraham in the Bible, the same as his grandfather Abraham. It was "Abe" for short; if his mother called in the dark, "Is that you, Abe?" he answered, "Yes, Mammy, it's me." The name of the family he belonged to was "Lincoln" or "Linkun," though most people called it "Linkern" and it was sometimes spelled "Linkhorn."

The family lived there on Knob Creek farm, from the time Abe was three or so till he was past seven years of age. Here he was told "Kaintucky" meant the state he was living in; Knob Creek farm, the Rock Spring farm where he was born, Hodgenville, Elizabethtown, Muldraugh's Hill, these places he knew, the land he walked on, was all part of Kentucky.

Yet it was also part of something bigger. Men had been fighting, bleeding, and dying in war, for a country, "our country"; a man couldn't have more than one country any more than he could have more than one mother; the name of the mother country was the "United States"; and there was a piece of cloth with red and white stripes having a blue square in its corner filled with white stars; and this piece of cloth they called "a flag." The flag meant the "United States." One summer morning his father started the day by stepping out of the front door and shooting a long rifle into the sky; and his father explained it was the day to make a big noise because it was the "Fourth of July," the day the United States first called itself a "free and independent" nation.

His folks talked like other folks in the neighborhood. They called themselves "pore" people. A man learned in books was "eddicated." What was certain was "sartin." The syllables came through the nose; joints were "jints"; fruit "spiled" instead of spoiling; in corn-planting time they "drapped" the seeds. They went on errands and "brung" things back. Their dogs "follered" the coons. Flannel was "flannen," a bandanna a "bandanner," a chimney a "chimbly," a shadow a "shadder," and mosquitoes plain "skeeters." They "gethered" crops. A creek was a "crick," a cover a "kiver."

A man silent was a "say-nothin'." They asked, "Have ye et?" There were dialogues, "Kin ye?" "No, I cain't." And if a woman had an idea of doing something she said, "I had a idy to." They made their own words. Those who spoke otherwise didn't belong, were "puttin' on." This was their wilderness lingo; it had gnarled bones and gaunt hours of their lives in it.

Words like *independent* bothered the boy. He was hungry to understand the meanings of words. He would ask what *independent* meant and when he was told the meaning he lay awake nights thinking about the meaning of the meaning of *independent*. Other words bothered him, such as *predestination*. He asked the meaning of that and lay awake hours at night thinking about the meaning of the meaning.

Seven-year-old Abe walked four miles a day going to the Knob Creek school to learn to read and write. Zachariah [1] Riney and Caleb [2] Hazel were the teachers who brought him along from A B C to where he would write the name "A-b-r-a-h-a-m L-i-n-c-o-l-n" and count numbers beginning with *one, two, three,* and so on. He heard "twice two is four."

The schoolhouse was built of logs, with a dirt floor, no window, one door. The scholars learned their lessons by saying them to themselves out loud till it was time to recite; alphabets, multiplication tables, and the letters of spelled words were all in the air at once. It was a "blab school"; so they called it.

The Louisville and Nashville pike running past the Lincoln cabin had many different travelers. Covered wagons came with settlers moving south and west, or north to Ohio and Indiana; there were peddlers with knickknacks to spread out and tell the prices of; Congressmen, members of the legislature meeting at Lexington, men who had visited Henry Clay at Ashland.

Coming back from a fishing trip, with one fish, Abe met a soldier who came from fighting in the Battle of New Orleans with General Jackson, and Abe, remembering his father and mother had told him to be good to soldiers, handed the soldier the one fish.

The Lincolns got well acquainted with Christopher Columbus Graham, a doctor, a scientist, who was beginning to study and write books about the rocks, flowers, plants, trees, and wild animals of Kentucky; Graham slept in the bed while the Lincolns slept on the floor of the cabin, more than once; he told in the evening talk about days camping with Daniel Boone, and running backward with Boone so as to make foot tracks pointing forward to mislead the

[1] **Zachariah** (zăk'*ȧ*·rī'*ȧ*).
[2] **Caleb** (kā'lĕb).

Indians; he talked about stones, leaves, bones, snakeskins he was carrying in a sack back to Louisville; he mentioned a young storekeeper at Elizabethtown, named John James Audubon, who had marvelous ways with birds and might someday write a great book about birds. The boy Abe heard traveling preachers and his father talk about the times when they held church meetings in cabins, and every man had his rifle by his side, and there were other men with rifles outside the cabin door, ready for Indians who might try to interrupt their Sabbath worship. And the boy never liked it when the talkers slung around words like *independent* and *predestination,* because he lay awake thinking about those long words.

Abe was the chore boy of the Knob Creek farm as soon as he grew big enough to run errands; to hold a pine knot at night lighting his father at a job; or to carry water, fill the woodbox, clean ashes from the fireplace, hoe weeds, pick berries, grapes, persimmons for beer-making. He hunted the timbers and came back with walnuts, hickory and hazel nuts. His hands knew the stinging blisters from using a hoe handle back and forth a summer afternoon, and in autumn the mash of walnut stain that wouldn't wash off with all the rinsing and scrubbing of Nancy Hanks's homemade soap. He went swimming with Austin Gollaher; they got their backs sunburned so the skin peeled off.

Wearing only a shirt – no hat nor pants – Abe rode a horse hitched to a "bull-tongue" plow of wood shod with iron. He helped his father with seed corn, beans, onions, potatoes. He ducked out of the way of the heels of the stallion and brood mares his father kept and paid taxes on.

The father would ride away to auctions, once coming home with dishes, plates, spoons, and a washbasin, another time with a heifer, and again with a wagon that had been knocked down to the highest bidder for eight and one-half cents.

Abe and his sister picked pails of currants and blueberries for Mother Nancy to spread in the sun to dry and put away for winter eating. There were wild grapes and pawpaws; there were bee trees with wild honey; there were wild crab apples and red haws. If it was a good corn year, the children helped shell the corn by hand and put it between two big flat stones, grinding it into corn meal. The creeks gave them fish to fry. Tom Lincoln took his gun and brought back prairie turkey, partridge, rabbit, sometimes a coon,[1] a bear, or a deer; and the skins of these big animals were tanned, cut, and sewed into shirts, trousers, moccasins; the coonskins made caps.

There were lean times and fat, all depending on the weather, the rains, or floods, how Tom Lincoln worked and what luck he had fishing and hunting. There were times when they lived on the fat of the land and said God was good; other times when they just scraped along and said they hoped the next world would be better than this one.

It was wilderness. Life dripped with fat and ease. Or it took hold with hunger and cold. All the older settlers remembered winter in the year 1795, when "cold Friday" came; Kentucky was "cold as Canada," and cows froze to death in the open fields. The wilderness is careless.

In the fall of the year 1816 Abe watched his father cut down trees, cut out logs, and fasten those logs into a

[1] **coon:** abbreviation of *raccoon.*

flatboat on Knob Creek. Abe ran after tools his father called for, sometimes held a hammer, a saw, and a knife in his hands ready to give his father the next one called for. If his father said, "Fetch me a drink of water," the boy fetched; his legs belonged to his father. He helped carry chairs, tables, household goods, and carpenter's tools, loading them on to the flatboat. These, with four hundred gallons of whisky, "ten bar'ls," Tom had loaded on to the boat, made quite a cargo. Tom Lincoln, who was not much of a drinking man, had traded his farm for whisky, which was a kind of money in that day, and twenty dollars cash.

Nancy Hanks and Sarah and Abe stayed on the farm while the husband and father floated down Knob Creek to Salt River and into the Ohio River. Tom was out of luck when the flatboat turned over so that the tool chest, household goods, and four barrels of whisky slid out of the boat. Most of the whisky and some of the other goods he managed to fish up from the river bottom. Then he crossed the Ohio River, landed on the Indiana side at Thompson's Ferry, and left his whisky and household goods at the house of a man called Posey.

He started off on foot into the big timbers of what was then Perry County, later divided into Spencer County. He decided to live and to farm on a quarter section [1] of land on Little Pigeon Creek; he notched the trees with his ax, cleared away brush and piled it, as the government land laws required. This was his "claim," later filed at the Land Office in Vincennes, Indiana, as the Southwest Quarter of Section Thirty-two, Town Four South, Range Five West, to be paid for at two dollars an acre. His Indiana homestead was now ready for a cabin and a family; he walked back to the Knob Creek home in Kentucky and told the family he reckoned they'd all put in the winter up in "Indianny."

They had fifty miles to go, in a straight line "as the crow flies," but about one hundred miles with all the zigzags and curves around hills, timbers, creeks, and rivers.

Pots, pans, kettles, blankets, the family Bible, and other things were put into bags and loaded on two horses. Nancy and Sarah climbed on one horse, Tom and Abe on the other. When it was hard going for the horses, the father and mother walked. Part of the way on that hundred-mile ride made little Abe's eyes open. They were going deeper into the wilderness. In Kentucky there were ten people to the square mile and in Indiana only three. As Abe sat on the horse plodding along, he saw miles and miles of beeches, oaks, elms, hard and soft maples, hung and run over with the scarlet streamers and the shifting gray hazes of autumn.

Then they came to the Ohio River. The Frenchmen years before named it "La Belle Riviere," [2] meaning it was a sheen of water as good to look at as a beautiful woman. There she lay – the biggest stretch of shining water his eyes had ever seen. And Abe thought how different it was from Knob Creek, which he could walk across on a log – if he didn't let his feet slip from under. They crossed the river, and at the house of the man called Posey they got a wagon, loaded the barrels of whisky and the household goods, and drove sixteen miles to their "claim." The trail was so

[1] **quarter section:** A section is a square mile. A quarter section is one-fourth of that, or one hundred and sixty acres.

[2] **La Belle Riviere** (lȧ bĕl rē·vyĕr′): The Beautiful River.

narrow that a few times Tom Lincoln got off the wagon with an ax and cut brush and trees so the wagon could pass through. It was a hired wagon and horses they came with, and the wagon and horse team were taken back to Posey.

Tom Lincoln, his wife, boy, and girl, had arrived on a claim at Little Pigeon Creek, without a horse or a cow, without a house, with a little piece of land under their feet and the wintry sky high over. Naked they had come into the world; almost naked they came to Little Pigeon Creek, Indiana.

The whole family pitched in and built a pole shed or "half-faced camp." On a slope of ground stood two trees about fourteen feet apart, east and west. These formed the two strong corner posts of a sort of cabin with three sides, the fourth side open, facing south. The sides and the roof were covered with poles, branches, brush, dried grass, mud; chinks were stuffed where the wind or rain was trying to come through. At the open side a log fire was kept burning night and day. In the two far corners inside the camp were beds of dry leaves on the ground. To these beds the sleepers brought their blankets and bearskins.

Here they lived a year. In the summertime and fair weather the pole shed was snug enough. When the rainstorms or wind and snow broke through and drenched the place, or when the south or southwest wind blew the fire smoke into the camp so those inside had to clear out, it was a rough life.

As Abe Lincoln, seven years old, going on eight, went to sleep on his bed of dry leaves in a corner of the pole shed there on Little Pigeon Creek, in Indiana, in the winter of 1816, he had his thoughts, his feelings, his impressions. He shut his eyes, and looking glasses began to work inside his head; he could see Kentucky and the Knob Creek farm again; he could see the Ohio River shining so far across that he couldn't begin to throw a stone from one side to the other.

And while his eyes were shut he could see the inside of the pole shed, the floor of earth and grass, the frying pan, the cooking pot, the water pail he and his sister carried full of water from the spring a mile away, and the log fire always kept burning. And sometimes his imagination, his shut eyes, and their quick-changing looking glasses would bring the whole outdoor sky and land indoors, into the pole shed, into the big shifting looking glasses inside of his head. The mystery of imagination, of the faculty of reconstruction and piecing together today the things his eyes had seen yesterday – this took hold of him and he brooded over it.

One night he tried to sleep while his head was working on the meaning of the heavy and mysterious words standing dark on the pages of the family Bible; the stories his mother told him from those pages; all the people in the world drowned, the world covered with water, even Indiana and Kentucky, all people drowned except Noah and his family; the man Jonah swallowed by a whale and after days coming out of the belly of the whale; the Last Day to come, the stars dropping out of the sky, the world swallowed up in fire.

And one night this boy felt the southwest wind blowing the log-fire smoke into his nostrils. And there was a hoot owl crying, and a shaking of branches in the beeches and walnuts outside, so that he went to the south opening of the shed and looked out on a winter sky with a high quarter-moon and a white shine of thin frost on the long open spaces of the sky.

And an old wonder took a deeper hold on him, a wonder about the loneliness of life down there in the Indiana wilderness, and a wonder about what was happening in other places over the world, places he had heard people mention, cities, rivers, flags, wars, Jerusalem, Washington, Baltimore.

He might have asked the moon, "What do you see?" And the moon might have told him many things.

That year of 1816 the moon had seen sixteen thousand wagons come along one turnpike in Pennsylvania, heading west, with people hungry for new land, a new home, just like Tom Lincoln. Up the Mississippi River that year had come the first steamboat to curve into the Ohio River and land passengers at Louisville. The moon had seen the first steamboat leave Pittsburgh and tie up at New Orleans. New wheels, wagons, were coming, an iron horse snorting fire and smoke. Rolling mills, ingots, iron, steel, were the talk of Pennsylvania; a sheet-copper mill was starting in Massachusetts.

When Napoleon sold to Jefferson the Great Plains between the Mississippi River and the Rocky Mountains, the moon saw only a few Indians, buffalo hunters and drifters, living there. The price for the land was fifteen million dollars; Jefferson had to argue with people who said the price was too high. Such things the moon had seen. Also, out of war-taxed and war-crippled Europe the moon could see steady lines of ships taking people from that part of the round world across the water to America. Also, lines of ships sailing to Africa with whisky, calico, and silk, and coming back loaded with Negroes.

And as the wagons, by thousands a year, were slipping through the passes of the Allegheny [1] Mountains, heading west for the two-dollar-an-acre government land, many steered clear of the South; they couldn't buy slaves; and they were suspicious of slavery; it was safer to go farming where white men did all the work. At first the stream of wagons and settlers moving west had kept close to the Ohio River. Then it began spreading in a fan shape up north and west.

The moon could see, along the pikes, roads, and trails heading west, broken wagon wheels with prairie grass growing up over the spokes and hubs. And near by, sometimes, a rusty skillet, empty moccasins, and the bones of horses and men.

In the hot dog days,[2] in the long rains, in the casual blizzards, they had stuck it out — and lost. There came a saying, a pithy, perhaps brutal folk proverb, "The cowards never started and the weak ones died by the way."

Such were a few of the many, many things the moon might have told little Abe Lincoln, nearly eight years old, on a winter night in 1816 on Little Pigeon Creek, in the Buckhorn Valley, in southern Indiana — a high quarter-moon with a white shine of thin frost on the long open spaces of the sky.

He was of the blood and breath of many of these things, and would know them better in the years to come.

During the year 1817 little Abe Lincoln, eight years old, going on nine, had an ax put in his hands and helped his father cut down trees and notch logs for the corners of their new cabin, forty yards from the pole shed where the

[1] **Allegheny** (ăl′ĕ·gā′nĭ).

[2] **dog days:** the sultry, close period of summer.

family was cooking, eating, and sleeping.

Wild turkey, ruffed grouse, partridge, coon, rabbit, were to be had for the shooting of them. Before each shot Tom Lincoln took a rifle ball out of a bag and held the ball in his left hand; then with his right hand holding the gunpowder horn, he pulled the stopper with his teeth, slipped the powder into the barrel, followed with the ball; then he rammed the charge down the barrel with a hickory ramrod held in both hands, looked to his trigger, flint, and feather in the touchhole – and he was ready to shoot, to kill for the home skillet.

Having loaded his rifle just that way several thousand times in his life, he could do it in the dark or with his eyes shut. Once Abe took the gun as a flock of wild turkeys came toward the new log cabin, and, standing inside, shot through a crack and killed one of the big birds; and after that, somehow, he never felt like pulling the trigger on game birds. A mile from the cabin was a salt lick where deer came; there the boy could have easily shot the animals, as they stood rubbing their tongues along the salty slabs or tasting of a saltish ooze. His father did the shooting; the deer killed gave them meat for Nancy's skillet; and the skins were tanned, cut, and stitched into shirts, trousers, mitts, moccasins. They wore buckskin; their valley was called the Buckhorn Valley.

After months the cabin stood up, four walls fitted together with a roof, a one-room house eighteen feet square, for a family to live in. A stick chimney plastered with clay ran up outside. The floor was packed and smoothed dirt. A log fire lighted the inside; no windows were cut in the walls. For a door there was a hole cut to stoop through. Bedsteads were cleated to the corners of the cabin; pegs stuck in the side of a wall made a ladder for young Abe to climb up in a loft to sleep on a hump of dry leaves; rain and snow came through chinks of the room onto his bearskin cover. A table and three-legged stools had the top sides smoothed with an ax, and the bark side under, in the style called "puncheon."

A few days of this year in which the cabin was building, Nancy told Abe to wash his face and hands extra clean; she combed his hair, held his face between her two hands, smacked him a kiss on the mouth, and sent him to school – nine miles and back – Abe and Sally hand in hand hiking eighteen miles a day. Tom Lincoln used to say Abe was going to have "a real eddication," explaining, "You air a-goin' to larn readin', writin', and cipherin'."

He learned to spell words he didn't know the meaning of, spelling the words before he used them in sentences. In a list of "words of eight syllables accented upon the sixth," was the word *incomprehensibility*. He learned that first, and then such sentences as "Is he to go in?" and "Ann can spin flax."

Some neighbors said, "It's a pore make-out of a school," and Tom complained it was a waste of time to send the children nine miles just to sit with a lot of other children and read out loud all day in a "blab" school. But Nancy, as she cleaned Abe's ears in corners where he forgot to clean them, and as she combed out the tangles in his coarse, sandy black hair, used to say, "Abe, you go to school now, and larn all you kin." And he kissed her and said, "Yes, Mammy," and started with his sister on the nine-mile walk through timberland where bear, deer, coon, and wildcats ran wild.

Fall time came with its early frost and

they were moved into the new cabin, when horses and a wagon came breaking into the clearing one day. It was Tom and Betsy Sparrow and their seventeen-year-old boy, Dennis Hanks, who had come from Hodgenville, Kentucky, to cook and sleep in the pole shed of the Lincoln family till they could locate land and settle. Hardly a year had passed, however, when both Tom and Betsy Sparrow were taken down with the " milk sick," beginning with a whitish coat on the tongue. Both died and were buried in October on a little hill in a clearing in the timbers near by.

Soon after, there came to Nancy Hanks Lincoln that white coating of the tongue; her vitals burned; the tongue turned brownish; her feet and hands grew cold and colder, her pulse slow and slower. She knew she was dying, called for her children, and spoke to them her last choking words. Sarah and Abe leaned over the bed. A bony hand of the struggling mother went out, putting its fingers into the boy's sandy black hair; her fluttering guttural words seemed to say he must grow up and be good to his sister and father.

So, on a bed of poles cleated to the corner of the cabin, the body of Nancy Hanks Lincoln lay, looking tired . . . tired . . . with a peace settling in the pinched corners of the sweet, weary mouth, silence slowly etching away the lines of pain and hunger drawn around the gray eyes where now the eyelids closed down in the fine pathos of unbroken rest, a sleep without interruption settling about the form of the stooped and wasted shoulder bones; looking to the children who tiptoed in, stood still, cried their tears of want and longing, whispered " Mammy, Mammy," and heard only their own whispers answering; looking to these little ones of her brood as though new secrets had come to her in place of the old secrets given up with the breath of life.

And Tom Lincoln took a log left over from the building of the cabin, and he and Dennis Hanks whipsawed [1] the log into planks, planed the planks smooth, and made them of a measure for a box to bury the dead wife and mother in. Little Abe, with a jackknife, whittled pine-wood pegs. And then, while Dennis and Abe held the planks, Tom bored holes and stuck the whittled pegs through the bored holes. This was the coffin, and they carried it the next day to the same little timber clearing near by, where a few weeks before they had buried Tom and Betsy Sparrow. It was in the way of the deer run leading to the saltish water; light feet and shy hoofs ran over those early winter graves.

So the woman, Nancy Hanks, died, thirty-six years old, a pioneer sacrifice, with memories of monotonous, endless, everyday chores, of mystic Bible verses read over and over for their promises, and with memories of blue wistful hills and a summer when the crab-apple blossoms flamed white and she carried a boy child into the world.

She had looked out on fields of blue-blossoming flax and hummed " Hey, Betty Martin, tiptoe, tiptoe "; she had sung of bright kingdoms by and by and seen the early frost leaf its crystals on the stalks of buttonweed and redbud; she had sung:

You may bury me in the East,
You may bury me in the West,
And we'll all rise together in that morning.

Some weeks later, when David Elkin, elder of the Methodist church, was in that neighborhood, he was called on to

[1] **whipsawed:** sawed with a special long slender saw.

speak over the grave of Nancy Hanks. He had been acquainted with her in Kentucky, and to the Lincoln family and a few neighbors he spoke of good things she had done, sweet ways she had of living her life in this Vale of Tears, and her faith in another life yonder past the River Jordan.

The " milk sick " took more people in that neighborhood the same year, and Tom Lincoln whipsawed planks for more coffins. One settler lost four milch cows [1] and eleven calves. The nearest doctor for people or cattle was thirty-five miles away. The wilderness is careless.

Lonesome and dark months came for Abe and Sarah. Worst of all were the weeks after their father went away, promising to come back.

Elizabethtown, Kentucky, was the place Tom Lincoln headed for. As he footed it through the woods and across the Ohio River, he was saying over to himself a speech – the words he would say to Sarah Bush Johnston, down in Elizabethtown. Her husband had died a few years before, and she was now in Tom's thoughts.

He went straight to the house where she was living in Elizabethtown, and, speaking to her as " Miss Johnston," he argued: " I have no wife and you no husband. I came a-purpose to marry you. I knowed you from a gal and you knowed me from a boy. I've no time to lose; and if you're willin' let it be done straight off."

Her answer was, " I got debts." She gave him a list of the debts; he paid them; a license was issued; and they were married on December 2, 1819.

He could write his name; she couldn't write hers. Trying to explain why the two of them took up with each other so quickly, Dennis Hanks at a later time said, " Tom had a kind o' way with women, an' maybe it was somethin' she took comfort in to have a man that didn't drink an' cuss none."

Little Abe and Sarah, living in the lonesome cabin on Little Pigeon Creek, Indiana, got a nice surprise one morning when four horses and a wagon came into their clearing, and their father jumped off; then Sarah Bush Lincoln, the new wife and mother; then John, Sarah, and Matilda Johnston, Sarah Bush's three children by her first husband. Next off the wagon came a feather mattress, feather pillows, a black-walnut bureau, a large clothes chest, a table, chairs, pots and skillets, knives, forks, spoons.

Abe ran his fingers over the slick wood of the bureau, pushed his fist into the feather pillows, sat in the new chairs, and wondered to himself, because this was the first time he had touched such fine things, such soft slick things.

" Here's your new mammy," his father told Abe as the boy looked up at a strong, large-boned, rosy woman, with a kindly face and eyes, with a steady voice, steady ways. The cheekbones of her face stood out and she had a strong jawbone; she was warm and friendly for Abe's little hands to touch, right from the beginning. As one of her big hands held his head against her skirt, he felt like a cold chick warming under the soft feathers of a big wing. She took the cornhusks Abe had been sleeping on, piled them in the yard, and said they would be good for a pigpen later on; and Abe sunk his head and bones that night in a feather pillow and a feather mattress.

Ten years pass with that cabin on Little Pigeon Creek for a home, and that farm and neighborhood the soil for

[1] **milch** (mĭlch) **cows:** cows giving milk.

growth. There the boy Abe grows to be the young man, Abraham Lincoln.

Ten years pass and the roots of a tree spread out finding water to carry up to branches and leaves that are in the sun; the trunk thickens, the forked limbs shine wider in the sun, they pray with their leaves in the rain and the whining wind; the tree arrives, the mystery of its coming, spreading, growing, a secret not even known to the tree itself; it stands with its arms stretched to the corners the four winds come from, with its murmured testimony, "We are here, we arrived, our roots are in the earth of these years," and beyond that short declaration, it speaks nothing of the decrees, fates, accidents, destinies, that made it an apparition of its particular moment.

Abe Lincoln grows up. His father talks about the waste of time in "eddication"; it is enough "to larn readin', writin', cipherin'"; but the stanch, yearning stepmother, Sarah Bush Lincoln, comes between the boy and the father. And the father listens to the stepmother and lets her have her way.

When he was eleven years old, Abe Lincoln's young body began to change. The juices and glands began to make a long, tall boy out of him. As the months and years went by, he noticed his lean wrists getting longer, his legs too, and he was now looking over the heads of other boys. Men said, "Land o' Goshen, that boy air a-growin'!"

As he took on more length, they said he was shooting up into the air like green corn in the summer of a good corn year. So he grew. When he reached seventeen years of age, and they measured him, he was six feet, nearly four inches, high, from the bottoms of his moccasins to the top of his skull.

These were years he was handling the ax. Excepting in spring-plowing time and the fall fodder pulling, he was handling the ax nearly all the time. The insides of his hands took on callus thick as leather. He cleared openings in the timber, cut logs and puncheons, split firewood, built pigpens.

He learned how to measure with his eye the half-circle swing of the ax so as to nick out the deepest possible chip from off a tree trunk. The trick of swaying his body easily on the hips so as to throw the heaviest possible weight into the blow of the ax — he learned that.

On winter mornings he wiped the frost from the ax handle, sniffed sparkles of air into his lungs, and beat a steady cleaving of blows into a big tree — till it fell — and he sat on the main log and ate his noon dinner of corn bread and fried salt pork — and joked with the gray squirrels that frisked and peeped at him from high forks of near-by walnut trees.

He learned how to make his ax flash and bite into a sugar maple or a sycamore. The outside and the inside look of black walnut and black oak, hickory and jack oak, elm and white oak, sassafras, dogwood, grapevines, sumac — he came on their secrets. He could guess close to the time of the year, to the week of the month, by the way the leaves and branches of trees looked. He sniffed the seasons.

Often he worked alone in the timbers, all day long with only the sound of his own ax, or his own voice speaking to himself, or the crackling and swaying of branches in the wind, and the cries and whirs of animals; of brown and silver-gray squirrels; of partridges, hawks, crows, turkeys, sparrows, and the occasional wildcats.

The tricks and whimsies of the sky, how to read clear skies and cloudy weather; the creeping vines of ivy and wild grape; the recurrence of dogwood blossoms in spring; the ways of snow, rain, drizzle, sleet, the visitors of sky and weather coming and going hour by hour — he tried to read their secrets; he tried to be friendly with their mystery.

So he grew, to become hard, tough, wiry. The muscle on his bones and the cords, tendons, cross weaves of fiber, and nerve centers — these became instruments to obey his wishes. He found with other men he could lift his own end of a log — and more too. One of the neighbors said he was strong as three men. Another said, " He can sink an ax deeper into wood than any man I ever saw." And another, " If you heard him fellin' trees in a clearin', you would say there was three men at work by the way the trees fell."

He was more than a tough, long, rawboned boy. He amazed men with his man's lifting power. He put his shoulders under a new-built corncrib one day and walked away with it to where the farmer wanted it. Four men, ready with poles to put under it and carry it, didn't need their poles. He played the same trick with a chicken house; at the new, growing town of Gentryville near by they said the chicken house weighed six hundred pounds, and only a big boy with a hard backbone could get under it and walk away with it.

A blacksmith shop, a grocery, and a store had started up on the crossroads of the Gentry farm. And one night after Abe had been helping thresh wheat on Dave Turnham's place, he went with Dennis Hanks, John Johnston, and some other boys to Gentryville, where the farm hands sat around with John Baldwin, the blacksmith, and Jones, the storekeeper, passed the whisky jug, told stories, and talked politics and religion and gossip. Going home late that night, they saw something in a mud puddle alongside the road. They stepped over to see whether it was a man or a hog. It was a man — drunk — snoring — sleeping off his drunk — on a frosty night outdoors in a cold wind.

They shook him by the shoulders, doubled his knees to his stomach; but he went on sleeping, snoring. The cold wind was getting colder. The other boys said they were going home; and they went away, leaving Abe alone with the snoring sleeper in the mud puddle. Abe stepped into the mud, reached arms around the man, slung him over his shoulders, carried him to Dennis Hanks's cabin, built a fire, rubbed him warm, and left him sleeping off the whisky.

And the man afterward said Abe saved his life. He told John Hanks, " It was mighty clever of Abe to tote me to a warm fire that night."

So he grew, living in that Pigeon Creek cabin for a home, sleeping in the loft, climbing up at night to a bed just under the roof, where sometimes the snow and the rain drove through the cracks, eating sometimes at a table where the family had only one thing to eat — potatoes. Once at the table, when there were only potatoes, his father spoke a blessing to the Lord for potatoes; the boy murmured, " Those are mighty poor blessings." And Abe made jokes once when company came and Sally Bush Lincoln brought out raw potatoes, gave the visitors a knife apiece, and they all peeled raw potatoes and talked about the crops, politics, religion, gossip.

Days when they had only potatoes to eat didn't come often. Other days in the year they had " yaller-legged chicken " with gravy, and corn dodgers with shortening, and berries and honey. They tasted of bear meat, deer, coon, quail, grouse, prairie turkey, catfish, bass, perch.

Abe knew the sleep that comes after long hours of work outdoors, the feeling of simple food changing into blood and muscle as he worked in those young years clearing timberland for pasture and corn crops, cutting loose the brush, piling it and burning it, splitting rails, pulling the crosscut saw and the whipsaw, driving the shovel plow, harrowing, planting, hoeing, pulling fodder, milking cows, churning butter, helping neighbors at house raisings, logrollings, cornhuskings.

He found he was fast, strong, and keen when he went against other boys in sports. On farms where he worked, he held his own at scuffling, knocking off hats, wrestling. The time came when around Gentryville and Spencer County he was known as the best "rassler" of all, the champion. In jumping, foot racing, throwing the maul,[1] pitching the crowbar, he carried away the decisions against the lads of his own age always, and usually won against those older than himself.

He earned his board, clothes, and lodgings, sometimes working for a neighbor farmer. He watched his father, while helping make cabinets, coffins, cupboards, window frames, doors. Hammers, saws, pegs, cleats, he understood firsthand, also the scythe and the cradle for cutting hay and grain, the corn-cutter's knife, the leather piece to protect the hand while shucking corn, and the horse, the dog, the cow, the ox, the hog. He could skin and cure the hides of coon and deer. He lifted the slippery two-hundred-pound hog carcass, head down, holding the hind hocks up for others of the gang to hook, and swung the animal clear of the ground. He learned where to stick a hog in the underside of the neck so as to bleed it to death; how to split it in two and carve out the chops, the parts for sausage-grinding, for hams, for "cracklings."

Farmers called him to butcher for them at thirty-one cents a day — this when he was sixteen and seventeen years old. He could "knock a beef in the head," swing a maul and hit a cow between the eyes, skin the hide, halve and quarter it, carve out the tallow, the steaks, kidneys, liver.

And the hiding places of fresh spring water under the earth crust had to be in his thoughts; he helped at well digging; the wells Tom Lincoln dug went dry one year after another; neighbors said Tom was always digging a well and had his land "honeycombed"; and the boy Abe ran the errands and held the tools for the well digging.

When he was eighteen years old, he could take an ax at the end of the handle and hold it out in a straight horizontal line, easy and steady — he had strong shoulder muscles and steady wrists early in life. He walked thirty-four miles in one day, just on an errand, to please himself, to hear a lawyer make a speech. He could tell his body to do almost impossible things, and the body obeyed.

Growing from boy to man, he was alone a good deal of the time. Days came often when he was by himself all the time except at breakfast and supper hours in the cabin home. In some years more of his time was spent in loneliness than in the company of other people. It happened, too, that this loneliness he knew was not like that of people in cities who can look from a window on streets where faces pass and repass. It was the wilderness loneliness he became acquainted with; solved; filtered through

[1] **maul** (môl): a heavy hammer, used for driving the wedges with which logs were split.

body, eye, and brain; held communion with in his ears, in the temples of his forehead, in the works of his beating heart.

He lived with trees; with the bush wet with shining raindrops; with the burning bush of autumn; with the lone wild duck riding a north wind and crying down on a line north to south, the faces of open sky and weather, the ax which is an individual one-man instrument – these he had for companions, books, friends, talkers, chums of his endless changing soliloquies.

His moccasin feet in the wintertime knew the white spaces of snowdrifts piled in whimsical shapes against timber slopes or blown in levels across the fields of last year's cut cornstalks; in the summertime his bare feet toughened in the gravel of green streams while he laughed back to the chatter of bluejays in the red-haw trees or while he kept his eyes ready in the slough quack grass [1] for the cow snake, the rattler, the copperhead.

He rested between spells of work in the springtime when the upward push of the coming out of the new grass can be heard, and in autumn weeks when the rustle of a single falling leaf lets go a whisper that a listening ear can catch.

He found his life thrown in ways where there was a certain chance for a certain growth. And so he grew. Silence found him; he met silence. In the making of him as he was, the element of silence was immense.

It was a little country of families living in one-room cabins. Dennis Hanks said at a later time, "We lived the same as the Indians, 'ceptin' we took an interest in politics and religion."

Cash was scarce; venison hams, bacon slabs, and barrels of whisky served as money; there were seasons when storekeepers asked customers, "What kind of money have you today?" because so many sorts of wildcat dollar bills [2] were passing around. In sections of timberland wild hogs were nosing out a fat living on hickory nuts, walnuts, acorns; it was said the country would be full of wild hogs if the wolves didn't find the litters of young pigs a few weeks old and kill them.

Farmers lost thirty and forty sheep in a single wolf raid. Toward the end of June came "fly time," when cows lost weight and gave less milk because they had to fight flies. For two or three months at the end of summer, horses weakened, unless covered with blankets, under the attacks of horseflies; where one lighted on a horse, a drop of blood oozed; horses were hitched to branches of trees that gave loose rein to the animals, room to move and fight flies.

Men and women went barefoot except in the colder weather; women carried their shoes in their hands and put them on just before arrival at church meetings or at social parties.

Rains came, loosening the topsoil of the land where it was not held by grass roots; it was a yellow clay that softened to slush; in this yellow slush many a time Abe Lincoln walked ankle-deep; his bare feet were intimate with the clay dust of the hot dog days, with the clay mud of spring and fall rains; he was at home in clay. In the timbers with his ax, on the way to chop, his toes, heels, soles, the balls of his feet, climbed and slid in banks and sluices of clay. In the corn-

[1] **slough** (slōō) **quack grass:** a tough, coarse grass growing in sloughs, or muddy, swampy places.

[2] **wildcat dollar bills:** paper money without adequate security behind it and so not worth its face value.

fields, plowing, hoeing, cutting, and shucking, again his bare feet spoke with the clay of the earth; it was in his toenails and stuck on the skin of his toe knuckles. The color of clay was one of his own colors.

In the short and simple annals of the poor it seems there are people who breathe with the earth and take into their lungs and blood some of the hard and dark strength of its mystery. During six and seven months each year in the twelve fiercest formative years of his life, Abraham Lincoln had the pads of his foot soles bare against clay of the earth. It may be the earth told him in her own tough gypsy slang one or two knacks of living worth keeping. To be organic with running wildfire and quiet rain, both of the same moment, is to be the carrier of wave lines the earth gives up only on hard usage.

He took shape in a tall, long-armed cornhusker. When rain came in at the chinks of the cabin loft where he slept, soaking through the book Josiah Crawford lent him, he pulled fodder two days to pay for the book, made a clean sweep, till there wasn't a blade left on a cornstalk in the field of Josiah Crawford.

His father was saying the big boy looked as if he had been roughhewn with an ax and needed smoothing with a jack plane. "He was the ganglin'est, awkwardest feller that ever stepped over a ten-rail snake fence; he had t' duck to git through a door; he 'peared to be all j'ints."

His stepmother told him she didn't mind his bringing dirt into the house on his feet; she could scour the floor, but she asked him to keep his head washed or he'd be rubbing the dirt on her nice whitewashed rafters. He put barefoot boys to wading in a mud puddle near the horse trough, picked them up one by one, carried them to the house upside down, and walked their muddy feet across the ceiling. The mother came in, laughed an hour at the foot tracks, told Abe he ought to be spanked – and he cleaned the ceiling so it looked new.

The mother said, "Abe never spoke a cross word to me in his life since we lived together." And she said Abe was truthful; when Tilda Johnston leaped onto Abe's back to give him a scare on a lonely timber path, she brought the big axman to the ground by pulling her hands against his shoulders and pressing her knee into his backbone. The ax blade cut her ankle, and strips from Abe's shirt and Tilda's dress had to be used to stop the blood. By then she was sobbing over what to tell her mother. On Abe's advice she told her mother the whole truth.

As time went by, the stepmother of Abe became one of the rich, silent forces in his life. Besides keeping the floors, pots, pans, kettles, and milk crocks spick and span, weaving, sewing, mending, and managing with sagacity and gumption, she had a massive, bony, human strength backed with an elemental faith that the foundations of the world were mortised by God with unspeakable goodness of heart toward the human family. Hard as life was, she was thankful to be alive.

Once she told Abe how her brother Isaac, back in Hardin County, had hot words with a cowardly young man who shot Isaac without warning. The doctors asked Isaac if they could tie him down while they cut his flesh and took out the bullet. He told them he didn't need to be tied down; he put two lead musket balls in between his teeth and ground his teeth on them while the doctors cut a slash nine inches long and one inch deep till they found the bullet and brought it out. Isaac never let out a moan or a whimper; he set his teeth into the musket balls, ground them into flat sheets, and spat them from his mouth when he thanked the doctors.

Sally Bush, the stepmother, was all of a good mother to Abe. If he broke out laughing when others saw nothing to laugh at, she let it pass as a sign of his thoughts working their own way. So far as she was concerned, he had a right to do unaccountable things; since he never lied to her, why not? So she justified him. When Abe's sister, Sarah, married Aaron Grigsby and a year after died with her newborn child, it was Sally Bush who spoke comfort to the eighteen-year-old boy of Nancy Hanks burying his sister and the wraith of a child.

A neighbor woman sized him up by saying, "He could work when he wanted to, but he was no hand to pitch in like killing snakes." John Romine made the remarks: "Abe Lincoln worked for me, but was always reading and thinking. I used to get mad at him for it. I say he was awful lazy. He would laugh and talk – crack his jokes and tell stories all the time; didn't love work half as much as his pay. He said to me one day that his father taught him to work, but he never taught him to love it."

A misunderstanding came up one time between Abe Lincoln and William Grigsby. It ended with Grigsby so mad he challenged Abe to a fight. Abe looked down at Grigsby, smiled, and said the fight ought to be with John Johnston, Abe's stepbrother. The day was set for the fight; each man was there with his seconds; the mauling began, with the two fighters stripped to the waist, beating and bruising each other with bare knuckles.

A crowd stood around, forming a ring, cheering, yelling, hissing, till after a while they saw Johnston getting the worst of it. Then the ring of people forming the crowd was broken as Abe Lincoln shouldered his way through, stepped out, took hold of Grigsby and threw that fighter out of the center of the fight ring.

Then Abe Lincoln called out, "I'm the big buck of this lick." And looking around so his eyes swept the circle of the crowd he let loose the challenge, "If any of you want to try it, come on and whet your horns." A riot of wild fist fighting came then between the two gangs and for months around the Jones grocery store there was talk about which gang whipped the other.

After a fox chase with horses, Uncle Jimmy Larkin was telling how his horse won the race, was the best horse in the world, and never drew a long breath; Abe didn't listen; Uncle Jimmy told it again, and Abe said, "Why don't you tell us how many short breaths he drew?" It raised a laugh on Jimmy, who jumped around threatening to fight, till Abe said quietly, "Now, Larkin, if you don't shut up I'll throw you in that water."

Asked by Farmer James Taylor if he could kill a hog, he answered, "If you will risk the hog I'll risk myself."

He had the pride of youth that resents the slur, the snub, besides the riotous blood that has always led youth in reckless exploits. When he was cutting up didoes one day at the Crawford farmhouse, Mrs. Crawford asked, "What's going to become of you, Abe?" And with mockery of swagger, he answered, "Me? I'm going to be President of the United States."

Driving a horse at the mill, he was sending the whiplash over the nag and calling, "Git up, you old hussy; git up, you old hussy." The horse let fly a hind foot that knocked down the big boy just as he yelled, "Git up." He lay bleeding, was taken home, washed, put to bed, and lay all night unconscious. As his eyewinkers opened the next day and he came to, his tongue struggled and blurted, "You old hussy," thus finishing what he started to say before the knockdown.

The farm boys in their evenings at Jones's store in Gentryville talked about how Abe Lincoln was always reading, digging into books, stretching out flat on his stomach in front of the fireplace, studying till midnight and past midnight, picking a piece of charcoal to write on the fire shovel, shaving off what he wrote, and then writing more – till midnight and past midnight. The next thing Abe would be reading books between the plow handles, it seemed to them. And once, trying to speak a last word, Dennis Hanks said, "There's suthin' peculiarsome about Abe."

He wanted to learn, to know, to live, to reach out; he wanted to satisfy hungers and thirsts he couldn't tell about, this big boy of the backwoods. And some of what he wanted so much, so deep down, seemed to be in the books. Maybe in books he would find the answers to dark questions pushing around in the pools of his thoughts and the drifts of his mind. He told Dennis and other people, "The things I want to know are in books; my best friend is the man who'll get me a book I ain't read." And sometimes friends answered, "Well, books ain't as plenty as wildcats in these parts o' Indianny."

This was one thing meant by Dennis when he said there was "suthin' peculiarsome" about Abe. It seemed that Abe made the books tell him more than they told other people. All the other farm boys had gone to school and read *The Kentucky Preceptor,* but Abe picked out questions from it, such as "Who has the most right to complain, the Indian or the Negro?" and Abe would talk about it, up one way and down the other, while they were in the cornfield pulling fodder for the winter. When Abe got hold of a storybook and read about a boat that came near a magnetic rock, and how the magnets in the rock pulled all the nails out of the boat so it went to pieces and the people in the boat found themselves floundering in water, Abe thought it was funny and told it to other people. After Abe read poetry, especially Bobby Burns's poems, Abe began writing rhymes himself. When Abe sat with a girl, with their bare feet in the creek water, and she spoke of the moon rising, he explained to her it was the earth moving and not the moon – the moon only seemed to rise.

John Hanks, who worked in the fields barefooted with Abe, grubbing stumps, plowing, mowing, said, "When Abe and I came back to the house from work, he used to go to the cupboard, snatch a piece of corn bread, sit down, take a book, cock his legs up high as his head, and read. Whenever Abe had a chance in the field while at work, or at the house, he would stop and read." He liked to explain to other people what he was getting from books; explaining an idea to someone else made it clearer to him. The habit was growing on him of reading out loud; words came more real if picked from the silent page of the book and pronounced on the tongue; new balance and values of words stood out if spoken aloud. When writing letters for his father or the neighbors, he read the words out loud as they got written. Before writing a letter he asked questions, such as, "What do you want

To Exercise Multiplication

There were 40 men concerned in payment
a sum of money and each man paid 127 l
how much was paid in all ——

If 1 foot contain 12 inches I demand how many there
are in 126 feet ——

Of Compound Division

Q What is compound Division

A When several numbers of Divers Denomination
are given to be divided by 1 common divisor this called
Compound Division ——

Abraham Lincoln His Book

A page signed " Abraham Lincoln His Book," showing young Abe's exercises in multiplication and division. (Oliver R. Barrett Collection) to say in the letter? How do you want to say it? Are you sure that's the best way to say it? Or do you think we can fix up a better way to say it? "

As he studied his books, his lower lip stuck out; Josiah Crawford noticed it was a habit and joked Abe about the "stuck-out lip." This habit, too, stayed with him.

He wrote in his sum book, or arithmetic, that compound division was "When several numbers of Divers [1] Denominations are given to be divided by 1 common divisor," and worked on the exercise in multiplication — "If 1 foot contain 12 inches I demand how many there are in 126 feet." Thus the schoolboy.

What he got in the schools didn't satisfy him. He went to three different schools in Indiana, besides two in Kentucky — altogether about four months of school. He learned his A B C; how to spell, read, write. And he had been with the other barefoot boys in butternut jeans learning "manners" under the schoolteacher, Andrew Crawford, who had them open a door, walk in, and say "Howdy do?" Yet what he tasted of books in school was only a beginning, only made him hungry and thirsty, shook him with a wanting and a wanting of more and more of what was hidden between the covers of books.

He kept on saying, "The things I want to know are in books; my best friend is the man who'll git me a book I ain't read." He said that to Pitcher, the lawyer over at Rockport, nearly twenty miles away, one fall afternoon, when he walked from Pigeon Creek to Rockport and borrowed a book from Pitcher. Then when fodder-pulling time came a few days later, he shucked corn from early daylight till sundown along with his father and Dennis Hanks and John Hanks; but after supper he read the book till midnight, and at noon he hardly knew the taste of his corn bread because he had the book in front of him. It was a hundred little things like these which made Dennis Hanks say there was "suthin' peculiarsome" about Abe.

Besides reading the family Bible and figuring his way all through the old arithmetic they had at home, he got hold of *Aesop's Fables, The Pilgrim's Progress, Robinson Crusoe,* and Weems's *The Life of Francis Marion.* The book of fables, written or collected thousands of years ago by the Greek slave known as Aesop, sank deep in his mind. As he read through the book a second and third time, he had a feeling there were fables all around him, that everything he touched and handled, everything he saw and learned had a fable wrapped in it somewhere. One fable was about a bundle of sticks and a farmer whose sons were quarreling and fighting.

There was a fable in two sentences which read: "A coachman, hearing one of the wheels of his coach make a great noise, and perceiving that it was the worst one of the four, asked how it came to take such a liberty. The wheel answered that from the beginning of time creaking had always been the privilege of the weak." And there were shrewd, brief incidents of foolery such as this: "A waggish, idle fellow in a country town, being desirous of playing a trick on the simplicity of his neighbors and at the same time putting a little money in his pocket at their cost, advertised that he would on a certain day show a wheel carriage that should be so contrived as to go without horses. By silly curiosity the rustics were taken in, and each succeeding group who came out from the show

[1] **Divers** (dī'vẽrz): various.

were ashamed to confess to their neighbors that they had seen nothing but a wheelbarrow."

The style of the Bible, of Aesop's fables, the hearts and minds back of those books, were much in his thoughts. His favorite pages in them he read over and over. Behind such proverbs as "Muzzle not the ox that treadeth out the corn" and "He that ruleth his own spirit is greater than he that taketh a city," there was a music of simple wisdom and a mystery of common everyday life that touched deep spots in him, while out of the fables of the ancient Greek slave he came to see that cats, rats, dogs, horses, plows, hammers, fingers, toes, people – all had fables connected with their lives, characters, places. There was, perhaps, an outside for each thing as it stood alone, while inside of it was its fable.

One book came, titled *The Life of George Washington,* "with Curious Anecdotes, Equally Honorable to Himself and Exemplary to His Young Countrymen. Embellished with Six Steel Engravings, by M. L. Weems, formerly Rector of Mt. Vernon Parish." It pictured men of passion and proud ignorance in the government of England driving their country into war on the American colonies. It quoted the far-visioned warning of Chatham to the British Parliament, "For God's sake, then, my lords, let the way be instantly opened for reconciliation. I say instantly; or it will be too late forever."

The book told of war, as at Saratoga. "Hoarse as a mastiff of true British breed, Lord Balcarras was heard from rank to rank, loud-animating his troops; while on the other hand, fierce as a hungry Bengal tiger, the impetuous Arnold precipitated heroes on the stubborn foe. Shrill and terrible, from rank to rank, resounds the clash of bayonets – frequent and sad the groans of the dying. Pairs on pairs, Britons and Americans, with each his bayonet at his brother's breast, fall forward together faint-shrieking in death, and mingle their smoking blood." Washington, the man, stood out, as when he wrote: "These things so harassed my heart with grief that I solemnly declared to God, if I know myself, I would gladly offer myself a sacrifice to the butchering enemy if I could thereby insure the safety of these my poor distressed countrymen."

The Weems book reached some deep spots in the boy. He asked himself what it meant that men should march, fight, bleed, go cold and hungry for the sake of what they called "freedom."

"Few great men are great in everything," said the book. And there was a cool sap in the passage: "His delight was in that of the manliest sort, which, by stringing the limbs and swelling the muscles, promotes the kindliest flow of blood and spirits. At jumping with a long pole, or heaving heavy weights, for his years he hardly had an equal."

Such book talk was a comfort against the same thing over again, day after day, so many mornings the same kind of water from the same spring, the same fried pork and corn meal to eat, the same drizzles of rain, spring plowing, summer weeds, fall fodder pulling, each coming every year, with the same tired feeling at the end of the day, so many days alone in the woods or the fields or else the same people to talk with, people from whom he had learned all they could teach him. Yet there ran through his head the stories and sayings of other people, the stories and sayings of books, the learning his eyes had caught from books; they were a comfort; they were good to have because they were good by themselves; and they were still better to have because they broke the chill of the lonesome feeling.

He was thankful to the writer of Aesop's fables because that writer stood by him and walked with him, an invisible companion, when he pulled fodder or chopped wood. Books lighted lamps in the dark rooms of his gloomy hours. . . . Well — he would live on; maybe the time would come when he would be free from work for a few weeks, or a few months, with books, and then he would read. . . . Yes, then he would read. . . . Then he would go and get at the proud secrets of his books.

His father — would he be like his father when he grew up? He hoped not. Why should his father knock him off a fence rail when he was asking a neighbor, passing by, a question? Even if it was a smart question, too pert and too quick, it was no way to handle a boy in front of a neighbor. No, he was going to be a man different from his father. The books — his father hated the books. His father talked about " too much eddication "; after readin', writin', 'rithmetic, that was enough, his father said. He, Abe Lincoln, the boy, wanted to know more than the father, Tom Lincoln, wanted to know. Already Abe knew more than his father; he was writing letters for the neighbors; they hunted out the Lincoln farm to get young Abe to find his bottle of ink with blackberry-brier root and copperas [1] in it, and his pen made from a turkey-buzzard feather, and write letters. Abe had a suspicion sometimes his father was a little proud to have a boy that could write letters, and tell about things in books, and outrun and outwrestle and rough-and-tumble any boy or man in Spencer County. Yes, he would be different from his father; he was already so; it couldn't be helped.

[1] **copperas** (kŏp'ĕr·ăs): a chemical used in making ink.

Keeping Facts in Mind

1. Which came first, the Knob Creek farm or the farm on Little Pigeon Creek? Hodgenville or Gentryville? the cornshuck bed or the featherbed? (Unless a page number is referred to in the question, try to answer without turning back to the text.)
2. For all Abe's love of learning, how many months of schooling did he have? Can you name five or six books he read as a young man? What was a " blab school "? What was his father's attitude toward education? his mother's and later, his stepmother's? How do you account for the difference?
3. What animals abounded in the Buckhorn Valley country? what game birds?
4. What objects sometimes served as money, and why?

Going Behind the Facts

1. The wilderness seemed to be filled with game animals, but sometimes the settlers almost starved. Why?
2. On page 265 the author says that looking glasses began to work inside Abe's head. What does he mean?
3. What were the main topics of conversation mentioned on page 271? Why were these particular things talked about?
4. How do you suppose the term " snake fence " got its name?
5. At the time Abe was a young man of seventeen or eighteen, people said that he was fun-loving, eager to learn, honest, witty, determined, lazy — and that he loved a good fist fight. How do you explain his laziness?
6. What is Sandburg's attitude toward Lincoln? Is he mainly factual and objective? Is he sympathetic or admiring? critical? Does he seem to hide faults? Read passages to support your answers.

Thinking It Over

1. Explain what the author means by calling Nancy Hanks a " pioneer sacrifice."
2. Make a list of the forces, people, situations, and experiences that molded Lincoln's

youth and show what was the influence of each.

3. " There's suthin' peculiarsome about Abe." Was there? Or was it just that in some respects he was different from the others? It is quite natural to think people who are different from us are " peculiarsome." How was Abe like all the other pioneers? How was he different? You will answer, " He read and studied and wanted to learn." Yes, that is one way; but there is another that is closely related and yet more important. He used his mind to think. Prove that he did.

4. Make a collection of Lincoln anecdotes. If a number of pupils contribute their favorites, let one pupil act as editor and, discarding duplicates, have the rest typed by some girl who is taking commercial work. Make them into a booklet. Perhaps someone will like to design a cover for it.

For Your Vocabulary

WORD BUILDING: The word *pike,* meaning " highway," has an interesting background. It is a shortened form of *turnpike.* Originally a turnpike (*turn* + *pike,* a sharp point) was a turnstile at the end of a toll road. You paid your toll, and the pike was turned to let you through. Do you know any roads that are still called turnpike or pike? Are they toll roads? What do you think is the original meaning of *highway*?

Words bothered Abe — words like *independent* and *predestination.* A *pendant* hangs around your neck; *dependents* " hang upon " someone else for support; the *independent* person stands without help. Find out what *predestination* means.

UNCOMMON WORDS: Sandburg likes to mix up literary and common words, as in the phrase " sagacity and gumption " (p. 274). What definitions can you give for both words? Why is this combination of formal and informal language appropriate when applied to Abe Lincoln? The word *mortised,* in the same paragraph, has a French origin meaning " securely fastened." Perhaps someone who is taking woodwork can explain what a mortised joint is by drawing one on the blackboard. When Sandburg said that Abe helped bury his sister and her " wraith of a child," he meant merely that the child was ghostlike. A *wraith* — the word comes from Scotland — is a ghostly appearance of a living person supposedly indicating that the person will die soon.

RENÉ KRAUS

Problem Child: Winston Churchill

Throughout the blackest years of World War II, the steady, courageous voices of two great men, broadcast all over the world, gave strength to the weak, faith to the faltering, and comfort to the oppressed. One of those men was Franklin Delano Roosevelt, and the other his friend and comrade, the dogged, determined English warrior, Winston S. Churchill. " Our Winnie " they called him in his own country, and he was to the hard-pressed British,

"Problem Child" from *Winston Churchill* by René Kraus, published by J. B. Lippincott Company. Reprinted by permission of the publisher.

as someone has said, "an abiding presence — a pillar of cloud by day and a pillar of fire by night."

Winston Churchill was the son of Lord Randolph Churchill and an American woman, Jennie Jerome, whose father was publisher and coeditor of the New York *Times*. Lord Randolph was a brilliant and sometimes unpredictable political leader in the English government when Winston was a boy. The son longed to follow his father's career and eventually did. During World War II he was Prime Minister of England and even today, in his late seventies, he leads the Conservative party in the House of Commons.

Certainly none of Churchill's early schoolmasters would have predicted for him a great career. He was sulky, stubborn, an erratic student, and generally troublesome. As you read the following biographical sketch by René Kraus,[1] you will note, however, that many of the characteristics which made him a problem in his childhood turned out to be assets when his country needed a tough, aggressive leader.

AND with a withering volley he shattered the enemy's line." . . .

Baby was now four years old. Baby had slightly bat ears; he was a funny rather than a beautiful baby. No matter, slightly bat ears might make it easier to drink in the music of these grandiose words. Sixty years later Winston Churchill can still hear the tones in which the old gentleman in his red uniform, glittering gold, uttered the magic-sounding sentence, "And with a withering volley . . ." His Grace, Grandfather, was unveiling the Lord Gough[2] statue. It was the first impression that has survived in Winston Churchill's life. Even as a four-year-old, Baby was receptive to magic words. No wonder he has become the greatest living word-wizard in the English language.

The first winter of his eventful life "Winnie," as he was to be called for the next few decades, spent at Blenheim[3] Palace. Then his parents moved to the town house at 50 Grosvenor[4] Square, in London, where the child remained largely under the care of Mrs. Everest the nurse. She was the first friend Winston Churchill ever had, and for long years the only one. Today her picture hangs on the wall of his studio in Chartwell, as it did in the bachelor flat he used to occupy in Mayfair.

Mrs. Everest had a sister living in Ventnor whose husband was a prison warden. He told the lad about prison revolts, and how he himself had often been attacked and injured by the convicts. The sympathy that these tales aroused in the budding revolutionary was naturally directed toward the convicts. In later years Churchill recalled that these stories had remained vividly in memory when he became Home Secretary and thus responsible for the English penal system. They led him to an inclusive prison reform.

With the warden of Ventnor little Winston often went walking along the cliffs. One day they saw a splendid ship passing by with all sails set, only two or three miles from shore. "The *Eurydice*,"[5] said his companion proudly, "the training ship." Suddenly the heavens darkened. Such a hurricane broke loose as occurs but once a century in those temperate climes. The boy got

[1] **René Kraus** (rĕ·nā′ krous).
[2] **Lord Gough** (gŏf): a British general.
[3] **Blenheim** (blĕn′ĕm) **Palace:** the country estate of the Churchills, in Oxfordshire.
[4] **Grosvenor** (grōv′nẽr).
[5] **Eurydice** (ū·rĭd′ĭ·sē).

home wet to the skin. Next day he heard that the *Eurydice* had capsized and gone to the bottom with three hundred soldiers and sailors on board. The divers went down to bring up the corpses; some of the men fainted at seeing the fish eating the drowned. Winston had nightmares; he saw ghosts at night. He was a high-strung child.

Next came learning to read and write. There would be a governess — the boy awaited her as some figure of dread. Mrs. Everest, the nurse, tried to soften the shock. She brought in a book, *Reading without Tears,* which the lad was to study in preparation for the lessons with the governess. But there was no reading without tears. The child fought desperately against the crooked, senseless shapes that were pounded into him, the letters and numbers. The letters were tolerable at a pinch; after a while they would take on shape, and assume some silly meaning or other. But figures? Never! Even in the nursery he showed that all through his school career he was going to fail in mathematics.

When the dreaded governess finally arrived, the boy ran out of the house and hid away in the woods. It took hours to catch him. Then he was put to the treadmill. In vain he appealed to his beautiful mother. Mamma had no time. She quite agreed with the governess's strict methods. Besides, the horse was already neighing impatiently at the door. On big, aristocratic thoroughbreds of the finest strain Jennie and her lord hunted through the Irish woods. Children belonged at home, under supervision. " She made a brilliant impression on my childhood's eye," Churchill remembered of his mother. " She shone for me like the evening star. I loved her dearly — but at a distance."

Thus lonely children grow up, timid and scared amid viceregal [1] pomp. For that matter, the pomp even then was rather superficial. Clouds, dark and menacing, descended even on Winnie's nursery. He was seven years old, and now it came time to take leave of the magic lantern, the real steam engine, and the thousand lead soldiers, wearing the uniforms of all the British services and regiments, that were more his playmates than his playthings. Off to school!

He would simply love school. There would be a great many other little boys, and wonderful adventures besides. Some boys grew so fond of school that they hated to come home for the holidays. Just ask your older cousins!

The cousins said nothing, but grinned.

He started on the journey of life with fourteen pairs of socks and three half crowns. With these possessions his beautiful Mamma delivered him to St. James's School, Ascot. She had scarcely taken leave of the headmaster, frozen in respect, before the latter's manner changed. He drew himself up as well as his stoop would allow. His wrinkled face darkened into an utterly authoritarian glare: " Have you any money with you? " The three half crowns vanished into a drawer. True, Winnie was carefully given a receipt. Then they handed him his first Latin book. He must learn to decline *mensa.*

So far as education went, St. James's School was the last gasp of an antediluvian era.[2] It had electric light, a revolutionary innovation at that time. It had a carefully chosen student body, with only ten boys in each form, all aspirants for Eton; it had the manner of Eton; its

[1] **viceregal** (vīs'rē'găl) **pomp:** dignity and splendor such as the establishment of a viceroy, or governor ruling as the representative of his king, would have.

[2] **antediluvian** (ăn'tē·dĭ·lū'vĭ·ăn) **era:** antiquated, old-fashioned period of time.

masters wore cap and gown. The school was fashionable and expensive. Each week in the library a number of boys were flogged until they were raw. Discipline demanded it.

The very first day, Winnie came dangerously close to the library. *Mensa,* vocative,[1] his form master explained, meant "O table!" "You would use that in addressing a table," he said.

"But I never do," replied the boy.

"Next time you will be punished very, very severely!" With these words ended his introduction to the humanities.[2]

Little Winston was not to be cowed. Never would he learn Latin, he vowed.

Of course they tried to introduce him by means of the cane to the beauties of the classical world. Once when he was thrashed too roughly he kicked the headmaster's hat to pieces. They beat him again. He was impertinent, stubborn, sulky. Why, the child even stole. Flogging again. His naughtiness became legendary.

Here the antidisciplinarian was born. Traces still remain. H. G. Wells [3] said of him many years later: "There are times when the evil spirit comes upon him, and then I can only think of him as an intractable little boy, a mischievous, dangerous little boy, a knee-worthy little boy. Only by thinking of him in that way can I go on liking him."

Untamable fury was stored up in the lad when discipline grew yet stricter. He would have revenge. When he was bigger he would come back to Ascot and publicly chastise the headmaster. He was still far too small for his great rage. After two years – the only two unhappy years of his life, as he later described them – he had a complete physical breakdown.

One question kept gnawing at his soul: Why did not his father come to deliver him? After all, his father was the greatest and handsomest man in the world; he could come striding like a god. But his father was long since in the grip of politics. Politics will devour even the greatest and handsomest man in the world. Not until a serious illness attacked the child did his parents take him from the terrible boarding school.

Lord Randolph had evidently forgotten his own school days. He regarded his underdeveloped son with a troubled eye. To a friend he introduced him with the words, "Not much of a boy yet – but he's a good'n, a good'n – "

A summer trip with his parents to Bad Gastein,[4] the Austrian spa,[5] restored the boy's health to some extent. But his condition still required rest and care. He was therefore sent to Brighton, where the family physician, the then celebrated Dr. Robson Roose, was in practice. The child had to be under constant medical supervision. At the same time he was put into a school conducted by two elderly ladies of Brighton. This was a much more unpretentious boarding school; there was neither the electric light nor the caning library of St. James's School. Instead there was an atmosphere of friendliness and sympathy quite new to the boy. For a little while he remained obdurate. Eva Moore the actress, who was teaching dancing at Brighton just then, recalls Winston with the words: "A small, red-headed pupil, the naughtiest small boy in the world. He was cheeky in a specially annoying way, but smart. Games did not attract him, but theatricals. He constructed a

[1] **vocative** (vŏc'á·tĭv): case denoting, in Latin, that which is addressed.
[2] **humanities** (hû·măn'ĭ·tĭz): classical studies.
[3] **H. G. Wells:** famous English novelist and historian.
[4] **Bad Gastein** (bät gä·stīn').
[5] **spa** (spä): a place having mineral springs.

toy theater and produced *Aladdin*."

Indeed it was at this time that the histrionic[1] element awoke which distinguished Churchill for years. Today it is long since extinct. But it cannot be denied that until quite late in his youth he felt most at ease in the glare of the lights. He had his first dramatic success in a school performance of Colman's *Heir at Law,* in which he played Dick Dowles. His elocutionary gifts attracted general attention, though he did lisp slightly. This impediment gave him a good deal of trouble later. Like Demosthenes,[2] Churchill, the greatest orator of his land and age, had to struggle painfully for speech.

Other early arts and sciences now came to him like a breeze. In French classes he did not have to say " O table! " Consequently he learned French very easily. Verses stuck in his youthful memory if he but read them once or twice. History began to fascinate him.

An attack of double pneumonia put the lad in bed. At that time double pneumonia was still a fatal disease, especially when the patient was a weak, delicate child. But Winston pulled through. " He has a charmed life," said the doctor. The phrase was to follow Churchill wherever he went.

During his convalescence the nine-year-old began to take an interest in politics. He came to it in an odd way, a regular Churchill way. To occupy him on Sundays he was allowed to look through the old volumes of *Punch*.[3] He not only looked them through, he devoured them. He was most deeply fascinated by the cartoons. Here he met the world, its great figures and events.

[1] **histrionic** (hĭs′trĭ·ŏn′ĭk): dramatic, characterizing an actor.
[2] **Demosthenes** (dê·mŏs′thê·nēz): Athenian orator who had a speech defect.
[3] **Punch:** an English humorous magazine.

In the course of his career Churchill himself became the favorite of the cartoonists. Not hundreds but thousands of drawings and caricatures show him with his two trade-marks, one of which is the wart-shaped nose — which, however, is nothing but a malicious yet ineradicable invention. The other is a tiny hat on an excessively broad skull. The wart nose that they have attached to him Churchill might endure. But he has grave objections to the hat. He tells how the hat legend originated. There is no denying that he once wore a hat too small for him by mistake while walking with his wife on the beach at Southport. Unfortunately a news photographer was on hand. From that day forward the cartoonists sealed the fate of Churchill's head and hat. In vain he points out tirelessly that his headgear is furnished by the best hatter in London. He has his trade-mark and his idiosyncrasy. At bottom he does not mind. A statesman no longer assaulted by the cartoonists is done for, he thinks with worldly wisdom.

Even while he was educating himself on *Punch* he remained an ill-behaved boy, self-willed and refractory. The school paper that he founded before he was nine was of course called *The Critic.* Only one number appeared, however. He demonstrated his critical talent when he met Rider Haggard at the home of his aunt, Lady Leslie. Rider Haggard, the author of *She* and *King Solomon's Mines,* was then at the height of his fame. Young Winston, however, was by no means awe-struck in his presence. " What do you mean by this passage in your new book? " asked the boy, quite without shyness. " I don't understand it."

Mr. Haggard examined the passage and did not understand it either. Of course a masculine friendship at once

Harrow is one of the oldest and most exclusive English schools. Since 1571, it has trained aristocratic young English gentlemen to be social and political leaders. (*Combine*)

developed out of that incident. Rider Haggard sent Winnie his newest work, and the latter thanked him with a most gracious holograph: "Thank you so much for sending me *Allan Quatermain.* It was so good of you. I like it better than *King Solomon's Mines;* it is more amusing. I hope you will write a great many more books."

An untamed, arrogant, presumptuous child, people said. No wonder – he was the son of the most conspicuous man in England.

After the Easter holidays of 1888 he took his entrance for Harrow. He had been intended for Eton; but the climate there, with its everlasting fogs, was too unhealthy for the sickly boy. He was a little hurt by what he considered discrimination in the choice of schools. That the examination was no great success seemed to him less tragic. He had hoped to shine in his favorite subjects – history, poetry, and essay-writing. Instead the examiners were painfully curious about his knowledge of Latin and mathematics. In the Latin paper, alas, he could not answer a single question. His mathematics did not seem to be much better. But Winston had the good fortune to find in the head of Harrow a great teacher with a deep knowledge of the boy soul. At this time Dr. Welldon, later Bishop of Calcutta and Dean of Durham, and for many years young Churchill's friend, was headmaster. Dr. Welldon was not unreasonable about his students' Latin prose at the expense of everything else. He knew a personality when he saw it, even in embryo form. Of his favorite pupil he was later to write: "Winston Churchill was not perhaps a boy who distinguished himself in the popularly accepted lines of public-school life. He was not prominent in Latin and Greek scholarships, or in mathematics, or in natural science, nor again was he a prominent athlete as a cricketer or football player. But not long after his entrance he attracted notice by his historical knowledge and his literary power, and he was, among the Harrow boys of my time, the most expert in the use of the foils.[1] It would be wrong to pretend that he did not give the masters a good deal of trouble, but I think I may claim to have always felt, as I feel now, a great faith in him. I do not mean that I anticipated the full brilliance of his future life, but it is my deliberate judgment that he showed in his school days at Harrow the unmistakable promise of distinction."

One did need the kind heart of a Dr. Welldon to feel this promise of distinction immediately. For in the beginning Winston was ranked among the worst pupils. He stood but two from the bottom of the whole school. And as these two disappeared almost immediately, he was soon the last in order.

He managed to make the best of even this setback. It is an especially characteristic Churchill feature that bad always turns out to be good for him. At least he is able to interpret it so. Since he remained so long in the lowest form, his more gifted companions were taught Latin and Greek and similar splendors, while he was constantly taught English, and English again. And in the person of a Mr. Sommerville he found an English teacher of uncommon stature. They continually practiced English analysis. And when in later years his more gifted companions who had got prizes for Latin verses and Greek prosody could not write a simple English sentence to earn their bread and make their way, Winston Churchill could not quite keep a grin off his broad face.

Even in childhood he could see his own path marked out ahead, with all its wanderings and diversions. The visionary gift that was later to distinguish him, more than any other quality, from the great mass of mankind must already have been developed at least in rudimentary form by the time he said, at twelve: "Of course I will become a soldier while there is any fighting to be done. After that I shall have a shot at politics." Quite independently he went to the great throat specialist, Sir Felix Semon. He must lose his lisp: "Cure the impediment in my speech, please. Of course I am going into the army first. But as a Minister later, I can't be haunted every time by the idea that I must avoid every word beginning with an *s*."

Lord Randolph Churchill was Chancellor of the Exchequer[2] and leader of the House of Commons. His whole life was a struggle with ill-health. He smoked cigarettes "till his tongue was sore" to soothe himself. He was capable of feats requiring uncommon strength, but in reaction suffered grave fits of exhaustion and despondency. "He gallops till he falls," his wife said of him, remembering their early years of riding together.

His mother, the Duchess of Marlborough, wrote after his early death: "He had a wonderful faculty of making firm friends, who remained through his life devoted to him. He was very constant and decided in his attachments, and outspoken — often imprudently — in his likes and dislikes. This enabled him to succeed in life, but also often brought

[1] **foils:** light swords used in fencing.

[2] **Chancellor of the Exchequer** (ĕks·chĕk′ẽr): officer in charge of public moneys.

him into trouble. . . . Alas, had I been a clever woman, I would have had more ability to curb and control his impulses, and I should have taught him patience and moderation. Yet at times he had extraordinary good judgment, and it was only on rare occasions that he took the bit between his teeth, and then there was no stopping him."

These lines read as if written about young Winston Churchill, not about his father. An almost uncanny likeness unites the two men. Words cannot tell how the boy Winston wanted to help his father in every fight, on every march. But naturally Lord Randolph gave him no opportunity; he was still far too young. The battles for which the lad already felt the call had to be fought on the football field, where he raged with the war cry, " St. George, St. Dunstan, and the Devil! " He let out all his pent-up energy in riding, swimming, and fencing. It was all simply a release, not boyish delight in play; so much he himself knew. Still, he had no objection to a good game of Indians. Once the redskins, two elder cousins, chased him across a bridge. The paleface could escape only by jumping off the bridge, which was held at both ends by the foe. In falling he would grab the branches of a tree, he hoped. He hoped in vain. He fell thirty feet, and landed on stones.

Once again he proved to have a charmed life. By rights he should have shattered his skull. Instead he merely broke his right shoulder. True, he did have to wear plaster casts for six months, and his shoulder has never been right since. But when a man is lucky, even an accident is good fortune. A few years later, at the celebrated Omdurman [1] cavalry assault, he was unable to use his sword. And so, while cavalry sabers flashed around him, he shot his way out with a brand-new Mauser pistol. No howling dervish [2] with the curved scimitar [3] of the Prophet ventured too near him.

Winston Churchill spent three of his four and a half years at Harrow in the Army Class. That he was to enter the service was soon decided. Lord Randolph was pained to think that his boy was too dull for the bar, which would really have been his paternal desire. The father was faced with a puzzle: Why was Winston, a noisy, alert lad, so feeble in his scholastic performances? He wrote excellent compositions. Sometimes he wrote too pointedly. *The Harrovian,* the school paper, had to censor one of his contributions radically because his language was not suited for publication. But his Latin translation he had to get done by a classmate. In return he dictated the latter's English essays to him.

The headmaster, Dr. Welldon, took a personal interest in the promising lad who unfortunately was such a backward scholar. Three times a week he gave him private tuition before evening prayers.

But when the time arrived for the entrance examinations for Sandhurst, the English West Point, Winston Churchill failed. He failed a second time. At the third attempt he felt safe in English and chemistry. French seemed tricky to him, although he had a natural talent for the language. He spent six months in a grim effort to master mathematics, his weakest subject. Up and at the enemy where he is most dangerous, was his watchword even then. All at once sines, co-

[1] **Omdurman** (ŏm'dẽr·măn'): a city in the Anglo-Egyptian Sudan, south of Egypt. The cavalry assault referred to here took place in 1898, during a Sudanese uprising.

[2] **dervish** (dûr'vĭsh): a follower of the Mohammedan leader of the Sudanese uprising.

[3] **scimitar** (sĭm'ĭ·tẽr): a curved sword, used mainly by Moslems, or followers of Mohammed (the Prophet).

sines, and tangents [1] became his daily pabulum.[2] According to his own confession he has heard not a word of these specters since Sandhurst. They vanished from his memory as suddenly as he had conjured them up.

Once again a stroke of luck decided the outcome. He knew that in the third examination, just ahead of him, he would have to draw from memory the map of some part of the Empire. Unfortunately the British Empire is truly great, and consists of many parts. He put bits of paper into his hat, each bearing the name of a dominion or a crown colony. With eyes closed he drew the slip marked New Zealand. New Zealand he studied.

In the examination the examiner said, "Draw us a map of New Zealand on the board."

Thinking It Over

1. The story of Winston Churchill is that of a boy from a wealthy and aristocratic English family who rose to the most responsible position his country could give him. Compare his life with that of Abraham Lincoln, the great American, in terms of his birth, early surroundings, education, physical powers or handicaps, mental traits, and public life.

2. Was Churchill really backward as a child? Why did he appear so? How did some of his early unpromising characteristics turn out to be assets in later life? What were the faults of his education? How does present-day American education differ from the schooling described here?

3. You can probably find in your library a clipping file about Churchill. Find out from that file something about the part he played in the military strategy of World War II and in the planning for world peace and security.

[1] **sines** (sīnz), **cosines** (kō′sīnz), **and tangents** (tăn′jĕntz): terms used in higher mathematics.
[2] **pabulum** (păb′ū·lŭm): food, in the sense of items in one's diet; in this case, mental nourishment.

4. Churchill is writing a powerful history of World War II, of which four volumes have appeared so far: *The Gathering Storm; Their Finest Hour; The Great Alliance;* and *The Hinge of Fate.* In a speech concerning these books Churchill said:

"The English language, its great writers, the great riches and treasures which it possesses – among which, of course, the Bible and Shakespeare stand alone on the highest platform – this literature is one of our greatest sources of inspiration and of strength. The English language is the language of the English-speaking people, and no such combination, so powerful and so fertile and so living, exists anywhere else on the surface of the globe.

"Thus, by being lovers of the English language, admirers of it and all its strength and variety, we shall not only improve and elevate and preserve our literature, but we shall make ourselves more intimate and effective members of that great English-speaking world with whom, if it is wisely guided, the future of mankind will largely rest."

Read what Mrs. Roosevelt says on the same subject (p. 253). What are you doing to prepare yourself for this tremendous responsibility?

For Your Vocabulary

CONTEMPORARY LANGUAGES: Winston Churchill is one of the most eloquent writers and orators of modern times. He has always advocated English as a world language. What languages are used officially in the U.N. today? Can you defend or attack the idea of English as a world language? He also supported the movement for Basic English. Find out all you can about Basic English. What are the arguments for and against it?

SYNONYMS: Tell whether the second in each pair of words below is *like* or *unlike* the first (taken from this selection):

1. grandiose – flowery
2. receptive – antagonistic
3. superficial – shallow
4. authoritarian – official
5. presumptuous – cautious
6. antidisciplinarian – rebel
7. obdurate – inconstant
8. malicious – evil

TOWARD RICHER EXPERIENCE

KATHRYN FORBES

Mama and Big Business

Among the hardy people of many lands who came here seeking opportunity as well as freedom were the Norwegians, many of whom settled on the broad farms and in the cities of the West. *Mama's Bank Account,* from which this incident is taken, is a story of the Americanization of a Norwegian family living in San Francisco. The real heroine of the story is Mama, with her goodness, her humor, and her wisdom; but you will be interested in Katrin, who was beginning high school and got her first job in a drugstore.

" Katrin " is Kathryn Forbes, the author. Her warm and richly human story of her family — Papa, brother Nels, sisters Christine and Dagmar, and above all, Mama — has become a modern classic of its kind. Under the title *I Remember Mama* this biography was made into a delightful stage play as well as a successful movie.

THE family suffered (the younger members not in silence) during the weeks that followed my graduation. The weeks that I was in the employ of Schiller & Son, Druggists. A. Schiller, Prop.

Overnight I became an authority on all medical matters. At home, Latin phrases rolled glibly from my tongue. I never said " distilled water." No. It was " Aqua Distillati," [1] the way it was printed on the square bottles in the drugstore. Nels knew some Latin, but I caught him on Aqua Menthapep,[2] and Aqua Auranti Flora.[3]

" My goodness," I crowed, " imagine not knowing that they mean peppermint- and orange-flower water! "

I ignored Nels's disgusted snort, and bragged endlessly concerning my importance, my indispensability, to Mr. Schiller. Nor was I above wondering, often and audibly, how he had ever got along without me.

I think that if it had been left to Mrs. Schiller she would have continued getting along without me. She had disapproved of Mr. Schiller's hiring me in the

[1] **Aqua Distillati** (ȧk′wȧ dĭs′tĭl·ä′tē).

[2] **Aqua Menthapep** (ȧk′wȧ mĕn′thȧ·pĕp).

[3] **Aqua Auranti Flora** (ȧk′wȧ ō·rän′tē flō′rȧ).

first place. Even when Mr. Schiller pointed out that it would mean that she wouldn't have to give up her afternoons to working in the store, and having *that* to complain of, she just got crosser. It was Mrs. Schiller who decreed that I must work one month before getting any salary.

I worked at the drugstore for three hours every afternoon and all of Saturday morning. At first I simply shined the showcases and dusted the displays, lingering long and rapturously over the candy counter.

Then I was allowed to fill capsules. Quinine. In two-, three-, and five-grain doses. Even the fact that the quinine had a way of lingering on my hands for hours afterward and imparting a bitter taste to anything I might eat did not diminish my tremendous feeling of importance.

Next I was allowed to fill bright yellow boxes with boracic [1] acid or Epsom salts and label them accordingly. And every Saturday morning it was my job to mix and bottle the citrate of magnesia.

This was an absorbing process, and I immediately imagined myself a famous woman chemist as I measured into the graduate so many ounces of the citric-acid solution, so much simple sirup, so much aqua distillati. The bottles were then corked and labeled. When sold, we would add the potassium-bicarbonate tablet and then seal the bottle with a metal cap. The corks were put back into a special box to be used over again the next Saturday.

Mr. Schiller was patient with me, and very kind, but fussy about details such as saving the magnesia corks, putting labels on straight, and never wasting paper or string. Also, alas, about his young clerk sampling the candy bars. Privately I considered this to be carrying thrift too far. Didn't he have a whole showcase full — *full* of Hershey bars, Tootsie Rolls, and those perfect, luscious things called Hoeffler's Centennials?

My hours in the drugstore soon became my whole existence. I arrived early and stayed late. I learned so many things. About the bottle of hydrocyanic [2] acid that was kept locked up because just one whiff of it could kill a person. How to mark the merchandise with the queer symbols that showed how much each item had cost wholesale. I learned how to make change, and the rudiments of salesmanship. If someone bought a washcloth, you immediately showed them the new soap display. Should they purchase calomel, you automatically fixed and wrapped up a bottle of citrate of magnesia so that they would not become something called "salivated" — which had to do with teeth getting black and falling out.

It was not long until I was sure that I knew everything.

Then I was trusted to stay alone in the store while Mr. Schiller went home to a hot lunch. From one until two o'clock, every afternoon, I was Schiller's drugstore and telephoned to Mr. Schiller's home only if a prescription came in.

Carmelita fell into the habit of coming by to visit with me during this hour. If a customer came in, Carmelita would pretend to be buying a magazine. We worked up quite a routine.

"Look through the racks again, madam," I would say to her in a businesslike tone. "Perhaps you will find one you like better. I will be right back, madam, just as soon as I've waited on this customer."

When alone again, we would resume our conversation — leaning idly on the candy counter, Carmelita in front, I at

[1] **boracic** (bō·răs′ĭk).

[2] **hydrocyanic** (hī′drō·sī·ăn′ĭk).

the back. For the first week we contented ourselves with gazing at the gorgeous display, choosing mentally the kind of candy we would buy if we had five dollars.

Sometimes the whole hour would be spent in this way. Always, though, our imaginary purchases contained a majority of Hoeffler's Centennials. They were Carmelita's favorites as well as mine. Creamy, delicately rum-flavored, one perfect chocolate in a brown cardboard box. Other candies might be larger, we conceded, might give you more for your money — but, ah, there was something so infinitely rich and satisfying about the Centennial's expensive elegance!

If Carmelita or I possessed a nickel we would purchase one and share it, I conscientiously ringing up the sale on the cash register. If we didn't have a nickel we would just gaze.

But not for long. Came the day when we took two whole Centennials out of the case and ate them! By devious ways we had arrived at a compromise with our consciences.

First, two little old candy bars among so many would hardly be missed, would they? Then, too, didn't I work overtime almost every day? Without any pay? Didn't Carmelita devote her time to coming up and staying with me?

Of course, Mr. Schiller was old-fashioned, and probably wouldn't approve of his clerk's having company during working hours. But what about Mrs. Schiller's constant dread of holdups? Certainly, we assured each other, it was far safer that the two of us be there in the store. If a robber came in, Carmelita could run for a policeman while I pretended I didn't know how to open the register.

We comfortably concluded that Carmelita was practically insurance for Schiller's drugstore, and it was no more than right that she and I should be paid one — perhaps two Hoeffler Centennials daily.

However, the concrete evidence of our self-administered pay became a problem. We couldn't put the empty boxes into the wastepaper basket, because Mrs. Schiller had a peculiar habit of inspecting that at every opportunity. We couldn't throw the boxes out into the street, because Mr. Schiller swept the sidewalks in front of the store several times a day; and we didn't want him to start wondering at the sudden and brisk sale in candy.

We finally solved the disposal problem by tossing the empty boxes up into the dark recess over the big street window, the one that had the big colored jars in it. A perfect hiding place, we assured each other.

Perfect, that is, until the Saturday the window dresser came to change the window decorations and climbed up to the cubbyhole to get the pink crepe paper he'd stored there the month before.

"Hey, Schiller," I heard him yell, "what you collecting these empty Hoeffler boxes for?"

He began to toss them down, one by one. Dusty, some of them crumpled or whole. Before my horrified eyes descended a cloud of empty candy boxes.

I moaned softly. Oh, surely Carmelita and I had never in the world consumed that many! Time stopped, along with my heart, while I watched the growing evidence of my guilt.

I looked up once at Mr. Schiller's surprised but still kind face. I gulped noisily, and he might have spoken; but some evil wind took that moment to blow Mrs. Schiller in through the front door and, from then on, nobody else had a chance to speak.

Her tight little eyes took in the situa-

A scene from the film version of "I Remember Mama," with Irene Dunne as Mama, Barbara Bel Geddes as Katrin, and Philip Dorn as Papa. (RKO Radio Pictures from Culver)

tion immediately. Her voice rose and fell in scathing denunciation, and the ugly words made me shiver. No one — ever — had talked to me like that, and the next few minutes became the most desolate of my life.

It was as if her tongue had been dipped in the acid that Mr. Schiller kept in a rubber-topped bottle on the back of the shelf because a drop of it could sear off your flesh.

Mrs. Schiller's most frequent — and mildest — word was Thief. Thief, capitalized and set in big, screaming letters.

I was not only a dirty, rotten, sneaking, low-down thief that should be sent to the juvenile-delinquency court; but I was no good, never would be any good, and nobody in the whole world would ever trust me again.

Mrs. Schiller said so. Mrs. Schiller said so again and again and louder and louder until, in pity for us both, Mr. Schiller made her go to the back of the store.

He finally let me go; and I rushed home to Mama, sobbing wretchedly, carrying the newspaper-wrapped package of empty Hoeffler boxes that Mrs. Schiller had commanded me to take to her.

It was some time before Mama could understand what I tried to tell her. Even then she did not seem to grasp the full import of my degradation, because she only said, "First you must stop sobbing so, my Katrin."

Her words were so loving I had to weep anew. Poor, poor Mama, to have such a child as I. A disgrace. A — a thief!

Mama dampened the towel by the sink and wiped my face, holding the coolness against my aching head.

"There now," she said, "there now."

And, big girl though I was, she made me sit in her lap while she rocked me gently.

Haltingly I told her of my crime. And when I got to the part about Mrs. Schiller she stopped rocking and just held me — tight.

I waited for Mama's answer. Mama could be strict, even stern, when we children had done wrong. I knew that I had sinned dreadfully, and now it was only right and just that I be punished.

Mama stood up so quickly I almost fell. She walked over to the sink and took a drink of water. Her back was so straight, so rigid, I started to cry again.

"Oh, please," I begged. "Please, Mama, don't you be angry too."

She turned and hurried to me, took my shaking hand in hers.

"Not with you, Katrin," she said earnestly. "It is with — but, yes, that can wait. Now — look at me, Daughter."

I looked into her quiet face, watched her mouth try to smile.

"This is important, my Katrin. Perhaps I cannot explain it so well, but you must not ever feel here" — she touched me — "in your heart, that you are what you said. A — a thief. A bad girl."

"But, Mama, I did take them — and Mrs. Schiller said —"

"Katrin, believe me, you are not a thief. You are a good girl."

I shook my head.

"You have been foolish, yes; you have done wrong. But no great wrong. You are still so young — so greedy for sweets, as all young things are."

"Mama, you just don't understand."

"But I do, that is why —" And Mama's laugh rang out suddenly, richly.

I stared at her. "Mama! You laughed!"

"As you must laugh, Daughter. Unless you" — Mama seemed to search for words — "unless you cripple something inside of you. Something that makes you lift your head after you have made a mistake. Something that makes you go on — with — with pride, Katrin."

I lowered my head. "But, Mama," I whispered, "whenever I think of it, oh, Mama, I am so ashamed!"

"Is good to be ashamed," Mama said briskly. "That makes it sure you will not do such a thing again. But cannot you see, Katrin, that with the shame and the sorrow there must also be the saving laughter?"

"I — I guess so."

"Listen, Daughter. Let me tell you why I understand, why I laughed. When Papa was courting me I lived, as you know, with your Aunt Jenny. Every Sunday evening Papa came to call. We did not have much money, but somehow Jenny could always contrive refreshments. Cookies, or a cake.

"Once she was able to make a fancy cake and pile it high with rich white frosting. It was, I believe, the most beautiful cake I had ever seen. I was young — it seemed that never did I get enough of sweets . . ."

Mama's eyes were misty, remembering.

"Well," she continued, "I kept tasting the frosting, sneaking into Jenny's pantry for just one more bite, until — oh, Katrin — until I'd eaten every speck of frosting on that cake!"

I found myself laughing with Mama at the story.

"Then what happened?"

"Jenny was cross, and with reason. So she served the cake that night and told Papa exactly why it looked so bare."

" And what did Papa do? "

Mama smiled a secret smile. " He married me," she said, " anyhow."

I leaned against Mama, relaxed, comforted.

Mama touched my cheek. " So can you smile now," she asked, " and believe that this – this thing you have done is not the end of the world? That you can go on without a voice in your heart ever crying ' Thief '? "

I nodded. " My goodness, though, wasn't I – "

" Foolish," Mama supplied. " And very naughty. And you must pay for the candy you ate. But you are not – bad."

" No, Mama, I guess I'm not bad."

" Is good. Now you will peel the potatoes for dinner and set the table. I " – Mama's gentle voice hardened – " I have a call to make."

And Mama wasn't smiling a bit as she marched out the door.

Thinking It Over

1. What do you like about Mama? What part of the incident shows that Mama has a stronge sense of family loyalty and pride?

2. How did Mama show great wisdom in dealing with her daughter? Was Katrin really a thief? How do you distinguish between foolishness and wickedness?

3. To rationalize is to try to prove to yourself or to someone else that the thing you *want* to do is the thing you *ought* to do. Have you ever caught yourself doing it? Give an example. How did Katrin and Carmelita rationalize their taking the candy bars?

4. Was it a good thing or not that Mrs. Schiller happened to come in at just the moment she did? What might have happened if the case had been left entirely to Mr. Schiller? What, then, might have been the effect on Katrin?

5. Find the place where Katrin says, " Please, Mama, don't you be angry, too." Note Mama's answer. What was going on in her mind at that moment? At the very end, where was Mama going when she marched out the door?

6. You noticed that Katrin was not afraid to tell her mother about her disgrace. She was ashamed, but not afraid. Have you ever discussed such an issue with your parents? If you have a Parent-Teacher Association in your school, perhaps your teacher could arrange a panel discussion on parent-child relations at one of their meetings with both parents and children represented. Be prepared with intelligent suggestions.

7. Another good class discussion might be held on the subject of jobs. Many young people take part-time jobs in order to earn money while completing their education. How should they prepare themselves for such work? What responsibilities must they be prepared to take? What temptations will beset them? Are part-time jobs, in the long run, good or bad for high school pupils?

For Your Vocabulary

WORD BUILDING: If something is *dispensable,* then one can *dispense* with it or do without it. The girl in this selection was proud of her *indispensability* to the druggist. What does this word mean? *Degradation* means " moving from a higher to a lower position "; the verb is *degrade,* and the adjective is *degrading.* What is the basic word? the prefix? How do they fit together to make this definition? When Mrs. Schiller's voice rose in *scathing denunciation,* she was sharply and bitterly *denouncing* the girl. *Denunciation* comes from the Latin *de-* (down) + *nunciare* (to announce), hence a down-announcement. What definition do you get from this analysis of the word? Note the difference in spelling of the verb and the noun. You find it also in pro*nounce* – pro*nun*ciation.

LOUIS BROMFIELD

Grandma Moses

If you had been in Albany, New York, on a certain day in September 1950, you might have been fortunate enough to attend a rather unusual public party given for a spry little old lady who was celebrating her ninetieth birthday. Her name was Mrs. Anna Mary Robertson Moses, but everyone called her Grandma Moses. She had come to Albany for the opening of a formal exhibition of her paintings — sixty of them. The year before, she had been named one of the ten outstanding women of America; and not long after that birthday party, she was acclaimed " Grandmother of the Nation." That tickled her. " I'm getting to be as famous as flying saucers," she said. " I hope all those grandchildren won't want Christmas presents."

Yes, Grandma Moses is quite a person. She didn't even *begin* to paint until she was seventy-six, yet she has painted more than a thousand pictures and is regarded as one of the most important artists in this country. Recently she was awarded her second Doctor of Arts degree. Grandma Moses is known as a *primitive* artist, which means " natural and untaught." Her drawing is childlike and sometimes almost crude, but unlike some modern paintings you don't have to hold her pictures upside down to try to make sense out of them. Every picture tells a story. Her colors are as clear and bright as her own philosophy of life, which is simple, wholesome, and wise. She has the shrewd humor of the country-bred and takes her honors easily with the humility of the truly great. America may well be proud of Grandma Moses. In the following pages the well-known writer, Louis Bromfield, tells you something about her work; and then you will have the pleasure of seeing a reproduction of one of her paintings and reading Grandma Moses' own account of the country fair it depicts.

About six or seven years ago I began hearing from friends living near Williamstown, Massachusetts, stories about a wonderful old woman who lived on a farm and painted pictures which she sold along with the jams and preserves she " put up " during the summer. She was, they said, prouder of her preserves than of her pictures, and when she was asked the prices of her paintings she countered with a question: " What size do you want? " The price depended on the size.

I would have suspected that the pictures were like the mediocrities [1] exhibited at the average Middle Western county fairs but for one fact: my friends said the pictures were remarkable and I respected their opinions because they had the background, the culture, the taste, and the understanding to know a real picture, a good picture, from a mediocrity or an affectation.[2] They were not impressed by any artistic snobbery [3] concerning "primitives" nor were they people to be entrapped by any nostalgic [4] feeling for quaintness and the "good old days." They were buying Grandma Moses' pictures and had even ordered some in advance, priced, at her insistence, according to size.

And then I saw my first "Grandma Moses" and I understood their enthusiasm. What struck me immediately about the picture, and indeed about all the other "early Grandma Moses" which I saw, was the decorative quality and a kind of design and composition that I found in the Persian and Moslem Indian paintings I had seen in the East. In the pictures of Grandma Moses there was less formality, less smoothness, less minute attention to details but there was in both the New England and the Indian pictures the same sense of space and "of the whole" and above all a sense of the painter's intimate feeling for children and animals and color and the delights which only those can know who share an intimate feeling for nature and have found for themselves a satisfactory relationship with the universe. As in the Indian pictures, each figure, animal or human, painted by Grandma Moses, was caught in an arrested moment of action . . . children skating, dogs running and barking, horses galloping and rearing. Clearly these were the pictures of someone who had loved and been loved and had borne children and lived close to animals and had had a busy, happy life. I knew, without ever seeing her, that Grandma Moses was a wise, shrewd, happy old lady and that she painted for her own pleasure because she loved life and color and felt the necessity of communication to others through the medium, first of all of color, her own sense of the richness of life. It was clear that never in all her life had she known a bored moment. . . . Her small world, whether viewed from her bedroom window, or from the window of a bus driving along the road, was at once a cosy and limitless universe which contained the keys to the knowledge of good living and understanding.

In those earlier pictures she often painted crudely, but this defect could not stifle the overwhelming sense of her satisfaction in life and her adjustment to the immense scheme of creation itself.

It is one of the remarkable things about Grandma Moses that after beginning to paint seriously late in life, she has gone on steadily learning and improving.

In the beginning she had to find her own way. She had to learn the kind of composition which gave her pleasure and satisfaction. She had to learn how to achieve the effects of color which so delighted her. She had even to learn about the materials and the tools she used and which ones permitted her to

[1] **mediocrities** (mē·dĭ·ŏk′rĭ·tĭz): things of very ordinary merit.
[2] **affectation** (ăf′ĕk·tā′shŭn): a pretense; in this case, a painting of pretended simplicity.
[3] **artistic snobbery:** desire to keep up with fashions in art regardless of true merit.
[4] **nostalgic** (nŏs·tăl′jĭk): homesick; recalling with affection.

Grandma Moses at home. (George Burns)

realize to the greatest degree the feeling she had inside her. She learned that a base of lustrous white, carefully prepared by her own methods after much experimentation, gave her pictures luminosity [1] and even brilliance. She had to learn painfully and slowly how to achieve the hazy, constantly changing beauty of the distant Vermont hills and skies which she conveys so skillfully in her pictures. In fact she had to learn, herself, without help or advice, how to become a painter. As a result she paints like herself.

I confess that for me many of Grandma Moses' pictures have a philosophical and at times even a literary appeal. She knows what country life feels like, and she conveys to the beholder the joy that is in a running colt, the singing beauty of a blossoming peach tree, the soothing peace of a clear, running brook. She does not paint any of these things separately, for themselves, but in a pattern, each in its proper relation to all the others. It is a pattern filled with the satisfaction of those who understand that any farm is a small but complete fragment of the universe in which all the laws of nature are constantly in play, affecting the lives, the philosophy, and the faith of those who inhabit it.

There have been and are today many technically skillful artists who paint farm scenes and rural landscapes, but nearly all of them simply paint "pictures," adroit and sophisticated [2] perhaps in design and color but without that luminosity, enthusiasm, and understanding which one finds in Grandma Moses' pictures. Too many of them are flat in spirit, with the smell of the studio about them. They reveal little inwardness or real warmth. They are simply pictorial, revealing or interpreting little or nothing.

A good farmer looking at most of the farm pictures and landscapes painted in our time might say "a pretty picture" or "no farm ever looked like that" and move on to the next one. In front of a Grandma Moses he would stop and chuckle and smile and sigh, for in it he would find not only every detail painted with satisfaction and understanding, but he would know at once that Grandma Moses understood his whole small world with its glories and hard work and those quick, deep inarticulate gusts of emotion which sweep over him at the sight of a newly born calf or a blossoming pear tree or at the smell of deep, rich soil, freshly turned to the warm sun in spring. He would recognize that Grandma Moses understood these fundamental things which make the good husbandman [3] a part of the earth and the fullness thereof and make him invulnerable to the petty miseries and misfortunes which complicate and torment the lives of city-dwellers. . . .

At least that is what I find in a Grandma Moses picture, and I have seen the same satisfaction in the eyes of others standing before one of her paintings, studying the figures of a strutting tom turkey, or a rearing colt, or a blossoming tree, or a child skating on the ice of the clear little river she loves so well and paints so often.

[1] **luminosity** (lū′mĭ·nŏs′ĭ·tĭ): the quality of being full of light or of reflecting light.
[2] **adroit** (ȧ·droit′) **and sophisticated** (sô·fĭs′tĭ·kāt′ĕd): clever and worldly.
[3] **husbandman:** a farmer.

MY FIRST FAIR

GRANDMA MOSES

This is a photograph of Grandma Moses' painting "The Country Fair." Grandma Moses describes her trip to a state fair in the following excerpt from her autobiography. Her writing is like her painting, simple, unaffected, and completely natural. Grandma Moses received little formal education, so that her style — given here exactly as she herself writes — is not the formal English you are accustomed to reading. Yet you will discover that it is colorful and expressive. (Photo by permission, Grandma Moses Properties, Inc.)

THERE was a time when I would look forward from one fall to another just to go to the fair, and summer picnics. Those were about all the recreations we had in those days, and we would work the year through saving our money and our clothing.

The first fair I ever went to, was the State Fair in the year of 1876, the grounds were between Troy and Albany. It was called a very nice fair, and I was invited by the president, a Mr. Edwin Throne. We left South Cambridge on the 10th of September going as far as Johnsonville on the steam cars; this was the first time I had ever been on a train, and I was very car sick before we reached Johnsonville. There we changed cars, and had to wait. I saw my Father at the lumber yard and asked Mrs. Whiteside if I could go over where he was and ride home with him and stay home till she came back, and she said no! How would you look riding on a load of lumber on the highway. So I had to go on, but was not car sick no more.

We reached West Troy about one o'clock and had a nice dinner; there were a lot of young people from out Galway. After dinner we all went down the street and crossed the ferry to the fair grounds. The first building we went through was the flower building, and oh was not that grand, we had a lovely flower garden at home, but not like that, oh it was so sweet, and delightful in there. We stayed there till sun down.

The next morning we all went back to the fair and this time we went through the poultry house, there were all kinds of feathered fowls. We were greeted as we opened the gate, "how do, how do, Polly wants a cracker"; Polly could speak very plain, that was the first time I had ever seen a parrot. From there we went through the stove building, a long house not so wide, with plenty of light, all along one side were cast iron cooking stoves of every description, behind every stove was a cook or chef and a table, and as you passed the stove some one would pass out to you some of the food that they were cooking on or in that stove, sometimes it would be hot rolls nicely buttered, then the next stove hot ginger bread or pies, and so forth; we did not have to go home for dinner, nor could we eat all that we got, and everything was the best. Oh those were the days – no hot dogs or sandwiches, that one never knows what the contents is!

From the stove building we went to the music hall, a large octagon building full of musical instruments, there you could not hear yourself think, but it was grand. From there part of us went to see the stock, and the rest to see the horses on exhibition. I liked that where the ladies rode on side saddles with long skirts and jumped hurdles; the horse racing was exciting but I did not understand it: – Take it all in all it was three delightful days.

Thinking It Over

1. In order to get the full benefit of Mr. Bromfield's analysis of Grandma Moses' paintings, you really need at least half a dozen examples of her pictures in color. Perhaps you can get some of the widely distributed Christmas cards which reproduce several of her paintings. Your art teacher may have some in her files. Try the clipping file in the library, too. While you are in the library, look for some of the newspaper and magazine articles about the artist. As you may well suppose, Grandma Moses is good journalistic "copy." Everything she does or says seems to be of interest. With several pictures to look at, or even if you have only the one in this book, read Louis Bromfield's article again and do these things:

a. Find examples of "arrested" action, caught as if by a camera.

b. Find evidence of the artist's love and understanding of children.

c. Find similar evidence of her affection for and knowledge of animals. (Could an artist have one without the other?)

d. Find examples of the realistic detail that pleases and amuses farmers and other country people.

2. How did Grandma Moses teach herself?

3. How does her work differ from that of other painters of country life?

4. In one place Mr. Bromfield mentions the "literary appeal" of Grandma Moses' pictures. Look into two or three poetry anthologies and see how many poems you can find that are related in some way to the things she paints. Find, for example, A. E. Housman's "Loveliest of Trees"; Tennyson's "The Brook"; and "The Pas-

ture," by Robert Frost. Do you think any of Grandma Moses' pictures would tie up with short stories in this book?

5. What do you learn of Grandma Moses' personality from the excerpt here given from her autobiography? Look carefully at the painting "The Country Fair." How much of her wealth of memories has she been able to transfer to canvas?

6. You note that since Grandma Moses has had very little school education, her way of expressing herself in words is as simple and "primitive" as her painting. What do you like about it? Do you think it would be better had it been rewritten in grammatical, formal English before publication? Give reasons for your answer.

FOOTPRINTS ON THE SANDS OF TIME

Suggestions for Free Reading

Andrews, Mary Raymond Shipman, *The Perfect Tribute* (Scribner, 1906)
Short but beautiful story about Lincoln.

Andrews, Roy Chapman, *Under a Lucky Star* (Viking, 1943)
Interesting life of an explorer with restless feet.

Baden-Powell, Sir Robert, *Lessons of a Lifetime* (Holt, 1943)
Memories of the man who founded the Boy Scouts.

Benét, Laura, *Enchanting Jenny Lind* (Dodd, 1937)
Great Swedish singer who took the world by storm one hundred years ago.

Burnett, Constance, *Shoemaker's Son* (Random, 1941)
Fascinating story of Hans Christian Andersen.

Chase, Genevieve, *Four Young Teachers* (Dodd, 1947)
Four girls interested in teaching are taken to visit different types of schools to see what it's like from the other side of the teacher's desk.

Considine, Bob, *The Babe Ruth Story* (Dutton, 1948)
A tough kid becomes a national sports hero.

Cornell, Katharine, *I Wanted to Be an Actress* (Random House, 1939)
From stock company to stardom.

Daché, Lily, *Talking Through My Hats* (Coward-McCann, 1946)
Boys won't care for this one. Tell them who she is, girls.

Davis, Kenneth Sydney, *Soldier of Democracy: a Biography of Dwight Eisenhower* (Doubleday, 1945)
An excellent biography of the man who led the Allied Forces to victory in World War II.

Daugherty, James, *Daniel Boone* (Viking, 1939)
Strong, homespun story of a great pioneer. Read *Poor Richard,* too – about Ben Franklin.

Day, Clarence, *Life With Father, Life With Mother* (Knopf, 1935)
Hilarious stories that will never grow old.

DiMaggio, Joe, *Lucky to Be a Yankee* (Greenberg, 1946)
The Yankee Clipper tells his story.

Eaton, Jeanette, *Leader by Destiny* (Harcourt, 1938)
Excellent biography of Washington; makes him a living personage. Read also *Gandhi: Fighter Without a Sword* (Morrow, 1950)

Embree, Edwin R., *13 Against the Odds* (Viking, 1944)
Achievements of thirteen Negroes in different walks of life.

Everson, George, *The Story of Television; the Life of Philo T. Farnsworth* (Norton, 1949)
Did you know that a high school *freshman* first dreamed of television? Read about it. It's true.

Ewen, David, *The Story of George Gershwin* (Holt, 1943)
The man who wrote "Rhapsody in Blue."

Garland, Hamlin, *Son of the Middle Border* (Macmillan, 1917)
Interesting memories of pioneer days.

Garst, Shannon, *Will Rogers, Immortal Cowboy* (Messner, 1950)
The mule-roping, broncho-busting, roving life of America's great humorist, whose homely wit and good sense made him famous.

Gibson, Katharine, *The Goldsmith of Florence* (Macmillan, 1929)
A truly lovely book if you are interested in art. Magnificent illustrations. The goldsmith is Benvenuto Cellini.

Gorsline, Douglas W., *Farm Boy* (Viking, 1950)

Every boy who has ever lived on a farm, or wanted to, will like this book.

Gray, Elizabeth, *Young Walter Scott* (Viking, 1935)
What was the creator of *Ivanhoe* like when he was young?

Jackson, Phyllis Wynne, *Golden Footlights* (Holiday, 1949)
Story of a famous comedienne, Lotta Crabtree.

Lagerlöf, Selma, *Mårbacka* (Doubleday, 1924)
Home life of the author in Sweden.

Lawrence, Gertrude, *A Star Danced* (Doubleday, 1945)
Famous actress tells her story.

Levinger, Elma Ehrlich, *Albert Einstein* (Messner, 1949)
True and human story of the great scientist. (Surprise! He didn't like to go to school!)

Lovelace, Delos W., *Rockne of Notre Dame* (Putnam, 1931)
Story of the big-hearted football coach, Knute Rockne.

Lindsay, Martin, *The Epic of Captain Scott* (Putnam, 1934)
Supplements the Scott story (p. 401).

Malvern, Gladys, *Dancing Star* (Messner, 1942)
Life of Anna Pavlova, world-renowned Russian ballerina. Girls who like dancing will enjoy this one.

Masani, Shakuntala, *Nehru's Story* (Oxford, 1949)
Adds to your knowledge of the great leader of India.

Meigs, Cornelia L., *Invincible Louisa* (Little, 1933)
Readable life of Louisa M. Alcott.

Morrow, Honoré Willsie, *Forever Free* (Morrow, 1927)
Novel based on the Lincoln period.

Nesbitt, Henrietta, *White House Diary* (Doubleday, 1948)
Entertaining story of the housekeeping job in the White House, especially under the Roosevelts.

Nicolay, Helen, *MacArthur of Bataan* (Appleton-Century, 1942)
Story of the great general in the heartbreaking days of World War II.

North, Sterling, *So Dear to My Heart* (Doubleday, 1948)
Gay and pleasant story of a boy's life in Indiana not too long ago.

Olmstead, Karsten, *The World at My Finger Tips* (Bobbs, 1942)
Boy faces blindness with courage.

Pace, Mildred Maston, *Juliette Low* (Scribner, 1947)
Interesting biography of the woman who founded the Girl Scouts.

Purdy, Clare, *He Heard America Sing* (Messner, 1940)
Moving story of Stephen Foster, whose songs were written in sorrow.

Reynolds, Quentin, *The Wright Brothers; Pioneers of American Aviation* (Random, 1950)
Famous war correspondent tells a thrilling story of American initiative.

Robinson, Jackie, *My Own Story* (Greenberg, 1948)
First Negro to play on a major-league team tells his story.

Romulo, Col. Carlos P., *I Saw the Fall of the Philippines* (Doubleday, 1942)
Firsthand account of a tragedy by the man who later became president of the United Nations General Assembly.

Roosevelt, Eleanor, *This Is My Story* (Harper, 1937)
A long and detailed account of Mrs. Roosevelt's life, from girlhood to her role as " Mrs. President."

Roosevelt, Eleanor, and Ferris, H., *Partners — the United Nations in Action* (Doubleday, 1950)
A description of the organization, functions, and aims of the U.N.

Rourke, Constance, *Audubon* (Harcourt, 1936)
Young artists and bird lovers will like the story of the great bird painter.

Steffens, Lincoln, *Boy on Horseback* (Harcourt, 1931)
How a boy learned to take care of himself and be independent.

Stevenson, O. T., *The Talking Wire* (Messner, 1947)
How Alexander Graham Bell gave us the telephone.

Undset, Sigrid, *Happy Times in Norway* (Knopf, 1942)
Happy memories of a famous novelist.

Yates, Elizabeth, *Amos Fortune, Free Man* (Aladdin, 1950)
Forty years a slave, Amos purchased his freedom and died a respected landowner.

Cathedral in Huehuetenango, Guatemala, courtesy United Fruit Co.

Lyrics from Many Lands

TRULY the world today is growing smaller and smaller. More than ever before there is a need for people of all nations to understand each other better. Stories, essays, and biographies give an insight into the lives and customs, the hopes and discouragements, of people in other lands; yet nowhere in literature do these feelings of people appear so plainly and intensely as in poetry, especially in lyric poetry. Lyric poetry is the special language of song. It is the outpouring of the heart about matters that are very personal; it is the songlike utterance of ideas that carry great emotion.

Reading Lyric Poetry

A lyric poem is usually written to praise or " celebrate " something – a season of the year, a place, a person, one's homeland, a noble action, or just an idea. It may also be a passionate denouncement of a great wrong, or simply an attempt to amuse the listener or reader. Unlike narrative poetry, a lyric poem does not usually attempt to tell a story. It is less concerned with telling about outside events or incidents than it is with describing some personal feeling or idea that the poet has.

Since a lyric poem is a personal expression of the poet, it will usually reflect a definite *mood.* You should be able to tell whether a poem is sorrowful or angry, whether it is thoughtful, reverent, happy, spirited, hopeful, or mysterious. You should be able to detect, too, whether it is complaining or boastful, solemn or whimsical. Possibly you will find other terms to describe the mood of the various poems in this section. Sensing the mood is important in poetry because it helps you to determine the full meaning of a poem. And if you are reading a lyric aloud, you will have to know the mood in order to give the lines their proper accent and emphasis.

POEMS FROM FAR PLACES

In this section you will take a quick tour around the world on the wings of lyric poetry. The first and longest stop will be in England, because that country is the main source of our American literary heritage. Then you will go to other lands, other places. Perhaps you will notice that although the scenery changes in these poems, they all reflect the universal feelings of men. People in England or Ireland, in Israel or India or China, are likely to share certain common attitudes toward life and all its pleasures and problems. Of course we have to depend on translations for those poems written in foreign languages, but someday you may be able to read some of them in the original.

SILVER

WALTER DE LA MARE

Walter de la Mare * is an English writer who in this poem shows us a calm, sleeping world by the light of the moon. " Silver " is one of the best possible pieces for reading aloud. Use a quiet, mysterious-sounding monotone; enunciate carefully and keep the rhythm slow and even. In this way you will get full value out of the liquid-sounding *l*'s and *s*'s which help to establish a sleepy, dreamlike mood.

Slowly, silently, now the moon
Walks the night in her silver shoon;°
This way, and that, she peers, and sees
Silver fruit upon silver trees;
One by one the casements catch 5
Her beams beneath the silvery thatch;
Couched in his kennel, like a log,
With paws of silver sleeps the dog;
From their shadowy cote° the white breasts peep
Of doves in a silver-feathered sleep; 10
A harvest mouse goes scampering by,
With silver claws and a silver eye;
And moveless fish in the water gleam,
By silver reeds in a silver stream.

* **De la Mare** (dĕ lȧ mâr′). 2. **shoon:** shoes.

9. **cote** (kōt): coop.

For Your Vocabulary

CLOSE ATTENTION TO WORDS: Much of the beauty of this poem is created by the use of one word, *silver*. Do you think the poet could use any other color with as great effect? Why or why not? If you wondered why the word *silver* never appears at the end of a line (though it appears ten times in the poem), the answer is that *silver* is one of the few words in the English language that cannot be rhymed exactly. Prove this to yourself. Are you acquainted with the *thesaurus,* a special kind of dictionary which enables you to pay close attention to words? Get one from the library and get acquainted with the information it offers. Find out how much fun you can have with words by looking up their *synonyms* (words of similar meaning) and *antonyms* (words of opposite meaning).

SONG

CHRISTINA ROSSETTI

Christina Rossetti was the sister of a famous nineteenth-century English poet and painter, Dante Gabriel Rossetti. " Song " is a very popular love poem that has been often imitated by modern writers. Probably nothing is rarer than an original love poem — but here is one.

When I am dead, my dearest,
  Sing no sad songs for me;
Plant thou no roses at my head,
  Nor shady cypress tree:
Be the green grass above me 5
  With showers and dewdrops wet;
And if thou wilt, remember,
  And if thou wilt, forget.

I shall not see the shadows,
  I shall not feel the rain; 10
I shall not hear the nightingale
  Sing on, as if in pain;
And dreaming through the twilight
  That doth not rise nor set,
Haply I may remember, 15
  And haply may forget.

How Well Did You Read?

1. People who are very much in love often ask each other to promise to remember forever, if one should be taken from the other. How is the speaker in this poem different? What reason is given in the second stanza for not exacting such a promise?

2. Explain lines 5 and 6. Does *haply* in lines 15 and 16 mean *happily?* If not, what does it mean?

WHEN ICICLES HANG BY THE WALL

WILLIAM SHAKESPEARE

You know of Shakespeare as a writer of plays, but did you know that scattered through his plays there are many charming songs? Some are sung by a single character, as is " Ariel's Song " in *The Tempest,* and some by a group of characters, as in *A Midsummer Night's Dream.* The following song is from *Love's Labor's Lost.*

When icicles hang by the wall,
  And Dick the shepherd blows his nail,
And Tom bears logs into the hall,
  And milk comes frozen home in pail,
When blood is nipped, and ways be foul, 5
Then nightly sings the staring owl,
  To-whit!
To-who! — a merry note,
While greasy Joan° doth keel° the pot.

When all aloud the wind doth blow, 10
  And coughing drowns the parson's saw,
And birds sit brooding in the snow,
  And Marian's nose looks red and raw,
When roasted crabs° hiss in the bowl,
Then nightly sings the staring owl, 15
  To-whit!
To-who! — a merry note,
While greasy Joan doth keel the pot.

9. **Joan** (jōn); **keel:** stir. 14. **crabs:** crab apples.

How Well Did You Read?

1. What is the picture that you get of the church through line 11? A *saw*, in this case, is a wise saying or a much-repeated one.

2. What took place when Dick the shepherd blew his *nail*? You've done this too on a cold day.

3. What is Shakespeare celebrating here — a scene, a season, or a person? What is the mood of the poem?

Song from DRAKE

ALFRED NOYES

It is perhaps natural that the modern English poet Alfred Noyes should write about the sea, for England has been a seafaring nation for hundreds of years. If you don't feel the rugged, virile quality of this poem, then your soul indeed needs tuning up! These stanzas are from a long poem about Sir Francis Drake, the admiral who sailed around the world in the service of Queen Elizabeth. Try to decide what is the " real " gold that attracts men to the high seas.

The moon is up, the stars are bright,
  The wind is fresh and free!
We're out to seek for gold tonight
  Across the silver sea!
The world was growing gray and old;
  Break out the sails again! 6
We're out to seek a Realm of Gold
  Beyond the Spanish Main.

We're sick of all the cringing knees,
  The courtly smiles and lies. 10
God, let Thy singing Channel breeze
  Lighten our hearts and eyes!
Let love no more be bought and sold
  For earthly loss or gain.
We're out to seek an Age of Gold 15
  Beyond the Spanish Main.

Beyond the light of far Cathay,°
  Beyond all mortal dreams,
Beyond the reach of night and day
  Our El Dorado° gleams, 20
Revealing — as the skies unfold —
  A star without a stain,
The Glory of the Gates of Gold
  Beyond the Spanish Main.

17. **Cathay** (kȧ·thā′): China. 20. **El Dorado** (ĕl dŏ·rä′dō): an imaginary place abounding in gold, supposedly in South America.

How Well Did You Read?

1. What is the " Realm of Gold " that the men seek? Is it the gold in Spanish ships? How would you describe the speakers in the poem? What did they hate about the life at court? What kind of life did they prefer? Why?

2. The phrase " the Spanish Main " should awaken in your mind suggestions of other great sailors and famous events. What do you know about the buccaneers and privateers in the days of " Good Queen Bess "? Why was it the Spanish Main instead of the English Main, and what do you think is the literal meaning of the word *main*?

LONE DOG

IRENE RUTHERFORD McLEOD

This English lyric poem has long been a favorite of readers who like their poetry rhythmic and marching in sound, as well as vigorous and powerful in mood. Its philosophy is one which should appeal to those who want to face the world squarely on its own terms. The poem is popular with verse-speaking groups. If you read it aloud, be sure to emphasize the adjectives that stand out, such as *lean, keen, wild,* and *lone.* Read crisply, slowing down only for the last line of each stanza.

I'm a lean dog, a keen dog, a wild dog, and lone;
I'm a rough dog, a tough dog, hunting on my own;
I'm a bad dog, a mad dog, teasing silly sheep;
I love to sit and bay the moon, to keep fat souls from sleep.

I'll never be a lap dog, licking dirty feet, 5
A sleek dog, a meek dog, cringing for my meat,
Not for me the fireside, the well-filled plate,
But shut door, and sharp stone, and cuff and kick, and hate.

Not for me the other dogs, running by my side,
Some have run a short while, but none of them would bide. 10
Oh, mine is still the lone trail, the hard trail, the best,
Wide wind, and wild stars, and hunger of the quest!

How Well Did You Read?

1. This poet certainly has in mind something very definite. Can you put it into a few words? Try to find comparisons between this poem and "Song" from *Drake.*

2. How do you interpret *fat souls* in line 4 and *bide* in line 10?

3. How are some people like lone dogs? Are such people really happy or popular? What is your idea of friendliness? Discuss.

INVICTUS

WILLIAM ERNEST HENLEY

No modern poet had more need for an "unconquerable soul" than the English writer William Ernest Henley. Handicapped by continued ill-health, he nevertheless created a tremendous amount of literature, including many beautiful short poems. "Invictus" is his best known, chiefly because of its powerful argument for the triumph of courage over circumstance.

Out of the night that covers me,
Black as the Pit from pole to pole,
I thank whatever gods may be
For my unconquerable soul.

In the fell° clutch of circumstance 5
I have not winced nor cried aloud.
Under the bludgeonings of chance
My head is bloody, but unbowed.

Beyond this place of wrath and tears
Looms but the horror of the shade,
And yet the menace of the years 11
Finds, and shall find, me unafraid.

It matters not how strait° the gate,
How charged with punishments the scroll,
I am the master of my fate; 15
I am the captain of my soul.

5. **fell:** cruel. 13. **strait:** narrow.

How Well Did You Read?

1. This is a poem to memorize, not only because it is one of the most famous poems in the English language, but also because it will come to mind many times in your life when the "bludgeonings of chance" seem too much for you. What spirit of mind does the poet celebrate here? Can you find a word that exactly describes the mood of the poem? Weigh your choices carefully.

2. Compare "Invictus" with Christina Rossetti's "Song" and Irene McLeod's "Lone Dog." In what way are they alike? In each poem, with whom is the speaker most concerned? What is his attitude toward the world in general? Man is a social being; he must learn to live with other men. How can a person be a good member of society and still remain an individual? Discuss this point.

For Your Vocabulary

WORD ORIGINS: The title of this poem comes from the Latin. Perhaps you remember the famous phrase that the Roman Caesar used in describing his conquest of Gaul: *veni, vidi, vici* — "I came, I saw, I conquered." By adding the prefix *in-*, which gives a negative meaning to the base word, the word *invictus* means "not conquered."

SYMBOLIC WORDS: In line 2 "the Pit" is a symbol of a place of eternal punishment. Notice that the symbol of life after death is carried throughout the poem. In line 10 "the shade" means the unknown darkness beyond life. In line 13 there is the word *strait,* which means narrow. To what would this narrow gate lead? What is the *scroll,* in line 14, that contains a list of a man's sins or the punishments due him?

KITTY OF COLERAINE

CHARLES DAWSON SHANLY

"Kitty of Coleraine" * is far different in mood and subject matter from the other poems in this section. It is a type of poetry called light verse, for it concerns neither a serious topic nor a deep emotion. At once you will sense the Irish lilt in the lines. If you read it aloud, rhyme *McCleary* with *dairy, leave* with *gave,* and *again* with *plain* and *pain.* An Irish lad and lass would probably pronounce the words this way!

As beautiful Kitty one morning was tripping
  With a pitcher of milk for the fair of Coleraine,
When she saw me she stumbled, the pitcher down tumbled,
  And all the sweet buttermilk watered the plain.
"Oh, what shall I do now? 'Twas looking at you now! 5
  I'm sure such a pitcher I'll ne'er see again.
'Twas the pride of my dairy. Oh, Barney McCleary,
  You're sent as a plague to the girls of Coleraine."

I sat down beside her, and gently did chide her
  That such a misfortune should give her such pain; 10
A kiss then I gave her, and before I did leave her
  She vowed for such pleasure she'd break it again.
'Twas the haymaking season — I can't tell the reason —
  Misfortunes will never come single, 'tis plain!
For very soon after poor Kitty's disaster 15
  The devil a pitcher was whole in Coleraine.

* **Coleraine** (kōl·rān′).

A RED, RED ROSE

ROBERT BURNS

Few men are so well loved and well remembered as the Scottish poet, Robert Burns, whose songs live in the hearts of men everywhere. On New Year's Eve, when everyone joins in singing "Auld Lang Syne," then it's the magic of Bobbie Burns's poetry — as well as the music — that draws people closer together. Here is another of his famous poems that has been put to music.

O, my luve's like a red, red rose,
  That's newly sprung in June;
O, my luve's like the melodie
  That's sweetly played in tune.

As fair art thou, my bonnie lass, 5
  So deep in luve am I;
And I will luve thee still, my dear,
  Till a' the seas gang dry.

Till a' the seas gang dry, my dear,
  And the rocks melt wi' the sun; 10
And I will luve thee still, my dear,
  While the sands o' life shall run.

And fare thee well, my only luve!
  And fare thee well awhile!
And I will come again, my luve, 15
  Though it were ten thousand mile.

How Well Did You Read?

1. Can you see why these lines will be remembered longer than most of the popular songs of today? Try to point out some great differences between a recent "hit" and the song by Robert Burns.

2. From the context, what do you think is the meaning of *gang*, lines 8 and 9? The last stanza gives a clue to the occasion for the writing of the poem. What is it?

3. The "language of love" in all countries is full of exaggerations. Point out some of the exaggerations in this poem. They are of a kind sometimes known as "little white lies." Why? Do lovers really mean or believe all they tell each other? How would you, as the girl spoken to, regard these promises?

4. Is the poet's "luve" in stanza 1 his emotion or the person he loves? Why do you think so? What is the situation, hinted at in the last stanza, that causes the poem to be written? Refer to the section "Reading Lyric Poetry" on page 305 and see whether you can find a word that correctly names the mood of this poem.

WHEN I AM WITH MY OWN ADORED

HEINRICH HEINE

The songs of Heinrich Heine,* a great German poet of the nineteenth century, match closely the feeling and expression of those by Robert Burns. However, because we must depend on translation, what we read of Heine in English loses something of its original charm. The following translation by the American poet and editor, Louis Untermeyer, fortunately retains the sincere feeling of the original and gives us a beautiful, rich sound of words, as well.

When I am with my own adored,
  Oh then my heart leaps high;
I am as rich as any lord,
  The world is mine to buy!

But every time I leave her, then 5
  My wealth, that seemed secure,
Is spent — and I am once again
  The poorest of the poor.

Louis Untermeyer, Translator

* **Heinrich Heine** (hīn′rĭk hī′nĕ).

THE SPELL OF THE YUKON

ROBERT W. SERVICE

This poem about the gold country of northern Canada is especially popular with boys. The lines have a vigorous songlike quality and the pictures are vivid. The author recognizes the perils as well as the pleasures of the Yukon.

I wanted the gold, and I sought it;
  I scrabbled and mucked like a slave.
Was it famine or scurvy — I fought it;
  I hurled my youth into a grave.
I wanted the gold, and I got it — 5
  Came out with a fortune last fall —
Yet somehow life's not what I thought it,
  And somehow the gold isn't all.

No! There's the land. (Have you seen it?)
  It's the cussedest land that I know,
From the big, dizzy mountains that screen it 11
  To the deep, deathlike valleys below.
Some say God was tired when he made it;
  Some say it's a fine land to shun;
Maybe; but there's some as would trade it 15
  For no land on earth — and I'm one.

The summer — no sweeter was ever;
  The sunshiny woods all athrill;
The grayling aleap in the river,
  The bighorn asleep on the hill. 20
The strong life that never knows harness;
  The wilds where the caribou call;
The freshness, the freedom, the farness —
  O God! how I'm stuck on it all.

The winter! the brightness that blinds you, 25
  The white land locked tight as a drum,
The cold fear that follows and finds you,
  The silence that bludgeons you dumb.
The snows that are older than history,
  The woods where the weird shadows slant; 30
The stillness, the moonlight, the mystery,
  I've bade 'em good-by — but I can't.

There's a land where the mountains are nameless,
  And the rivers all run God knows where;
There are lives that are erring and aimless, 35
  And deaths that just hang by a hair;
There are hardships that nobody reckons;
  There are valleys unpeopled and still;
There's a land — oh, it beckons and beckons,
  And I want to go back — and I will.

There's gold, and it's haunting and haunting; 41
  It's luring me on as of old;
Yet it isn't the gold that I'm wanting
  So much as just finding the gold.
It's the great, big, broad land 'way up yonder, 45
  It's the forests where silence has lease;
It's the beauty that fills me with wonder,
  It's the stillness that fills me with peace.

How Well Did You Read?

1. Point out the lines that have good figures of speech in them. What details of description clearly reveal that the Yukon is

Poets find inspiration in many different lands: above, *A sunny corner in Ireland,* below, *The cold splendor of Alaska.* (Above, *Consulate General of Ireland,* below, *Ewing Galloway*)

a wild country of the Far North?

2. Which stanza most successfully tells the charms of the Yukon? Which best tells its hardships? Point out some similarities between the lure of the gold in this poem and in the one by Alfred Noyes.

For Your Vocabulary

UNCOMMON WORDS: Some words are fun. In line 28 there is the word *bludgeons.* Get your dictionary and find out whether you would be able to walk off in a high *dudgeon* if a mean old *curmudgeon* should hit you with a *bludgeon.* In Browning's famous poem "Pied Piper of Hamelin" you may remember the word *nuncheon.* Look that word up also and see if you could eat a *truncheon* at a *nuncheon* while wondering what in the world a *puncheon* is.

THE SAIL

MIKHAIL LERMONTOV

"The Sail" by Mikhail Lermontov * is a thought-provoking poem, although on the surface it appears very simple. At one time or another most of us have probably watched a boat in the distance and have idly wondered where it was going, what cargo it carried, who was on it. This Russian poet of more than a century ago asks, and answers, a deeper question. See if you can find it.

A lonely sail is dimly whitening
Within the ocean's azure dome.
What does it seek on the horizon?
What has it left behind at home?

The glad waves play, the glad wind
whistles, 5
The mast is bending like a tree . . .
Alas, it does not seek for gladness,
And not from gladness does it flee.

The sea is brighter than light azure,
In golden light the sky is drest — 10
But it is asking for the tempest,
As if in tempest there is rest.

J. J. Robbins, Translator

* **Mikhail Lermontov** (myĭ·ĸŭ·ēl′ lyär′mŭn·tôf)

How Well Did You Read?

1. The poet says that the "sail" is seeking for something. Obviously, the sail itself cannot seek for anything, so it must be a sign or symbol of something else. What does it stand for? What word in the second stanza is used in the same way? What does "it" mean in the last stanza?

2. What is the antecedent of *it* in line 11? Here is an interesting idea — that the tempest brings peace. Do you agree that this could be so? Can you show how human "tempests" sometimes bring peace by clearing the air, as it were?

TRAINING

DEMETRIO HERRERA S.

Demetrio Herrera S.* is a poet from Panama who ingeniously compares a harbor scene with a boxer's training camp. Notice that each short line gives a different mental picture, and each sentence is either a completely developed idea or figure of speech. Like "Spring & Co." this is a *free verse* poem; that is, it doesn't have a regular pattern of rhyme or even meter. The lines move along without being bound by any prescribed form and with an easy swing.

The sea — quick pugilist —
uses for a pun-
ching
ball
the restless little boats. 5

* **Demetrio Herrera** (dē·mā′trē·ō ĕr·rĕ′rä) **S.: The** *S* **stands for Servillano, Mr. Herrera's last name, which he rarely uses.**

On the other side of the earth: above, *The exotic setting of an Indian bazaar,* below, *Chinese junk in Hong Kong Harbor.* (Above, *Monkmeyer,* below, *Ewing Galloway*)

With the towel of the wind,
evening rubs down the boxer's
sweaty body.

The buildings —
ringside fans — 10
crowd close to watch
the big training.

(The dock is whispering
with a smoking ship . . .)

And the surf's applause 15
makes the tower stand on tiptoe
with its watch in hand
to keep the time.

Stray kids,
the sea birds 20
sneak in through the roof.

How Well Did You Read?

1. What lines would you pick out to show that this picture is the work of a poet rather than that of a sports writer?

2. Since this is a *free verse* poem, it has a highly irregular line length. The lines do not rhyme either. You may wonder why it is called a poem at all. See if you can discover what it is that makes the lines poetry rather than prose. Why are lines 2 to 4 set up in this manner? Point out the comparison that is drawn in lines 13 and 14, and explain line 17.

IN THE BAZAARS OF HYDERABAD

SAROJINI NAIDU

From Central America to India is a far jump across the Pacific, but Mme. Sarojini Naidu * takes us to Hyderabad † in a rich, colorful picture of the city market places, where vendors cry out their exotic wares. Notice the vivid, bright pictures. Here is a true lyric poem again, one with rhyme and rhythm and regular line lengths. The poem is well designed for reading aloud. The questions might be read by a single voice, with the replies spoken by the rest of the class. Look carefully at the pronunciations, even of such common words as *azure* and *perfume*.

* **Sarojini Naidu** (så·rō′jē·nē nä′ī·do͞o). † **Hyderabad** (hī′dĕr·å·băd′).

What do you sell, O ye merchants?
Richly your wares are displayed.
Turbans of crimson and silver,
Tunics of purple brocade,
Mirrors with panels of amber, 5
Daggers with handles of jade.

What do you weigh, O ye vendors?
Saffron° and lentil and rice.
What do you grind, O ye maidens?
Sandalwood, henna,° and spice. 10
What do you call, O ye pedlars?
Chessmen and ivory dice.

What do you make, O ye goldsmiths?
Wristlet and anklet and ring,
Bells for the feet of blue pigeons, 15
Frail as a dragonfly's wing,
Girdles of gold for the dancers,
Scabbards of gold for the king.

What do you cry, O ye fruitmen?
Citron,° pomegranate,° and plum. 20
What do you play, O musicians?
Cithār,° sarangi,° and drum.
What do you chant, O magicians?
Spells for aeons° to come.

8. **Saffron** (săf′rŭn): a substance used for yellow dye and for food flavor. 10. **henna** (hĕn′å): a shrub, the leaves of which yield a reddish-orange dye. 20. **Citron** (sĭt′rŭn); **pomegranate** (pŏm·grăn′ĭt). 22. **Cithār** (sĭth′âr); **sarangi** (sä′rŭng·gē). 24. **aeons** (ē′ŏnz): ages.

What do you weave, O ye flower girls
With tassels of azure and red? 26
Crowns for the brow of a bridegroom,
Chaplets° to garland his bed,
Sheets of white blossoms new-gathered
To perfume the sleep of the dead. 30

28. **Chaplets** (chăp'lĕtz): wreaths of flowers.

For Your Vocabulary

CONTEXT: This is a good poem by which to determine how well you have learned to get the meaning of words from their context. Even though the words *citron, pomegranate, cithār,* and *sarangi* are strange and unusual, how can you tell in general what they refer to? Look up these words now and get their exact meanings. How do you know for sure that *chessmen* are objects used in a game? To determine meaning of words from context requires a close attention to such details as punctuation. For example, are the *tassels,* line 26, a part of the costume of the flower girls or a part of what they are weaving? What effect would a comma after the word *girls* have on the meaning?

AN OLD SONG

SOLOMON BLOOMGARDEN

This poem is truly international. The writer has taken an old Japanese song and by writing in Yiddish has employed a language that is a modified German dialect with Hebrew letter characters! And of course you are reading the poem in an English translation.

In the blossom-land Japan
Somewhere thus an old song ran.
Said a warrior to a smith,
" Hammer me a sword forthwith.
Make the blade 5
Light as wind on water laid.
Make it long
As the wheat at harvest song.
Supple, swift
As a snake, without rift, 10
Full of lightnings, thousand-eyed!
Smooth as silken cloth and thin
As the web that spiders spin.
And merciless as pain, and cold."

" On the hilt what shall be told? " 15

" On the sword's hilt, my good man,"
Said the warrior of Japan,
" Trace for me
A running lake, a flock of sheep 19
And one who sings her child to sleep."

Marie Syrkin, Translator

How Well Did You Read?

1. *Without* using the poet's figures of speech, make a sentence containing the adjectives that describe the blade of the sword which is to be made. Which is more effective – the prose statement, or the poetic? Why?

2. The directions for the hilt and the blade are far different. There may be some special significance in the scenes to be inscribed on the hilt. What is it?

SAILING HOMEWARD

CHAN FANG-SHENG

Home is a magic word to all weary travelers. This poem, dating back hundreds of years, is about a man of ancient China returning to his own country and finding comfort in its familiar sights.

Cliffs that rise a thousand feet
Without a break,
Lake that stretches a hundred miles
Without a wave.
Sands that are white through all the
year

Without a stain, 6
Pine-tree woods, winter and summer
Evergreen,
Streams that forever flow and flow
Without a pause, 10
Trees that for twenty thousand years
Your vows have kept,
You have suddenly healed the pain of a traveler's heart,
And moved his brush to write a new song.

Arthur Waley, Translator

THE DONKEY

GILBERT KEITH CHESTERTON

This poem by an English author serves as a close link to the selection that follows it. Here the beast of burden, the humble donkey, tells how he is scorned by the world. Yet he has the memory of one proud moment.

When fishes flew and forests walked
And figs grew upon thorn,
Some moment when the moon was blood
Then surely I was born.

With monstrous head and sickening cry
And ears like errant wings, 6
The devil's walking parody
Of all four-footed things.

The tattered outlaw of the earth,
Of ancient crooked will; 10
Starve, scourge, deride me: I am dumb,
I keep my secret still.

Fools! For I also had my hour;
One far fierce hour and sweet:
There was a shout about my ears, 15
And palms before my feet.

How Well Did You Read?

1. What do you think is the purpose of the first stanza? Try to put the idea of this stanza into a prose statement of your own. Why could you not understand that stanza until you had finished the poem?
2. *Errant wings* means " wings that have wandered far from their proper place." How can a donkey be a *parody*? You may have to look up this word.
3. The last two lines give a clue to the donkey's one hour of fame. Do you know what scene in the Bible is referred to?

FROM CHAPTER XII,

ECCLESIASTES

A large part of the Bible is true poetry. Many of the *Psalms*, for example, have been set to music. The following passage from *Ecclesiastes,* whose original form is prose, is here printed as a poem. You should recognize at once that the rich figures of speech are in the language of poetry, not prose. Although the lines do not have a definite meter, they read smoothly and rhythmically.

Remember also thy Creator in the days of thy youth,
Or ever the evil days come,
And the years draw nigh, when thou shalt say,
" I have no pleasure in them ";

Or ever the sun, and the light, 5
And the moon, and the stars, be darkened,
And the clouds return after the rain:
In the day when the keepers of the house shall tremble,
And the strong men shall bow themselves,
And the grinders cease because they are few, 10
And those that look out of the windows be darkened,
And the doors shall be shut in the street;
When the sound of the grinding is low,
And one shall rise up at the voice of a bird,
And all the daughters of music shall be brought low; 15
Yea, they shall be afraid of that which is high,
And terrors shall be in the way;
And the almond tree shall blossom,
And the grasshopper shall be a burden,
And the caper-berry shall fail: 20
Because man goeth to his long home,
And the mourners go about the streets:
Or ever the silver cord be loosed,
Or the golden bowl be broken,
Or the pitcher be broken at the fountain, 25
Or the wheel broken at the cistern;
And the dust return to the earth as it was,
And the spirit return unto God who gave it.

How Well Did You Read?

1. What one word would we ordinarily use instead of *or ever* in lines 2 and 5?

2. If you look closely, you can find hints of both pestilence and famine in this selection. Can you point out the specific lines that indicate each?

3. For the best understanding of lines 23 to 26, go back to the very first line.

4. This selection is a bit of advice or warning to do something before certain other things happen. Write a sentence or two which clearly sums up the entire idea.

Thinking Over Poems from Far Places

1. Consider yourself, for a moment or two, the editor of this section of poems. If you were to arrange these poems by their theme, or subject matter, what order of selections would you make? If you were to arrange them by mood, what would be your order? Review what was said about *mood* on page 305.

2. How do you explain the fact that so many parts of the Bible can be considered poetry, yet are printed as prose? What effect does putting poetry into a definite line or stanza pattern have on the reader? Someone may wish to look up the well-known edition of the Bible which actually prints much of it in a poetic form, *The Bible Designed to be Read as Living Literature,* by Sutherland Bates.

3. Try to find other Shakespearean songs besides the one given here. Perhaps some of you will read to the class these or your favorite Robert Burns song.

4. Describe in a paragraph of prose or a piece of free verse a scene or section of your own country that affects you strongly. Reread " The Spell of the Yukon " and " Sailing Homeward " first and use these poems as models.

5. Try to catch the feeling of a scene of the year in free verse. Don't copy the method of " Training," but use a specific tree and season as a starting point. Begin with " The willow tree – " or " The apple

tree — " and see where your imagination leads you. Be sure your lines read smoothly, but do not worry about rhyme or meter.

6. Of the various love poems in this section, which do you think is the best? Explain your reasons.

7. Write a short co-operative class poem. As a model look at the pattern of questions and answers in the poem " In the Bazaars of Hyderabad." Take a county fair or a game or a market scene with which you are familiar as a setting. Each of you can write a first line; then the class can vote on which is best, so that it can be put on the board. Then everyone writes a second line, and so on. This kind of work is fun, and with everyone helping you may be able to compose a pretty good class poem.

For Your Vocabulary

WORD HISTORY: The *azure* tassels in the poem " In the Bazaars of Hyderabad " were the deep blue of the sky. *Azure* came to the English language from an Old French word, which came from the Arabic, which came from the Persian. Here it crops up in a poem written in English by a woman of India. The warrior in " An Old Song " asks that his sword be made without *rift.* This is a rather unusual use of the word, which is of Scandinavian origin and usually means a " crevice " or a " splitting apart." Probably *flaw* would be a better word, for *rift* indicates a serious defect. However, translations are difficult to manage, especially where rhyme must be considered.

WIT AND NONSENSE

Satire and humor are the spices that add flavor to all forms of writing. Satire is a sharp form of criticism usually aimed at social customs, manners, morals, politics, literary fads, and so on. " Mycilla Dyes Her Locks " and " Bought Locks " are satirical poems, for example, written by two early Roman writers. These quatrains very neatly make fun of a feminine vanity that even today will bear a little humorous criticism. Somewhat different is " The Crow and the Fox," one of the old, familiar Aesop fables which a famous French writer has put into poetic form. " A Llyric of the Llama " (what's wrong with the spelling?) and " A Lay of Ancient Rome " are humorous poems whose only purpose is to amuse. A *lay,* by the way, is a song; and the title of this poem is a playful variation on *Lays of Ancient Rome,* the title of a famous group of poems about Roman heroes, written by the English historian, Thomas Babington Macaulay.

MYCILLA DYES HER LOCKS

GAIUS LUCILLIUS *

Mycilla° dyes her locks, 'tis said,
But 'tis a foul aspersion;°
She buys them black, they therefore need
No subsequent immersion.°

William Cowper, Translator

* **Gaius Lucillius** (gā'yŭs lû·sĭl'ĭ·ŭs). 1. **Mycilla** (mī·sĭl'ȧ). 2. **foul aspersion** (ȧs·pûr'shŭn): dirty slur. 4. **subsequent immersion:** further soaking or dipping.

BOUGHT LOCKS

MARCUS VALERIUS MARTIALIS *

The golden hair that Gulla wears
Is hers: who would have thought it?
She swears 'tis hers, and true she swears,
For I know where she bought it.

Sir John Harington, Translator

* **Marcus Valerius Martialis** (mär'kŭs vȧ·lē̦r'ĭ·ŭs mär'shĭ·āl'ĭs): better known by the shortened form of his name — Martial (mär'shȧl).

THE CROW AND THE FOX

JEAN DE LA FONTAINE *

A crow sat perched upon an oak,
And in his beak he held a cheese.
A fox sniffed up the savory breeze,
And thus in honeyed accent spoke:
"O Prince of Crows, such grace of mien
Has never in these parts been seen. 6
If but your song be half as good,
You are the phoenix of the wood!"
The Crow, beside himself with pleasure,
And eager to display his voice, 10
Opened his beak, and dropped his treasure.
The Fox was on it in a trice.
"Learn, sir," said he, "that flatterers live
On those who swallow what they say.
A cheese is not too much to give 15
For such a piece of sound advice."
The Crow, ashamed to have been such easy prey
Swore, but too late, he shouldn't catch him twice.

Edward Marsh, Translator

* **Jean de la Fontaine** (zhäɴ d' lȧ fôɴ·tĕn').

A LAY OF ANCIENT ROME

THOMAS YBARRA *

Oh! the Roman was a rogue,
He erat, was, you bettum;
He ran his automobilis
And smoked his cigarettum:
He wore a diamond studibus, 5
An elegant cravattum,
A maxima cum laude shirt,
And such a stylish hattum!

He loved the luscious hic — haec — hoc,
And bet on games and equi; 10
At times he won; at others, though,
He got it in the nequi;
He winked (quo usque tandem?)
At puellas on the Forum,
And sometimes even made 15
Those goo-goo oculorum!

He frequently was seen
At combats gladiatorial,
And ate enough to feed
Ten boarders at Memorial; 20
He often went on sprees
And said, on starting homus,
"Hic labor —opus est,
Oh, where's my hic — hic — domus?"

* **Ybarra** (ĭ·bär'ȧ).

LLYRIC OF THE LLAMA

BURGES JOHNSON

Behold how from her lair the youthful llama
  Llopes and llightly scans the llandscape o'er.
With llusty heart she llooks upon llife's drama,
  Relying on her llate-llearnt worldly llore.

But llo! Some llad, armed with a yoke *infama* 5
  Soon llures her into llowly llabor's cause;
Her wool is llopped to weave into pajama,
  And llanguidly she llearns her Gees and Haws.

My children, heed this llesson from all llanguishing young lllamas,
If you would lllive with lllatitude, avoid each llluring lllay; 10
And do not lllightly lllleave, I beg, your llllonesome, lllloving mammas,
And llllast of allll, don't spellllll your name in such a sillllllly way.

Monkmeyer

"Llyric of the Llama" from *Bashful Ballads* by Burges Johnson, published by Harper & Brothers. Reprinted here by permission of the author.

LYRICS FROM MANY LANDS

Suggestions for Free Reading

Barnouw, Adriaan I., *Coming After, an Anthology of Poets from the Low Countries* (Rutgers Press, 1948)
Translations of Dutch and Flemish poetry with a distinct flavor of those countries.

Daringer, H. F., and Eaton, A. T., *The Poet's Craft* (World, 1935)
Very helpful for the beginning reader of poetry.

De la Mare, Walter, *Come Hither* (Knopf, 1923)
A lyric poet gives you his favorites.

Dickinson, Emily, *Poems for Youth* (Little, 1948)

Guiterman, Arthur, *Death and General Putnam, and 101 Other Poems* (Dutton, 1935)
Mr. Guiterman writes an easily flowing verse that somehow sticks in the mind.

Hoagland, Kathleen, ed., *1000 Years of Irish Poetry* (Devin-Adair, 1947)
A rich collection of all types of Irish wit and thoughtfulness in verse, including fables, stories, folk songs, and lyrics.

Hulme, Francis Pledger, *Come Up the Valley* (Rutgers Press, 1949)
Mountain songs make up the first part of this little book.

Kilmer, Joyce, *Trees, and Other Poems* (Doran, 1914)
Some well-loved poems by an appealing young writer who died in World War I.

Kipling, Rudyard, *A Choice of Kipling's Verse* (Scribner's, 1943)
A fine selection of Kipling's enjoyable ballads and poems.

Lomax, John Avery, *Cowboy Songs and Other Frontier Ballads* (Macmillan, 1938)
You probably never thought there were as many songs of this kind! There is music for many of them.

Macaulay, Thomas Babington, *Lays of Ancient Rome*
A famous series of ballads about long-ago days and heroes.

McNeil, Horace J., and Zimmer, Dorothy S., *Living Poetry* (Globe, 1950)
A revision of *Poems for a Machine Age.*

Millay, Edna St. Vincent, *Poems Selected for Young People* (Harper, 1929)
You will be sure to like this collection!

Noyes, Alfred, *Forty Singing Seamen* (Stokes, 1930)
Boys have always liked these six sea poems.

Sechrist, Elizabeth H., *One Thousand Poems for Children* (Macrae-Smith, 1946)
Poems for teen-agers are in Part II. There are good decorative drawings.

Teasdale, Sara, *Rainbow Gold* (Macmillan, 1922)
A selection of poems old and new, especially for young people.

Van Doren, Mark, *A Junior Anthology of World Poetry* (Boni, 1929)
Poems from all countries – a book designed especially for school-age readers.

WIT AND NONSENSE

Crane, Nathalia, *The Janitor's Boy, and Other Poems* (Seltzer, 1924)
A very talented eleven-year-old wrote these poems that have sparkling rhyme, rhythm, and imagination, and a wisdom far beyond the writer's age.

Daly, T. A., *McAroni Ballads* (Harcourt, 1919); and *Late Lark Singing* (Harcourt, 1946)
Chiefly humorous poems, some in Italian dialect.

De la Mare, Walter, *Stuff and Nonsense* (Holt, 1927)

Fishback, Margaret, *I Take It Back* (Dutton, 1935)
You will be greatly amused by this bright and airy nonsense.

Guiterman, Arthur, *Lyric Laughter* (Dutton, 1939)
You will find these poems to be humorous, entertaining, and thoughtful comments on many subjects.

Lindsay, Vachel, *Every Soul Is a Circus* (Macmillan, 1929)
This is fantastic foolery written for young people in particular.

McCann, Rebecca, *Cheerful Cherub* (Covici-Friede, 1930)
You like short poems? Each of these is just four lines long, each is on a page, each has a drawing.

McCord, David T., *What Cheer* (Coward-McCann, 1945)
One of the best collections of American and British fun and wit.

Ewing Galloway

The Curtain Rises

LET'S pretend. From childhood to old age, there is magic in those words. Everyone likes to be in a play, even those of us who are not expert actors. It is fun to pretend to be a different person – to imitate a tone of voice, a gesture, a way of walking. Some people have a real gift for this art of make-believe or interpretation, and they become our professional actors. Most of us, of course, will remain only part of an audience. But whether we are taking part, or looking on, or simply reading a play silently, a magic quality surrounds the drama as it does no other form of literature.

Part of this magic or mystery lies in the glamour of the theater itself. There we find the dimming house lights, the spotlights playing on a shadowed stage, the clever settings that take us in an instant to a New England parlor or a Pennsylvania Dutch kitchen, a college dormitory, or a temple in Tibet. Mainly, however, drama holds our attention because of what the dramatist has to tell us, the beautiful or bitter things that he has to say about life. In reading or seeing plays, we tend to recognize, in the characters or situations portrayed, the people and events of the life around us.

This close relationship of drama to life itself is perhaps the strongest part of the magic. The drama has been called a "mirror held up to life." We watch the characters as they display all their whims and jealousies, their weaknesses and their ambitions – and they don't see us! We laugh at them and worry with them, or we wink back the tears and swallow the lumps in our throats, as we see them caught up in the emotions and complications of some dramatic event. When an audience experiences a powerful emotion, the persons who have laughed or shuddered together feel better for having done so. In reading plays, too, there is a real value in talking over and sharing our impressions with others.

A few pointers will help you to read plays with more enjoyment. Long and short plays have much in common, but length makes them differ considerably in some ways. A one-act play usually runs no longer than thirty minutes in playing time. Such short plays correspond roughly to short stories in form. The main character is introduced early, and the reader soon learns that a struggle or complication is going to take place. Also, as in the short story, there is usually only one major action or idea developed during the course of the play.

Longer plays of two or more acts, on the other hand, correspond roughly to novels. Here the dramatist has enough space to create several characters fully. Instead of a single major action as in the one-act play, there are several different complications developed between the various characters; in other words, there is a main plot, together with one or more subplots. The plays in this book, however, are all of the one-act type (except the television play, which is not divided strictly by acts), and each of them consequently centers on a single main dramatic situation.

In general, plays may be said to affect us either happily or unhappily. In a tragedy we are saddened as we watch the main character lose his struggle (and often die), while in a comedy we are gladdened when the characters overcome their problems and " live happily ever after." This is a simple way of classifying plays, but a good one. As a reader of plays you will want to talk about drama with some assurance. Keep in mind a few of the accepted dramatic terms. *Characters* are the persons who are involved in the action of the play. An *incident* is something that happens; and a series of incidents makes up the *action* of a play. The *climax* is the highest, or most intense, point of the action; after the climax is passed, the play clears up loose ends and comes to a conclusion. The time and place in which a play occurs are, of course, the *setting*.

And now you are ready to be introduced to the setting of the first of these plays. If you have the opportunity to read aloud in class, try to imagine that you *are* the character you portray. Get acquainted with the character – with what happens to him, with the reasons for his behavior. Try to imagine how he would look and act; what kind of voice he would use in certain situations; how he would react under the pressure of fear, excitement, pleasure, or anger. If you will do these things, your skill in reading will be increased, as well as your enjoyment in drama.

The potent magic of the theater begins at the opening of the velvet curtain. Lights down . . . the curtain rises. . . .

ONE-ACT PLAYS

S. SYLVAN SIMON

Trouble in Tunnel Nine

Have you ever read in newspaper headlines or heard a radio announcer tell the dramatic story of miners trapped far underground while teams of weary rescuers work frantically to reach them? If so, you may have wondered what you would do, or how you would act, under similar circumstances. Perhaps, too, when you hear of such disasters you realize more clearly what dangerous lives many workers lead and what a heavy price they sometimes pay in order that we may all be secure and comfortable.

In "Trouble in Tunnel Nine," there are only four characters, three of whom belong to one family. The main theme of the play is to be found in the way each character meets a mine disaster when it strikes. There is, however, a second theme – that of the family conflict. Many of our miners have come to America from a foreign country. They face special problems of education, recreation, and living conditions. Note which of these problems causes the particular conflict in this play, and how it is finally solved for one of the characters at least.

For Better Reading . . . Understanding human character – why people act as they do – is one of the most interesting parts of reading plays. By observing the speeches and actions of the people in a play you can tell whether they are good or bad, strong or weak, wise or foolish. Most of them, you will find, are mixtures of several qualities. Frequently a character is shown in only one light early in a play. Later, other sides of his nature are exposed as he meets various situations. In reading this play, keep alert for *changes* in the behavior and personalities of the characters. Take a particular character like Pete, for example; see what you can learn about him not only from what he says and does, but from what others say about him. Jan, the father, is interesting too. In the beginning you do not like him, but you change your opinion somewhat as you learn why he behaves as he does and as he himself shows a willingness to change.

Characters

JAN NOVAK, a coal miner
DAVE, his elder son
PETE, the younger son
JOE, another miner

SCENE. *Cross section of a tunnel in a coal mine; about twenty feet wide downstage and narrows to approximately twelve feet at upstage end. Tunnel makes right-angle turn upstage so that backdrop is the tunnel wall. Huge chunks of coal and ore lie here and there. Left side of tunnel wall is damp and wet. Walls shored up with timbers which support ceiling beams. From center of these beams runs an electric-light wire that turns right upstage* [1] *and apparently continues down tunnel. Two electric lights glow dimly in the tunnel.*

TIME. *Just before noon.*

AT RISE. JOE *and* PETE, *the younger* NOVAK, *are leaning on their picks, boondoggling* [2] *a bit. Lunch pails rest against the tunnel wall downstage.*

PETE. What's the matter, Joe?

JOE (*wiping his face with a bright red bandanna*). The sweat. All the time she gets in my eyes.

PETE (*with a short laugh*). Well, take it easy, what's the rush?

JOE (*shaking his head*). Plenty rush, Pete. Boss . . . he say, Joe, you lazy bum. All time you lean on pick. Get move on or . . . (*Makes gesture signifying hasty exit.*)

PETE (*impatiently*). Oh, never mind him. Pop wouldn't be happy unless he were bellyaching about something.

JOE (*blandly*). What? What you say he do?

PETE. I said that . . . Oh never mind . . . skip it.

[*Both men continue work in silence. Finally* JOE *pauses and again wipes his forehead.*]

JOE. What time you say it is?

PETE (*gruffly*). I didn't say.

JOE. I know. What time you make heem now?

PETE (*glancing at watch*). Quarter to twelve.

JOE (*dubiously*). Your watch. Your sure she go? She not stop?

PETE. No. It's going all right. (*Winds it to make sure.*) I checked it this morning.

JOE (*weakly*). Okay, okay. . . . (*Starts working with pick.*)

PETE (*gives elaborate yawn and stretches luxuriously*). Hmmm . . . ! (PETE *picks up lunch pail and sits down on pile of slag. He opens pail and pulls out a sandwich.*)

JOE (*interested*). What you do?

PETE. Me? I'm going to have lunch. Any objections?

JOE (*puzzled*). You eat him now? So soon?

PETE. Sure. Why not?

JOE (*shaking his head*). Not twelve o'clock. Boss no like. He see red like crazy bull.

PETE. Well, what if he does. I can take it. Besides there's something special I want to do today.

[PETE *hesitates a moment and then takes a book from his pocket and starts reading it while, with the other hand, he holds a sandwich which he munches.*]

JOE (*still leaning on pick*). Pretty soft for you, I think.

PETE (*looking up*). What's that?

JOE. Pretty soft. You boss's son. You

[1] **upstage:** In reading stage directions, think of *upstage* as toward the back of the stage and *downstage* as toward the front or near the footlights. *Exit* means "he (or she) goes out"; *exeunt* means "they go out."

[2] **boondoggling** (bo͞on′dôg′lĭng): wasting time.

do what you like. Pretty easy.

PETE (*angrily*). Hey, where do you get that stuff?

JOE (*taken aback*). Your name is Pete Novak same as his. They tell me you his boy. Pretty soft.

PETE. Sure, my old man's a foreman. But listen, if you think that makes it any easier for me, you're crazy. Why, he treats me rougher than anyone else on this level. If anybody gets favors around here, it's Dave.

JOE (*puzzled*). Dave?

PETE. Sure. My brother. He's been working here in this same pocket with us. You know — that big guy.

JOE (*enlightened*). Beeg. Beeg strong back. Lika that? Black hair?

PETE. Yeah. That's Dave. All back and no brains.

JOE. I think I eat my lunch now. I see what my Maria [1] put up for me.

[JOE *gets pail and sits down, investigating the contents with childlike pleasure.* PETE *continues to read and eat.*]

JOE (*in a talkative mood*). Where they go?

PETE (*looking up, bored*). Who?

JOE. The boss.

PETE. Oh, there was some sort of trouble near the old shaft. Pop took Dave along with him to see what it was. A lot of good Dave would be.

JOE (*interested*). Trouble? What kinda trouble?

PETE. I don't know. Somebody smelt coal gas. There must be coal damp around here or something.

JOE (*alarmed*). Coal gas? I don't like that.

PETE. Who does like it? But what do you expect in an old mine like this? Everything's out of date. Look at the equipment. Look at those electric lights.

[1] **Maria** (mä·rē′ä).

JOE (*puzzled*). What's wrong wit de electric lights?

PETE. Nothing. Except they're all strung on one circuit. If one blows out, they all blow out.

JOE. Blows out? Humph. That's bad. How you know so much about electric lights? You talka like Meester Edison.

PETE. Sure. I know about electricity. (*Tapping book*) I got a book here. It tells all about it. Receivers and condensers and magnetic poles and oh, a lotta stuff I'm interested in.

JOE (*shaking head and taking a huge bite of bread*). My sister married a Pole. He no good. No good at all.

PETE (*laughing*). I don't mean that kind of a pole. This tells about wave lengths and receiving messages. Gee! It's interesting.

JOE. Why? Why you read all dat stuff?

PETE. Gosh, Joe. I wanta learn something. I want to get somewhere. I don't want to be a miner all my life.

JOE. Why not? You get good pay. You got place to sleep. You got plenty to eat. By and by you marry and have nice wife. Plenty kids. Not bad.

PETE (*fiercely*). That's just it. I don't want to marry and live here in the mines. Suppose I did have kids. What would happen to them? They'd go to work here too just the way I did. They'd never have a chance.

JOE. Sure they have fine chance. Just the same as you or me.

PETE (*bitterly*). Sure. They have a chance to stop school when they're fourteen. They have a chance to spend all their life underground in a damp tunnel. They have a chance to work day in and day out. Never to see the sunlight or to be anybody or go anywhere. Joe?

JOE. What?

PETE. Why did you leave Italy?

JOE. Me? Oh, I had too bigga family.

Too many brothers. Too many sisters. Never enough food to go around. So I take ship and come to America. Things better here.

PETE. But don't you ever miss it? I mean don't you ever want to go home?

JOE. Sure. Sure. I save up money. I go home sometime.

PETE (*wistfully*). Gee, I wish I could go to Italy. I saw some pictures of it last Saturday.

JOE. You did? Where?

PETE. In the movies. It was one of those travel pictures. You know, done in colors and everything? There was the Bay of Naples and a big mountain and people out in little boats singing. Gee, it was swell!

JOE. Napoli! Napoli! [1] (*Breaking into song*) Oh, Santa Lucia! [2]

PETE (*excited*). Yeah. That was the song they were singing. How did you know?

JOE (*laughing*). Sure. That is Neapolitan song. I used to sing him.

PETE. You did?

JOE. Yes. I come from Sorrento. That's — (*trying to illustrate with his hands*) that's thisa big. When I was a leetle keed — four, five years old, I sleep in sun all day long. Justa bambino! [3] That song maka me homesick.

PETE. And now you never see the sun. Gee, that's tough! That's why I got to study and be somebody.

JOE (*munching contentedly*). Why? Why you study?

PETE (*eagerly*). I want to travel. I want to see places and know something.

JOE (*amused*). Travel? That take plenty money. Plenty money.

PETE. Yeah. I know it does. But not the way I'm going. I'm going to learn all about radio and get a job on a boat.

JOE (*unimpressed*). What kinda job?

PETE (*getting enthusiastic*). A radio operator. They get good pay and they go all over the world. Only you've got to have brains to hold down a job like that.

JOE (*nodding sagely*). Sure. Radio fellas plenty smart.

PETE. It's all in this book here. Only it's awful hard for me to get to understand it. You see, Pop won't let me go to school.

JOE. He no let you go to school?

PETE. No. He thinks schools are waste of time. He never went and he don't want me to go.

JOE (*sympathetically*). Too bad! You smart boy, Pete. You should go to school like other keeds.

PETE. Pop says no. He won't even let me study at home. If he catches me with a book he licks the tar outa me. I got to do everything on the sly.

[*During this conversation,* DAVE, *a hulking young miner of eighteen or twenty, has rounded the bend in the tunnel. He stands listening to* PETE *with sardonic amusement. When* PETE *finishes he snatches the book from his hand.*]

DAVE. Caught you that time.

PETE (*enraged*). Give me that book. That's mine.

DAVE (*holding book out of reach*). Oh yeah? So what?

PETE. Let me have that.

DAVE (*sneering*). Oh, so you wanta go to school, heh? You wanta be highbrow, do you? I suppose we ain't good enough for you.

PETE. Give me my book. (*Makes effort to grab it.*)

DAVE. Lay off. Lay off. Do you want

[1] **Napoli** (nä′pȯ·lė): Naples, a city in Italy.
[2] **Santa Lucia** (sän′tä lo͞o·chē′ä): a popular Neapolitan (nē′ȧ·pŏl′ĭ·tăn: belonging to Naples) song.
[3] **bambino** (bäm·bē′nȯ): a child; a baby.

A miner's equipment today includes electric torch on his helmet and drill to help him work. Here a father and son are intent on their job. (*National Film Board, Canada*)

me to smear you all over the floor?

JOE (*placatingly*). Give him his book. It's his.

DAVE (*sidling up to him*). So what? Going to get tough, are you?

[*As soon as* DAVE'*s attention is divided,* PETE *makes a dive for his book.* DAVE, *with a stiff right, sends* PETE *sprawling on the floor.*]

DAVE. I told you to lay off.

[PETE, *sobbing with rage, struggles to his feet and starts for* DAVE *again.* DAVE *calmly knocks him down a second time.* JOE *reaches over and raises his pick.* NOVAK *enters unobserved by the contestants.*]

NOVAK (*angrily*). Hey. What's all this? Cut it out. (*To* DAVE) What you fighting your brother for?

DAVE (*sullenly*). I ain't fighting. I took his book away and he started hollering.

NOVAK (*to* PETE). So? That's it? You ain't got nothing better to do with your time than to read high-falutin' books. Get busy there on that slag heap. (*Starts to destroy book.*)

PETE. Hey, you can't do that. That's my book. I paid for it out of my own money.

NOVAK. Is that so? Well, I'll show you who's boss around here. (*Rips book in half.*) There ain't gonna be no scholars in this family. Get back to work.

[PETE, *in brooding silence, takes up his pick.*]

DAVE (*admiringly*). That's telling him, Pop.

NOVAK (*gruffly*). That means you too, all of you.

JOE. Okay, okay.

[JOE *gobbles down an enormous chunk of sandwich, wipes his mouth with the back of his hand and shambles back to his former position. For a while all work in silence, then* PETE *lowers his pick.*]

NOVAK (*suspiciously*). Hey, what's the matter there?

PETE. I don't know . . . but it don't sound right.

NOVAK. What don't sound right?

PETE (*perplexed*). The wall. There's a funny sort of trembling when the pick strikes. I think we're getting too close to that other tunnel.

NOVAK (*sourly*). You do, eh? Say, who's foreman here, you or me?

PETE (*dully*). You are. Do you want me to keep on going?

NOVAK. I ain't heard myself changing any orders, did you?

PETE (*returning to work*). No.

NOVAK. Okay. Then keep on going.

DAVE (*tauntingly*). That's what happens when you read books. You get funny ideas.

NOVAK. Don't you worry about that. I'll see that he don't do no more reading.

[*Sound of timber cracking.*]

DAVE. Hey, hear that noise?

NOVAK. That's nothing. Them timbers are always cracking.

JOE. Say, boss, that don't sound right to me.

NOVAK (*angrily*). Who's boss around here? Get back to your work.

JOE (*philosophically*). Okay. Okay.

[*Sound of louder, more ominous, crack, overhead beam near upstage end of tunnel quivers.*]

PETE (*pointing*). Look at that beam. It's cracking.

DAVE (*in fear*). I'm getting outa here. Come on. Scram!

JOE. You betcha.

[JOE, DAVE, *and* PETE *start upstage, bumping against each other in fright.*]

NOVAK (*shouting*). Trying to run out on me, are you? Come back here.

[*They stop at the menace in his shouted command and turn. Standing in this tableau they hear a louder cracking, and the beam falls upstage side of them, just missing them.*]

DAVE (*gasp*). Gee. That almost got me.

JOE (*terrified voice*). Boss or no boss, I'm goin'.

NOVAK (*realizing the danger*). Go ahead. Climb over that beam. We've got to get outa here.

[*They climb over and crawl under the beam shouting to each other and yelling for* JOE *to hurry.* JOE *is last momentarily. He has leaned against the wall. Suddenly he screams in terror and points to the wall.*]

JOE (*in a panic*). Look! The wall she trembles. The whole mine, she ees comin' down on us.

SHOUTS. Look out! Get away from the wall, boys! She's sliding! That's dangerous! Get back!

DAVE (*screams*). It's a cave-in!

[*As* DAVE *shouts, the lights flicker out. There is a roar and crash of falling rock and timbers. Gradually this dies away. The lights flicker on again. The four men look at each other with dazed faces.* DAVE *is the first to speak.*]

DAVE. Well, it didn't get us this time! What happened, Pop?

NOVAK. Don't know yet. Got to find out.

[*The men, with the exception of* JOE, *who is now silently praying, hasten upstage to the turn of the tunnel. As they walk there is another short rumble and suddenly the bend is blocked with debris; rock dust floats in the air. They stop short, mouths agape.*]

NOVAK (*repressed, tragic voice*). Look! We're buried!

DAVE. It's a good thing we was in this pocket.

NOVAK (*recovering composure*). Yep. That's the only thing that saved us.

DAVE (*nervously*). What are we going to do? How are we going to get out of here?

NOVAK. We ain't going to get out. We got to stay here until they dig us out.

DAVE. That may be a couple of days.

NOVAK (*stolidly*). Or longer. I was trapped in the old mine once for over a week.

DAVE. And they got to you.

NOVAK. Sure. But it was no picnic, waiting in the dark for 'em to get to us. You got to keep cool.

PETE. We're lucky the lights are still going.

DAVE. A lotta good an electric-light bulb is gonna be to you.

PETE. It's better than being in the dark.

DAVE. Oh, a wise guy! I suppose you learned that in a book, too.

NOVAK. Cut it out, you two.

DAVE. He thinks he knows so much. I was just telling him that —

NOVAK. Never mind. Quit quarreling and save your breath. The air ain't gonna be any too good in here in a coupla hours.

PETE (*who has been investigating a crack in the tunnel wall upstage*). A little air is coming in here.

DAVE (*pointing to* JOE *who is praying audibly*). Make him quit, Pop. He's using up more air than anybody.

NOVAK (*curtly*). Joe. Cut it out!

[JOE *nods in a dazed way. He continues to pray but the words are now inaudible.*]

PETE (*sniffing near where he has examined the tunnel crack*). What's that?

NOVAK (*sniffs*). Oh that . . . (*A worried look comes over his face. He sniffs again, and is silent.*)

DAVE (*impatiently*). Well, what is it?

NOVAK (*in a strange voice*). Boys, you was asking me how long it was going to be before they come and dug us out and I said it would be forty-eight hours.

PETE AND DAVE. Yes . . . sure —

NOVAK (*slowly*). Well, it ain't gonna be that long.

BOTH. What's that?

NOVAK. You're both men and got to learn to face facts like men. You ain't going to last that long.

BOTH (*excitedly*). Why? What's happened?

NOVAK. Because WHAT YOU SMELL IS COAL GAS!

[*The stage darkens slowly to show a passage of time. When the lights go up again the men are all in the same relative positions except that they are all listlessly sitting.* JOE *is lying on the ground, his head pillowed on his arm as though asleep.*]

DAVE (*turning to look at* JOE). Do you suppose Joe's all right? He's been that way for an awful long time.

NOVAK (*after a pause, looks at* JOE). Yeah, he's all right. You can tell by the breathing.

PETE (*thoughtfully*). Poor Joe! I guess he won't get back to Italy after all.

NOVAK (*shaking his head*). Not this trip.

PETE. It was funny. We was talking about Italy just before this happened.

NOVAK (*not much interested*). What was he saying?

PETE. All about the sunshine and lying under the trees when he was a kid. And the Bay of Naples. I could see it just as plain. I wish I could have got there.

DAVE (*irritated*). Cut it out, will yuh? Quit it!

NOVAK (*still calm*). Let him talk. He ain't doin' any harm.

DAVE. What's the use of talking of all them foreign places? We're here, ain't we? Trapped in a mine.

NOVAK. Might as well talk. There ain't nothing else we can do.

DAVE (*starting up, almost hysterical*). We got to do something. I ain't gonna die down here. We got to do something.

NOVAK. Easy there. Take it easy.

DAVE (*running around like a trapped animal*). I gotta get out of here. I tell you, I can't stand it. Somebody's got to do something. (*Holding his hands like a megaphone and shouting.*) Help! Help!

NOVAK (*slowly*). That won't do no good. Nobody can hear you.

DAVE. They gotta hear me. They can't let us die down here in this hole. They got to do something.

NOVAK. Pipe down. There ain't nothing we can do. (*Disgusted*) I thought you was the man of the family and here you are acting like a baby. You got to face things.

DAVE. It's all right for you to talk. You're old. You've lived your life. With me it's different. I'm young. I don't want to die. Not like this. (*Throws himself on the ground and sobs hysterically.*) I can't stand it, I tell you. I can't stand it.

[NOVAK *and* PETE *turn and look at each other.* PETE'*s face is filled with sympathy. There is a silence broken only by* DAVE'*s muffled sobbing.*]

NOVAK (*shaking his head*). I'm ashamed of Dave. I thought he had more guts.

PETE. He can't help it.

NOVAK (*surprised*). Why not? He's a big, husky boy. Why, he's twice the size you are. (*In a hurt voice*) Funny, I always sorta relied on Dave.

PETE (*thoughtfully*). I know you did, Pop.

NOVAK (*more to himself*). You was the one I thought would break. You was a strange youngster. Always studying and trying to be superior. You weren't like the rest of us.

PETE. I wasn't trying to be superior, Pop.

NOVAK (*not convinced*). Well, maybe not. I guess you take after your ma. She looked down on me, too.

PETE. Did she, Pop? I didn't know that.

NOVAK. Yep. She was teaching school here in the mine country when I married her. She hated the mines and she hated me for being so ignorant. She was always trying to improve me.

PETE (*interested*). What happened?

NOVAK. Nothing happened. Nothing that is, except quarreling and unhappiness. I guess you was too young to remember.

PETE (*shaking his head*). No, I don't remember.

NOVAK. So when she dies, I says to myself, if these boys is goin' to be like her, I'll whale it outa them. My sons ain't growin' up to look down on Jan Novak.

PETE. I wasn't lookin' down on you, Pop.

NOVAK. You didn't have no chance. I pulled you out of school and stuck you down in the mines. That's why it made me mad when you was always reading.

PETE (*nodding*). I see.

[NOVAK *gives a faint cough.*]

PETE (*anxiously*). You all right, Pop?

NOVAK. Yeah. It's just the gas. It's getting down in my lungs.

PETE. Pop?

NOVAK. Yeah. What is it?

PETE. Do you suppose they know about the coal gas? The rescuers might think we're all right.

NOVAK. They don't know nothing. I just found out about the leak myself a short while ago.

PETE. But if they knew about the gas they could do something. They could run a pipe through to us from the old shaft and give us fresh air.

NOVAK. But they don't know, I tell you. What's the use of talking?

PETE (*stubbornly*). Yet there must be some way of letting them know.

NOVAK. How? Are yuh figurin' on writing 'em a letter? No, I tell you they'll get down to us when they're good and ready.

PETE. But it may be too late.

NOVAK (*shrugs*). Can't be helped.

PETE. Gee! There must be something we can do.

NOVAK. Yeah. What?

PETE. I don't know. I was just thinking —

NOVAK. What good is thinking goin' to do you?

PETE (*in a wondering voice*). When boats at sea get into trouble they send a wireless message.

NOVAK. Yeah, but a mine ain't no boat.

PETE. But a boat is cut off from people too and they get help. If we had some way of sending a message —

NOVAK. There ain't no way, so forget it.

PETE (*puzzling*). Something that would connect us with the outside . . . a wave length or a wire — or a — (*jubilantly*) I've got it! I've got it! *The lights!*

NOVAK (*bewildered*). What about the lights?

PETE. That same wire runs all over the mine. (*Points.*) Thank God, it's all on one circuit.

NOVAK (*coughs*). I don't get it. Suppose it is all one circuit. (*He leans weakly against the tunnel wall. Gas is getting him.*) You — you can't talk over an electric-light wire. It — ain't — no — telephone.

PETE (*coughs and chokes a bit*). You can't talk over it but you can send a message. Look, like this — (PETE *reaches to pull himself up onto a jagged piece of rock from which he can reach the electric light. He unscrews the bulb. The stage goes dark. Then as* PETE *screws the bulb tight the light goes on again. He twists it. Light flickers on and off.*) See — it works! A short one for a dot! A long one for a dash! Look — (*switching lights as he does so*) C—O—A—L . . . COAL; —G—A—S . . . GAS;—N—E—E—D . . . NEED;—A—I—R . . . AIR. (*Triumphantly*) They'll get it. They'll send a pipe through.

NOVAK. But it don't make sense. Them flashes don't mean a thing.

PETE. Sure it does. It's the Morse code. It's what they use on boats.

NOVAK (*surprised*). It is?

PETE (*continuing to flash the light so that it flickers over their two attentive faces*). Sure.

NOVAK (*puzzled*). How did you happen to know this — this here combination?

PETE. That's what I've been studying. I wanted to be a radio operator. (*Proudly*) And I will be, too.

NOVAK (*humbly*). Do you guess they'll get your message? (*Coughs.*)

PETE. I'll keep on till they do.

DAVE (*rousing himself*). Hey, what — what's going on?

NOVAK (*proudly*). It's Pete. He's sending a message through to the outside.

DAVE (*coughs — incredulous*). Well, for the love of mike — how's he doing it?

NOVAK (*contemptuous*). With the lights, you numskull.

DAVE. Lights?

NOVAK. Sure. He's making words. He's telling 'em we need air.

DAVE. Gee! Here, let me help you.

NOVAK. Leave him alone. He's doing all right.

JOE (*gasping and sitting up*). What's alla this?

NOVAK. It's Pete. He's calling for help.

[JOE *slumps back again uncomprehendingly. There is a moment of darkness and then the lights start winking.*]

NOVAK (*bewildered*). What's going on?

PETE (*triumphant*). I knew it. I knew it.

DAVE. Knew what? What is it?

PETE (*shouting*). They got our message. They're answering!

DAVE. What do they say? Are they coming?

JOE (*still uncomprehending*). The lights, they talk?

NOVAK (*impatiently*). Shut up. Shut up. (*To* PETE) What are they saying?

PETE. Wait . . . wait. (*Spelling out words*) G–O–T . . . Got . . . message . . . sending . . . down . . . pipe . . . (*The lights now burn steadily.*) Do you hear that? We've reached 'em. We're saved!

DAVE. Yeah, but when? (*Interrupted by a fit of coughing*) We can't hold out much longer.

NOVAK. We just got to wait. That's all.

DAVE. We can't wait. We'll be dead before they get here.

JOE (*looking around*). They make hole through wall?

DAVE. Of course not. It's just a gag. That's all. They just want to make us feel good.

PETE. Maybe we could help 'em if we started digging from this end . . . ?

NOVAK. It's no use. We don't know where the pipe's coming through.

[*There is an apprehensive* [1] *silence broken only by* DAVE'S *coughing and despairing groans from* JOE.]

DAVE (*excitedly*). Listen! What's that I hear?

NOVAK. I don't hear nothing.

[*They are silent. Faint tapping sound of drilling.*]

DAVE. It sounds like drilling.

NOVAK (*excited now*). Where?

DAVE (*pointing to wall just at the bend upstage*). There! There in the wall.

NOVAK (*exultant*). They're coming for us. They're trying to get through. (*Grabbing up pick*) Let me at that wall.

[*Lights remain on as* PETE *gets down and joins* DAVE *to watch* NOVAK *as he excitedly picks at the wall.*]

DAVE. Lemme help.

NOVAK. No. This is my job.

[*All are coughing at intermittent periods.*]

PETE (*peering over* DAVE'S *shoulder*). Go ahead. Hurry. (*He clings weakly to* DAVE, *who is in little better shape.* NOVAK'S *movements grow slower and slower as his strength evaporates.*) Hurry . . . Pop . . . hurry.

NOVAK (*grunts as he gives the wall a whack*). . . . and . . . What's this?

ALL. What is it?

[NOVAK *has his nose pressed against the wall breathing deeply.* JOE *staggers to his feet and reels to them.*]

NOVAK (*croaking in joy — almost beside himself*). Air . . . fresh air! Do

[1] **apprehensive** (ăp′rē·hĕn′sĭv): **filled with fear.**

you smell it? (*Suddenly the drilling is quite loud and then it stops. There is the noise of a clanking of iron. Tap . . . tap . . . tap . . . and the end of a pipe comes through the wall.*) They've got to us. We're saved!

DAVE (*taking* PETE'S *hand*). Smart – work – kid. You're not so dumb after all.

JOE (*chokingly*). He bright boy. How long we stay here now?

DAVE. I don't care how long it is. Now I can breathe.

[*Takes deep breath. There is the sound of drilling much louder than before and the constant beat of picks.*]

NOVAK. Listen, they're getting closer. You can hear the picks cutting into the slide.

[JOE *and* DAVE *make their way to the blocked end of the tunnel and press their ears against the wall, leaving* PETE *and his father alone downstage center.*]

NOVAK (*self-consciously*). I guess we owe something to you, Pete. Dave, Joe, and myself.

PETE (*embarrassed*). Okay, Pop. Forget it.

NOVAK. You know, I was thinking while you was workin' that trick with them lights –

PETE. Yeah?

NOVAK. I was thinking that them radio fellers on those boats must be kinda smart to send messages in the air that way.

PETE (*eagerly*). Oh they are, Pop. That's why I was studying so hard.

NOVAK. Well, I'd hate to have their standin' lowered by any son of mine. A son who could turn out to be a heap smarter radio feller than them what's on the boats.

PETE (*incredulous*). What do you mean, Pop?

NOVAK (*hand on* PETE'S *shoulder*). I mean I'm sending you back to school.

[*They smile in mutual understanding and clasp hands as the sound of the rescue party grows louder and is answered by the triumphant, glad shouts of encouragement from* DAVE *and* JOE.]

[CURTAIN]

Observing Character in a Play

1. In what way do you learn that conflicts existed between Pete and his father and between Pete and Dave? How do conflicts like these reveal the basic nature of the persons involved?

2. Find speeches of Pete's which show that he is somewhat scornful and intolerant. Find others which prove him sympathetic and ambitious.

3. Point out those actions and speeches which show that there are weak spots in Dave's outward show of hardness.

4. Did your opinion of any character change before the play ended? What caused the change? What difference occurs in Novak's attitude toward Pete? toward Dave? in Pete's attitude toward Dave?

Thinking It Over

1. What is the theme or subject of this play? What point do you consider the climax?

2. Why does the author mention the lighting system in the mine fairly early in the play? In this connection, look up the word *foreshadowing.*

3. What conditions and events in his life made Pete's father reject education and call it a waste of time? Perhaps you have known uneducated persons who scorned learning. You may wish to write a character sketch of one of them. How did Pete prove that he would profit by the education that he wanted so much?

4. In what states are most of our coal mines located? What do you know about dangerous conditions in mines? about safety devices? about living conditions in

mining towns? Since coal mining is so important to our industrial life, those of us who are merely consumers should know more about it. Make a list of questions about mining that occur to you and appoint a committee to find the answers. The encyclopedia will furnish a great deal of information, but there are excellent books on the subject, too. Try the card catalogue.

For Your Vocabulary

WORD RECOGNITION: In each series below, match the italicized word with the one closest to it in meaning. Then use the italicized word in a sentence.

1. *blandly* — quickly, definitely, boastfully, agreeably
2. *dubiously* — hopefully, doubtfully, shyly, brazenly
3. *munching* — chewing, gulping, nibbling, swallowing
4. *sagely* — bitterly, quietly, wisely, hesitatingly
5. *placatingly* — irritably, maliciously, quizzically, with a desire to please
6. *repressed* — restated, restored, restrained, reproved
7. *stolidly* — busily, wonderingly, stupidly, unexcitedly
8. *listlessly* — indifferently, attentively, joyfully, sadly
9. *incredulous* — inedible, inaudible, unbelieving, inflexible
10. *intermittent* — interchangeable, intermingled, constant, at intervals

GWEN PHARIS

The Courting of Marie Jenvrin

" The Courting of Marie Jenvrin " is a delightful comedy about an unusual romance. According to the song writers, romance is supposed to flourish best in the month of June, under a sympathetic moon, with an orchestra in the distance playing a haunting tune. It doesn't always work out that way, however. Up in the Northwest Territories where buckskin boots and heavy woolen parkas are fashionable, where it's dark at 3:30 on a February afternoon, and where dogsleds are more useful than convertibles — up there people fall in love just as frequently, and quarrel and pretend to ignore each other just as unsuccessfully, as they do in any other quarter of the globe. A romantic play requires only a hero and a heroine — and sometimes a villain for good measure. This play has all three — and a cow!

The idea for " The Courting of Marie Jenvrin " occurred to the author while she was studying her new cookbook, looking for desserts that did *not* need whipped cream. " In this barren land," she says, " fresh milk and cream come to have a dreamlike significance symbolizing all the glamorous joys of the world ' outside.' "

"The Courting of Marie Jenvrin" by Gwen Pharis from *International Folk Plays* edited by Samuel Selden, published by the University of North Carolina Press. Reprinted by permission of the publisher.

For Better Reading . . . Here is a play with many comic situations and lines to bring laughter from an audience. In addition, a great deal of humor can be created by actors themselves through gestures, facial expressions, other bits of " stage business," and the expression they give to the reading of their lines. If you give the play in class, try to think how you would behave if you were one of the characters. Recall good actors of stage and screen whom you have seen playing similar roles. Incidentally, some of the fun in the play lies in its use of French expressions. Don't avoid these; make use of the footnotes and try pronouncing the words aloud.

Characters

MR. WERNECKE,[1] proprietor of the Beaverlodge Hotel
MRS. WERNECKE, his wife
MARIE JENVRIN [2]
LOUIS HÉBERT,[3] a young miner
FATHER LE BEAU,[4] a flying priest
MR. DINSMORE, a businessman
MICHAEL LORRIGAN, a miner

THE SCENE. *The combined lunchroom and sitting room of the Beaverlodge Hotel in Yellowknife, Northwest Territories, Canada.*

THE TIME. *The Present. A late afternoon in February.*

The curtain rises on the combined lunchroom and sitting room of the Beaverlodge Hotel in Yellowknife, Northwest Territories. A bear rug on the floor, a mounted caribou head, some heavily beaded mukluks [5] *of Indian fashion, and a man's parka* [6] *with heavily furred hood – this last hanging near the door – are some tangible evidence of the Northern setting. Less colorful but essential furniture in the room includes a good-sized wood or oil heater at the left, two old leather armchairs, a small stand-table for magazines and papers, a table with three painted chairs grouped round it, and a narrow counter at the right with three or four wooden stools in front of it. In the rear wall two windows and a door look out on the main street of the mining town. Up left is a door leading to the rooms upstairs and down right is a door that leads outside through the kitchen.*

Our first glimpse of life in the Beaverlodge Hotel comes at about 3:30 on a February afternoon. Darkness comes early in the North, and the shadows are deepening in the room. It is a slack time, since the miners do not come off shift until after 4 o'clock.

We discover a rather apologetic-looking little man seated on the floor in front of the large chair right of the stove, surrounded by three pulp magazines and a strange assortment of screws, coils, and machinery, the largest piece looking much like a food chopper. In the armchair left of the stove a large, placid-looking woman with the rather gaudy beauty of a great sunflower is dozing peacefully, a box of chocolates beside her. These good people are MR. *and* MRS. WERNECKE, *proprietors of the Inn. Behind the counter, folding paper napkins and tidying the cigarette and gum boxes on the shelf, is* MARIE JENVRIN.

MARIE JENVRIN *is perhaps nineteen, with a vivid little face, framed by dark,*

[1] **Wernecke** (vâr'nĕ·kĕ).
[2] **Marie Jenvrin** (má·rē' zhôɴ·vrăɴ').
[3] **Louis Hébert** (lwē' ā·bâr').
[4] **Father LeBeau** (lĕ·bō').
[5] **mukluks** (mŭk'lŭkz): knee-high buckskin or caribou boots like moccasins, often elaborately trimmed with fur, embroidery, or bead work.
[6] **parka:** a long heavy woolen coat with a hood attached.

curly hair. She wears a flared skirt, a blouse graced with a demure little collar and tiny bow tie. Around her waist is a flared apron as gay as fancy can conceive.

MR. WERNECKE *is muttering to himself as he ecstatically assembles his machinery.*

WERNECKE. She won't fit. His directions is wrong. (*He refers to one of the magazines.*) He says it fits but I make it and it don't fit. (*He takes up the paper and addresses it politely.*) Your directions are just plain wrong, Mr. Beasley. You don't ought to publish such directions.

MARIE. You work at a new invention, *Monsieur?*[1]

WERNECKE. Yes, Marie, but that Beasley makes a mistake. (*The light dawns.*) Wait! No, he don't! She fits. I have the wrong side. See, now she fits perfect. (*He holds up a coil which fits inside a circle of steel.*)

MARIE. *C'est bon.*[2] What is this – invention, *Monsieur?*

WERNECKE. Ah, a surprise! You will know tomorrow. I have one more part to come in by the plane.

MARIE. I think the plane does not get in after all. It is 3:30 and getting dark. The storm has kept him.

WERNECKE. If it is BQQ it will not come. If it is BVY it will come – you see. That BQQ is a bad plane. She looks good but she won't go. I don't like that BQQ. Twice I have been held up on an invention, waiting for that plane.

ANNABELLA (MRS. WERNECKE) (*stirring drowsily*). Fiddlesticks. I have gone outside in both. BQQ is better. I don't get sick in BQQ.

WERNECKE. Women don't know about airplanes. She looks nice so you think she is nice. I tell you BQQ is no good.

MARIE (*taking a glass of paper napkins over to the table*). Father LeBeau was to come in today. I hope the storm has not forced them down and they have lost themselves.

WERNECKE. No need to worry about the Father, Marie. He knows the North from McMurray to Aklavik. He has gone down to Aklavik alone with three dogs.

MARIE (*at the window*). Louis Hébert stands on the airplane dock. How foolish to stand shivering in such cold.

WERNECKE. Perhaps while Father LeBeau is here you will marry with Louis, Marie.

MARIE (*turning from the window and beginning to light the lamp on the table*). And perhaps I will not, Monsieur. I have no mind to marry Louis Hébert.

WERNECKE. Then what of Ed McArthy or William Shumlett or Michael Lorrigan?

MARIE. Michael Lorrigan! Such a man! *Non,*[3] Monsieur Wernecke, I prefer to work in your hotel, please.

ANNABELLA. We will give Father LeBeau the green room. It is warmer.

WERNECKE. He can have his choice of rooms – if he comes.

ANNABELLA. Well, he must come sometime. If not today, tomorrow.

WERNECKE. If it is BQQ I shall not be surprised if he never comes. (*The droning of a plane is heard quite close.*)

MARIE (*excitedly*). *Écoutez!*[4] The plane! I hear it. (*They all listen. Their faces light up.*)

[*Now the engine of the plane can be heard distinctly. All three are excited*

[1] **Monsieur** (mẽ·syû'): Sir.
[2] **C'est bon** (sĕ bôɴ'): That's good.
[3] **Non** (nôɴ): No.
[4] **Écoutez** (ā·kōō·tā'): Listen.

and hurry toward the window. MR. WERNECKE *takes time to thrust his invention into a box, which he pushes under the table. Their voices rise with pleasure.*]

WERNECKE (*gathering up his invention*). It is a plane! BVY has come through the storm.

MARIE. There it is! See, *Madame.*[1] He circles above the bay.

ANNABELLA. It is dark to land.

WERNECKE. Hah! That BVY can land any place.

MARIE. Michael Lorrigan says the ice is not safe by the Hudson Bay dock. There is a current there.

WERNECKE. It is time a plane got in. Now I can finish my invention. (*He comes to the window where the women are watching.*)

ANNABELLA. My new silk dress will be on it – and slippers for Wernecke.

MARIE. *Oui, et une lettre de ma mère.*[2]

WERNECKE. He brings her down fast. No nonsense. I like to see a good plane brought down fast.

MARIE. *Attention!*[3] He is about to land.

ANNABELLA. That is BQQ or I'm not Annabella.

MARIE. I think you are right, Madame. Voilà[4] – he is on the ice. That is a good landing. He is on the ice and no bumps.

ANNABELLA (*triumphantly*). And it is BQQ. I can see from here. So, Wernecke, BQQ cannot come in a storm.

WERNECKE. There is some mistake. I could swear it was the other.

ANNABELLA. Now what have you to say?

WERNECKE (*with dignity as he dons his parka*). I say nothing. I go to meet the guests. If it is BQQ, I expect no guests – they have probably fallen out the bottom.

ANNABELLA. What stubbornness! Soon you must invent an airplane, I suppose.

WERNECKE. I have thought of it.

ANNABELLA. Now, hurry, Wernecke. They will be getting out in a minute.

WERNECKE. They can get out without me, Mrs. Wernecke. (*With offended dignity, he leaves.*)

MARIE. Father LeBeau has come. I see him.

ANNABELLA. Shaking hands with the Mounted Policeman.

MARIE. And there is Madame Barnett. Her husband and little girl are kissing her.

ANNABELLA. Marie, isn't that Mr. Dinsmore – getting off now?

MARIE. *Ma foi,*[5] he only went outside last week.

ANNABELLA. He's a queer one. I wonder where he makes his money. Certainly not in that jewelry store of his.

MARIE. It takes much money to fly back and forth so often.

ANNABELLA. Michael Lorrigan says he's a crook.

MARIE. There is someone else. Oh, it is only Louis talking to the pilot. Now he is running up here. (*Giggling a little*) Wherever he goes, Louis must run like a scared rabbit.

ANNABELLA. I'd better go up and make sure the green room is ready.

MARIE. And I must finish my pie.

[*They turn from the window.* ANNABELLA *takes a chocolate as she starts upstairs.*]

ANNABELLA. Why don't you eat a chocolate, Marie? Michael left them for you.

[1] **Madame** (mȧ·dȧm′): Madam.
[2] **Oui, et une lettre de ma mère** (wē′, ā ün lĕ′-trĕ dẽ mȧ mâr′): Yes, and a letter from my mother.
[3] **Attention** (ȧ·tôɴ·syôɴ′): Look out now!
[4] **Voilà** (vwȧ·lȧ′): There!

[5] **Ma foi** (mȧ fwȧ′): My goodness!

MARIE. I do not eat chocolate. Besides, how do I know he leaves them for me?

ANNABELLA. I suppose a handsome young miner leaves chocolates about for Mrs. Wernecke.

MARIE. Michael Lorrigan speaks only insults. No man can speak insults to Marie Jenvrin.

ANNABELLA (*placidly as she lumbers upstairs*). Pride falls, Marie, pride falls. I was like you once. Now, as you see, I am a slave to Wernecke. (*She goes off.*)

MARIE (*patting the caribou head affectionately*). Such foolishness they talk, *mon petit.*[1] As if Marie must marry tomorrow or be forever left.

[MARIE *moves behind the counter. As she begins rolling out a pie crust which is already mixed,* LOUIS HÉBERT *pokes his head in cautiously through the door at back.* LOUIS HÉBERT *is a dapper young man, not very tall, dark and rather good-looking. He is excitable and far from levelheaded. The romance of the North is in his soul only as far as clothes are concerned. He wears a heavily furred parka, elaborately embroidered mitts, and mukluks with huge red tassels, and is indeed a colorful sight.*]

LOUIS. Marie! Are you there? I bring you something.

MARIE. Of course I am here, Louis Hébert. Don't you see me?

LOUIS (*coming into the room*). Marie, do you know what day this is?

MARIE. Tuesday, *mon petit chou!* [2]

LOUIS. Ah, but is something else, also. February 14 – that is Saint Valentine's. And I have sent to Edmonton for a valentine for Marie Jenvrin. It comes by the airplane. (*He presents her with a large red envelope.*)

MARIE. You should not spend your money on me, Louis.

LOUIS. Aren't you going to open it?

MARIE (*as she opens it*). It is a very big valentine. So much lace and ribbon.

LOUIS (*unable to wait for her to open it, he takes it from her*). Look, this is best of all. When you open this little red heart – there is my picture. *Voilà!* (*He demonstrates.*)

MARIE (*with a little throaty giggle*). *Oui,* it is you all right and looking very solemn.

LOUIS. You like it, Marie?

MARIE. *Mais oui, c'est beau.*[3] But, Louis, you should not give it to me. I am not your valentine.

LOUIS. Marie, could you not love me a little bit? Louis Hébert would serve you like a slave. Even when you are angry you are beautiful, Marie. In my mind I call you *La Belle du Nord.*[4]

MARIE. Your tongue says fine things, Louis. No wonder Cécile Rideau lies awake weeping for love of you.

LOUIS. Cécile Rideau! [5]

MARIE. Go to her, Louis. Have I not said a hundred times – four hundred times – I will not marry you?

LOUIS. If I fall down the mine shaft or get eaten up by huskies, you will be sorry then.

MARIE (*returning to her pie*). No man gets eaten up by huskies for love, Louis Hébert. Only for lack of brains.

LOUIS. Two years I stay in this wild country of rock only because of you, Marie. Two years I work in the mine. Two years I set myself down on the shore of a lake, one thousand miles from any place. And no way to get ex-

[1] **mon petit** (môɴ p'tē'): my little one.
[2] **mon petit chou** (môɴ p'tē shōō'): sweetheart (literally, my little cabbage).
[3] **Mais oui, c'est beau** (mā wē', sē bō'): Why, of course, it is beautiful.
[4] **La Belle du Nord** (là bĕl' dü nôr'): the beautiful one from the North.
[5] **Cécile Rideau** (sā·sēl' rē·dō').

cept by those airplane which make me so sick. And still you do not love me!

MARIE. When the ice melts there will be a boat. You can go outside then.

LOUIS. What is outside for me if you are not there? *Non,* if you must stay by this frozen lake beside the North Pole, then Louis Hébert stays too.

MARIE. Louis, Louis, it is no use. I will never love you – not for all the gold in Yellowknife.

LOUIS. I know – I am what they call – a dope. But I stay.

MARIE. *Très bien.*[1] If you must stay, you stay. But what if I tell you there is a whisper of love – just a small stirring – in my heart for someone else?

LOUIS. I will fight him.

MARIE. *C'est impossible.*[2] Besides, he does not love me.

LOUIS. Then he is a fool with no eyes. I can fight him.

MARIE. He is twice as big as you. Anyway, perhaps I do not love him. Perhaps I hate him. *Mais, j'ai mal au cœur,*[3] Louis.

LOUIS (*solemnly*). *Moi, aussi.*[4] We French suffer, Marie.

MARIE (*with a big sigh*). *Oui, nous souffrons.*[5] (*For a brief period these very young people suffer. Then* MARIE *turns briskly back to her pie.*) There, it is ready for the oven. See how beautiful, Louis.

LOUIS. You are wonderful.

MARIE (*complacently*). I make good pies. Outside where I have cream to pile on top, I take prizes for my pie. But enough talk. Be a good boy and go down to the lake and bring me two pails of water.

LOUIS. Every day I cut holes in the ice to bring you water.

MARIE. I know Louis. (*She smiles at him.*) You are very good, *mon cher.*[6]

[*She hands him the pails, but before he leaves* MR. WERNECKE *enters with* FATHER LE BEAU. FATHER LE BEAU *is a rosy little priest with twinkling eyes.*]

MARIE. Père LeBeau! *Vous êtes ici.*[7] (*She runs to him and gives him both her hands.*)

FATHER LE BEAU. Marie – Louis. *Comment allez-vous, mes enfants?*[8] Marie grows prettier each week, *n'est-ce pas,*[9] Louis? (*He pats her cheek and shakes hands with* LOUIS.)

MARIE (*her eyes shining*). *C'est vous à la fin, mon père.*[10] We are so glad to see you.

LOUIS. *Oui,* it is good to have you here, Père LeBeau.

FATHER LE BEAU. Your welcome warms my heart, my children. Now I will take my things upstairs – but I will be down again soon to eat one of your fine pies, Marie.

WERNECKE. I will lead the way, Father.

FATHER LE BEAU. Thank you, Mr. Wernecke. This hotel always seems like home to me.

WERNECKE. I am honored, Father.

FATHER LE BEAU. Have you been inventing lately?

WERNECKE. A new one – a surprise. See, the last part came in with you. (*He displays the treasured parcel.*)

[1] **Très bien** (trĕ byăɴ′): Very well.
[2] **C'est impossible** (sĕ tăɴ·pô·sē′bl′): That's impossible.
[3] **Mais, j'ai mal au cœur** (mā, zhā mȧ lō kûr′): But I am heartsick.
[4] **Moi, aussi** (mwȧ, ō·sē′); Me, too.
[5] **Oui, nous souffrons** (wē′, nōō sōō·frôɴ′): Yes, we suffer.
[6] **mon cher** (môɴ shâr′): my dear.
[7] **Père LeBeau! Vous êtes ici** (pâr lĕ·bō′, vōō-zĕt zē·sē′): Father LeBeau! You are here.
[8] **Comment allez-vous, mes enfants** (kô·mänɴ-tȧ·lā·vōō′, mĕ·zäɴ·făɴ′): How are you, my children?
[9] **n'est-ce pas** (nĕ·spȧ′): doesn't she?
[10] **C'est vous à la fin, mon père** (sĕ vōō·zȧ·lȧ făɴ′, môɴ pâr′): It really is you, Father.

FATHER LE BEAU. I shall be glad to see it. (*They go upstairs.*)

LOUIS (*once more taking up his water pails*). Père LeBeau is here. There are rings at Dinsmore's. If you loved me, Marie, we could marry. As it is I am as lonely as — (*He searches for a simile.*) as one rabbit's track in the snow.

[*He adjusts his parka hood, pulls on his fine mitts, and is about to leave when* R. S. DINSMORE *enters from the street.* R. S. DINSMORE, *jeweler, is a stocky gentleman with an unctuous* [1] *manner and sharp, suspicious eyes. He wears a large fur coat.*]

DINSMORE. Well, well, get two Frenchies together and the talk flies like crows in a cornfield. How are you behaving yourself, Miss Jenvrin?

MARIE (*coldly*). Did you wish something, *Monsieur?*

DINSMORE. Only to see old Wernecke. No hurry. (*He shakes the snow off his coat carelessly.*)

LOUIS (*without warmth*). You were not long in Edmonton.

DINSMORE. Just a little business trip, my boy. Some of us have to keep a foot on the ladder, you know.

LOUIS (*as he goes out the door*). You should take care you make no false steps, *Monsieur.*

DINSMORE (*after* LOUIS *has shut the door*). I see you've got your boy friend working.

MARIE (*ignoring the remark*). Monsieur Wernecke should be down very soon.

DINSMORE. I can wait. Would you care to take a little walk after you're through tonight?

MARIE. A walk? What for?

DINSMORE. Why — just a walk — over to my shop maybe. To get out.

MARIE. I have been out. When I walk in twenty below zero, I have a purpose.

DINSMORE. Perhaps you'd like to see the moving picture?

MARIE. Thank you, *Monsieur,* you will excuse me but I do not care to go.

DINSMORE. As you like. You know, Miss Jenvrin, I've been thinking of opening a restaurant here. With your help the restaurant would become a very paying proposition.

MARIE. I have no wish to change jobs, *Monsieur.*

DINSMORE. You don't understand. You see, I'm a man of some means. I realize my position may seem rather out of reach to you, but I've been keeping my eye on you this last three months and —

[MICHAEL LORRIGAN *enters from outside. He is a tall, homely, and thoroughly attractive young man of great vitality.*]

MICHAEL. Well, Marie Jenvrin, have you a kiss for Michael Lorrigan, the hardest working hard-rock miner in the town of Yellowknife? On second thought I'll not kiss you. You've painted your mouth like a signboard. I'll have a cup of coffee instead.

MARIE. You'll have no kiss from me, Michael Lorrigan, and you pay for your coffee.

MICHAEL. Ten cents for cold coffee. No wonder I must go around in a ragged shirt.

DINSMORE (*turning*). Look here, my good man, you're interrupting —

MICHAEL. The name's Lorrigan, Mr. Dinsmore, and I'm nobody's man but my own.

DINSMORE. Prickly today, aren't you?

MICHAEL. I've been waiting for you to get back.

DINSMORE. Really?

[1] **unctuous** (ŭngk'tū̦·ŭs): oily; seeking favor by insincerity and pretense.

MICHAEL. I understand you lent old Carl Swanson money to pay his poker debts, after getting him that drunk he didn't know what he was doing. He's been drunk ever since, but I got that much out of him.

DINSMORE. I lent him the money. Poor old codger. He shouldn't have sat in on a game with that bunch down at Joe's. They cleaned him.

MICHAEL. Did you take any security?

DINSMORE. Don't be funny. What security has Swanson got to give?

MICHAEL. I wouldn't know, Mr. Dinsmore, but I think you might. Carl keeps jabbering about some paper he signed.

DINSMORE. Oh, that, it's nothing. Tell him to come in and see me. I'll explain it to him in words of one syllable.

MICHAEL. He's soberin' up in my room now.

DINSMORE. Pleasant friends he has, eh, Miss Jenvrin?

MICHAEL. I wouldn't like to see old Carl cheated, Mr. Dinsmore.

DINSMORE. Tell him to keep away from the crowd that hang around Joe's, then.

MICHAEL. I'll tell him that – from you.

DINSMORE. Look here, Lorrigan, I felt sorry for the old soak. I lent him some money. What's the matter with that?

MICHAEL. If you did it out of kindness, I'll beg your pardon, Mr. Dinsmore. If not – (*He breaks off, puts a coin on the table, and speaks to* MARIE, *turning away from* DINSMORE.) I did your coffee an injustice, Colleen. It's lukewarm. You're doin' better.

MARIE. There is your change. You are welcome to go now.

[MICHAEL *lights a cigarette and gazes nonchalantly at the smoke rings which he blows at the ceiling.*]

MICHAEL. I was just thinking –

MARIE. There is small use digging for gold where no gold is, *Monsieur.*

MICHAEL. You'd be almost a pretty girl, Marie, if you controlled your tongue. Your nose is snub, of course, and there's too much red stuff on your lips, but you'd get by, if you didn't talk. Too bad. (*He shakes his head.*)

[MR. *and* MRS. WERNECKE *come downstairs and into the room, arguing vociferously.* ANNABELLA *carries a tall, rangy plant.*]

ANNABELLA. I tell you, Wernecke, it is the B_1 tablets that have made this begonia plant grow.

WERNECKE. B_1! The plant was withering away to a shadow until I invented my plant food – all its growing is because of my plant food.

ANNABELLA. Nonsense! Your plant food didn't help the geraniums. They died. B_1 is necessary to plant life.

WERNECKE (*irritated*). B_1 be hanged, Mrs. Wernecke. My plant food has made the begonia blossom like the pines of Lebanon.[1] Am I right, Marie?

MARIE. Perhaps it is the soil Louis brings me for my garden that makes the begonia grow so tall.

ANNABELLA. Michael. I appeal to you – I read about B_1 and I try it. Immediately this plant shoots up two feet. Now Wernecke claims all the glory for his plant food. It is unreasonable!

WERNECKE. Every time I invent an invention around here somebody makes slams. Give me that begonia – I'll throw it out the window!

ANNABELLA. So, indeed! I will put it in my own sitting room where you can't ruin it with your plant food. Credit taker! (*She glares at him, then takes a chocolate.*)

[1] **Lebanon** (lĕb′*ȧ*·nŭn): a country near Palestine – but the pines, or cedars, of Lebanon grow in other countries.

MICHAEL (*getting up*). Plant food alone cannot account for this wonderful plant, Mrs. Wernecke. B_1 alone might account for half of it. It is the combination. I am going upstairs. I'll leave it in your sitting room.

[*With a courtly smile,* MICHAEL *relieves* MRS. WERNECKE *of the begonia plant.*]

ANNABELLA (*noticing that* WERNECKE *is grimly starting upstairs with his box*). Where are you taking that?

WERNECKE. To the green room. Intelligent people, like Father LeBeau, are interested – very interested in the things I invent. (ANNABELLA *gives an elaborate sniff.*)

DINSMORE. I don't suppose you could spare a minute from plant foods and such junk to rent me a room, Wernecke. No time for business, I guess.

ANNABELLA (*between chocolates*). The yellow room is ready, Wernecke.

WERNECKE (*pausing at the foot of the stairs*). I'm sorry. I have no rooms.

ANNABELLA. Why, Wernecke!

WERNECKE (*firmly, though it is an effort*). I have no room for Mr. Dinsmore.

ANNABELLA. Wernecke, the yellow room –

WERNECKE (*politely*). I'm sorry. You will have to go elsewhere.

DINSMORE. Look here, everybody knows you are not full. That priest and I were the only –

WERNECKE. I own this hotel. Perhaps everybody does not know that.

DINSMORE. Why won't you give me a room?

WERNECKE (*advancing and speaking in a very gentle voice*). Well, I will tell you. I just don't like you, Mr. Dinsmore. I never have liked you. I never will like you. So, when you ask me for a room, I suddenly decide I have no rooms. Now you know as much about it as I do.

ANNABELLA. Why, Wernecke, you've never acted like this before.

WERNECKE. I know. It surprises me too.

DINSMORE (*belligerently*). I suppose I can't eat in your lunchroom?

WERNECKE (*considering*). Yes, you may have your supper here.

ANNABELLA. Wernecke, are you quite well?

WERNECKE. Quite well, Annabella, thank you. You will excuse me, Mr. Dinsmore. (*With a little bow he goes through the door leading upstairs.*)

ANNABELLA (*solemnly*). You shouldn't have called his invention junk, Mr. Dinsmore. He will be a great man some day. Inventing is a passion with him – a pure passion.

DINSMORE. What a hotel! What a way to run a business! I'll take away every customer –

[MICHAEL *reappears from upstairs.*]

MICHAEL. Well, the begonia plant is safe in your sitting room, Mrs. Wernecke. I put it in the window.

ANNABELLA. Ah! There is a draft in that window. It will freeze. Excuse me, sir. (*She brushes past* DINSMORE *and hurries out.*)

MICHAEL. Are you fond of begonias, Marie? (*He gets in her way.*)

MARIE (*moving to the table with two glasses of water*). Of course. But I am not fond of people who waste my time. *Allez!*[1] (*She places the water on the table.*)

MICHAEL (*in a startled tone*). Marie, let me see the backs of your hands – quick.

[*Obediently* MARIE *extends her hands, palms down, lifting startled eyes to his. With a flourish,* MICHAEL *places a glass of water on each hand and walks*

[1] **Allez** (à·lā'): Run along now!

A scene at Yellowknife, on Great Slave Lake, the wilderness setting for the comedy, "The Courting of Marie Jenvrin." A group of the inhabitants stand around watching while a consignment of food is unloaded at the Hudson's Bay Company. (National Film Board, Canada)

off whistling "They're hanging Danny Deever."]

MARIE. Take them off, you hear. Take them off at once.

MICHAEL. Never act without thinking, my pet. You can take my advice as that of an uncle.

MARIE. Better I have advice from that stuffed caribou! Take them off, I tell you —

DINSMORE. Permit me, Miss Jenvrin. (*He removes the glasses.*) A poor joke, sir.

MARIE. Thank you. Go now, Michael Lorrigan, or I will throw the kettle at you.

MICHAEL. 'Twould do less damage than one of your pies, my sweet.

MARIE. You dare! I win prizes for my pies — many times.

MICHAEL. Still, if I want good pie I go to the Chinaman's down the street.

MARIE. Listen to him! If I had beautiful, fresh cream from the cow, *Monsieur,* I could make a pie that would set you dreaming of heaven. And a dream is as near as you will get.

MICHAEL. Cream! Listen to her! You're lucky to have cream in tin cans.

MARIE. That! It tastes like gasoline.

MICHAEL. Perhaps you think they should fly a cow in here for you, my grand lady. That's one thing even you can't have while you stay in the North, little Buttercup.

MARIE. So, you know everything. I could have a cow next week.

MICHAEL. Indeed! Could you now? (LOUIS HÉBERT *enters with his pails of water.*) Hear that, Louis. Marie Jenvrin can have a cow flown in!

LOUIS. You are only talking, Marie.

MARIE. *Fermez la bouche,*[1] Louis Hébert.

LOUIS. If you would marry me, we could go outside and Louis Hébert would buy you a cow.

MICHAEL. A grand idea. Marry Louis and go outside!

MARIE (*goaded beyond all reason*). Marry, marry, marry! I am sick of this talk about marriage. I will marry the man who brings me a cow on the noose to that door there, and no other. I swear it! Now, there is your answer. Get out, all of you!

LOUIS. Do you mean it, Marie – truly? About the cow?

MARIE. I have said it, haven't I?

DINSMORE. Foolishness. What would you feed a cow here?

MARIE. Carrots, *Monsieur,* that I raise in my garden.

DINSMORE. So, you have a garden? Very enterprising.

LOUIS. You bet. Marie is the true French *Canadienne.* Even in this godforsaken rock she must have a garden. Seven of us carried dirt in pails from three miles to make a garden for Marie.

MICHAEL. I'm the only free man left in camp.

LOUIS. I will get the cow, Marie, and then we will marry and –

MICHAEL. You take the first plane out, Louis. Get yourself to a duckpond. The quacking would be restful after the clacking of her tongue.

LOUIS. You do not insult Marie! We will settle now.

MARIE. You do not, Louis. He would break you in two.

MICHAEL. Hold your whist, Marie Jenvrin. This is men's talk. (*To* LOUIS) Forget it, Louis, I feel no malice toward you.

LOUIS. So, you will not fight. Very well. My honor is satisfied.

MARIE. I die of boredom with all this talk, talk, talk.

LOUIS. I am going now to the Canadian Airways, Marie, to see about the cow.

MARIE. Louis, I didn't mean –

LOUIS (*exuberantly*). A cow – you will see, it is nothing to Louis Hébert.

MARIE. But Louis – *attendez! Vous ne comprenez*[2] –

MICHAEL. She's trying to tell you she didn't mean it, Louis. She talks only to fill silence –

MARIE. Who are you to know what I mean? Of course I mean it.

MICHAEL. I suppose then you'd put it in writing?

MARIE. Perhaps I would –

MICHAEL. And sign your name to it? Oh, no, my sweet, you are not that foolish!

MARIE. Foolish, is it? You think I could not have a cow. You think no man would care enough to buy a cow for Marie Jenvrin.

MICHAEL. Not even enough to buy a teeny weeny little calf. (*He measures a calf as big as a mouse.*)

LOUIS. I would, Marie.

MICHAEL. She was only joking, Louis. She knows you can't fly cows for nothing.

MARIE. Joking, was I? I will show you. (*To* DINSMORE). Give me your pencil, *Monsieur.* (*He does so.*) Now, Michael Lorrigan, look with your eyes at this. (*She writes on the back of the valentine.*) "I, Marie Jenvrin, promise to marry the man who brings a cow to Yellowknife to me. – Signed, Marie Jen-

[1] **Fermez la bouche** (fâr·mā lȧ bo͞osh′): Keep still.

[2] **attendez! Vous ne comprenez** (ȧ·tôɴ·dā′ vo͞o n'kôɴ·prĕ·nā′): Listen! You do not understand.

vrin." What do you say now?

MICHAEL. You must have witnesses.

MARIE (*doubtfully*). And what are those?

DINSMORE. It makes it legal, Miss Jenvrin. See — I write " witnessed by R. S. Dinsmore." (*He does so.*)

MICHAEL (*enjoying himself*). One is not enough.

MARIE. Write your name, Louis. (LOUIS *does so.*) So — I do not mean it, Monsieur Lorrigan. (*Triumphantly*) Now it is — what you say? (*She turns to* DINSMORE.)

DINSMORE. Legal.

MARIE. That's it — legal. I will put it up here. (*She places it in a prominent place on the counter. To* MICHAEL) I expect you feel very small now. (*She smiles contentedly; then with a sudden burst of anger leans toward him, measuring with her fingers.*) Like a teeny weeny calf, you feel small, I hope.

MICHAEL (*bursting into a roar of laughter*). Ah, Marie Jenvrin, you should listen to your Uncle Michael's advice. All the camp will hear of this. (*He goes over, gets a newspaper, and sits down to read.*)

LOUIS. I will order a Jersey cow, Marie. They have a very kind face. And a Jersey would fly best. They have good digestion.

MARIE (*crossly*). Always you talk too much, Louis.

LOUIS. Do not argue, *chérie.*[1] (*He puts on his fine mitts.*) I know many brands of cow, and the Jersey, it is the kindest. *Au 'voir, mes amis.*[2] (*He goes out in high spirits.*)

DINSMORE. What a fool! No wonder he wearies you, Marie.

MARIE. Speak no ill of Louis, *Monsieur.* He is my greatest friend.

DINSMORE. Excuse me. You know this business of the cow — it isn't so foolish as it first appears. There are children in this camp. Parents would pay fifty cents a quart for milk for their children. Some cows might be a good investment.

MICHAEL (*looking up from his paper*). You smell money like a rat smells cheese, Mr. Dinsmore. Milk for babes seems a little out of your line.

DINSMORE (*getting up*). Look here, Lorrigan, a man can express an opinion. You will excuse me, Marie. I'll be back later. (*He puts on his coat.*)

MARIE. Very well.

DINSMORE. Perhaps you will reconsider my invitation to the moving picture?

MARIE. Perhaps — in one hundred thousand leap years!

DINSMORE. These young girls must have their jokes, eh, Lorrigan?

MICHAEL. Be on your way, sir. Miss Jenvrin is busy.

DINSMORE. She is happiest when busy; I see that. And it is charming, Marie, charming. (*He goes out highly pleased with his compliment.*)

MICHAEL (*muttering to himself*). Blatherskite! A havering blatherskite.[3]

[*There is a moment's silence while* MARIE *continues setting the table and* MICHAEL *reads his paper.* MARIE *takes up a heavy coal bucket and starts to put some in the stove.*]

MICHAEL (*angrily*). Here, you, put that down. (*He gets up and takes the heavy bucket from her.*) Have you no more sense than a daft mud hen? (*He puts the coal in the stove as* MARIE *moves out of the way.*)

MARIE. To whom do you speak, *Monsieur?*

[1] **chérie** (shâ·rē'): darling.
[2] **Au 'voir, mes amis** (ō vwär', mā·zà·mē'): good-by, my friends.
[3] **havering blatherskite** (hā'vĕr·ĭng blăth'ĕr-skīt): a babbling chatterer.

MICHAEL. To a lass who will sell herself for a cow on a noose — and because a poor Irish hard-rocker says her pie is not so good as the Chinaman's down the street.

MARIE. Keep your tongue to yourself, Michael Lorrigan. You are no more to me than — than a mouse in a field!

MICHAEL. Never mind, little bird. Perhaps old Dinsmore will have a fine cow flown in for you.

MARIE (*startled*). Oh, no —

MICHAEL (*returning to his chair*). Why not? He's pinched his ill-gotten pennies till he's squeezed dollars out of them.

MARIE. But, Michael, he's old — and there is greed in his face.

MICHAEL. Then I'll lend the money to Louis Hébert. You shall have your cow.

MARIE (*stung by his indifference*). To hear you boast of lending money is to hear wind in an empty chimney. Have I not heard how Michael Lorrigan gets drunk on a Saturday and gives his money to the Indians?

MICHAEL. Better an Indian papoose should have it than a French vixen!

MARIE. How dare you call names at me, Marie Jenvrin?

MICHAEL (*genuinely angry*). Who are you to say whether I can lend two hundred dollars or not? So, you think I'm a no-good wanderer with no thought for day after tomorrow. I'll show you. I'll lend the money to Black Oscar. Then you'll have to marry him and live in that dirty shack with eighteen huskies.

MARIE. I will marry whom I choose.

MICHAEL. Did you or did you not promise to marry the man who brings you a cow?

MARIE (*close to tears*). You drove me to it, by your insults.

MICHAEL. I thought it time you were taught a lesson. The world is not your oyster, my pretty goose.

MARIE (*shouting*). Take yourself out of the door! For a million dollars every day in golden money I wouldn't have you around for an hour. You and your two hundred dollars! Two hundred cents is more like it — and that is more than you are worth!

MICHAEL (*at the door*). If I had two hundred dollars and I have — I tell you, I wouldn't marry you if I got a gold brick for a premium.

MARIE. Or I you for *two* gold bricks.

[FATHER LE BEAU *comes in. He looks at the two reproachfully.*]

FATHER LE BEAU. Children, children!

MARIE. He could do penance for twenty years, Father, and not receive forgiveness for the wickedness of his tongue.

MICHAEL. Have I or have I not two hundred dollars, Father? Am I one to scatter money to the waves? Answer me that!

FATHER LE BEAU. Marie — Michael — This is no way. Control your —

MICHAEL. Control — I have not lost my temper in ten years — but this, this —

MARIE. Make him go away, Father. How can you stand up for him? He falls asleep at Mass; I've seen him.

MICHAEL. Don't worry, I'm going, and if I never come back it is too soon. I mean soon enough. You hear me — never!

[*He takes up his cap and miner's lamp and goes out.*]

MARIE (*following him*). Go, go, go! I would rather see the back of your heels than the face of a blessed angel!

FATHER LE BEAU (*as* MICHAEL *closes the door*). Marie, it is not good to get so angry.

MARIE. I am sorry, Father, if I blasphemed. (*She is very meek.*)

FATHER LE BEAU (*who has been looking at the document*). What is this? "I, Marie Jenvrin promise to marry . . ." (*He reads the rest in silence.*) Marie!

MARIE (*a little frightened at his disapproval*). That Michael, Père LeBeau, he jokes about my pie, and I make a polite wish for cream and –

FATHER LE BEAU. It is not seemly to joke about marriage, Marie.

MARIE (*anxious to agree*). I know. You should talk gravely to that Michael, Father. He causes all this trouble. (*Almost ready to weep*) Now I am in so much of a mix-up and all the camp will laugh at Marie Jenvrin. *C'est horrible!* [1] Already Louis goes to get a cow. I wish to die.

FATHER LE BEAU (*smiling in spite of himself*). Louis would make a good husband.

MARIE. But I do not love him.

FATHER LE BEAU. What of Michael Lorrigan? He is a good man.

MARIE. To you, maybe. To me he is a werewolf in a sheepskin.

FATHER LE BEAU (*patting her shoulder*). Things may arrange themselves, my child. It costs much money to bring a cow by plane.

MARIE (*restored to cheerfulness*). Then you are not angry, *mon père?*

FATHER LE BEAU. No, Marie, but you must guard your tongue more carefully.

[LOUIS HÉBERT *comes in, breathless and disconsolate.*]

LOUIS. Marie, you do not mean it about the cow. It costs two hundred dollars to fly one cow to this place. I have seventeen dollars, Marie.

MARIE (*smiling radiantly*). I would be a bad wife, Louis. I would throw things and lie in bed in the mornings.

LOUIS. What is it about a cow that you want so much?

MARIE. Cream, *mon petit chou,* cream. Do not feel bad, Louis. Cécile – why, I forgot to tell you – Cécile sends you a scarf. Madame Wernecke has it.

LOUIS (*stubbornly*). I do not wear it.

MARIE. What are you saying? Cécile has been knitting that scarf for two months. (*Smugly*) Cécile is a very bad knitter, of course.

LOUIS (*mumbling*). Always you push, push, push me at Cécile Rideau. Sometime I will allow myself to be pushed. A man can't be strong of mind forever.

[*He is about to go upstairs as* MR. DINSMORE *comes in.*]

DINSMORE. Well, Louis, I hear you had some difficulty with your Jersey.

LOUIS (*crossly*). Your ears are too long, *Monsieur.*

DINSMORE. Better long ears than a short pocketbook, eh, Father LeBeau? (*He is very much pleased with himself.*)

LOUIS (*going out*). Scarves. I hate scarves!

DINSMORE. Marie, my girl, everything has been arranged for your satisfaction.

MARIE. I do not understand you, *Monsieur.*

DINSMORE. No need to be coy with me, young lady. You'll be in charge of the restaurant.

MARIE. You must be mad. I work in nobody's restaurant unless it pleases me.

DINSMORE. Of course not, until we are married.

MARIE. Married? I – marry *you?*

DINSMORE. I have paid the money and you are to have your cow. I wired for it to come on Monday. We will sell milk at fifty cents –

MARIE (*stricken*). You – you have bought a cow?

DINSMORE. To be flown in on the next

[1] **C'est horrible** (sĕ·tô·rēbl"): It is horrible.

plane. Two hundred dollars, it cost me, above the price of the cow, but we will soon make it up.

MARIE. Oh, no! Father –

DINSMORE. Two hundred dollars is a lot of money, but I am not worried.

MARIE. *Monsieur,* you did not understand. I was joking – I –

DINSMORE. I believe in striking while the iron's hot.

MARIE. *Monsieur,* you make a big mistake. I have no wish to marry.

FATHER LE BEAU. Surely you are not serious, Mr. Dinsmore. After all –

DINSMORE. Marie swore to marry the man who brings a cow to Yellowknife. I am doing this. We can be married on Tuesday.

MARIE (*frightened and pleading*). Please, *Monsieur,* it was a foolish vow. You would not want me for a wife. My temper – it is very bad.

DINSMORE. So was the first Mrs. Dinsmore's. Temper never bothers me. Perhaps you'd like to come in on Sunday to clean up our rooms a bit.

MARIE. Never.

DINSMORE. I've got an idea. I'll just run over to my shop and get you a ring – to wear until Tuesday.

MARIE. I won't have your ring.

DINSMORE. Now, now, no need to be foolish. We'll make our fortune, my girl, our fortune. (*He turns to go.*)

[MRS. WERNECKE *comes downstairs.*]

ANNABELLA. I'll give you a hand with supper, Marie.

DINSMORE. I've just done the Beaverlodge Hotel out of a good cook, Mrs. Wernecke. But to the victor the spoils, eh, Father? (*He goes out the door at the rear.*)

MARIE (*sinking down in a disconsolate heap*). Oh, I am so much a fool! *Qu'est-ce que je vais faire?* [1] *Qu'est-ce que je vais faire?*

ANNABELLA. Marie, you are crying. What has happened?

MARIE. *Oh, je suis désolée. Je veux mourir.* [2]

FATHER LE BEAU (*worried*). Come, Marie, you mustn't cry. We must think. You see, Mrs. Wernecke, Marie made a foolish vow to marry the man who brings her a cow – (*He hands* ANNABELLA *the document.*)

ANNABELLA. A cow? Here?

MARIE. And that Dinsmore has bought one. Oh, I wish to die, somewhere in the snow – alone!

FATHER LE BEAU. If only you hadn't signed a paper.

ANNABELLA. Don't cry, Marie. Wernecke is clever. He will help us.

MARIE. Nobody can help. I have nobody, nothing. I will be a prisoner in those awful rooms of Dinsmore's.

ANNABELLA. You shall not, Marie. Wernecke will –

MARIE. There is no time. Even now he brings me a ring. My heart is broken, broken.

FATHER LE BEAU. You might get into a rage, Marie, and throw things until he is frightened to marry you. (*Apologetically*) It is only a suggestion –

MARIE. The vow is – what they call – legal. *Oh, mon cœur, mon cœur!* [3]

[LOUIS *comes rushing in in great excitement, followed by* MR. WERNECKE.]

LOUIS. Marie! Monsieur Wernecke has invented the most beautiful, the most wonderful machinery. It is machinery to

[1] **Qu'est-ce que je vais faire?** (kĕs·kĕ′ zhĕ vā fâr′): What shall I do?

[2] **Oh, je suis désolée. Je veux mourir.** (ō zhĕ swē dā·zō·lā′. zhĕ vû mōō·rēr′): Oh, I am heartbroken. I wish to die.

[3] **Oh, mon cœur, mon cœur** (ō môɴ kûr′, môɴ kûr′): Oh, my heart, my heart.

FATHER LE BEAU (*sitting*). Well, I am quite exhausted. I'll soon be ready for some of your pie, Marie.

MICHAEL (*as if the subject had never come up before*). Say, Father, if you want good pie you ought to try Long Jim's. Best pie I ever ate.

MARIE. *Mon Dieu,* listen to him! I can't think – I cannot put on my lip rouge – I cannot speak English – I cannot cook – nothing I do is good –

MICHAEL (*calmly*). That's right. You're a bad-tempered, willful, spoiled brat with no mind of what you want. Crying for a cow like a baby for the moon. There's three hundred dollars. Now don't say Michael Lorrigan never saves any money. You buy your cow and live alone in your garden and frighten the children with your sputtering. (*He places a roll of bills on the counter before her.*)

MARIE. Three hundred dollars! You insult me with your money.

MICHAEL. I give it to you, with no strings attached – except peace from your havering.

MARIE. Oh, you are a – a – a devil! I call all the saints in heaven to see how I treat your money! (*She throws it at him.*) Take it, and take that, too, you – you – blatherskite! (*She takes up a dipper of water and throws it over him.*)

ANNABELLA. Marie!

FATHER LE BEAU. Child, you mustn't.

MICHAEL (*very quietly*). So, you threw water on me. You spoiled my clean shirt that I ironed myself. All right, Marie Jenvrin. Now, none of you interfere, you understand?

MARIE. What are you going to do? I – I didn't mean –

MICHAEL. I'm going to give you something you've needed for a long time. I'm lucky to find a weapon at hand. (*He rolls up a magazine.*)

MARIE. Father!

FATHER LE BEAU. Michael, this is not –

MICHAEL. I said there's to be no interfering, Father. (*He takes up* MARIE *as if she were a flour sack and puts her over his knee.*) I'll give you twenty. One for each year. You can count them in French if you like. One! (*There is a resounding smack.*)

MARIE. Ouch! You let me go, Michael Lorrigan. Let me go. (*She kicks vigorously.*)

MICHAEL. Two, three, four, five.

MARIE. Ow! *Diable!*[1] Father, he's hurting me. I'll bite your hand off.

MICHAEL. Six, seven, eight.

MARIE. *Mon Dieu,* he's killing me. You let him kill me!

MICHAEL. Nine, ten, eleven – Ouch, you vixen, would you take a piece out of my knee? Twelve, thirteen, fourteen.

MARIE. Enough, enough! I will never be angry again. I will – (*She beats on him.*) Fiend, devil, put me down, I tell you!

MICHAEL. Fifteen, sixteen.

[LOUIS HÉBERT *comes in carrying a very large book.*]

LOUIS. The encyclopedia says – (*He stops short.*) Marie! (*He starts toward* MARIE *but* ANNABELLA *stops him.*)

ANNABELLA. No, Louis. Stay there.

[LOUIS *starts to go on, but* FATHER LE-BEAU *lays his hand on his shoulder.*]

FATHER LE BEAU. She is right, Louis. It is better so.

MICHAEL. Eighteen, nineteen, twenty. There! (*He sets* MARIE *on her feet.*) Now pick up that money and put it in a tidy roll.

MARIE (*in a small voice*). I won't.

MICHAEL. What's that you say?

MARIE. Yes, Michael. (*She kneels to*

[1] **Diable** (dē-ä'bl'): devil.

take up the bills. There is a pause.)

ANNABELLA (*suddenly decisive*). Wernecke, go and get the mail.

WERNECKE. Yes, Annabella. (*He goes quietly.*)

ANNABELLA. And Father, you and Louis must come up and see the begonia plant. It has grown so you wouldn't know it.

FATHER LE BEAU. Yes. It's amazing how the begonia plant grows, Mrs. Wernecke. (*He follows her toward the door.*)

ANNABELLA. Come, Louis.

LOUIS. Marie, do you want me to look at the begonia plant?

MARIE (*gently*). It is better so, Louis.

LOUIS. *Très bien,* Marie. I am – sorry. (LOUIS, *as he turns, starts winding a scarf around his neck.*)

MARIE. What is that on your neck, Louis?

LOUIS. It is the scarf that Cécile knit for me.

MARIE (*sadly*). *C'est bon.* You look very handsome. Cécile will be proud.

LOUIS. Father. Mrs. Wernecke. Wait for me. I come to look at the begonia. (*He follows the procession out sadly.*)

[*There is a painful pause.* MARIE *puts the money into a neat roll and tidies herself a little.* MICHAEL *continues to read.*]

MARIE (*in a very little voice*). I have picked up the money, Michael.

MICHAEL. Good.

MARIE. I feel very small. (*She measures.*)

MICHAEL (*without looking up*). Good.

MARIE. Michael – that spanking you gave me. It hurt me very bad.

MICHAEL (*still reading*). Very good.

MARIE (*drawing a little nearer, shyly*). Michael, was that – would you say that was the spanking of an – uncle?

MICHAEL (*looking at her doubtfully*). What else? What other kind of spanking would it be?

MARIE (*very small*). It is strange. I only thought – it reminds me so much of the spanking my sister Rose receives from her – husband.

MICHAEL. Indeed.

MARIE (*daring a quivering little smile*). It wouldn't be that kind, would it, Michael?

MICHAEL. And if it were? What would you have to say? (*He gets up and puts down his newspaper.*) Come here and tell me.

MARIE (*approaching a few steps*). I am here, Michael.

MICHAEL. Well! You're a small thing to cause a man's heart to flutter. But Michael Lorrigan is no coward. Look at me, Marie Jenvrin. (*He smiles at her as he tilts her chin up.*) Will we be getting married before the Lenten season?

MARIE (*burying her head in his shoulder*). Michael! Michael, I'm crying.

MICHAEL. You've had a hard day. (*He dries her eyes with his handkerchief.*) Come, now. Shall we buy a cow with the money there?

MARIE. *Non, non.* I never want to see a cow! But Mr. Wernecke will make us a cream machine – and we will buy a little house with the money.

MICHAEL. 'Tis settled then. We'll tell Father tonight. One more thing; I'm to be boss in the household, Marie Jenvrin. There'll be no doubt of that. You understand. None of this "Michael this, and Michael that."

MARIE. *Oui,* I understand.

MICHAEL. Good. (*He kisses her lightly. Her hand goes up to trace his kiss as she looks at him.*)

MARIE (*with a sigh*). Michael.

MICHAEL. You're happy, Marie Jenvrin?

MARIE. I'm so happy. I could – (*She*

searches for words.) I could eat up the sky! (*Breaking away*) But it is near supper time. I must hurry.

MICHAEL. I'll get a fresh shirt. (*He turns to go.*)

MARIE. Michael, if it would not be – if you don't mind. You see, the wood box – it is entirely empty. And it is so late, I thought –

MICHAEL (*unaware of the web into which he has fallen*). Sure, I'll fill it for you, Marie. No trouble at all.

[FATHER LE BEAU *appears in the doorway. They do not see him.* MARIE *runs to* MICHAEL *with the box. As she gives it to him she lays her head against his shoulder for a moment.*]

MARIE. You will be a wonderful husband, Michael. (*Her eyes are shining as she looks into the future.*) I know it!

[FATHER LE BEAU *smiles benignly.*[1]]

[CURTAIN]

Enjoying Comic Situations

1. What elements of humor did you find in the following? (*a*) The arrival of the airplane; (*b*) Marie's predicament; (*c*) the characterization of Louis Hébert; (*d*) Wernecke's inventions; (*e*) Louis's departure at the very end of the play; (*f*) Michael's filling the woodbox.

2. In addition to these general situations there were many humorous lines or speeches, all carefully calculated to draw audience laughter. In the language of the theater, these are " punch " lines. Find the punch lines in the following: (*a*) Marie's refusal to go walking with Dinsmore; (*b*) Wernecke's refusal to rent Dinsmore a room; (*c*) the speech of Marie to Dinsmore as she tries to get out of marriage when she first learns he has ordered a cow; (*d*) one line in the final scene when Marie and Michael are left alone together.

[1] **benignly** (bê·nīn'lĭ): kindly; approvingly.

Thinking It Over

1. Most of us do not know much about our French-Canadian neighbors, though they live just across the border from us. You have discovered, at least, that they can be very entertaining. What other qualities do they possess, judging from the play? This would be a good time to exchange class notes with each other about books you have read or movies you have seen dealing with life in the country that lies north of us.

2. Did you notice all the important little speeches that gave clues to later events? Tell what was in Annabella's mind when she said of Dinsmore: " I wonder where he makes his money." Why wouldn't Marie eat the chocolates that Michael left for her? Of whom was she thinking when she told Louis that there was just a " whisper of love " in her heart for someone else? Why was she so startled when Michael said that Dinsmore might really fly a cow in?

3. What do you think of Marie? and Michael? Which one of them do you think will dominate the other in their married life? What speech of Marie's stings Michael into proving that the Irish can be thrifty? What course of action does he take in handling Marie? Does Marie actually think that he is cruel? What lines show his real tenderness? Did you feel a little sorry for Louis Hébert? Which of the two – Louis or Michael – would make the better husband for Marie?

4. Everyone but Dinsmore is in the room when Michael administers the spanking to Marie. By what tried and tested stage device does the author manage to get rid of the other characters, so that the lovers may be left alone finally?

5. To heighten the comedy and dramatic intensity in a play like this one, playwrights frequently show a young couple who *ought* to be in love in the midst of antagonism and bickering. Shakespeare did this in *The Taming of the Shrew*, for example, and the same device is used again and again in radio, movies, and television. In what ways do Michael and Marie do and say things that put them further apart? Is Mr. Dinsmore's " document " something that would be possible in real life, or just an artificial invention of the author?

For Your Vocabulary

CONTEXT: You learned long ago that one good way to determine the meaning of an unfamiliar word is by context; that is, by the way it is related to the words and phrases that precede or follow it. Can you make a working definition for *complacently* (page 343)? This is in a stage direction for Marie, but the speech by Louis, as well as Marie's response, should furnish the clue. Even if you don't know exactly what *vociferously* means, when you read that Mr. and Mrs. Wernecke enter the room *arguing vociferously* you have a pretty good idea. Can you give a synonym? When you learn (page 351) that Louis enters the room *disconsolate,* you might be temporarily puzzled. His speech, however, makes the word clear. How *does* Louis feel? It might be a good idea to look up the word *disconsolate* and see if you think it is the best possible word to use here considering the speech that follows.

HOLWORTHY HALL
AND ROBERT MIDDLEMASS

The Valiant

The grim, gray walls of our prisons hold many a strange and dark secret. Once behind those forbidding walls, after the routine of interviews, the fingerprinting, and the donning of the hated prison stripes, the prisoner enters his cell and the door clangs shut behind a once free man. Prisoner No. 14228. Only a number now. What did he leave behind him? a good mother? a wife and children? a comfortable home? a prosperous business? In what dark moment did he surrender all that made life worth living and exchange his freedom for a prison cell, or even perhaps for the electric chair? What circumstances, or what weaknesses of character, caused him to commit a crime against society, thereby proving himself unworthy to live in freedom? The prison wardens wonder. The chaplains wonder. Teachers and social leaders are concerned with these questions too, because to help create preventive measures they must know why people take the wrong path.

" The Valiant " turns the spotlight upon just such a prisoner. It helps us to see how the crime of one man affects the lives of others. It also shows the bitter loneliness of the prisoner about to die in " Murderers' Row." When a man begins to walk his " last mile," he still has two choices. He may die a coward's death or he may accept his punishment with courage. Dyke, the condemned man in " The Valiant " has that choice to make.

Characters

WARDEN HOLT, about 60
FATHER DALY, the prison chaplain
JAMES DYKE, the Prisoner
JOSEPHINE PARIS, the Girl, about 18
DAN, a jailer
AN ATTENDANT

SCENE. *The* WARDEN'S *office in the State's Prison at Wethersfield, Connecticut.*

TIME. *About half-past eleven on a rainy night.*

The curtain rises upon the WARDEN'S *office in the State's Prison at Wethersfield, Connecticut. It is a large, cold, unfriendly apartment, with bare floors and staring, whitewashed walls; it is furnished only with the* WARDEN'S *flat-topped desk and swivel chair, with a few straight-backed chairs, one beside the desk and others against the walls, with a water cooler and an eight-day clock. On the* WARDEN'S *desk are a telephone instrument, a row of electric push-buttons, and a bundle of forty or fifty letters. At the back of the room are two large windows, crossed with heavy bars; at the left there is a door to an anteroom, and at the right there are two doors, of which the more distant leads to the office of the deputy*[1] *warden, and the nearer is seldom used.*

WARDEN HOLT, *dressed in a dark brown sack suit, is seated at his desk, reflectively smoking a long, thin cigar. He is verging on sixty, and his responsibilities have printed themselves upon his countenance. His brown hair and bushy eyebrows are heavily shot with gray; there are deep wrinkles at the corners of his mouth and innumerable fine lines about his eyes. He is no sentimentalist, but he believes that in each of us there is a constant oscillation*[2] *of good and evil; and that all evil should be justly punished in this world, and that all good should be generously rewarded — in the next.*

Behind the WARDEN, *the prison chaplain stands at one of the barred windows, gazing steadily out into the night.* FATHER DALY *is a slender, white-haired priest of somewhat more than middle age; he is dressed in slightly shabby clerical clothes. His face is calm, intellectual, and inspiring; but just at this moment it gives evidence of a peculiar depression.*

The WARDEN *blows a cloud of smoke to the ceiling, inspects the cigar critically, drums on the desk, and finally peers over his shoulder at the chaplain. He clears his throat and speaks brusquely.*

THE WARDEN. Has it started to rain?

FATHER DALY (*answers without turning*). Yes, it has.

THE WARDEN (*glaring at his cigar and impatiently tossing it aside*). It would rain tonight. (*His tone is vaguely resentful, as though the weather had added a needless fraction to his impatience.*)

FATHER DALY (*glances at a big silver watch*). It's past eleven o'clock. (*He draws a deep breath and comes slowly to the center of the room.*) We haven't much longer to wait.

THE WARDEN. No, thank God! (*He gets up, and goes to the water cooler; with the glass halfway to his lips he pauses.*) Was he quiet when you left him?

FATHER DALY (*a trifle abstractedly*). Yes, yes, he was perfectly calm and I believe he'll stay so to the very end.

THE WARDEN (*finishes his drink, comes back to his desk, and lights a fresh cigar*). You've got to hand it to him, Father; I never saw such nerve in all my

[1] **deputy** (dĕp'ū·tĭ): substitute.

[2] **oscillation** (ŏs'ĭ·lā'shŭn): swinging back and forth.

life. It isn't bluff, and it isn't a trance, either, like some of 'em have — it's plain nerve. You've certainly got to hand it to him. (*He shakes his head in frank admiration.*)

FATHER DALY (*sorrowfully*). That's the pity of it — that a man with all his courage hasn't a better use for it. Even now, it's very difficult for me to reconcile his character, as I see it, with what we know he's done.

THE WARDEN (*continues to shake his head*). He's got my goat, all right.

FATHER DALY. Yes, and he's got mine, too.

THE WARDEN. When he sent for you tonight, I hoped he was going to talk.

FATHER DALY. He did talk, very freely.

THE WARDEN. What about?

FATHER DALY (*smiles faintly, and sits beside the desk*). Most everything.

THE WARDEN (*looks up quickly*). Himself?

FATHER DALY. No. That seems to be the only subject he isn't interested in.

THE WARDEN (*sits up to his desk, and leans upon it with both elbows*). He still won't give you any hint about who he really is?

FATHER DALY. Not the slightest. He doesn't intend to, either. He intends to die as a man of mystery to us. Sometimes I wonder if he isn't just as much of a mystery to himself.

THE WARDEN. Oh, he's trying to shield somebody, that's all. James Dyke isn't his right name — we know that; and we know all the rest of his story is a fake, too. Well, where's his motive? I'll tell you where it is. It's to keep his family and his friends, wherever they are, from knowing what's happened to him. Lots of 'em have the same idea, but I never knew one to carry it as far as this, before. You've certainly got to hand it to him. All we know is that we've got a man under sentence; and we don't know who he is, or where he comes from, or anything else about him, any more than we did four months ago.

FATHER DALY. It takes moral courage for a man to shut himself away from his family and his friends like that. They would have comforted him.

THE WARDEN. Not necessarily. What time is it?

FATHER DALY. Half-past eleven.

THE WARDEN (*rises and walks over to peer out of one of the barred windows*). I guess I'm getting too old for this sort of thing. A necktie party didn't use to bother me so much; but every time one comes along nowadays, I've got the blue devils beforehand and afterward. And this one is just about the limit.

FATHER DALY. It certainly isn't a pleasant duty even with the worst of them.

THE WARDEN (*wheels back abruptly*). But what gets *me* is why I should hate this one more than any of the others. The boy is guilty.

FATHER DALY. Yes, he killed a man, "willfully, feloniously, and with malice aforethought."

THE WARDEN. And he pleaded guilty. So he deserves just what he's going to get.

FATHER DALY. That is the law. But has it ever occurred to you, Warden, that every now and then when a criminal behaves in a rather gentlemanly fashion to us, we instinctively think of him as just a little less of a criminal?

THE WARDEN. Yes, it has. But, all the same, this front of his makes me as nervous as the devil. He pleaded guilty all right, but he don't *act* guilty. I feel just as if tonight I was going to do something every bit as criminal as he did. I can't help it. And when I get to feeling like that, why, I guess it's pretty nearly time I sent in my resignation.

FATHER DALY (*reflectively*). His whole attitude has been very remarkable. Why, only a few minutes ago I found myself comparing it with the fortitude that the Christian martyrs carried to their death, and yet —

THE WARDEN. He's no martyr.

FATHER DALY. I know it. And he's anything in the world but a Christian. That was just what I was going to say.

THE WARDEN. Has he got any religious streak in him at all?

FATHER DALY. I'm afraid he hasn't. He listens to me very attentively, but — (*He shrugs his shoulders.*) It's only because I offer him companionship. Anybody else would do quite as well — and any other topic would suit him better.

THE WARDEN. Well, if he wants to face God as a heathen, *we* can't force him to change his mind.

FATHER DALY (*with gentle reproach*). No, but we can never give up trying to save his immortal soul. And his soul tonight seems as dark and foreboding to me as a haunted house would seem to the small boys down in Wethersfield. But I haven't given up hope.

THE WARDEN. No — you wouldn't.

FATHER DALY. Are you going to talk with him again yourself?

THE WARDEN (*opens a drawer of his desk, and brings out a large envelope*). I'll have to. I've still got some government bonds that belong to him. (*He gazes at the envelope, and smiles grimly.*) That was a funny thing — when the newspaper syndicate offered him twenty-five hundred for his autobiography, he jumped at it so quick I was sure he wanted the money for something or other. (*He slaps the envelope on the desk.*) But now the bonds are here, waiting for him, he won't say what to do with 'em. Know why? (FATHER DALY *shakes his head.*) Why, of course you do! Because the story he wrote was pure bunk from start to finish and the only reason he jumped at the chance of writing it was so's he could pull the wool over everybody's head a little farther. He don't want the bonds, but I've got to do *something* with 'em. (*He pushes a button on the desk.*) And besides, I want to make one more try at finding out who he is.

FATHER DALY. Shall I go with you to see him or do you want to see him alone?

THE WARDEN (*sits deliberating with one hand at his forehead, and the other hand tapping the desk*). Father, you gave me a thought — I believe I'm going to do something tonight that's never been done before in this prison — that is to say — not in all the twenty-eight years that *I've* been warden.

FATHER DALY. What's that?

THE WARDEN (*who has evidently come to an important decision, raps the desk more forcibly with his knuckles*). Instead of our going to see him, I'll have that boy brought into this office and let him sit here with you and me until the time comes for us all to walk through that door to the execution room.

FATHER DALY (*startled*). What on earth is your idea in doing a thing like that?

THE WARDEN. Because maybe if he sits here awhile with just you and me, and we go at him right, he'll loosen up and tell us about himself. It'll be different from being in his cell; it'll be sort of free and easy, and maybe he'll weaken. And then, besides, if we take him to the scaffold through this passageway, maybe I can keep the others quiet. If they don't know when the job's being done, they may behave 'emselves. I don't want any such yelling and screeching tonight as we had with that Greek. (*A* JAILER *in blue uniform enters from the deputy's room and stands waiting.*) Dan, I want you to get Dyke and bring him to me here. (*The* JAILER *stares blankly at him and the* WARDEN's *voice takes on an added note of authority.*) Get Dyke and bring him here to me.

THE JAILER. Yes, sir. (*He starts to obey the order but halts in the doorway and turns as the* WARDEN *speaks again. It is apparent that the* WARDEN *is a strict disciplinarian of the prison staff.*)

THE WARDEN. Oh, Dan!

THE JAILER. Yes, sir?

THE WARDEN. How nearly ready are they?

THE JAILER. They'll be all set in ten or fifteen minutes, sir. Twenty minutes at the outside.

THE WARDEN (*very sharp and magisterial*). Now, I don't want any hitch or delay in this thing tonight. If there is, somebody's going to get in awful Dutch with me. Pass that along.

THE JAILER. There won't be none, sir.

THE WARDEN. When everything's ready — not a second before — you let me know.

THE JAILER. Yes, sir.

THE WARDEN. I'll be right here with Dyke and Father Daly.

THE JAILER (*eyes widening*). Here?

THE WARDEN (*peremptorily*). Yes, here!

THE JAILER (*crushes down his astonishment*). Yes, sir.

THE WARDEN. When everything and everybody is ready, you come from the execution room through the passage — (*He gestures toward the nearer door on the right.*) open that door quietly, and stand there.

THE JAILER. Yes, sir.

THE WARDEN. You don't have to say anything, and I don't *want* you to say anything. Just stand there. That all clear?

THE JAILER. Yes, sir.

THE WARDEN. That'll be the signal for us to start — understand?

THE JAILER. Yes, sir.

THE WARDEN (*draws a deep breath*). All right. Now bring Dyke to me.

THE JAILER. Yes, sir. (*He goes out dazedly.*)

FATHER DALY. What about the witnesses and the reporters?

THE WARDEN. They're having their sandwiches and coffee now — the deputy'll have 'em seated in another ten or fifteen minutes. Let 'em wait. (*His voice becomes savage.*) I'd like to poison the lot of 'em. Reporters! Witnesses! (*The telephone bell rings.*) Hello — yes — yes — what's that? — Yes, yes, right here — who wants him? (*To* FATHER DALY) Father, it's the Governor! (*His expression is tense.*)

FATHER DALY (*His voice also gives evidence of incredulity and hope*). What! (*He walks swiftly over to the desk.*) Is it about Dyke?

THE WARDEN. Ssh. (*He turns to the telephone.*) Yes, this is Warden Holt speaking. Hello — oh, hello, Governor Fuller, how are you? Oh, I'm between grass and hay, thanks. Well, this isn't my idea of a picnic exactly — yes — yes — Oh, I should say in about half an hour or so — everything's just about ready. (*His expression gradually relaxes, and* FATHER DALY, *with a little sigh and shake of the head, turns away.*) Oh, no, there won't be any slip-up — Yes, we made the regular tests, one this afternoon and another at nine o'clock tonight — Oh, no, Governor, nothing can go wrong — Well, according to the law I've got to get it done as soon as possible after midnight, but you're the Governor of the state — How long? — Certainly, Governor, I can hold it off as long as you want me to — What say? — A *girl!* — You're going to send her to me? — You *have* sent her! — She ought to be here by this time? — All right, Governor, I'll ring you up when it's over. Good-by. (*He hangs up the receiver, mops his forehead with his handkerchief, and turns to* FATHER DALY *in great excitement.*) Did you get *that?* Some girl thinks Dyke's her long-lost brother, and she's persuaded the old man to let her come out here tonight — he wants me to hold up the job until she's had a chance to see him. She's due here any minute, he says — in his own car — escorted by his own private secretary! Can you beat it?

FATHER DALY (*downcast*). Poor girl!

THE WARDEN (*blots his forehead vigorously*). For a minute there I thought it was going to be a reprieve at the very least. Whew!

FATHER DALY. So did I.

[*The door from the deputy's room is opened, and* DYKE *comes in, followed immediately by the* JAILER. DYKE *halts just inside the door and waits passively to be told what to do next. He has a lean, pale face, with a high forehead, good eyes, and a strong chin; his mouth is ruled in a firm straight line. His wavy hair is prematurely gray. His figure has the elasticity of youth, but he might pass among strangers either as a man of forty, or as a man of twenty-five, depending upon the mobility of his features at a given moment. He is dressed in a dark shirt open at the throat, dark trousers without belt or suspenders, and soft slippers. The* JAILER *receives a nod from the* WARDEN, *and goes out promptly, closing the door behind him.*]

THE WARDEN (*swings halfway around in his swivel chair*). Sit down, Dyke. (*He points to the chair at the right of his desk.*)

DYKE. Thanks. (*He goes directly to the chair and sits down.*)

THE WARDEN (*leans back, and surveys him thoughtfully.* FATHER DALY *remains in the background*). Dyke, you've been here under my charge for nearly four months and I want to tell you that from first to last you've behaved yourself like a gentleman.

DYKE. (*His manner is vaguely cynical without being in the least impertinent.*) Why should I make you any trouble?

THE WARDEN. Well, you *haven't* made me any trouble, and I've tried to show what I think about it. I've made you every bit as comfortable as the law would let me.

DYKE. You've been very kind to me. (*He glances over his shoulder at the chaplain.*) And you, too, Father.

THE WARDEN. I've had you brought in here to stay from now on. (DYKE *looks inquiringly at him.*) No, you won't have to go back to your cell again. You're to stay right here with Father Daly and me.

DYKE (*carelessly*). All right.

THE WARDEN (*piqued* [1] *by this cool reception of the distinguished favor*). You don't seem to understand that I'm doing something a long way out of the ordinary for you.

DYKE. Oh, yes, I do, but maybe *you* don't understand why it doesn't give me much of a thrill.

FATHER DALY (*comes forward*). My son, the warden is only trying to do you one more kindness.

DYKE. I know he is, Father, but the warden isn't taking very much of a gamble. From now on, one place is about the same as another.

THE WARDEN. What do you mean?

DYKE (*His voice is very faintly sarcastic*). Why, I mean that I'm just as much a condemned prisoner here as when I

[1] **piqued** (pēkt): annoyed.

was in my cell. That door (*He points to it.*) leads right *back* to my cell. Outside those windows are armed guards every few feet. You yourself can't get through the iron door in that anteroom (*He indicates the door to the left.*) until somebody on the outside unlocks it; and I know as well as you do where *that* door (*He points to the nearer door on the right.*) leads to.

THE WARDEN (*stiffly*). Would you rather wait in your cell?

DYKE. Oh, no, this is a little pleasanter. Except –

THE WARDEN. Except what?

DYKE. In my cell, I could smoke.

THE WARDEN (*shrugs his shoulders*). What do you want – cigar or cigarette?

DYKE. A cigarette, if it's all the same.

[*The* WARDEN *opens a drawer of his desk, takes out a box of cigarettes, removes one and hands it to* DYKE. *The* WARDEN, *striking a match, lights* DYKE'S *cigarette and then carefully puts out the match.*]

DYKE (*smiles faintly*). Thanks. You're a good host.

THE WARDEN. Dyke, before it's too late I wish you'd think over what Father Daly and I've said to you so many times.

DYKE. I've thought of nothing else.

THE WARDEN. Then – as man to man – and this is your last chance – who are you?

DYKE (*inspects his cigarette*). Who am I? James Dyke – a murderer.

THE WARDEN. That isn't your real name and we know it.

DYKE. You're not going to execute a name – you're going to execute a *man*. What difference does it make whether you call me Dyke or something else?

THE WARDEN. You had another name once. What was it?

DYKE. If I had, I've forgotten it.

FATHER DALY. Your mind is made up, my son?

DYKE. Yes, Father, it is.

THE WARDEN. Dyke.

DYKE. Yes, sir?

THE WARDEN. Do you see this pile of letters? (*He places his hand over it.*)

DYKE. Yes, sir.

THE WARDEN (*fingers them*). Every one of these letters is about the same thing, and all put together we've got maybe four thousand of 'em. These here are just a few samples.

DYKE. What about them?

THE WARDEN. We've had letters from every state in the Union and every province in Canada. We've had fifteen or twenty from England, four or five from France, two from Australia, and one from Russia.

DYKE. Well?

THE WARDEN (*inclines toward him*). Do you know what every one of those letters says – what four thousand different people are writing to me about?

DYKE. No, sir.

THE WARDEN (*speaks slowly and impressively*). Who *are* you – and are you the missing son – or brother – or husband – or sweetheart?

DYKE (*flicks his cigarette ashes to the floor*). Have you answered them?

THE WARDEN. No, I couldn't. I want you to.

DYKE. How's that?

THE WARDEN. I want you to tell me who you are. (DYKE *shakes his head.*) Can't you see you *ought* to do it?

DYKE. No, sir, I can't exactly see that. Suppose you explain it to me.

THE WARDEN (*suddenly*). You're trying to shield somebody, aren't you?

DYKE. Yes – no, I'm not!

THE WARDEN (*glances at* FATHER DALY *and nods with elation*). Who is it? Your family?

DYKE. I said I'm not.

THE WARDEN. But first, you said you were.

DYKE. That was a slip of the tongue.

THE WARDEN (*has grown persuasive*). Dyke, just listen to me a minute. Don't be narrow, look at this thing in a big, broad way. Suppose you should tell me your real name, and I publish it, it'll bring an awful lot of sorrow, let's say, to *one* family, *one* home, and that's your own. That's probably what you're thinking about. Am I right? You want to spare your family and I don't blame you. On the surface, it sure would look like a mighty white thing for you to do. But look at it *this* way: suppose you came out with the truth, flat-footed, why, you might put all that sorrow into *one* home — your own — but at the same time you'd be putting an immense amount of relief in four thousand — others. Don't you get that? Don't you figure you owe something to all these other people?

DYKE. Not a thing.

FATHER DALY (*has been fidgeting*). My boy, the warden is absolutely right. You do owe something to the other people — you owe them peace of mind — and for the sake of all those thousands of poor, distressed women, who imagine God knows what, I beg of you to tell us who you are.

DYKE. Father, I simply can't do it.

FATHER DALY. Think carefully, my boy, think very carefully. We're not asking out of idle curiosity.

DYKE. I know that, but please don't let's talk about it any more. (*To the* WARDEN) You can answer those letters whenever you want to, and you can say I'm not the man they're looking for. That'll be the truth, too. Because I haven't any mother — or father — or sister — or wife — or sweetheart. That's fair enough, isn't it?

FATHER DALY (*sighs wearily*). As you will, my son.

THE WARDEN. Dyke, there's one more thing.

DYKE. Yes?

THE WARDEN. Here are the government bonds (*He takes up the large envelope from his desk.*) that belong to you. Twenty-five hundred dollars in real money.

DYKE (*removes the bonds and examines them*). Good-looking, aren't they?

THE WARDEN (*casually*). What do you want me to do with them?

DYKE. Well, I can't very well take them with me, so, under the circumstances, I'd like to put them where they'll do the most good.

THE WARDEN (*more casually yet*). Who do you want me to send 'em to?

DYKE (*laughs quietly*). Now, Warden Holt, you didn't think you were going to catch me that way, did you?

THE WARDEN (*scowls*). Who'll I send 'em to? I can't keep 'em here, and I can't destroy 'em. What do you want to do with 'em?

DYKE (*ponders diligently and tosses the envelopes to the desk*). I don't know. I'll think of something to do with them. I'll tell you in just a minute. Is there anything else?

THE WARDEN. Not unless you want to make some sort of statement.

DYKE. No, I guess I've said everything. I killed a man and I'm not sorry for it — that is, I'm not sorry I killed that particular person. I —

FATHER DALY (*raises his hand*). Repentance —

DYKE (*raises his own hand in turn*). I've heard that repentance, Father, is the sickbed of the soul — and mine is very well and flourishing. The man deserved to be killed; he wasn't fit to live. It was my duty to kill him, and I did it. I'd never struck a man in anger in all my life, but when I knew what that fellow had done, I knew I had to kill him, and I did it deliberately and intentionally — and carefully. I knew what I was doing, and I haven't any excuse — that is, I haven't any excuse that satisfies the law. Now, I learned pretty early in life that whatever you do in this world you have to pay for in one way or another. If you kill a man, the price you have to pay is this (*He makes a gesture which sweeps the entire room.*) and that (*He points to the nearer door on the right.*) and I'm going to pay it. That's all there is to that. And an hour from now, while my body is lying in there, if a couple of angel policemen grab my soul and haul it up before God —

FATHER DALY (*profoundly shocked*). My boy, my boy, please —

DYKE. I beg your pardon, Father. I don't mean to trample on anything that's sacred to you, but what I do mean to say is this: If I've got to be judged by God Almighty for the crime of murder, I'm not afraid, because the other fellow will certainly be there, too, won't he? And when God hears the whole story and both sides of it, which *you* never heard and never will — and they never heard it in the courtroom, either — why, then, if he's any kind of a God at all, I'm willing to take my chances with the other fellow. That's how concerned I am about the hereafter. And, if it'll make you feel any better, Father, why I *do* rather think there's going to be a hereafter. I read a book once that said a milligram [1] of musk will give out perfume for seven thousand years, and a milligram of radium will give out light for *seventy* thousand. Why shouldn't a soul — mine, for instance — live more than twenty-seven? But if there *isn't* any hereafter — if we just die and are dead and that's all — why, I'm still not sorry and I'm not afraid, because I'm quits with the other fellow — the law is quits with me, and it's all balanced on the books. And that's all there is to that.

[*An attendant enters from the anteroom.*]

THE WARDEN. Well? What is it?

THE ATTENDANT. Visitor to see you, sir. With note from Governor Fuller. (*He presents it.*)

THE WARDEN (*barely glances at the envelope*). Oh! A young woman?

THE ATTENDANT. Yes, sir.

THE WARDEN. Is Mrs. Case there?

THE ATTENDANT. Yes, sir.

THE WARDEN. Have the girl searched, and then take her into the anteroom and wait till I call you.

THE ATTENDANT. Yes, sir. (*He goes out.*)

THE WARDEN. Dyke, a young woman has just come to see you — do you want to see her?

DYKE. I don't think so. What does she want?

THE WARDEN. She thinks maybe she's your sister, and she's come a thousand miles to find out.

DYKE. She's wrong. I haven't any sister.

THE WARDEN (*hesitates*). Will I tell her that, or do you want to tell it to her yourself?

DYKE. Oh, you tell her.

THE WARDEN. All right. (*He starts to rise but resumes his seat as* DYKE *speaks.*)

DYKE. Just a second — she's come a thousand miles to see me, did you say?

THE WARDEN. Yes, and she's got special permission from the Governor to talk to you — that is, with my O.K.

DYKE. A year ago, nobody'd have crossed the street to look at me, and

[1] **milligram** (mĭl'ĭ·grăm): a thousandth of a gram.

now they come a thousand miles!

FATHER DALY. This is one of your debts to humanity, my boy. It wouldn't take you two minutes to see her, and, if you don't, after she's made that long journey in hope and dread and suffering –

DYKE. Where can I talk with her – here?

THE WARDEN. Yes.

DYKE. Alone? (*The* WARDEN *is doubtful.*) Why, you don't need to be afraid. I haven't the faintest idea who the girl is, but if she happens to be some poor misguided sentimental fool, with a gun or a pocketful of cyanide of potassium,[1] she's wasting her time. I wouldn't cheat the sovereign state of Connecticut for anything in the world – not even to please a young lady.

THE WARDEN. Dyke, there's something about you that gets everybody.

DYKE. How about the jury?

THE WARDEN. You've got a sort of way with you –

DYKE. How about that spread-eagle district attorney?

THE WARDEN. I'm going to let you talk with that girl in here – alone.

DYKE. Thanks.

THE WARDEN. It's a sort of thing that's never been done before, but if I put you on your honor –

DYKE (*cynically*). My honor! Thank you, so much.

FATHER DALY. Warden, are you sure it's wise?

DYKE. Father, I'm disappointed in you. Do you imagine I'd do anything that could reflect on Warden Holt – or you – or the young lady – or *me*?

THE WARDEN. Father, will you take Dyke into the deputy's room? I want to speak to the young lady first.

FATHER DALY. Certainly. Come, my boy. (FATHER DALY *and* DYKE *start toward the deputy's room.*)

THE WARDEN. I'll call you in just a couple of minutes.

DYKE. We promise not to run away. (*They go out together.*)

THE WARDEN (*calls*). Wilson! (*The* ATTENDANT *enters from the left.*)

THE ATTENDANT. Yes, sir.

THE WARDEN. Is the girl there?

THE ATTENDANT. Yes, sir.

THE WARDEN. Frisked? [2]

THE ATTENDANT. Yes, sir.

THE WARDEN. Everything all right?

THE ATTENDANT. Yes, sir.

THE WARDEN (*throws away his cigar*). Bring her in.

THE ATTENDANT. Yes, sir. (*He speaks through the door at the left.*) Step this way, Miss. This here's the warden.

[*A young girl appears on the threshold, and looks about in mingled curiosity and apprehension. She is fresh and wholesome, and rather pretty. She wears a blue tailored suit with deep white cuffs and a starched white collar, and a small blue hat which fits snugly over her fluffy hair. Her costume is not quite conservative enough to be literally old-fashioned, but it hints at the taste and repression of an old-fashioned home.*

She is neither timid nor aggressive; she is self-unconscious. She looks at the WARDEN *squarely, but not in boldness, and yet not in feminine appeal; she has rather the fearlessness of a girl who has lost none of her illusions about men in general. Her expression is essentially serious; it conveys, however, the idea that her seriousness is due to her present mission, and that ordinarily she takes an active joy in the mere pleasure of existence.*]

[1] **cyanide of potassium** (sī'ȧ·nīd of pō·tăs'ĭ·ŭm): a kind of poison.

[2] **frisked:** searched.

THE WARDEN (*He had expected a very different type of visitor, so that he is somewhat taken aback.*) All right, Wilson.

THE ATTENDANT. Yes, sir. (*He goes out.*)

THE WARDEN (*with grave deference, half rises*). Will you sit down?

THE GIRL. Why — thank you very much. (*She sits in the chair beside the desk and regards him trustfully.*)

THE WARDEN (*He is affected by her youth and innocence, and he is not quite sure how best to proceed, but eventually he makes an awkward beginning.*) You've had an interview with the Governor, I understand?

THE GIRL. Yes, sir. I was with him almost an hour.

THE WARDEN. And you want to see Dyke, do you?

THE GIRL. Yes, sir. I *hope* I'm not — too late.

THE WARDEN. No, you're not too late. (*He is appraising her carefully.*) But I want to ask you a few questions beforehand. (*Her reaction of uncertainty induces him to soften his tone.*) There isn't anything to get upset about. I just want to make it easier for you, not harder. Where do you live?

THE GIRL. In Ohio.

THE WARDEN (*very kindly*). What place?

THE GIRL. In Pennington, sir. It's a little town not far from Columbus.

THE WARDEN. And you live out there with your father and mother?

THE GIRL. No, sir — just my mother and I. My father died when I was a little baby.

THE WARDEN. Why didn't your mother come here herself, instead of sending you?

THE GIRL. She couldn't. She's sick.

THE WARDEN. I see. Have you any brothers or sisters?

THE GIRL (*slightly more at ease*). Just one brother, sir — this one. He and I were the only children. We were very fond of each other.

THE WARDEN. He was considerably older than you?

THE GIRL. Oh, yes. He's ten years older.

THE WARDEN. Why did he leave home?

THE GIRL. I don't really know, sir, except he just wanted to be in the city. Pennington's pretty small.

THE WARDEN. How long is it since you've seen him?

THE GIRL. It's eight years.

THE WARDEN (*his voice is almost paternal*). As long as that? Hm! And how old are you now?

THE GIRL. I'm almost eighteen.

THE WARDEN (*repeats slowly*). Almost eighteen. Hm! And are you sure after all this time you'd recognize your brother if you saw him?

THE GIRL. Well — (*She looks down, as if embarrassed to make the admission.*) of course I *think* so, but maybe I couldn't. You see, I was only a little girl when he went away — he wasn't a bad boy, sir, I don't think he could ever be really bad — but if this *is* my brother, why he's been in a great deal of trouble and you know that trouble makes people look different.

THE WARDEN. Yes, it does. But what makes you think this man Dyke may be your brother — and why didn't you think of it sooner? The case has been in the papers for the last six months.

THE GIRL. Why, it wasn't until last Tuesday that Mother saw a piece in the *Journal* — that's the Columbus paper — that he'd written all about himself, and there was one little part of it that sounded so like Joe — like the funny way he used to say things — and then there was a picture that looked the least little *bit* like him — well, Mother just wanted me to come East and find out for sure.

THE WARDEN. It's too bad she couldn't come herself. She'd probably know him whether he'd changed or not.

THE GIRL. Yes, sir. But I'll do the best I can.

THE WARDEN. When was the last time you heard from him, and where was he, and what was he doing?

THE GIRL. Why, it's about five or six years since we had a letter from Joe. He was in Seattle, Washington.

THE WARDEN. What doing?

THE GIRL. I don't remember. At home, though, he worked in the stationery store. He liked books.

THE WARDEN (*suspiciously*). Why do you suppose he didn't write home?

THE GIRL. I — couldn't say. He was just — thoughtless.

THE WARDEN. Wasn't in trouble of any kind?

THE GIRL. Oh, *no!* Never. That is — unless he's — here now.

THE WARDEN (*deliberates*). How are you going to tell him?

THE GIRL. I don't know what you mean.

THE WARDEN. Why, you say maybe you wouldn't know him even if you saw him — and I'll guarantee this man Dyke won't help you out very much. How do you think you're going to tell? Suppose he don't want to be recognized by you or anybody else? Suppose he's so ashamed of himself he —

THE GIRL. I'd thought of that. I'm just going to talk to him — ask him questions — about things he and I used to do together — I'll watch his face, and if he's my brother, I'm sure I can tell.

THE WARDEN (*with tolerant doubt*). What did you and your brother ever use to do that would help you out now?

THE GIRL. He used to play games with me when I was a little girl, and tell me stories — that's what I'm counting on mostly — the stories.

THE WARDEN. I'm afraid —

THE GIRL. Especially Shakespeare stories.

THE WARDEN. Shakespeare!

THE GIRL. Why, yes. He used to get the plots of the plays — all the Shakespeare plays — out of a book by a man named Lamb, and then he'd tell me the stories in his own words. It was wonderful!

THE WARDEN. I'm certainly afraid he —

THE GIRL. But best of all he'd learn some of the speeches from the plays themselves. He liked to do it — he was sure he was going to be an actor or something — he was in all the high school plays, always. And then he'd teach some of the speeches to me, and we'd say them to each other. And one thing — every night he'd sit by the side of my bed, and when I got sleepy there were two speeches we'd always say to each other, like good night — two speeches out of *Romeo and Juliet*, and then I'd go to sleep. I can see it all. (*The* WARDEN *shakes his head.*) Why do you do that?

THE WARDEN. This boy isn't your brother.

THE GIRL. Do you think he isn't?

THE WARDEN. I *know* he isn't.

THE GIRL. How do you?

THE WARDEN. This boy never heard of Shakespeare — much less learned him. (*He presses a button on his desk.*) Oh, I'll let you see him for yourself, only you might as well be prepared. (*The* ATTENDANT *enters from the anteroom.*) Tell Dyke and Father Daly to come in here — they're in the deputy's room.

THE ATTENDANT. Yes, sir. (*He crosses behind the* WARDEN, *and goes off to the right.*)

THE WARDEN. If he turns out to be your brother — which he won't — you can have, say, an hour with him. If he don't, you'll oblige me by cutting it as short as you can.

THE GIRL. You see, I've got to tell Mother something perfectly definite. She's worried so long about him, and — and *now* the suspense is perfectly terrible for her.

THE WARDEN. I can understand that. You're a plucky girl.

THE GIRL. Of course, it would be awful for us if this *is* Joe, but even that would be better for Mother than just to stay awake nights, and wonder and wonder, and never *know* what became of him.

[*The* ATTENDANT *opens the door of the deputy's room, and when* DYKE *and* FATHER DALY *have come in, he crosses again behind the* WARDEN, *and is going out at the left when the* WARDEN *signs to him and he stops.*]

THE WARDEN (*gets to his feet*). Dyke, this is the young lady that's come all the way from Pennington, Ohio, to see you.

DYKE (*who has been talking in an undertone to* FATHER DALY, *raises his head quickly*). Yes, sir?

THE WARDEN. I've decided you can talk with her here — alone.

[*The* GIRL *has risen, breathless, and stands fixed;* DYKE *inspects her coldly from head to foot.*]

DYKE. Thank you. It won't take long.

THE WARDEN (*has been scanning the girl's expression; now, as he sees that she has neither recognized* DYKE *nor failed to recognize him, he makes a little grimace in confirmation of his own judgment*). Father Daly and I'll stay in the deputy's office. We'll leave the door open. Wilson, you stand in the anteroom with the door open.

DYKE (*bitterly*). My honor!

THE WARDEN. What say?

DYKE. I didn't say anything.

THE WARDEN (*to the* GIRL). Will you please remember what I told you about the time?

THE GIRL. Oh, yes, sir.

THE WARDEN. Come, Father. (*They go off into the deputy's room, and the* ATTENDANT, *at a nod from the* WARDEN, *goes off at the left.*)

[DYKE *and the* GIRL *are now facing each other;* DYKE *is well-poised and gives the impression of complete indifference to the moment. The* GIRL, *on the other hand, is deeply agitated and her agitation is gradually increased by* DYKE'S *own attitude.*]

THE GIRL (*after several efforts to speak*). Mother sent me to see you.

DYKE (*politely callous*). Yes?

THE GIRL (*compelled to drop her eyes*). You see, we haven't seen or heard of my brother Joe for ever so long, and Mother thought — after what we read in the papers —

DYKE. That I might be your brother Joe?

THE GIRL (*obviously relieved*). Yes, that's it.

DYKE. Well, you can easily see that I'm not your brother, can't you?

THE GIRL (*stares at him again*). I'm not sure. You look a little like him, just as the picture in the paper did, but then again, it's so long — (*She shakes her head dubiously.*) and I'd thought of Joe so differently —

DYKE (*His manner is somewhat indulgent, as though to a child.*) As a matter of fact, I couldn't be *your* brother, or anybody else's brother, because I never had a sister. So that rather settles it.

THE GIRL. Honestly?

DYKE. Honestly.

THE GIRL (*unconvinced, becomes more appealing*). What's your real name?

DYKE. Dyke — James Dyke.

THE GIRL. That's sure enough your name?

DYKE. Sure enough. You don't think I'd tell a lie at this stage of the game, do you?

THE GIRL (*musing*). No, I don't believe you would. Where do you come from — I mean where were you born?

DYKE. In Canada, but I've lived all over.

THE GIRL. Didn't you ever live in Ohio?

DYKE. No. Never.

THE GIRL. What kind of work did you do — what was your business?

DYKE. Oh, I'm sort of Jack-of-all-trades. I've been everything a man *could* be — except a success.

THE GIRL. Do you like books?

DYKE. Books?

THE GIRL. Yes — books to read.

DYKE. I don't read when there's anything better to do. I've read a lot here.

THE GIRL. Did you ever sell books — for a living, I mean?

DYKE. Oh, no.

THE GIRL (*growing confused*). I hope you don't mind my asking so many questions. But I —

DYKE. No — go ahead, if it'll relieve your mind any.

THE GIRL. You went to school somewhere, of course, — high school?

DYKE. No, I never got that far.

THE GIRL. Did you ever want to be an actor? Or *were* you ever?

DYKE. No, just a convict.

THE GIRL (*helplessly*). Do you know any poetry?

DYKE. Not to speak of.

THE GIRL (*delays a moment, and then, watching him very earnestly, she recites just above her breath*).

Thou knowst the mask of night is on my face
Else would a maiden blush bepaint my cheek
For that which —

(*Realizing that* DYKE's *expression is one of utter vacuity she falters, and breaks off the quotation, but she continues to watch him unwaveringly.*) Don't you know what that is?

DYKE. No, but to tell you the truth, it sounds sort of silly to *me*. Doesn't it to you?

THE GIRL (*Her intonation has become slightly forlorn, but she gathers courage, and puts him to one more test.*)

Good night, good night, parting is such sweet sorrow
That I shall say good night till it be morrow.

DYKE (*his mouth twitches in amusement*). Eh?

THE GIRL. What comes next?

DYKE. Good Lord, *I* don't know.

THE GIRL (*Gazes intently, almost imploringly, at him as though she is making a struggle to read his mind. Then she relaxes and holds out her hand.*) Goodby. You — you're *not* Joe, are you? I — had to come and find out, though. I hope I've not made you too unhappy.

DYKE (*ignores her hand*). You're not going now?

THE GIRL (*spiritless*). Yes. I promised the — is he the warden? — that man in there? — I said I'd go right away if you weren't my brother. And you aren't, so —

DYKE. You're going back to your mother?

THE GIRL. Yes.

DYKE. I'm surprised that she sent a girl like you on a sorry errand like this, instead of —

THE GIRL. She's very sick.

DYKE. Oh, that's too bad.

THE GIRL (*twisting her handkerchief*).

No, she's not well at all. And most of it's from worrying about Joe.

DYKE. Still, when you tell her that her son isn't a murderer — at least, that he isn't *this* one — that'll comfort her a good deal, won't it?

THE GIRL (*reluctantly*). Yes, I think maybe it will, only —

DYKE. Only what?

THE GIRL. I don't think Mother'll ever be *really* well again until she finds out for certain where Joe is and what's become of him.

DYKE (*shakes his head compassionately*). Mothers ought not to be treated like that. I wish I'd treated *mine* better. By the way, you didn't tell me what your name is.

THE GIRL. Josephine Paris.

DYKE (*is suddenly attentive*). Paris? That's an unusual name. I've heard it somewhere, too.

THE GIRL. Just like the name of the city — in France.

DYKE (*knitting his brows*). And your brother's name was Joseph?

THE GIRL. Yes — they used to call us Joe and Josie — that's funny, isn't it?

DYKE (*thoughtfully*). No, I don't think it's so very funny. I rather like it. (*He passes his hand over his forehead as if trying to force his memory.*)

THE GIRL. What's the matter?

DYKE (*frowning*). I was thinking of something — now, what on earth was that boy's name! Wait a minute, don't tell me — wait a minute — I've got it! (*He punctuates his triumph with one fist in the palm of the other hand.*) Joseph Anthony Paris!

THE GIRL (*amazed*). Why, that's his name! That's Joe! How did you ever —

DYKE (*his manner is very forcible and convincing.*) Wait! Now listen carefully to what I say, and don't interrupt me, because we've only got a minute, and I want you to get this all straight, so you can tell your mother. When the war came along I enlisted and I was overseas with the Canadians. Early one morning we'd staged a big raid, and there was an officer who'd been wounded coming back, and was lying out there in a shell hole under fire. The Jerries were getting ready for a raid of their own, so they were putting down a box barrage [1] with light guns and howitzers [2] and a few heavies. This officer was lying right in the middle of it. Well, all of a sudden a young fellow dashed out not far from where I was, and went for the officer. He had to go through a curtain of shells and, more than that, they opened on him with rifles and machine guns. The chances were just about a million to one against him, and he must have known it, but he went out just the same. He got the officer in his arms and started back, but he'd only gone a few yards when a five point nine landed right on top of the two of them. Afterward, we got what was left — the identification tag was still there — and that was the name — Joseph Anthony Paris!

THE GIRL (*carries both hands to her breast*). Oh!

DYKE. If that was your brother's name, then you can tell your mother that he died like a brave man and a soldier, three years ago, in France.

THE GIRL. Joe — my brother Joe — is dead?

DYKE. On the field of battle. It was one of the wonderful, heroic things that went almost unnoticed, as so many of them did. If an officer had seen it, there'd have been a decoration for your mother to keep and remember him by.

THE GIRL. And you were there — and saw it?

[1] **barrage** (bȧ·räzh′): concentrated gunfire.
[2] **howitzers** (hou′ĭt·sẽrz): light cannon.

DYKE. I was there and saw it. It was three years ago. That's why you and your mother haven't heard from him. And if you don't believe what I've said, why, you just write up to Ottawa [1] and get the official record. Of course (*He shrugs his shoulders contemptuously.*) those records are in terribly poor shape, but at least they can tell you what battalion he fought with, when he went overseas. Only you mustn't be surprised no matter whether they say he was killed in action, or died of wounds, or is missing, or even went through the whole war with his outfit, and was honorably discharged. They really don't know what happened to half the men. But I've told you the truth. And it certainly ought to make your mother happy when she knows that her boy died as a soldier, and not as a criminal.

THE GIRL (*is transfigured*). Yes, yes, it will!

DYKE. And does that make you happy, too?

THE GIRL (*nods repeatedly*). Yes. So happy — after what we were both afraid of — I can't even cry — yet. (*She brushes her eyes with her handkerchief.*) I can hardly wait to take it to her.

DYKE (*struck by a sudden inspiration*). I want to give you something else to take to her. (*He picks up from the desk the envelope containing the government bonds and seals it.*) I want you to give this to your mother from me. Tell her it's from a man who saw your brother die, so it's a sort of memorial for him. (*He touches her arm as she absently begins to tear open the envelope.*) No, don't you open it — let *her* do it.

THE GIRL. What is it? Can't I know?

DYKE. Never mind now, but give it to her. It's all I've got in the world and it's too late now for me to do anything else

[1] **Ottawa** (ŏt′ȧ·wȧ): capital of Canada.

with it. And have your mother buy a little gold star to wear for her son — and you get one, too, and wear it — here — (*He touches his heart.*) Will you?

THE GIRL. Yes — I will. And yet somehow I'll almost feel that I'm wearing it for you, too.

DYKE (*shakes his head soberly*). Oh, no! You mustn't ever do that. I'm not fit to be mentioned in the same breath with a boy like your brother, and now I'm afraid it *is* time for you to go. I'm sorry, but — you'd better. I'm glad you came before it was too late, though.

THE GIRL (*gives him her hand*). Good-by, and thank you. You've done more for me — and Mother — than I could possibly tell you. And — and I'm so sorry for you — so *truly sorry* — I wish I could only do something to make you a tiny bit happier, too. Is there anything I could do?

DYKE (*stares at her and by degrees he becomes wistful*). Why — yes, there is. Only I — (*He leaves the sentence uncompleted.*)

THE GIRL. What is it?

DYKE (*looks away*). I can't tell you. I never should have let myself think of it.

THE GIRL. Please tell me. I want you to. For — for Joe's sake, tell me what I can do.

DYKE (*His voice is low and desolate.*) Well — in all the months I've been in this hideous place, you're the first girl I've seen. I didn't ever expect to see one again. I'd forgotten how much like angels women look. I've been terribly lonesome tonight, especially, and if you really do want to do something for me — for your brother's sake — you see, you're going to leave me in just a minute and — and I haven't any sister of my own, or anybody else, to say good-by to me — so, if you could — *really* say good-by — (*She gazes at him for a moment, understands, flushes, and then slowly moves into his outstretched arms. He holds her close to him, touches his lips to her forehead twice, and releases her.*)

DYKE (*thickly*). Good-by, my dear.

THE GIRL. Good night. (*She endeavors to smile, but her voice catches in her throat.*) Good-by.

DYKE (*impulsively*). What is it?

THE GIRL (*shakes her head*). N-nothing.

DYKE. Nothing?

THE GIRL (*clutches her handkerchief tight in her palm*). I was thinking — I was thinking what I used to say to my brother — for good night. (*She very nearly breaks down.*) If I *only* could have — have said it to him just once more — for good-by.

DYKE. What was it?

THE GIRL. I — I told it to you once, and you said it was silly.

DYKE (*softly*). Say it again.

THE GIRL (*She cannot quite control her voice.*)

Good night, good night, parting is such sweet sorrow
That I shall say good night till it be morrow.

[*She goes uncertainly toward the anteroom, hesitates, almost turns back, and then with a choking sob she hurries through the door and closes it behind her. For several seconds* DYKE *stands rigidly intent upon that door; until at length, without changing his attitude or his expression, he speaks very tenderly and reminiscently.*]

Sleep dwell upon thine eyes, peace in thy breast;
Would *I* were sleep and peace, so sweet to rest.

[*The* WARDEN *and* FATHER DALY *come in quietly from the deputy's room; and as they behold* DYKE, *how rapt and unconscious of them he is, they look at each other questioningly. The* WARDEN *glances at the clock and makes as though to interrupt* DYKE'S *solitary reflections but* FATHER DALY *quietly restrains him. The* CHAPLAIN *sits down in one of the chairs at the back wall; the* WARDEN *crosses on tiptoe and sits at his desk; he is excessively nervous and he continually refers to the clock.* DYKE *turns, as though unwillingly, from the door; there are depths in his eyes, and his thoughts are evidently far away. He sits in the chair to the right of the* WARDEN'S *desk and leans outward, his right hand on his knee. He puts his left hand to his throat as though to protect it from a sudden pain. He gazes straight ahead into the unknown and speaks in reverie.*]

Of all the wonders that I yet have heard,
It seems to me most strange that men should fear;
Seeing that death, a necessary end,
Will come when it will come.

[*He stops and muses for a time, while the* WARDEN *glances perplexedly at* FATHER DALY *to discover if the priest can interpret what* DYKE *is saying.* FATHER DALY *shakes his head. Abruptly* DYKE'S *face is illumined by a new and welcome recollection; and again he speaks, while the* WARDEN *tries in vain to comprehend him.*]

Cowards die many times before their death;
The valiant never taste of death but once.

[*He stops again and shudders a trifle; his head droops and he repeats, barely above a whisper.*]

The valiant never taste of death but once.

[*The nearer door on the right is opened noiselessly and the* JAILER, *in obedience to his instructions, steps just inside the room and stands there mute.*

The skillful use of lighting is a key factor in the success of a play presented through any medium — stage, film, television, or radio. (*Culver*)

FATHER DALY *and the* WARDEN *glance at the* JAILER, *and with significance at each other, and both rise, tardily. The* WARDEN'S *hand, as it rests on his desk, is seen to tremble. There is a moment of dead silence; presently* DYKE *lifts his head and catches sight of the motionless* ATTENDANT *at the open door. With a quick intake of his breath, he starts half out of his seat and stares, fascinated; he sinks back slowly, and turns his head to gaze first at* FATHER DALY *and then at the* WARDEN. *The* WARDEN *averts his eyes, but* FATHER DALY'S *expression is of supreme pity and encouragement. Involuntarily,* DYKE'S *hand again goes creeping upward toward his throat, but he arrests it. He grasps the arms of his chair and braces himself; he rises then, and stands very erect, in almost the position of a soldier at attention.*]

THE WARDEN (*swallows hard*). Dyke!

FATHER DALY (*brushes past the* WARDEN, *his right hand lifted as though in benediction*). My son!

DYKE (*regards them fixedly; his voice is low and steady*). All right, let's go.

[*He faces about, and with his head held proud and high, and his shoulders squared to the world, he moves slowly toward the open door.* FATHER DALY, *with the light of his calling in his eyes, steps in line just ahead of* DYKE. *The* WARDEN, *his mouth set hard, falls in behind. When they have all gone forward a pace or two,* FATHER DALY *begins to speak, and* DYKE *to reply.* FATHER DALY'S *voice is strong and sweet; and* DYKE *speaks just after him not mechanically, but in brave and unfaltering response.*]

FATHER DALY. "I will lift up mine eyes unto the hills ——"

DYKE. "The valiant never taste of death but once."

FATHER DALY. "From whence cometh my help."

DYKE. "The valiant never taste of death but once."

FATHER DALY (*has almost reached the door; his voice rises a semitone, and gains in emotion*). "My help cometh from the Lord which made Heaven and earth."

DYKE. "The valiant never taste of death – but once."

[*When the* WARDEN, *whose hands are tightly clenched, has passed the threshold, the* JAILER *follows and closes the door behind him. There is a very brief pause and then*]

[CURTAIN]

Thinking It Over

1. Read again those lines that gave such comfort to James Dyke, ending with "The valiant never taste of death but once." What did Shakespeare mean by this passage? What does the word *valiant* mean?

2. There are several audience and reader clues early in the play pointing to Dyke's identity. Were these clues in the speeches or stage directions? Point them out.

3. You have no doubt seen movies or followed radio series based on the work of the Bureau of Missing Persons. What do you know about its methods and successes? What causes, other than concealing crime, might account for the disappearance of some persons?

4. What special power does the governor of a state have with regard to condemned prisoners? Why are witnesses required at an execution?

5. How does Warden Holt show that he has not become hardened by his years of service at the State's Prison?

6. In another melodrama, "Trouble in Tunnel Nine," there are several characters who at the end are seen in a different light from that in which they are shown at the beginning. In this play the main interest centers on the prisoner. In what way does Dyke change during the course of the play?

7. What are some of the circumstances that start a boy along the road to a prison sentence? Which ones seem to have operated in Dyke's case? What did you learn about his early life and education? Why do you suppose he never went back home?

8. What is Dyke's idea of courage? What is the difference between physical and moral courage? Where in the play does Dyke show moral courage? At what point does he exhibit the greatest self-control?

9. What is your guess as to the nature and circumstances of Dyke's crime? Discuss his defense of his deed. Was the law just in requiring him to pay for it?

10. A great many people do not believe in the death penalty for any kind of crime. The question has long been the subject of earnest debate. You probably have an opinion yourself. Can you support that opinion by facts and arguments in debate? Discuss the matter at home, with teachers, with clergymen; find out what people think of the legal, moral, and religious aspects of the question. See what you can find in the library. You might challenge some other class to a debate. Or, if you prefer, write a composition supporting your own opinion.

For Your Vocabulary

WORD RECOGNITION: As before, pick the word that most nearly matches the word in italics. Write five of the italicized words in meaningful sentences.

1. *verging on* – overhanging, preaching, approaching, poaching
2. *brusquely* – abruptly, rapturously, busily, complainingly
3. *peremptorily* – perilously, penitently, temptingly, sharply
4. *prematurely* – obviously, too early, tardily, disturbingly
5. *diligently* – meekly, industriously, carefully, devoutly
6. *cynically* – curtly, pessimistically, boldly, bashfully
7. *illusions* – references, plans, worries, false impressions

TELEVISION PLAY

ROBERT LOUIS STEVENSON

The Sire de Maletroit's Door

Adapted for television by MARY ORR *and* REGINALD DENHAM

Now that television has become an important part of our entertainment, script-writers are haunting the libraries in search of literature that can be transformed into TV plays. (You would be surprised to know how many modern jobs require you to be *very* well-read.) To be sure, radio writers, to say nothing of movie playwrights, have already combed the shelves, but the television writers, undaunted, follow suit. It seems inevitable that some of them should discover the possibilities in Robert Louis Stevenson, whose stories have always been sure-fire romance. The play that follows is adapted from Stevenson's famous story " The Sire de Maletroit's [1] Door."

Television is a new and exciting medium for drama. At one time, of course, plays could be seen only on the stages of theaters. When motion pictures were invented, plays moved from the narrow limits of a stage to all the varied and sweeping scenes to which a movie camera could take the audience. Shortly afterward, radio broadcasting was made practical and, though radio was dependent solely on sound, it did bring plays right into the living rooms of our homes. Now comes television, which can combine the best features of all the earlier forms of play presentation! A television play is not restricted to a single set, like a stage play; it may use several different sets, the cameras shifting from one to another as in a movie. And like radio, television brings drama into our homes, where it may be enjoyed more frequently, more economically, and more comfortably than anywhere else.

" The Sire de Maletroit's Door," is, as you shall see, well suited to television performance. It has plenty of rousing action – sword fighting on the streets of a medieval town, the threat of danger in a strange castle. It also has some characters you will enjoy visualizing in the flesh – a dashing young nobleman, a beautiful but frightened young girl, and the devilishly clever and dangerous Sire de Maletroit. Flick on the set and make yourself comfortable.

Reading a Television Script . . . Try reading this play as if you were a cast member studying the script under the direction of a stage manager. Read the lines while at the same time you imagine the physical movements and gestures you would make. If you are reading the parts aloud in class, someone should be assigned to read the various camera directions as a running commentary on the play. (No doubt you've heard such commentaries in radio plays.)

[1] **Sire de Maletroit** (sēr dĕ măl·trwä).

Keep in mind that this is a play that is *seen* as well as heard. The camera directions are most important. Here are a few definitions that will explain technical terms used in the camera directions:

Dissolve to, fade in, fade out: different techniques for shifting the cameras from one scene or person or object to another.

Close-up shot, long shot: instruction for placing the camera at close or far distance from the scene.

Change angle: instruction for moving the cameras to different position, either high or low, or to one side.

Superimpose, rotate over: methods for showing printed captions over a background of scenery. Credit lines and commercials are often so used.

SETTINGS

(*The action of the story takes place in France in the Fifteenth Century.*)

Main Sets. (1) Grand Hall in the Sire de Maletroit's Château.[1] (2) Outside the Sire de Maletroit's Château

Small Sets. (1) Corner of a French Fifteenth-Century Tavern. (2) The Enclosed Porch of the Sire de Maletroit's Château

CHARACTERS

Main Parts

DENIS OF BEAULIEU,[2] a handsome aristocratic English soldier of twenty-five years, an expert swordsman

THE SIRE DE MALETROIT, a venerable French aristocrat of sixty-five years. He has gray hair and a neatly trimmed white beard and mustache. In spite of a benign smile, there is something sinister in his eyes. Like most well-born Frenchmen of his day, he speaks English practically without an accent.

BLANCHE DE MALETROIT, his niece, a beautiful French girl of seventeen. Her beauty is innocent — spiritual. She too has been taught to speak English and has only a trace of accent.

Small Parts

THE PRIEST (Maletroit's private chaplain), well-fed and worldly

INNKEEPER, a stout French peasant. Speaks English with an accent.

Walk-on Parts

Burgundian[3] Soldiers

Pikemen (Maletroit's armed retainers)

Choristers (unseen boy singers)

Fade in camera on a photograph or etching of the medieval[4] walled city of Carcassonne,[5] France. Superimpose and rotate over the picture, the following:

FRANCE: 1428 A.D.

HENRY THE FIFTH HAD WON THE BATTLE OF AGINCOURT.[6] A LARGE PART OF FRANCE HAD BEEN CONQUERED BY THE BRITISH. THE TROOPS OF BURGUNDY AND ENGLAND RULED SIDE BY SIDE UNDER AN UNEASY TRUCE.

Dissolve to a painting of Joan of Arc in full armor.

Superimpose:

HOWEVER, THIS STATE OF ARMED NEUTRALITY WAS TO BE SHORT-LIVED. A YEAR LATER, JOAN OF ARC WOULD DON HER ARMOR AND DRIVE THE HATED ENGLISH BACK ACROSS THE CHANNEL.

[1] **Château** (shă·tō′): a feudal castle.

[2] **Beaulieu:** pronounced "Bewley," as an English name.

[3] **Burgundian** (bûr·gŭn′dĭ·ăn): belonging to the old Duchy of Burgundy (bûr′gŭn·dĭ) in the south of France.

[4] **medieval** (mē′dĭ·ē′văl): pertaining to the Middle Ages.

[5] **Carcassonne** (kȧr·kȧ·sôn′).

[6] **Agincourt** (ȧ·zhăɴ·kōōr′; *Eng.*, ăj′ĭn·kōrt).

Dissolve to two banners flying in the breeze — the oriflamme[1] *of France and the cross of St. George of England.*

Superimpose:

BUT THAT IS TO ANTICIPATE HISTORY. THE ORIFLAMME OF FRANCE AND THE CROSS OF ST. GEORGE OF ENGLAND STILL FLUTTERED OVER THE CITADEL OF THE WALLED TOWN OF CHÂTEAU LANDONNE[2] DURING THE NIGHT THIS STRANGE ROMANTIC TALE TOOK PLACE.

Dissolve to a tavern sign. On it is painted a black horse and underneath it the words:

LE CHEVAL NOIR[3]

Dissolve to interior of the tavern. All that need be seen is a corner of the room. DENIS OF BEAULIEU, *a young English aristocrat, is sprawling nonchalantly in a large oak armchair. In front of him is a table on which is a stone flagon*[4] *and a half-filled glass. He is a soldier. His coat of chain mail shimmers in the flickering firelight. His sword and belt hang over the back of his chair. He wears spurs. He is young, handsome, and, at the moment, the picture of boredom. He drains off the glass, then raps on the table . . .*

DENIS. Landlord! . . . Landlord! . . .

[*A fat French* INNKEEPER *comes into camera. He has bristling mustachios*[5] *and speaks good English with an accent . . .*]

INNKEEPER. Monsieur?

DENIS. Your cellar boasts an excellent cordial. Where was it brewed?

INNKEEPER. At the abbey of Fécamp. The Benedictine monks distill it.

DENIS. I must take a sample back with me to England, when my mission is accomplished. Can you secure me a cask?

INNKEEPER. With ease, Monsieur.

DENIS. Good! . . . Just the same, this priests' potion does not compensate for the lack of company. How does a stranger allay boredom in your benighted town?

INNKEEPER. Pardon, Monsieur, but if the stranger is English — and wise — he will retire safely to his bed. It is dangerous to be on the streets of Château Landonne, alone, after curfew.

DENIS. Pox on you, man! France and England are no longer at war — and I am here on safe conduct.

INNKEEPER. What use are safe-conduct papers in the dark? It is only the kings who have made this peace, not their subjects. I regret, Monsieur, but there is little love between my people and yours. Every night the Burgundian soldiers, drunk with wine, roam the byways. They search for trouble — trouble in the shape of an English accent with a sword.

DENIS (*rising scornfully*). You insult me, landlord. Do you think I cannot defend myself? Do you think I fear your Burgundians? One Englishman is worth a half a dozen of those tattered mercenaries.[6] King Harry proved that on the field of Agincourt.

INNKEEPER (*groveling*). Pardon — I didn't mean to offend Monsieur. I had one thought alone — your safety.

DENIS (*softening*). I am obliged for

[1] **oriflamme** (ŏr′ĭ·flăm): a red silk banner, the battle flag of the early French kings, as the cross of St. George was the battle flag of the English kings.
[2] **Landonne** (län·dôn′).
[3] **Le Cheval Noir** (lẽ shē·văl nwâr′): The Black Horse.
[4] **flagon** (flă′gŭn): a jug or bottle for liquor.
[5] **mustachios** (mŭs·tä′shōz): pointed mustaches on either side of the face.
[6] **mercenaries** (mûr′sē·nĕr′ĭz): hired soldiers.

The walls of the medieval city of Carcassonne. (*French Embassy — Information Division*)

your concern. Nevertheless I intend to venture forth tonight. Otherwise I shall drown myself in that sticky Benedictine brew . . . Tell me, mine host, where can a gentleman find a game of cards?

INNKEEPER. The English officers are billeted at the southwest corner of the town — at the *Auberge Normande,*[1] below the Keep.[2] Doubtless they would furnish you with a game.

DENIS. I devoutly hope so! Now give me my sword! (*The landlord does so and helps him to buckle it on.*) How does one reach this hostelry?

INNKEEPER. Walk a thousand roods [3] due east, then turn north by the walls of the Sire de Maletroit's château. You cannot fail to recognize it, even in the dark.

[1] **Auberge Normande** (ō·běrj′ nôr·mänd′): an inn.
[2] **the Keep:** a dungeon.
[3] **a thousand roods:** between three and four miles.

You will see the round stern of a chapel on the opposite corner. The *Auberge* lies at the end of this lane.

[*They walk toward the door.* DENIS *puts on his cloak and hat.*]

DENIS (*the typical patronizing aristocrat*). You speak English uncommonly well — for a snail-eating Frenchie.

INNKEEPER (*bowing low*). Monsieur is too gracious! . . . My father taught me your language. This has been a hundred years' war between our countries, Monsieur. (*With a meaningful smile*) English soldiers have come to this inn — and gone — many times.

[DENIS *looks at him and laughs good-humoredly. He opens the door and departs.*]

Dissolve to outside the Sire de Maletroit's château. Long shot. What we see is an L*-shaped stone wall. In the short part of the* L *is an imposing Norman door, heavily carved in massive oak. The Maletroit coat of arms is on a large shield over the door. There is a striking gargoyle*[1] *over the shield.*

The long arm of the L *is supported by three projecting buttresses. The corners formed by these supports are in complete darkness. But the wall itself and the cobblestone street in front of it are streaked with moonlight.*

Three drunken Burgundian soldiers coming from the direction in which the door stands stagger along the streets. They wear steel helmets and breastplates, and are armed with swords. They are singing a French marching song of the period. They stop, pass a flagon around, and assuage their thirst from it. Then they draw their swords, wave them wildly toward the heavens, and curse the English.

THE SOLDIERS (*together*). *À bas, les Anglais!*[2] . . . etc., etc.!

[*They drink again, then link arms and stagger out of the picture. A moment or so later,* DENIS *comes along the lane from the same direction. He walks warily, obviously keeping his eye on the drunken men ahead of him. Suddenly their singing, which has been growing fainter, crescendos*[3] *again, indicating that they have wheeled around and are returning his way.*

Seeing that he will come face to face with these men if he pursues his present route, DENIS *darts into the shadow of the center buttress and flattens himself against the wall. Except for a faint gleam on his chain mail, he is completely hidden from sight.*

The three Burgundians return. They pass where DENIS *is concealed. Inadvertently, he shifts his position. His sword clatters against the stone walls. The three Burgundians hesitate, turn, and stare into the shadows.*]

BURGUNDIAN SOLDIER. *Qui v'là?*[4] . . .

[*He lurches into the shadows and drags* DENIS *into the light.* DENIS *immediately whips out his sword.*]

DENIS. Filthy French offal! Out of my way! . . .

BURGUNDIAN SOLDIER. *Parbleu! Un Anglais!*[5] . . .

[*The three Burgundians draw their swords and scream a volley of oaths at* DENIS. *Then they hurl themselves upon him.* DENIS *takes on the three, confident that his superior, and sober, swordsmanship will see him through. He overcomes the first two after a hard but brief exchange of swords. They writhe on the ground, severely wounded. The third Burgundian proves to be a better swordsman and gives him considerable difficulty.*

The clank of steel is heard by other soldiers in the neighborhood. Three more dash to the scene. They immediately whip out their swords and enter the fray. DENIS *is now tiring, outnumbered, and in danger of being killed. He is forced to take the defensive. He retreats down the street in the direction of the door. The soldiers follow, lunging at him the while. He finds*

[1] **gargoyle** (gär′goil): a strangely shaped carved animal figure, projecting from the upper part of a building and serving as a waterspout.

[2] **À bas, les Anglais!** (ȧ·bä′ lā·zäɴ·glā′): Down with the English!

[3] **crescendos** (krĕ·shĕn′dōz): becomes louder.

[4] **Qui v'là?** (kē v'lȧ′): Who goes there?

[5] **Parbleu! Un Anglais!** (pȧr·blû′ ûɴ·näɴ·glā′): By Heaven! An Englishman!

Doorway of mansion: Fifteenth-century France. (Guillumette)

himself against the door. It gives under his weight. Just as the leading Burgundian is about to deliver him a fatal blow, he kicks the door further open, slips behind it, and slams it in his opponent's face.

The Burgundians curse, then batter on the door wildly. They find it will not budge. Eventually they give up, return to their wounded comrades, who are groaning on the cobblestones, and carry them off.]

Cut to SMALL SET. *A small enclosed stone porch. On one side of it is the Maletroit door. Facing this door is a little staircase leading up to another door. It is bare of any furniture or trappings.* DENIS *is leaning against the door he has entered, breathing heavily and listening intently. He hears the Burgundians batter on the other side of the door. Their voices eventually recede and there is silence.*

DENIS *wipes the blood from his sword with his kerchief and returns it to its scabbard. Satisfied that it will now be safe to regain the street, he tries to find the latch to the door. To his amazement, there is neither latch nor handle nor bolt. Suddenly, while he is occupied in trying to pry it open in some fashion, the other door, the one at the top of the stairs, creaks ajar very slightly. He turns swiftly and draws his sword again, but there is no person to be seen. All that meets his eye is a faint edge of light outlining the door. Very cautiously, he tiptoes up the stairs, then slowly opens this door.*

Cut to MAIN SET. *Grand hall in the Sire de Maletroit's château. This is a large pentagonal*[1] *room — obviously part of a five-sided turret — with walls of polished stone. Various banners, tapestries, and standards adorn them. Across one corner is a large chimney piece carved with the arms of the Maletroits. Oaken love seats face each other beneath it. There is a large window looking down into a courtyard. In the wall on the opposite side of the room there is an arras*[2] *covering a Norman archway to a chapel. When this tapestry is pulled aside, it is only necessary to see a suggestion of an altar, and a tiny stained glass window. A low, tiny oak door is beside the mantelpiece leading to an anteroom. The door through which* DENIS *has entered is not seen until a mo-*

[1] **pentagonal** (pĕn·tăg′ō·năl): five-sided.
[2] **arras** (ăr′ăs): tapestry or wall hanging.

The massive interior of a medieval hall. (New York Public Library)

ment or two later. There is an imposing oak table in the center of the hall and a high armchair behind it. The table is littered with parchments, quill pens, an inkwell, and a receptacle for holding sand to sprinkle on parchment as a blotter. A small earthenware bowl holds a gay bunch of camellias.

The camera moves around the room, then finally rests on the SIRE DE MALETROIT *himself. He is standing by a large wooden bird cage, hanging from a bracket on the wall. In it there is a small falcon.*[1] *He is feeding the bird shreds of meat.* ALAIN DE MALETROIT *is a venerable-looking old man. His white beard and mustache are neatly trimmed. Only an almost comically evil look in his eyes betrays something greedy, maybe brutal, in his nature.*

Camera on DENIS. *He is standing inside the door. Seeing no one more alarming than an apparently harmless old man, he sheathes his sword.*

[1] **falcon** (fôl'kŭn): a hawk trained for hunting.

DENIS. Your pardon, Sire, for this intrusion.

MALETROIT. Pray step in. I have been expecting you all the evening.

DENIS (*much puzzled*). You have been what, Sire?

MALETROIT. I will explain further, when I have finished feeding Merlin his supper. A bird of unique spirit. My constant companion. One of nature's better efforts. His body an arrow — death in his wings. (*He closes one eye and cocks his head to one side.*) As in your sword, young man.

DENIS. You saw that skirmish outside your walls?

[*Close shot.* MALETROIT. *He covers Merlin's cage with a cloth. He then moves over to* DENIS. *He rubs his frail hands together in relish.*]

MALETROIT. I can never resist a good fight. I heard the clash of steel and watched from a turret window. You are a brave man. Your swordsmanship was better than I would have expected from a fop of an Englishman.

[DENIS's *hand goes swiftly to his sword. He half draws it, then sheathes it again.*]

DENIS. Only your venerable gray hairs, Sire, prevent my avenging that insult.

[MALETROIT *cackles malevolently.*]

MALETROIT. Tut, tut! We are hot-tempered, are we not? Pray be seated. Cool your heels, together with your head. I had no intention to anger you. Put yourself entirely at your ease. We shall arrange our affairs in good time.

DENIS. Sire, I guess you to be the Master of Maletroit.

MALETROIT (*sarcastically*). How clever of you!

DENIS. Then there can be nothing to settle between us. We are strangers. This is merely a chance encounter. I found myself against your door. It happened to be open. I sought temporary refuge behind it. When I wanted to reenter the street, it remained fast.

MALETROIT (*with a benign smile*). Ah, yes! My door! An excellent example of French ingenuity, eh? By your own admission you were anxious to avoid my acquaintance. (*Nodding his head wisely*) Well, what of that? We old ones look for such reluctance now and then. But when it touches our honor, we cast about until we find some way of overcoming it. You arrived uninvited — but you are welcome. (*With a sly wink*) *Very* welcome!

DENIS. You persist in error, Sire. How can any affairs of mine **touch** your honor? This is my first night in your countryside. I was on my way to the *Auberge Normande* for a game of cards with some of my King's officers. I had already passed your abode when I was forced to retreat, by those Burgundian scum.

MALETROIT (*unbelievingly*). Indeed?

DENIS. I am not accustomed to having my word doubted, Sire. (*He stands proudly.*) I am the elder son of Sir Roland of Beaulieu. Our rich acres stretch from the Port of Southampton to the Forest of Brockenhurst. The land was a grant to my grandsire from Edward the Third, for valor at the battle of Crécy.[1]

MALETROIT. A happy surprise! It is some satisfaction to know that your pocket is well lined.

DENIS (*thoroughly aroused*). Sire, you persist in making a fool of me. I waste my time conversing with a lunatic. There is no power under God that will make me stay here any longer. If I cannot make my way out in a peaceful fashion, I will hack a hole in your door with my sword.

[*He draws his sword and walks toward the entrance by which he came.*]

MALETROIT (*in a sudden harsh voice*). Sit down — *nephew.*

DENIS (*wheeling around — amazed*). Nephew?! . . .

[*The old man shakes with silent laughter as* DENIS *continues to stare at him.*]

MALETROIT. You rogue! Do you fancy that when I made my little contrivance for the door, I stopped short with that?

[*The old man claps his hands. Camera moves swiftly to the door to the vestibule. Four men in armor carrying pikes (large spears with diamond-shaped points) appear and stand waiting* MALETROIT*'s orders.*]

[1] **Crécy** (krā'sē').

MALETROIT (*suavely*). Now, my dear nephew, if you wish to remain a free young buck, agreeably conversing with an old – lunatic (*He chuckles at this sally.*), sit as I command, in peace; and God be with you.

DENIS (*slowly*). Do you mean – I'm a prisoner?

MALETROIT (*with a wave of his delicate hand*). I leave that conclusion to your natural wits – not that they are plentiful in English heads.

[DENIS *controls his boiling indignation and sits.* MALETROIT *shakes with laughter again.*]

DENIS. What do you want of me?

MALETROIT (*in utter scorn*). As if you did not know! . . . (*He turns to the pikemen at the door.*) Wait by the outer door. This man is not to leave without my permission.

[*The pikemen depart.* MALETROIT *crosses to the arras covering the arch to the chapel and pulls the tapestry aside.*]

MALETROIT (*calling inside*). Father, I wish to speak with you.

[*After a moment a tall, robed priest comes forth.*]

PRIEST. Yes, Messire? [1]

MALETROIT (*with a twisted smile – pointing to* DENIS). Behold! The young gallant has arrived! Indeed, so anxious was he to steal the prize from under my roof that he literally fought his way in.

PRIEST (*looking* DENIS *over*). I am relieved, Sire. I had expected someone much less presentable.

[*They cease staring at* DENIS.]

MALETROIT. And how is my niece? In a better frame of spirit?

PRIEST. More resigned, Messire.

[1] **Messire** (mĕ·sēr′): your lordship; my lord.

MALETROIT (*sneering*). The Lord help her, she is hard to please! What more would she have than a likely stripling of her own choosing?

PRIEST. A young damsel is prone to blushes, Messire. And the situation *is* unusual.

MALETROIT. Heaven knows it was none of *my* making. *She* began this dance, and she shall finish it. . . . Bring her hither. (*Again with a sneer*) And bid her dry those foolish tears. . . .

[*The priest bows and goes behind the arras.* MALETROIT *crosses to* DENIS.]

MALETROIT. Come, come, Monsieur, Paris should not look so sourly when he meets his Helen.[2]

[*Camera on the arras. The priest returns, leading by the hand a singularly beautiful young girl of seventeen,* BLANCHE DE MALETROIT. *She is considerably distressed. Her face is deathly pale. Her eyes betray that she has been crying for hours. She appears with extreme reluctance. Her eyes are cast downward; she stands staring at the floor. She is attired as a bride in the costume of the period.*

Close shot. DENIS. *He rises slowly, deeply struck by her beauty and tragic appearance.*

Close shot. MALETROIT.]

MALETROIT (*softly – insinuatingly*). Blanche – I have brought a friend to see you. Come forward, my little chick, and give him your pretty hand. It is good to be modest, but necessary to be polite. (*Sharply*) Come, my niece! . . .

[2] **Paris . . . Helen:** According to Greek legend, the goddess of love promised Paris, son of the Trojan king, that if he would judge her the most beautiful of the goddesses she would give him the most beautiful woman in the world. This was Helen, wife of the king of Sparta.

[*Close shot on* BLANCHE. *Very slowly she leaves the priest and moves to* DENIS. *Camera rolls back as she moves. She still cannot bring herself to raise her eyes. She stares at his feet, trembling.* DENIS *is staring breathlessly at her.*
Camera on BLANCHE. *She has now raised her head and is staring at* DENIS. *Her eyes meet his. Shame gives place to horror and terror in her looks. With a piercing scream she covers her face with her hands and sinks to the floor.*
Change angle. MALETROIT *comes quickly to her side, kneels, and raises her to her feet. She gazes at him piteously.*]

BLANCHE. My uncle, this is not the man! . . .

[MALETROIT'S *lips curl in an unbelieving smile.*]

BLANCHE (*frantically*). I tell you, Uncle, this is not the man.

MALETROIT (*chirping agreeably*). Of course not! I had expected you to say that. Just as you pretended you did not know his name.

BLANCHE. You must believe me. I have never seen this person until this moment. Never so much as set my eyes upon him. And I never wish to see him again. (*She turns to* DENIS.) Monsieur — if you are a gentleman, you will bear me out. Have I ever seen you? Have you ever seen me — before this dreadful hour?

DENIS. You are correct! I have never seen you before — such is my bad fortune. . . . Sire de Maletroit, this is the first time that I have met your engaging niece. I will swear it — (*pointing to the arras*) on that altar — if you so desire.

BLANCHE (*with a profound sigh of relief*). Thank you, Monsieur. You have earned my eternal gratitude.

[*Close shot.* MALETROIT *and the priest. They exchange a look.*]

MALETROIT. Distressing, is it not, Father?

PRIEST. Alas, yes, Messire! (*With a beatific smile*) But the barrier is not insurmountable.

MALETROIT. My point of view, exactly. I had little acquaintance with my poor late wife before I wedded her. Impromptu marriages are sometimes the best in the long run.

[DENIS *comes into the picture belligerently.*]

DENIS. Sire, you are proposing to marry me to your niece? Would you ignore my voice in such a matter?

MALETROIT. Not entirely. I will give you a few moments of leisure to make up for lost time — before we proceed with the ceremony.

[MALETROIT *proceeds toward the little door by the mantelpiece, the priest toward the chapel.* BLANCHE *rushes frantically after her uncle, flings herself on the ground, and clutches him by the knees.*]

BLANCHE. Sire — Uncle — have pity on me! I declare before God I will stab myself rather than be forced on that young man. My heart rebels against it. God forbids such marriages. You dishonor your gray hairs. You —

MALETROIT (*breaking in harshly*). Witness this talk about dishonor. It is you yourself, Blanche, who have besmirched the name of Maletroit. You have forfeited your right to question my designs.

BLANCHE. But I have done nothing. Nothing! . . .

MALETROIT. Had your father been alive, I doubt if he would have agreed with you. His was the hand of iron. He would have turned you from his doors. You may bless your stars you now have only to deal with a hand of velvet, Mademoiselle.[1]

[*He caresses her hair with his thin hand. She flinches.*]

BLANCHE. Any woman in the world would prefer death to such a marriage.

[MALETROIT *takes her sternly by the shoulders and lifts her to her feet again.*]

MALETROIT. I have finished arguing with you, Blanche. After your scandalous behavior, it is my duty to get you married without delay. Out of pure kindness of heart, I have tried to find your own gallant for you. I still believe I have succeeded. If I have failed, I care not one jackstraw. So I recommend you make yourself agreeable to this young man. If you do not, your next groom may not be so — presentable. When either one of you decides to admit your duplicity,[2] knock on this door. I shall be waiting in my anteroom.

[*He goes, shutting the door behind him. Change angle. The priest is standing by the arras.* BLANCHE *goes to him in supplication.*]

BLANCHE. Can you not help me, Father?

PRIEST. My child, your duty is clear. You must obey your uncle.

[*At this moment, in the distance, some boy choristers can be heard chanting a "Plain Song" in Latin.*]

PRIEST. Listen! The choristers are practicing your nuptial hymn. . . .

[1] **Mademoiselle** (måd·mwå·zĕl'): Miss.
[2] **duplicity** (dů·plĭs'ĭ·tĭ): deception; double-dealing.

[*He goes. There is an embarrassed silence.* BLANCHE *hangs her head again. After a moment,* DENIS *crosses to her slowly.*]

DENIS. Mademoiselle, it grieves me to see you so distressed.

BLANCHE (*flashing him a look of disdain*). I can scarcely believe that — seeing your presence has added to my woes. Why are you here? What is the meaning of all this?

DENIS. God knows! I find myself a prisoner in a house of mad people. As to everything else, I am completely in the dark.

BLANCHE. Then how did you come here?

DENIS. By accident. I was driven within during a street brawl that was none of my seeking. (*He goes a little closer to her.*) Now it is my turn to ask questions. Why are *you* in this predicament? I cannot believe that anyone so innocent — so lovely — has brought dishonor to her family.

BLANCHE (*with a grateful look*). That is true. My uncle wrongs me. At the worst I have been a little — unmaidenly.

DENIS. Tell me. You can trust me.

BLANCHE (*searching his eyes*). I believe I can. I have been without father and mother, Monsieur — oh, for as long as I can recollect. Indeed, I have been lonely and unhappy for most of my life. Until three months ago! . . . Tell me, Monsieur, is it wrong to smile? If so, then I am much to blame.

DENIS. How can I tell whether it is wrong? Alas, I have never seen your smile.

[*She tries to favor him with one, but it is only a pathetic flicker.*]

BLANCHE. It was in church. A young captain — an Englishman like yourself —

began to stand near me every Sunday. I could see that I pleased him. He smiled at me. I smiled back. I was so touched that anyone should like me.

DENIS (*with an understanding grin*). And then one day he secretly passed you a note.

BLANCHE (*in innocent surprise*). Yes. You know him? He has told you?

DENIS. No. But I have known young men like him. It has been done before. And it will be done again, as long as there are beautiful damsels – like you – to inspire such an action.

BLANCHE (*gravely*). You are very wise in the ways of the world, Monsieur! . . .

DENIS. It does not take wisdom to know how to court a chaperoned [1] maiden. That springs from instinct! . . . May I ask what was in the note?

BLANCHE. He asked me to leave the wall door open, so that we might speak together upon the stairs.

DENIS. And did you?

BLANCHE. No. I knew my uncle trusted me. . . . This officer has since besieged me with notes with the same request. I have always ignored them.

DENIS. Then you have never so much as even spoken to this man?

BLANCHE. Alas, no!

[DENIS *looks at the door behind which* MALETROIT *left and takes a pace or two about the floor.*]

DENIS. Your uncle is a disgrace to mankind. (*He comes to* BLANCHE'S *side again.*) How did he find out?

BLANCHE. That I do not know. He is very shrewd. This morning, when we came from Mass, he took my hand in his, forced it open, and read my little billet.[2] He gave it back to me with great politeness.

[1] **chaperoned** (shăp′ẽr·ōnd): accompanied and guarded, as it were, by an older person.
[2] **billet** (bĭl′ĕt): a note.

DENIS. Did it contain another request to leave the door open – this evening?

BLANCHE. Yes. I fear that is what has been the downfall of us. . . . My uncle kept me strictly in my room all day. Then he ordered me to dress myself in this – as you see me. My mother's bridal gown!

DENIS. How does it happen that he does not know your young man's name?

BLANCHE (*after a slight hesitation*). He never told it to me. The notes were signed – (*shyly*) "One who worships from afar." Even if he *had* disclosed his name, I would not have told my uncle, for how could I know whether the gentleman would be willing to take me for a wife. He might have been trifling with me.

DENIS. I understand! Everything now is clear! . . . Mademoiselle, you have honored me with your confidence. It remains for me to prove it that I am not unworthy of the honor. We will call your uncle.

[*He moves over to the little door. He raps on it sharply.*]

DENIS (*calling*). Sire de Maletroit, my interview with your niece is at an end.

[MALETROIT *re-enters.*]

DENIS (*assuming his most confident manner*). Sire – I believe it is customary for a man to have some say in the ordering of his marriage. Therefore, let me tell you, I will be no party to forcing my hand on this lady. Had she offered herself freely to me, I should have been proud to accept. (*He turns to* BLANCHE *and looks at her with growing admiration.*) For, unlike yourself, I judge her to be as good as she is beautiful. However, things being as they are, I am reluctantly forced to refuse her hand.

Coleen Gray as the beautiful heroine in a television performance of "The Sire de Maletroit's Door." (*Columbia Broadcasting Studios*)

[*Close-up of* BLANCHE'S *reaction to his statement. Her eyes shine with gratitude.*

Close shot. MALETROIT. *His smile grows.*]

MALETROIT. I am afraid, Monsieur de Beaulieu, you do not understand the choice I am offering you. . . . Follow me to this window . . .

[*Change angle.* MALETROIT *crosses to the window followed by* DENIS. MALETROIT *flings it wide open and points.*]

Observe, Monsieur, there is an iron ring in the upper masonry; and reeved [1] through it, a very stout rope.

[*Close-up of a hangman's noose dangling from a buttress above the window.*]

MALETROIT'S VOICE. Now, mark my words! If you persist in refusing to marry my beautiful niece, I shall have you hanged by this rope at sunrise.

[*Close shot.* BLANCHE. *She gasps in horror as she puts her hands to her cheeks.*]

DENIS (*aghast*). You would not dare! . . .

MALETROIT. You know little of what a Maletroit does, or does not, dare — particularly where an Englishman is concerned. Not that your death is my *primary* desire. Indeed, the picture of your spurs — (*He looks down at* DENIS'S *legs.*) dangling in the breeze below my windows, would be middling distasteful to me; and mar the view of my beautiful garden.

DENIS. But this is sheer murder. Even a lowly peasant is given a trial.

MALETROIT. Not murder — expiation! The erasing of a stain! The honor of my house has been compromised. I believe you to be the guilty person. Furthermore, even if you were one of my own countrymen — if you sprang from Charlemagne [2] himself — you cannot refuse the hand of a Maletroit with impunity.[3]

DENIS. Neither can you hang a Beaulieu! . . . (*He draws his sword.*) If you or any of your minions attempt to lay a hand on me, I will drench this floor with blood.

MALETROIT (*laughing scornfully*). Put up your sword! Hot-headed nonsense! Would you fight the world? . . . You have seen my pikemen. They still stand behind that door. Others await my summons in the anteroom, there. (*He points to the little door.*) Still another band stands at arms in the chapel. They are all eager to make mincemeat of you. . . .

[*Close shot.* BLANCHE.]

BLANCHE. Uncle, will you permit me to speak with this gentleman? I would not —

MALETROIT (*in a voice of doom*). Silence, girl! I am doing the speaking! And these are my final words on this subject. (*He moves over to his desk, where he picks up the hourglass.*) Monsieur de Beaulieu — look well on this hourglass! When these sands have run three times from top to bottom, it will be daybreak. Three hours of life are always three hours. Even the course of history has been changed in shorter time. Three little hours! I give them to you — for reflection. A wife may be a millstone round the neck — but not so deadly a one as yonder noose. (*He hobbles to the little door and turns.*) Besides, my niece appears to have something still to say to you. Do not disfigure your last moments by a want of courtesy.

[1] **reeved:** passed through.

[2] **Charlemagne** (shär'lĕ·mān): ruler of an empire which later became France.

[3] **impunity** (ĭm·pū'nĭ·tĭ): freedom from punishment.

[*He goes. Camera on* BLANCHE. *She looks after her uncle, then goes over to* DENIS *in desperation.*]

BLANCHE. Monsieur, you shall not die! You shall marry me after all.

DENIS. Do you think I stand in that much fear of death?

BLANCHE. Oh, no, no! I do not believe you to be a coward! It is for my own peace of spirit that I offer myself. I could not have it on my conscience that you were slain for such a scruple.

DENIS. Mademoiselle, you do not perceive the core of the problem. What you offer — in pity, I must refuse — in pride. In this impulsive moment of generosity, you forget what you owe to another.

BLANCHE. But I must do something to help you.

DENIS. Believe me, Mademoiselle, there is no young man in England, or France, who would not be glad to die in doing you a service.

BLANCHE. Must someone die — because I smiled?

[*She suddenly bursts into tears, walks away from him, flings herself into her uncle's chair behind the desk, and buries her head in her arms. After a moment, she speaks through her tears.*]

BLANCHE. If my uncle persists in carrying out his threat, I will hide myself from the world.

[*Camera on* DENIS. *He stands looking down at her for a moment. Her sobs distress him considerably. As they continue, he turns quietly away and walks over to the window, where he stares at the noose.*
Close-up on BLANCHE. *After a moment, camera moves from her to the hourglass on the desk beside her. The sands are trickling slowly from the upper part to the lower.*]

[*Fade out.*]

Fade in. Camera still on the hourglass. The sands have run out. DENIS's *hand comes into camera and turns glass over. The sands begin to trickle again.* DENIS *is standing staring down at* BLANCHE, *who is still sobbing. He puts his hand gently on her shoulder.*

DENIS. Mademoiselle — an hour has passed and you still weep. Will you not reflect on the little time I have before me? Spare me the sight of your distress.

[BLANCHE *manages to stop sobbing and looks up at him.*]

BLANCHE. I am very selfish, Monsieur. I will try to be brave — for your sake. (*She shivers.*) I am cold! . . . Shall we not sit by the fire? (*They go to the fireplace, to the love seats.*) Seat yourself opposite me, Monsieur. (DENIS *does so.*) Put it in my power to do something more for you than weep. If — if you are determined to die — have you no family to whom I could carry your farewells?

DENIS (*shaking his head*). My father fell in battle. My mother has married again and has a young family to tend. My only brother, Neville de Beaulieu, will inherit my estates. (*Bitterly*) If I am not in error, that will amply compensate him for my passing. (*She hangs her head again.*) Do not look so sad, Mademoiselle! What is life but a little vapor that passeth away?

BLANCHE. Have you no friends?

DENIS. But few. And once I am beneath the sod I shall have none.

BLANCHE. You are wrong, Monsieur. You forget Blanche de Maletroit. She will think of you until she, too, is in her grave.

DENIS. You have a sweet nature, Mademoiselle, and estimate my little service beyond its worth.

BLANCHE. It is not that! I say so, because you are the noblest man I have ever met.

DENIS (*mockingly*). Have you met so many?

BLANCHE (*with her first smile*). You are pleased to tease me, Monsieur.

DENIS. I had hoped to make you smile — and I succeeded.

BLANCHE (*Blushing shyly, she changes the subject*). Let us talk of things other than my unfortunate smile: that led us into our sad predicament. . . . What brought you to France — and this ill-fated town?

DENIS (*slapping his thigh*). By the Lord Harry — you remind me of my mission. I had forgotten it in the presence of your distress — and your beauty. (*He stands and unbuckles a pouch from his belt.*) I am a courier from the Master of the English Fleet. (*Pointing to pouch*) In this is a sealed missive to the Governor of Calais.[1] My country needs more ships to expand her trade to the Indies. . . . Is it in your power to have it delivered?

BLANCHE (*holding out her hand*). I promise it shall reach its destination.

[*He gives it to her.*]

DENIS. Thank you, Mademoiselle.

[*He continues to gaze at her in frank admiration. She returns his look for a moment, then lowers her eyes.*]

BLANCHE (*talking to cover her embarrassment*). Monsieur — tell me something of your island. Though I have been taught to speak your tongue, I have never been beyond the walled gates of this town.

DENIS (*in quiet rapture*). England! Where shall I begin? . . . In the springtime? . . . I wish you could see our countryside in the spring! The meadows yellow with daffodils. The sky-blue hyacinths carpeting the woods. The banks of primroses . . . And our lazy streams; the Test River[2] that flows through my land, drenched in the morning mist; the still herons roosting like purple sentinels in the willows.

[*His voice fades.*]

DENIS (*continuing*). Near the castle of Beaulieu is a vast forest of stalwart oaks rich in deer — that same forest where King William the Red was slain by an arrow as he —

[*Picture fades with his voice.*]

Fade in: DENIS *is still talking. But he is now seated beside* BLANCHE, *holding her hand. She is looking up at him with wide adoring eyes and listening with rapt attention.*

DENIS. . . . and for that small feat, the king awarded me an additional twenty thousand acres. I assure you it was undeserved. It was the luck of battle.

BLANCHE. I cannot believe that, Monsieur. Do not forget, I have seen a sample of your courage.

[*This remark brings them back to a state of reality. There is a momentary silence.* DENIS *looks down and they both realize that he is holding her hand. She tries to withdraw it, but he does not let go.*]

[1] **Calais** (kă·lā′): a city of France.

[2] **Test River:** a river in Hampshire, in southern England.

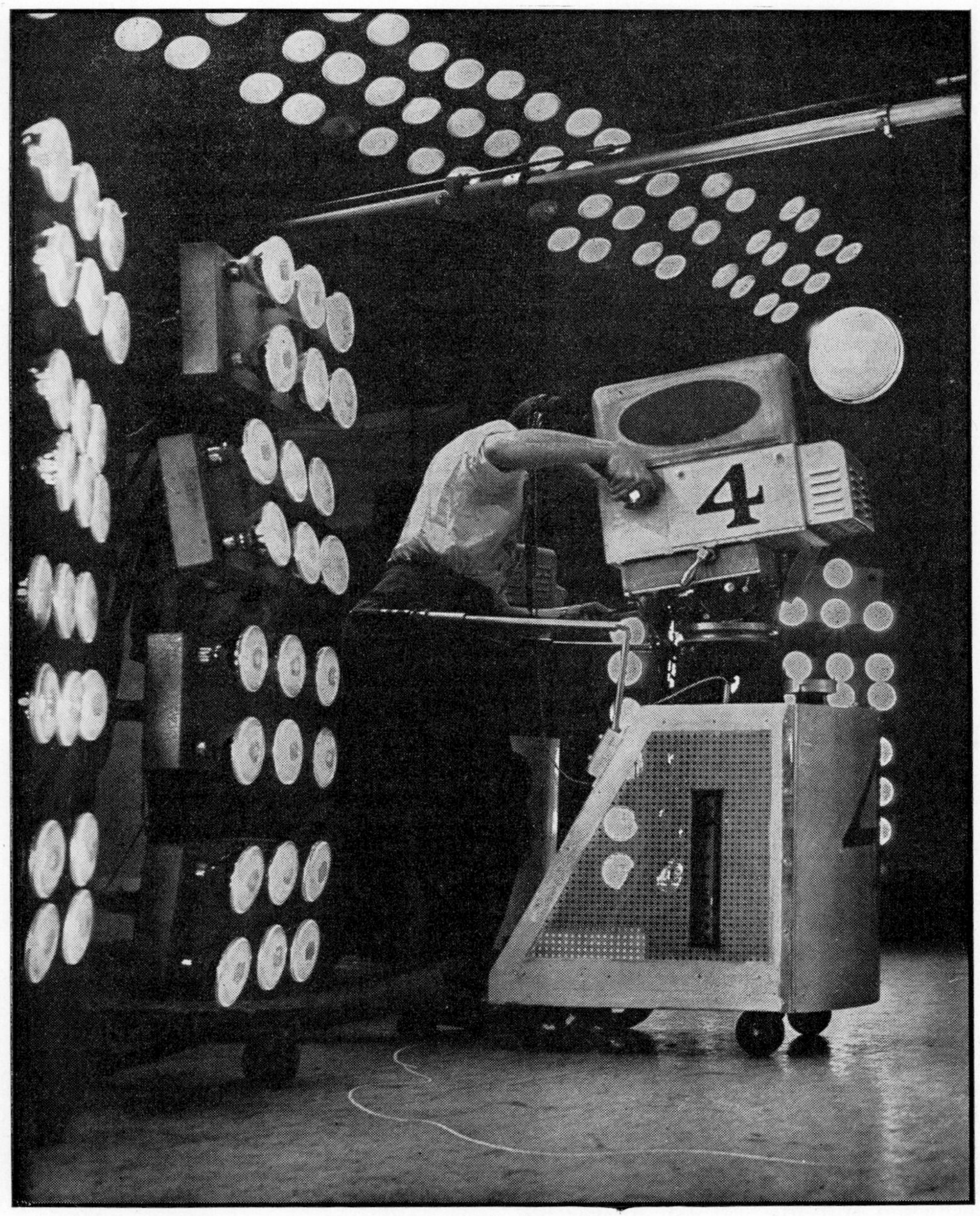

Television camera in action. (Black Star)

DENIS. Mademoiselle, forgive my chattering tongue. And my idle boasts. I have babbled shamelessly of my country, my thoughts, and my deeds in battle. How I must have wearied you! Why did you not stop me?

BLANCHE. Because I was enchanted by your every word! Never has a night passed so quickly. (*She points to the hourglass.*) Why, look — the hourglass!

[*Cut to close-up of the hourglass. The sands have run out.*]

BLANCHE'S VOICE. We forgot to turn it. We do not even know what o'clock it is.

DENIS. It is late enough! . . . Too late.

[*She rises as if she would go to the hourglass to turn it upside down again. He jumps quickly to his feet and detains her by putting his arm around her shoulder.*]

DENIS. No, Blanche! Let it lie.

[*Something arresting in his voice and manner causes her to turn back to him.*]

There are moments when time stands still: you cannot measure their length by sand.

[*Close-up.* BLANCHE. *Her face becomes gradually transfigured by love.*]

BLANCHE. Then, while the clock waits, let me tell you something I became aware of, whilst you held my hand. It is only right that you should go to your death, knowing . . . When I asked you to marry me, it was not only because I respected and admired you. It was because — I loved you. From the first moment you took my part against my uncle, I loved you.

DENIS (*deeply moved*). Blanche! Blanche! You know I would never force myself on you without your free consent. But since you —

BLANCHE'S VOICE (*breaking in*). No, hear me out! Although I have revealed the secret of my heart, I cannot forget your first sentiments toward me. Nor can I forgive them. You chose the noose rather than my hand. So, if you have it in mind to go back on your word, know this! I would no more marry you now than I would my uncle's groom. I, too, have pride.

[*After a pause,* DENIS *sighs deeply. His spirits seem to droop. He points to the window.*]

DENIS. Look! The dawn is creeping in! Any moment now your uncle will be here. . . . (*He takes her gently by the shoulders and looks into her eyes.*) Blanche — can you not read my eyes? You must also know by now that I too loved you. Are we to lose each other because we are both tangled in pride?

BLANCHE. But it is impossible. There is another reason why I cannot wed you. I — I lied to you.

[DENIS'S *grip on her arms tightens jealously.*]

DENIS. Don't tell me that, after all, you *did* meet that impertinent sender of notes?

BLANCHE. No, no! But I lied when I said I did not know his name. I sent my serving maid to the *Auberge Normande* to seek it out. It was — Percy of Warbecke.

[DENIS'S *jealousy evaporates as suddenly as it came.*]

DENIS. Little goose, is that all?

BLANCHE. You do not despise me?

DENIS. For being feminine? Of course not! Besides, it is so easy to blot his name from our memory.

[*Without waiting for her permission, he kisses her on the lips.*
There is a discreet cough behind them. Camera on MALETROIT *and the priest standing at the anteroom door.* MALETROIT *is smiling and rubbing his hands.*]

MALETROIT. A touching scene! Are you kissing farewell or sealing a betrothal?

[DENIS *and* BLANCHE *break apart.*]

DENIS (*with an elaborate bow*). Sire — we have decided to accede to your wishes.

[*The priest and* MALETROIT *exchange satisfied glances. The priest goes quickly toward the chapel.*]

DENIS. Furthermore, I owe you an apology, Sire. I *was* the man — all the time.

[*Camera moves in to a very close shot as* DENIS *bends to kiss her again. He whispers into her ear.*]

Now we are equal in lies.

[*The sound of the bridal chant floats into the room.*]

[*Fade out.*]

Thinking It Over

1. Find the original Stevenson story and compare it with the TV script. How closely does the script follow the original story? In what ways is fiction able to give you a better presentation of a story than drama? In what ways is drama more effective?

2. This is a play in which *pride* governs many of the actions of the various characters, getting them into complications that are sometimes dangerous, sometimes humorous. Give several good examples of pride as exhibited by the innkeeper, Denis, the Sire de Maletroit, and Blanche. In what way can a person be *too* proud? How can your pride sometimes hurt others? These are important questions for you to consider in relation to your own personality and behavior.

3. The Sire de Maletroit contrived an elaborate and supposedly foolproof trick to force Blanche into a marriage. How was he himself tricked in the end? Why was the massive door without apparent hinges or handles?

4. If you read the first part of the script carefully, you should be able to tell a little about the time and place of the story. How is it that the characters know both English and French? How were the English driven from Burgundy and other parts of France at this time in history? Look up the locale of the story on a map.

5. Try writing a TV play as a class project. Follow the example of actual scriptwriters and do some extensive research in the library until you find a suitable play. Use the script you have just read as a model in form. Note that there are instructions for setting the scenes, for the gestures and movements of the actors, and for the movement of the cameras. Don't forget to look up such details as appropriate speech and costuming, if your play is historical, rather than present-day, in setting. The musicians in the class can suggest appropriate musical scores; and the artists can make sketches for scenery and design costumes.

For Your Vocabulary

WORD BUILDING: The stage directions say that Maletroit *cackles malevolently* at one place — that is, his laugh has a sneering and cruel sound. *Malevolent* comes originally from the Latin *male* (ill) + *volens* (wishing). Does that prefix suggest anything about the name Stevenson has given one of the main characters? *Impromptu* marriages, which Maletroit says sometimes turn out best, are unplanned marriages. How does the meaning of this word relate to *prompt?*

Maletroit says Denis's death is not his *primary desire. Primary* here means "first in importance." Whenever the stem *prime* is used, it conveys a quality either of firstness or of major importance. In the *primary* grades, you *primarily* read *primers*. What meaning can you give to *prima donna, prime minister, primitive?* When Maletroit said that his house had been *compromised*, he meant that the honor of his family had been lowered. Another meaning for the word *compromise* is " mutual agreement or adjustment." In this sense the two parts of the word have a good bit of meaning — *com-* + *promise*. Can you explain, from these two parts, how the word obtains its meaning?

THE CURTAIN RISES

Suggestions for Free Reading

Anderson, Maxwell, *The Eve of St. Mark* (Anderson House, 1942)
An American boy, the girl he loves, and an old legend.

Banning, Nina Lloyd, *Pit Pony* (Knopf, 1947)
A boy and his pony in a Welsh coal mine.

Brink, Carol Ryrie, *Caddie Woodlawn* (Macmillan, 1945)
A play based on the popular book of the same name.

Cohen, Helen Louise, *One-act Plays by Modern Authors* (Harcourt, 1934)

Corwin, Norman L., *Thirteen by Corwin* (Holt, 1942)
Modern plays by an original radio writer.

Crownfield, Gertrude, *Angelique* (Crowell, 1941)
Simple, pleasant story of French-Canadian life.

Dunsany, Lord, *Five Plays* (Little, 1917–18)
Fantastic and mysterious one-act plays. *Plays of Gods and Men* (J. W. Luce, 1917) is similar in content.

Fox, D. R., and Schlesinger, A. M., eds., *Cavalcade of America* (Bradley, 1937; Series Two, 1938)

Gillette, William, *Sherlock Holmes* (Doubleday, 1935)
A play about the great detective and his friend, Dr. Watson.

Goldsmith, Clifford, *What A Life* (Dramatists' Play Service, 1939)
Farce-comedy about high school life.

Griffith, Francis, and Mersand, Joseph, *Modern One-Act Plays* (Harcourt, 1950)

Hackett, Walter, *Radio Plays for Young People* (Plays, Inc., 1950)
Fifteen famous stories adapted for radio, including " The Necklace " by De Maupassant.

Hark, Mildred, and McQueen, Noel, *Special Plays for Special Days* (Plays, Inc., 1947)
Easy non-royalty holiday plays.

Hemon, Louis, *Maria Chapdelaine* (Macmillan, 1921)
Popular romance of the French-Canadian country.

Housman, Louis, and Koehler, Edward Thomas, *Footlights Up!* (Harper, 1935)
Easy practical plays with directions for costuming and staging.

Jagendorf, M., *Twenty Non-Royalty Mystery Plays* (Greenberg, 1944)

Knickerbocker, Edwin V., *Short Plays* (Holt, 1931)

Kozlenko, William, ed., *One Hundred Non-Royalty Radio Plays* (Greenberg, 1941)

Lass, McGill, and Axelrod, *Plays from Radio* (Houghton, 1948)

Leonard, Sterling A., *Atlantic Book of Modern Plays* (Little, 1934)

Mayorga, Margaret, *Representative One-Act Plays by American Authors* (Little, Brown and Dodd, Mead, published annually since 1937)
Miss Mayorga apparently reads every play written and puts the best into her anthologies.

Miller, Helen Louise, *On Stage for Teen-Agers* (Plays, Inc., 1948)
Twenty-two one-act comedies, royalty-free.

Nicholson, Kenyon, *Appleton Book of Short Plays* (Appleton-Century-Crofts, 1926)

Rinehart, Mary Roberts, *The Bat* (Samuel French, 1932)
Excellent mystery play.

Saunders, Louise, *The Knave of Hearts* (Longmans, 1926)
Romantic one-act play — good for St. Valentine's Day.

Schauffler, Robert H., and Sanford, A. P., eds., *Plays for Our American Holidays* (Dodd, 1928)

Sherwood, Robert Emmet, *Abe Lincoln in Illinois* (Scribner, 1939)

Dramatic episodes in the pre-presidential life of Lincoln.

Simon, S. Sylvan, *Thrillers* (Samuel French, 1937)

Struther, Jan, *Mrs. Miniver* (Dramatic Pub. Co., Chicago)

Adapted from Miss Struther's book about England in World War II.

Tarkington, Booth, *Monsieur Beaucaire,* dr. by Ethel Hale Freeman (Walter H. Baker Co., 1916)

A costume play with mystery and romance — hoop skirts, wigs, and buckled shoes, and a duel for a lady.

Thomas, Charles Swain, *Atlantic Book of Junior Plays* (Little, Brown, 1924)

Good plays for acting or reading.

Ullman, Samuel S., *Plays of America's Achievements; Plays of America's Growth* (Dodd, 1940)

Dramatic moments in American history, invention, and research.

Walker, Stuart, *Portmanteau Plays* (Stewart and Kidd Co., 1917)

You can put the scenery for these in a suitcase.

BOOKS ABOUT PLAY PRODUCTION

Bendick, Jeanne, and Bendick, Robert, *Television Works Like This* (McGraw, 1949)

Answers nearly any question you may have on television.

Daugherty, Charles M., *Let 'Em Roll* (Viking, 1950)

If you are interested in movies, you will like this one.

Korn, Terry, and Korn, Elizabeth P., *Trailblazer to Television* (Scribner, 1950)

Naumberg, Nancy, *We Make the Movies* (Norton, 1937)

Information by specialists in each branch of moviemaking.

Henle from Guillumette

The Spirit of Adventure

THE title of this section is a high-sounding phrase, no doubt, but it stands for something real. Ask yourself these questions: What lies behind the urge to explore and the desire to discover more and more of knowledge? What sustains the sheer human will to accomplish the seemingly impossible? It can be nothing less than this thing we call the spirit of adventure.

Since the earliest times, when most of the world was hidden from view and inaccessible to men, a spirit of adventure has led them to conquer the wilderness, to settle new lands, to build nations and empires, and to industrialize and civilize whole continents. Behind the map of today's world is the story of people who were willing to pioneer and investigate, to explore the unknown.

Even in our daily lives, in our ordinary experiences, we can sense adventure. We can hardly cease to be interested in ourselves and others; we can hardly fail to discover something new almost every moment. Think of it this way: all of us take part in a personal adventure. We enjoy the humor and ponder the tragedy of human experience as it unfolds before us, from childhood to the time of youth, to adulthood, and even to old age. Heroic or not, this too is adventure.

Now adventure finds its way into literature in several forms. Fiction writers and dramatists invent imaginary incidents and complications to give their readers a feeling of suspense and excitement. But not all the adventures in reading are imaginary. Many of them are recordings of fact and actual experience; they are, in short, nonfictional. You are already acquainted with biography, which is the factual recording of a person's life. In the selections that follow you can read another kind of nonfiction in the form of personal narratives as well as articles and essays.

Personal narratives, like Fitzroy Maclean's exciting account of his exploits in Persia, are found in the literature of practically all ages and all nations. Marco Polo, in the fourteenth century, wrote a book about his trip to the Far

East that is still read, not only as a source book for historians but also for the keen reading enjoyment it affords. You may remember, too, that the first book about America was the personal narrative of Captain John Smith, who wanted to tell his fellow Englishmen what it was like in the new land.

Articles and essays are an equally familiar kind of nonfiction writing. Actually, there isn't much distinction between the two. We think of articles, which usually occur in newspapers and magazines, as presenting various kinds of information or discussions of issues and ideas of current interest. There is almost no limit to the subject matter of articles. They may discuss the economic situation in China today, or the styles of women's clothes in 1900, or perhaps give glimpses of outstanding personalities in public life. An essay may cover the same subject matter, but it is likely to be less direct and factual and more personal in tone than the usual magazine article. For example, you will soon read an essay by the American humorist Robert Benchley, in which he gives us his conception of the " good, old-fashioned Christmas." His writing is light and informal, and his purpose, like that of most essayists, is not mainly to inform but to entertain in a highly personal style.

Articles and essays are popular reading fare today, as you know if you look at current publications. Americans are inclined to like their reading material fresh, crisp, and brief. They keep up with the daily news through their newspapers, and with the world of thought and ideas through magazines. In both they find a wide variety of interesting material, realistic, scientific, humorous, and critical. As you read the selections that follow, you will see how such writing bridges the gap between one mind and another and helps you to share in another kind of adventure.

EXPLORING THE UNKNOWN

THOMAS R. HENRY

The South Pole

For many years it was the dream of scientists and lovers of adventure to reach the unexplored area of the South Pole. Explorers from various countries fitted out expeditions and made daring attempts to reach the pole, each man hoping to plant there the flag of his native land and claim for his country the great Antarctic region. Of these, two men especially claim our attention, one for his success, and the other for his heroic failure. The following essay, from *The White Continent* by Thomas R. Henry, tells the story of these two men who pitted their courage and their fortitude against the elements – one to conquer, the other to die.

For Better Reading . . . Making comparisons and noting contrasts between persons, real or fictitious, adds to our understanding of all people – and of ourselves. Try to keep track of any important likenesses or differences in the characteristics of the two famous explorers, Scott and Amundsen. At the end you should be able to tell what qualities of greatness they had, quite apart from their actual accomplishments.

THE South Pole, the mathematical bottom of the world, is in the middle of a depression, about five hundred feet deep, very close to the center of the great polar plateau. This point, above which the sun stands still through most of the ninety-day Antarctic summer, has been reached four times by man – twice by land and twice by air. The pole has absolutely no distinguishing characteristic in the seemingly infinite desolation of whiteness. On his last flight, however, Admiral Byrd reported that the sastrugi[1] – wind-piled windrows[2] of snow which cover the plateau – seemed a little less prominent there, indicating milder winds, and all who have reached the pole have reported excellent weather. It may be that this particular spot lies beyond the tempests.

Attainment of the mathematical

[1] **sastrugi** (sȧs·trōō′gĭ).
[2] **windrows:** ridges.

point where every direction is north is no longer of any particular scientific interest, but the pole will remain for all time a symbol of human courage and endurance. There, within a few days of each other in the Antarctic summer of 1911–12, arrived the Norwegian sailor, Roald Amundsen,[1] and the British naval officer, Sir Robert Falcon Scott, after a dramatic race through a vast unknown of haunted blizzards. For one the race ended in death. To the other it brought only a continuation of lifelong frustration.

Scott, then a thirty-five-year-old Royal Navy captain, led his first Antarctic expedition under the auspices of the Royal Geographic Society in 1901. After an easy passage through the Ross Pack his wooden ship *Discovery* was frozen in at McMurdo Sound for the winter. This expedition accomplished little, but the commander returned to England with the virus of the green southern lights in his blood and the determination to be the first man to stand at the bottom of the world. Appealing to the patriotism of Englishmen and obtaining a small government grant, he succeeded in raising funds for the purchase of the large Dundee whaler *Terra Nova* and in enlisting a group of able scientists and sailors.

Scott reached Melbourne on October 12, 1910. There he heard for the first time that the Norwegian explorer Roald Amundsen, first man to sail through the Northwest Passage and an Antarctic veteran who had served as mate on a Belgian expedition twelve years before, also was on his way to the Ross Sea and planned a sledge dash to the South Pole.

The dream of discovering the North Pole had dominated Amundsen's life from the time he read of the exploits of British and American expeditions which braved the Arctic in the forties and fifties in search of the lost English explorer Sir John Franklin. With an unshakable singleness of purpose virtually every act of his life was directed toward standing on the top of the world. He flew over it at long last, but with only a brief glimpse of the long-sought goal far below. Most men who knew him agreed that to the day he crashed to his death on a rescue mission over the Arctic north of Spitsbergen, Amundsen was a thwarted, unhappy man. He never considered the South Pole more than a steppingstone to the North Pole.

As a youth he had rebelled at working in his father's shipping office at Oslo. For two years he attended medical school at the urging of his mother, but without interest. Then, the first step on his way to the North Pole, he went to sea as a common sailor on a Norwegian freighter. In 1895 this ship put in at Antwerp, where Amundsen heard of a Belgian expedition to the Antarctic which was being organized, in the face of mounting financial difficulties, by a former artillery officer, Captain Adrien de Gerlache.[2] The twenty-three-year-old Norwegian sailor, obtaining letters of introduction from his celebrated countryman Fridtjof Nansen,[3] secured for himself the position of first mate.

For thirteen months the expedition's ship, the *Belgica*,[4] was frozen in the pack and drifted helplessly over the fog-covered Sea of Bellingshausen.[5] Scurvy and insanity attacked the crew. Gerlache was incapacitated; Lieutenant Danco, second in command, died,

[1] **Roald Amundsen** (rō′äl ä′mo͝on·sĕn).

[2] **Adrien de Gerlache** (ȧ·drē·äɴ′ dē zhĕr·lȧsh′).

[3] **Fridtjof Nansen** (frĭt′yŏf nän′sĕn): Arctic explorer.

[4] **Belgica** (bĕl′jĭ·kȧ).

[5] **Bellingshausen** (bĕl′ĭngz·hou′z′n).

and Amundsen found himself essentially in command.

The *Belgica* expedition provided Amundsen's education as a polar explorer, but he thought of applying it only to the great quest of his life at the other end of the earth. He returned to Europe and established himself at Hamburg, where he purchased, largely with promissory notes,[1] the forty-seven-ton sloop *Gjoa*[2] for a projected expedition to the North Magnetic Pole. Promised contributions were not forthcoming, however, and Amundsen was pestered with note collectors. One morning the *Gjoa* and its crew were missing — the explorer had fled from his creditors toward the open sea where they could not follow him. For three years they were left to worry about their money.

During this time Amundsen sailed through the Northwest Passage, thus finally bringing the dreams of the Cabots, Frobisher, and Henry Hudson to reality. Incidentally, he "fixed the position" of the magnetic pole, a claim which experts on the earth's magnetism would smile at today. It is noteworthy that Amundsen, like his great contemporary, Sir Ernest Shackleton, was cynical in his relations to science. He never evidenced any devotion to it except when he was attempting to raise money. To him adventure, wild beauty in action, was its own excuse.

By lecturing, writing, and collecting on promises Amundsen was able to settle the debts from which he had fled. The time had come for the greatest adventure of all — to sail northward in the Arctic explorer Nansen's old ship, the *Fram,* allow himself to be frozen in the ice, and drift across the North Pole. It would cost a great deal of money.

Again Amundsen went begging with pleas "for the sake of science." This time, because of his larger reputation, the gods of the market place were kinder, but still funds were forthcoming with discouraging reluctance. Then, in 1909, came a crushing blow — news that the American, Admiral Robert E. Peary, had planted the Stars and Stripes on the top of the world.

Amundsen met this with the most astounding move in the history of exploration. He was still ill-financed, ill-staffed, ill-equipped. But the *Fram* was in seaworthy condition, and, confiding his intentions only to his brother, he set sail, presumably in conformity with the plans outlined to his backers. The *Fram* went south instead of north. At Madeira the captain told his crew the real situation — they were on their way to the South Pole.

His reasoning was even more surprising than the decision itself: If he could reach the bottom of the world the publicity value would be so great that he would have no trouble raising fresh funds to resume his expedition to the top of the world. Otherwise he counted the attainment of the South Pole as of no importance; the Antarctic was simply a barrier to be crossed on the way to the Arctic.

When Amundsen made his extraordinary decision he was well aware that Scott was on the point of sailing south, but he rationalized the situation to his own satisfaction. Discovery of the South Pole, he said, was only one of the announced objectives of the British and, to judge from previous announcements, not the chief one; the expedition had a quite varied program of exploration and scientific research upon which he had not the slightest intention of intru-

[1] **promissory** (prŏm'ĭ·sō'rĭ) **notes:** written promises to pay certain sums upon demand.
[2] **Gjoa** (yû'ȧ).

sion. His single purpose was to reach the pole and return to civilization as soon as possible.

Thus the stage was set for one of the epic tragedies of history.

Scott encountered a far more difficult pack on his second trip and was greatly delayed in reaching McMurdo Sound, where he established the expedition's base camp on Cape Evans. While the camp was being set up, the *Terra Nova* skirted eastward along the barrier edge to the Bay of Whales. There the commander's worst fears were confirmed. Amundsen had already arrived in the *Fram*, and his men were busy building Framheim,[1] the base camp near Little America. The Norwegians were sixty-nine miles closer to the pole than the British at Cape Evans.

Clearly it was to be a race for glory between two explorers and two flags.

The winter night closed down on the rival camps, and both parties toed the mark for a head start as soon as the sun rose again over the hummocked ice. Amundsen finally got underway on October 19, 1911. Scott started from McMurdo Sound thirteen days later. He planned to follow rather closely the path onto the high continental plateau which had been blazed a few years earlier by his former associate, Ernest Shackleton.

Scott's plan looked excellent on paper. He proposed to advance toward the pole by easy stages with two supporting parties, laying down a supply depot with sufficient food and fuel for six weeks every sixty-five miles along the 922-mile route.

At the outset all the supplies were to be carried on motor sledges. In these the commander had little confidence; they bogged down in the snow and were essentially useless in areas of rough ice and crevasses. However, they could be expected to bear most of the load for the first stages of the trip over the smooth surface of the shelf and could be sent back after the remaining supplies had been reloaded on sledges drawn by Manchurian ponies. Two dog teams accompanied the expedition for emergencies.

The ponies were expected to haul the supplies to the foot of the great Beardmore glacier, probably Antarctica's mightiest ice river, which forms a broad highway between towering mountain ranges to the polar plateau. Each pony dragged 650 pounds; once a cache was set up, the animal was to be killed and its flesh stored to augment the food supply. When the mouth of the Beardmore was reached, the last pony was to be slaughtered and the second supporting party sent back with the dogs. On the trek up the glacier and across the plateau the remaining supplies were to be hauled on hand-drawn sledges by the four men chosen to accompany Scott to the pole.

Bad luck dogged the realization of this program. Three of the ponies drowned when sea ice broke up beneath them near Cape Evans before the start of the polar dash. In the middle of the shelf the party was marooned in a four-day blizzard, followed by unprecedented warm weather with the temperature barely at the freezing point. The ice surface was covered with slush eighteen inches deep. Through this Antarctic morass the party waded and wallowed for fourteen days.

On December 16, nearly seven weeks after the start from Cape Evans and long after the last pony had been slaughtered, hard "blue ice" was

[1] **Framheim** (frȧm'hīm).

reached at an elevation of three thousand feet up the glacier. Thenceforth the pace was more rapid and the polar party emerged on the plateau, 6,800 feet above the level of the Ross Shelf, five days later.

On January 4 the last supporting party turned back and Scott with his four companions started the final lap of their outward journey, a distance which they estimated at about 145 miles. Skies were clear and weather excellent . . . the men had every reason to believe that their hard luck had run out. Of even more significance, they felt that they had won the race with Amundsen; they had seen no trace of the Norwegians along the trail. The flag of England would be the first at the bottom of the world.

They were due for a rude awakening. Less than sixty miles from the South Pole, after crossing latitude 88, Scott's party came upon fresh sledge tracks. There could be only one interpretation: Their rivals were at least several days ahead of them. Their seventy-five days of weary, painful trudging over barrier, glacier, and plateau had been in vain. A little later, on January 17, they sighted a tent above which flew the flag of Norway. Inside the tent Amundsen had left a letter for Scott, together with an account of his exploit to be forwarded to the king of Norway that his triumph might be recognized in the event he himself perished on the return journey to Framheim. He had written:

Polheim
15 December, 1911

DEAR CAPT. SCOTT:

As you are probably the first to reach this area after us I will ask you kindly to forward this letter to King Haakon VII. If you can use any of the articles left in this tent please do not hesitate to do so. The sledge left outside may be of use to you. With best regards I wish you safe return.

Yours truly,
ROALD AMUNDSEN

Perhaps no man ever suffered a more bitter disillusion than did Scott at the South Pole on January 18, 1912. The proof of his rival's triumph was indisputable; Amundsen had won the race with less planning, less expense, less equipment. The Englishman could not understand, and did not when he died, how it had been done. For him the flag of the Norwegians was the banner of death. He was far behind schedule, and even with the best of luck his party could not hope to reach the shelter of Cape Evans, more than nine hundred miles away, before the onset of the Antarctic autumn with its rapidly lengthening black nights and blizzards.

Scott lingered only long enough to fix the precise position of the bottom of the earth. The spot agreed upon was less than a half mile from that established by Amundsen — a remarkable example of the accuracy of both men, considering the difficulty of solar observation in the Antarctic.

With heavy hearts the five Englishmen started their return journey on January 19, wearily dragging their heavy sledge behind them through the sand-like snow which covers the plateau.

It was an uphill road away from the pole; the mathematical southernmost point of the world lies in a five-hundred-foot depression in the surface of the plateau. The heavy haul was especially difficult because of the thin air at an altitude of ten thousand feet above sea level. Add to this the fact that the men were already badly weakened by the hardships they had experienced and had been brought to a nerve-shattering climax by the sight of Amundsen's flag.

Four of the party were tough little men — physically, mentally, and morally tough and resilient. The fifth, Petty Officer Edgar Evans of the British navy, was a two-hundred-pound six-footer and a veteran sledge man. He had been the wheelhorse of the expedition, the man always called for when any job required exceptional physical strength; because of this he was picked especially for the polar dash. This probably was one of Scott's worst mistakes. Had he chosen a small man there is at least a possibility that the party might have returned safely. Paradoxical as it may seem, history shows rather clearly that big, strong men are not well equipped to be explorers — they seldom show the stamina necessary in emergencies.

Almost from the start of the return trip Evans, who until then had been a cheery fellow, began to complain and drop behind. It was obvious to the others that he was breaking fast; the man was sick. His feet and hands were badly frostbitten. He no longer could pull his share of the burden and finally had to be relieved altogether. Very likely this unhappy change could be interpreted as due to food deficiency; Evans could not fuel his big body on the rations sufficient for the smaller men.

Then came the day when he stumbled on the hummocked ice of the Beardmore glacier and sustained a brain concussion. There was an emergency council. By this time all realized that the chances of getting back alive were very small at best, and essentially nonexistent if the party was burdened with a sick man; the decision, however, was not to abandon Evans. The tent was pitched and Scott reconciled himself to a long and probably fatal delay until the sailor was able to travel again. But that night the injured man died without regaining consciousness, thus giving his companions one more chance to push ahead. It grew colder and colder as they stumbled and staggered toward the mouth of the Beardmore through white darkness and blizzard. All now suffered intensely from frostbite and were constantly growing weaker. It was then that Scott ordered the medical officer and second in command of the party, Dr. E. A. Wilson, whose accomplishments on the expedition rate second only to those of the commander himself, to do what they had agreed upon from the beginning if the worst came — distribute the opium tablets. If anyone felt he could endure no more he had only to swallow one of these white pills and fall into a sleep from which he would not awake.

The man now in the worst physical condition was Captain L. E. G. Oates of the British army. His feet and hands were frozen and at times he became delirious. In these last hours he thought bitterly that he had brought the disgrace of failure on the regiment he represented — the ultra-swanky Iniskillin Dragoons. He knew also that he was a burden, and would constantly become a worse burden, on the others. He continually asked the doctor's advice.

"Slog on, keep slogging on," was all Wilson could answer.

One night when the four were holed up in the tent during a blizzard, Oates told the others he was going for a walk. He stepped out in the storm and was never seen again. The men knew his purpose and did not try to stop him.

The three survivors, Scott, Dr. Wilson, and Lieutenant H. R. Bowers of the British Marines, crawled heroically on over the crevassed ice. Their one remaining hope was to reach One Ton

Two scenes from the movie " Scott of the Antarctic." Above, *Captain Scott pauses before the grave of the seaman Vince, one of the first casualties in his ill-fated expedition.* Below, *a sledge party moving across an " infinite desolation of whiteness."* (*Ealing Studios from J. Arthur Rank, Inc.*)

Camp, a cache of food and fuel left on the shelf about halfway between the mouth of the Beardmore and their home base.

Oates had died on March 17, his birthday. The others crept forward two or three more days, covering about twenty miles. Their supplies were nearly exhausted. They still had eleven miles to go when a blizzard broke around them and they pitched their tent for the last time. Even if they had been able to reach the supply depot it is doubtful if they could have gone farther; their feet were frozen now.

So when they crawled into the tent there was little doubt in their minds that it would be their grave. Perhaps they were not too uncomfortable in their last hours. Their sleeping bags were stiff with ice which melted with the warmth of their bodies as long as any warmth was left and the canvas protected their faces from the screaming blizzard outside.

How long they survived in the tent nobody knows — ten or eleven days at best. Scott remained busy to the last. He wrote letters to Dr. Wilson's wife and to Lieutenant Bowers' mother in England. For himself he wrote to Sir James Barrie: [1]

We are in a desperate state, feet frozen, etc. No fuel and a long way from food, but it would do your heart good to be in our tent, to hear our songs and the cheery conversation as to what we will do when we get to Hut Point.

Later: We are very near the end but have not and will not lose good cheer. We have had four days of storm in our tent and nowhere's food and fuel. We did intend to finish ourselves when things proved like this but we have decided to die naturally in the track.

One of the dying explorer's last acts was to scribble with frozen fingers the following apology to his countrymen for what he regarded as his failure as a British empire builder:

The causes of the disaster are not due to faulty organization, but to misfortune in all risks which had to be undertaken.

The loss of pony transport in March 1911 obliged me to start later than I had intended and obliged the limits of the stuff to be transported to be narrowed.

The weather throughout the outward journey, and especially the long gale in 83 south, stopped us. We fought these untoward events with a will and conquered, but it cut into our provision reserves.

Every detail of our food supplies, clothing, and depots made on the interior ice sheet and over that long stretch of nine hundred miles to the pole and back worked out to perfection. The advance party should have returned to the glacier in fine form and with a surplus of food but for the astonishing failure of the man whom we had least expected to fail. Edgar Evans was thought the strongest man of the party.

The Beardmore glacier is not difficult in fine weather. but on our return we did not get a single completely fine day; this, with a sick companion, enormously increased our difficulties. As I have said elsewhere, we got into frightfully rough ice and Edgar Evans received a concussion of the brain — he died a natural death but left us a shaken party with the season unduly advanced.

But all the facts enumerated above were as nothing compared to the surprise that awaited us on the barrier. I maintain that our arrangements for returning were quite adequate and that no one in the world would have expected the temperature and

[1] **Barrie:** famous Scottish writer, author of several novels, including *The Little Minister* and *Sentimental Tommy,* and a long list of plays — *Peter Pan, Quality Street,* etc.

surfaces we encountered at this time of year. On the summit in latitude 85–86 we had minus 20, minus 30. On the barrier in latitude 82, 10,000 feet lower, we had minus 30 in the day, minus 47 at night pretty regularly, with a constant headwind during our day marches. It is clear that these circumstances came on very suddenly, and our wreck is certainly due to this sudden advent of severe weather which does not seem to have any satisfactory cause.

I do not think human beings ever came through such a month as we have come through, and we should have got through in spite of the weather but for the sickening of a second companion, Captain Oates, and a shortage of fuel in our depots for which I cannot account, and finally but for the storm which had fallen upon us within thirteen miles of the depot at which I had hoped to secure final supplies. Surely misfortune could scarcely have exceeded this last blow.

We arrived within thirteen miles of One Ton Camp with fuel for one hot meal and food for two days. For four days we have been unable to leave the tent – the gale howling about us. We are weak, writing is difficult, but for my own sake I do not regret this journey, which has shown that Englishmen can endure hardships, help one another, and meet death with as great a fortitude as ever in the past. We took risks; we knew we took them; things have come out against us; and therefore we have no cause for complaint but bow to the will of Providence, determined still to do our best to the last.

But if we have been willing to give our lives to this enterprise which is for the honor of our country, I appeal to our countrymen to see that those who depend on us are properly cared for. Had we lived I should have had a tale to tell of the hardihood, courage, and endurance of my companions which would have stirred the heart of every Englishman. These rough notes and our dead bodies must tell the tale, but surely a great rich country like ours will see that those who are dependent on us are properly provided for.

R. Scott

Scott, Dr. Wilson, and Lieutenant Bowers died in the tent on the ice about 150 miles from the McMurdo Sound base on or about March 29. Eight months later, at the start of the Antarctic summer, a search party found the bodies, together with the commander's notes and diaries. These constitute the greatest of all epics of polar exploration.

Robert Falcon Scott had failed in his mission from his own time-circumscribed point of view.[1] Through a series of adverse circumstances – perhaps, despite his dying protests, through his own inadequate preparations to some extent – he had been beaten in the race to the bottom of the world by a more practical and less temperamental man. But in the long sweep of history he had succeeded with a measure of success far greater than would have come with the mere attainment of a mathematical point on the surface of the globe before anybody else.

With their frozen footprints down the cascading ice of the mighty Beardmore, and across the ridged, crevassed [2] barrier, Scott and his men wrote a story of human fortitude and heroism for which history shows few equals and which will be an inspiration for all who follow them.

Thirty-five years after the tragedy, a United States Navy plane was soaring

[1] **time-circumscribed point of view:** Encircled by his own immediate and pressing day-by-day problems, he could not foresee that in the long slow march of time, he would become famous even in defeat.

[2] **crevassed** (krĕ·văst′): with deep openings or fissures.

John Mills as Captain Scott – even Scott's boundless courage and determination could not bring him success. (*Ealing Studios from J. Arthur Rank, Inc.*)

over the barrier on its way to explore the mountains west of the Ross Sea, many of which had been named by Scott but upon whose towering majesty he and his companions had only looked from afar.

It was uncomfortably warm in the cockpit. Lieutenant George H. Anderson, the pilot, started to raise a window.

"George," quietly remarked Commander William M. Hawkes, the commander of the flight, "do you realize that we are complaining about the heat almost exactly above the spot where a party of very brave men froze to death?"

Hawkes had been a lifelong admirer of Scott. To him this featureless, unmarked, and unmarkable spot in the great ice desert – longitude 169.15 east, latitude 79.38 south – was holy ground. He had kept careful watch for it ever since the mission had left Little America.

Thus men fly in relative comfort and safety today where Scott and his men crawled through the blizzard and the night to their doom.

The Norwegians made their first start for the pole on September 8 with eight men, seven sleds, and ninety dogs. After three days in blinding snow, with the temperature sinking at one time to 108 below zero Fahrenheit, they were obliged to turn back. From the failure, however, Amundsen gained invaluable experience. Impatiently he and his party waited at Framheim for signs of the Antarctic spring, the reappearance of birds and seals around the Bay of Whales. When the first of the colony of Weddell seals that live among the pressure ridges crawled out of their home in a crevasse, he accepted the animals' judgment that winter was done. The second start was made on October 19, nearly two weeks before Scott was able to get underway with his sleds drawn by ponies. This time Amundsen and four companions went across the shelf with four sleds, each drawn by thirteen dogs. The sleds were lightly loaded. Provisions sufficient for four months already had been cached at the foot of the Axel Heiberg[1] glacier.

Across the barrier and up the glacier they fought through fog and blizzard. Their ascent of the Axel Heiberg to the plateau was one of the most difficult feats yet accomplished by Antarctic explorers. It has sometimes been charged that Amundsen had all the luck with weather while Scott got all the bad breaks, but this was only partly true. One party met about as nasty weather as the other, but the Norwegians encountered it on their way to the pole when they were in good physical condition and spurred by enthusiasm, the Englishmen on their way back when they were exhausted from their long journey and low in spirits.

Once on the plateau, Amundsen's troubles were over. The party entered a period of sunny, almost windless days. Both the men and the remaining dogs were in excellent shape after their ordeal of crevasses and tempests. Perhaps most important of all, they found that their days of climbing were over; the ice sheet either was a level plain or, as proved the case as they neared the pole, it sloped gently downward.

Amundsen left as little to luck as possible. Snow beacons, to be used as guides on the way back, were set up every three miles. A cache with provisions for four days was left every sixty miles. For eleven days they moved inland from the head of the Axel Heiberg. The average day's march was about fifteen miles; one day they traveled twenty-eight miles. On December 8 they crossed latitude 88 degrees, 88 minutes south, the farthest point attained by Sir Ernest Shackleton three years earlier.

On the afternoon of December 14 they reached "the spot where the sun stands still." This physical observation entranced Amundsen: the solar disk was continuously directly overhead. It was a bright day with a temperature of 41 below zero. There were no signs of the Englishmen. Amundsen felt briefly the high exultation that comes with a great accomplishment – and then in the northern heavens flashed his star. If he got back to civilization alive he would be the greatest explorer in the world; what he wanted would be his for the asking. In his mind he was already halfway to the North Pole.

The Norwegians stayed four days at the earth's bottom, fixing accurately the position of the pole. They raised the Norse flag and named the entire continental plateau after their sovereign, Haakon[2] VII. They were 870 miles from Framheim and had been fifty-seven days on the way. The return journey was almost a picnic; weather continued nearly perfect and they were able to observe Christmas Eve on the glacier in high spirits, smoking cigars which one member of the party had carried all the way to the Pole for just this occasion. In thirty-eight days they were back at their base, all in excellent condition and with no further reason for remaining in the Antarctic. Meanwhile Scott was struggling through blizzards on the Beardmore.

There has been endless debate on why the Norwegians succeeded while the more experienced English so dismally failed. The difference has been attributed to pure luck, to the fact that Amundsen relied entirely on dogs for transportation, to the shorter route, to the earlier start, to better planning. Probably all these played a part. But all are encompassed in the singleness

[1] **Axel Heiberg** (ăk′s'l hī′bûrg).

[2] **Haakon** (hô′kôn).

of Amundsen's purpose — to get to the pole and back again in the shortest possible time.

He returned to Norway in 1913 — again engaged in pursuit of the real ambition of his life which was to drift with the ice across the North Pole. This time he was thwarted by the start of World War I. Only in 1918 was he able to get underway in the specially constructed ship *Maud,* but the expedition was a failure — the ice did not drift according to his calculations. The war had brought aviation to the fore, and on his fourth attempt in 1926 Amundsen crossed the pole, flying from Spitsbergen to Point Barrow, Alaska, in the semi-rigid dirigible *Norge,* built in Italy. He was accompanied by the American explorer Lincoln Ellsworth.

Making Character Comparisons

1. What characteristics did Scott and Amundsen have in common? In what ways were they different?

2. How did Amundsen regard his South Pole exploit? Why? What view did Scott take of Amundsen's success and of his own failure?

3. Make two columns on a sheet of paper, labeling one "Scott" and the other "Amundsen." List the characteristics of each, underlining those which you think are similar.

4. Aside from the two leaders, compare the rival groups which made the dash to the Pole. Take into consideration their purpose, preparation, experience, difficulties, success, and that elusive factor called "luck."

Thinking It Over

1. What was at stake in the race between Scott and Amundsen, for them personally as well as for their backers? Does the essay suggest that Norway in any way benefited from Amundsen's claim to the South Pole? If you will check the book from which this selection is taken, *The White Continent,* you can find out the present state of national claims to the South Pole.

2. In what way do you think the Scott and Amundsen explorations were valuable scientifically? Incidentally, perhaps one of the science-minded members of the class can explain how it is that all directions from the South Pole are north. What do we now know about Antarctic exploration that neither Scott nor Amundsen knew? Find out what you can about Admiral Byrd's expeditions and about various experiments made by the American armed forces in the Antarctic regions.

3. You have learned that conflict is what holds your interest in many types of writing. How many kinds of conflict (man against man, man against the elements, man against himself, man in competition with others of his group, etc.) can you find in this account? Illustrate your answer by naming specific people and circumstances.

For Your Vocabulary

CONTEXT CLUES: Explain, as best you can from the context, the italicized words in the phrases below; then check with your dictionary.

1. "seemingly *infinite* desolation of whiteness" (p. 401)

2. "a continuation of lifelong *frustration*" (p. 402)

3. "under the *auspices* of the Royal Geographic Society" (p. 402)

4. "he *rationalized* the situation to his own satisfaction" (p. 403)

5. "to *augment* the food supply" (p. 404)

6. "*unprecedented* warm weather" (p. 404)

7. "*Paradoxical* as it may seem, history shows" (p. 406)

8. "fought these *untoward* events" (p. 408)

9. "all are *encompassed* in the singleness of Amundsen's purpose" (p. 411)

OSA JOHNSON

Lion Hunting with Truck and Camera

Some people hunt with high-powered rifles; others think it more sporting to stalk their prey with cameras. Among the most famous camera hunters were Osa and Martin Johnson, who spent years in the African jungles photographing wild animals in their native habitats. In a highly entertaining book called *I Married Adventure,* Osa Johnson tells of their many exciting encounters in the African jungle, such as the one in the following selection. They collected a series of pictures that are unique: lions, tigers, water buffaloes, gorillas, and other untamed beasts, often photographed at close range.

Martin Johnson was killed in an airplane crash in 1937, but his wife has carried on. She has since set forth again on safari, taking with her several automobiles, fourteen persons variously trained for different duties, apparatus for technicolor photography, a helicopter for jungle exploration, and even equipment with which to broadcast from the jungle. Mrs. Johnson, who is only five feet tall, is as great in courage as she is small in stature, as you will soon discover.

LIONS! For a year we lived with them in what Carl Akeley [1] had called the "lions' den," that area some five hundred miles square in Tanganyika Territory [2] to which Carl had taken us shortly before the illness which was to end his life. We worked with lions; we ate and slept with their roars all round us. At times, and with good reason, we feared the great tawny cats, but in the end we grew, as Carl said we would, to respect and love them.

Our equipment consisted roughly of five tents, two water stills,[3] ten motion-picture cameras, eleven still cameras, one hundred thousand feet of film, medical stores, food stuffs, a typewriter and even a phonograph, and guns, of course. In all there was something like four tons of stuff, and our big touring car, together with four trucks, carried the lot.

I drove the touring car with four natives hanging on wherever they could.

[1] **Carl Akeley:** American explorer and sculptor who made several expeditions to Africa for museum specimens. He had died in Africa a few months before the Johnsons started on the expedition which is the subject of this selection.

[2] **Tanganyika** (tăng′găn·yē′kȧ) **Territory:** a large territory in East Africa.

[3] **water stills:** equipment for distilling water.

Martin took the wheel of one of the trucks, which carried two tons of supplies and six boys, while the next truck, equally overloaded, was driven by Urg, our newly acquired Swahili [1] mechanic.

As we rolled into this vast and almost immeasurable domain that is the lion's "happy hunting ground," I thought of Carl Akeley's resentment against the caging of these beautiful beasts. Here, the lion has an abundance for his every need from food and air to freedom, and restraint is probably the one thing he cannot comprehend. Yet for thousands of years, he has been hunted and captured and caged to satisfy the vanity of man. I am deeply in sympathy with those enlightened zoos, such as that at San Diego, dedicated to education rather than to entertainment, which are willing to appropriate sufficient ground to give their lion prizes some of the liberty and color of their native home.

Although the lion has counted more than any other factor in man's dread of Africa, curiously enough man is the only enemy the lion really fears. Hunters from the days of the ancient Ptolemies [2] and before have ranged the plains of Africa with all manner of weapons which were too much even for his magnificent strength and speed and cunning, and it has always surprised me that lions did not somehow remember and that they would trust us at all.

Government has now reduced the menace of the hunter as much as possible by high license fees and other protections, but there is still considerable wanton killing. Martin and I have always done all we could to encourage the setting aside of game preserves, and it was one of his special hopes to see the Serengetti [3] Plains made into a protected area where lions could be hunted only with the camera, which now has finally become a fact. . . .

For the most part, the lion is a thoroughly agreeable personage. He lives a most leisurely existence, loafs and sleeps a great deal, has just as playful moods as a house cat and just as decided a personality. He minds his own business, is very fond of his family, and takes his duties as family protector and provider very seriously. As a youngster he usually attaches himself to a pride or "gang" of young males, and they roam about together, sometimes for years, having a hilarious time, sharing their food and their fun, until he finally settles down to domestic bliss and the raising of a family. When he becomes a grandfather and too old to keep up with his family and friends, he is ejected from the pride and left to roam about alone, and it is then that he often becomes a "rogue," probably a neurasthenic [4] condition not unfamiliar to humans.

Naturally, being of the cat family, he is carnivorous.[5] He kills to eat. Except in self-defense, he seldom disturbs a living thing, although I have known him to attack without provocation and have always been careful not to startle or annoy him. When attacked or wounded, he never retreats, but fights as long as there is a spark of life in his magnificent body. . . .

Martin had the complacent look of a man who has just finished a large and thoroughly satisfactory meal. What he had just finished, however, was not a

[1] **Swahili** (swä·hē′lē): member of an African tribe living chiefly in Zanzibar.
[2] **Ptolemies** (tŏl′ĕ·mĭz): kings of Egypt from the third century B.C. to the first century A.D.
[3] **Serengetti** (sĕr′ĕn·gĕt′ē).
[4] **neurasthenic** (nū′răs·thĕn′ĭk): caused by emotional disturbances.
[5] **carnivorous** (kär·nĭv′ō·rŭs): meat-eating.

meal but an afternoon's photography in the midst of fourteen lions. The big beasts had been as indifferent to us as we, in turn, might have been to a couple of field mice; and while this attitude on their part gave us a comfortable enough feeling, I can't say it was exactly flattering.

My husband had exposed several magazines of film and was about to put still another into the camera.

"Well, my gracious," I said, "haven't you got about enough?"

Martin grinned at me a little sheepishly. "Oh, I guess so," he said, "but, golly, aren't they wonderful?"

He looked fondly at the sleek, lovely animals. For hours they had boxed and mauled one another. When tired they had slept, usually on their backs with their feet in the air and snoring mightily. They had been through this routine several times. There were perhaps eight or nine lionesses among them, but very little ill temper or jealousy was displayed, and in fact, a better-mannered or more amiable group – man or beast – could not be imagined.

"Of course they're wonderful," I replied, "but they've eaten nothing in hours. Suppose they suddenly decide they're hungry?"

I stepped on the starter and began backing away, whereupon one of the husky young males decided to challenge our departure. He bristled, his eyes sharpened with excitement, and he started to follow us, measuring his sinewy, menacing stride exactly to the roll of our car. There was only one safe thing to do, and that was to stop, because a lion, like any other member of the cat family, finds a retreating object almost irresistible. Martin trained his gun on the animal's great head.

Looking up at us in mild surprise that we should have stopped, and a little disappointed, I think, at our taking the fun out of his little game of pursuit, the lion sniffed at our left front tire, then bit it gently. The taste of rubber was new to him, apparently, and he wrinkled his nose, not quite sure that he liked it. Then he tried again. Persuaded this time that it was nothing he cared particularly to eat, but that it might be worth playing with, he began mouthing and growling over it in the manner of a puppy with a rubber ball. The other lions moved up as if on cue, and stood lazily watching this performance.

My husband looked a little anxious. "A puncture wouldn't be a very healthy thing right now," he said, his voice lowered to a cautious key. The more he thought about this possibility, the less he liked it. "The explosion right in his teeth might make him mad, too," he added.

"How about racing the motor?" I offered.

Martin nodded. "Yes. Try it. It might distract him."

I did so. The lion forgot the tire, as we hoped he would, and, cocking his head, listened attentively. So far, so good, I thought, and pushed a little harder on the accelerator. The racing engine now gave off a cloud of noxious fumes, and taking advantage of the astonished sniffs and distaste, which all the lions suddenly exhibited, I backed away, jockeyed out of sight around a huge rock, and streaked off across the plain.

In order to obtain a really complete pictorial history of the lion, it became apparent that we must photograph his nocturnal as well as his daylight habits.

Fortunately, Martin had experimented at length and successfully with night camerawork and knew all the mechanical requirements. Contrary to his usual procedure, however, of rigging up the flashlights and cameras and letting the mechanical devices do the work, he decided that he would probably have better results with lion if we stationed ourselves in our car and he operated the camera himself.

The method followed was to set four flash lamps on firmly planted poles about six feet above the ground, then to fasten the cameras securely to solid platforms three feet in front of and below each lamp. These were connected with dry batteries and controlled by a long "firing" wire. The cameras, especially made for this purpose, took pictures automatically at a speed of one three-hundredths of a second when the light from the flash was at its maximum. . . .

The wretched hyenas[1] were invariably the first to find our bait.[2] Sometimes a well-aimed rock would disperse them, but when they came in packs and seemed on the point of eating all the bait, we were usually forced to shoot one or two to show them that we were in earnest.

"If only the lions would eat the darned old hyenas," Martin grumbled, "everything would be fine."

"Shhh," I whispered. "I think I hear something."

"Oh, there won't be anything doing tonight," my husband said drowsily. "I wish I were in bed." This said, he promptly went to sleep.

The sky was overcast; there was no moon and the darkness was black and thick and cold. I remembered how quietly lions moved on their padded paws. I also derived what comfort I could from the fact that we had sat in open cars many times before, with lions all around us, and that so far we had not been eaten.

Then I heard a tearing sound, and a chewing and gulping and crunching and, along with this, a sort of purring growl.

I nudged Martin, but he was too fast asleep for gentle methods to have effect. I pinched him. He said "ouch"; the crunching, accompanied only by a deep growl, went steadily on.

"Golly!" my husband said. He turned on his electric torch and there, sitting right in front of us and wearing one of the finest manes I have ever seen, was surely the king himself – the king of all the Tanganyika lions. Lifting his great head slowly the big animal looked disdainfully straight into our light. . . .

My husband now put our flashlight and cameras into operation. The lion dropped his piece of meat, bared his teeth and roared, and then, with an abruptness that left me trembling and with my gun still pointed at his head, he went back to his feast.

Others of his family joined him. Several of them were his wives, apparently, and the smaller ones might have been his half-grown sons. They were a fine-looking lot and formed a perfect picture.

"Oh, that's great! That's great!" I heard Martin whispering to himself. He pressed the button. Nothing happened. Again he pressed it with all his might, and there was no sign of a flash. Frantically he pulled the wires from the button and touched them together, but still without result.

"Well," he said, "I guess there's nothing else to do."

[1] **hyenas** (hī·ē′nȧz): large, strong, but cowardly animals.

[2] **bait:** In a previous passage, Mrs. Johnson tells of placing zebra meat in the area of the cameras to attract the lions.

He was looking straight out to where the lions were feeding.

I knew what he meant, but I wouldn't believe him. "What do you mean?" I demanded.

"I've got to get out there and fix it, that's all."

He was out of the car before I could stop him. I caught him by the collar.

"You're crazy," I said, half crying.

"Give me the sawed-off gun," was all he said.

So I drove the lions off the kill by throwing the powerful searchlight of our car in their faces, tooting the auto horn and yelling, covering Martin the while with my gun. The lions retreated about twenty yards, and in a few brief minutes, which seemed like an eternity, my husband found the loose connection, and returned to the car.

"Don't you ever do that again!" I said, practically in collapse.

Martin went straight to work, though I saw that he was shaking a little.

The lion king, having eaten his fill, apparently decided now to investigate the flashlights and cameras. He even gave one of the cameras an experimental bite.

"You let that camera alone!" my husband yelled, completely beside himself.

The majestic cat glanced our way indifferently, then began chewing at the base on which the camera was fastened. The whole thing went over.

Martin got out of the car again and began throwing rocks and anything else that came to hand. To add to the complication, one of the younger lions now decided to follow the cue of the older one, and seizing one of the wires, tugged at it until he had torn it and several other wires from their fastenings.

We sat there throwing rocks, shooting our guns into the air, yelling until we were hoarse, but not until those two lions had pulled down every wire, battery, and camera, and pole of our equipment were they satisfied. Then they strolled off, their tails waving proudly, and our night of flashlight photography was definitely at an end.

A few days later we came upon a large pride of young males resting under a cluster of trees and we stopped to watch. They were extremely curious and began edging up to look us over. They were so playful and frisky that Martin obtained some new and very valuable film. We decided to lunch there and climbed out through the aperture at the top of the truck and sat down to enjoy our sandwiches and to watch.

At the sight of our food, the lions came up close to the car and sat down like a bunch of hungry beggars. I threw them some partridge legs, which they tasted and then licked their chops as much as to say, "Pretty high-toned food for a jungle lion."

For an hour they played about us, within a few feet of the car, bit at the tires, and nipped at one another and had a rowdy time. . . .

Perhaps it was experiences of this sort that made us a little reckless; that had us thinking of the huge felines [1] in terms of fireside tabbies. At any rate, we were on foot one very hot day, our camera and gunbearers were with us, of course, when we turned a sort of corner past a jagged rock and there, not twenty yards from us, was a sleeping lion.

The big creature was on his feet almost instantly and facing us. He drew his ears back, switched his tail, and snarled – three signs I didn't at all like. My husband proceeded busily, however, to set up his camera.

"I don't like his looks, Martin," I said

[1] **felines** (fē'līnz): cats.

cautiously. At the same time I signaled for my gun.

"Oh, he's all right," my husband said. "A little cranky, maybe, but just bluffing." He started to crank the camera.

Then, with a low growl, the lion started slowly toward us, his tail lashing from side to side. How at such a moment I could notice, and sharply at that, the ripple of his hard shoulder muscles under his shining yellow coat, I don't know.

"He's going to charge, Martin – I tell you he is!"

"I don't think so," my husband said, biting hard on his cigar.

The lion, crouching tensely now, stared at us in what seemed to be an all-consuming hatred. Then he charged.

Martin's hand continued mechanically to crank the camera.

The animal looked as large as a bull as he leaped toward us – his mane flying, fangs bared. I seemed to be watching in a prolonged, timeless sort of daze, and then, without really being aware of what I was doing, I shot. Afterward I couldn't even recall taking aim.

The lion seemed to hesitate in mid-air and then fell just thirteen feet from the camera's tripod.

To give an adequate picture of our almost innumerable encounters with lions of the Tanganyika region would require many weeks to tell. There were triumphs and disappointments. We worked long hours under the most discouraging conditions. We saw the leonine prototypes[1] of the entire human race; the clown, the outcast, the misfit, the arrogant, the tragic, the noble, the dictator, yes, and even the flirt, and we made photographic records of all of these in their natural habitat.

Sometimes our adventures were exciting; other times they were plain drudgery. Much of the time we were happy and comfortable; some of the time as on all our *safaris,* we went through almost unbearable hardships. It was the sum total that mattered to us both, however, and there was an immense satisfaction in being able to present the true picture of this noble animal to the millions of people who had thought of him as a vicious, treacherous, bloodthirsty beast.

[1] **leonine prototypes** (lē′ō·nīn prō′tō·tīps): lion-like counterparts or likenesses.

Thinking It Over

1. What do you think about this kind of hunting? What rewards does it offer? What are its special dangers?
2. The Johnsons preferred to shoot with a camera but on the occasion described here they had to kill. Why?
3. What evidence is there that the Johnsons were happily married and worked well as a team? How did they show courage and resourcefulness each in his own way? What seemed to you Mrs. Johnson's most unusual skill?
4. If you have a camera enthusiast among you, perhaps he can describe the photographic equipment necessary for work like the Johnsons'. Why were water stills a part of their jungle equipment?
5. What is the advantage of the helicopter in jungle exploration? How could Martin have used it in the situation described on page 416?
6. At one point the statement is made that "man is the only animal which the lion really fears," yet this narrative does not show lions being frightened. How do you account for this?
7. Pretend that you are broadcasting from Mrs. Johnson's camp in East Africa. Tell what you can see from your jungle broadcasting station and describe some of the incidents related by Mrs. Johnson. Prepare a regular script, time it, and read it, using a dummy "mike" if you have no broadcasting equipment in your school.

For Your Vocabulary

REBUILDING CONTEXTS: From the following list of italicized words, select — and explain — the words which properly complete the phrases below as they occur in the story:

aperture	nocturnal
complacent	pride
disdainfully	provocation
disperse	sinewy
domain	wanton

1. " his immeasurable ——— "
2. " ——— killing "
3. " attaches himself to a ——— "
4. " attack without ——— "
5. " had the ——— look of a man who . . ."
6. " measuring his ———, menacing stride "
7. " his ——— habits "
8. " sometimes a well-aimed rock would ——— them "
9. " looked ——— right into our light "
10. " the ——— at the top of the truck "

ROBERT P. TRISTRAM COFFIN

Cap'n Bibber's Biggest Fish

Fish stories are probably as old as man himself. We can imagine, many thousands of years ago, some grinning Stone Age man arriving at the tribal camp and, pointing to his string of scaly fish, enunciating for the first time those immortal words: " But you ought to have seen the one that got away! "

No present-day writer seems to enjoy the sea more than Robert P. Tristram Coffin, a poet, essayist, and novelist whose many books give us a picture of the coast of Maine where he spent his childhood. In the book *Yankee Coast,* from which this account of Cap'n Bibber is taken, he tells of yachts and dories, of lighthouses and bell buoys, of clammers, lobstermen, sardine fishers, and master mariners, of white yachts and dark little dories " hobnobbing on the bobbing waves," and of eating lobsters hot from the spruce embers of a seashore fire. Because he is a poet, these pictures come alive for us, especially when we read lines like " a hundred herons stand and dream in a hundred coves, up to their blue feathers in crystal." The good clean smells of salt and tar blow through his picturesque pages.

How much of Cap'n Bibber's story is poetic imagination and how much is fact, you can decide for yourself. Cap'n Bibber is a real Maine coast character — but maybe that doesn't guarantee that all this happened!

My friend, Cap'n Cyrus Bibber, has caught a lot of big fish in his time. He has wrestled eight-hundred-pound tunas [1] and brought them home, by the scores. He has caught a sight of big fish, I tell you. But the biggest one he ever met up with got away. And wasn't Cap'n Bibber glad of it!

"There wan't no fish house on this bay that could house that baby." That's the way Cy sums it up. "He'd go fifty tons, easy."

It was this way. Cy was out with some schoolmarms. One of the captain's best hauls is schoolmarms. Summers. Schoolmarms love the Maine coast and love roughing it on salt water almost as much as upcountry clerks who work in a bank.

Speaking of bank clerks, there is that whole bankful of them who are lying now out somewhere, under the Brown Cow or Sequin, in fifty fathoms of water. That's another story, and a sad one. One of the thousand sad tales the rugged bottom of the coast of Maine could tell if deep water could talk. The bays are full of unsolved mysteries.

These bank clerks I was speaking of, girls and men, were off to make a day of it, though it was a hide-and-seek summer Sunday, and you could walk from reef to reef, in places, on the fog. It was their annual field day, and they wouldn't let fog stop them. They were hankering for codfishing and hot lobsters. They put out of Thief Jones's Cove in a boat that had a bad reputation. The *Eve*. The *Eve* was a killer. She had tipped her first owner over and drowned her second. She was narrow where she shouldn't be, topheavy in her cabin, skittish and cranky, and too fast for her own good in heavy going. Her skipper was a young featherweight of an amateur lobsterman. You couldn't tell him a thing, and most people didn't try to.

There were twenty-odd bank clerks to the party. They put out singing *There's a Long, Long Trail* bright and early in the morning, and no one ever saw one of them again. Except the numbskull of a skipper. And he didn't have anything to say. He had been under a week. He came ashore with his leg fouled in a rope, and the empty water keg on the end of it. Oh, yes, and a collie dog. Seems to me he was washed up, too. They had a mass funeral, up in that upcountry town, but there weren't any caskets to put flowers on. One clerk, a girl, showed up the morning after her people had heard she was lost. She had missed her ride to the coast and had spent the night at the home of a friend. She was lucky to miss that boat.

They never found hide or hair of the *Eve*. Did she hit a reef and sink? How could all those strong young men and women, some of them good swimmers, die in that summer water? Cap'n Bibber believes she shipped a wave, with her speed, and they all screamed, landlubber-like, and ran into the cabin, got on one side, put her out of trim, so over she went. They were all trapped in that mahogany coffin. All but her skipper. He took the keg for a life preserver, and lit out. He had sense enough for that. And the collie. But they swam blind in the fog, tuckered out, and went down. That's Cap'n Bibber's theory. Cap'n Bibber swears that if you rigged him up in a diving suit, he could go right down smack upon the *Eve* — he's that sure of his theory and that sure of the bottom of the whole bay. She lies, he says, just in the lee of

[1] **tunas** (tōō'nəz): large, oily, mackerel-like fish.

Brown Cow Reef. It is where there is a mean current sweeping around from Cape Small Point. They are all there in the cabin together. It was a blame shame. The seagulls cry lonesome out there. It makes Cy Bibber sad every time he sails over that spot.

But I was telling you about the big fish and the schoolmarms. Cap'n Bibber always has a mess of them to take out deep-sea fishing summers. He can't go after a lobster trap but what one of these teaching ladies goes with him, steering the boat or getting tangled up in the flywheel of his Palmer Cos-Cob.[1] It doesn't so much matter about the steering, for Cap'n Bibber can always steer himself all right aft, where he stands by the engine. All he does is to take hold of the rope under the rail and keep her headed where he wants her to go, in spite of the schoolteacher. He never lets her know but what she is doing all the steering with the wheel she's playing with.

But this day the boat was loaded down with teachers, and they were a special, de luxe lot. I think they were from Jersey and Massachusetts. Cy runs to Jersey and Massachusetts ones on his best days. Anyway, they were up-and-coming ones, I'm telling you, and they wanted their money's worth of the Atlantic and local color. Cap'n Cy had fishlines for them all, plenty of clams shelled out, and kelp mussels.[2] He planned to go out where the big fellows grew. Cy was in a gala mood. He was all set to give these women local color by the bailerful.

It was a lovely August day, the cut-glass kind of day that comes maybe just once a summer. Sizzling hot, but cool as cucumbers on the water. Offshore breeze, and the sky like a bluebell. Nice on the water. Whitecaps running like young puppies. Not rough enough to wet everybody down, but kicking up just enough chop to keep a boat sweet and all hands happy.

Cap headed her right out beyond Halfway before he hove anchor. There's a codfish feeding ground off there, east by south of the light, where the cod are thick as boys around the lemonade at a church picnic, when the wind is offshore and it's a sunshiny day. Not many people know about that ground but Cy. He knows the whole bottom out fifty-sixty miles as well as he knows his own back pants pocket.

Cy cut his spark and let go with the anchor. He shocked[3] all the schoolmarms a big clam apiece, or a mussel, and baited them all up. The girls paid out the lines to the bottom. Cap'n showed them how to hold the lead[4] four feet off bottom and loop the line around the first finger, wait for the yank, and then jerk up and set that hook deep. The pretty brown-haired schoolmarm got the first nibble. She like to threw her arm out, she yanked so. But she hooked him. He came up like a big one, she kept her tension all the way, just as Cy had showed her, stood up, sawing. He came so fast, he went five feet in the air, and came down spank in Cy's lap. It was an eight-pound cod, pretty as a picture, with his bronze spots shining, and a nice whisker on his chin.

Another teacher got a sculpin,[5] all thorns and growling. He growled till Cy put his jackknife into his ugly head

[1] **Palmer Cos-Cob:** the trade name of his boat.
[2] **kelp mussels:** shellfish found in kelp or seaweed.

[3] **shocked:** shucked; removed the shell.
[4] **lead** (lĕd): a lead weight attached to a line.
[5] **sculpin** (skŭl′pĭn): a large-headed, prickly, scaleless fish.

and stopped him. Somebody snaked up a hake[1] good enough for anyone's chowder. Cy unreeled his own line and came right up with a codfish to match the brown-haired teacher's. The fish were biting pretty. Everybody but one or two who couldn't have caught a kelp[2] got something. The bottom of the boat was flopping with fish. Cy kept landing them. Young Brown-Hair kept landing them, too. She kept right abreast of Cy. She was a fishing schoolmarm from 'way back. She could have shipped in a Grand Banks crew and held her own with the best old-timers with full sets of whiskers. She was from Massachusetts. Schoolmarms from Massachusetts come like that sometimes. The young Brown-Head went two ahead of Cap'n Bibber. But Cy had most of the hooks for the others to bait up, of course, and he had to take their fish off for them. That slowed him up. He didn't mind Brown-Hair's luck, he was glad of it.

They were so busy, they never thought about the root beer and sandwiches. It was a master blue-and-golden day. The boat was filling up with cod, and some hake and pollock.[3] Yet somehow there was a tension in the air. As though this was too good fishing to be true. As though it couldn't last. As though something was going to happen. Maybe dogfish coming. Any minute, up might come a line, and only the head of the cod left, the rest sliced off by a dogfish. It was August, dogfish were around. Anyway, something was going to happen. Cap'n Bibber sensed it. He is tuned to such things.

It came. All at once, it came.

"Cap'n Bibber," Brown-Head said, low but tense-like, "what would you say if I said I just saw a fish come up about ten times bigger than this boat?"

"Say?" said Cy Bibber. "I'd say we'd better yank up our mudhook."

And the captain jumped to the bow, spat on his hands, and started pulling the anchor hand over fist.

But before Cy could get her in, the Atlantic Ocean did a funny thing. It up and tipped right up sidewise. All the islands to the nor'ard tipped, too, and the whole skyline. Cy and the schoolmarms and the boat slid downhill sideways a long, long ways before they touched bottom. Then they saw what had done it. A thing like a continent broke water on their starboard. It was all of five times the length of the boat. It made the boat look like a peapod. It was humped in the middle and a dirty gray color. It was alive. It fetched a vast sigh, and half the Atlantic, says Cy, blew up in a thin spray in their faces.

It was a whale.

"Moby Dick!" breathed the young Massachusetts schoolmarm.

"Yeah," said Cy, sawing away at the anchor again, "and ain't he playful! Pull in your lines, girls. Time we was going home."

The whale tipped on end, waved something as big as two barn doors, and went under. The water was like buttermilk around them. Cy got the anchor in at last. He jumped to the flywheel, and spun her. The engine coughed and choked. Cy spun her again, giving her the whole works with the primer[4] full out. The Palmer hiccupped and burst into a roar. They went off with the planking vibrating so it shook all their eyeteeth. Cy headed her for Small Point Harbor.

[1] **hake:** a codlike fish.
[2] **kelp:** a piece of seaweed.
[3] **pollock** (pŏl'ŭk): food fish.
[4] **primer** (prīm'ẽr): ignition part of the engine.

The schoolmarms sat in a tangle of fishlines and big-eyed cod. Their eyes were like the cods'. They didn't say a word. They couldn't. They'd swallowed their cuds. They just sat there and left their fingerprints in the oak rail on the boat. The boat picked up speed and got her bone in her mouth. Cap'n Bibber gave her all the gas she could swallow. They tore for the reefs and shoal water, where a whale would scrape the barnacles off his belly if he tried to follow.

The ocean rose up on their port. It and the sky slanted over, there was that sudden mountain again, they keeled over and slid down it.

This time, Cy says, that whale was so close they could count his eyewinkers.[1] And a whale's eyewinkers are not big things. His eyes aren't any bigger than Cy's. But mean. When the whale waved good-by with his flukes,[2] Cy and his schoolmarms got a faceful of ocean. He just nicked the tip of their prow. The Atlantic boiled and subsided.

Cap'n Bibber thought next time would be it. They were bracketed [3] for fair now. Cy had been in the Coast Artillery in his younger days. He knew. He knew all about bracketing a target. He gave her more gas. The schoolmarms had lost the tan of their whole summer.

But Moby Dick fooled Cy Bibber. This time the ocean tipped up astern, and they went bow-first downhill and buried their nose in a welter of water. Cy grit his teeth and yanked the rudder rope hard to port. He thought the whale was going to roll over on them. But he only blew his nose hard, drenched them, and went under.

There ought to be a law, says Cy, to force whales to use a handkerchief!

That whale was taking his sweet time. He was having a lot of fun out of it. He was having a barrel of fun. But he meant business after he had played with them all he wanted to.

Cy figured out where Moby would come up next. He was smart. He thought to himself, "Where would I come up if I was a whale?" And, by golly! he figured it out right! The whale came up there. But Cy wasn't there any more. For just before the whale rose, he wrenched the tiller rope and swung her nose forty degrees. Up came Moby where Cy should have been but wasn't. The whale was hopping mad. He went down wicked, like an island sinking.

It was the closest Moby had come. Cy swears he could see what that whale'd had for his breakfast. It wasn't a pretty sight. And his breath didn't smell any too sweet, either. The whale was doing the double bracket on them.

But Cy had his dander up now. No whale could make a fool of him, this way. He waited till his hunch hit him, then yanked her hard aport with the rudder rope. The schoolmarms all went to their knees in the bilge [4] and spoiled their nylons, but they were still alive.

Sure enough, up came Moby a few inches off. Not more than seven or eight. But he missed them. Cy could have tickled his sulphur-colored belly with an oar, and a short one. After the ocean tipped back level again, Cy zigzagged three times in a minute. He had been a student of the evasive tactics [5] in this war. He was up on naval science.

[1] **eyewinkers:** eyelashes.
[2] **flukes** (flo͞okz): parts of the whale's tail.
[3] **bracketed:** Cap'n Bibber is comparing the whale's performance to the practice of bracketing in artillery firing. To bracket a target, the gun is fired first beyond the target, then short of it, to determine the proper position for the gun.

[4] **bilge:** dirty water.
[5] **evasive tactics:** clever dodging devices.

Northeaster *by Winslow Homer (Metropolitan Museum of Art)*

This time Moby broke water at port again. He was close – so close he seared Cyrus's cheek. But it was still a miss. He went under with a snort like ten foghorns. He was plain puzzled. But his dander was up, too, now. And he was hopping, hopping mad. Cy could see that by the light in his starboard eye. That eye was mean. Next time it would be do or die.

It wasn't, though. Cy fooled him. He kept her straight all the time. The whale came up alongside, but a good boat's length off. He stayed still there a long time, thinking mean thoughts and looking them over as he ran alongside. Oh, Cy knew what he was thinking, what he was up to. The whale wanted to take a good look at what was making such a fool of him. He wanted to see how it ticked, so next time he could not miss, even with his eyes closed, but hit fair and make kindling of them. His eyes, says Cy, were like two coals of fire. He went under slow and quiet.

The next time would tell the story. For Cy and his schoolmarms were in where the reefs were humping up higher now. The bold water was shallowing up. Moby would have just one more chance at them without smashing his brains out on granite. The engine was giving all she had. She didn't want to die yet, even though she was a 1918 model. They were tearing for dear life. The schoolmarms were saying nothing.

Cy says it was the nearest he ever came to sheer genius. As the spirit moved him at last, he put her about completely and raced seaward. He guessed right. A continent hissed up astern where his bow should have been. It rose sheer. It rubbed all the patina [1]

[1] **patina** (păt′ĭ·nȧ): a soft film deposited by age or use – in this case, probably the action of salt water.

off Cy's propeller. But the propeller was still there. The continent rolled over on them. But Cy quartered away and swung a vast circle again toward land. Moby spouted the sky full of fog, groaned like a whole herd of dying elephants, submerged, and came after them. But it was too late. The reefs were under them.

Cy swears he heard it. Heard that whale hit. The whole continent, he says, shook. He felt it. It must have knocked the wind out of the whale completely. Cy says he will hear that thud to his dying day.

Anyway, Moby Dick never rose again. Cy and the teachers, rattling at every tooth, slid through the narrows and into sanctuary in Small Point Harbor.

Cap'n Bibber says he had no starch left in his knees when they got in. He just sat there for ten minutes on end. He wasn't able to stand.

"Jehoshaphat![1] – You could have knocked me flat with a feather!"

Cap'n Bibber looked hard at the brown-haired schoolteacher from Roxbury, Massachusetts. He expected to find her completely white. But she wasn't. Her hair was as brown as ever. You can't, says Cyrus, beat a Massachusetts schoolmarm.

Thinking It Over

1. Why do you suppose schoolteachers and bank clerks like to spend their vacations "roughing it on salt water"? What was Cap'n Bibber's explanation of the brown-haired teacher's skill? Your own teacher may tell you that after handling a schoolroom class for a year, even a whale has no terrors.

2. Did you note the rather casual manner in which the story of the bank clerks' drowning is related? Why do men who follow the sea have such a realistic and impersonal attitude toward life and death? Does the tale of the drowned clerks really belong in this story? Why do you suppose it was included?

3. What characteristics of a good boat did you learn from reading about the bad points of the *Eve*? What did you learn about salt-water fishing? Did you pick up any information about handling a boat in an emergency?

4. Why did the Massachusetts schoolmarm call the whale "Moby Dick"?

5. Write a letter from the brown-haired schoolmarm to someone back home in Massachusetts. Try to make your letter as picturesque as Cap'n Bibber's story.

6. Look in the library for some other good sea stories. Find some by Joseph C. Lincoln. The state of Maine can offer some very famous names in the literary world. See what you can find by Gladys Hasty Carroll, Kenneth Roberts, Robert Frost, Sarah Orne Jewett, Edwin Arlington Robinson, Edna St. Vincent Millay, and Mary Ellen Chase. Get a book about American painting and see what pictures you can find of the Maine coast. Look for pictures by Winslow Homer and Rockwell Kent.

For Your Vocabulary

TECHNICAL TERMS: Perhaps you were already familiar with many of the technical terms in this story. If you were puzzled by a word not given in the footnotes, try to decide the meaning from context, or if that is unclear, check in a dictionary. Here are several sailing and boat terms you may have puzzled over: *aft; lee; hove anchor; paid out the lines; nor'ard; starboard; astern; barnacles; keeled over; hard to port, hard aport; quartered away.*

FIGURES OF SPEECH: Your enjoyment of this narrative depends to some extent upon your appreciation of Mr. Coffin's style of writing. When he writes that "Cy and his schoolmarms got a *faceful* of ocean," or that the boat picked up speed and "got her bone in her mouth," he is using colorful figures of speech that invoke for us pictures of the sea and the movement of the boat. Find other figures of speech in the narrative.

[1] **Jehoshaphat** (jê·hŏsh'ȧ·făt): the name of a king of Judah, often used as an exclamation.

DAVID E. LILIENTHAL

The Friendly Atom

The history of man upon this earth has been marked by great discoveries and inventions. We speak of the Iron Age, the Steel Age, the Age of Electricity, and now in our own times, the Atomic Age. The discovery that the atom, once thought to be the smallest unit of matter, can be divided and used in such a way as to produce tremendous force and energy has opened infinite possibilities for progress in science, industry, medicine, and almost all areas of living. But the possibilities for destruction are great also. The atomic bomb may be used for warfare more terrifying than the world has ever before seen. The choice is between good and evil. Few men in modern American life are more aware of this than David E. Lilienthal, who was Chairman of the United States Atomic Energy Commission from 1947 to 1950. In the following radio speech, delivered the year he took office, Lilienthal reminds his listeners of the *constructive* aspects of atomic energy. He urges them to realize that not only scientists but all educated people must take an interest in this important discovery and make sure that it is explored and employed for the benefit of all mankind.

For Better Reading . . . Since speeches are primarily intended to be listened to, not read silently, it might be well to give this one the "delivery" test to find out how it sounds. Of course, you will want to read it silently first. Here are a few simple rules for best results in speech delivery: *Read slowly, at about half the speed of usual silent reading. Pay particular attention to the punctuation while speaking, for it gives you a clue on how to group phrases and where to let your voice rise or fall. Give every important word or phrase special emphasis with your voice.* You may find that in reading this speech aloud, you will understand better the difficult ideas it contains and you will grasp the complicated use of words more readily.

No one underestimates the importance of atomic energy as a weapon that has shaken previous military and diplomatic concepts to their foundations. But it is equally important to understand that atomic energy and atomic bombs are not synonymous.[1]

There is nothing of a physical nature

[1] **synonymous** (sĭ·nŏn′ĭ·mŭs): having the same or nearly the same meaning.

that is more friendly to man, or more necessary to his well-being, than the sun. From the sun you and I get every bit of our energy, the chemical energy, energy that gives life and sustains life; that builds skyscrapers, and churches; that writes poems and symphonies. In its rays is the magic stuff of life itself.

As familiar as all of this is to everyone, it is very close to the subject of atomic energy. For the life-giving sun is itself a huge atomic energy factory. The energy the sun pours forth has its origin in a process within the sun by which there is released for our benefit the forces within the atomic nucleus, within the atom of the familiar substance known as hydrogen.

The forces, then, within the atom are not new. Far from it. Without the atomic energy released by the sun, this country would be a lifeless crater.

What *is* new is this: that in our generation, knowledge has so increased that we are now actually on the long road to understanding atomic energy and making it serve man's needs.

These atomic forces are still not well understood by even the most learned scientists. But here are two towering facts of greatest importance to every living human being the world over:

First: Mankind has probably learned more in the past thirty years about atomic forces than in all the preceding centuries.

Second: Within the next few years – a decade perhaps – we should be in a position to unlock new knowledge about life and matter so great that wholly new concepts of human life will follow in the wake of this new knowledge.

Just as the sun is fundamental to human life, so are the forces within the atom. It is our fortune, yours and mine, and that of our children, to live in that fragment of historical time when knowledge of the very cornerstone and foundation of life may be opened to human understanding. Atomic energy has already brought changes in the treatment of human suffering, and is at this moment adding to knowledge to be used in fighting cancer, heart ailments, and many other diseases. Radioactive materials from the Commission's plant at Oak Ridge are throwing a clear light upon some of the oldest mysteries of life. For example, how does a stalk of growing corn use the rays of the sun to manufacture its products into energy-giving food substances? How does a plant absorb fertilizer from the soil, and just what happens within the plant? It is fair to say that the entire investment in the atomic energy project, now nearly two and a half billion dollars, may be more than repaid by the benefits to agriculture and to human nutrition. Atomic treatment of familiar metals and new knowledge of little-known metals open up great prospects in industry. At Commission laboratories work proceeds so that some day the energy released by the splitting of the atoms of uranium and plutonium will provide a new source of electricity and heat. New professions for your young people, new hope for the afflicted, new understanding of how science can serve for peace – these are among the items on the agenda of the present and immediate future.

But these things are but a beginning. No one can predict just what changes will come of knowledge that goes to the root of all things physical. For bear in mind that every living being is composed of atoms, and the nuclear forces we are talking about are within each of these atoms. Remember, too, that every bit of matter, this desk, the walls of this chapel, the mountains and the seas are likewise composed of atoms and their nuclei. We are, therefore, throwing light upon the very nature of the structure of the world we live in. What is important to understand is not just what the precise effect of knowledge of these basic forces will be, which is necessarily speculative, but rather that important changes will come, which is as certain as anything in this world can be.

The primitive man who first beheld fire was probably terrified by this strange and destructive force he knew so little about. He could not predict that fire would change the life of every mortal from that early day to this, nor could he possibly know that the forces that he saw lay waste the forest and consume his enemies would some day be accepted as one of the most friendly and helpful forces at man's command.

What we should be concerned about, and what we should make sure of, is that the changes that are coming shall be fitted into the American way of doing things; that they shall not be so imposed upon us that individual freedom is impaired. We must make sure that the American people will have a decisive say-so in the adjustments these discoveries will bring in community life, in our agricultural, educational, industrial, and military institutions. You must make dead sure that your public servants in all branches of your government, civil and military, legislative and executive, all understand clearly that atomic energy *is* your business, the people's business.

Now I must warn you that this will not be easy. But it is vitally important to you here in this community and all other communities, large and small, that you keep the decisions, the broad decisions, in your hands. For science and technical matters will become more and more important in determining peace and security, important in industry and jobs, in health, in farming, in education, in community affairs in thousands of cities and towns and villages all through the country. More and more things of your daily life, and in the factory, school, and farm will be affected by the discoveries and applications of science. Atomic science will stimulate a whole new world of other discoveries. This is already happening and it will continue. And it can be made pretty much to the good for peace and decency and human freedom. But you must not at your peril let these new technical advances get out of your power to control and direct. I warn you that this must not happen or the essence of the American scheme of things will be lost.

What is needed is not knowledge and judgment about scientific or engineering matters. You don't have that and couldn't take the time to acquire it. The technical forces associated with the Atomic Energy Commission can do that, and are doing a good job of it. The quality of that job is being constantly checked by independent advisory boards of distinguished scientists. But the kind of judgment that I am talking about is, for example, a sense of what things people will accept as right and sensible and workable. What is needed is sense about human relations, about standards of fairness, about principles of self-government and of self-education. These judgments turn on the weight to be given to concern for the individual as compared to concern for the state. The issues call for the kind of over-all judgment that is summed up when your neighbor says: "That makes sense to me."

Nothing could weaken the security of our country in the atomic field more

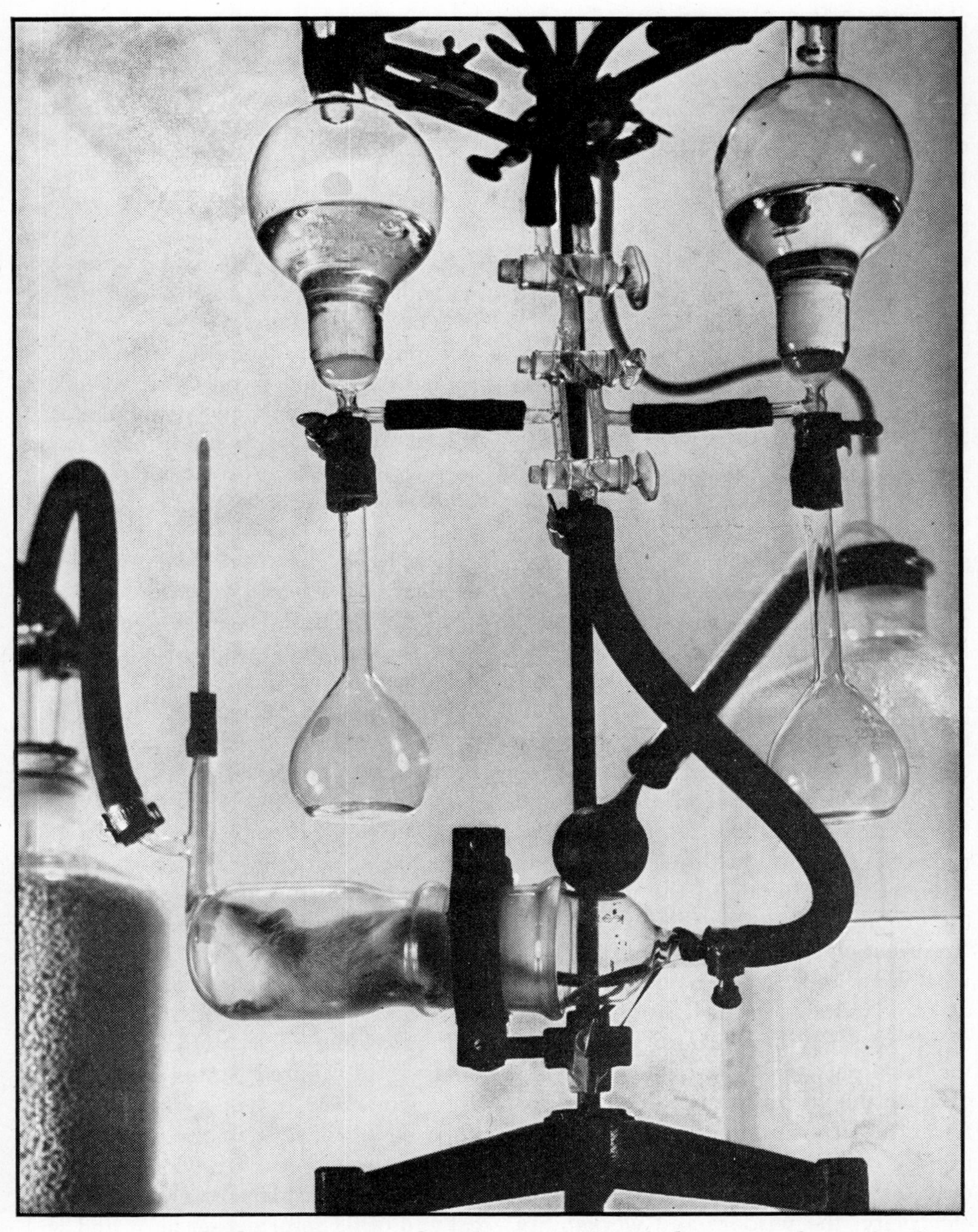

Medical science uses radioactivity to test food absorption: the rat has been fed fatty foods containing radioactive carbon. As his body consumes this fat, he breathes out radioactive carbon dioxide, which rises through the tubes to the flasks above, where it is measured. (*By* Life *photographer Albert Fenn,* © Time, *Inc.*)

quickly, nor more surely slow up research in cancer control, say, than to permit science and scientists to be kicked around by the organized forces of ignorance and demagoguery,[1] and petty politics. You don't have to have scientific training to sense that this would be bad for you, bad for the country. This sort of thing is a real danger to our scientific progress, for as the old Hoosier saying has it, "There are some men who would play peanut politics with the multiplication table and the Ten Commandments." There is only one real protection against the harm selfish and ignorant and fanatical [2] men can do and that is an informed public.

There are many other broad issues where your judgment will be essential, and your interest vital. These might include such matters as the proposals for international control of atomic weapons; the conditions under which the present government monopoly in this field can safely be changed to private competitive production; the share of the national budget that should be devoted to scientific research; the adequacy of protection against health hazards from radioactive materials in the air and on the ground; the proper relation of civilian direction to the military, in this field; what kind and size of navy, army, and air force we need in the light of developments in scientific warfare; what sense the proposals make that we go underground; the workability of decentralization of cities as a defense measure; how rapidly atomic fuel may supplement coal, oil, and water power as a source of electricity; the wisdom and workability of censorship of the press and radio as a means of maintaining secrecy in this field, under peacetime conditions. Such a list of policy issues could be extended almost indefinitely.

You need to watch your public servants, to keep an eye on us, whether in the executive branch, the military, or in Congress. And to do so effectively, your views and judgments must be based upon some knowledge of the background of facts.

How can you acquire sufficient information to make you effective? As to *what* you should know, remember that the information you need to have is *not* secret technical information. Nor is it highly complicated. The essentials of atomic energy, even on the scientific side, are actually not difficult, not nearly as difficult as those who would like to keep the decisions to themselves would lead you to believe. For what technical information you need, try your nearby colleges or your local high schools, and if their science teachers don't know enough about the subject to be able to explain it simply to the average layman, then you know there is something wrong with the teaching going on around you, and that is worth something in itself. As for the public issues, there, too, the colleges and the schools can assemble and boil down the relevant facts for the use of your civic organizations.

In providing information about atomic energy, the United States Atomic Energy Commission has a responsibility, imposed by law. It is our hope that it can be discharged with good sense and restraint. A considerable area of technical and other information must and will be kept secret under present conditions, and elaborate precautions are being taken to this end. The Commission must provide some guidance on such matters, of course, and will from time to time be

[1] **demagoguery** (dĕm′ȧ·gŏg′ẽr·ĭ): attempts by a speaker to gain political influence by arousing discontent.
[2] **fanatical** (fȧ·năt′ĭ·kăl): excessively or unreasonably enthusiastic.

prepared to release new information that can be made public without prejudice to security. But by and large, the sources of information on public issues are already open. Much of the information has already been published.

The problem is chiefly one of getting nonsecret information into a form for your consideration that will be clear, interesting, and without bias.[1] And for this you can properly expect great things of the press of the United States, the radio, and the magazines. These, together with motion pictures, constitute one of the greatest educational forces in human history.

It is important that the facts and analysis of policies should come to you from a variety of sources, not from only one, and above all that they should not come solely from official sources. This variety gives you a chance to check one version against another and draw your own conclusions.

Such help as this from the outside is necessary, and can be very useful. But try to keep this as close to home as possible, when you come to your analysis and your discussion of these things. Don't be content to take ideas that have been predigested for you at some distant place. Put this on the programs of your Chamber of Commerce, the Boy Scouts, the unions, the Parent-Teacher Association, Rotary, the League of Women Voters, 4-H Clubs, the local veterans' organizations, the business and professional women's organizations, the bar association and county medical society, etc.

These are your organizations. You can speak your mind in your own town. You don't need a brand-new organization for this purpose. Make use of the many fine civic, fraternal, educational, professional, and religious organizations you now have in your community.

Don't make this a crusade, a " drive," full of ardor and zing for a couple of weeks and then it's all over. This is not a " campaign." This subject will be with you for a long time, so take it as part of your community responsibilities.

[1] **bias** (bī'ăs): prejudice.

Noting the Characteristics of Speeches

Most speeches are made for the following purposes: to entertain, to instruct, to persuade, or to move to action. Once in awhile there is a combination of these. What is the main purpose of this speech? Can you specifically support your answer? Considering that the speech was delivered to an unseen and uncounted audience of persons of varying ages and experience, how well did the speaker succeed in keeping within the ability of the average person to understand his subject? Frequently a speaker makes a humorous introduction to his main subject in order to secure the attention of his audience and perhaps make it favorably disposed toward him. Why do you suppose Mr. Lilienthal does not begin with a humorous anecdote or some light remarks? How does *he* attempt to capture attention?

Thinking It Over

1. What are some of the responsibilities of the educated citizen in this matter of atomic energy, according to Mr. Lilienthal? If citizens are not alert to the possibilities and dangers of atomic energy, how can it be used against their own interests?

2. There are several suggestions here for making atomic information known to the general public. Check those on this page and determine whether your own community and school has promoted interest and understanding in the problem of atomic energy control. How have newspapers, popular magazines, radio, movies, and television promoted public understanding of atomic power?

3. Appoint an " Atomic Energy Board " from those among you who are especially interested in chemistry or general science. Make a list of questions that you would like

to have them answer. When the Board is ready to report, be prepared to take notes and ask further questions for discussion. This is a chance to combine your work in English with your general science course. Pay particular attention to the words relating to atomic energy mentioned in the following section on vocabulary.

4. A speech or essay like this one is informative; that is, it contains definite information that the listener or reader is expected to obtain. Try writing a précis (prā·sē′) or condensation of this speech, using about 300 words, and see how many important points you can cover.

For Your Vocabulary

TECHNICAL WORDS: There are a number of words in this speech that are probably not familiar to you unless you have a special interest in science and particularly in chemistry and physics. Try to get good working definitions of the following words: *atomic, radioactive, uranium, nuclear, nuclei, plutonium, fission.* Words like these, technical words that apply to a particular science or vocation, are hard to understand from context. It is not often that you can guess at their meanings. You will have to go to a dictionary for a satisfactory definition.

WALDEMAR KAEMPFFERT

Miracles You'll See in the Next Fifty Years

Think of a time fifty years from now. What kind of place will you be living in? What kind of transportation will you use? The answers to these and similar questions you might ask may be so unusual, so fantastic, that you could not possibly anticipate them *now.* Of course, it is fascinating to speculate on the kind of life science will enable us to achieve as this rapidly moving age goes on. David Lilienthal, in the preceding essay, speaks of some possible improvements in the coming world; and in the following article, Waldemar Kaempffert, the science editor for the New York *Times,* also does some looking into a crystal ball. Take a look over his shoulder.

WHAT will the world be like in A.D. 2000? You can read the answer in your home, in the streets, in the trains and cars that carry you to your work, in the bargain basement of every department store. You don't realize what is happening because it is a piecemeal process. The jet-propelled plane is one piece, the latest insect killer is another. Thousands of such pieces are automatically dropping into their places to form the pattern of tomorrow's world.

The best way of visualizing the new world of A.D. 2000 is to introduce you to the Dobsons, who live in Tottenville, a hypothetical metropolitan suburb[1] of 100,000. There are parks and playgrounds and green open spaces not only around detached houses but also around apartment houses. The heart of the town is the airport. Surrounding it are business houses, factories, and hotels. In concentric circles beyond these lie the residential districts.

Thanks to alloys, plastics, and other artificial materials, houses differ from those of our own time. The Dobson house has light metal walls only four inches thick. There is a sheet of insulating material an inch or two thick with a casing of sheet metal on both sides.

This Dobson air-conditioned house is not a prefabricated structure, though all its parts are mass-produced. Metal, sheets of plastic, and aerated clay (clay filled with bubbles so that it resembles petrified sponge) are cut to size on the spot. In the center of this eight-room house is a unit that contains all the utilities — air-conditioning apparatus, plumbing, bathrooms, showers, electric range, electric outlets. Around this central unit the house has been pieced together. Some of it is poured plastic — the floors, for instance. By 2000, wood, brick, and stone are ruled out because they are too expensive.

It is a cheap house. With all its furnishings, Joe Dobson paid only $5,000 for it. Though it is galeproof and weatherproof, it is built to last only about 25 years. Nobody in 2000 sees any sense in building a house that will last a century.

Everything about the Dobson house is synthetic in the best chemical sense of the term. When Joe Dobson awakens in the morning he uses a depilatory.[2] No soap or safety razor for him. It takes him no longer than a minute to apply the chemical, wipe it off with the bristles, and wash his face in plain water.

This Dobson house is not as highly mechanized as you may suppose, chiefly because of the progress made by the synthetic chemists. There are no dishwashing machines, for example, because dishes are thrown away after they have been used once, or rather put into a sink where they are dissolved by superheated water. Two dozen soluble plastic plates cost a dollar. They dissolve at about 250 degrees Fahrenheit, so that boiling-hot soup and stews can be served in them without inviting a catastrophe.[3] The plastics are derived from such inexpensive raw materials as cottonseed hulls, oat hulls, Jerusalem artichokes, fruit pits, soy beans, straw, and wood pulp.

When Jane Dobson cleans house she simply turns the hose on everything. Why not? Furniture (upholstery included), rugs, draperies, unscratchable floors — all are made of synthetic fabric or waterproof plastic. After the water has run down a drain in the middle of the floor (later concealed by a rug of synthetic fiber) Jane turns on a blast of hot air and dries everything. A detergent in the water dissolves any rēsistant dirt. Tablecloths and napkins are made of woven paper yarn so fine that the untutored eye mistakes it for linen. Jane Dobson throws soiled "linen" into the incinerator. Bed sheets are of more substantial stuff, but Jane Dobson has only to hang them up and wash them down with a hose when she puts the bedroom in order.

[1] **hypothetical metropolitan suburb** (hī′pō·thĕt′ĭ·kăl mĕt′rō·pŏl′ĭ·tăn sŭb′ûrb): an imaginary community on the outskirts of a city.

[2] **depilatory** (dē·pĭl′ȧ·tō′rĭ): a hair remover.

[3] **catastrophe** (kȧ·tăs′trō·fē): a serious accident; a sudden calamity.

Cooking as an art is only a memory in the minds of old people. A few die-hards still broil a chicken or roast a leg of lamb, but the experts have developed ways of deep-freezing partially baked cuts of meat. Even soup and milk are delivered in the form of frozen bricks.

This expansion of the frozen-food industry and the changing gastronomic habits of the nation have made it necessary to install in every home the electronic industrial stove which came out of World War II. Jane Dobson has one of these electronic stoves. In eight seconds a half-grilled frozen steak is thawed; in two minutes more it is ready to serve. It never takes Jane Dobson more than half an hour to prepare what Tottenville considers an elaborate meal of several courses.

Some of the food that Jane Dobson buys is what we miscall "synthetic." In the middle of the twentieth century statisticians were predicting that the world would starve to death because the population was increasing more rapidly than the food supply. By 2000, a vast amount of research has been conducted to exploit principles that were embryonic[1] in the first quarter of the twentieth century. Thus sawdust and wood pulp are converted into sugary foods. Discarded paper table "linen" and rayon underwear are bought by chemical factories to be converted into candy.

Of course the Dobsons have a television set. But it is connected with the telephones as well as with the radio receiver, so that when Joe Dobson and a friend in a distant city talk over the telephone they also see each other. Businessmen have television conferences. Each man is surrounded by half a dozen television screens on which he sees those taking part in the discussion. Documents are held up for examination; samples of goods are displayed. In fact, Jane Dobson does much of her shopping by television. Department stores obligingly hold up for her inspection bolts of fabric or show her new styles of clothing.

By 2000, supersonic planes cover a thousand miles an hour, but the consumption of fuel is such that high fares have to be charged. In one of these supersonic planes the Atlantic is crossed in three hours. Nobody has yet circumnavigated the moon in a rocket space ship, but the idea is not laughed down.

Corporation presidents, bankers, ambassadors, and rich people in a hurry use the 1000-mile-an-hour rocket planes and think nothing of paying a fare of $5,000 between Chicago and Paris. The Dobsons take the cheaper jet planes.

This extension of aerial transportation has had the effect of distributing the population. People find it more satisfactory to live in a suburb like Tottenville, if suburb it can be called, than in a metropolis like New York, Chicago, or Los Angeles. Cities have grown into regions, and it is sometimes hard to tell where one city ends and another begins. Instead of driving from Tottenville to California in their car — teardrop in shape and driven from the rear by a high-compression engine that burns cheap denatured alcohol — the Dobsons use the family helicopter, which is kept on the roof. The car is used chiefly for shopping and for journeys of not more than twenty miles.

The railways are just as necessary in 2000 as they are in 1950. They haul chiefly freight too heavy or too bulky for air cargo carriers. Passenger travel by rail is a mere trickle. Even commuters go to the city, a hundred miles away,

[1] **embryonic** (ĕm'brĭ·ŏn'ĭk): in the very first stages of development; hardly begun.

The world of the future comes gradually. This modern home may very well represent the functional house of the future. (*Designed by Architect Paul Beidler, courtesy Museum of Modern Art, New York*)

in huge aerial busses that hold two hundred passengers. Hundreds of thousands make such journeys twice a day in their own helicopters.

Fast jet- and rocket-propelled mail planes made it so hard for telegraph companies all over the world to compete with the postal service that dormant facsimile-transmission systems [1] had to be revived. It takes no more than a minute to transmit and receive in facsimile a five-page letter on paper of the usual business size. Cost? Five cents. In Tottenville the clerks in telegraph offices no longer print out illegible words. Everything is transmitted by phototelegraphy [2] exactly as it is written – illegible spelling, blots, smudges, and all. Mis-

[1] **dormant facsimile** (făk·sĭm′ĭ·lē)**-transmission systems:** inactive systems for sending exact copies.

[2] **phototelegraphy** (fō′tō·tē·lĕg′ră·fĭ): sending pictures by telegraph.

takes are the sender's, never the telegraph company's.

When the Dobsons are sick they go to the doctor, in a hospital, where he has only to push a button to command all the assistance he needs.

In the middle of the twentieth century, doctors talked much of such antibiotics [1] as penicillin,[2] streptomycin,[3] aureomycin [4] and about fifty others that had been extracted from soil and other molds. It was the beginning of what was even then known as chemotherapy [5] — cure by chemical means. By 2000, physicians have several hundred of these chemical agents or antibiotics at their command. Tuberculosis in all of its forms is cured as easily as pneumonia was cured at mid-century.

In that wonderful year, 2000, any marked departure from what Joe Dobson and his fellow citizens wear and eat and how they amuse themselves will arouse comment. If old Mrs. Underwood, who lives around the corner from the Dobsons and who was born in 1920, insists on sleeping under an old-fashioned comforter instead of a blanket of glass puffed with air so that it is as light as thistledown, she must expect people to talk about her "queerness." It is astonishing how easily the great majority of us fall into step with our neighbors. Some people dislike standardization, of course, but most of us could take a good deal of it in order to have a house like Joe Dobson's.

[1] **antibiotics** (ăn′tĭ·bī·ŏt′ĭks): substances produced by living organisms and used to fight bacteria.
[2] **penicillin** (pĕn′ĭ·sĭl′ĭn).
[3] **streptomycin** (strĕp′tō·mī′sĭn).
[4] **aureomycin** (ô′rē·ō·mī′sĭn).
[5] **chemotherapy** (kĕm′ō·thĕr′ȧ·pĭ).

Thinking It Over

1. Not all the speculations made by the author should seem entirely foreign, or even fantastic, to a person living in the 1950's. Take a number of the predictions he makes about (a) building materials, (b) house architecture, (c) foods, and see if you can find things in our present-day world that already suggest such new developments.

2. You ought to take pleasure in imagining that some day you will have some of the conveniences described here. Which ones please you most? What advantages would they give you?

3. The author paints a rosy picture unquestionably, but there are other things to consider than material advancements. What in our present life suggests to you that while we have made great strides in science, we have failed or faltered in other realms of human endeavor? Is there a mention of this in the essay "The Friendly Atom"?

THE PERSONAL ADVENTURE

It would certainly be a dull world if adventure were possible only for those few people who accomplish grand and daring deeds. Fortunately, however, adventure is to be found everywhere — if you know how to look for it.

In a delightful essay, the American writer Logan Pearsall Smith once described the simple act of getting ready to leave one's house. In a dramatic manner, full of suspense, he told how he put on his coat, reached for his umbrella, felt in his pocket for the house key, and then — armed and momentously ready for whatever would come — closed the door and stepped into the street. He very cleverly made the reader realize that almost anything we do can be a personal adventure. All we need is a little curiosity and a good imagination.

You will realize this truth as you read the following short articles and magazine sketches, which suggest the great variety of human experience and give you a glimpse of several human beings absorbed in their own personal adventures.

FITZROY MACLEAN

A Passage to Persia

Fitzroy Maclean is not a man to let life go idly and uneventfully by, as you will discover in reading this account of his strange adventure during World War II. His book *Escape to Adventure* is one of the great true adventure stories of modern times. Before the war, as a brilliant young diplomat, Maclean gave up his comfortable post in the British embassy at Paris to ask for service at Moscow. When he got to Russia he amazed his colleagues – and the Russians, who never quite knew how to stop him – by traveling into the remotest regions of that secretive and little-known land. Later, the British Foreign Office refused to release him from the diplomatic service so that he might enlist in the army. He got around this refusal by running for Parliament and, as soon as he was elected, resigning his office to join the Scottish Highlanders as a private. During World War II he made secret forays behind the German lines in Egypt and at one time became Winston Churchill's personal envoy to the famous guerrilla leader, Marshal Tito, in the mountains of Yugoslavia.

His adventure in Persia is an almost incredible story. Persia (which has been called Iran since 1935) was neither on the German nor the Allied side during World War II. Russian troops were in the north, a few scattered British troops were in the south, and German spies were everywhere. To lose control of Persia would have been a desperate blow to the Allies, yet neither Britain nor other Allied nations had enough strength to hold the country by armed force. The situation was ticklish. It got worse when the British learned that the Germans had succeeded in winning the support of a certain Persian general in the south. Somehow, some way, the general had to be removed without a military attack – but how? The job was given to Fitzroy Maclean and he carried it out with boldness and imagination – and with the sheer luck that seems to follow him wherever he goes.

For Better Reading . . . You need to use imagination for practically anything you read. In the following selection, for example, you will miss much of the excitement and interest unless you try to visualize the setting and the circumstances surrounding the action. Actually, because the situation described here *is* true, its dramatic effect is heightened and sharpened. Try to put yourself in the narrator's place by visualizing all the circumstances surrounding his experiences.

I FOUND General Baillon at the British Legation in conference with the Minister, Sir Reader Bullard. They told me that they had a job for me. For some time past, they said, there had been signs that some kind of trouble was brewing in south Persia. The tribes, the Qashgai[1] and the Bakhtiari,[2] had German agents living among them and seemed likely to rise at any moment, just as they had risen in 1916, when their rebellion had caused us a disproportionate amount of trouble. Were this to happen, our supply route to the Persian Gulf might be cut. There was also discontent in Isfahan[3] and other towns, largely caused by the hoarding of grain by speculators, which we were unable to prevent. This discontent might at any moment flare up into open rebellion. Worse still, if there were trouble, the Persian troops in south Persia were likely to take the side of the rioters.

A sinister part was being played in all this by a certain General Zahidi,[4] who was in command of the Persian forces in the Isfahan area. Zahidi was known to be one of the worst grain hoarders in the country. But there was also good reason to believe that he was acting in co-operation with the tribal leaders and, finally, that he was in touch with the German agents who were living in the hills and, through them, with the German High Command in the Caucasus.[5] Indeed, reports from secret sources showed that he was planning a general rising against the Allied occupation force, in which his troops and those of the Persian general in the Soviet-occupied northern zone would take part and which would coincide with a German air-borne attack on the Tenth Army, followed by a general German offensive on the Caucasus front. In short, General Zahidi appeared to be behind most of the trouble in south Persia.

The situation was a delicate one. The Allied forces of occupation in northern Persia had been reduced to a minimum, in order to meet demands from the fighting fronts; there were practically no Allied troops in south Persia at all. The nearest British troops to the seat of the trouble were at Qum,[6] two hundred miles north of Isfahan. There was very real danger that any sudden movement of British troops in a southward direction might provoke a general rising which we should have serious difficulty in containing[7] with the small forces at our disposal. On the other hand, if we allowed events to take their course, the results would be equally disastrous.

In short it was essential to nip the trouble in the bud, while avoiding a full-scale showdown. General Baillon and Sir Reader Bullard had decided that this could best be achieved by the removal of General Zahidi, and it was this task that they had decided to entrust to me. How it was to be done they left me to work out for myself. Only two conditions were made: I was to take him alive

[1] **Qashgai** (käsh'gī). [2] **Bakhtiari** (bäk·tyär'ē). [3] **Isfahan** (ĭs'fȧ·hän). [4] **Zahidi** (zä·hē'dē).
[5] **Caucasus** (kô'kȧ·sŭs): a mountain range in southern Soviet Russia between the Black and the Caspian seas.

[6] **Qum** (ko͞om): a city in Iran.
[7] **containing**: checking; restraining.

Isfahan in Iran (Persia), the scene of Fitzroy Maclean's daring adventure. (Henri Cartier-Bresson from Magnum)

and I was to do so without creating a disturbance.

My first step was to go to Isfahan and see for myself how the land lay. That city's mosques [1] and palaces, unrivaled in the whole of Asia, provided an excellent pretext for visiting it. I let it be known in Teheran [2] that I was going to spend a few days' leave sight-seeing in the south, and set out.

I reached Isfahan the same night after driving all day across a bleak plateau fringed with distant snow-capped mountains. Flickering lights shone out of the darkness, showing two or three dim figures squatting in a doorway, drinking their tea and smoking their long pipes; then a group of houses; then some shops; and then we were in the main street in a seething stream of carts, donkeys, and camels, whose owners turned round to stare at the first jeep and the first British uniforms to make their appearance in Isfahan.

I drove to the British Consulate,[3] where I was welcomed by the Consul, John Gault. Soon Duncan and I, in the time-honored phrase of the British soldier, had "our knees under the table," and were making good progress with a brace of the local brand of partridge, washed down by delicious wine from the town of Shiraz,[4] which, according to some, disputes with Xeres [5] the honor of being the birthplace of sherry.[6]

Over dinner I disclosed to my host, a robust young man who gave the impression of being equally alert both mentally and physically, the true purpose of my visit. He was delighted. General Zahidi, he said, though pleasant to meet, was a really bad lot: a bitter enemy of the Allies, a man of unpleasant personal habits, and, by virtue of his grain-hoarding activities, a source of popular discontent and an obstacle to the efficient administration of south Persia. He, too, had heard that he was plotting with the Germans and with the tribal leaders. Indeed, according to information which had reached him, one of the opening moves in General Zahidi's plot was to be the liquidation [7] of the British Consul in Isfahan, a piece of news which completely outweighed all the General's personal charm, as far as he was concerned.

I asked Gault where Zahidi lived. He said he would show me, and after dinner we strolled out of the Consulate, across a narrow many-arched bridge, and along a broad avenue of plane trees, until we came to a massive pair of gates, set in a high stone wall and flanked by a sentry box and guardroom. Outside, a Persian infantryman was marching up and down while others, all well armed, slouched at the door of the guardroom. We took a turn round the back premises, where the surrounding wall was pierced by another gate, guarded by another sentry. This was the General's residence. Then we continued our stroll along the avenue under the trees. A few hundred yards farther along we came to a large modern barracks, which according to Gault contained the greater part of the garrison of Isfahan, ready to rush to the assistance of their commander in case of trouble. It did not look as though a frontal attack by a small raiding party

[1] **mosques** (mŏsks): places of worship of the Mohammedan religion.
[2] **Teheran** (tĕ'hĕ·rän'): the capital of Iran.
[3] **Consulate** (kŏn'sů·lât): the office or premises of a consul, an officer appointed by his country to care for the interests of his countrymen in a foreign city.
[4] **Shiraz** (shē·räz'): a city in southwestern Iran.
[5] **Xeres** (shā'râs): a city in Spain, now called Jerez (hâ·rāth').
[6] **sherry** (shĕr'ĭ): a white wine.
[7] **liquidation** (lĭk'wĭ·dā'shŭn): complete destruction or wiping out.

would have much chance of succeeding.

If Zahidi could not conveniently be winkled out of his place of residence, the obvious alternative was to ambush him when he was away from home, traveling from one point to another. I ascertained from Gault that at the same time every morning he crossed the bridge on his way to his headquarters. Would it not be possible to take advantage of the narrow bottleneck formed by this ancient monument to hold up his car, drag him out of it, and make off with him?

I gave this plan careful consideration, but there were two serious objections to it. In the first place Zahidi was reputed to go nowhere without a heavily armed bodyguard, whom it would be necessary to overcome by force. Secondly, even assuming that we managed to avoid a pitched battle with the bodyguard, we were unlikely to succeed in kidnapping a general in broad daylight in the middle of so populous a town as Isfahan without attracting a good deal of attention. The two of us driving peacably along in the jeep had been a sufficiently novel spectacle to hold up the traffic in the main street of Isfahan; the same party with the addition of a struggling general and his bereaved bodyguard could scarcely fail to introduce into the proceedings that very element of uproar which my superiors were so anxious to avoid. I went to sleep that night with the feeling that the problem before me was not as simple as it had at first sight appeared.

Next day, after further thought and another talk with Gault, I came to the conclusion that, unless I was prepared to risk a serious incident which might have unforeseeable repercussions,[1] I should have to rely primarily on some kind of a ruse in order to get my man. In short, what was needed was a Trojan horse.[2]

Once I had started thinking on these lines, it was not long before there began to shape in my mind a plan which seemed to offer a better chance of neatly and successfully eliminating the source of the trouble without setting light to the powder magazine of south Persia. That afternoon I sent off a cipher telegram to Teheran giving my proposals for Operation "Pongo," which was the code name I had chosen for the abduction of the General.

The first thing was to find a pretext for introducing myself into Zahidi's house. I suggested that I should be given authority to assume for the occasion a brigadier's[3] badges of rank; that I should then ring up the house and announce myself as a senior staff officer from Baghdad[4] who wished to pay his respects to the General. If the latter agreed, I would drive up in a staff car, accompanied by Duncan and one or two other resourceful characters, hold him up at the point of the pistol, hustle him into the car, and drive away with him out of Isfahan before the alarm could be given. I also asked for a platoon of infantry to lend a hand in case anything went wrong. I undertook to work out some means of introducing these into Isfahan in such a way as to attract as little attention as possible.

Having sent off my telegram, I spent two agreeable days making a detailed

[1] **repercussions** (rē′pẽr·kŭsh′ŭnz): resultant actions or effects.

[2] **Trojan horse:** according to classical myth, a wooden horse filled with soldiers, used during the siege of Troy; in modern usage, agents "planted" in another country for spying or sabotage.

[3] **brigadier** (brĭg′ȧ·dēr′): in the British army, an officer of any rank who is placed in command of a brigade.

[4] **Baghdad** (băg′dăd): a city in Iraq (ē·räk′), an independent Arab country south of Turkey.

reconnaissance [1] of the city, with special attention to the best line of withdrawal in case of an emergency, and at the same time enjoying its peerless beauty.

The arrival of an urgent message from GHQ.[2] in reply to my telegram, submitting my proposals and requesting instructions, brought me back to the realities of World War II. My plan was approved in principle and I was instructed to go ahead with my preparations. Only one item of my highly unorthodox program stuck in the throats of the well-trained staff officers at the other end. It was not possible, they said, to authorize an officer of my age and seniority (I was a captain) to masquerade, even for a day, as a brigadier. Rather than allow this, they would place at my disposal, for a limited period of time, a genuine brigadier, for use as bait or for any other purpose within reason. Moreover this officer, for the purposes of the operation, would receive his instructions from me. For administrative purposes I was directed to report to General Anderson, the corps [3] commander at Qum, some two hundred miles from Isfahan, who had been asked to furnish the brigadier and also such troops, equipment, and transport as I might require.

I lost no time in reporting to Corps Headquarters, where I was provided with a platoon of Seaforth Highlanders,[4] who were told that they had been specially selected for training in commando tactics.[5] As surprise was clearly essential to the success of our enterprise, secrecy was of the utmost importance, and at this stage practically no one except the corps commander and I was aware of our real objective. The Seaforths were equipped with tommy guns and hand grenades and we repaired to a secluded part of the desert near Qum to rehearse our act.

I had decided that the Seaforths should only be used in case of an emergency. My plan was that on the appointed day they should arrive in Isfahan in two covered trucks, disguised as far as possible to look like civilian vehicles, shortly before I set out for the General's house. One would draw up under the plane trees on the far side of the avenue, opposite the main entrance to the house, and stay there. The other would take up a position covering the back entrance. The men, clutching their tommy guns and hand grenades, would remain in the back of the trucks, out of sight. Only if they heard firing or a prearranged signal of three blasts on the whistle would they emerge from their hiding place, overpower the guard, and force an entrance, after which their task would be to cover the withdrawal of the party in the staff car, which it was hoped would include Zahidi whatever happened. If, on the other hand, all went well, the two trucks would simply wait until the staff car drove out with Zahidi in it, and then fall in behind and escort us out of Isfahan to a point in the desert where an aircraft would be waiting, ready to fly our prisoner out of the country.

For our rehearsals I chose a ruined fort in the desert. Again and again the two trucks took up their positions outside; the staff car drove in; the whistle sounded; the Seaforths poured out of the trucks and into the fort; an imaginary victim was bundled unceremoniously into the car, and all three vehicles

[1] **reconnaissance** (rē·kŏn′ĭ·săns): a survey or examination to gain military information about a region.

[2] **GHQ.:** General Headquarters.

[3] **corps** (kōr): a large unit of an army, usually made up of at least two divisions.

[4] **Seaforth Highlanders:** a Scottish regiment.

[5] **commando tactics:** the methods used by commandos (specially trained raiding groups).

drove off in triumph, the occupants tossing dummy hand grenades out of the back at imaginary pursuers, as they went. The Seaforths gave a splendidly realistic performance. Indeed their enthusiasm was such that my only anxiety was lest on the day itself they would emerge from their place of concealment, whether things went well or badly, and massacre [1] a number of harmless Persians out of sheer ebullience.[2]

It now only remained to fix the day. This was done after a further exchange of signals with GHQ. Baghdad and with the Foreign Office via Teheran. I also extracted from the authorities, not without difficulty, permission to shoot General Zahidi, should he be armed and resist capture.

Our D day [3] was fixed, and on D minus one we set out from Qum. I had decided that the Seaforths should spend the night well out of sight in the desert about ten miles from Isfahan. Next day, while the main party entered the town in the two trucks, smaller parties were detailed to cut the telegraph wires connecting Isfahan with the neighboring Persian garrisons. Meanwhile I collected the Brigadier, a distinguished officer whose well-developed sense of humor caused him to enter completely into the spirit of the somewhat equivocal [4] role that had been allotted to him, and set out for the British Consulate.

On our arrival a telephone call was put through to the General's house and an appointment made for the same afternoon. After a copious lunch we took our places in the staff car, which was flying a large Union Jack. A reliable NCO,[5] armed to the teeth, occupied the seat next the driver, while Guardsman Duncan and a Seaforth Highlander, both carrying tommy guns, crouched in the luggage compartment at the back, under a tarpaulin. Gault followed in his own car. As we approached Zahidi's house, I was relieved to see our two trucks, their tarpaulin covers concealing the battle-hungry Seaforths, drawn up in their appointed places. At the gate the Persian sentry was deep in conversation with Laurence Lockhart, a Persian linguist from RAF [6] Intelligence, whose services I had enlisted for the occasion. So far everything had gone according to plan.

On our appearance, the sentry at the gate reluctantly put out the cigarette which Lockhart had given him, broke off his conversation, and presented arms. We drove on up the drive and drew up in front of the house immediately outside a large pair of open French windows. A servant ushered us in and went off to fetch the General.

When, a couple of minutes later, General Zahidi, a dapper figure in a tight-fitting gray uniform and highly polished boots, entered the room, he found himself looking down the barrel of my Colt automatic. There was no advantage in prolonging a scene which might easily become embarrassing. Without further ado, I invited the General to put his hands up and informed him that I had instructions to arrest him and that, if he made any noise or attempt at resistance, he would be shot. Then I took away his pistol and hustled him through the window into the car which was waiting outside with the engine running. To my relief there was no sign of the much-advertised bodyguard. As we passed the guardroom, the sentry once again inter-

[1] **massacre** (măs′ȧ·kẽr): slaughter.
[2] **ebullience** (ê·bŭl′ĭ·ĕns): high spirits.
[3] **D day:** a military term for the day of attack. "D minus one" is the day before D day.
[4] **equivocal** (ê·kwĭv′ô·kăl): questionable.
[5] **NCO:** noncommissioned officer.
[6] **RAF:** Royal Air Force.

rupted his conversation to present arms, and the General, sitting bolt upright, with my pistol pressed against his ribs and Duncan breathing menacingly down his neck, duly returned the salute. The two "plain vans," with their occupants now bitterly disappointed, fell in behind; and the whole convoy swept at a brisk pace over the bridge and into the main avenue leading out of Isfahan.

Some miles outside the town we passed a large barracks, full of General Zahidi's troops, but the telephone wire from the town had duly been cut by the wire-cutting party, and there was no sign that the alarm had been given. Meanwhile Zahidi continued to sit bolt upright and to assure me that there was a very good explanation of any aspects of his conduct which might at first sight have seemed at all suspicious. Soon we reached the point in the desert where we had spent the night, and here I handed over my captive to an officer and six men who were standing by to take him by car to the nearest landing ground, where an airplane was waiting to fly him to Palestine. This was the last I saw of General Zahidi, but, reading my newspaper not long ago, I was amused to see an announcement that he had returned to Persia and once again been placed in command of the south Persian military district.

Having said good-by to the Brigadier, whose duties were now at an end, and sent a signal to General Wilson announcing the completion of Operation "Pongo," I went back into town to clear up any outstanding points, taking a few Seaforths with me. My first objective was Zahidi's headquarters, which I entered at the head of six Seaforths carrying tommy guns. Gault had told me that Zahidi's Chief of Staff was also very hostile to the Allies, and, in addition to this, extremely truculent in manner. The exaggerated amiability with which this dignitary now greeted me accordingly left me in no doubt that news of what had occurred had already got out. Taking him with me, I returned to Zahidi's house, which I proceeded to search methodically. In the General's bedroom I found a collection of automatic weapons of German manufacture and a large number of letters and papers which I took back with me to the Consulate.

That night the Seaforths camped in the Consulate garden in case there was trouble, and Gault and I sat down to examine Zahidi's correspondence. One of the first letters that caught our eye was a recent communication from a gentleman styling himself "German Consul General for South Persia," and apparently resident in the hills somewhere to the south. He spoke of Zahidi's activities in terms of general approval and, like all agents living in the hills, asked for more supplies. His letter left no doubt that the General's arrest had not come a moment too soon.

Visualizing the Circumstances

Maclean's daring capture of the Persian general is not just a solitary act. It is part of a whole set of circumstances. To fully appreciate this account you had to understand what these circumstances were and how they affected Maclean's exploit. If you were able to visualize the setting and the whole atmosphere of danger and intrigue, your reading was made more enjoyable and meaningful.

1. What was the situation in Persia so far as the Allies were concerned? In what way was General Zahidi's part a "sinister one," as the author says on page 438?

2. Was kidnapping the only possible plan to follow? Why was a military attack on the town or on the General's house not practical?

3. How well did you visualize the actual setting and happenings? Skim through the

paragraph beginning " I asked Gault where Zahidi lived," then describe in your own words the general's residence and surroundings. Perhaps you can draw a sketch on the blackboard.

Thinking It Over

1. Intelligence agents must undergo hard and precise training. What instances in this selection make you realize this? What are some of their duties?

2. We sometimes appreciate success better if we realize the consequences of failure. What would have happened if Captain Maclean's kidnapping project had failed? Try to reason this out by referring again to the whole set of circumstances surrounding the incident.

3. Why were the captain's superior officers so horrified at the idea of his masquerading as a brigadier? What evidence of official " red tape " did you discover?

For Your Vocabulary

COMMON WORDS: Find the paragraph beginning " If Zahidi could not conveniently be *winkled out* of his place of residence." A *winkle* is a *periwinkle,* a small snail. The snails are boiled – in the shell – and the one who eats them has to pull them out of their curved spiral shell with a bent pin or similar instrument. *Winkled out* is a good phrase! A *copious* lunch is a large or full one. It comes from the Latin *copia,* meaning " abundant." The Latin *cornu* means " horn "; *cornucopia,* " horn of plenty." This is a symbolic representation of plenty, and you see it often in pictures of Thanksgiving scenes. One of the persons involved in the ruse was a Persian *linguist,* that is, a person skilled in languages and especially the Persian language. *Linguist* comes from the Latin *lingua,* meaning " tongue " or " language." Many persons come from *bilingual* homes. Have you any idea what the term means? When the whole *convoy* swept over the bridge safely, you undoubtedly understood the author to mean the general's car, the jeep, and the trucks. Ordinarily we think of a convoy as a group of ships traveling together for protection. Actually, one armed ship can convoy another. Convoys can travel by land, sea, or air. Note that the word can be used as a noun and as a verb.

CHARLES LAUGHTON

Storytelling

Whoever has seen the movie *Mutiny on the Bounty* will remember the exciting scene in which Charles Laughton, in the character of Captain Bligh, bellows his rage at the mutineers on his ship. American movie, stage, and radio audiences have been thrilled for years by this English actor (now an American citizen). His deep but sensitive voice is known to millions. But Laughton is known not only as an actor. He has revived the art of " reading aloud " – a phrase Laughton doesn't use himself, incidentally – and has

"Storytelling" by Charles Laughton from *The Atlantic Monthly,* June, 1950. Reprinted by permission of the author.

traveled around the country reading Abraham Lincoln's Gettysburg Address, selections from Dickens' novels, sketches by James Thurber, and works from many other writers. During one trip he made fifty-two one-night stands, being greeted everywhere by large audiences who came to enjoy the oldest of entertainments – listening to a storyteller. In this essay, Charles Laughton tells about his career as a modern storyteller practicing an old art.

For Better Reading . . . Most articles you read in a magazine or newspaper present *facts;* they are mainly written to inform the reader. Usually, an informational article presents facts in a one-two-three order. The main idea of the article is stated, examples and details are given point by point to support the main idea, and then a conclusion is drawn. But in an essay like the following selection, the purpose is not only to give information but also to suggest the personality and tastes of the essayist himself. The writing is therefore indirect and rambling in approach, somewhat like a conversation between friends. Because of this the important ideas in the essay are not stated directly. See if you can determine the author's main ideas on the subject of storytelling.

WAY back in the late twenties at the Haymarket Theater in London I was rehearsing a play which was called *Mr. Pickwick,* founded on Charles Dickens' *Pickwick Papers.* We were rehearsing the famous Christmas scene at Dingley Dell farm – the scene of the mistletoe and the wassail [1] and the old lady and the fat boy and the blazing log fire and the dancing – and I found that I and it were dull and spiritless. Over the week end I went to visit my home town, and during the train ride to Scarborough and back I reread Dickens' book, and the language jigged and swirled and was breathless and peaceful by turns, and I remember thinking, even that long ago, that Dickens' text was complete of itself and that the mistake of our play was that it could not be transferred to any other medium without taking away its excitement. And I remember thinking then that I would like to work on this passage and read it aloud many times so that I could convey to people what Dickens' text did to me.

[1] **wassail** (wŏs'l): a spiced drink used for toasts at a festive time like Christmas.

About that time, too, I had a beautiful little book of Hans Andersen's story "The Nightingale" (it had illustrations by Edmund Dulac, and I have never been able to find the edition since) and I remember thinking that I would like to spend months learning how to tell that story to large numbers of people, as if I were the author inventing the story for the first time. I knew very clearly that it would be a long hard process. I knew that the smallest part of the labor would be the learning of these stories by heart.

I met Norman Corwin. My wife Elsa Lanchester and I did two shows with him on a program which he had in New York then, "The Pursuit of Happiness." One program was a condensation of Stephen Vincent Benét's *John Brown's Body;* the other was extracts from the work of Thomas Wolfe. Again with Norman I did a program of Sandburg, one of Wolfe, one of Walt Whitman; and I found the old ambition raging.

During the recent war I was in Hollywood. I was not actively in the war and I was restless. I had a heavy contract at a movie studio, and apparently I was be-

Charles Laughton, actor and storyteller.

having badly around the house. Elsa, who understands me only too well, said, "You're an out-of-work man and a nuisance around the house; get out of here and work." I was angry – very angry – but as usual, after two or three days I knew she was right. I was being paid a lot of money, but movie acting is no complete job. In a year it will absorb only four to five months of your time, and a tenth of a man's energy. I was in a still department one day, up at Universal, I think. There were two wounded men from Birmingham Hospital and I asked what the fellows did of an evening. They said, "Nothing," and I asked them if they would be interested in anybody's coming and reading to them a couple of times a week for two hours or so. They said they would, so I had a full occupation.

I read Dickens, Aesop, Shakespeare, Walt Whitman, Maupassant, James Thurber, Hans Andersen, Washington Irving, and what all. One day I picked up a Bible, and they protested. They did not want to hear anything from a dull book. The Bible was not dull to me, but I had to prove to them that it was not dull to me, and I used every trick that I had learned and they liked it and asked for more. We had a pleasant time. There is something about reading aloud to a group of people, however scarred, that turns them into children. These men would sit and listen to fairy stories. They found a reflection of their sufferings, which they had thought to be unique, in the tragedies of Shakespeare, and felt better. I lost my actor's nerves. I taught dozens of them how to read aloud to their wives and children. The whole affair is one of the good memories of my life.

One evening when I went home to Elsa I said that I believed people want this thing that I am doing; we are all disturbed and unsettled and seem to like sitting down and hearing about the same things that have happened to people in the past and which have been set down by great writers. I found that people all had — contrary to what I had been told in the entertainment industry — a common shy hunger for knowledge. I found that when I went home after one of these sessions I slept like a log — I am not normally a sound sleeper. I then began to read about reading aloud. I read of two famous tours of Charles Dickens; of Fanny Kemble and of the Chautauqua circuit; [1] and learned that I had invented nothing, but was carrying on an American tradition.

It is a friendly thing to read from great books to large numbers of people. I have always been a nervous actor and scared of appearing before audiences. I have never yet been scared when I have had a bundle of books under my arm.

I have been asked which of the great authors people seem to like best. I have read to audiences varying in size from several hundred to six thousand or so, and the main impression that I have taken away is that people have just liked hearing things out of real books. Sometimes they had said, "I liked Dickens best" (it may have been snowing outside — it was in Detroit); sometimes James Thurber (they wanted to laugh together); sometimes a Psalm (they wanted to be solemn together); and sometimes Shakespeare's magic wood from *A Midsummer Night's Dream* (they were indulging in magic together). There has been no preference. I have been moved by their acceptance of things particularly loved. And that is an interesting thing about people in theaters — doing things together. That is the beauty of being in a theater. That we all — fifteen hundred or so of us in a big room — do the same thing together at the same moment — laugh or wonder or pity — and we feel good and safe because the people around us are the same as we are.

I have thought about this a lot — what theater is — and I think this is a good part of what it is. And when we agree, as we mostly do, that a play is a good or a bad play, what we are saying is that it had the truth or it did not have the truth to fuse us then and there. And the communion that happens in a theater is one of the best things we have in life.

I have been asked about the techniques of reading aloud. I had better tell you something of my experiences in the hospitals when the men came to me and asked me to teach them to read love poems to their wives or Mother Goose stories to their children. They would first of all start by imitating my English accent. I had to get them back to speaking in the accents of the place they came from. People always speak most beautifully in the accents of their home towns — I, by the way, do not think that standard speech is the most alive speech. Then they would go downtown to some store and make recordings of their voices and I would have to tell them they had to learn to tell stories or poems to another person and that if they wanted to learn to read aloud well they must learn to seek the response in somebody else's eyes as they read; and so I would get them reading to each other. After that, it's a question of practice; a lot of practice. There are laws, to obey the rhythms laid down by the poet. The verse of Shakespeare has always made nonsense to me unless one follows strict-

[1] **Chautauqua circuit** (shȧ·tô′kwȧ sûr′kĭt): a traveling educational organization.

ly his iambic pentameter:[1] *de-dum, de-dum, de-dum, de-dum, de-dum;* but the whole thing is bound up in wanting to communicate something you like to others and have them like it too.

I know that some people could be angry about the remark about standard speech. I know someone who is a friend of mine who may be disappointed that I have made it. Her name is Margaret Pendergast McClean. She is a speech teacher and she has taught our Shakespeare class about the control of our voices. I know that standard speech is necessary in professional acting; otherwise in great centers such as New York and Chicago no plays could be put together if all the actors were speaking in the several accents of their home towns, but still I would like to hear *Julius Caesar* in Iowa in the speech of the Middle West, which is strong. And *Julius Caesar* in Oregon in the speech of the Far West, and *Julius Caesar* in New Orleans in the soft and lovely speech of the South. This would not work if your point of view is that *Julius Caesar* is chiefly about ancient Rome, but I think *Julius Caesar* is more about man as a political animal in the town in which it is being played in that year and at that moment. I hope Mrs. McClean will understand this, and will know that we are not ungrateful for what she has so usefully and patiently taught us.

I find myself objecting every time I either say or hear the phrase "reading aloud." Stories were told and retold for hundreds of years before they were set down, and these are the best stories, the stories which were told before they were written, and not written before they were read. This is so of the stories in the Bible. As an actor, it is easy for me to understand that they are for the voice. There are places to go loud and places to go soft and places to go fast and places to go slow. And any good actor is likely to go loud and soft and fast and slow in the same places all by himself. That is what I want to be — a storyteller. I would like to be the man who knows all the stories, who has on his back a bag full of stories, as bottomless as Santa Claus's bag of toys. But that can never be, because no man could ever know all the stories even if he were to live to be a thousand years old. I shall never even know all the stories in that way that I like best — but it is a good thing to want to go on living longer than possible. It is better than wishing you were dead.

[1] **iambic pentameter** (ī·ăm′bĭk pĕn·tăm′ê·tẽr): a line of verse having five beats, each consisting of two syllables, the second of which is accented.

Restating the Main Ideas

Try to complete the following main ideas — in your own words, if not the author's:

1. Some great authors' stories are written so well that . . .
2. Learning stories by heart is . . .
3. Storytelling in public is an old . . .
4. Reading from great books to large numbers of people is . . .
5. Audiences like to hear . . .
6. One of the best things in life is the communion . . .
7. The natural speech of an area is . . .
8. The best stories for reading aloud are . . .

Thinking It Over

1. There are so many important things in Mr. Laughton's article to talk about that you may not have time for them all. There is, for example, the whole question of storytelling and its place in handing down tradition from one generation to another; the loss of personal contact between the audience and the actor in movies, radio, and television; and the art of the actor in building a bridge from great writers to a listening audience. How does Mr. Laughton feel about all of these things? What do you

learn of his personal qualities and his interests from the essay? What kind of person emerges from this writing?

2. Make a list of all the persons mentioned by Mr. Laughton. You will find poets, actors, novelists, playwrights, and others, living and dead, on the list. Divide the work and look up the names in biographical reference books. Then report to the class. Don't forget to look up Mr. Laughton himself.

For Your Vocabulary

WORD DISTINCTIONS: The word *communion* means "sharing with others," and almost all the other words which have this *commun-* beginning also contain the idea of sharing. Only when the word is capitalized does it refer to the religious celebration of the Lord's Supper, which is also a sharing experience. A *community* is a group of people having the same common dwelling place, sharing the same general living conditions. *Communicate* means "to tell to others." Thus the knowledge becomes common; it is shared with others. How does the word *communism* apply here? Many *communal* groups, usually of a religious order, have existed from time to time in this country. Do you know about any of them?

RED SMITH

Ben Hogan

Americans are sports-minded. A good many men pick up the newspaper, glance hastily at the headlines to see if the world has collapsed since the last edition, and then turn quickly to the sports section. A surprising number of women read the sports pages, too, and write letters to the editor about figures in the sports world. People who have never seen a game of golf, for example, will follow with intense interest the story of a thrilling national championship contest, especially if there is some human interest "angle." Such a contest occurred one June day in 1950, and one of America's best sports writers was there to report it. Red Smith, a Notre Dame alumnus and sports columnist for the New York *Herald Tribune* (his real name is Walter Wellesley Smith, but no one calls him anything but Red), told the story in his column next day. This is excellent writing and typical of the style of so many sports reporters who have become recognized creative writers: Ring Lardner, John Kieran, Gene Fowler, and many others. Note the short sentences, the economy of words. A lesser writer might have said too much.

For Better Reading . . . Being able to summarize – to pick out a main point and the evidence or ideas that support or illustrate it – is one of the marks of an expert reader. Try your skill on this highly condensed selection.

To say there never has been another achievement in competitive sports comparable to Ben Hogan's victory in the National Open golf championship is not mere understatement; it is practically an insult to language. We shall not live to see anything like it again.

When Ben talked to the press after the title playoff at the Merion Golf Club outside Philadelphia, he asked the newspapermen to play down references to the automobile accident that destroyed everything save his life and his will sixteen months ago. He wanted them to ignore a story which will be told to succeeding generations as long as games are played. He thought the tale of what happened in those four days at Merion should be written simply as a golf story. He did not see that it is something immeasurably bigger than that — the story of a man.

Sporting literature is studded with stories of men who succeeded in spite of grave physical handicaps. But what Hogan accomplished was not merely a physical victory, a demonstration of extraordinary recuperative powers. Maybe once in the lifetime of any of us it is possible to say with accuracy and without mawkishness,[1] "This was a spiritual victory, an absolute triumph of will." This is that one time.

Ben Hogan always was tough. They call him "Little Ben," but he is a very big little man, all whalebone and rawhide, and as tough in mind as in body. To get his first job on a golf course, he had to whip the best scrapper among the caddies. To make his way on the tournament circuit, he had to whip bad luck and failure and his own temper and comparative poverty.

In a slugging game, he had to outslug men far bigger and more powerful than he. By mastering every stroke in the game, he became the most nearly perfect golfer of his time; by mastering himself, the most nearly perfect competitor.

Then a bus smashed his car and him to pieces. There was doubt that he could live, but he lived. It was questionable whether he would walk again. As for playing golf — well, with the single exception of balk-line billiards, there is no other game which demands such tyrannical control of muscles and nerves, such strength and delicacy of touch, such power of concentration, such domination of the imagination, as big league golf. And Ben's bones were shattered, muscles torn, nerves ripped.

Before he could learn to walk again, he had to stand. After the months of doctoring, there were months of daily massage, hour upon hour. Then he took a step. Then he walked around the room. Then around the block. Standing in his room, he jogged, up and down, up and down, up and down, clenching and relaxing his fingers with a rubber ball in each fist, rebuilding every muscle, commanding every nerve.

Before he was strong enough to remain long on his feet, he was back in tournament golf — resting on a chair between shots. When he played in the Open, there was still a stiffness in his gait. On the course he used a golf club as a cane. In the hotel lobby he stood straight, but always with his back against a pillar.

Merion is an exacting, constricted course whose par of 70 defeated splendid golfers like Sam Snead and Jimmy Demaret and Cary Middlecoff. Congested as it was during the Open, a succession of sweltering bottlenecks from clubhouse to eighteenth green, it was a difficult place merely to get around.

[1] **mawkishness** (môk'ĭsh·nĕs): weak or foolish sentimentality.

Above, *Ben Hogan (in the dark sweater) sinks a final putt at the Merion Golf Club in Ardmore, Pennsylvania, to win the 1950 National Open Golf championship.* (Wide World)

Left, *The champion!* (Wide World)

Healthy spectators came back bushed after walking eighteen holes in the punishing sun.

Hogan played eighteen holes on Thursday, eighteen on Friday, thirty-six on Saturday – the first double round he had attempted in two years – and eighteen on Sunday.

He is a golfer who knows exactly what he can do with every club in his bag in every circumstance. That is why he asked the press to play down his injuries. He dislikes to be pictured as a handicapped golfer because he feels, rightly, that he still has all the strokes. The only thing he wasn't sure he had was the necessary stamina, and on Saturday he showed himself that he did.

Yet when the job was done that day, he still had to go eighteen holes against two fine golfers – Lloyd Mangrum and George Fazio. So he went on, playing the same game he had played from the first tee on the first day.

It was a studied game, an intellectual game. Every shot he made was calculated to match par exactly. Not many missed. He scored 72 – 69 – 72 – 74 – 69. He beat everybody and every thing.

Watching, one thought of the wartime slogan of the Seabees: "The impossible takes a little longer." It took Ben sixteen months.

Summarizing the Main Point

Summarize this article in one sentence. After you have a satisfactory statement of perhaps twenty or twenty-five words, reduce the whole idea to a brief newspaper headline type of statement. Use the present tense in the verb. Pretend that you are a "rewrite man" who has been told to cut this article to save space. Pick out six or seven of the most important points and make each one into a sentence. The more points you can condense into one sentence, the more you can use. Cut out all unnecessary words. Precede these points with a sentence that serves as an introduction, and end them with a sentence giving a general conclusion.

Thinking It Over

1. After reading that story you can hardly fool yourself into thinking that you have a good excuse for cutting gym. What does Red Smith mean by saying that Ben Hogan's winning of the contest was a "spiritual victory"? What qualities does he attribute to Hogan? What has been Mr. Hogan's record since 1950?

2. Mr. Smith says that sporting literature is studded with stories of men who succeeded in spite of grave physical handicaps. This is a good time to recall and exchange some of those stories if you know them. Look for others.

3. Try your hand at sports writing yourself. Cover the next school game or some local or national event, possibly one you have seen on television. Study the style of different sports columnists and reporters and try to imitate their *best* features, such as vigorous, colorful language and directness and brevity of statement.

For Your Vocabulary

CONTEXT: Try to decide the meaning of the italicized words from the setting in which they are found.

1. "a demonstration of extraordinary *recuperative* power"

2. "such *domination* of the imagination"

3. "an exacting, *constricted* course"

4. "The thing he wasn't sure he had was the necessary *stamina*."

ZULMA STEELE

Friend of Every Friendless Beast

If a dog is run over by a car, or a cat climbs to the top of a tall tree and refuses to come down, someone usually hurries to the telephone and calls up the ASPCA, often called the Humane Society. He would find the telephone number under American Society for the Prevention of Cruelty to Animals, an organization for which many an animal lover has had occasion to be grateful. The man who founded it deserves to be remembered. It takes one kind of courage to brave a lion and quite another to interfere with a man who is beating his own horse. Henry Bergh's adventures in his fight against such cruelty make an inspiring story.

For Better Reading . . . Try, as you read, to separate the important facts from the less important. For example, after you have read through a third or a half of the story, think back to the opening incidents and decide whether they are really important — and if so, in what way. Since this article is mainly about Henry Bergh in his role as a reformer, try to judge which particular facts about him are important in helping you to understand his career.

It happened in the New York of 1866 — a city of horsecars and hansom cabs. A weary truck horse pulled up to the curb and quivered under the driver's whip. The truckman shouted "C'mon you —— " and laid on the lash.

Suddenly, the flickering light of a street lamp outlined a man in Prince Albert coat and top hat.

"Stop, my friend!" he said to the driver. "You can't do that."

"Can't beat my own horse?" sneered the truckman. "Who says I can't?" And the lash flicked out again at the weary horse.

The top-hatted gentleman raised his cane to call a nearby policeman. "Arrest this driver," he said. "The charge is cruelty to animals."

In court the driver, still muttering about "meddling swells," paid a fine of $10. It was one of the first convictions secured by the new Society for the Prevention of Cruelty to Animals, which was founded in that same year of 1866 by the same impeccable gentleman, Henry Bergh.

Today, kindness to animals is an axiom everywhere. Animal owners practice it — or else — the "else" meaning that the ASPCA gets after them. But in bygone days the devoted dog, the faithful horse, received no more protection than a man's umbrella.

When Henry Bergh set out to apply his hard-won anticruelty law, he met with sneers and catcalls. Yet the Great Meddler, as he was called, carried on almost singlehanded. Why did this sensitive, wealthy crusader persist? The answer lies in the strange career of one of the most colorful reformers in American history.

Young Bergh, scion [1] of a shipbuilding family, was educated in the arts, then took the fashionable Grand Tour abroad. When he was appointed by Abraham Lincoln as Secretary to the United States legation in St. Petersburg, he sported gold lace and a Napoleonic hat.

One day, while driving in the Czar's capital, Bergh saw a horse fall to its knees beneath the lash of a Russian cabby. Leaping from the legation carriage, he snatched the upraised whip. The cabman, cowed by the air of authority, began to bow and scrape.

"At last I've found a use for my gold braid," Bergh told the court — and shortly resigned from the diplomatic service.

Bergh, it seemed, had glimpsed a new goal in life. Borrowing the scheme for his humane society from England's Royal SPCA, he hurried home to America. Two years later, in 1866, he founded the first American Society for the Prevention of Cruelty to Animals.

Peter Cooper, John Jacob Astor, Jr., August Belmont, C.V.S. Roosevelt, Horace Greeley — charter members of the Society — joined him in the extravagant pledge "that the blood-red hand of cruelty shall no longer torture dumb beasts with impunity."

More than fine words, however, were needed to combat the brutal conditions of Bergh's day. Cities were run by horsepower, and the horse-railway companies by political influence. "Sportsmen" indulged in dogfighting, cockfighting, and live pigeon shoots. Butchers and dairymen, running their businesses strictly for profit, had no time for kindness to animals.

When Bergh set out from ASPCA headquarters to patrol the streets, New Yorkers shrugged off the elegant eccentric [2] as just another "crank." The newspapers ignored him. What he needed was a device to make people sit up and take notice of his crusade. The break came when the schooner *Active*, loaded with turtles, docked at an East River pier.

In the hold of the ship, Bergh found a hundred turtles half-dead, blood oozing from their flippers where holes had been drilled and rope run through them. Arresting the captain and his crew, Bergh marched them to the Tombs, followed by a boisterous mob.

In court, defense counsel argued that the new laws were made for animals, not turtles. What then, asked Bergh, *was* the turtle? Surely not mineral or vegetable? He lost the case midst cynical laughter, but gained his point, for the New York *Herald* devoted six columns to the trial. Next day a million people knew about his aims.

Soon Bergh began to employ uniformed agents, armed with powers of arrest. Fewer blows rained down upon the backs of overburdened horses. Ridicule gave way to respect as carters and butcher boys found the fashionable "toff" [3] and his helpers did not flinch at oaths or recoil from brickbats. In court, Bergh used his political influence to see

[1] **scion** (sī'ŭn): descendant.

[2] **eccentric** (ĕk·sĕn'trĭk): a queer, odd person.
[3] **toff** (tŏf): British slang for a fine gentleman; a dandy.

that judges weighted the anticruelty law with fines.

After four years' work, the ASPCA badge had won recognition through most of New York City, yet Bergh had made no headway against the transit companies that abused their horses. One blizzardy afternoon, at a downtown corner, he stepped onto the tracks, right in the path of an overloaded car being dragged by two tired nags.

"Unload!" he ordered, turning back the lapel of his coat to show the Society badge.

"Get out of the way!" cried the driver, doubling his fists. Swiftly, the six-foot Bergh pulled the man from his seat and tossed him headlong into a snowbank.

The car behind stopped, and the next, and the next. Soon a blockade extended a quarter mile, while chilly passengers fumed. The streetcar company tried to send cars up Fourth Avenue, but ASPCA agents stopped them at the Bowery. For two hours, Bergh kept his finger pressed on the main arteries of the city's rush-hour traffic.

Finally, at 7 P.M., the company gave in. As soon as Bergh saw doubled horse teams on the downtown route – four animals instead of two to pull a car – the lines began to move again. Next day, the ASPCA was the talk of the town.

Bergh invaded one abattoir[1] where hogs were being thrown into boiling water. "The laws of God and man are against this cruelty to helpless animals," he told the butchers. "I appeal to your manhood to help me in saving unnecessary suffering."

The men fell back, baffled. Slaughterhouse "rings" fought his interference in court. But ensuing publicity brought down on their heads the rules of enlightened health boards.

[1] **abattoir** (ăb'ȧ·twär'): a slaughterhouse.

As the influence of the Society grew, Henry Bergh watched anxiously over his diminishing funds. One night, working late over figures, he glanced about his dingy attic office. There were not even enough chairs to seat the agents who carried on his work! Something must be done. But what?

Like an answer to prayer came a knock on the ASPCA door. Would Mr. Bergh visit a sick man in the hospital? Wondering, Bergh went to the bedside of Louis Bonard,[2] a Frenchman who had made a fortune trading with the Indians. The old man's gaunt face lighted.

"You will go far!" he said, and began pouring out admiration of Bergh's work in an excitable mixture of French and English.

"Perhaps," said Bergh sadly. And then he confessed that his society could not go on without help.

"*Mon ami,*" said the trader, "I shall help you! Only promise that if ever you have the power, you will extend your protection to the wild things of forest and plain."

Bonard died soon afterward, leaving $100,000 to the Society. This sum, plus other contributions which followed, enabled the ASPCA to acquire larger offices and to spread the word through a countrywide campaign. Eventually, Bonard's dream of helping the animals whose pelts and feathers had built his fortune came true with today's wildlife conservation program and the Audubon Society, of which Bergh was vice-president.

Bergh lived to become a prophet not without honor, though always a paradox. One might have expected the animals' champion to surround himself with pets, yet at home no puppy ran to greet him. Still he loudly praised "man's

[2] **Louis Bonard** (lwē bô·när').

best friend." No pet canary perched on Bergh's well-tailored shoulder, yet he crusaded in defense of the pesky English sparrow and raged against those who recommended that the birds be killed and made into potpies. Reportedly, Bergh had no love for cats, yet he sneaked bits of food for stray felines from his table at Delmonico's.[1]

Bergh seemed not even especially fond of horses, for whose cause his society did so much, although he retired a stableful of New York hacks to quiet old age at his estate on Lake Mahopac.[2] He was never seen to fondle a handsome steed, yet he did not consider it beneath him to bring hay and water with manicured hands to a horse fallen on icy streets.

As the years caught up with him, Bergh brooded: "I hate to think what may befall this society when I am gone." He need not have worried. So firm was its foundation – morally and financially – that practically every branch of humane work now carried on for animals had its roots in the farseeing vision of Henry Bergh.

Each year in New York City, the ASPCA investigates almost as many cases of cruelty to animals as the more than twelve thousand covered during the twenty-two years of Bergh's leadership. Its five shelters handle more than two hundred fifty thousand animals a year.

The thirty-three societies he inspired throughout the country have grown to more than six hundred. What's more, their influence is felt today in every home and classroom, in every poultry market, pet shop, dog pound, race track, stable, circus – even in Hollywood where a humane agent looks out for the safety of animal actors in the movies.

"Age is a point I am very tender upon," Bergh once remarked. "I'm never going to be more than forty-five!"

Thirty years over his deadline, however, in his seventy-fifth year, he ended an amazing career at dawn of New York's famous blizzard of '88. For the first time in twenty-two years, the animal's friend failed to command the ASPCA as agents worked to rescue snowbound animals.

While the ASPCA became a household word, the name of Henry Bergh vanished with the snowflakes. Yet he won poetic immortality in Longfellow's lines:

> Among the noblest of the land,
> Though he may count himself the least,
> That man I honor and revere,
> Who, without favor, without fear,
> In the great city dares to stand
> The friend of every friendless beast!

[1] **Delmonico's** (dĕl·mŏn′ĭ·kōz): a famous restaurant in New York City during the nineteenth century.

[2] **Lake Mahopac** (mā′ō·păk): a lake in New York State, about 50 miles north of New York City.

Recognizing the Important Facts

1. Why does the author begin with a dramatic incident? Where does the article proper actually begin?

2. Pick out the statements that build up the character of Henry Bergh. Name two or three of his most important characteristics.

3. Among the statements below, five are very important and five of only minor significance. Discuss these statements and when you have found the five of greatest importance, tell why each one is worthy of note.

a. Bergh was called the Great Meddler.

b. Bergh was not fond of pets.

c. Bergh knew of England's Royal SPCA.

d. Louis Bonard left $100,000 to the Society.

e. Bergh won the help of the New York *Herald.*

f. In Russia, Bergh wore gold lace and a Napoleonic hat.

g. The streetcar company gave in to Bergh.

h. Bergh owned an estate on Lake Mahopac.

i. There are now over 600 ASPCA branches.

Thinking It Over

1. What do you know about the work of the SPCA in your community? Is there a junior branch in your school? How would it be possible for high school pupils to further the work of the organization?
2. In what ways do well-meaning people who actually love their pets sometimes ill-treat them? What persons or groups were opposed to Bergh's movement and why?
3. Read the names of the charter members again. All of those men became famous. See if you can find out why. Also, find out what you can about the Audubon Society.
4. Write or tell an incident involving cruelty to animals which you yourself have observed.

For Your Vocabulary

WORD BUILDING: The term *paradox* comes from the Greek and means " a contradiction " or " two opposing ideas." It was a *paradox,* therefore, that Henry Bergh was a champion of helpless animals, yet he . . . (You complete the statement.)

Two Latin words meaning " godlike " or " not mortal " give us the term *immortality.* Today this usually means " unending fame," and the word is often loosely applied. Even during his lifetime one knew that Babe Ruth had achieved baseball *immortality.* But does your school football hero, making a touchdown in the last minute of a game, win *immortality?* What if this were the last game of the season and for a championship?

A *legation* is any group of persons who legally act for others. A foreign minister and his staff are a legation. Under what circumstances might a group of pupils act as a legation?

Manicure, the noun, means " hand care " and especially " care of the nails." Have you any idea what *pedicure* might mean? The word *pedal* might give you a clue.

ROBERT BENCHLEY

A Good Old-fashioned Christmas

Robert Benchley was one of the best-loved of our modern humorists. His long list of witty and entertaining books, his frequent contributions to current magazines, and the hilarious movie " shorts " in which he appeared, playing himself, made him a familiar figure on the American scene even after his death in 1945. As a rule, all we ask of a humorist is that he be funny. We don't usually investigate the sources of his material — we just enjoy it. When we come to examine Mr. Benchley's sketches, however, we are surprised to note how many of them are actually a kind of exaggerated autobiography of practically any typical American. Benchley was able, in a phrase, to make us see the humor in the ordinary and conventional ideas and habits of us all. In this essay he suggests that all the talk about the "good old days" needs to be taken with a grain of Benchley, who is a very special kind of literary salt.

For Better Reading . . . Humor is created in many different ways, three of which are illustrated very well in this essay. *Irony* is a form of humor that Mr. Benchley uses frequently. An *ironical* statement is a usually humorous sarcasm in which an author says the opposite of what he means. When you say, "Well, I like that!" with an emphasis on "that," you are being ironical. *Exaggeration,* another form of humor, is simply stretching the truth beyond reason. A third form is *absurdity,* the putting together of ideas which are unexpected and nonsensical. Keep these kinds of humor in mind as you go through the essay — you'll recognize them between smiles and laughs!

SOONER or later at every Christmas party, just as things are beginning to get good, someone shuts his eyes, puts his head back, and moans softly: "Ah, well, this isn't like the old days. We don't seem to have any good old-fashioned Christmases any more." To which the answer from my corner of the room is: "All right! That suits me!"

Just what they have in mind when they say "old-fashioned Christmas" you never can pin them down to telling. "Lots of snow," they mutter, "and lots of food." Yet, if you work it right, you can still get plenty of snow and food today. Snow, at any rate.

Then there seems to be some idea of the old-fashioned Christmas being, of necessity, in the country. It doesn't make any difference whether you were raised on a farm or whether your ideas of a rural Christmas were gleaned from pictures in old copies of *Harper's Young People,* you must give folks to understand that such were the surroundings in which you spent your childhood holidays. And that, ah, me, those days will never come again!

Well, supposing you get your wish sometime. Supposing, let us say, your wife's folks who live up in East Russet, Vermont, write and ask you to come up and bring the children for a good old-fashioned Christmas, "while we are all still together," they add cheerily with their flair for putting everybody in good humor.

Hurray, hurray! Off to the country for Christmas! Pack up all the warm clothes in the house, for you will need them up there where the air is clean and cold. Snowshoes? Yes, put them in, or better yet, Daddy will carry them. What fun! Take along some sleigh bells to jangle in case there aren't enough on the pung.[1] There must be jangling sleigh bells. Now we're off! Good-by, all! Good-by! JANGLE-JANGLE-JANGLE-Jangle-Jangle-Jangle-jangle-jangle-jangle-jangle-jangle-jangle!

In order to get to East Russet you take the Vermont Central as far as Twitchell's Falls and change there for Torpid River Junction, where a spur line takes you right into Gormley. At Gormley you are met by a buckboard which takes you back to Torpid River Junction again. By this time a train or something has come in which will wait for the local from Besus. While waiting for this you will

[1] **pung** (pŭng): a box sled.

have time to send your little boy to school, so that he can finish the third grade.

At East Russet Grandpa meets you with the sleigh. The bags are piled in, and Mother sits in front with Lester in her lap while Daddy takes Junior and Ga-Ga in back with him and the luggage. Giddap, Esther Girl!

Esther Girl giddaps, and two suitcases fall out. Heigh-ho! Out we get and pick them up, brushing the snow off and filling our cuffs with it as we do so. After all, there is nothing like snow for getting up one's cuffs. Good clean snow never hurt anyone. Which is lucky, because after you have gone a mile or so, you discover that Ga-Ga is missing. Never mind, she is a self-reliant little girl and will doubtless find her way to the farm by herself. Probably she will be there waiting for you when you arrive.

The farm is situated on a hill about eleven hundred miles from the center of town, just before you get into Canada. If there is a breeze in winter, they get it. But what do they care for breezes, so long as they have the Little Colonel oil heater in the front room, to make everything cozy and warm within a radius of four inches! And the big open fireplace with the draft coming down it! Fun for everybody!

You are just driving up to the farmhouse in the sleigh, with the entire right leg frozen where the lap robe has slipped out. Grandma is waiting for you at the door and you bustle in, all glowing with good cheer. "Merry Christmas, Grandma!" Lester is cross and Junior is asleep and has to be dragged by the hand upstairs, bumping against each step all the way. It is so late that you decide that you all might as well go to bed, especially as you learn that breakfast is at four-thirty. It usually is at four, but Christmas being a holiday everyone sleeps late.

As you reach the top of the stairs you get into a current of cold air which has something of the quality of the temperature in a nice well-regulated crypt.[1] This is the Bed Room Zone, and in it the thermometer never tops the zero mark from October fifteenth until the middle of May. Those rooms in which no one sleeps are used to store perishable vegetables in, and someone has to keep thumbing the tomatoes and pears every so often to prevent their getting so hard that they crack.

The way to get undressed for bed in one of Grandpa's bedrooms is as follows: Starting from the foot of the stairs where it is warm, run up two at a time to keep the circulation going as long as possible. Opening the bedroom door with one hand, tear down the curtains from the windows with the other, pick up the rugs from the floor, and snatch the spread from the top of the bureau. Pile all these on the bed, cover with the closet door which you have wrenched from its hinges, and leap quickly underneath. It sometimes helps to put on a pair of rubbers over your shoes.

And even when you are in bed, you have no guarantee of going to sleep. Grandpa's mattresses seem to contain the overflow from the silo, cornhusks, baked-potato skins, and long, stringy affairs which feel like pipe cleaners. On a cold night, snuggling down into these is about like snuggling down into a bed of damp pine cones out in the forest.

Then there are Things abroad in the house. Shortly after you get into bed, the stairs start snapping. Next something runs along the roof over your head. You say to yourself: "Don't be

[1] **crypt** (krĭpt): an underground burial chamber.

silly. It's only Santa Claus." Then it runs along in the wall behind the head of the bed. Santa Claus wouldn't do that. Down the long hall which leads into the ell of the house you can hear the wind sighing softly, with an occasional reassuring bang of a door.

The unmistakable sound of someone dying in great pain rises from just below the window sill. It is a sort of low moan, with just a touch of strangulation in it. Perhaps Santa has fallen off the roof. Perhaps that story you once heard about Grandpa's house having been a hangout for Revolutionary smugglers is true, and one of the smugglers has come back for his umbrella. The only place at a time like this is down under the bedclothes. But the children become frightened and demand to be taken home, and Grandpa has to be called to explain that it is only Blue Bell out in the barn. Blue Bell has asthma, and on a cold night they have to be very patient with her.

Christmas morning dawns cloudy and cold, with the threat of plenty more snow, and, after all, what would Christmas be without snow? You lie in bed for one hour and a quarter trying to figure out how you can get up without losing the covers from around you. A glance at the water pitcher shows that it is time for them to put the red ball up for skating. You think of the nice warm bathroom at home, and decide that you can wait until you get back there before shaving.

This breaking the ice in the pitcher seems to be a feature of the early lives of all great men which they look back on with tremendous satisfaction. "When I was a boy, I used to have to break the ice in the pitcher every morning before I could wash," is said with as much pride as one might say, "When I was a boy I stood at the head of my class." Just what virtue there is in having to break ice in a pitcher is not evident, unless it lies in their taking the bother to break the ice and wash at all. Any time that I have to break ice in a pitcher as a preliminary to washing, I go unwashed, that's all. And Benjamin Franklin and U. S. Grant and Rutherford B. Hayes can laugh as much as they like. I'm nobody's fool about a thing like that.

Getting the children dressed is a lot of fun when you have to keep pumping their limbs up and down to keep them from freezing out stiff. The children love it and are just as bright and merry as little pixies when it is time to go downstairs and say "Good morning" to Grandpa and Grandma. The entire family enters the dining room purple and chattering and exceedingly cross.

After breakfast everyone begins getting dinner. The kitchen being the only warm place in the house may have something to do with it. But before long there are so many potato peelings and turkey feathers and squash seeds and floating bits of pie crust in the kitchen that the womenfolk send you and the children off into the front part of the house to amuse yourselves and get out of the way.

Then what a jolly time you and the kiddies and Grandpa have together! You can either slide on the horsehair sofa, or play "The Wayside Chapel" on the piano (the piano has scrollwork on either side of the music rack with yellow silk showing through), or look out the window and see ten miles of dark gray snow. Perhaps you may even go out to the barn and look at the horses and cows, but really, as you walk down between the stalls, when you have seen one horse or one cow you have seen them all. And besides, the cold in the barn has an added flavor of damp harness leather and musty carriage upholstery which eats into your very marrow.

Of course, there are the presents to be distributed, but that takes on much the same aspect as the same ceremony in the new-fashioned Christmas, except that in the really old-fashioned Christmas the presents weren't so tricky. Children got mostly mittens and shoes, with a sled thrown in sometimes for dissipation. Where a boy today is bored by three o'clock in the afternoon with his electric grain elevator and miniature pond with real perch in it, the old-fashioned boy was lucky if he got a copy of *Naval Battles of the War of 1812* and an orange. Now this feature is often brought up in praise of the old way of doing things. "I tell you," says Uncle Gyp, "the children in my time never got such presents as you get today." And he seems proud of the fact, as if there were some virtue accruing to him for it. If the children of today can get electric grain elevators and tin automobiles for Christmas, why aren't they that much better off than their grandfathers who got only wristlets? Learning the value of money, which seems to be the only argument of the standpatters, doesn't hold very much water as a Christmas slogan. The value of money can be learned in just about five minutes when the time comes, but Christmas is not the season.

But to return to the farm, where you and the kiddies and Gramp' are killing time. You can either bring in wood from the woodshed, or thaw out the pump, or read the books in the bookcase over the writing desk. Of the three, bringing in the wood will probably be the most fun, as you are likely to burn yourself thawing out the pump, and the list of reading matter on hand includes *The Life and Deeds of General Grant, Our First Century, Andy's Trip to Portland,* bound volumes of the Jersey Cattle Breeders' Gazette, and *Diseases of the Horse.* Then there are some old copies of *Round the Lamp* for the years 1850–54 and some colored plates showing plans for the approaching World's Fair at Chicago.

Thus the time passes, in one round of gaiety after another, until you are summoned to dinner. Here all caviling[1] must cease. The dinner lives up to the advertising. If an old-fashioned Christmas could consist entirely of dinner without the old-fashioned bedrooms, the old-fashioned pitcher, and the old-fashioned entertainments, we professional pessimists wouldn't have a turkey leg left to stand on. But, as has been pointed out, it is possible to get a good dinner without going up to East Russet, Vt., or, if it isn't, then our civilization has been a failure.

And the dinner only makes the aftermath seem worse. According to an old custom of the human race, everyone overeats. Deliberately and with considerable gusto you sit at the table and say pleasantly: "My, but I won't be able to walk after this. Just a little more of the dark meat, please, Grandpa, and just a dab of stuffing. Oh, dear, that's too much!" You haven't the excuse of the drunkard, who becomes oblivious to his excesses after several drinks. You know what you are doing, and yet you make light of it and even laugh about it as long as you *can* laugh without splitting out a seam.

And then you sit and moan. If you were having a good new-fashioned Christmas you could go out to the movies or take a walk, or a ride, but to be really old-fashioned you must stick close to the house, for in the old days there were no movies and no automobiles and

[1] **caviling** (kăv'ĭl·ĭng): frivolous faultfinding.

Drawing by Gluyas Williams in The Early Worm, *by Robert Benchley, 1927.*

if you wanted to take a walk you had to have the hired man go ahead of you with a snow shovel and make a tunnel. There are probably plenty of things to do in the country today, and just as many automobiles and electric lights as there are in the city, but you can't call Christmas with all these improvements "an old-fashioned Christmas." That's cheating.

If you are going through with the thing right, you have got to retire to the sitting room after dinner and *sit*. Of course, you can go out and play in the snow if you want to, but you know as well as I do that this playing in the snow is all right when you are small but a bit trying on anyone over thirty. And anyway, it always began to snow along about three in the afternoon of an old-fashioned Christmas day, with a cheery old leaden sky overhead and a jolly old gale sweeping around the corners of the house.

No, you simply must sit indoors, in front of a fire if you insist, but nevertheless with nothing much to do. The children are sleepy and snarling. Grandpa is just sleepy. Someone tries to start the conversation, but everyone else is too gorged with food to be able to move the lower jaw sufficiently to articulate. It develops that the family is in possession of the loudest-ticking clock in the world and along about four o'clock it begins to break its own record. A stenographic report of the proceedings would read as follows:

"Ho-hum! I'm sleepy! I shouldn't have eaten so much."

"Tick-tock-tick-tock-tick-tock-tick-tock—"

"It seems just like Sunday, doesn't it?"

" Look at Grandpa! He's asleep."

" Here, Junior! Don't plague Grandpa. Let him sleep."

" Tick-tock-tick-tock-tick-tock — "

" Junior! Let Grandpa alone! Do you want Mamma to take you upstairs? "

" Ho-hum! "

" Tick-tock-tick-tock-tick-tock — "

Louder and louder the clock ticks, until something snaps in your brain and you give a sudden leap into the air with a scream, finally descending to strangle each of the family in turn, and Grandpa as he sleeps. Then, as you feel your end is near, all the warm things you have ever known come back to you, in a flash. You remember the hot Sunday subway to Coney, your trip to Mexico, the bullfighters of Spain.

You dash out into the snowdrifts and plunge along until you sink exhausted. Only the fact that this article ends here keeps you from freezing to death, with an obituary the next day reading:

" DIED suddenly, at East Russet, Vt., of an old-fashioned Christmas."

Recognizing the Elements of Humor

Do you recall these choice bits of humor: the roundabout way of getting to the farm; sending the little boy to school; losing the little girl and not stopping for her; the distance of the farm from the town; the heat made by the oil heater; the fun from the drafty fireplace; the frozen leg; late breakfast because of the holiday; the temperature of the bedrooms; thumbing the pears and tomatoes; directions for going to bed. What other incidents or descriptions struck you as funny? Do you think you could fit these to the definitions of *exaggeration*, *irony*, and *absurdity*, as given on page 459? How would you apply these terms to comic strips and slapstick movies?

Thinking It Over

1. Do you think Robert Benchley ever actually experienced anything like what he described? Allowing for exaggeration, which parts sound true? Would any parts fit your own family experience?

2. Now and then there is a bit of good common sense to be found in Mr. Benchley's wild mental ramblings. At one point he says: " The value of money can be learned in just about five minutes when the time comes, but Christmas is not the season." Write two or three paragraphs on one of these topics: " My Attitude Toward Christmas Spending," or " When I Learned the Value of Money."

3. Find in the library books by other American humorists such as Mark Twain, John Kendrick Bangs, James Whitcomb Riley, Ellis Parker Butler, Frank R. Stockton, Oliver Herford, Don Marquis, Clarence Day, and Carolyn Wells. Somebody on the list ought to give you a laugh or two. Stephen Leacock is a Canadian, but he also belongs on that list.

THE SPIRIT OF ADVENTURE

Suggestions for Free Reading

Adams, Franklin P., *Innocent Merriment* (McGraw-Hill, 1942)
Humor selected by F. P. A., American columnist and humorist.

Amundsen, Roald, *The South Pole* (Keedick, 1913)
The Norwegian explorer's own story of his discovery of the South Pole. Read also *My Life as an Explorer* (Doubleday, 1927)

Andrews, Roy Chapman, *Ends of The Earth* (Putnam, 1920)
Expeditions and travels of the curator of the New York Museum of Natural History.

Asimov, Isaac, *Pebble in the Sky* (Doubleday, 1950)
Popular science-fiction. Shall earth be ruled by men from another world?

Berg, Victor, and Lanier, Henry W., *The Pearl Diver* (Doubleday, 1930)
Pearl-diving, cannibals, and head-hunters.

Bleiler, Everett F., and Dikty, T. E., *Best Science Fiction Stories* (Fell Science Fiction Library, 1949)

Burr, W. Leyson, *Modern Wonders and How They Work* (Dutton, 1949)

Atomic fission, rockets, jets, supersonic speed, radar, television. Watch imprint date in books like this. They get out of date fast.

Campbell, Captain William, *Arctic Patrols* (Bruce, 1936)
Color adventure with Royal Canadian Mounted Police.

Coffin, Robert P. Tristram, *Yankee Coast* (Macmillan, 1947)
For lovers of sailing and fishing.

Collins, Dale, *Shipmates Down Under* (Holiday, 1950)
Shipwreck on uncharted coral reef.

Collins, Jimmy, *Test Pilot* (Doubleday, 1935)
They take 'em up and try 'em.

Conklin, Graff, *Treasury of Science Fiction* (Crown, 1948)
A wide range of science stories.

Ellsberg, Edward, *Thirty Fathoms Deep* (Dodd, 1930)
Search for sunken treasure off coast of Peru. Read also *The Cruise of the Jeannette*, about a North Pole expedition (Dodd, 1949)

Fenimore, Stephen, *Bush Holiday* (Doubleday, 1949)
American boy in Australian bush. Ever meet a duckbilled platypus?

Flaherty, John J., *Men Without Fear* (Lippincott, 1940)
Thrills and hazards of most dangerous occupations. Read also *Aviation from the Ground Up* (Lippincott, 1950)

Furnas, Clifford Cook, *The Next Hundred Years; The Unfinished Business of Science* (World, 1942)

Gilbert, Kenneth, *Arctic Venture* (Holt, 1950)
Walrus hunting, treachery, trading with Eskimos. Exciting.

Heimlein, Robert, *Space Cadet* (Scribner, 1948)
Jet propulsion, rocket ships, and the " Interplanetary Patrol."

Henry, Thomas H., *The White Continent* (Sloane, 1951)
Stories of Arctic exploration.

Heyerdahl, Thor, *Kon-Tiki* (Rand, McNally, 1950)
Thrilling story of six men and their journey from Peru to Polynesia on a 45-foot balsa raft — one of the finest adventure stories of modern times.

Hubbard, Rev. Bernard R., S.J., *Cradle of the Storms* (Dodd, 1935); *Mush, You Malemutes* (American Press, 1932)
A missionary has exciting scientific adventures in Alaska and the Aleutians.

Johnson, Martin Elmer, *Safari* (Putnam, 1928); *Congorilla* (Harcourt, 1939)
Adventures of Martin and Osa Johnson in Africa.

Kjelgaard, Jim, *Buckskin Brigade* (Holiday, 1947)
Trail blazers of the American continent.

Lent, Henry B., *Aviation Cadet* (Macmillan, 1941)
The Coast Guard Air Patrol in peace and war.

Ley, Willy, *The Conquest of Space* (Viking, 1950)

Lindsay, Martin, *The Epic of Captain Scott* (Putnam, 1934)
The story of Robert Falcon Scott, part of whose story is told in this book.

Meader, Stephen, *Trap-Lines North* (Dodd, 1936)
Men live dangerously to provide ladies with furs.

Montague, Sydney R., *North to Adventure* (McBride, 1939)
Three years with the Canadian Mounted Police.

Nordhoff, Charles B., and Hall, James N., *Men Against the Sea* (Little, 1934)
If you like your sea stories tough, read this one and *Mutiny on the Bounty* (Little, 1932)

O'Brien, John S., *By Dog Sled for Byrd* (Follet, 1931)
Sixteen hundred miles across antarctic ice. Longest dog trip ever made.

Sokoloff, Boris, *The Miracle Drugs* (Ziff-Davis, 1940)

Stefansson, Vilhjalmur, *Hunters of the Great North* (Harcourt, 1922)
Heroic adventure in northern wilds.

Thurber, James, *The Thurber Carnival* (Harper, 1945)
The text is as funny as the drawings.

Untermeyer, Louis, *Treasury of Laughter* (Simon & Schuster, 1946)
Fun in prose and poetry.

From *Rio Grande, River of Destiny*, by Laura Gilpin, pub. by Duell, Sloan and Pearce

American Songs and Sketches

THE folk songs of America and the picture poems of her everyday scenes and people tell a great deal about our way of life, for the popular songs of America reflect the wide-ranging spirit of the peoples who came to her shores from many lands. These songs express the story of their labor and their fun, their dreams as well as their disappointments. Names of the writers have often been lost, but the songs live on and on.

More artistic than the folk songs are the pictures or sketches which poets have created. With words for their brushes and paints, the poets have given us scenes of both country and town, and a bright gallery of great and little-known Americans – the men and women who fought battles, tilled the soil, built cities, and made the nation strong. Here, in these songs and sketches, is part of the vivid and unforgettable story of America.

We usually think of " folk " songs as being poems created in the early days of a people's history, long before printing was known or education was widespread. In this sense, there are not many folk songs that are actually native to America. Our history and tradition do not go back far enough in this country to include songs like the old English and Scottish ballads, although variations of many of these ballads can be found in some parts of America.

Yet there are some poems that are truly American, songs created over the years out of the talk and humor and singing of the common people – songs that are similar to the old folk ballads. Nowhere else but here can you find the singing poetry of the Indian, the cowboy, and the Negro, or the many ditties that were sung along a young nation's wagon trails, canals, and railroads. Even tramps and hoboes, the "knights of the road," have their own characteristic ballads to sing as they ride the rails or gather in their " jungles " to build a comforting fire and cook an uncertain meal. Such songs constitute a part of our American folklore.

AMERICAN SONGS

A TRIP ON THE ERIE CANAL

At one time America's waterways provided her chief transportation, and canals were very important, but the railroads put most of the canals out of business. In a way this was unfortunate, because the canals and the people who traveled them were both colorful in their own way. Canal traffic was slow and hot, and the rough canalmen (or *canawlers,* as they called themselves) had lots of time for singing and joking and even fighting now and then – for there was always the struggle for first position at a lock. Here you see something of their rough-and-ready humor. We wonder if the cook really appreciated it!

You may talk about pleasures
  And trips on the lake;
But a trip on the Erie,
  You bet, takes the cake.
With the beefsteak as tough   5
  As a fighting dog's neck
And the flies playing tag
  With the cook on the deck.

The cook, she's a daisy;
  She's dead gone on me.   10
She has fiery red hair;
  And she's sweet twenty-three.
She's cross-eyed and freckled;
  She's a darling and a pet.
And we use her for a headlight   15
  At night on the deck.

So haul in your towline
  And pull in your slack;
Take a reef in your trousers,
  And straighten your back.   20
And mind what I say,
  Driver, never forget
To touch the mules gently
  When the cook's on the deck.

How Well Did You Read?

1. What is the visual picture that you get from lines 7 and 8? American humor of a hundred years ago was full of exaggeration. Can you point out a good example?

2. All of the third stanza is addressed to one person. Who is this person, and why is it addressed to him?

OH, BURY ME NOT ON THE LONE PRAIRIE

Nobody knows who wrote this cowboy song, but it is based on an old sea chantey. This may seem strange unless you know that many unemployed sailors in the old days drifted out West and became cowboys. Ballads like this one, usually sung by lumberjacks, cowboys, sailors, and other men far away from home, are frequently sorrowful and sentimental. The singer often accompanies himself on a guitar or banjo.

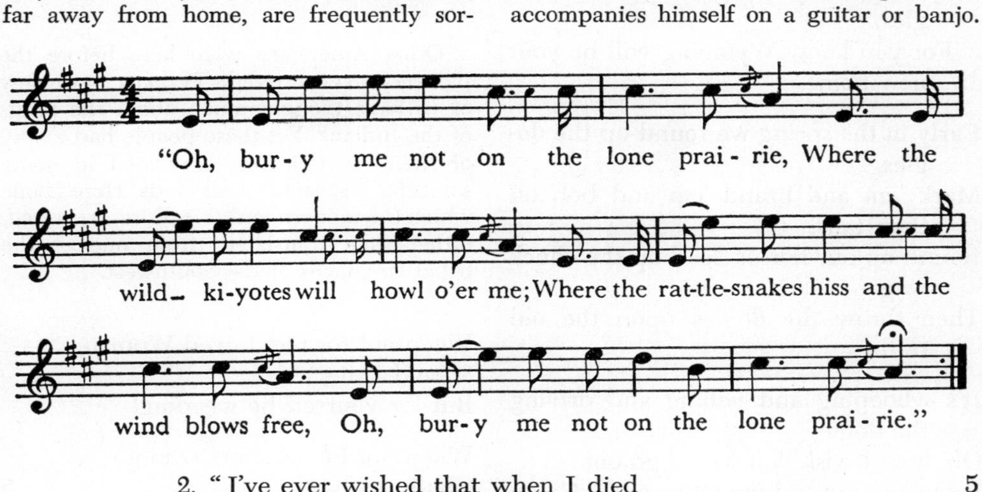

2. "I've ever wished that when I died
My grave might be on the old hillside;
Let there the place of my last rest be –
Oh, bury me not on the lone prairie! 5

3. "O'er my slumbers a mother's prayer
And a sister's tears will be mingled there; 10
For 'tis sad to know that the heart throb's o'er,
And that its fountain will gush no more.

4. "In my dreams I say" – but his voice failed there;
And they gave no heed to his dying prayer;
In a narrow grave six feet by three, 15
They buried him there on the lone prairie.

WHOOPEE TI YI YO

"Whoopee Ti Yi Yo" is a trail song, and dogies * are the herd calves that have been separated from their mothers. In this song you see dogies being driven north to the grasslands of Wyoming and Idaho for fattening. The scene is one you have often viewed in the movies – the men on horses, the cattle stirring up a cloud of dust, and the chuck wagon with provisions bouncing along behind.

* **dogies** (dō′gĭz).

As I walked out one morning for pleasure,
I spied a cowpuncher a-ridin' alone;
His hat was throwed back and his spurs was a-janglin',
As he approached me a-singin' this song,

Whoopee ti yi yo, git along, little dogies, 5
It's your misfortune, and none of my own.

Whoopee ti yi yo, git along, little dogies,
For you know Wyoming will be your new home.

Early in the spring we round up the dogies,
Mark 'em and brand 'em and bob off their tails; 10
Round up our horses, load up the chuck wagon,
Then throw the dogies upon the old trail.

It's whooping and yelling and driving the dogies;
Oh, how I wish you would go on!
It's whooping and punching and "Go on little dogies, 15
For you know Wyoming will be your new home."

Your mother she was raised way down in Texas,
Where the jimson weed and sandburs grow;
Now we'll fill you up on prickly pear and cholla°
Till you are ready for the trail to Idaho.

Oh, you'll be soup for Uncle Sam's Injuns; 21
"It's beef, heap beef," I hear them cry.
Git along, git along, git along, little dogies,
You're going to be beef steers by and by.

Whoopee ti yi yo, git along, little dogies, 25
It's your misfortune, and none of my own.
Whoopee ti yi yo, git along, little dogies,
For you know Wyoming will be your new home.

19. cholla (chōl'yä): a cactus.

WARRIOR'S SONG

Other Americans were here before the pioneers ever arrived. Perhaps very few of us have thought much about the songs of the Indians. Yet these people had a way of life, too, that was expressed in many songs for occasions of all kinds. Here is one which the modern author calls *re-expressed*, rather than translated, from one of the tribal languages of the Southwest.

Weep not for me, Loved Woman,
Should I die;
But for yourself be weeping!

Weep not for warriors who go
Gladly to battle. 5
Theirs is to revenge
Fallen and slain of our people;
Theirs to lay low
All our foes like them,
Death to make, singing. 10

Weep not for warriors,
But weep for women!
Oh, weep for all women!

Theirs to be pitied
Most of all creatures, 15
Whose men return not!
How shall their hearts be stayed
When we are fallen?

Weep not for me, Loved Woman,
For yourself alone be weeping! 20

Re-expressed by Mary Austin

How Well Did You Read?

1. This selection presents an entirely masculine point of view. Can you make a statement of this viewpoint beginning, "The warrior tells his wife . . ."? What is your reaction to the idea expressed?

2. What is the antecedent of *them* in line 9? What word is omitted in line 8, and what words in line 10?

GO DOWN MOSES

Of all the great Negro spirituals, "Go Down Moses" is one of the best loved. The spirituals sprang from the deeply religious nature of a people whose music is said to be the most original, most truly American that we have.

"Go Down Moses" from *American Negro Songs and Spirituals* edited by John W. Works, published by Crown publishers.

Thinking Over American Songs

1. If you find folk ballads like these interesting or amusing, you will want to look at Carl Sandburg's *The American Songbag,* as well as James Weldon Johnson's *The Book of American Negro Poetry.* America has a wealth of folk songs, many of them available on recordings. A committee of the class might wish to get together a small collection of records including songs from different sections of the country. Present them to the group after doing some research on the backgrounds to the songs; make an oral presentation of each record, pointing out the typical characteristics of the ballad.

2. Old-fashioned country dances have become popular in recent years. A number of radio programs feature folk music. If someone in your class can play a violin or guitar, you can plan an interesting program of American folk music. A " hobo jungle " number would be interesting with a group of hoboes cooking supper and singing songs of the road.

For Your Vocabulary

SPECIAL WORDS: If you have ever worked as a carpenter's or plumber's helper, you know that there are many words used in certain kinds of jobs that do not appear often in common speech. In " A Trip on the Erie Canal " you will find several nautical terms. What do lines 17 and 18 mean? Can you explain the meaning of *reef,* line 20, from the context? *Dogies* is another special word with an interesting origin. Try to find out how it came to be used by cowboys, and look up the term *maverick* also.

SLANG: Changes in American slang are always interesting. See if you can substitute contemporary slang for these phrases in " A Trip on the Erie Canal ": " she's a daisy "; " she's dead gone on me "; and " takes the cake."

AMERICAN SKETCHES

Visitors to our shores often comment that no people are more curious about their own land and their own national personality than Americans. This keen interest in ourselves is not egotistical or self-centered. Rather, it probably stems from the fact that America is still today a " new " country. We have not yet finished exploring the breadth of our great land or the variety of nationalities that have made a new life here.

Certainly the poets have shown a curious and sharp interest in the character of Americans. They have drawn pictures, too, of the multitude of scenes that make up America – scenes of nature and home life, views of the countryside and the city streets. Here you will have a chance to glimpse briefly the moving scenes that poets have sketched in for us with their colorful use of " sound and sense."

Quiet moment: descendants of the first Americans (*From* Rio Grande, River of Destiny, *by Laura Gilpin, pub. by Duell, Sloan and Pearce*)

THE PIONEER

WILLIAM B. RUGGLES

Here is a picture-poem of a time when this country was very slowly spreading westward, when the canals were few and the railroads had not yet stretched their steel bands across the prairies.

He could not breathe in a crowded place –
He wanted his air and his open space –
He watched while civilization neared
On the path through the wilderness Boone had cleared,
Saw highways hiding the Indian trails:
West fled the bear and the elk and the deer – 6
"I've got to go," said the Pioneer.
He whistled to his dog and called to his wife,
Loaded his rifle and sharpened his knife,
Tossed in his wagon a pan or two – 10
Texas-bound, to a land plumb new.
They watched him go, and shook each head –
"Shiftless fool – better stay," they said.
Not a sign they saw that might denote
That a Nation rode in his coonskin coat. 15

How Well Did You Read?

1. What is your interpretation of line 4? In your reading of the poem, did you decide that it was a *path* or a *wilderness* that Boone had cleared? One makes better sense than the other.
2. Poetry frequently suggests a great deal in a few words. Explain the idea in lines 14 and 15.
3. Do you think that both his dog and his wife followed him? What does that line suggest about pioneer wives?

THOMAS JEFFERSON

ROSEMARY AND STEPHEN VINCENT BENÉT

By all means, try reading this poem aloud. If you do it in a group, the girls might read the stanzas *not* in quotation marks, with the boys giving the responses. All might read the last stanza, with the girls saying "He" instead of "I."

Thomas Jefferson,
What do you say
Under the gravestone
Hidden away?

"I was a giver, 5
I was a molder,
I was a builder
With a strong shoulder."

Six feet and over,
Large-boned and ruddy, 10
The eyes gray-hazel
But bright with study.

The big hands clever
With pen and fiddle
And ready, ever, 15
For any riddle.

From buying empires
To planting 'taters,
From Declarations
To trick dumb-waiters. 20

"I liked the people,
The sweat and crowd of them,
Trusted them always
And spoke aloud of them.

"I liked all learning 25
And wished to share it
Abroad like pollen
For all who merit.

" I liked queer gadgets
And secret shelves, 30
And helping nations
To rule themselves.

" Jealous of others?
Not always candid?
But huge of vision 35
And open-handed.

" I got no riches.
I died a debtor.
I died free-hearted
And that was better." 40

How Well Did You Read?

1. What were some of the things that Thomas Jefferson helped to build? Be as specific as you can.

2. What do lines 17 and 19 refer to? Possibly someone who has visited or read about Monticello,* Jefferson's home near Charlottesville, Virginia, can explain line 20 and tell about some other features of the place.

3. What is suggested about Jefferson's character in lines 33 and 34? How are these lines " answered " in the two lines that follow?

* Monticello (mŏn′tĭ·sĕl′ō)

A FARMER REMEMBERS LINCOLN

WITTER BYNNER

In the following poem Witter Bynner pictures Abraham Lincoln through the eyes of a simple, plain-speaking farmer. The awkwardly phrased language, which has a conversational quality, helps to strengthen the impression of Lincoln's kind, unaffected, neighborly spirit. This kind of poem is called a dramatic monologue – that is, the spoken words of one person telling of some important or dramatic incident.

" Lincoln? –
Well, I was in the old Second Maine,
The first regiment in Washington from the Pine Tree State.
Of course I didn't get the butt of the clip;°
We was there for guardin' Washington – 5
We was all green.

" I ain't never ben to but one theater in my life –
I didn't know how to behave.
I ain't never ben since.
I can see as plain as my hat the box where he sat in 10
When he was shot.
I can tell you, sir, that was a panic
When we found our President was in the shape he was in!
Never saw a soldier in the world but what liked him.

" Yes, sir. His looks was kind o' hard to forget. 15
He was a spare man,
An old farmer.

4. butt of the clip: the heavy end of the blow; that is, the farmer didn't get into the main action of the war.

Everything was all right, you know,
But he wa'n't a smooth-appearin' man at all —
Not in no ways; 20
Thin-faced, long-necked,
And a swellin' kind of a thick lip like.

"And he was a jolly old fellow — always cheerful;
He wa'n't so high but the boys could talk to him their own ways.
While I was servin' at the hospital 25
He'd come in and say, 'You look nice in here,'
Praise us up, you know.
And he'd bend over and talk to the boys —
And he'd talk so good to 'em — so close —
That's why I call him a farmer. 30
I don't mean that everything about him wa'n't all right, you understand,
It's just — well, I was a farmer —
And he was my neighbor, anybody's neighbor.

"I guess even you young folks would 'a' liked him."

How Well Did You Read?

1. A dramatic monologue presents one person talking, but you have the feeling that he is carrying on a conversation with others. How does the first line give this impression?
2. The farmer is afraid that his listener will think he is criticizing Lincoln. Can you point out lines that show this fear?
3. What quality in Lincoln is the speaker trying to describe? Why is this an important quality for all of us to have? What happens when a businessman, a clerk, a factory worker, an office worker — or a high school student — lacks this quality?

ACHILLES DEATHERIDGE

EDGAR LEE MASTERS

In "Achilles Deatheridge"* we are given a battlefield picture of General Grant. You will notice that the form of the poem is different from the preceding one in several respects. Since it is a conversation, it is well designed for group reading. Either a single boy with a deep voice, or the entire group of girls in the class, might read the part of the officer who speaks first. The boys should read the lines of the young recruit.

* **Achilles Deatheridge** (ȧ·kĭl′ēz dĕth′ẽr·ĭj).

"Your name is Achilles Deatheridge?
How old are you, my boy?"
"I'm sixteen past and I went to the war
From Athens, Illinois."

"Achilles Deatheridge, you have done
A deed of dreadful note." 6
"It comes of his wearing a battered hat,
And a rusty, wrinkled coat."

"Why, didn't you know how plain he is?
And didn't you ever hear, 10
He goes through the lines by day or night
Like a sooty cannoneer?

"You must have been half dead for sleep,
For the dawn was growing bright."
"Well, Captain, I had stood right there
Since six o'clock last night. 16

"I cocked my gun at the swish of the grass,
And how am I at fault
When a dangerous-looking man won't stop
When a sentry hollers halt? 20

"I cried out halt and he only smiled,
And waved his hand like that.
Why, any Johnny could wear the coat,
And any fellow the hat.

"I hollered halt again and he stopped,
And lighted a fresh cigar. 26
I never noticed his shoulder badge,
And I never noticed a star."

"So you arrested him? Well, Achilles,
When you hear the swish of the grass,
If it's General Grant inspecting the lines
Hereafter let him pass." 32

SPANISH JOHNNY

WILLA CATHER

"Spanish Johnny" is a memorable picture of earlier days when violence was common and justice was frequently administered by a mob. This is a character sketch of a rough, daring man who nonetheless had tender songs in his heart. How do you account for a man like Spanish Johnny? Read the poem with this question in mind, noting how he appeared to a child.

The old West, the old time,
The old wind singing through
The red, red grass a thousand miles —
And, Spanish Johnny, you!
He'd sit beside the water ditch 5
When all his herd was in,
And never mind a child, but sing
To his mandolin.

The big stars, the blue night,
The moon-enchanted lane; 10
The olive man who never spoke,
But sang the songs of Spain.
His speech with men was wicked talk —
To hear it was a sin;
But those were golden things he said 15
To his mandolin.

The gold songs, the gold stars,
The world so golden then;
And the hand so tender to a child
Had killed so many men. 20
He died a hard death long ago
Before the Road came in —
The night before he swung, he sang
To his mandolin.

How Well Did You Read?

1. Try to account for the contradictory character of Spanish Johnny. Where was he probably working when the child listened to his playing? What was his job? What do you think his past had been? What lines tell you that he was not all bad?

2. Just to be certain, what is the meaning of line 23? What does "the Road" refer to?

For Your Vocabulary

SOUND PATTERNS: If you remember what was said about reading poetry on page 160, you know that poets make special uses of words. It is especially important to realize that poets are concerned not only with the sense, or meaning, of words but also with their sounds. In "Spanish Johnny," Willa Cather makes repeated use of *repetition* and *alliteration* of sounds. In the first line of the poem there is a repetition of the word *old.* What other examples can you find? Alliteration is the repetition of the same consonant at the beginning of words, as in the line " The *b*ig stars, the *b*lue night." Can you find other lines having alliteration? In what way do you think the line " But sang the songs of Spain " includes *both* repetition and alliteration? See if you can find examples of both sound patterns in other poems in this section.

JAZZ FANTASIA CARL SANDBURG

Carl Sandburg has caught the spirit of America's farms, her cities, and her workers in rugged free-verse poetry which often looks much like prose. Here he sets down the feelings and pictures aroused by an old-time jazz band. Notice the sounds, the changing moods, and the use of slang or even inexact grammar! If you read this aloud, you should adjust your reading speed and voice volume to the mood.

Drum on your drums, batter on your banjos, sob on the long cool winding saxophones. Go to it, O jazzmen.

Sling your knuckles on the bottoms of the happy tin pans, let your trombones ooze, and go husha-husha-hush with the slippery sandpaper.

Moan like an autumn wind high in the lonesome treetops, moan soft like you wanted somebody terrible, cry like a racing car slipping away from a motorcycle-cop, bang-bang! you jazzmen, bang altogether drums, traps, banjos, horns, tin cans — make two people fight on the top of a stairway and scratch each other's eyes in a clinch tumbling down the stairs.

Can the rough stuff . . . Now a Mississippi steamboat pushes up the night river with a hoo-hoo-hoo-oo . . . and the green lanterns calling to the high soft stars . . . a red moon rides on the humps of the low river hills . . . Go to it, O jazzmen.

How Well Did You Read?

1. Can you explain why " batter on your banjos " is better than *drum* or *strum*? How do you account for the *happy* tin pans and the trombones that *ooze*? Perhaps someone who plays in an orchestra can explain the *slippery sandpaper*.
2. Point out several uses of poor grammar. What is meant by " Can the rough stuff "? Try to justify Sandburg's use of slang and poor grammar in this poem.
3. Judging the poem as a whole, what do you think Sandburg is trying to express? How well does he succeed?
4. Following Sandburg's pattern, try writing a modern " fantasia," using current terms for this type of music.

SAND DUNES ROBERT FROST

Probably there is no greater American poet of the last half century than Robert Frost, most of whose poetry clearly shows a New England background and character. The last two stanzas of this poem carry a quiet message of courage. Can you interpret it? Note, as you read, the number of simple, one-syllable words.

Sea waves are green and wet,
But up from where they die,
Rise others vaster yet,
And those are brown and dry.

Jazzmen (Gendreau)

They are the sea made land 5
To come at the fisher town,
And bury in solid sand
The men she could not drown.

She may know cove and cape,
But she does not know mankind 10
If by any change of shape,
She hopes to cut off mind.

Men left her a ship to sink:
They can leave her a hut as well;
And be but more free to think 15
For the one more cast-off shell.

How Well Did You Read?

1. There is an interesting adventure book called *Men against the Sea.* How has man always been in conflict with the sea? What dangers are faced by coastal villages? How does the sea "make land"? What weapons does the poet suggest that man uses against his enemy? What is his most powerful weapon? Look for the answer in line 12. See if you can explain the idea suggested there.

2. It is possible to learn something about poetic art from this poem. For example, it doesn't take big words to state big ideas. That is one reason why the poem seems more simple than it actually is.

THE SUN

EMILY DICKINSON

Emily Dickinson is regarded as one of our most gifted American poets, though few of her writings were published during her lifetime. "The Sun" is one of her brightest fancies, a whimsical little sketch of sunrise and sunset.

I'll tell you how the sun rose —
A ribbon at a time.
The steeples swam in amethyst,
The news like squirrels ran.
The hills untied their bonnets, 5
The bobolinks begun.
Then I said softly to myself,
"That must have been the sun!"

But how he set, I know not.
There seemed a purple stile 10
Which little yellow boys and girls
Were climbing all the while,

Till when they reached the other side,
A dominie in gray
Put gently up the evening bars, 15
And led the flock away.

For Your Vocabulary

FIGURES OF SPEECH: The preceding poem is a good example of figurative language. See if you can find examples of similes and metaphors. What was the news that ran like squirrels? How could hills look as if they were untying their bonnets? A *stile* is a set of steps used in climbing a fence. What would look like a purple stile at sunset? A *dominie* is a minister (or, in a broad sense, a teacher). What does the poet mean by the dominie, and what is his flock?

AFTERNOON ON A HILL

EDNA ST. VINCENT MILLAY

"Afternoon on a Hill" is a graceful little lyric poem that is a picture of a mood more than anything else. Have you ever felt as happy and contented as this? Note again what can be done with very short words.

I will be the gladdest thing
  Under the sun!
I will touch a hundred flowers
  And not pick one.

I will look at cliffs and clouds 5
With quiet eyes,
Watch the wind bow down the grass,
And the grass rise.

And when lights begin to show
Up from the town, 10
I will mark which must be mine,
And then start down!

AT THE AQUARIUM

MAX EASTMAN

Ever since people have put fish into bowls and aquariums so that they could stare at them, the fish have been staring right back! In this poem the poet is half humorously, but half seriously, too, suggesting a likeness between the fishes on display and the people who stare at them. See if you can discover that likeness. If you have seen any of those recently popular books of cartoons like *Zoo's Who,* in which visitors to the zoo are shown to look very like the inhabitants, you will be able to use your own imagination on this poem.

Serene the silver fishes glide,
Stern-lipped, and pale, and wonder-eyed!
As, through the aged deeps of ocean,
They glide with wan and wavy motion.
They have no pathway where they go,
They flow like water to and fro, 6
They watch with never-winking eyes,
They watch with staring, cold surprise,
The level people in the air,
The people peering, peering there: 10
Who wander also to and fro,
And know not why or where they go,
Yet have a wonder in their eyes,
Sometimes a pale and cold surprise.

STEAM SHOVEL

CHARLES MALAM

" Steam Shovel " is a modern sketch that could have its setting almost anywhere. As you read the poem you will be struck by the fact that poets see and feel things that many persons miss. Has a machine ever reminded *you* of a person – or an animal?

The dinosaurs° are not all dead.
I saw one raise its iron head
To watch me walking down the road
Beyond our house today.
Its jaws were dripping with a load 5
Of earth and grass that it had cropped.
It must have heard me where I stopped,
Snorted white steam my way,
And stretched its long neck out to see,
And chewed, and grinned quite amiably. 10

1. **dinosaurs** (dī′nō·sôrz): huge animals of prehistoric times. Find a picture of a dinosaur, and you will see why the poet likens it to a steam shovel.

THE CHILDREN'S HOUR

HENRY WADSWORTH LONGFELLOW

" The Children's Hour " is one of the best-loved poems of one of America's early and still best-loved poets. It is a picture of home life that is both whimsical and tender. If you read it with sympathetic understanding, you will be struck by one pretty important idea: No matter how the world changes, home and love of family don't change.

Between the dark and the daylight,
When the night is beginning to lower,
Comes a pause in the day's occupations,
That is known as the Children's Hour.

I hear in the chamber above me 5
The patter of little feet,
The sound of a door that is opened,
And voices soft and sweet.

From my study I see in the lamplight,
Descending the broad hall stair, 10
Grave Alice, and laughing Allegra,°
And Edith with golden hair.

A whisper, and then a silence:
Yet I know by their merry eyes
They are plotting and planning together
To take me by surprise. 16

A sudden rush from the stairway,
A sudden raid from the hall!
By three doors left unguarded
They enter my castle wall! 20

They climb up into my turret
O'er the arms and back of my chair;
If I try to escape, they surround me;
They seem to be everywhere.

They almost devour me with kisses, 25
Their arms about me entwine,
Till I think of the Bishop of Bingen
In his Mouse-Tower on the Rhine!

Do you think, O blue-eyed banditti,°
Because you have scaled the wall, 30
Such an old mustache as I am
Is not a match for you all!

I have you fast in my fortress,
And will not let you depart,
But put you down into the dungeon 35
In the round-tower of my heart.

And there will I keep you forever,
Yes, forever and a day,
Till the walls shall crumble to ruin,
And moulder in dust away! 40

11. Allegra (ä·lĕg′rȧ): a name taken from the Italian, meaning merry and gay. **29. banditti** (băn·dĭt′ĭ): the Italian form for the plural of the word *bandit*.

How Well Did You Read?

1. Do you think this is a poem about real children and about Longfellow himself? A little library research may turn up some interesting answers. What clue in line 9 will help you answer the question?

2. The writer seems to be surrounded by "blue-eyed banditti," but near the end of the poem he turns the tables and captures them. Can you point out the stanza that shows the change from whimsy to seriousness? In which mood is he writing in the last stanza?

3. What picture of family life does Longfellow present here? Compare it with contemporary home life. What moments in your own family life are comparable?

4. Look up the word *lower* in line 2. It actually does rhyme with *hour,* and it is not the word you probably think it is.

THE SNOW-STORM

RALPH WALDO EMERSON

Once in a great while some particular poem is stated in lines so memorable that it earns a lasting place in a nation's literature. Here is one of those poems. If you live in a part of the country that has little or no snow, you will receive here an impression of what a New England snowstorm must be like. Be sure to notice the variety and highly colorful figures of speech throughout – the picture would be bare without them!

Announced by all the trumpets of the sky,
Arrives the snow, and, driving o'er the fields,
Seems nowhere to alight: the whited air
Hides hills and woods, the river, and the heaven,
And veils the farmhouse at the garden's end. 5
The sled and traveler stopped, the courier's feet
Delayed, all friends shut out, the housemates sit

"The frolic architecture of the snow" (*Don Knight*)

Around the radiant fireplace, inclosed
In a tumultuous privacy of storm.

Come see the north wind's masonry. 10
Out of an unseen quarry evermore
Furnished with tile, the fierce artificer°
Curves his white bastions with projected roof
Round every windward stake, or tree, or door.
Speeding, the myriad-handed, his wild work 15
So fanciful, so savage, naught cares he
For number or proportion. Mockingly,
On coop or kennel he hangs Parian° wreaths;
A swanlike form invests the hidden thorn;
Fills up the farmer's lane from wall to wall, 20
Mauger° the farmer's sighs; and at the gate
A tapering turret overtops the work.
And when his hours are numbered, and the world
Is all his own, retiring, as he were not,
Leaves, when the sun appears, astonished Art 25
To mimic in slow structures, stone by stone,
Built in an age, the mad wind's night-work,
The frolic architecture of the snow.

12. **artificer** (är·tĭf′ĭ·sẽr): a skillful worker.
18. **Parian** (pâr′ĭ·ăn): marble; Paros was an island in the Mediterranean noted for its beautiful marble.

How Well Did You Read?

1. What does line 6 tell you about transportation at the time the poem was written? *Housemates* in line 7 is an interesting word.

21. **Mauger** (mô′gẽr): in spite of.

Are the people who are shut in by the storm all of one family?

2. Can you tell why the farmer would sigh, line 21? (His lane, if the word *walls* bothers you, has stone fences on either side.)

3. Lines 23 to 28 are the only ones in this poem which are very troublesome. Their difficulty lies in the fact that they say a great deal in a complicated, condensed style. Here is how they might have been more directly, but less poetically, expressed:

> "And when this furiously working laborer, the north wind, is nearly exhausted, and the world has been completely made over according to his ideas, he leaves the scene as if he had never existed. But his work still remains at daybreak – astonishing, artful likenesses of marble castles that would take centuries to create. Yet the frenzied wind, working only one night, left all these fanciful buildings of snow."

Now that it is explained, try to read the passage aloud just for the enjoyment of the word pictures and the beautiful-sounding language.

For Your Vocabulary

FIGURATIVE LANGUAGE: This poem is exceptionally rich in word pictures made by figures of speech. The very first line contains a metaphor. What are the "trumpets of the sky" that announce the coming storm? Notice that the *whited air* "hides" and "veils" the scene and gives the friends a feeling of being closed in. Have you ever seen the word *whited* before? How can you find out if this is a word created by the poet himself? *Tumultuous privacy* is a contradictory phrase but a highly descriptive one. In what way is it contradictory?

Notice too that in lines 10 through to the end of the poem, the poet uses one metaphor throughout. Explain how these words and phrases are all part of the same figure of speech: *north wind's masonry; unseen quarry; furnished with tile; fierce artificer; white bastions; Parian wreaths; tapering turret; frolic architecture of the snow.*

SONG OF THE SETTLERS

JESSAMYN WEST

In this section of American Songs and Sketches you have journeyed forward, then backward again, through America's rich, changing patterns, its varied scenes, and its many peoples. But although this poem deals with the early settlers, it leaves us with a challenge for the future.

Freedom is a hard-bought thing –
A gift no man can give,
For some, a way of dying,
For most, a way to live.

Freedom is a hard-bought thing – 5
A rifle in the hand,
The horses hitched at sunup,
A harvest in the land.

Freedom is a hard-bought thing –
A massacre, a bloody rout, 10
The candles lit at nightfall,
And the night shut out.

Freedom is a hard-bought thing –
An arrow in the back,
The wind in the long corn rows, 15
And the hay in the rack.

Freedom is a way of living,
A song, a mighty cry.
Freedom is the bread we eat;
Let it be the way we die! 20

Thinking Over American Sketches

1. What character traits were needed by the explorers, hunters, traders, trappers, and homesteaders who opened up and settled our land? Summarize in half a dozen sentences some book you have read that deals with these pioneers.

2. Find other poems about Lincoln and

have a committee present several to the class, comparing them with each other and with the Witter Bynner poem included here. Some of the best-known Lincoln poems are: " O Captain! My Captain! " by Walt Whitman; " The Master " by Edwin Arlington Robinson; " Lincoln, Man of the People " by Edwin Markham; " Abraham Lincoln Walks at Midnight " by Vachel Lindsay; and " Lincoln's Grave " by Maurice Thompson.

3. Someone in the class should report on Robert Frost's life, especially his early career, showing how the message in his " Sand Dunes " might have an autobiographical basis.

4. Try writing a free-verse descriptive sketch about an animal, a bird, a building, a machine, a section of a city, a street, a store, a hill, or an interesting person. If you choose the last suggestion, consider as a possible subject some worker who has a very humble job that is usually taken for granted.

5. Write a storm poem of your own. Try to invent a good figure of speech for the first line, and then follow up the idea. Here are some suggestions for the first line:

Here came the wind like a . . .
The wind now wrapped his . . .
And now the ribbons of the wind . . .

AMERICAN SONGS AND SKETCHES

Suggestions for Free Reading

Barnes, Ruth A., *I Hear America Singing* (Winston, 1937)
You will like this wide selection of native American songs and ballads. There's some good folk poetry here.

Benét, Rosemary and Stephen Vincent, *A Book of Americans* (Farrar and Rinehart, 1933)
Here are some famous personalities — Washington, Cotton Mather, Jesse James, Woodrow Wilson. You'll find it hard to lay aside this little book, and you'll wish there were more like it.

Bone, D. W., *Capstan Bars* (Porpoise Press, 1931)
If you like sea chanteys, this collection is certain to interest you.

Bontemps, Arna Wendell, *Golden Slippers* (Harper, 1941)
This is a fine anthology of Negro poetry — religious, humorous, lyric, and narrative.

Coatsworth, Elizabeth, *Country Poems* (Macmillan, 1942)
Girls more than boys will probably be interested in this little book. Here are good, honest sketches of country life.

Coffin, Robert P. T., *Primer for America* (Macmillan, 1943)
Places, people, and customs that are distinctly parts of our American heritage come to life in these ballads and poems.

Frost, Robert, *Come In, and Other Poems* (Holt, 1943)
This is a selection for youth, beautifully illustrated. There are many explanatory introductions.

Guiterman, Arthur, *I Sing the Pioneer* (Dutton, 1926)
Ballads and lyrics tell the story of the making of the nation. You'll like the sketches of young George Washington, Dan Boone, Kit Carson, and others.

Hurd, Harry Elmore, *Yankee Boundaries* (Day, 1949)
New England scenes and people vividly described in brief word sketches.

Johnson, James Weldon, *God's Trombones* (Viking, 1927)
These Negro folk poems make good companion pieces to the spirituals.

Keller, Martha, *Brady's Bend, and Other Poems* (Rutgers, 1946)
A fine, frank slice of America that is as honest as homemade bread. Boys will like this little book, which contains some World War II poems.

Lomax, J. A. and Alan, *Folk Songs: U.S.A.* (Duell, 1948)
Here are words and music on large, attractive pages.

Morley, Christopher, *Chimneysmoke* (Doran, 1921)
You will recognize some of your surroundings and your ideas, too, in these pleasant, casual verses.

Rickaby, Franz, *Ballads and Songs of the Shanty-Boy* (Harvard, 1926)
These are lumberjack songs — with music. There are excellent notes on the background of the songs.

Sarett, Lew, *Collected Poems* (Holt, 1941)
Sketches of the people of the tall timber country — Indians, French Canadians, lumberjacks.

Scene from film version of *Great Expectations* (Culver)

Great Expectations

A NOVEL

WHEN you first leafed through the pages of this anthology, curious to know what was in store for you, you may have noted the long section entitled *Great Expectations.* Well, there are great expectations in store for you in reading this novel by Charles Dickens. You may expect to be entertained as rarely before; you may expect to be rewarded richly and lastingly by a great book. *Great Expectations* has excitement, adventure, romance, comedy, tragedy, and mystery. You can hardly ask for more from reading a novel!

A novel is fiction, of course, just as a short story is. It is a prose story in which fictitious characters behave as real people would in the situations created by the author. The main difference between novels and short stories is *length.* A short story may usually be read at one sitting and runs to no more than fifteen thousand words. A novel, however, may run anywhere from this number to a half million words or more: it is simply a long story.

Interestingly enough, the word *novel* means "new." People have been telling stories for centuries (the *Odyssey* is more than two thousand years old), but until the eighteenth century stories were told either in the form of narrative poems or plays. About three hundred years ago a *new* kind of storytelling became popular – and it was called the novel. You may be surprised to learn that *Robinson Crusoe,* written in 1719, was one of the earliest novels written in English.

Like all stories a novel is first of all interesting for a reader because it concerns people. In *Great Expectations* you will become acquainted with an orphan boy named Pip and a proud and beautiful girl brought up to hate all men. You will meet a madwoman, an escaped convict, and a surprising assortment of crooks, swindlers, and murderers. You will find some good people, too, particularly Joe Gargery, the simple, honest blacksmith, and Herbert, Pip's loyal friend. This invention of fictitious people is called *characterization,* and it is an important part of all novels.

Dickens created unforgettable characters. His remarkable memory and his sensitive imagination helped him to create a whole gallery of people who come to life the moment they speak or act in his pages. If Dickens had not become a writer, he almost certainly would have become an actor — and a good one, too. He had a natural flair for dramatics. In fact, his tendency to " dress up " a scene often resulted in melodrama and caricature, which are the *exaggeration* of happenings and personalities in fiction. Yet it is this quality of exaggeration that has endeared him to so many generations of booklovers. His readers know just what to expect when they come upon such obvious villains as Pecksniff, Gradgrind, Fagin, and Ebenezer Scrooge.

Of course none of us is interested in people just because they exist. We like to know what people think, how they act, what they do, and how they stand in relation to each other. In reading *Great Expectations* you will keep asking, " What is going to happen next? " or, " How will these characters solve their problems and get out of their difficulties? " The story keeps moving forward from one event to another, building up suspense. It is this movement in a novel that is called the *plot*. The plot is especially important in *Great Expectations* because it is, actually, a mystery story. This novel is a book with no loose ends: it is closely knit, well organized. Dickens practically defies you to solve the entanglements until the very end. (You'll be cheating yourself if you look at the last pages. That spoils everything!)

Besides the people and the happenings in a novel — the characterization and the plot — there is still another important part of its writing. Every novel has a *setting:* the story is set in a certain place and at a certain time. In this novel the setting is England in the 1830's and 1840's, about a hundred years ago. You will recognize the setting quickly in such details as the fact that Pip travels between his native village and the great city of London by stagecoach, stopping at old-fashioned inns. You will get a notion of the times by observing, for instance, the schools and the prison system that Dickens describes. The book progresses through many scenes of both city and country; the dismal slums, the dark little taverns and swarming water front, as well as the country lanes and hedges, the chalk cliffs, and the wide, lonely marshes along the river.

But from your point of view, as the reader, the most important thing about a novel is its *theme,* or the meaning or ideas it leaves with you. *Great Expectations* is much more than a clever mystery. Here Dickens presents a man's life from his early years to his adulthood. He shows you the events that shape this man's character, the people who help or hinder him, and the involved pattern of his relations with these people. All this seems intensely personal because Pip tells his own story. Dickens discovered that in some of his novels he could write more naturally in the first person. So here you will find Pip speaking directly to you, the reader, telling you about his life, from the first terrifying experience in the graveyard through all the joys, fears, disappointments, and turmoils that came with his "great expectations."

At first you will probably feel sorry for Pip. Later you may become exasperated with him almost to the point of dislike. But don't judge him too hastily. You are looking at a person's life. It could be your own. The really vital thing is not the mistakes a person makes, but how he comes to know that he is wrong, how he reacts to the knowledge, and what he does to set things right. There are usually forces that influence us, causing us in some way to act as we do. Watch for the motivation of Pip's behavior – and of the beautiful Estella's, and of other characters in this novel. Discover what motivates, or causes, them to take certain actions or hold certain attitudes. You will find that what the characters *do* in a novel is always interesting, but what *makes them do it* is still more important.

Charles Dickens

WHILE reading the books of Dickens – so intricate in plot, so rich in detail, and so understanding of human nature – it is impossible not to become curious about the man himself. How did he learn all he knew? The life of Charles Dickens is as interesting as that of almost any character he created. His childhood experiences, especially, furnished him with a wealth of material. He said himself that he could remember every little incident and even slight looks and words of his childhood days. Many of the people he met or observed in those days turned up later as characters in his books – often decidedly caricatured.

Dickens was born in Portsmouth, England, in 1812. He did not have much formal schooling in his early years. His mother taught him to read and write and gave him the rudiments of Latin, but she had a large family to care for and could not spend much time on Charles alone. Later on he went to a small school, but most of his education he got from books, identifying himself with their characters and peopling his own imaginative world with others of his own creation. When his irresponsible, debt-ridden father (the original of Mr. Micawber in *David Copperfield*) moved his family to London, Charles was very lonely. He had no friends of his own age and was left to his own amusements. Soon he began to prowl about the London slums and the river front. Here he found much misery and poverty which aroused his compassion, while at the same time the wickedness, crime, and mystery of the city kindled his ever active fancy.

When Charles was twelve years old, his father, John Dickens, was arrested for debt and sent to prison. Then began a period in which Charles became familiar with pawnshops and miserable lodgings. He was obliged to work long hours in a warehouse, where he had the wretched job of pasting paper covers on jars of blacking. Eventually the whole family went to live with the father at the Marshalsea prison, in accordance with the strange custom in those days, although Charles remained in a tiny attic room in the neighborhood. Many of the odd characters he met at this time appear in *Oliver Twist, Dombey and Son,* and *The Old Curiosity Shop.*

When his father was finally released and got a fairly good job, Charles went to school at Wellington House Academy for a couple of years. His previous lack of schooling did not hold him back, and he ended up as " first boy " of the school and winner of a number of prizes. It was evident quite early that he had some gift for writing. He began to write plays, and with another boy he edited a little newspaper.

After leaving school, he became the office boy for a law firm. He kept his eyes and ears open at this job; many of the details of Mr. Jaggers' unusual business in *Great Expectations* probably stem from that experience. At about the same time, he became friendly with a boy of his own age with whom he traveled about London, visiting inns and the homes of friends much as Pip and Herbert Pocket do in this novel. He fell in love, too, and the girl was just as capricious and heartless as Estella, who makes Pip's life so miserable. He loved the girl deeply and was utterly wretched during the whole affair, which eventually came to nothing.

By this time Dickens had become a newspaper reporter, and a good one. He continued to study; he read diligently in the British Museum. He even took lessons in acting, having always harbored a longing to go on the stage. But the most rewarding thing he did was to send some short articles and stories to a monthly magazine, using the pen name of "Boz." They were accepted, and Dickens walked on air. However, he received from the first writings nothing more than the satisfaction of seeing them in print. Later on, as people began to read his stories and as his reputation grew, he was well paid for his work and eventually became prosperous.

Dickens' first great success was the book *The Pickwick Papers.* In Mr. Pickwick he created a character that appealed to all classes of readers. The hilarious adventures of Mr. Pickwick and his friends, Mr. Tupman, Mr. Winkle, and Mr. Snodgrass, made happy reading for many thousands of nineteenth-century readers, and the name of Sam Weller became a household word. After this success, words seemed literally to flow from Dickens' inexhaustible pen. He wrote *Oliver Twist, Barnaby Rudge,* and *Nicholas Nickleby,* all of which appeared serially, and his mind teemed with ideas for more books.

In 1842, Dickens came to America. He had a widespread audience in this country, where his books were as well known as in England. His poor wife cried every time he spoke of plans for the dangerous trip, but she finally had to go. They had a terrible crossing in a little 1,154-ton steamboat which fought a storm and ended up on a mudbank near Halifax. But what a reception they received from Americans, who were as ready a century ago as today to idolize an actor or an author! There had never before been a reception like that in Dickens' honor – and he loved it.

Things did not stay so pleasant, however. At that time copyright laws for books were not enforced between nations, and Dickens complained, justly enough, of the pirating of his works in this country. He suggested that he be paid the royalties that were due him for the thousands of his books sold in this country. He criticized slavery, too – a very touchy issue on this side of the water at that time. Worst of all, he spoke harshly of American table manners and social behavior. Heartily sick of the flattery that he at first had enjoyed, he went home and wrote *Martin Chuzzlewit,* a devastating satire on life in the United States. What his American readers thought of his criticisms is best described by an English writer who said that it "caused all Yankee-doodledom to fizz like one universal soda-water bottle."

After his return to England, Dickens wrote *A Christmas Carol* and *Dombey and Son,* in which little Paul Dombey dies in an unforgettably sorrowful scene. The sentimental Americans shed gallons of tears and forgave Dickens for *Martin Chuzzlewit.* His popularity continued, and he seemed tireless in activity. He edited a weekly newspaper for nine years and wrote a succession of books, including *A Tale of Two Cities,* one of the most popular of his novels, and *Great Expectations,* which was among the last of his works. His children grew up and went out into the world, most of them having inherited some measure of their father's cleverness and versatility. The lonely, unhappy child had become a man loved and honored the world over.

In 1867, Dickens returned to America and was received with almost as much acclaim as on his first visit, but he was getting older and the trip was harder for him. After his return he felt constantly ill. Nevertheless, he continued to give dramatic readings, chiefly of scenes from his own books. Since each program was a full evening's entertainment, the readings were a greater strain on his health than he realized. On June 9, 1870, he died after a brief illness, and the voice of a great storyteller was stilled.

Few novelists have been so widely read, so greatly beloved, or so long remembered. His popularity was a publishing sensation in his own time, and it has persisted to the present day. He was a man of so many talents and so many interests that his books appeal to readers of all ages and temperaments. He had tremendous powers of invention, a delightful sense of humor, and abiding sympathy for the common people who make up the world. Like Shakespeare, Charles Dickens has enriched the pleasure of readers of the English language for all time to come.

Great Expectations

Great Expectations is probably a new kind of reading experience for you. No doubt you have read other novels, but perhaps none that was constructed exactly like this one.

First of all, keep in mind that the story is told in the *first person,* that is, by Pip himself. Whatever you learn about the events of the story, or about the other characters, is limited to what Pip himself knows at any particular time. Keep in mind, too, that Pip's views of events and people are colored by his own feelings and attitudes. Anticipate the possibility that sometimes you may have a different view from his.

Second, you will discover that the working out of the plot is very important in this novel. The plot is revealed only bit by bit, as Pip discovers things. Keep alert for any *hints or forewarnings* of what is to come, because this will heighten the suspense of the story for you.

Third, get accustomed to the *episodic* form of the novel; it is told in a series of scenes or episodes. The action shifts rapidly from the country village to London. Don't be disturbed if just as things get going at one place, the action is moved to another place. Actually, the story keeps going in a straight line; only the scenes are shifted, like the changing of sets on a stage.

There are quite a few characters in *Great Expectations*. Maybe this partial list of them will help you keep them straight at the beginning:

PIP (PHILIP PIRRIP): *main character*
MRS. JOE GARGERY: *Pip's sister*
JOE GARGERY: *blacksmith*
MISS HAVISHAM: *wealthy recluse (hermit)*
ESTELLA: *ward of Miss Havisham*
MR. WOPSLE: *church warden, friend of Joe*
MR. PUMBLECHOOK: *Joe's uncle, a tradesman*

These are just a few of the people you will meet at the beginning of the novel. There are several others, later on, whom you will identify with the London setting. As you read you may wish to refer to this list.

Because *Great Expectations* is, in the original, an extremely long novel — so long that we would not have space to include it as such in this anthology — the version you are about to read has been shortened considerably. No important characters or incidents have been omitted, but a great deal of elaborate description has been cut. You will want to read some of Dickens' books in complete editions in order to get the full flavor of his highly personal style, and his wonderful humor.

CHAPTER I

My father's family name being Pirrip, and my Christian name Philip, my infant tongue could make of both names nothing more explicit than Pip. So I called myself Pip, and came to be called Pip.

I gave Pirrip as my father's family name, on the authority of his tombstone and my sister — Mrs. Joe Gargery, who married the blacksmith. I never saw my father or my mother, and never saw a picture of either of them.

We lived in the marsh country, down by the river, within twenty miles of the sea. My first vivid impression of things seems to me to have been gained on a memorable raw afternoon toward evening. At such a time I found out for certain that this bleak place was the churchyard; that Philip Pirrip, late of this parish, and Georgiana, his wife, were dead and buried here. I knew that the dark flat wilderness beyond was the marshes; that the low leaden line beyond them was the river; that the distant savage lair from which the wind was rushing was the sea; and that the small bundle of shivers growing afraid of it all and beginning to cry was Pip.

"Hold your noise!" cried a terrible voice, as a man started up from among the graves. "Keep still, you little devil, or I'll cut your throat!"

A fearful man, all in coarse gray, with a great iron on his leg. A man with no hat, and with broken shoes, and with an old rag tied round his head. A man who had been soaked in water, and smothered in mud, and lamed by stones, and cut by flints, and stung by nettles, and torn by briers; who limped, and shivered, and glared, and growled; and whose teeth chattered in his head as he seized me by the chin.

"Oh! Don't cut my throat, sir," I pleaded in terror. "Pray don't do it, sir."

"Tell us your name!" said the man. "Quick!"

"Pip, sir."

"Once more," said the man, staring at me. "Give it mouth!"

"Pip. Pip, sir."

"Show us where you live," said the man. "Point out the place!"

I pointed to where our village lay, a mile or more from the church.

The man, after looking at me for a moment, turned me upside down and emptied my pockets. There was nothing in them but a piece of bread. He ate the bread ravenously.

"You young dog," said the man, licking his lips. "What fat cheeks you ha' got. Darn me if I couldn't eat 'em, and if I han't half a mind to't!"

I held tighter to the tombstone on which he had put me; partly, to keep myself upon it; partly, to keep myself from crying.

"Now lookee here!" said the man. "Where's your mother and father?"

"There, sir!" said I, pointing to the tombstones.

He started, made a short run, and stopped and looked over his shoulder.

"Ha!" he muttered. "Who d'ye live with — supposin' you're kindly let to live, which I han't made up my mind about?"

"My sister, sir — Mrs. Joe Gargery — wife of Joe Gargery, the blacksmith, sir."

"Blacksmith, eh?" said he. And looked down at his leg.

After darkly looking at his leg and at me several times, he came closer, took me by both arms, and tilted me back as far as he could hold me.

"Now lookee here," he said, "the question being whether you're to be let to live. You know what a file is?"

"Yes, sir."

"And you know what wittles [1] is?"

"Yes, sir."

After each question he tilted me over a little more, so as to give me a greater sense of helplessness and danger.

"You get me a file." He tilted me again. "And you get me wittles." He tilted me again. "You bring 'em both to me." He tilted me again. "Or I'll have your heart and liver out."

I was dreadfully frightened, and so giddy that I clung to him with both hands, and said, "If you would kindly please to let me keep upright, sir, perhaps I shouldn't be sick, and perhaps I could attend more."

He gave me a most tremendous dip and roll. Then he held me by the arms in an upright position and went on in these fearful terms:

"You bring me, tomorrow morning early, that file and them wittles to that old Battery [2] over yonder. You do it, and you never dare to say a word or dare to make a sign concerning your having seen such a person as me, or any person

[1] **wittles:** victuals, food. (There are a number of other words in this book in which "v" is pronounced like "w" — a common speech habit of certain characters in this novel.)

[2] **Battery** (băt′ẽr·ĭ): a bank of earth on which large guns are mounted.

sumever, and you shall be let to live. You fail, or you go from my words in any partickler, no matter how small it is, and your heart and your liver shall be tore out, roasted, and ate. Now, I ain't alone, as you may think I am. There's a young man hid with me. That young man hears the words I speak. That young man has a secret way of getting at a boy, and at his heart, and at his liver. It is in wain for a boy to attempt to hide himself from that young man. A boy may lock his door, may be warm in bed, may tuck himself up, may draw the clothes over his head, may think himself comfortable and safe, but that young man will creep his way to him and tear him open. I am a-keeping that young man from harming of you at the present moment, with great difficulty. I find it wery hard to hold that young man off of your inside. Now, what do you say?"

I said that I would get him the file, and I would get him what broken bits of food I could, and I would come to him at the Battery, early in the morning.

"Say, Lord strike you dead if you don't!" said the man.

I said so, and he took me down.

"Now," he pursued, "you remember what you've undertook, and you remember that young man, and you get home."

He hugged his shuddering body in both his arms and limped toward the low church wall. He got over it, like a man whose legs were numbed and stiff, and then turned round to look for me. I looked all around for the horrible young man, and could see no signs of him. But now I was frightened again, and ran home without stopping.

CHAPTER II

My sister, Mrs. Joe Gargery, was more than twenty years older than I, and had established a great reputation with herself and the neighbors because she had brought me up "by hand."[1] Knowing her to have a hard and heavy hand, and to be much in the habit of laying it upon her husband as well as upon me, I supposed that Joe Gargery and I were both brought up by hand.

She was not a good-looking woman, my sister; and I had a general impression that she must have made Joe Gargery marry her by hand. Joe was a fair man, with curls of flaxen hair on each side of his smooth face, and with eyes of a very undecided blue. He was a mild, good-natured, sweet-tempered, easygoing, foolish, dear fellow — a sort of Hercules[2] in strength, and also in weakness. My sister, Mrs. Joe, with black hair and eyes, was tall and bony, and always wore a coarse apron, fastened over her figure behind with two loops.

Joe's forge adjoined our house, which was a wooden house, as many of the dwellings in our country were. When I ran home from the churchyard, the forge was shut up, and Joe was sitting alone in the kitchen. Joe and I being fellow sufferers, he warned me the moment I raised the latch of the door and peeped in at him.

"Mrs. Joe has been out a dozen times, looking for you, Pip."

"Has she?"

"Yes, Pip," said Joe, "and what's worse, she's got Tickler with her."

At this dismal news, I twisted the only button on my waistcoat round and round, and looked dejectedly at the fire. Tickler was a wax-ended piece of cane, worn smooth by collision with my frame.

"She sot down," said Joe, "and she

[1] **by hand:** by personal looking-after and responsibility.

[2] **Hercules** (hûr'kū·lēz): a mythological hero noted for his strength.

got up, and she made a grab at Tickler, and she Ram-paged[1] out. That's what she did," said Joe, " she Ram-paged out, Pip."

" Has she been gone long, Joe? " I always treated him as a larger child, and as no more than my equal.

" Well," said Joe, " she's been on the Ram-page, this last spell, about five minutes, Pip. She's a-coming! Get behind the door, old chap."

I took the advice. My sister, Mrs. Joe, throwing the door wide open, and finding an obstruction behind it, immediately applied Tickler. She concluded by throwing me at Joe, who passed me next to the chimney and quietly fenced me up there with his great leg.

" Where have you been, you young monkey? " said Mrs. Joe, stamping her foot. " Tell me directly what you've been doing to wear me away with fret and fright and worry, or I'd have you out of that corner if you was fifty Pips, and he was five hundred Gargerys."

" I have only been to the churchyard," said I, from my stool, crying and rubbing myself.

" Churchyard! " repeated my sister. " If it warn't for me you'd have been to the churchyard long ago, and stayed there. Who brought you up by hand? "

" You did," said I.

" And why did I do it, I should like to know? " exclaimed my sister.

I whimpered, " I don't know."

" *I* don't! " said my sister. " I'd never do it again! I know that. It's bad enough to be a blacksmith's wife, and him a Gargery, without being your mother."

My thoughts strayed from the question as I looked disconsolately at the fire. I fancied I saw the fugitive out on the marshes with the ironed leg, the mysterious young man, the file, the food I was about to steal, rise before me in the avenging coals.

Our supper was soon ready and my sister, as was her custom, sawed a very thick round off the loaf and hewed it into two halves, of which Joe got one, and I the other. Though I was hungry, I dared not eat my slice. I felt that I must have something in reserve for my dreadful acquaintance and his ally, the still more dreadful young man. I resolved to put my hunk of bread-and-butter down the leg of my trousers.

Joe was about to take a bite when his eye fell on me, and he saw that my bread-and-butter was gone.

The wonder and consternation with which Joe stopped and stared at me were too evident to escape my sister's observation.

" What's the matter now? " said she.

" I say, you know! " muttered Joe, shaking his head at me in a very serious remonstrance. " Pip, old chap! You'll do yourself a mischief. It'll stick somewhere. You can't have chawed it, Pip."

" What's the matter *now?* " repeated my sister, more sharply than before.

" If you can cough any trifle of it up, Pip, I'd recommend you to do it," said Joe, all aghast. " Manners is manners, but still your 'elth's your 'elth."

By this time, my sister was quite desperate, so she pounced on Joe, and, taking him by the two whiskers, knocked his head for a little while against the wall behind him while I sat in the corner, looking guiltily on.

" Now, perhaps you'll mention what's the matter," said my sister, out of breath, " you staring great stuck pig."

Joe looked at her in a helpless way; then took a helpless bite and looked at me again.

[1] **Ram-paged:** Joe is giving added emphasis to the word *rampage,* which means to storm about wildly.

"Been bolting his food, has he?" cried my sister.

"You know, old chap," said Joe, "I bolted, myself, when I was your age, but I never see your bolting equal yet, Pip."

My sister made a dive at me, and fished me up by the hair, saying nothing more than the awful words, "You come along and be dosed."

Some medical beast had revived tar-water in those days as a fine medicine, and Mrs. Joe always kept a supply of it in the cupboard. The urgency of my case demanded a pint of this mixture, which was poured down my throat, while Mrs. Joe held my head under her arm.

Conscience is a dreadful thing. I suffered the guilty knowledge that I was going to rob Mrs. Joe – I never thought I was going to rob Joe, for I never thought of any of the housekeeping property as his. This and the necessity of always keeping one hand on my bread-and-butter as I sat, or when I was ordered about the kitchen on any small errand, almost drove me out of my mind.

It was Christmas Eve, and I had to stir the pudding for next day, with a copper-stick. I tried it with the load upon my leg (and that made me think afresh of the man with the load on *his* leg), and found it quite unmanageable, so I slipped away, and deposited that part of my conscience in my garret bedroom.

"Hark!" said I, when I had done my stirring, and was taking a final warm in the chimney corner before being sent up to bed. "Was that great guns, Joe?"

"Ah!" said Joe. "There's another conwict off."

"What does that mean, Joe?" said I.

"There was a conwict off last night," said Joe, "after sunset-gun. And they fired warning of him. And now it appears they're firing warning of another."

"*Who's* firing?" said I.

"Drat that boy," interposed my sister, frowning at me over her work, "what a questioner he is. Ask no questions, and you'll be told no lies."

"Mrs. Joe," said I, after a long silence, "I should like to know – if you wouldn't much mind – where the firing comes from?"

"Drat that boy!" exclaimed my sister again. "From the Hulks!"

"And please what's Hulks?" said I.

"That's the way with this boy!" exclaimed my sister, pointing me out with her needle and thread, and shaking her head at me. "Answer him one question, and he'll ask you a dozen directly. Hulks are prison ships, right 'cross the marshes."

"I wonder who's put into prison ships, and why they're put there?" said I, in a general way, and with quiet desperation.

It was too much for Mrs. Joe, who immediately rose. "I tell you what, young fellow," said she, "I didn't bring you up by hand to badger people's lives out. People are put in the Hulks because they murder, and because they rob, and forge, and do all sorts of bad; and they always begin by asking questions. Now, you get along to bed!"

I was never allowed a candle to light me to bed, and, as I went upstairs in the dark, I was in mortal terror of the young man who wanted my heart and liver; I was in mortal terror of the man with the iron leg; I was in mortal terror of myself, from whom an awful promise had been extracted.

As soon as it was dawn, I got up and went downstairs, every board upon the way, and every crack in every board, calling after me, "Stop thief!" and "Get up, Mrs. Joe!" I had no time to spare. I stole some bread, some rind of cheese, and about half a jar of mincemeat (which I tied up in my pocket handkerchief with my last night's slice). I took some brandy from a stone bottle, diluting the stone bottle from a jug in the kitchen cupboard. Lastly, I took a meat bone with very little on it, and a beautiful round compact pork pie.

There was a door in the kitchen leading to the forge; I unlocked and unbolted that door and got a file from among Joe's tools. Then I put the fastenings as I had found them, opened the door at which I had entered when I ran home last night, shut it, and ran for the misty marshes.

CHAPTER III

It was a very damp morning. On every rail and gate, wet lay clammy, and the marsh mist was thick. However fast I went, I couldn't warm my feet, to which the damp cold seemed riveted as the iron was riveted to the leg of the man I was running to meet. I knew my way to the Battery, because I had been down there with Joe, who had told me that when I was apprenticed to him, we would have such larks [1] there! I had just crossed a ditch which I knew to be very near the Battery, and had scrambled up the mound beyond, when I saw the man sitting before me. His back was toward me, and he had his arms folded and was nodding forward, heavy with sleep, so I went forward softly and touched him on the shoulder. He instantly jumped up, and it was not the same man, but another man!

And yet this man was dressed in coarse gray, too, and had a great iron on his leg, and was lame, and hoarse, and cold, and everything that the other man was except that he had not the same face, and had a flat, broad-brimmed, low-crowned felt hat on. He swore an oath at me and then he ran into the mist, stumbling twice as he went.

"It's the young man!" I thought, feeling my heart shoot as I identified him. I dare say I should have felt a pain in my liver, too, if I had known where it was.

I was soon at the Battery, and there was the right man – hugging himself and limping to and fro, as if he had never all night left off hugging and limping – waiting for me. He was awfully cold, to be sure. His eyes looked awfully hungry, too. He did not turn me upside down this time, but left me right side upward while I opened the bundle and emptied my pockets.

"What's in the bottle, boy?" said he.

"Brandy," said I.

He was already handing mincemeat down his throat in a violent hurry, but he left off to take some of the liquor. He shivered all the while violently.

"I think you have got the ague," [2] said I.

"I'm much of your opinion, boy," said he.

"It's bad about here," I told him. "You've been lying out on the marshes."

"I'll eat my breakfast afore they're the death of me," said he. "I'd do that if I was going to be strung up to that there gallows over there, directly afterward. I'll beat the shivers so far, *I'll* bet you."

He was gobbling mincemeat, meat bone, bread, cheese, and pork pie, all at once; staring distrustfully while he did so at the mist all around us, and often stopping to listen. Some real or fancied sound, some clink upon the river or breathing of beast upon the marsh, now gave him a start, and he said, suddenly:

[1] **larks:** fun; in the sense of "going on a lark."

[2] **ague** (ā'gū): a fever accompanied by chills and shaking.

"You're not a deceiving imp? You brought no one with you?"

"No, sir! No!"

"Well," said he, "I believe you. You'd be but a fierce young hound indeed, if at your time of life you could help to hunt a wretched creature, hunted as near death as this poor wretched creature is!"

Something clicked in his throat as if he had works in him like a clock, and was going to strike. And he smeared his ragged rough sleeve over his eyes.

Pitying him, I made bold to say, "I am glad you enjoy it."

"Thankee, my boy. I do."

"I am afraid you won't leave any of it for him," said I, timidly. "There's no more to be got where that came from."

"Leave any for him? Who's him?" said my friend, stopping in his crunching of piecrust.

"The young man. That you spoke of. That was hid with you."

"Oh, ah!" he returned, with something like a gruff laugh. "Him? Yes, yes! *He* don't want no wittles."

"I thought he looked as if he did," said I.

The man stopped eating, and regarded me with the keenest scrutiny and the greatest surprise.

"Looked? When?"

"Just now."

"Where?"

"Yonder," said I, pointing; "over there, where I found him nodding asleep, and thought it was you."

He held me by the collar, and stared at me so that I began to think his first idea about cutting my throat had revived.

"Dressed like you, you know, only with a hat," I explained, trembling; "and — and" — I was very anxious to put this delicately — "and with — the same reason for wanting to borrow a file. Didn't you hear the cannon last night?"

"When a man's alone on these flats, with a light head and a light stomach, perishing of cold and want, he hears nothin' all night but guns firing, and voices calling. But this man — did you notice anything about him?"

"He had a badly bruised face," said I.

"Not here?" exclaimed the man, striking his left cheek.

"Yes, there!"

"Where is he?" He crammed what little food was left into the breast of his gray jacket. "Show me the way he went. I'll pull him down, like a bloodhound. Curse this iron on my sore leg! Give us hold of the file, boy."

He was down on the rank wet grass, filing at his iron like a madman, and not minding me or minding his own leg, which had an old chafe upon it and was bloody, but which he handled as roughly as if it had no more feeling in it than the file.

I was very much afraid of him again, now that he had worked himself into this fierce hurry, and I was likewise very much afraid of keeping away from home any longer. I told him I must go, but he took no notice, so I thought the best thing I could do was to slip off. The last I saw of him, his head was bent over his knee and he was working hard at his fetter, muttering at it and at his leg. The last I heard of him, I stopped in the mist to listen, and the file was still going.

CHAPTER IV

I fully expected to find a constable in the kitchen, waiting to take me up. But not only was there no constable there, but no discovery had yet been made of the robbery. Mrs. Joe was prodigiously [1]

[1] **prodigiously** (prô·dĭj′ŭs·lĭ): extremely; remarkably.

busy in getting the house ready for the festivities of Christmas.

"And where the deuce ha' *you* been?" was Mrs. Joe's Christmas salutation.

I said I had been down to hear the carols. "Ah! well!" observed Mrs. Joe. "You might ha' done worse." Joe secretly crossed his two forefingers, and exhibited them to me as our token that Mrs. Joe was in a cross temper.

We were to have a superb dinner, consisting of a leg of pickled pork and greens, and a pair of roast stuffed fowls. A handsome mince pie had been made yesterday morning (which accounted for the mincemeat not being missed), and the pudding was already on the boil. My sister, having so much to do, was not going to church, but Joe and I were going. In his working clothes, Joe was a well-knit, characteristic-looking blacksmith; in his holiday clothes, he was more like a scarecrow than anything else. Nothing that he wore then fitted him or seemed to belong to him. As for me, when I was taken to have a new suit of clothes, the tailor had orders to make them like a kind of reformatory, and on no account to let me have the free use of my limbs. Joe and I going to church, therefore, must have been a moving spectacle for compassionate minds. Yet what I suffered outside was nothing to what I underwent within. I was filled with terrors whenever Mrs. Joe went near the pantry, and I was remorseful under the weight of my wicked secret.

Mr. Wopsle, the clerk[1] at church, was to dine with us; and Mr. Hubble, the wheelwright, and Mrs. Hubble; and Uncle Pumblechook, who was a well-to-do grain merchant in the nearest town, and drove his own carriage. The dinner hour was half-past one. When Joe and I got home, we found the table laid, and Mrs. Joe dressed, and the dinner dressing, and the front door unlocked (it never was at any other time) for the company to enter by, and everything most splendid. And still, not a word of the robbery.

The time came, without bringing with it any relief to my feelings, and the company came. Mr. Wopsle, besides a Roman nose and a large, shining, bald forehead, had a deep voice which he was uncommonly proud of. In church his reading of the psalms was a performance of dramatic vigor, and he was moreover somewhat given to competition with the minister. He punished the *amens* tremendously; and when he started the psalm he always looked around the congregation first, as much as to say, "You have heard our friend overhead; oblige me with your opinion of this style!"

I opened the door to the company, first to Mr. Wopsle, next to Mr. and Mrs. Hubble, and last of all to Uncle Pumblechook. (*I* was not allowed to call him "uncle," under the severest penalties.)

"Mrs. Joe," said Uncle Pumblechook — a large, hard-breathing, middle-aged, slow man, with a mouth like a fish, dull staring eyes, and sandy hair standing upright on his head, so that he looked as if he had just been all but choked, and had that moment come to — "I have brought you as the compliments of the season — I have brought you, mum, a bottle of sherry wine — and I have brought you, mum, a bottle of port wine." Every Christmas Day he presented himself, as a profound novelty, with exactly the same words, and carrying the two bottles like dumbbells.

We dined on these occasions in the kitchen, and adjourned, for the nuts and oranges and apples, to the parlor. Among this good company I should

[1] **clerk** (klärk): an official (though not a minister) in the Church of England.

have felt myself, even if I hadn't robbed the pantry, in a false position. I should not have minded that if they would only have left me alone. But they wouldn't leave me alone. They seemed to think the opportunity lost if they failed to point the conversation at me, every now and then, and stick the point into me.

It began the moment we sat down to dinner. Mr. Wopsle said grace with theatrical declamation [1] and ended with the proper hope that we might be truly grateful. Upon which my sister fixed me with her eye, and said, in a low reproachful tone, "Do you hear that? Be grateful."

"Especially," said Mr. Pumblechook, "be grateful, boy, to them which brought you up by hand."

Joe always aided and comforted me when he could, in some way of his own, and he always did so at dinnertime by giving me gravy, if there were any. There being plenty of gravy today, Joe spooned into my plate, at this point, about half a pint.

"He was a world of trouble to you, ma'am," said Mrs. Hubble, sympathizing with my sister.

"Trouble?" echoed my sister. "Trouble?" And then entered on a fearful catalogue of all the illnesses I had been guilty of, and all the acts of sleeplessness I had committed, and all the high places I had tumbled from, and all the low places I had tumbled into, and all the injuries I had done myself, and all the times she had wished me in my grave, and I had stubbornly refused to go there. Everybody looked at me with indignation and abhorrence.

"Have a little brandy, uncle," said my sister, presently.

O Heavens, it had come at last! He would find it was weak, he would say it was weak, and I was lost! I held tight to the leg of the table with both hands and awaited my fate.

My sister went for the stone bottle, came back with the stone bottle, and poured his brandy out: no one else taking any. The wretched man trifled with his glass — took it up, looked at it through the light, put it down — prolonged my misery. All this time Mrs. Joe and Joe were briskly clearing the table for the pie and pudding.

I couldn't keep my eyes off him. I saw the miserable creature finger his glass playfully, take it up, smile, throw his head back, and drink the brandy off. Instantly, the company was seized with unspeakable consternation, owing to his springing to his feet, turning round several times in an appalling whooping-cough dance, and rushing out at the door; he then became visible through the window, making the most hideous faces and apparently out of his mind.

I held on tight, while Mrs. Joe and Joe ran to him. I didn't know how I had done it, but I had no doubt I had murdered him somehow. In my dreadful situation, it was a relief when he was brought back, and, surveying the company all round as if *they* had disagreed with him, sank down into his chair with the one significant gasp, "Tar!"

I had filled up the bottle from the tar-water jug!

"Tar!" said my sister, in amazement. "Why, how ever could tar come there?"

But Uncle Pumblechook, who had the complete run of our kitchen, wouldn't hear the word, wouldn't hear of the subject, imperiously waved it away with his hand, and asked for hot gin-and-water. My sister now had to employ herself actively in getting the gin, the hot water, the sugar, and the lemon peel, and mix-

[1] **declamation** (dĕk'lȧ·mā'shŭn): high-flown speech in the manner of an oration.

ing them. For the time at least, I was saved. I still held on to the leg of the table, but clutched it now with the fervor of gratitude.

By degrees, I became calm enough to release my grasp, and partake of pudding. Mr. Pumblechook partook of pudding. All partook of pudding. I began to think I should get over the day, when my sister said to Joe, "Clean plates — cold."

I clutched the leg of the table again immediately. I foresaw what was coming, and I felt that this time I really was gone.

"You must taste," said my sister, addressing the guests with her best grace, "you must taste, to finish with, a pie; a savory pork pie."

My sister went out to get it. I heard her steps proceed to the pantry. I saw Mr. Pumblechook balance his knife. I heard Joe say, "You shall have some, Pip." I felt that I could bear no more, and that I must run away. I released the leg of the table and ran for my life.

But I ran no farther than the house door, for there I ran head foremost into a party of soldiers with their muskets, one of whom held out a pair of handcuffs to me, saying: "Here you are, look sharp, come on!"

CHAPTER V

The strange sight of a file of soldiers ringing down the butt ends of their loaded muskets on our doorstep caused the dinner party to rise from table in confusion, and caused Mrs. Joe, re-entering the kitchen empty-handed, to stop short and stare in her wondering lament of "Gracious goodness gracious me, what's gone — with the — pie!"

The sergeant and I were in the kitchen when Mrs. Joe stood staring. It was the sergeant who had spoken to me, and he was now looking round at the company, with his handcuffs in his right hand, and his left on my shoulder.

"Excuse me, ladies and gentlemen," said the sergeant, "but I want the blacksmith."

"You see, blacksmith," said the sergeant, who had by this time picked out Joe with his eye, "we have had an accident with these, and I find the lock of one of 'em goes wrong. As they are wanted for immediate service, will you throw your eye over them?"

Joe threw his eye over them and pronounced that the job would necessitate the lighting of his forge fire, and would take nearer two hours than one. "Will it? Then will you set about it at once, blacksmith?" said the offhand sergeant, "as it's on His Majesty's service." With that he called to his men, who came trooping into the kitchen one after another and piled their arms in a corner.

I was still in an agony of fear; but seeing that the handcuffs were not for me, and that the pie had been for the moment forgotten, I collected a little of my scattered wits.

"How far might you call yourselves from the marshes, hereabouts? Not above a mile, I reckon?"

"Just a mile," said Mrs. Joe.

"That'll do. We begin to close in upon 'em about dusk. That'll do."

"Convicts, sergeant?" asked Mr. Wopsle, in a matter-of-course way.

"Ay!" returned the sergeant, "two. They're pretty well known to be out on the marshes still, and they won't try to get clear of 'em before dusk. Anybody here seen anything of any such game?"

Everybody, myself excepted, said no, with confidence. Nobody thought of me.

"Well," said the sergeant, "they'll find themselves trapped in a circle. Now, blacksmith! If you're ready, His Majesty the King is."

Joe had got his coat and waistcoat and cravat[1] off, and his leather apron on, and passed into the forge. One of the soldiers opened its wooden windows, another lighted the fire, another turned to at the bellows, the rest stood round the blaze, which was soon roaring. Then Joe began to hammer and clink, hammer and clink, and we all looked on.

At last Joe's job was done, and the ringing and roaring stopped. As Joe got on his coat, he mustered courage to propose that some of us should go down with the soldiers and see what came of the hunt. Mr. Wopsle said he would go, if Joe would. Joe said he was agreeable and would take me.

The sergeant took a polite leave of the ladies, and his men resumed their muskets and fell in. Mr. Wopsle, Joe, and I received strict charge to keep in the rear and to speak no word after we reached the marshes. When we were all out in the raw air and were steadily moving toward our business, I whispered to Joe, " I hope, Joe, we shan't find them." And Joe whispered to me, " I'd give a shilling if they had escaped, Pip."

We were joined by no stragglers from the village, for the weather was cold and threatening, the way dreary, the footing bad, darkness coming on, and the people had good fires indoors, and were keeping the day. We struck out on the open marshes, through the gate at the side of the churchyard. A bitter sleet came rattling against us here on the east wind, and Joe took me on his back.

Now that we were out upon the dismal wilderness where I had been only eight or nine hours before, and had seen both men hiding, I considered for the first time, with great dread, if we should come upon them, would my particular convict suppose that it was I who had brought the soldiers there? He had asked me if I was a deceiving imp, and he said I should be a fierce young hound if I joined the hunt against him. Would he believe that I was both imp and hound in treacherous earnest, and had betrayed him?

It was of no use asking myself this question now. There I was, on Joe's back, and there was Joe beneath me, charging at the ditches like a hunter. The soldiers were in front of us, extending into a pretty wide line with an interval between man and man.

With my heart thumping at Joe's broad shoulder, I looked all about for any sign of the convicts. I could see none, I could hear none. The soldiers were moving on in the direction of the old Battery, and we were moving on a little way behind them, when, all of a sudden, we all stopped. For there had reached us, on the wings of the wind and rain, a long shout. It was repeated. The sergeant, a decisive man, ordered that the sound should not be answered, but that the course should be changed, and that his men should make toward it " at the double."

It was a run indeed now. Down banks and up banks, and over gates, and splashing into dikes, and breaking among coarse rushes, no man cared where he went. As we came nearer to the shouting, it became more and more apparent that it was made by more than one voice. After awhile, we could hear one voice calling " Murder! " and another voice, " Convicts! Runaways! Guard! This way for the runaway convicts! " Then both voices would seem to be stifled in a struggle, and then would break out again. And when it had come to this, the soldiers ran like deer, and Joe too.

The sergeant ran in first, and two of

[1] **cravat** (krȧ·văt′): a necktie.

his men ran in close upon him. Their pieces were cocked and leveled when we all ran in.

"Here are both men!" panted the sergeant, struggling at the bottom of a ditch. "Surrender, you two! and confound you for two wild beasts! Come asunder!"

Water was splashing, and mud was flying, and oaths were being sworn, and blows were being struck, when some more men went down into the ditch to help the sergeant, and dragged out, separately, my convict and the other one. Both were bleeding and panting and swearing and struggling; but of course I knew them both immediately.

"Mind!" said my convict, wiping blood from his face with his ragged sleeves, and shaking torn hair from his fingers; "*I* took him! *I* give him up to you! Mind that!"

"It's not much to be particular about," said the sergeant. "It'll do you small good, my man, being in the same plight yourself. Handcuffs there!"

"I don't expect it to do me any good. I don't want it to do me more good than it does now," said my convict, with a greedy laugh. "I took him. He knows it. That's enough for me."

The other convict, in addition to the old bruised left side of his face, seemed to be bruised and torn all over. He could not so much as get his breath to speak, until they were both separately handcuffed, but leaned upon a soldier to keep himself from falling.

"Take notice, guard — he tried to murder me," were his first words.

"Tried to murder him?" said my convict, disdainfully. "Try, and not do it? I took him, and giv' him up; that's what I done. I not only prevented him getting off the marshes, but I dragged him here. He's a gentleman if you please, this villain. Now the Hulks has got its gentleman again, through me. Murder him? When I could do worse and drag him back?"

The other one still gasped, "He tried — he tried — to — murder me. Bear — bear witness."

"Lookee here!" said my convict to the sergeant. "Singlehanded I got clear of the prison ship; I made a dash and I done it. I could ha' got clear of these death-cold flats likewise — look at my leg: you won't find much iron on it — if I hadn't made discovery that *he* was here. Let *him* go free? Let *him* profit by means as I found out? Let *him* make a tool of me afresh and again? Once more? No, no, no. If I had died at the bottom there," and he made an emphatic swing at the ditch with his manacled[1] hands, "I'd have held to him with that grip, that you should have been safe to find him in my hold."

The other fugitive, who was evidently in extreme horror of his companion, repeated, "He tried to murder me. I should have been a dead man if you had not come up."

"He lies!" said my convict, with fierce energy. "He's a liar born, and he'll die a liar. Look at his face; ain't it written there? Let him turn those eyes of his on me. I defy him to do it."

The other looked at the soldiers, and looked about at the marshes and at the sky, but certainly did not look at the speaker.

"Do you see him?" pursued my convict. "Do you see what a villain he is? Do you see those groveling and wandering eyes? That's how he looked when we were tried together. He never looked at me."

The other, turning his eyes restlessly about him far and near, did at last turn

[1] **manacled** (măn′*ȧ*·k'ld): chained; handcuffed.

"'Here are both men!' panted the sergeant."

them for a moment on the speaker, with the words, " You are not much to look at," and with a half-taunting glance at the bound hands. At that point, my convict became so frantic that he would have rushed upon him but for the interposition of the soldiers. " Didn't I tell you," said the other convict then, " that he would murder me, if he could? " And anyone could see that he shook with fear, and that there broke out upon his lips curious white flakes, like thin snow.

" Enough of this! " said the sergeant. " Light those torches."

As one of the soldiers, who carried a basket, went down on his knee to open it, my convict looked round him for the first time, and saw me. I had alighted from Joe's back on the brink of the ditch when we came up, and had not moved since. I looked at him eagerly when he looked at me, and slightly moved my hands and shook my head. I had been waiting for him to see me, that I might try to assure him of my innocence. He gave me a look that I did not understand, and it all passed in a moment. But he looked at me closely, and I knew I could not fail to remember his face ever afterward.

The soldier with the basket soon lighted three or four torches. Before we departed from that spot, four soldiers, standing in a ring, fired twice into the air. Presently we saw other torches kindled at some distance behind us, and others on the marshes on the opposite bank of the river. " All right," said the sergeant. " March."

We had not gone far when three cannon were fired ahead of us with a sound that seemed to burst something inside my ear. " You are expected on board," said the sergeant to my convict. " They know you are coming. Don't struggle, my man. Close up here."

The two were kept apart, and each walked surrounded by a separate guard. I had hold of Joe's hand now, and Joe carried one of the torches. Mr. Wopsle had been for going back, but Joe was resolved to see it out, so we went on with the party. The two prisoners limped along in the midst of the muskets. We could not go fast, because of their lameness; and they were so spent, that two or three times we had to halt while they rested.

After an hour or so, we came to a rough wooden hut and a landing place. Then we went into the hut, where there was a smell of tobacco and whitewash, and a bright fire, and a lamp.

My convict never looked at me, except that once. While we stood in the hut, he turned to the sergeant, and remarked:

" I wish to say something respecting this escape. It may prevent some persons laying under suspicion because of me."

" You can say what you like," returned the sergeant, standing coolly looking at him with his arms folded, " but you have no call to say it here. You'll have opportunity enough to say about it, and hear about it, before it's done with, you know."

" I know, but this is another matter. A man can't starve; at least *I* can't. I took some wittles, up at the village over yonder — "

" You mean stole," said the sergeant.

" And I'll tell you where from. From the blacksmith's."

" Halloa! " said the sergeant, staring at Joe.

" Halloa, Pip! " said Joe, staring at me.

" It was some broken wittles — that's what it was — and a dram of liquor, and a pie."

" Have you happened to miss such an article as a pie, blacksmith? " asked the sergeant, confidentially.

"My wife did, at the very moment when you came in. Don't you know, Pip?"

"So," said my convict, turning his eyes on Joe in a moody manner, and without the least glance at me; "so you're the blacksmith, are you? Then I'm sorry to say, I've eat your pie."

"God knows you're welcome to it—so far as it was ever mine," returned Joe, with a saving remembrance of Mrs. Joe. "We don't know what you have done, but we wouldn't have you starved to death for it, poor miserable fellow creature. Would us, Pip?"

The something that I had noticed before clicked in the man's throat again, and he turned his back. The boat had returned, and his guard were ready, so we followed him to the landing place, and saw him put into the boat, which was rowed by a crew of convicts like himself. No one seemed surprised to see him, or interested in seeing him, or glad to see him, or sorry to see him, or spoke a word, except that somebody in the boat growled as if to dogs, "Give way, you!" which was the signal for the dip of the oars. By the light of the torches, we saw the black Hulk lying out a little way from the mud of the shore, like a wicked Noah's ark. Cribbed and barred and moored by massive rusty chains, the prison ship seemed in my young eyes to be ironed like the prisoners. We saw the boat go alongside, and we saw him taken up the side and disappear. Then, the ends of the torches were flung hissing into the water, and went out, as if it were all over with him.

And so far as I could know it was all over with him, for I never mentioned him, or my pilfering in his behalf, to a living soul. I loved Joe—perhaps for no better reason in those days than because the dear fellow let me love him—and it was much on my mind that I ought to tell Joe the whole truth. Yet I did not, for I feared he would think me worse than I was. The fear of losing Joe's confidence tied my tongue. In a word, I was too cowardly to do what I knew to be right, just as I had been too cowardly to avoid doing what I knew to be wrong.

CHAPTER VI

When I was old enough, I was to be apprenticed to Joe, and until I could assume that dignity I was not to be what Mrs. Joe called "Pompeyed," or (as I render it) pampered. Therefore, I was not only odd boy about the forge, but if any neighbor happened to want an extra boy to frighten birds, or pick up stones, or do any such job, I was favored with the employment. A money box was kept on the kitchen mantel shelf, into which it was publicly made known that all my earnings were dropped, but I had no hope of any personal claim to the treasure.

Mr. Wopsle's great-aunt kept an evening school in the village. She was a ridiculous old woman who used to go to sleep from six to seven every evening, in the company of youth who paid twopence[1] per week each for the improving opportunity of seeing her do it. She rented a small cottage, and Mr. Wopsle had the room upstairs, where we students used to overhear him reading aloud in a most dignified and terrific manner, and occasionally bumping on the ceiling. There was a pretense that Mr. Wopsle "examined" the scholars, once a quarter. What he did on those occasions was to turn up his cuffs, stick up his hair, and give us Mark Antony's

[1] **twopence** (tŭp′ĕns): an amount equaling about four cents in American money.

oration over the body of Caesar.[1]

Mr. Wopsle's great-aunt, besides keeping this educational institution, kept — in the same room — a little general shop. She had no idea what stock she had, or what the price of anything in it was; but there was a little greasy memorandum book kept in a drawer, which served as a catalogue of prices, and by this list Biddy arranged all the shop transactions. Biddy was Mr. Wopsle's great-aunt's granddaughter. She was an orphan like myself; like me, too, she had been brought up by hand. Her hair always wanted brushing, her hands always wanted washing, and her shoes always wanted mending and pulling up at heel.

More by the help of Biddy than of Mr. Wopsle's great-aunt, I struggled through the alphabet as if it had been a bramblebush, getting considerably worried and scratched by every letter. After that, I fell among those thieves, the nine figures, who seemed every evening to do something new to disguise themselves and baffle recognition. But at last I began, in a groping way, to read, write, and cipher,[2] on the very smallest scale.

One night, I was sitting in the chimney corner with my slate, expending great efforts on the writing of a letter to Joe. I think it must have been a full year after our hunt upon the marshes, for it was a long time after, and it was winter and a hard frost. With an alphabet on the hearth at my feet for reference, I contrived in an hour or two to print and smear this epistle:

mI deEr JO i opE U r krWitE wEll i opE i shAl soN B haBelL 4 2 teeDge U JO aN theN wE shOrl b sO glOdd aN wEn i M preNgtD 2 u JO woT larX an blEvE ME inF xn PiP.

There was no necessity for my writing Joe a letter, inasmuch as he sat beside me and we were alone. But I delivered this written communication (slate and all) with my own hand, and Joe received it as a miracle of learning.

"I say, Pip, old chap!" cried Joe, opening his blue eyes wide, "what a scholar you are! Ain't you?"

"I should like to be," said I, glancing at the slate as he held it, with a misgiving that the writing was rather hilly.

"Why, here's a J," said Joe, "and a O equal to anythink! Here's a J and a O, Pip, and a J-O, Joe."

I had never heard Joe read aloud to any greater extent than this single word, and I had observed at church last Sunday, when I accidentally held our prayer book upside down, that it seemed to suit his convenience quite as well as if it had been all right. Wishing to find out whether, in teaching Joe, I should have to begin quite at the beginning, I said, "Ah! But read the rest, Joe."

"The rest, eh, Pip?" said Joe, looking at it with a slowly searching eye. "One, two, three. Why, here's three J's, and three O's, and three J-O, Joe's, in it, Pip!"

I leaned over Joe, and, with the aid of my forefinger, read him the whole letter.

"Astonishing!" said Joe, when I had finished. "You *are* a scholar."

"How do you spell Gargery, Joe?" I asked.

"I don't spell it at all," said Joe.

"But supposing you did?"

"It *can't* be supposed," said Joe. "Tho' I'm uncommon fond of reading, too."

"Are you, Joe?"

"Uncommon. Give me," said Joe, "a

[1] Mark Antony's oration is from Shakespeare's play, *Julius Caesar*.

[2] **cipher** (sī'fẽr): do sums in arithmetic.

good book, or a good newspaper, and sit me down afore a good fire, and I ask no better. Lord!" he continued, after rubbing his knees a little, "when you *do* come to a J and a O, and says you, 'Here, at last, is a J-O, Joe,' how interesting reading is!"

I derived from this last, that Joe's education was yet in its infancy. Pursuing the subject, I inquired:

"Didn't you ever go to school, Joe, when you were as little as me?"

"No, Pip."

"Why didn't you ever go to school, Joe, when you were as little as me?"

"Well, Pip," said Joe, taking up the poker, and settling himself to his usual occupation, when he was thoughtful, of slowly raking the fire between the lower bars, "I'll tell you. My father, Pip, he were given to drink, and when he were overtook with drink, he hammered away at my mother most unmerciful. My mother and me we ran away from my father several times; and then my mother she'd go out to work, and she'd say, 'Joe,' she'd say, 'now, please God, you shall have some schooling, child,' and she'd put me to school. But my father were that good in his heart that he couldn't a-bear to be without us. So, he took us home and hammered us. Which, you see, Pip," said Joe, "were a drawback on my learning."

"Certainly, poor Joe!"

"Though mind you, Pip," said Joe, "rendering unto all their due, and maintaining equal justice betwixt man and man, my father were that good in his heart, don't you see?"

I didn't see; but I didn't say so.

"'Consequence, my father didn't make objections to my going to work; so I went to work at my present calling, and I worked tolerable hard, I assure *you*, Pip. In time I were able to keep him, and I kept him till he went off in a purple leptic fit.[1] My mother, she were in poor 'elth, and quite broke. She weren't long of following, poor soul, and her share of peace come round at last."

Joe's blue eyes turned a little watery. "It were but lonesome then," said Joe, "living here alone, and I got acquainted with your sister. Now, Pip," Joe looked firmly at me, as if he knew I was not going to agree with him, "your sister is a fine figure of a woman."

I could not help looking at the fire, in an obvious state of doubt.

"Whatever family opinions, or whatever the world's opinions, on that subject may be, Pip, your sister is," Joe tapped the top bar with the poker after every word following, "a — fine — figure — of — a — woman!"

I could think of nothing better to say than "I am glad you think so, Joe."

"So am I," returned Joe. "When I offered to your sister to keep company, and to be asked in church, at such times as she was willing and ready to come to the forge, I said to her, 'And bring the poor little child. God bless the poor little child,' I said to your sister, 'there's room for *him* at the forge!'"

I broke out crying and hugged Joe round the neck. Joe dropped the poker to hug me, and to say, "Ever the best of friends; ain't us, Pip? Don't cry, old chap!"

When this little interruption was over, Joe resumed:

"Well, you see, Pip, and here we are! Now, when you take me in hand in my learning, Pip (and I tell you beforehand I am awful dull, most awful dull), Mrs. Joe mustn't see too much of what we're

[1] **purple leptic fit:** Joe probably means to say "apoplectic (ăp′ō·plĕk′tĭk)." Apoplexy is a sudden paralysis or loss of consciousness, sometimes called a "stroke."

up to. It must be done, as I may say, on the sly. I'll tell you why, Pip.

"Your sister ain't over partial to having scholars on the premises," Joe continued, "and in partickler would not be over partial to my being a scholar, for fear as I might rise. Like a sort of rebel, don't you see?"

Young as I was, I believe that I dated a new admiration of Joe from that night. We were equals afterward, as we had been before; but afterward, at quiet times when I sat looking at Joe and thinking about him, I had a new sensation of feeling conscious that I was looking up to Joe in my heart.

"However," said Joe, rising to feed the fire, "here's the Dutch clock a-working himself up to being equal to strike eight of them, and she's not home yet!"

Mrs. Joe made occasional trips with Uncle Pumblechook on market days to assist him in buying such household stuffs and goods as required a woman's judgment, Uncle Pumblechook being a bachelor. This was market day, and Mrs. Joe was out on one of these expeditions.

Joe made the fire and swept the hearth, and then we went to the door to listen for the carriage. It was a dry, cold night.

"Here comes the mare," said Joe, "ringing like a peal of bells!"

Mrs. Joe was soon landed, and Uncle Pumblechook was soon down too, and we were soon all in the kitchen, carrying so much cold air with us that it seemed to drive all the heat out of the fire.

"Now," said Mrs. Joe, unwrapping herself with haste and excitement, and throwing her bonnet back on her shoulders, where it hung by the strings, "if this boy ain't grateful this night, he never will be!"

I looked as grateful as any boy possibly could who was wholly uninformed why he ought to be grateful.

"It's only to be hoped," said my sister, "that he won't be Pompeyed. But I have my fears."

"She ain't like that, mum," said Mr. Pumblechook. "She knows better."

She? I looked at Joe, making the motion with my lips and eyebrows. "She?" Joe looked at me, making the motion with *his* lips and eyebrows. "She?" My sister catching him in the act, he drew the back of his hand across his nose with his usual air on such occasions, and looked at her.

"Well?" said my sister, in her snappish way. "What are you staring at? Is the house afire?"

"Some indiwidual," Joe politely hinted, "mentioned she."

"And she is a she, I suppose?" said my sister. "Unless you call Miss Havisham a he. And I doubt if even you'll go so far as that."

"Miss Havisham uptown?" said Joe.

"Is there any Miss Havisham downtown?" returned my sister. "She wants this boy to go and play there. And of course he's going. And he had better play there," said my sister, shaking her head at me as an encouragement to be extremely light and sportive, "or I'll work him."

I had heard of Miss Havisham uptown — everybody for miles round had heard of Miss Havisham uptown — as an immensely rich and grim lady who lived in a large and dismal house barricaded against robbers, and who led a life of seclusion.

"Well, to be sure!" said Joe, astounded. "I wonder how she comes to know Pip!"

"Noodle!" cried my sister. "Who said she knew him?"

"Some indiwidual," Joe again politely

hinted, "mentioned that she wanted him to go and play there."

"And couldn't she ask Uncle Pumblechook if he knew of a boy to go and play there? Isn't it just barely possible that Uncle Pumblechook may be a tenant of hers, and that he may sometimes go there to pay his rent? And couldn't she then ask Uncle Pumblechook if he knew of a boy to go and play there? And couldn't Uncle Pumblechook — being always considerate and thoughtful for us, though you may not think so, Joseph — then mention this boy that I have forever been a willing slave to?" My sister spoke in a tone of deepest reproach as if Joe were the most callous of nephews.

"Good again!" cried Uncle Pumblechook. "Well put! Good indeed! Now, Joseph, you know the case."

"No, Joseph," said my sister, in a reproachful manner, "you do not yet — though you may not think it — know the case. Uncle Pumblechook, being sensible that this boy's fortune may be made by his going to Miss Havisham's, has offered to take him into town tonight in his own carriage, and to keep him tonight and to take him with his own hands to Miss Havisham's tomorrow morning. And Lor-a-mussy me!" cried my sister, casting off her bonnet in sudden desperation, "here I stand talking, with Uncle Pumblechook waiting, and the mare catching cold at the door, and the boy grimed with crock and dirt from the hair of his head to the sole of his foot!"

With that she pounced on me, like an eagle on a lamb, and my face was squeezed into wooden bowls in sinks, and my head was put under taps of water butts, and I was soaped, and kneaded, and toweled, and thumped, and harrowed, and rasped, until I really was quite beside myself.

When my washing was completed, I was put into clean linen of the stiffest character, and was trussed up in my tightest and fearfulest suit. I was then delivered over to Mr. Pumblechook, who formally received me as if he were the sheriff, and who let off upon me the speech that I knew he had been dying to make all along; "Boy, be forever grateful to all friends, but especially unto them which brought you up by hand!"

"Good-by, Joe!"

"God bless you, Pip, old chap!"

I had never parted from him before, and what with my feelings and what with soapsuds, I could at first see no stars from the carriage. But they twinkled out one by one, without throwing any light on the question why on earth I was going to play at Miss Havisham's, and what on earth I was expected to play at.

CHAPTER VII

Upon reaching Mr. Pumblechook's grain and seed shop on the High Street of the market town, I was sent straight to bed in an attic with a sloping roof, which was so low in the corner where the bedstead was that I calculated the tiles as being within a foot of my eyebrows.

Mr. Pumblechook and I breakfasted at eight o'clock in the parlor behind the shop while his shopman took his mug of tea and hunk of bread-and-butter on a sack of peas in the front premises. I considered Mr. Pumblechook wretched company. Besides giving me as much crumb as possible in combination with as little butter, and putting a great quantity of warm water in my milk, his conversation consisted of nothing but arithmetic. On my politely bidding him good morning, he said pompously, "Seven times nine, boy?" And how should *I* be able to answer, dodged in that way, in a strange place, on an empty stomach! I was hungry, but before I had swallowed a morsel, he began a running sum that lasted all through the breakfast. "Seven?" "And four?" "And eight?" "And six?" "And two?" "And ten?" And so on.

I was very glad when ten o'clock came and we started for Miss Havisham's. Within a quarter of an hour we came to Miss Havisham's house, which was of old brick, and dismal, and had a great many iron bars to it. Some of the windows had been walled up; of those that remained, all the lower were rustily barred. There was a courtyard in front, and that was barred; so we had to wait, after ringing the bell, until someone should come to open it. While we waited at the gate, I saw that at the side of the house there was a large brewery. No brewing was going on in it, and none seemed to have gone on for a long time.

A window was raised, and a clear voice demanded, "What name?" To which my conductor replied, "Pumblechook." The voice returned, "Quite right," and the window was shut again, and a young lady came across the courtyard, with keys in her hand.

"This," said Mr. Pumblechook, "is Pip."

"This is Pip, is it?" returned the young lady, who was very pretty, and seemed very proud. "Come in, Pip."

Mr. Pumblechook was coming in also, when she stopped him with the gate.

"Oh!" she said. "Did you wish to see Miss Havisham?"

"If Miss Havisham wished to see me," returned Mr. Pumblechook, somewhat confused.

"Ah!" said the girl; "but you see she doesn't."

She said it so finally, that Mr. Pumblechook could not protest. But he eyed me severely — as if *I* had done anything to him! — and departed with the words reproachfully delivered: "Boy! Let your behavior here be a credit unto them which brought you up by hand!"

My young conductress locked the gate, and we went across the courtyard. It was paved and clean, but grass was growing in every crevice. The brewery beyond stood open, and all was empty and disused. The cold wind seemed to blow colder there than outside the gate; and it made a shrill noise in howling in and out at the open sides of the brewery, like the noise of wind in the rigging of a ship at sea.

"What is the name of this house, miss?"

"Its name was Satis; which is Greek, or Latin, or Hebrew, or all three — or all one to me — for enough."

"Enough House!" said I. "That's a curious name, miss."

"Yes," she replied, "but it means more than it says. It meant, when it was given, that whoever had this house, could want nothing else. They must have been easily satisfied in those days, I should think. But don't loiter, boy."

Though she called me "boy" so often, and with a carelessness that was far from complimentary, she was of about my own age. She seemed much older than I, of course, being a girl, and beautiful and self-possessed; and she was as scornful of me as if she had been one-and-twenty, and a queen.

We went into the house by a side door — the great front entrance had two chains across it outside — and the first thing I noticed was that the passages were all dark, and that she had left a candle burning there. She took it up, and we went through more passages and up

"'This is Pip, is it?'"

a staircase, and still it was all dark, and only the candle lighted us.

At last we came to the door of a room, and she said, " Go in."

I answered, more in shyness than politeness, " After you, miss."

To this she returned, " Don't be ridiculous, boy; I am not going in." And scornfully walked away, and — what was worse — took the candle with her.

This was very uncomfortable, and I was half afraid. However, the only thing to be done being to knock at the door, I knocked, and was told from within to enter. I entered, therefore, and found myself in a pretty large room, well lighted with wax candles. No glimpse of daylight was to be seen in it. It was a dressing room, as I supposed from the furniture. But prominent in it was a draped table with a gilded looking glass, and that I made out at first sight to be a fine lady's dressing table.

In an armchair, with an elbow resting on the table and her head leaning on that hand, sat the strangest lady I have ever seen, or shall ever see.

She was dressed in rich materials — satins, and lace, and silks — all of white. Her shoes were white. She had a long white veil hanging from her hair, and she had bridal flowers in her hair, but her hair was white. Some bright jewels sparkled on her neck and on her hands, and some other jewels lay sparkling on the table. Dresses and half-packed trunks were scattered about. She had not quite finished dressing, for she had but one shoe on — the other was on the table near her hand — her veil was but half arranged, her watch and chain were not put on, and her handkerchief and gloves, some flowers, and a prayer book lay all confusedly heaped about the looking glass.

But I saw that everything within my view which ought to be white had lost its luster, and was faded and yellow. I saw that the bride within the bridal dress had withered like the dress, and like the flowers, and had no brightness left but the brightness of her sunken eyes. I saw that the dress had been put upon the rounded figure of a young woman, and that the figure upon which it now hung loose had shrunk to skin and bone.

" Who is it? " said the lady at the table.

" Pip, ma'am."

" Pip? "

" Mr. Pumblechook's boy, ma'am. Come — to play."

" Come nearer; let me look at you. Come close."

It was when I stood before her, avoiding her eyes, that I took note of the surrounding objects in detail, and saw that her watch had stopped at twenty minutes to nine, and that a clock in the room had stopped at twenty minutes to nine.

" Look at me," said Miss Havisham. " You are not afraid of a woman who has never seen the sun since you were born? "

I regret to state that I was not afraid of telling an enormous lie in the answer, " No."

" Do you know what I touch here? " she said, laying her hands, one upon the other, on her left side.

" Yes, ma'am."

" What do I touch? "

" Your heart."

" Broken! "

She uttered the word with an eager look, and with strong emphasis, and with a weird smile that had a kind of boast in it.

" I am tired," said Miss Havisham. " I sometimes have sick fancies, and I have a sick fancy that I want to see some play. There, there!" with an impatient movement of the fingers of her right hand, "play, play, play!"

I stood looking at Miss Havisham in what I suppose she took for a stubborn manner, inasmuch as she said, when we had taken a good look at each other:

"Are you sullen and obstinate?"

"No, ma'am, I am very sorry for you, and very sorry I can't play just now. If you complain of me I shall get into trouble with my sister, so I would do it if I could; but it's so new here, and so strange, and so fine – and sad ——" I stopped, fearing I might say too much, or had already said it, and we took another look at each other.

Before she spoke again, she turned her eyes from me, and looked at the dress she wore, and at the dressing table, and finally at herself in the looking glass.

"So new to him," she muttered, "so old to me; so strange to him, so familiar to me; so sad to both of us! Call Estella."

As she was still looking at the reflection of herself, I thought she was still talking to herself, and kept quiet.

"Call Estella," she repeated, flashing a look at me. "You can do that. Call Estella. At the door."

I called, and the scornful young lady answered at last, and her light came along the dark passage like a star.

Miss Havisham beckoned her to come close, and took up a jewel from the table, and tried its effect against her pretty brown hair. "Your own, one day, my dear, and you will use it well. Let me see you play cards with this boy."

"With this boy! Why, he is a common laboring boy!"

I thought I overheard Miss Havisham answer – only it seemed so unlikely – "Well? You can break his heart."

"What do you play, boy?" asked Estella of me, with the greatest disdain.

"Nothing but beggar my neighbor, miss."

"Beggar him," said Miss Havisham to Estella. So we sat down to cards.

It was then I began to understand that everything in the room had stopped, like the watch and the clock, a long time ago. I noticed that Miss Havisham put down the jewel exactly on the spot from which she had taken it up. As Estella dealt the cards, I glanced at the dressing table again, and saw that the shoe upon it, once white, now yellow, had never been worn. I glanced down at the foot from which the shoe was absent, and saw that the silk stocking on it, once white, now yellow, had been trodden ragged.

Miss Havisham sat, corpselike, as we played at cards.

"He calls the knaves jacks, this boy!" said Estella with disdain, before our first game was out. "And what coarse hands he has! And what thick boots!"

I had never thought of being ashamed of my hands before; but her contempt for me was so strong that it became infectious, and I caught it.

She won the game, and I dealt. I misdealt, as was only natural when I knew she was lying in wait for me to do wrong; and she denounced me for a stupid, clumsy laboring boy.

"You say nothing of her," remarked Miss Havisham to me, as she looked on. "She says many hard things of you, yet you say nothing of her. What do you think of her?"

"I don't like to say," I stammered.

"Tell me in my ear," said Miss Havisham, bending down.

"I think she is very proud," I replied, in a whisper.

"Anything else?"

"I think she is very pretty."

"Anything else?"

"I think she is very insulting." (She was looking at me then with a look of supreme distaste.)

"Anything else?"

"I think I should like to go home."

"And never see her again, though she is so pretty?"

"I am not sure that I shouldn't like to see her again, but I should like to go home now."

"You shall go soon," said Miss Havisham aloud. "Play the game out."

I played the game to an end with Estella, and she won of me. She threw the cards down on the table when she had won them all, as if she despised them for having been won of me.

"When shall I have you here again?" said Miss Havisham. "Let me think. Come again after six days. You hear?"

"Yes, ma'am."

"Estella, take him down. Let him have something to eat, and let him roam and look about him while he eats. Go, Pip."

I followed the candle down, as I had followed the candle up, and she stood it in the place where we had found it.

"You are to wait here, you boy," said Estella. She disappeared and closed the door.

I took the opportunity of being alone to look at my coarse hands and my common boots. They had never troubled me before, but they troubled me now. I determined to ask Joe why he had ever taught me to call those picture cards jacks, which ought to be called knaves. I wished Joe had been better brought up, and then I should have been so too.

She came back, with some bread and meat and a little mug of beer. She put the mug down on the stones of the yard, and gave me the bread and meat without looking at me, as insolently as if I were a dog in disgrace. I was so humiliated, hurt, spurned, offended, angry, sorry, that tears started to my eyes. The moment they sprang there, the girl looked at me with a quick delight in having been the cause of them. This gave me power to keep them back and to look at her; so she gave a contemptuous toss – but with a sense, I thought, of having made too sure that I was so wounded – and left me.

But, when she was gone, I got behind one of the gates in the brewery lane, and leaned my sleeve against the wall there, and leaned my forehead on it, and cried. As I cried, I kicked the wall, and took a hard twist at my hair, so bitter were my feelings.

I got rid of my injured feelings for the time, by kicking them into the brewery wall, and twisting them out of my hair, and then I smoothed my face with my sleeve, and came from behind the gate. The bread and meat were acceptable, and the beer was warming and tingling.

Soon I saw Estella approaching with the keys to let me out. She gave me a triumphant glance in passing me, as if she rejoiced that my hands were so coarse and my boots were so thick, and she opened the gate and stood holding it. I was passing out without looking at her, when she touched me with a taunting hand.

"Why don't you cry?"

"Because I don't want to."

"You do," said she. "You have been crying till you are half blind, and you are near crying again now."

She laughed, pushed me out, and locked the gate upon me. I went straight to Mr. Pumblechook's, and was immensely relieved to find him not at home. So, leaving word with the shopman on what day I was wanted at Miss Havisham's again, I set off on the four-mile walk to our forge. As I went along, I thought on all I had seen, and that I was a common laboring boy; that my hands were coarse; that my boots were thick; that I was much more ignorant than I had considered myself last night; and generally that I was in a bad way.

CHAPTER VIII

When I reached home, my sister was very curious to know all about Miss Havisham's, and asked a number of questions. And I soon found myself getting heavily bumped from behind in the nape of the neck and the small of the back, and having my face shoved against the kitchen wall, because I did not answer those questions at sufficient length.

I felt convinced that if I described Miss Havisham's as my eyes had seen it, I should not be understood. Not only that, but I felt convinced that Miss Havisham too would not be understood. I felt that there would be something coarse and treacherous in my dragging her as she really was (to say nothing of Miss Estella) before the attention of Mrs. Joe. Consequently, I said as little as I could, and had my face shoved against the kitchen wall.

The worst of it was that bullying old Pumblechook, who had a devouring curiosity to be informed of all I had seen and heard. He came gaping over in his carriage at teatime, to have the details related to him.

"Well, boy," Uncle Pumblechook began, as soon as he was seated in the chair of honor by the fire. "How did you get on uptown?"

I answered, "Pretty well, sir," and my sister shook her fist at me.

"Pretty well?" Mr. Pumblechook repeated. "Pretty well is no answer. Tell us what you mean by pretty well, boy!"

My sister with an exclamation of impatience was going to fly at me — I had no shadow of defense, for Joe was busy in the forge — when Mr. Pumblechook interposed with "No! Don't lose your temper. Leave this lad to me, ma'am; leave this lad to me." Mr. Pumblechook then turned me toward him, as if he were going to cut my hair, and said:

"Boy! What is Miss Havisham like?" Mr. Pumblechook began again, folding his arms tight on his chest.

"Very tall and dark," I told him.

"Is she, uncle?" asked my sister.

Mr. Pumblechook winked assent, from which I at once gathered that he had never seen Miss Havisham, for she was nothing of the kind.

"Good!" said Mr. Pumblechook, conceitedly. "This is the way to have him! We are beginning to hold our own, I think, mum?"

"I am sure, uncle," returned Mrs. Joe, "I wish you had him always; you know so well how to deal with him."

"Now, boy! What was she a-doing of, when you went in today?" asked Mr. Pumblechook.

"She was sitting," I answered, "in a black velvet coach."

Mr. Pumblechook and Mrs. Joe stared at one another — as they well might — and both repeated, "In a black velvet coach?"

"Yes," said I. "And Miss Estella — that's her niece, I think — handed her in cake and wine at the coach window, on a gold plate. And we all had cake and wine on gold plates. And I got up behind the coach to eat mine, because she told me to."

Mr. Pumblechook and Mrs. Joe stared

at one another again, in utter amazement. I was perfectly frantic — a reckless witness under the torture — and would have told them anything.

"Did you ever see her in it, uncle?" asked Mrs. Joe.

"How could I," he returned, forced to tell the truth, "when I never see her in my life? Never clapped eyes upon her!"

"Goodness, uncle! And yet you have spoken to her?"

"Why, don't you know," said Mr. Pumblechook, testily, "that when I have been there, I have been took up to the outside of her door, and the door has stood ajar, and she spoken to me that way. What did you play at, boy?"

"We played with flags," I said. (I beg to observe that I think of myself with amazement, when I recall the lies I told on this occasion.)

"Flags!" echoed my sister.

"Yes," said I. "Estella waved a blue flag, and I waved a red one, and Miss Havisham waved one sprinkled all over with little gold stars, out at the coach window. And then we all waved our swords and hurrahed."

If they had asked me any more questions I should undoubtedly have betrayed myself, but Joe came in then to have a cup of tea, and my sister began to tell him of my pretended experiences.

Now, when I saw Joe open his blue eyes and roll them all round the kitchen in helpless amazement, I was overtaken by repentance. Toward Joe, and Joe only, I considered myself a young monster, while they sat debating what results would come to me from Miss Havisham's acquaintance and favor. They had no doubt that Miss Havisham would "do something" for me. My sister thought it would be "property." Mr. Pumblechook was in favor of a handsome premium [1] for binding me apprentice to some trade.

After Mr. Pumblechook had driven off, and when my sister was washing up, I stole into the forge to Joe, and remained by him until he had done for the night. Then I said, "Before the fire goes out, Joe, I should like to tell you something."

"Should you, Pip?" said Joe, drawing his shoeing stool near the forge. "Then tell us. What is it, Pip?"

"Joe," said I, taking hold of his rolled-up shirt sleeve, and twisting it between my finger and thumb, "you remember all that about Miss Havisham's?"

"Remember?" said Joe. "I believe you! Wonderful!"

"It's a terrible thing, Joe; it ain't true."

"What are you telling of, Pip?" cried Joe, falling back in the greatest amazement. "You don't mean to say it's ——"

"Yes, I do; it's lies, Joe."

As I fixed my eyes hopelessly on Joe, he looked at me in dismay. "Pip, old chap! This won't do, old fellow! I say! Where do you expect to go to?"

"It's terrible, Joe; ain't it?"

"Terrible?" cried Joe. "Awful! What possessed you?"

"I don't know what possessed me, Joe," I replied, letting his shirt sleeve go, and sitting down in the ashes at his feet, hanging my head; "but I wish you hadn't taught me to call knaves at cards jacks, and I wish my boots weren't so thick nor my hands so coarse."

And then I told Joe that I felt very miserable, and that I hadn't been able

[1] **premium** (prē′mĭ·ŭm): an initial fee paid to a master workman by a prospective apprentice. In former times, apprenticeship was the most common way to learn a trade. A boy (with his parents or guardian) signed a contract, called "indentures," by which he was bound to serve a master workman without pay for five to seven years. In return for this service, he was taught the workman's trade.

to explain myself to Mrs. Joe and Pumblechook, who were so rude to me, and that there had been a beautiful young lady at Miss Havisham's who was dreadfully proud, and that she had said I was common, and that I knew I was common, and that I wished I was not common, and that the lies had come of it somehow, though I didn't know how.

"There's one thing you may be sure of, Pip," said Joe, "namely, that lies is lies. However they come, they didn't ought to come, and they come from the father of lies, and work round to the same. Don't you tell me no more of 'em, Pip. *That* ain't the way to get out of being common, old chap. And as to being common, I don't make it out at all clear. You are uncommon in some things. You're uncommon small. Likewise you're a uncommon scholar."

"No, I am ignorant and backward, Joe."

"Why, see what a letter you wrote last night! Wrote in print even! I've seen letters — ah! and from gentlefolks! — that I'll swear weren't wrote in print," said Joe.

"I have learned next to nothing, Joe. You think much of me. It's only that."

"Well, Pip," said Joe, "you must be a common scholar afore you can be a uncommon one, I should hope!"

"You are not angry with me, Joe?"

"No, old chap. That's all, old chap, and don't never do it no more."

When I got up to my little room and said my prayers, my young mind was in a disturbed and unthankful state. I thought long how common Estella would consider Joe, a mere blacksmith, how thick his boots, and how coarse his hands. I thought how Joe and my sister were then sitting in the kitchen, and how I had come up to bed from the kitchen, and how Miss Havisham and Estella never sat in a kitchen, but were far above the level of such common doings. I fell asleep recalling what I "used to do" when I was at Miss Havisham's; as though I had been there weeks or months, instead of hours.

That was a memorable day to me, for it made great changes in me. But it is the same with any life. Imagine one selected day struck out of it, and think how different its course would have been. Pause, you who read this, and think for a moment of the long chain of iron or gold, of thorns or flowers, that would never have bound you, but for the formation of the first link on one memorable day.

CHAPTER IX

The idea occurred to me a morning or two later when I woke, that the best step I could take toward making myself uncommon was to get out of Biddy everything she knew. I mentioned to Biddy when I went to Mr. Wopsle's great-aunt's at night, that I had a particular reason for wishing to get on in life, and that I should feel very much obliged to her if she would impart all her learning to me. Biddy, who was the most obliging of girls, immediately said she would, and indeed began to carry out her promise within five minutes.

The educational scheme or course established by Mr. Wopsle's great-aunt may be summarized briefly. The pupils ate apples and put straws down one another's backs until Mr. Wopsle's great-aunt collected her energies and tottered at us with a birch rod. After receiving the charge with every mark of derision,[1] the pupils formed a line and buzzingly passed a ragged book from hand to hand. The book had an alphabet in it, some figures and tables, and a little

[1] **derision** (dē-rĭzh'ŭn): ridicule; disrespect.

spelling. Biddy gave out the number of the page, and then we all read aloud in a frightful chorus. Biddy led with a high shrill voice, and none of us had the least notion of, or respect for, what we were reading.

It appeared to me that it would take time to become uncommon under these circumstances; nevertheless, I resolved to try it, and that very evening Biddy entered on our special agreement by lending me, to copy at home, a large Old English *D* which she had imitated from the heading of some newspaper, and which I supposed, until she told me what it was, to be a design for a buckle.

Of course there was a public house in the village, and of course Joe liked sometimes to smoke his pipe there. I had received strict orders from my sister to call for him at the Three Jolly Bargemen that evening, on my way from school, and bring him home at my peril. To the Three Jolly Bargemen, therefore, I directed my steps.

I found Joe there, smoking his pipe in company with Mr. Wopsle and a stranger. Joe greeted me as usual with "Halloa, Pip, old chap!" and the moment he said that, the stranger turned his head and looked at me.

He was a secret-looking man whom I had never seen before. His head was all on one side, and one of his eyes was half shut up, as if he were taking aim at something with an invisible gun. He had a pipe in his mouth, and he took it out, and, after slowly blowing all his smoke away and looking hard at me all the time, nodded. So I nodded, and then he nodded again, and made room on the settle beside him that I might sit down there.

But, as I was used to sit beside Joe whenever I entered that place of resort, I said, "No, thank you, sir," and fell into the space Joe made for me on the opposite settle. The strange man, after glancing at Joe, and seeing that his attention was otherwise engaged, nodded to me again when I had taken my seat, and then rubbed his leg – in a very odd way, it struck me.

"You was saying," said the strange man, turning to Joe, "that you was a blacksmith. What'll you drink, Mr. Gargery? At my expense? To top up with?"

"Well," said Joe, "to tell you the truth, I ain't much in the habit of drinking at anybody's expense but my own."

"Habit? No," returned the stranger, "but once and away, and on a Saturday night too. Come! Put a name to it, Mr. Gargery."

"I wouldn't wish to be stiff company," said Joe. "Rum."

"Rum," repeated the stranger. "And the other gentleman?"

"Rum," said Mr. Wopsle.

"Three rums!" cried the stranger, calling to the landlord. "Glasses round!"

The stranger put his legs up on the settle that he had to himself. He wore a flapping broad-brimmed traveler's hat and under it a handkerchief tied over his head in the manner of a cap, so that he showed no hair.

"I am not acquainted with this country, gentlemen, but it seems a solitary country toward the river."

"Most marshes is solitary," said Joe.

"No doubt, no doubt. Do you find any gypsies, now, or tramps, or vagrants of any sort, out there?"

"No," said Joe; "none but a runaway convict now and then. And we don't find *them*, easy."

"Seems you have been out after such?" asked the stranger.

"Once," returned Joe. "Not that we wanted to take them, you understand; we went out as lookers on, me and Mr.

Wopsle, and Pip. Didn't us, Pip?"

"Yes, Joe."

The stranger looked at me again and said, "He's a likely young parcel of bones that. What is it you call him?"

"Pip," said Joe.

"Christened Pip?"

"No, not christened Pip."

"Surname Pip?"

"No," said Joe; "it's a kind of a family name what he gave himself when a infant, and is called by."

"Son of yours?"

"Well," said Joe, slowly —— "well – no. No, he ain't."

"Nevvy?"[1] said the strange man.

"Well," said Joe, "he is not – no, not to deceive you, he is *not* – my nevvy."

"What the blue blazes is he?" asked the stranger.

Mr. Wopsle then explained the ties between Joe and me, and all the while the strange man looked at nobody but me. He said nothing until the glasses were brought. Then he stirred his rum-and-water pointedly at me. And he stirred it not with a spoon that was brought to him, but *with a file.*

He did this so that nobody but I saw the file; and when he had done it, he wiped the file and put it in a breast pocket. I knew it to be Joe's file, and I knew that he knew my convict, the moment I saw the file. I sat gazing at him, spellbound. Joe got up to go, and took me by the hand.

"Stop half a moment, Mr. Gargery," said the strange man. "I think I've got a bright new shilling somewhere in my pocket, and if I have, the boy shall have it."

He looked it out from a handful of small change, folded it in some crumpled paper, and gave it to me. "Yours!" said he. "Mind! Your own."

[1] **nevvy:** nephew.

I thanked him, staring at him far beyond the bounds of good manners, and holding tight to Joe. On the way home I could think of nothing else but this strange meeting.

My sister was not in a very bad temper when we presented ourselves in the kitchen, and Joe was encouraged by that unusual circumstance to tell her about the bright shilling. "A bad un, I'll be bound," said Mrs. Joe triumphantly, "or he wouldn't have given it to the boy. Let's look at it."

I took it out of the paper, and it proved to be a good one. "But what's this?" said Mrs. Joe, throwing down the shilling and catching up the paper. "Two one-pound notes?"[2]

Joe caught up his hat again, and ran with them to the Jolly Bargemen to restore them to their owner. While he was gone I sat down on my usual stool and looked vacantly at my sister, feeling pretty sure that the man would not be there.

Presently Joe came back, saying that the man was gone, but that he, Joe, had left word at the Three Jolly Bargemen concerning the notes. Then my sister sealed them up in a piece of paper, and put them under some dried rose leaves in an ornamental teapot on the top of a press in the parlor. There they remained a nightmare to me many and many a night and day.

I had sadly broken sleep when I got to bed, through thinking of the strange man and of the guiltily coarse and common thing it was to be on secret terms of conspiracy with convicts – a feature in my low career that I had previously forgotten. I was haunted by the file too. A

[2] Two one-pound notes would be worth forty shillings, or almost ten dollars in American money in Dickens' time. It should be remembered that ten dollars was a considerable sum of money at that time.

dread possessed me that when I least expected it, the file would reappear. I coaxed myself to sleep by thinking of Miss Havisham's next Wednesday; and in my sleep I saw the file coming at me out of a door, without seeing who held it, and I screamed myself awake.

CHAPTER X

At the appointed time I returned to Miss Havisham's, and my hesitating ring at the gate brought out Estella. She took me to a small paved courtyard, the opposite side of which was formed by a detached dwelling house. There was a clock in the outer wall of this house. Like the clock in Miss Havisham's room, and like Miss Havisham's watch, it had stopped at twenty minutes to nine.

We went in at the door, which stood open, and into a gloomy room with a low ceiling, on the ground floor at the back. There was some company in the room, and Estella said, "You are to go and stand there, boy, till you are wanted." "There" being the window, I crossed to it, and stood "there," in a very uncomfortable state of mind, looking out.

The other occupants of the room had stopped conversation and were looking at me closely. There were three ladies in the room and one gentleman. Before I had been standing at the window five minutes, they somehow conveyed to me that they were all toadies and humbugs.

One lady, whose name was Camilla, was speaking of Miss Havisham, whom she called a "poor, dear soul" without much sympathy, I thought. Having nothing else to do but stand, nervously, I listened and discovered, from the conversation, that the gentleman in the room was this lady's husband. The two other ladies were Sarah Pocket and someone, who hardly spoke at all, named Georgiana. I discovered, also, that while they addressed each other as "Cousin," none seemed to approve of the others — and together they obviously disapproved of a gentleman named Cousin Matthew, who was not present.

The ringing of a distant bell, combined with the echoing of some cry or call along the passage by which I had come, interrupted the conversation and caused Estella to say to me, "Now, boy!" On my turning round they all looked at me with the utmost contempt, and as I went out, I heard Sarah Pocket say, "Well I am sure! What next!" and Camilla added, with indignation, "Was there ever such a fancy! The i-*de*-a!"

As we were going with our candle along the dark passage, Estella stopped all of a sudden, and facing round, said in her taunting manner, with her face quite close to mine:

"Well?"

"Well, miss," I answered, almost falling over her and checking myself.

She stood looking at me, and of course I stood looking at her.

"Am I pretty?"

"Yes; I think you are very pretty."

"Am I insulting?"

"Not so much so as you were last time," said I.

"Not so much so?"

"No."

She slapped my face with such force as she had.

"Now?" said she. "You little coarse monster, what do you think of me now?"

"I shall not tell you."

"Because you are going to tell upstairs. Is that it?"

"No," said I, "that's not it."

"Why don't you cry again, you little wretch?"

"Because I'll never cry for you again," said I. Which was, I suppose, as false a declaration as ever was made; for I was inwardly crying for her then, and I know what I know of the pain she cost me afterward.

We went on our way upstairs after this episode; and, as we were going up, we met a gentleman groping his way down.

"Whom have we here?" asked the gentleman, stopping and looking at me.

"A boy," said Estella.

He was a burly man of an exceedingly dark complexion, with an exceedingly large head. He took my chin in his large hand and turned up my face to have a look at me by the light of the candle. He was bald on the top of his head, and had bushy black eyebrows that wouldn't lie down, but stood up bristling. His eyes were set very deep in his head, and were disagreeably sharp and suspicious. He had a large watch chain, and strong black dots where his beard and whiskers would have been if he had let them grow. He was nothing to me, and I could have had no foresight then, that he ever would be anything to me, but it happened that I had this opportunity of observing him well.

"Boy of the neighborhood? Hey?" said he.

"Yes, sir," said I.

"How do *you* come here?"

"Miss Havisham sent for me, sir," I explained.

"Well! Behave yourself. I have a pretty large experience of boys, and you're a bad set of fellows. Now mind!" said he, biting the side of his great forefinger, as he frowned at me, "you behave yourself!"

With these words he released me — which I was glad of, for his hand smelt of scented soap — and went his way downstairs. We were soon in Miss Havisham's room. Estella left me standing near the door, and I stood there until Miss Havisham cast her eyes upon me from the dressing table.

"So!" she said, "the days have worn away, have they?"

"Yes, ma'am. Today is ——"

"There, there, there!" with the impatient movement of her fingers. "I don't want to know. Are you ready to play?"

I was obliged to answer in some confusion. "I don't think I am, ma'am."

"Not at cards again?" she demanded with a searching look.

"Yes, ma'am; I could do that, if I was wanted."

"Since this house strikes you old and grave, boy," said Miss Havisham, impatiently, "and you are unwilling to play, are you willing to work?"

I could answer this inquiry with a better heart than I had been able to find for the other question, and I said I was quite willing.

"Then go into that opposite room," said she, pointing at the door behind me with her withered hand, "and wait there till I come."

I crossed the staircase landing, and entered the room she indicated. From that room, too, the daylight was completely excluded, and it had an airless smell that was oppressive. Everything in it was covered with dust and mold, and dropping to pieces. The most prominent object was a long table with a tablecloth spread on it, as if a feast had been in preparation when the house and the clocks all stopped together. A centerpiece of some kind was in the middle of this cloth; at one time it must have been a wedding cake, but now it was so heavily overhung with cobwebs that its form was quite undistinguishable. I saw speckled-legged spiders with blotchy bodies running home to it, and running out from it.

I heard the mice, too, rattling behind the panels.

These crawling things had fascinated my attention, and I was watching them from a distance, when Miss Havisham laid a hand upon my shoulder. In her other hand she had a crutch-headed stick on which she leaned, and she looked like a witch.

"This," said she, pointing to the long table with her stick, "is where I will be laid when I am dead. They shall come and look at me here."

"What do you think that is?" she asked me, again pointing with her stick; "that, where those cobwebs are?"

"I can't guess, ma'am."

"It's a great cake. A bride cake. Mine!"

She looked all round the room in a glaring manner, and then said, leaning on me while her hand twitched my shoulder, "Come, come, come! Walk me, walk me!"

I made out from this, that the work I had to do was to walk Miss Havisham round and round the room. Accordingly, she leaned on my shoulder and we started away round and round the room.

Estella entered and became a spectator of our proceedings. With her she had brought the three ladies and the gentleman whom I had seen below.

"Dear Miss Havisham," said Miss Sarah Pocket. "How well you look!"

"I do not," returned Miss Havisham. "I am yellow skin and bone."

Camilla brightened when Miss Pocket met with this rebuff; and she murmured, as she plaintively contemplated [1] Miss Havisham, "Poor dear soul! Certainly not to be expected to look well, poor thing. The idea!"

"And how are *you*?" said Miss Havisham to Camilla. As we were close to Camilla then, I would have stopped as a matter of course, only Miss Havisham wouldn't stop. We swept on, and I felt that I was highly obnoxious to Camilla.

"Thank you, Miss Havisham," she returned. "I am as well as can be expected."

"Why, what's the matter with you?" asked Miss Havisham, with exceeding sharpness.

"Nothing worth mentioning," replied Camilla. "I don't wish to make a display of my feelings, but I have habitually thought of you more in the night than I am quite equal to."

"Then don't think of me," retorted Miss Havisham.

"Oh!" cried Camilla, "it's a weakness to be so affectionate, but I can't help it."

Miss Havisham and I kept going round and round the room; now brushing against the skirts of the visitors; now giving them the whole length of the dismal chamber.

"There's Matthew!" said Camilla. "Never mixing with any natural ties, never coming here to see how Miss Havisham is!"

When this same Matthew was mentioned, Miss Havisham stopped me and herself, and stood looking at the speaker. This change had a great influence in bringing Camilla's weeping manner to a sudden end.

"Matthew will come and see me at last," said Miss Havisham, sternly, "when I am laid on that table. That will be his place – there," striking the table with the stick, "at my head! And yours will be there! And your husband's there! And Sarah Pocket's there! And Georgiana's there! Now you all know where to take your stations when you come to

[1] **plaintively contemplated** (plān′tĭv·lĭ kŏn′tĕm·plāt·ĕd): sorrowfully gazed at.

"'It's a great cake. A bride cake. Mine!'"

feast upon me.[1] And now go!"

At the mention of each name, she had struck the table with her stick in a new place. She now said, "Walk me, walk me!" and we went on again.

While Estella was away lighting them down, Miss Havisham still walked with her hand on my shoulder, but more and more slowly. At last she stopped before the fire, and said, after muttering and looking at it some seconds:

"This is my birthday, Pip."

I was going to wish her many happy returns, when she lifted her stick.

"I don't permit it to be spoken of. I don't permit those who were here just now, or anyone, to speak of it. They come here on the day, but they dare not refer to it."

Of course *I* made no further effort to refer to it.

"On this day of the year, long before you were born, this heap of decay," stabbing with her crutched stick at the pile of cobwebs on the table, but not touching it, "was brought here. It and I have worn away together. The mice have gnawed at it, and sharper teeth than teeth of mice have gnawed at me."

She held the head of her stick against her heart as she stood looking at the table; she in her once white dress, all yellow and withered; the once white cloth all yellow and withered; everything around, in a state to crumble under a touch.

"When the ruin is complete," said she, with a ghastly look, "and when they lay me dead, in my bride's dress on the bride's table – which shall be done, and which will be the finished curse upon him – so much the better if it is done on this day!"

I remained quiet. Estella returned, and she too remained quiet. At length, Miss Havisham said, "Let me see you two play at cards; why have you not begun?" With that, we returned to her room, and sat down as before; I was beaten, as before and again, as before, Miss Havisham watched us all the time, directed my attention to Estella's beauty, and made me notice it the more by trying her jewels on Estella's breast and hair.

Estella, for her part, treated me as before, except that she did not condescend to speak. When we had played some half-dozen games, a day was appointed for my return, and I was taken down into the yard to be fed in the former dog-like manner. There, too, I was again left to wander about as I liked.

I strolled into the garden and found myself in the dismal corner which I had seen out of a window. Never questioning for a moment that the house was now empty, I looked in a window, and found myself, to my great surprise, exchanging a broad stare with a pale young gentleman with red eyelids and light hair.

This pale young gentleman quickly appeared beside me. He had been at his books when I had found myself staring at him, and I now saw that he was inky.

"Who let *you* in?" said he.

"Miss Estella."

"Who gave you leave to prowl about?"

"Miss Estella."

"Come and fight," said the pale young gentleman.

What could I do but follow him? I have often asked myself the question since; but, what else could I do? His manner was so final and I was so astonished that I followed where he led, as if I had been under a spell.

"Stop a minute, though," he said,

[1] That is, to collect their shares of her will after her death.

wheeling round before we had gone many paces. "I ought to give you a reason for fighting, too. There it is!" In a most irritating manner he instantly slapped his hands against one another, daintily flung one of his legs up behind him, pulled my hair, slapped his hands again, dipped his head, and butted it into my stomach.

I hit out at him, and was going to hit out again, when he said, "Aha! Would you?" and began dancing backward and forward in a manner quite unparalleled[1] within my limited experience.

"Laws of the game!" said he. Here, he skipped from his left leg on to his right. "Regular rules!" Here, he skipped from his right leg on to his left. "Come to the ground, and go through the preliminaries!" Here, he dodged backward and forward, and did all sorts of things while I looked helplessly at him.

I was secretly afraid of him when I saw him so skillful; but I followed him without a word to a retired nook of the garden. On his asking me if I was satisfied with the ground, and on my replying, "Yes," he obtained from the house a bottle of water and a sponge dipped in vinegar. "Available for both," he said, and fell to pulling off, not only his jacket and waistcoat, but his shirt too, in a manner at once light-hearted, businesslike, and bloodthirsty. Although he did not look very healthy, these dreadful preparations quite appalled me. I judged him to be about my own age, but he was much taller.

My heart failed me when I saw him squaring at me with every demonstration of mechanical skill. I never have been so surprised in my life as I was when I let out the first blow and saw him lying on his back, looking up at me with a bloody nose.

[1] **unparalleled** (ŭn·păr′ă·lĕld): unequaled.

But he was on his feet directly, and after sponging himself began squaring again. The second greatest surprise I have ever had in my life was seeing him on his back again, looking up at me out of a black eye.

His spirit inspired me with great respect. He seemed to have no strength, and he never once hit me hard, and he was always knocked down. He got heavily bruised, but he came again and again until at last he got a bad fall with the back of his head against the wall. Even after that, he got up and turned round confusedly a few times; but finally went on his knees to his sponge and threw it up, panting out, "That means you have won."

He seemed so brave and innocent that although I had not proposed the contest, I felt but a gloomy satisfaction in my victory. However, I got dressed and said, "Can I help you?" and he said, "No, thankee," and I said, "Good afternoon," and *he* said, "Same to you."

When I got into the courtyard, I found Estella waiting with the keys. But she neither asked me where I had been, nor why I had kept her waiting; and there was a bright flush upon her face, as though something had happened to delight her. Instead of going straight to the gate, too, she stepped back into the passage, and beckoned me.

"Come here! You may kiss me if you like."

I kissed her cheek as she turned it to me. I think I would have gone through a great deal to kiss her cheek. But I felt that the kiss was given to the coarse common boy as a piece of money might have been, and that it was worth nothing.

What with the birthday visitors, and what with the cards, and what with the fight, my stay had lasted so long that when I neared home the light off the point on the marshes was gleaming against a black night sky, and Joe's furnace was flinging a path of fire across the road.

CHAPTER XI

My mind grew very uneasy on the subject of the pale young gentleman. The more I thought of the fight, and recalled the pale young gentleman on his back, the more certain it appeared that something would be done to me. When the day came round for my return to the scene of the deed of violence, my terrors reached their height. However, go to Miss Havisham's I must, and go I did. And behold! nothing came of the late struggle. It was not mentioned in any way, and no pale young gentleman was to be seen anywhere.

On the broad landing between Miss Havisham's own room and that other room in which the long table was laid out, I saw a light chair on wheels. I entered, beginning with that day, on a regular occupation of pushing Miss Havisham in this chair (when she was tired of walking with her hand upon my shoulder) round her own room, and across the landing, and round the other room. Over and over and over again, we would make these journeys, and sometimes they would last as long as three hours at a stretch.

As we began to be more used to one another over a period of some eight or ten months, Miss Havisham talked more to me, and asked me such questions as what had I learned and what was I going to be? I told her I was going to be apprenticed to Joe, I believed; and I enlarged upon my knowing nothing and wanting to know everything, in the hope that she might offer some help toward that desirable end. But she did not; on the contrary, she seemed to prefer my being ignorant. Neither did she ever give me any money or anything but my daily dinner — nor even suggest that I should be paid for my services.

Estella was always about, and always let me in and out, but never told me I might kiss her again. Sometimes, she would be quite familiar with me; sometimes, she would tell me energetically that she hated me. Miss Havisham would often ask me in a whisper, or when we were alone, "Does she grow prettier and prettier, Pip?" And when I said, "Yes," (for indeed she did), would seem to enjoy it greedily. Also, when we played at cards Miss Havisham would look on, relishing Estella's moods, whatever they were. Sometimes, when her moods were so many and so contradictory that I was puzzled what to say or do, Miss Havisham would embrace her with lavish fondness, murmuring something in her ear that sounded like "Break their hearts, my pride and hope, break their hearts and have no mercy!"

Perhaps I might have told Joe of my adventures, had I not previously been betrayed into those enormous lies to which I had confessed. As it was, I reposed complete confidence in no one but Biddy; but I told poor Biddy everything. Why it came natural for me to do so, and why Biddy had a deep concern in everything I told her, I did not know then, though I think I know now.

Meanwhile, councils went on in the kitchen at home. That fool Pumblechook and my sister would pair off in nonsensical speculations about Miss Havisham, and about what she would do with me and for me. In these discussions, Joe bore no part. But he was often talked at, while they were in progress, by reason of Mrs. Joe's perceiving that he was not favorable to my being taken from the forge.

We went on in this way for a long time, when, one day, Miss Havisham stopped short as she and I were walking and said with some displeasure:

"You are growing tall, Pip!"

She said no more at the time, but she presently stopped and looked at me again; and after that looked frowning and moody. The next day she stayed me with a movement of her impatient fingers:

"Tell me the name again of that blacksmith of yours."

"Joe Gargery, ma'am."

"Meaning the master you were to be apprenticed to?"

"Yes, Miss Havisham."

"You had better be apprenticed at once. Would Gargery come here with you, and bring your indentures,[1] do you think?"

"At any particular time, Miss Havisham?"

"There, there! I know nothing about times. Let him come soon, and come along with you."

When I delivered this message at home, my sister "went on the Rampage," threw a candlestick at Joe, got out the dustpan – always a very bad sign – and fairly cleaned us out of house and home. It was ten o'clock at night before we ventured to creep in again – and all because Miss Havisham had asked for Joe and had not included my sister.

It was a trial to my feelings, on the next day but one, to see Joe arraying himself in his Sunday clothes to accompany me to Miss Havisham's. At breakfast time, my sister declared her intention of going to town with us, and being left at Uncle Pumblechook's, and called for "when we had done with our fine ladies."

The forge was shut up for the day, and Joe inscribed in chalk upon the door (as it was his custom to do on the very rare occasions when he was not at work) the monosyllable HOUT,[2] accompanied by a sketch of an arrow supposed to be flying in the direction he had taken. When we came to Pumblechook's, my sister bounced in and left us. As it was almost noon, Joe and I held straight on to Miss Havisham's house. Estella opened the gate as usual, and led us the way that I knew so well.

Estella told me we were both to go in, so I took Joe by the coat cuff and conducted him into Miss Havisham's presence. She was seated at her dressing table, and looked round at us immediately.

"Oh!" said she to Joe. "You are the husband of the sister of this boy?"

I could hardly have imagined dear old Joe looking so unlike himself or so like some extraordinary bird, standing, as he did, speechless, with his tuft of feathers ruffled, and his mouth open as if he wanted a worm.

"You are the husband," repeated Miss Havisham, "of the sister of this boy?"

It was very aggravating; but, throughout the interview, Joe persisted in addressing me instead of Miss Havisham. It was quite impossible for me to make him understand that he ought to speak to Miss Havisham. The more I made faces and gestures to him to do it, the more confidential, argumentative, and polite, he persisted in being to me.

"Have you brought his indentures with you?" asked Miss Havisham.

"Well, Pip, you know," replied Joe, as if that were a little unreasonable, "you yourself see me put 'em in my 'at, and

[1] **indentures** (ĭn·dĕn'tūrz): a contract binding an apprentice to a master.

[2] HOUT: out.

therefore you know as they are here." With which he took them out, and gave them, not to Miss Havisham, but to me. I am afraid I was ashamed of the dear good fellow — I *know* I was ashamed of him — when I saw that Estella laughed mischievously. I took the indentures out of his hand and gave them to Miss Havisham.

"You expected," said Miss Havisham, as she looked them over, "no premium with the boy?"

"Joe!" I remonstrated; for he made no reply at all. "Why don't you answer ——"

"Pip," returned Joe, cutting me short as if he were hurt, "which I meantersay that were not a question requiring a answer betwixt yourself and me, and which you know the answer to be full well 'No.' You know it to be 'No,' Pip, and wherefore should I say it?"

Miss Havisham glanced at him as if she understood what he really was, better than I had thought possible. She took up a little bag from the table beside her.

"Pip has earned a premium here," she said, "and here it is. There are five-and-twenty guineas [1] in this bag. Give it to your master, Pip."

Joe, even at this pass, persisted in addressing me. "This is very liberal on your part, Pip," said Joe, "and it is as such received and grateful welcome, though never looked for. And now, old chap," said Joe, "may you and me do our duty, one to another!"

"Good-by, Pip!" said Miss Havisham. "Let them out, Estella."

"Am I to come again, Miss Havisham?" I asked.

"No. Gargery is your master now. Gargery! One word!"

Thus calling him back as I went out of the door, I heard her say to Joe, in a distinct emphatic voice, "The boy has been a good boy here, and that is his reward. Of course, as an honest man, you will expect no other and no more."

In another minute we were outside the gate, and it was locked, and Estella was gone. When we stood in the daylight alone again, Joe backed up against a wall, and said to me, "Astonishing!" And there he remained so long, saying "Astonishing" at intervals, so often that I began to think his senses were never coming back. At length, he said, "Pip, I do assure *you* this is as-TON-ishing!" and so, by degrees, became conversational and able to walk away.

"Well!" cried my sister, addressing us both at once, when we arrived at Pumblechook's. "I wonder you condescend to come back to such poor society as this, I am sure I do! Well, what did she give this boy here?"

"To be partick'ler," said Joe, handing the bag to my sister; "it's five-and-twenty pound."

"It's five-and-twenty pound, mum," echoed that basest of swindlers, Pumblechook, rising to shake hands with her; "and it's no more than your merits (as I said when my opinion was asked), and I wish you joy of the money!"

"Goodness knows, Uncle Pumblechook," said my sister (grasping the money), "we're deeply beholden to you."

"Never mind me, mum," returned that diabolical [2] grain merchant. "A pleasure's a pleasure all the world over. But this boy, you know; we must have him bound. I said I'd see to it — to tell you

[1] **guinea** (gĭn'ĭ): a gold coin worth twenty-one shillings, a little over five dollars in American money at that time. See footnote on page 521.

[2] **diabolical** (dī'ȧ·bŏl'ĭ·kăl): literally, devilish; in this context, "scheming" is perhaps closer to Dickens' meaning.

the truth."

The justices were sitting in the town hall near at hand, and we at once went over to have me bound apprentice to Joe. I say, we went over, but I was pushed over by Pumblechook, exactly as if I had that moment picked a pocket or set a house afire. Indeed, it was the general impression in court that I had been taken red-handed; for, as Pumblechook shoved me before him through the crowd, I heard some people say, "What's he done?" and others, "He's a young 'un, too, but looks bad, don't he?" One person of pious appearance even gave me a pamphlet entitled, TO BE READ IN MY CELL.

When we had come out again, we went back to Pumblechook's. And there my sister became so excited by the twenty-five guineas that nothing would serve her but we must have a dinner at the Blue Boar, and that Mr. Pumblechook must go over in his cart, and bring the Hubbles and Mr. Wopsle.

My only remembrances of the great festival are that they wouldn't let me go to sleep, but whenever they saw me dropping off, woke me up and told me to enjoy myself and that when I got into my little bedroom, I was truly wretched, and had a strong conviction on me that I should never like Joe's trade. I had liked it once, but once was not now.

It is a most miserable thing to feel ashamed of home. Home had never been a very pleasant place to me, because of my sister's temper. But Joe had blessed it, and I believed in it. Within a single year all this was changed. Now, it was all coarse and common, and I would not have had Miss Havisham and Estella see it on any account.

How much of my ungracious condition of mind may have been my own fault, how much Miss Havisham's, how much my sister's, is now of no importance. The change was made in me; the thing was done. Well or ill done, it was done.

Once it had seemed to me that when I should at last roll up my shirt sleeves and go into the forge, Joe's 'prentice, I should be distinguished and happy. Now I only felt that I was dusty with the dust of the small coal, and that I had a weight upon my daily remembrance to which the anvil was a feather. There have been occasions in my later life when I have felt for a time as if a thick curtain had fallen on all its interest and romance, to shut me out from anything save dull endurance any more. Never has that curtain dropped so heavy and blank, as when my way in life lay stretched out straight before me through the newly entered road of apprenticeship to Joe.

But I am glad to know that I never breathed a murmur to Joe while my indentures lasted. It is about the only thing I *am* glad to know of myself in that connection. It was not because I was faithful, but because Joe was faithful, that I never ran away and became a soldier or a sailor. It was not because I had a strong sense of the virtue of industry, but because Joe did, that I worked with tolerable zeal against the grain. It is not possible to know how far the influence of any amiable, honest-hearted, duty-doing man flies out into the world, but I know right well that any good that intermixed itself with my apprenticeship came of plain, contented Joe, and not of restless, aspiring, discontented me.

What I dreaded most was that in some unlucky hour I, being at my grimiest and commonest, should lift up my eyes and see Estella looking in at one of the wooden windows of the forge. I was haunted by the fear that she would, sooner or later, find me out, with a black face and hands, doing the coarsest part of my work, and would exult over me and despise me. Often after dark, when I was pulling the bellows for Joe, I would fancy that I saw her just drawing her face away, and would believe that she had come at last.

After that, when we went in to supper, the place would have a more homely look than ever, and I would feel more ashamed of home than ever, in my own ungracious breast.

CHAPTER XII

As I was getting too big for Mr. Wopsle's great-aunt's room, my education under that ridiculous female ended; not, however, until Biddy had imparted to me everything she knew, from the little catalogue of prices to a comic song she had once bought for a halfpenny. Although the only coherent part of the latter piece of literature was the opening lines,

> When I went to Lunnon town, sirs,
> Too rul loo rul!
> Too rul loo rul!
> Wasn't I done very brown, sirs?
> Too rul loo rul!
> Too rul loo rul!

– still, in my desire to be wiser, I got this composition by heart with the utmost care. Moreover, in my hunger for information, I made proposals to Mr. Wopsle to bestow some intellectual crumbs upon me; with which he kindly complied. As it turned out, however, he wanted me only as a dramatic assistant for his reading of Shakespeare, to be contradicted and embraced and wept over and bullied and clutched and stabbed and knocked about in a variety of ways. I soon declined that course in instruction; though not until Mr. Wopsle in his poetic fury had severely mauled me.

Whatever I acquired, I tried to impart to Joe. This statement sounds so well that I cannot in my conscience let it pass unexplained. I wanted to make Joe less ignorant and common, that he might be worthier of my society and less open to Estella's reproach.

The old Battery out on the marshes was our place of study, and a broken slate and a short piece of slate pencil were our educational implements, to which Joe always added a pipe of tobacco. I never knew Joe to remember anything from one Sunday to another, or to acquire, under my tuition, any piece of information whatever. Yet he would smoke his pipe at the Battery with a far wiser air than anywhere else – even with a learned air – as if he considered himself to be advancing immensely. Dear fellow, I hope he did.

It was pleasant and quiet, out there with the sails on the river. Whenever I watched the vessels standing out to sea with their white sails spread, I somehow thought of Miss Havisham and Estella and the strange house and the strange life that was so picturesque. One Sunday I resolved to mention a thought concerning them that had been much in my head.

"Joe," said I, "don't you think I ought to pay Miss Havisham a visit?"

"Well, Pip," returned Joe, slowly considering. "What for?"

"What for, Joe? What is any visit made for?"

"There is some wisits p'r'aps," said Joe, "as forever remains open to the question, Pip. But in regard of wisiting Miss Havisham. She might think you wanted something – expected something of her."

I had thought of that too, and it was

very far from comforting to me to find that he had thought of it; for it seemed to render it more probable.

"But, Joe."

"Yes, old chap."

"Here am I, getting on in the first year of my time, and, since the day of my being bound I have never thanked Miss Havisham, or asked after her, or shown that I remember her."

"Well," said Joe, "if I was yourself, Pip, I wouldn't. No, I would *not*."

"But, Joe; what I wanted to say was, that as we are rather slack just now, if you would give me a half holiday tomorrow, I think I would go uptown and make a call on Miss Est – Havisham."

Joe decided that if I thought well of it, he thought well of it. But he insisted that if I were not received with cordiality, or if I were not encouraged to repeat my visit, then this experimental trip should have no successor. By these conditions I promised to abide.

Now, Joe kept a journeyman [1] at weekly wages whose name was Orlick. He was a broad-shouldered, loose-limbed, swarthy fellow of great strength, never in a hurry, and always slouching. He never even seemed to come to his work on purpose, but would slouch in as if by mere accident. He lodged at a sluice keeper's [2] out on the marshes, and on working days would come slouching in with his hands in his pockets and his dinner loosely tied in a bundle round his neck and dangling on his back.

This sullen journeyman had no liking for me. When I was very small and timid, he gave me to understand that the Devil lived in a black corner of the forge, and that he knew the fiend very well; also that it was necessary to make up the fire, once in seven years, with a live boy, and that I might consider myself fuel. When I became Joe's 'prentice, Orlick was perhaps confirmed in some suspicion that I should displace him and he liked me still less.

Orlick was at work and present, next day, when I reminded Joe of my half holiday. He said nothing at the moment, for he and Joe had just got a piece of hot iron between them, and I was at the bellows; but by and by he said, leaning on his hammer:

"Now, master! Sure you're not a-going to favor only one of us. If Young Pip has a half holiday, do as much for Old Orlick." I suppose he was about five-and-twenty, but he usually spoke of himself as an ancient person.

"Why, what'll you do with a half holiday, if you get it?" said Joe.

"What'll *I* do with it? What'll *he* do with it? I'll do as much with it as *him*," said Orlick.

"As to Pip, he's going uptown," said Joe.

"Well then, as to Old Orlick, *he's* a-going uptown," retorted that worthy. "Two can go uptown. 'Tain't only one wot can go uptown."

"Don't lose your temper," said Joe.

"Shall if I like," growled Orlick. "Now, master! Come. No favoring in this shop. Be a man!"

"Then, as in general you stick to your work as well as most men," said Joe, "let it be a half holiday for all."

My sister had been standing silent in the yard, within hearing – she was a most unashamed spy and listener – and she instantly looked in at one of the windows.

[1] **journeyman** (jûr'nĭ·măn): one who has learned a craft and is no longer an apprentice, but who still works for a master craftsman as an employee.

[2] **sluice** (slo͞os) **keeper:** the person in charge of a gate which regulates the flow of water in a sluice, a man-made stream used for drainage or irrigation purposes.

"Like you, you fool!" said she to Joe, "giving holidays to great idle hulkers like that. You are a rich man, upon my life, to waste wages in that way. I wish *I* was his master!"

"You'd be everybody's master if you durst," retorted Orlick, with an ill-favored grin.

"Let her alone," said Joe.

"I'd be a match for all noodles and all rogues," returned my sister, beginning to work herself into a mighty rage. "And I couldn't be a match for the noodles, without being a match for your master, who's the dunderheaded king of the noodles. And I couldn't be a match for the rogues, without being a match for you, who are the blackest looking and the worst rogue between this and France. Now!"

"You're a foul shrew,[1] Mother Gargery," growled the journeyman. "If that makes a judge of rogues, you ought to be a good 'un."

"Let her alone, will you?" said Joe.

"What did you say?" cried my sister, beginning to scream. "What did you say? What did that fellow Orlick say to me, Pip? What did he call me, with my husband standing by? Oh! Oh! Oh!" Each of these exclamations was a shriek. "Oh! Hold me! Oh!"

"Ah-h-h!" growled the journeyman, between his teeth, "I'd hold you, if you was my wife. I'd hold you under the pump, and choke it out of you."

"I tell you, let her alone," said Joe.

"Oh! To hear him!" cried my sister, with a clap of her hands and a scream together. "To hear the names he's giving me! That Orlick! In my own house! Me, a married woman! With my husband standing by! Oh! Oh!"

What could the wretched Joe do now, but stand up to his journeyman? They went at one another, like two giants. But if any man in that neighborhood could stand up long against Joe, I never saw the man. Orlick was very soon among the coal dust, and in no hurry to come out of it. Then Joe picked up my sister, who had fainted at the window, and carried her into the house. Afterward came that calm and silence which succeed all uproars — and I went upstairs to dress.

When I came down again, I found Joe and Orlick sweeping up, without any other traces of the fight than a slit in one of Orlick's nostrils. A pot of beer had appeared from the Jolly Bargemen, and they were sharing it by turns in a peaceable manner. Joe followed me out into the road to say, as an observation that might do me good, "On the Ram-page, Pip, and off the Ram-page, Pip — such is life!"

When I found myself again going to Miss Havisham's, I passed and repassed the gate many times before I could make up my mind to ring.

Miss Sarah Pocket came to the gate. No Estella.

"How, then? You here again?" said Miss Pocket. "What do you want?"

When I said that I only came to see how Miss Havisham was, Sarah let me in, and presently brought the sharp message that I was to "come up."

Everything was unchanged, and Miss Havisham was alone. "Well!" said she, fixing her eyes upon me. "I hope you want nothing? You'll get nothing."

"No indeed, Miss Havisham. I only wanted you to know that I am doing very well in my apprenticeship, and am always much obliged to you."

"There, there!" with the old restless fingers. "Come now and then; come on your birthday. — Ay!" she cried suddenly, turning herself and her chair toward

[1] **shrew:** noisy, scolding woman.

me. " You are looking round for Estella? Hey? "

I had been looking round – in fact, for Estella – and I stammered that I hoped she was well.

" Abroad," said Miss Havisham; " educating for a lady; far out of reach; prettier than ever; admired by all who see her. Do you feel that you have lost her? "

There was such a wicked enjoyment in her utterance of the last words, and she broke into such a disagreeable laugh, that I was at a loss what to say. She spared me the trouble of considering, by dismissing me. When the gate was closed upon me, I felt more than ever dissatisfied with my home and with my trade and with everything.

As I was loitering along the High Street, looking at the shop windows, and thinking what I would buy if I were a gentleman, who should come out of the bookshop but Mr. Wopsle. He was on his way to drink tea at the Pumblechookian parlor and insisted on my accompanying him. I made no great resistance; consequently, we turned into Pumblechook's just as the street and shops were lighting up.

It was a very dark night with a heavy mist when I set out with Mr. Wopsle on the walk home, and the turnpike lamp was a blur. Suddenly we came upon a man, slouching under the lee of the turnpike house.

" Halloa! " we said, stopping. " Orlick there? "

" Ah! " he answered, slouching out. " I was standing by a minute on the chance of company."

" You are late," I remarked.

Orlick not unnaturally answered, " Well? And *you're* late."

" We have been," said Mr. Wopsle, " indulging, Mr. Orlick, in an intellectual evening."

Old Orlick growled, as if he had nothing to say about that, and we all went on together. I asked him presently whether he had been spending his half holiday up and down town?

" Yes," said he, " all of it. I come in behind yourself. I didn't see you, but I must have been pretty close behind you. By the bye, the guns is going again."

" At the Hulks? " said I.

" Ay! There's some of the birds flown from the cages. The guns have been going since dark, about. You'll hear one presently."

We had not walked many yards farther when the well-remembered boom came toward us, deadened by the mist.

" A good night for cutting off in," said Orlick. " We'd be puzzled how to bring down a jailbird on the wing tonight." Orlick, with his hands in his pockets, slouched heavily at my side. I thought he had been drinking, but he was not drunk.

Thus we came to the village. We approached the Three Jolly Bargemen, which we were surprised to find – it being eleven o'clock – in a state of commotion, with the door wide open, and lights scattered about. Mr. Wopsle dropped in to ask what was the matter (thinking that a convict had been taken), but came running out in a great hurry.

" There's something wrong," said he, without stopping, " up at your place, Pip. Run all! "

" What is it? " I asked, keeping up with him. So did Orlick, at my side.

" I can't quite understand. The house seems to have been violently entered when Joe Gargery was out. Supposed by convicts. Somebody has been attacked and hurt."

We were running too fast to admit of more being said, and we made no stop until we got into our kitchen. It was full of people; the whole village was there or in the yard, and there was a surgeon, and there was Joe, and there was a group of women, all on the floor in the midst of the kitchen. The bystanders drew back when they saw me, and so I became aware of my sister — lying without sense or movement on the bare boards where she had been knocked down by a tremendous blow on the back of the head, dealt by some unknown hand when her face was turned toward the fire — destined never to be on the rampage again, while she was the wife of Joe.

Joe had been at the Three Jolly Bargemen, smoking his pipe, from a quarter after eight o'clock to a quarter before ten. While he was there, my sister had been seen standing at the kitchen door and had exchanged good night with a farm laborer going home. When Joe went home at five minutes before ten, he found her struck down on the floor, and promptly called in assistance.

Nothing had been taken away from any part of the house. But there was one remarkable piece of evidence on the spot. She had been struck with something blunt and heavy, on the head and spine; after the blows were dealt, something heavy had been thrown down at her with considerable violence, as she lay on her face. And on the ground beside her, when Joe picked her up, was a convict's leg iron which had been filed asunder.

Now, Joe, examining this iron with a smith's eye, declared it to have been filed asunder[1] some time ago. Officials from the Hulks testified that this leg iron had not been worn by either of two convicts who had escaped last night. Further, one of those two was already retaken, and had not freed himself of his iron.

Knowing what I knew, I believed the iron to be my convict's iron — the iron I had seen and heard him filing at, on the marshes — but my mind did not accuse him of having put it to its latest use. For I believed one of two other persons to have become possessed of it, and to have turned it to this cruel account. Either Orlick, or the strange man who had shown me the file.

Now, as to Orlick; he had gone to town exactly as he told us when we picked him up at the turnpike, he had been seen about town all the evening, he had been in several public houses, and he had come back with myself and Mr. Wopsle. There was nothing against him, save the quarrel; and my sister had quarreled with him, and with everybody else about her, ten thousand times. As to the strange man: if he had come back for his two bank notes there could have been no dispute about them, because my sister was fully prepared to restore them. Besides, there had been no argument; the assailant had come in so silently and suddenly that she had been felled before she could look round.

The constables were about the house for a week or two, searching for evidence by which to take the culprit. But they found nothing, and neither did they find the culprit. For a long time my sister lay ill in bed. Her sight was disturbed, so that she saw objects multiplied; her hearing was greatly impaired; her memory also; and her speech was unintelligible. It was necessary to keep my slate always by her, that she might indicate in writing what she could not indicate in speech.

However, her temper was greatly improved, and she was patient. We were at a loss to find a suitable attendant for

[1] **asunder** (ȧ·sŭn′dẽr): apart.

her, until a circumstance happened conveniently to relieve us. Mr. Wopsle's great-aunt died, and Biddy became part of our establishment. Biddy came to us with a small speckled box containing the whole of her worldly effects and became a blessing to the household. Above all she was a blessing to Joe, for the dear old fellow was sadly cut up by the constant sight of the wreck of his wife. Biddy instantly taking the cleverest charge of her, Joe became able in some sort to appreciate the greater quiet of his life, and to get down to the Jolly Bargemen now and then for a change that did him good.

Biddy's first triumph in her new office was to solve a difficulty that had completely puzzled me. Again and again and again, my sister had traced upon the slate a character that looked like a curious *T*, and then with the utmost eagerness had called our attention to it as something she particularly wanted. I had in vain tried everything that began with a *T*, from tar to toast and tub. At length it had come into my head that the sign looked like a hammer, and on my lustily shouting that word in my sister's ear, she had begun to hammer on the table and had confirmed my guess. Thereupon, I had brought in all our hammers, one after another, but without avail.

When my sister found that Biddy was very quick to understand her, this mysterious sign reappeared on the slate. Biddy looked thoughtfully at it, heard my explanation, looked thoughtfully at my sister, looked thoughtfully at Joe, and ran into the forge, followed by Joe and me.

"Why, of course!" cried Biddy with an exultant face. "Don't you see? It's *him!*"

Orlick, without a doubt! She had lost his name, and could only signify him by his hammer. We told him why we wanted him to come into the kitchen, and he slowly laid down his hammer, wiped his brow with his arm, took another wipe at it with his apron, and came slouching out.

I confess that I expected to see my sister denounce him, and that I was disappointed by the different result. She showed the greatest anxiety to be on good terms with him, was evidently much pleased by his being at length produced, and motioned that she would have him given something to drink. She watched his face as if she particularly hoped that he took kindly to his reception. After that, a day rarely passed without her drawing the hammer on her slate, and without Orlick's slouching in and standing doggedly before her, as if he knew no more than I did what to make of it.

CHAPTER XIII

I now fell into a regular routine of apprenticeship life, which was varied, beyond the limits of the village and the marshes, by no more remarkable circumstance than the arrival of my birthday and my paying another visit to Miss Havisham. The interview lasted but a few minutes, and she gave me a guinea when I was going, and told me to come again on my next birthday. I may mention at once that this became an annual custom. I tried to decline taking the guinea on the first occasion, causing her to ask me angrily if I expected more. After that, I took it. So unchanging was the dull old house, it bewildered me, and under its influence I continued at heart to hate my trade and to be ashamed of home.

Slowly I became conscious of a change in Biddy, however. Her shoes came up at the heel, her hair grew bright and neat, her hands were always clean. She was not beautiful — she was common, and could not be like Estella — but she was pleasant and wholesome and sweet-tempered. I observed to myself one evening that she had curiously thoughtful and attentive eyes; eyes that were very pretty and very good. I laid down my pen, and Biddy stopped in her needlework without laying it down.

"Biddy," said I, "how do you manage it? Either I am very stupid, or you are very clever."

"What is it that I manage? I don't know," returned Biddy, smiling.

She managed our whole domestic life, and wonderfully too; but I did not mean that, though that made what I did mean more surprising.

"How do you manage, Biddy," said I, "to learn everything that I learn, and always to keep up with me?" I was beginning to be rather vain of my knowledge, for I spent my birthday guineas on it and the greater part of my pocket money.

"I suppose I must catch it — like a cough," said Biddy, quietly; and went on with her sewing.

I looked at Biddy and began to think her rather an extraordinary girl.

"You are one of those, Biddy," said I, "who make the most of every chance. You never had a chance before you came here, and see how improved you are!"

Biddy looked at me for an instant, and went on with her sewing. "I was your first teacher, though, wasn't I?" said she, as she sewed.

"Yes, Biddy," I observed, "you were my first teacher, and that at a time when we little thought of ever being together like this, in this kitchen. I must consult you a little more, as I used to do. Let us have a quiet walk on the marshes next Sunday, Biddy, and a long chat."

My sister was never left alone now; but Joe undertook the care of her on that Sunday afternoon, and Biddy and I went out together. It was summertime and lovely weather. When we came to the riverside and sat down on the bank, I resolved that it was a good time and place for the admission of Biddy into my inner confidence.

"Biddy," said I, after binding her to secrecy, "I want to be a gentleman."

"Oh, I wouldn't, if I was you!" she returned. "I don't think it would be right."

"Biddy," said I, with some severity, "I have particular reasons for wanting to be a gentleman."

"You know best, Pip; but don't you think you are happier as you are?"

"Biddy," I exclaimed, impatiently, "I am not at all happy as I am. I am disgusted with my calling and with my life. Don't be absurd."

"Was I absurd?" said Biddy, quietly raising her eyebrows; "I am sorry for that; I didn't mean to be. I only want you to do well, and be comfortable."

"Well, then, understand once for all that I never shall or can be comfortable — or anything but miserable — there, Biddy! — unless I can lead a very different sort of life from the life I lead now."

"That's a pity!" said Biddy, shaking her head with a sorrowful air.

"If I could have settled down," I said to Biddy, "I know it would have been much better for me. Joe and I would perhaps have gone partners, and I might have grown up to keep company with you. Instead of that, see how I am going on. Dissatisfied, and uncomfortable, and — what would it signify to me, being coarse and common, if nobody had told me so!"

Biddy turned her face suddenly toward mine, and looked attentively at me.

"It was neither a very true nor a very polite thing to say," she remarked. "Who said it?"

"The beautiful young lady at Miss Havisham's, and she's more beautiful than anybody ever was, and I admire her dreadfully, and I want to be a gentleman on her account."

"Do you want to be a gentleman to spite her or to gain her over?" Biddy quietly asked me, after a pause.

"I don't know," I moodily answered.

"Because, if it is to spite her," Biddy pursued, "I should think — but you know best — that might be better and more independently done by caring nothing for words. And if it is to gain her over, I should think — but you know best — she was not worth gaining over."

"It may be all quite true," said I to Biddy, "but I admire her dreadfully."

I turned over on my face when I came to that, and got a good grasp on the hair on each side of my head, and wrenched it well. Biddy was the wisest of girls, and she tried to reason no more with me. She put her hand, which was a comfortable hand though roughened by work, on my shoulder in a soothing way, while with my face upon my sleeve I cried a little — exactly as I had done in the brewery yard long ago — and felt vaguely convinced that I was very much ill-used by somebody, or by everybody; I can't say which.

"I am glad of one thing," said Biddy, "and that is, that you have felt you could give me your confidence, Pip." So, with a quiet sigh for me, Biddy rose from the bank, and said, with a fresh and pleasant change of voice, "Shall we walk a little farther, or go home?"

"Biddy," I cried, getting up, putting my arm around her neck, and giving her a kiss, "I shall always tell you everything."

"Till you're a gentleman," said Biddy.

"You know I never shall be, so that's always. Not that I have any occasion to tell you anything, for you know everything I know — as I told you at home the other night."

"Ah!" said Biddy, quite in a whisper, and then repeated, with her former pleasant change, "shall we walk a little farther, or go home?"

We talked a good deal as we walked, and all that Biddy said seemed right. Biddy was never insulting, or changeable, or Biddy today and somebody else tomorrow; she would have derived only pain, and no pleasure, from giving me pain. I began to consider whether I was not happier in these circumstances, after all, than being despised by Estella. How could it be, then, that I did not like her much the better of the two?

"Biddy," said I, when we were walking homeward, "I wish you could put me right."

"I wish I could!" said Biddy.

"If I could only get myself to fall in love with you — you don't mind my speaking so openly to such an old acquaintance?"

"Oh dear, not at all!" said Biddy. "Don't mind me."

"If I could only get myself to do it, *that* would be the thing for me."

"But you never will, you see," said Biddy.

When we came near the churchyard, we had to cross an embankment and there started up, from the rushes, Old Orlick.

"Halloa!" he growled, "where are you two going?"

"Where should we be going, but home?"

"Well, then," said he, "I'm jiggered

if I don't see you home!"

Biddy said to me in a whisper, "Don't let him come; I don't like him." As I did not like him either, I took the liberty of saying that we thanked him, but we didn't want seeing home. He dropped back, but came slouching after us at a little distance.

Curious to know whether Biddy suspected him of having had a hand in that murderous attack of which my sister had never been able to give any account, I asked her why she did not like him.

"Oh!" she replied, glancing over her shoulder as he slouched after us, "because I — I am afraid he likes me."

"Did he ever tell you he liked you?" I asked indignantly.

"No," said Biddy, glancing over her shoulder again, "he never told me so; but he looks at me strangely whenever he can catch my eye."

I kept an eye on Orlick after that night. He had struck root in Joe's establishment, by reason of my sister's sudden fancy for him, or I should have tried to get him dismissed. He quite understood my distaste for him and returned it in good measure, as I had reason to know thereafter.

And now my mind was confused. At times, I would decide that my drawing away from dear old Joe and the forge was ended, and that I was growing up in a fair way to be partners with Joe and to keep company with Biddy — when all in a moment some remembrance of the Havisham days would fall upon me and scatter my wits again. Scattered wits take a long time picking up; and often, they would be dispersed in all directions by one stray thought, that perhaps after all Miss Havisham was going to make my fortune when my time was out.

If my time had run out, it would have left me still at the height of my perplexities, I dare say. It never did run out, however, but was brought to an early end, as I proceed to relate.

CHAPTER XIV

It was in the fourth year of my apprenticeship to Joe, and it was a Saturday night. There was a group assembled round the fire at the Three Jolly Bargemen, attentive to Mr. Wopsle as he read the newspaper aloud. Of that group I was one.

I became aware of a strange gentleman leaning over the back of the settle opposite me, looking on. There was an expression of contempt on his face, and he bit the side of a great forefinger as he watched the group of faces.

"Well!" said the stranger to Mr. Wopsle, when the reading was done, "you have settled it all to your own satisfaction, I have no doubt?"

The strange gentleman had an air of authority not to be disputed, and a manner expressive of knowing something secret about every one of us.

"From information I have received," said he, looking round at us as we all quailed before him, "I have reason to believe there is a blacksmith among you, by name Joseph — or Joe — Gargery. Which is the man?"

"Here is the man," said Joe.

The strange gentleman beckoned him out of his place, and Joe went.

"You have an apprentice," pursued the stranger, "commonly known as Pip? Is he here?"

"I am here!" I cried.

The stranger did not recognize me, but I recognized him as the gentleman I had met on the stairs, on the occasion of my second visit to Miss Havisham. I had known him the moment I saw him looking over the settle. I checked off again in detail his large head, his dark complexion, his deep-set eyes, his bushy black eyebrows, his large watch chain, his strong black dots of beard and whisker, and even the smell of scented soap on his great hand.

"I wish to have a private conference with you two," said he, when he had surveyed me at his leisure. "It will take a little time. Perhaps we had better go to your place of residence."

Amidst a wondering silence, we three walked out of the Jolly Bargemen, and in a wondering silence walked home. Joe went on ahead to open the front door. Our conference was held in the parlor, which was feebly lighted by one candle.

It began with the strange gentleman's sitting down at the table, drawing the candle to him, and looking over some entries in his pocketbook.

"My name," he said, "is Jaggers, and I am a lawyer in London. I am pretty well known. I have unusual business to transact with you, and I commence by explaining that it is not of my originating. If my advice had been asked, I should not have been here. It was not asked, and you see me here. What I have to do as the confidential agent of another, I do. No less, no more.

"Now, Joseph Gargery, I am the bearer of an offer to relieve you of this young fellow, your apprentice. You would not object to cancel his indentures at his request and for his good? You would want nothing for so doing?"

"Lord forbid that I should want anything for not standing in Pip's way," said Joe, staring.

"Lord forbidding is pious, but not to the purpose," returned Mr. Jaggers. "The question is, would you want anything? Do you want anything?"

"The answer is," returned Joe, sternly, "no."

I thought Mr. Jaggers glanced at Joe, as if he considered him a fool for his unselfishness. But I was too much bewildered between breathless curiosity and surprise, to be sure of it.

"Very well," said Mr. Jaggers. "Now, I return to this young fellow. And the communication I have got to make is that he has Great Expectations."

Joe and I gasped, and looked at one another.

"I am instructed to communicate to him," said Mr. Jaggers, throwing his finger at me sideways, "that he will come into a handsome property. Further, that it is the desire of the present possessor of that property that he be immediately removed from his present sphere of life and from this place, and be brought up as a gentleman – in a word, as a young fellow of great expectations."

My dream was out; my wild fancy was surpassed by sober reality; Miss Havisham was going to make my fortune on a grand scale.

"Now, Mr. Pip," pursued the lawyer, "I address the rest of what I have to say to you. You are to understand, first, that it is the request of the person from whom I take my instructions that you always bear the name of Pip. You will have no objection, I dare say, but if you have any objection, this is the time to mention it."

My heart was beating so fast, and there was such a singing in my ears, that I could scarcely stammer I had no objection.

"I should think not! Now you are to understand, secondly, Mr. Pip, that the name of the person who is your liberal benefactor remains a profound secret, until the person chooses to reveal it at firsthand by word of mouth to yourself. When or where that intention may be carried out, no one can say. It may be years hence. It is not important what the reasons of this prohibition are; they may be the strongest and gravest reasons, or they may be a mere whim. This is not for you to inquire into. The condition is laid down. Your acceptance of it, and your observance of it as binding, is the only remaining condition that I am charged with, by the person from whom I take my instructions. That person is the person from whom you derive your expectations, and the secret is solely held by that person and by me. If you have any objection to it, this is the time to mention it. Speak out."

Once more, I stammered that I had no objection.

"I should think not! Now, Mr. Pip, I have done with stipulations.[1] We come next to mere details of arrangement. You must know that although I have used the term 'expectations' more than once, you are not endowed with expectations only. There is already lodged in my hands a sum of money amply sufficient for your suitable education and maintenance. You will please consider me your guardian.

"Oh!" he said, just as I was going to thank him, "I tell you at once, I am paid for my services, or I shouldn't render them. It is considered that you must be better educated, in accordance with your altered position."

I said I had always longed for it.

"Never mind what you have always longed for, Mr. Pip," he retorted. "Keep to the record. If you long for it now, that's enough. Am I answered that you are ready to be placed at once under some proper tutor? Is that it?"

I stammered yes, that was it.

"There is a certain tutor who I think might suit the purpose," said Mr. Jaggers. "The gentleman I speak of is one Mr. Matthew Pocket."

Ah! I caught at the name directly. Miss Havisham's relation. The Matthew whom Mr. and Mrs. Camilla had spoken of. The Matthew whose place was to be at Miss Havisham's head when she lay dead in her bride's dress on the bride's table.

"You know the name?" said Mr. Jaggers, looking shrewdly at me. "What do you say of it?"

I said that I was much obliged to him for his mention of Mr. Matthew Pocket, and that I would gladly try that gentleman.

"Good. You had better try him in his own house. The way shall be prepared for you, and you can see his son first, who is in London. When will you come to London?"

I said (glancing at Joe, who stood looking on, motionless), that I supposed I could come directly.

"First," said Mr. Jaggers, "you should have some new clothes to come in, and they should not be working clothes. Say this day week. You'll want some money. Shall I leave you twenty guineas?"

He produced a long purse, with the greatest coolness, and counted them out on the table and pushed them over to me, and sat swinging his purse and eyeing Joe.

"Well, Joseph Gargery? You look dumfoundered?"

"I *am!*" said Joe, in a very decided manner.

"It was understood that you wanted nothing for yourself, remember?"

"It were understood," said Joe. "And it are understood. And it ever will be the same."

"But what," said Mr. Jaggers, swinging his purse, "what if it was in my instructions to make you a present, as compensation?"

[1] **stipulations** (stĭp′ū·lā′shŭns): conditions of agreement.

"As compensation what for?" Joe demanded.

"For the loss of his services."

Joe laid his hand upon my shoulder with the touch of a woman. "Pip is that hearty welcome," said Joe, "to go free with his services, to honor and fortun', as no words can tell him. But if you think as money can make compensation to me for the loss of the little child – what come to the forge – and ever the best of friends! ——"

O dear good Joe, whom I was so ready to leave and so unthankful to, I see you again, with your muscular blacksmith's arm before your eyes, and your broad chest heaving, and your voice dying away.

But I encouraged Joe at the time. I begged Joe to be comforted, for (as he said) we had ever been the best of friends, and (as I said) we ever would be so. Joe scooped his eyes with his wrist, but said not another word.

Mr. Jaggers, looking on at this, said, "Now, Joseph Gargery, I warn you this is your last chance. If you mean to take a present that I have in charge to make you, speak out, and you shall have it. If on the contrary you mean to say ——" Here, to his great amazement, he was stopped by Joe's suddenly assuming a fighting air.

"Which I meantersay," cried Joe, "that if you come into my place bull-baiting and badgering me, come out! Which I meantersay as sech if you're a man, come on!"

I drew Joe away, and he immediately became peaceful. Mr. Jaggers backed near the door and there delivered his last remarks:

"Well, Mr. Pip, I think the sooner you leave here the better. Let it stand for this day week,[1] and you shall receive my printed address in the meantime. You can take a coach at the stagecoach office in London, and come straight to me."

Something came into my head which induced me to run after him.

"I beg your pardon, Mr. Jaggers."

"Halloa!" said he. "What's the matter?"

"I wish to be quite right, Mr. Jaggers. Would there be any objection to my taking leave of anyone I know about here, before I go away?"

"No," said he, looking as if he hardly understood me.

"I don't mean in the village only, but uptown?"

"No," said he. "No objection."

I thanked him and ran home again, and there I found Joe seated by the kitchen fire with a hand on each knee, gazing intently at the burning coals. I too sat down before the fire and gazed at the coals, and nothing was said for a long time.

My sister was in her cushioned chair in her corner, and Biddy sat at her needlework before the fire, and Joe sat next Biddy.

At length I got out, "Joe, have you told Biddy?"

"No, Pip," returned Joe, "I left it to yourself, Pip."

"I would rather you told, Joe."

"Pip's a gentleman of fortun', then," said Joe, "and God bless him in it!"

Biddy dropped her work, and looked at me. Joe held his knees and looked at me. I looked at both of them. After a pause they both heartily congratulated me; but there was a certain touch of sadness in their congratulations that I rather resented.

I took it upon myself to impress Biddy (and through Biddy, Joe) with the grave obligation I considered my friends under, to know nothing and say nothing

[1] **this day week:** a week from today.

about the maker of my fortune. They said they would be very particular and then they congratulated me again, and went on to express so much wonder at the notion of my being a gentleman that I didn't half like it.

"Saturday night," said I, when we sat at our supper of bread-and-cheese and beer. "Five more days, and then the day before *the* day! They'll soon go."

"Yes, Pip," observed Joe, whose voice sounded hollow in his beer mug. "They'll soon go."

"I have been thinking, Joe, that when I go downtown on Monday and order my new clothes, I shall tell the tailor that I'll come and put them on there, or that I'll have them sent to Mr. Pumblechook's. It would be very disagreeable to be stared at by all the people here."

"Mr. and Mrs. Hubble might like to see you in your new genteel figure, too, Pip," said Joe. "So might Wopsle. And the Jolly Bargemen might take it as a compliment."

"That's just what I don't want, Joe. They would make such a business of it — such a coarse and common business — that I couldn't bear myself."

Biddy asked me here, "Have you thought about when you'll show yourself to Mr. Gargery, and your sister, and me? You will show yourself to us, won't you?"

"Biddy," I returned with some resentment, "you are so exceedingly quick that it's difficult to keep up with you. I shall bring my clothes here in a bundle one evening — most likely on the evening before I go away."

Biddy said no more. Handsomely forgiving her, I soon exchanged an affectionate good night with her and Joe, and went up to bed. When I got into my little room, I sat down and took a long look at it, as a mean little room that I should soon be parted from and raised above forever.

As I put the window open and stood looking out, I saw Joe come slowly forth at the dark door below, and take a turn or two in the air; and then I saw Biddy come, and bring him a pipe and light it for him. He never smoked so late, and it seemed to hint to me that he wanted comforting, for some reason or other. I drew away from the window and sat down in my one chair by the bedside, feeling it very sorrowful and strange that this first night of my bright fortunes should be the loneliest I had ever known.

I put my light out, and crept into bed; and it was an uneasy bed now, and I never slept the old sound sleep in it any more.

CHAPTER XV

Morning made a considerable difference in my general prospect of life. After breakfast, Joe brought out my indentures from the press in the best parlor, and we put them in the fire, and I felt that I was free.

After our early dinner, I strolled out alone. As I passed the church, I thought — with something akin to shame — of my companionship with the fugitive whom I had once seen limping among those graves. My comfort was that it happened a long time ago, and that he had doubtless been transported a long way off, and that he was dead to me, and might be dead into the bargain. I made my way to the old Battery, and, lying down there to consider the question whether Miss Havisham intended me for Estella, fell asleep.

When I awoke, I was much surprised to find Joe sitting beside me, smoking his pipe. He greeted me with a cheerful smile on my opening my eyes, and said:

"As being the last time, Pip, I thought I'd foller."

"And Joe, I am very glad you did so."

"Thankee, Pip."

"You may be sure, dear Joe," I went on, after we had shaken hands, "that I shall never forget you."

"No, no, Pip!" said Joe, in a comfortable tone, "*I'm* sure of that. Ay, ay, old chap!"

I told Joe of my former thoughts in this very place, that I had long wanted to be a gentleman. "It's a pity now, Joe," said I, "that you did not get on a little more when we had our lessons here, isn't it?"

"Well, I don't know," returned Joe. "I'm so awful dull. I'm only master of my own trade. It were always a pity as I was so awful dull; but it's no more of a pity now than it was – this day twelvemonth [1] – don't you see!"

What I had meant was that when I came into my property and was able to do something for Joe, it would have been much more agreeable if he had been better qualified for a rise in station. He was so perfectly unaware of my meaning, however, that I thought I would mention it to Biddy in preference.

So, when we had walked home and had had tea, I took Biddy into our little garden and said I had a favor to ask of her.

"And it is, Biddy," said I, "that you will not omit any opportunity of helping Joe on a little."

"How helping him on?" asked Biddy, with a steady sort of glance.

"Well! Joe is a dear good fellow – in fact, I think he is the dearest fellow that ever lived – but he is rather backward in some things. For instance, Biddy, in his learning and his manners."

"Oh, his manners! Won't his manners do, then?" asked Biddy, plucking a black-currant leaf.

"My dear Biddy, they do very well here ——"

"Oh! they *do* very well here?" interrupted Biddy, looking closely at the leaf in her hand.

"Hear me out – but if I were to remove Joe into a higher sphere, as I shall hope to remove him when I fully come into my property, they would hardly do him justice."

"And don't you think he knows that?" asked Biddy.

It was such a provoking question (for it had never in the most distant manner occurred to me) that I said, snappishly, "Biddy, what do you mean?"

"Have you never considered that he may be proud?"

"Proud?" I repeated, with disdainful emphasis.

"Oh! there are many kinds of pride," said Biddy, looking full at me and shaking her head; "pride is not all of one kind ——"

"Well? What are you stopping for?" said I.

"Not all of one kind," resumed Biddy. "He may be too proud to let anyone take him out of a place that he is competent to fill, and fills well and with respect."

"Now, Biddy," said I, "I am very sorry to see this in you. You are envious, Biddy, and grudging. You are dissatisfied on account of my rise in fortune, and you can't help showing it."

"If you have the heart to think so," returned Biddy, "say so. Say so over and over again, if you have the heart to think so."

"If you have the heart to be so, you mean, Biddy," said I, in a virtuous and superior tone. "Don't put it off upon me. I am extremely sorry to see this in you,

[1] **this day twelvemonth:** a year ago today.

Biddy, it's a — it's a bad side of human nature."

I walked away from Biddy, and Biddy went into the house, and I went out at the garden gate and took a dejected stroll until suppertime, again feeling it very sorrowful and strange that this, the second night of my bright fortunes, should be as lonely and unsatisfactory as the first.

But morning once more brightened my view. I went into town as early as I could hope to find the shops open, and presented myself before Mr. Trabb, the tailor, who was having his breakfast in the parlor behind his shop, and who did not think it worth his while to come out to me, but called me in to him.

"Well!" said Mr. Trabb, in a hail-fellow-well-met kind of way. "How are you, and what can I do for you?"

"Mr. Trabb," said I, "it's an unpleasant thing to have to mention, because it looks like boasting, but I have come into a handsome property."

A change passed over Mr. Trabb. He got up from the bedside, and wiped his fingers on the tablecloth, exclaiming, "Lord bless my soul!"

"I am going up to my guardian in London," said I, casually drawing some guineas out of my pocket and looking at them; "and I want a fashionable suit of clothes to go in. I wish to pay for them," I added, "with ready money."

"My dear sir," said Mr. Trabb, "may I venture to congratulate you? Would you do me the favor of stepping into the shop?"

Mr. Trabb's boy was the boldest boy in all that countryside. When I had first entered he was sweeping the shop, and he sweetened his labors by sweeping over me. He was still sweeping when I came out into the shop with Mr. Trabb, and he knocked the broom against all possible corners and obstacles, to express equality with any blacksmith, alive or dead.

"Hold that noise," said Mr. Trabb with the greatest sternness, "or I'll knock your head off! Do me the favor to be seated, sir. Now, sir," said Mr. Trabb, taking down a roll of cloth.

I selected the materials for a suit, and re-entered the parlor to be measured. When he had at last done and had arranged to send the articles to Mr. Pumblechook's, he said, "I know, sir, that London gentlemen cannot be expected to patronize local work, as a rule; but if you would give me a turn now and then I should greatly esteem it. Good morning, sir, much obliged. — Door!"

The last word was flung at the boy, who had not the least notion what it meant. But I saw him collapse as his master rubbed me out with his hands, and my first decided experience of the stupendous power of money was that it had morally laid upon his back Trabb's boy.

After this memorable event I went to the hatter's, and the bootmaker's, and the hosier's, and felt rather like Mother Hubbard's dog whose outfit required the services of so many trades. I also went to the coach office and took my place for seven o'clock on Saturday morning. When I had ordered everything I wanted, I directed my steps toward Pumblechook's, and, as I approached that gentleman's place of business, I saw him standing at his door.

He was waiting for me with great impatience. He had been out early with the carriage, and had called at the forge and heard the news. He had prepared a luncheon for me in the parlor, and he too ordered his shopman to "come out of the gangway" as my sacred person passed.

"To think," said Mr. Pumblechook, after snorting admiration at me for some moments, "that I should have been the humble instrument of leading up to this, is a proud reward."

I begged Mr. Pumblechook to remember that nothing was to be ever said or hinted on that point. I mentioned that I wished to have my new clothes sent to his house, and he was delighted on my so distinguishing him. I mentioned my reason for wishing to avoid observation in the village, and he lauded it to the skies.

There followed many glasses of wine, the drinking of which was constantly interrupted by Mr. Pumblechook's rising from his chair, extending a fervent hand, and clasping my own with the request that he might shake it.

There was nobody but himself, he intimated, worthy of my confidence. Then he asked me tenderly if I remembered our boyish games at sums, and how we had gone together to have me bound apprentice, and, in effect, how he had ever been my favorite fancy and my chosen friend. If I had taken ten times as many glasses of wine, I should have known that he never stood in that relation to me, and should in my heart of hearts have repudiated the idea.

Tuesday, Wednesday, and Thursday passed, and on Friday morning I went to Mr. Pumblechook's to put on my new clothes and pay my visit to Miss Havisham. My clothes were rather a disappointment, of course. Probably every new and eagerly expected garment ever put on fell a trifle short of the wearer's expectation. But after I had had my new suit on some half an hour, it seemed to fit me better.

I went to Miss Havisham's by all the back ways, and rang at the bell. Sarah Pocket came to the gate, and positively reeled back when she saw me so changed.

"You?" said she. "You? Good gracious! What do you want?"

"I am going to London, Miss Pocket," said I, "and want to say good-by to Miss Havisham."

I was not expected, for she left me locked in the yard while she went to ask if I were to be admitted. After a very short delay, she returned and took me up, staring at me all the way.

Miss Havisham was taking exercise in the room with the long table, leaning on her crutch stick. The room was lighted as usual, and at the sound of her entrance, she stopped and turned. She was then just abreast of the rotted bride cake.

"Don't go, Sarah," she said. "Well, Pip?"

"I start for London, Miss Havisham, tomorrow." I was exceedingly careful what I said. "And I thought you would kindly not mind my taking leave of you."

"This is a gay figure, Pip," said she, making her crutch stick play round me, as if she, the fairy godmother who had changed me, were bestowing the finishing gift.

"I have come into such good fortune since I saw you last, Miss Havisham," I murmured. "And I am so grateful for it, Miss Havisham!"

"Ay, ay!" said she, looking at the envious Sarah with delight. "I have seen Mr. Jaggers. *I* have heard about it, Pip. So you go tomorrow?"

"Yes, Miss Havisham."

"And you are adopted by a rich person?"

"Yes, Miss Havisham."

"Not named?"

"No, Miss Havisham."

"And Mr. Jaggers is made your guardian?"

"Yes, Miss Havisham."

She quite gloated on these questions and answers, so keen was her enjoyment of Sarah Pocket's jealous dismay. "Well!" she went on; "you have a promising career before you. Be good — deserve it — and abide by Mr. Jaggers' instructions." She looked at me, and looked at Sarah, and Sarah's face wrung out of her watchful face a cruel smile. "Good-by, Pip! — you will always keep the name of Pip, you know."

"Yes, Miss Havisham."

"Good-by, Pip!"

She stretched out her hand, and I went down on my knee and put it to my lips. I had not considered how I should take leave of her; it came naturally to me at the moment to do this. She looked at Sarah Pocket with triumph in her weird eyes, and so I left my fairy godmother, with both her hands on her crutch stick, standing in the midst of the dimly lighted room beside the rotten bride cake that was hidden in cobwebs.

And now, those six days which were to have run out so slowly had run out fast and were gone, and tomorrow looked me in the face more steadily than I could look at it. As the six evenings had dwindled away, I had become more and more appreciative of the society of Joe and Biddy. On this last evening, I dressed myself out in my new clothes for their delight and sat in my splendor until bedtime. We had a hot supper on the occasion, graced by the inevitable roast fowl. We were all very low, and none the higher for pretending to be in spirits.

I was to leave our village at five in the morning, and I had told Joe that I wished to walk away all alone. I am afraid that this purpose originated in my sense of the contrast there would be between me and Joe if we went to the coach together. I had pretended with myself that there was nothing of this taint in the arrangement; but when I went up to my little room on this last night, I felt compelled to admit that it was so, and had an impulse to go down again and entreat Joe to walk with me in the morning. I did not.

It was a hurried breakfast with no taste in it. I got up from the meal, saying with a sort of briskness, as if it had only just occurred to me, "Well! I suppose I must be off!" and then I kissed my sister, who was nodding and shaking in her usual chair, and kissed Biddy, and threw my arms around Joe's neck. The last I saw of them was when dear old Joe waved his strong right arm above his head, crying huskily, "Hooroar!" and Biddy put her apron to her face.

I walked away at a good pace, thinking it was easier to go than I had supposed it would be. The village was very peaceful and quiet, and all beyond was so unknown and great that in a moment with a strong heave and sob I broke into tears. I was better after I had cried than before — more sorry, more aware of my own ingratitude, more gentle. If I had cried before, I should have had Joe with me then.

When I was on the coach, and it was clear of the town, I deliberated with an aching heart whether I would not get down when we changed horses and walk back, and have another evening at home, and a better parting.

We changed horses after awhile and it was now too late and too far to go back, and I went on. And the mists had all solemnly risen now, and the world lay spread before me.

This Is the End of the First Stage of Pip's Expectations.

How Well Did You Read?

There are a number of unsettled matters or " mysteries " in your mind at this point in the story, naturally. If you read the first stage carefully, you noticed certain events and suggestions that will bear keeping in mind as you go on with the story:

1. The two convicts on the marsh: How much do you know about them? What other references to them are made up to the end of this stage?

2. The pale young gentleman: Is he a Havisham relative, or another boy brought in like Pip?

3. ESTELLA: What relation is she to Miss Havisham?

4. MISS HAVISHAM: How much of her story do you know at this point?

5. MRS. JOE'S ASSAILANT: Whom do you suspect? Why?

6. PIP'S ADOPTION: What are the stipulations under which Pip is to be supported and educated as a gentleman? What clues does Pip have as to his benefactor?

7. There are a few more important mysteries. Why does Miss Havisham want Pip around? Consider the significance of the remark which Pip fancies he has heard her make (p. 528): " Break their hearts, my pride and hope, break their hearts and have no mercy! " What reason might she have for saying that?

Already you may have noted some change in the characters, if you have really gotten to know them. During the course of the story so far, in what way has Pip changed? What changes, if any, have appeared in the behavior of Miss Havisham? Estella?

Thinking Over the First Stage

Dickens divided the story of Pip and his expectations into three stages. The first stage ends at the moment when Pip, on the stagecoach for London, has wiped away his tears of loneliness and turned his face toward the new world that lies before him.

1. Note that Pip *knows* he is ungrateful and is sorry for it, though his sorrow is not likely to change his conduct or last for very long. Have you ever behaved in this contradictory fashion – perhaps on leaving home for camp or school or for a holiday? You were annoyed at your parents' concern and at their many instructions, yet you were ashamed of being annoyed. Try to analyze what lies behind such behavior, using your experience as a guide and referring to Pip's experience also.

2. How does Dickens arouse your sympathy for both the boy and the convict in the opening scene? What was your impression of the convict? Why does Pip comply with the wishes of the convict?

3. What do you think about Joe? Is he really dull? When did you admire him most? Do you suppose anything will change his feeling for Pip?

4. Mrs. Joe is of course a strange character. Is she as strict with herself as she is with Joe and Pip? What incident reveals her strict sense of honesty? What makes her so ill-tempered, do you suppose?

5. With regard to Estella, what is happening to Pip? What conflicting feelings does Estella arouse in Pip? How do you think Biddy feels about Pip? In what ways will she be able to understand him even though Pip has left her kind of life?

6. What do you know about the system of apprenticing boys to master workmen? Does any such system exist today?

7. Who first uses the phrase " great expectations "? What does it mean as it is specifically used in this story?

8. Pip and Estella play an old card game, " Beggar My Neighbor," in which the goal is for one player to take all the other player's cards. What popular modern card game is probably most like it? When Miss Havisham tells Estella to " beggar him," what does she really mean? Why is Pip suddenly ashamed of his hands, his boots, and his speech? What does the word " gentleman " mean as Pip and the other characters in this novel use it? What does the word mean generally to you?

9. At what point does Pip first discover the enormous power of money to change the attitude of one person toward another? Is that power greater or less now than it was in Dickens' time? Does the possession of spending money give a high school student any advantage? What happens to the feelings and behavior of students who cannot compete on a money basis?

10. How does money affect the behavior of Miss Havisham's relatives? Have you

observed, in your other reading or from personal experience, the power of money to change people's lives? To discuss this, you may wish to wait until you see what happens to Pip next — but don't forget this question of money.

For Your Vocabulary

CONTEXT: Try to supply more common substitutes for the words in italics.

1. "*rank* wet grass"
2. "Mrs. Joe's Christmas *salutation*"
3. "a *moving spectacle* for *compassionate* minds"
4. "seized with unspeakable *consternation*"
5. "*expending* great efforts"
6. "a tone of deepest *reproach*"
7. "said Estella with *disdain*"
8. "when Mr. Pumblechook *interposed*"
9. "met with this *rebuff*"
10. "*nonsensical speculations*"
11. "*pious* appearance"
12. "her hearing was greatly *impaired*"
13. "should have *repudiated* the idea"

WORD BUILDING: The very first sentence in the story contains the word *explicit,* meaning plain or clear. It comes from the Latin *explicare,* to unfold or display. Other words built from the same Latin verb and having a similar meaning are *explicable, explicate, explication* and *explicatory.* Can you attempt the meanings of these words from knowing the Latin root? Try to pronounce *explicable* and *explicatory* with the accent on the first syllable.

The Second Stage of Pip's Expectations

CHAPTER XVI

The journey from our town to London was one of about five hours. It was a little past midday when the four-horse stagecoach in which I was passenger got into the ravel of traffic in London. If we Britons had not at one time decided that it was treasonable to doubt our having and our being the best of everything, I would have been scared by the immensity of London, and I think I might have had some faint doubts whether it was not rather ugly, crooked, narrow, and dirty.

Mr. Jaggers had sent me his address: it was in a section called Little Britain. I was soon taken there by hackney coach and deposited at certain offices with an open door, whereon was painted MR. JAGGERS.

I went into the front office and asked, was Mr. Jaggers at home?

"He is not," returned the clerk. "He is in court at present. Am I addressing Mr. Pip?"

I signified that he was addressing Mr. Pip.

"Mr. Jaggers left word would you wait in his room. He couldn't say how long he might be, having a case on. But it stands to reason, his time being valuable, that he won't be longer than he can help."

With those words, the clerk opened a door, and ushered me into an inner chamber at the back. Mr. Jaggers' room was lighted by a skylight only, and was a most dismal place. I sat wondering and waiting in Mr. Jaggers' close room, until I really could not bear the dust and grit that lay thick on everything, and got up and went out.

I told the clerk that I would take a turn in the air while I waited, and went out into the streets, where I saw the great black dome of Saint Paul's bulging at me from behind a grim stone building which a bystander said was Newgate Prison. Following the wall of the jail, I found a number of people standing about, smelling strongly of beer. I learned that the trials were on.

I dropped into the office to ask if Mr. Jaggers had come in yet, and I found he had not, and I strolled out again. I became aware that other people were waiting about for Mr. Jaggers, as well as I. There were two men of secret appearance lounging nearby, one of whom said to the other when they first passed me that "Jaggers would do it if it was to be done." There were two women standing at a corner, and one of the women was crying on her dirty shawl, and the other comforted her by saying, as she pulled her own shawl over her shoulders, "Jaggers is for him, 'Melia, and what more *could* you have?" These testimonies to the popularity of my guardian made a deep impression on me, and I admired and wondered more than ever.

At length I saw Mr. Jaggers coming across the road toward me. All the others who were waiting saw him at the same time, and there was quite a rush at him. Mr. Jaggers addressed himself to his followers.

First, he took the two secret men.

"Now, I have nothing to say to *you*," said Mr. Jaggers. "I told you from the first it was a tossup. Have you paid Wemmick?"

"Yes, sir," said both the men together.

"Very well; then you may go. If you say a word to me, I'll throw up the case."

"We thought, Mr. Jaggers ——" one of the men began, pulling off his hat.

"That's what I told you not to do," said Mr. Jaggers. "*You* thought! I think for you; that's enough for you."

"And now *you!*" said Mr. Jaggers, suddenly stopping, and turning on the two women with the shawls. "Once for all; if you come here, bothering about your Bill, I'll make an example of both your Bill and you, and let him slip through my fingers. Have you paid Wemmick?"

"Oh, yes, sir! Every farthing."

"Very well. Say another word – one single word – and Wemmick shall give you your money back." This terrible threat caused the two women to fall off immediately.

Without further interruption we reached the front door. My guardian then took me into his own room, and while he lunched, he informed me what arrangements he had made for me. I was to go to Barnard's Inn, to young Mr. Pocket's rooms, where a bed had been sent in for my accommodation; I was to remain with young Mr. Pocket until Monday; on Monday I was to go with him to his father's house on a visit. Also, I was told what my allowance was to be – it was a very liberal one – and had handed to me the cards of certain tradesmen with whom I was to deal for all kinds of clothes and such other things as I should want. "You will find your credit good, Mr. Pip," said my guardian, "but I shall by this means be able to check your bills, and to pull you up if I find you spending too much. Of course you'll go wrong somehow, but that's no fault of mine."

After I had pondered a little over this encouraging sentiment, I asked Mr. Jaggers if I could send for a coach. He said it was not worth while, I was so near my destination; Wemmick should walk round with me, if I pleased.

I then found that Wemmick was the clerk in the next room. I accompanied him into the street, after shaking hands with my guardian. We found a new set of people lingering outside, but Wemmick made a way among them by saying coolly yet decisively, "I tell you it's no use; he won't have a word to say to one of you"; and we soon got clear of them, and went on side by side.

Casting my eyes on Mr. Wemmick as we went along, to see what he was like in the light of day, I found him to be a dry man, rather short in stature, with a square wooden face. He wore his hat on the back of his head, and looked straight before him, walking in a self-contained way as if there were nothing in the streets to claim his attention.

"Do you know where Mr. Matthew Pocket lives?" I asked Mr. Wemmick.

"Yes," said he, nodding in the direction. "At Hammersmith, west of London."

"Is that far?"

"Well! Say five miles."

"Do you know him?"

"Why, you are a regular cross-examiner!" said Mr. Wemmick, looking at me with an approving air. "Yes, I know him. *I* know him!"

Soon he said here we were at Barnard's Inn. It was the dingiest collection of shabby buildings ever squeezed together in a rank corner as a club for tomcats. We entered a melancholy little square that looked to me like a flat burying ground. I thought it had the most dismal trees in it, and the most dismal sparrows, and the most dismal cats, and the most dismal houses that I had ever seen. The windows of the houses were in every stage of dilapidated [1] blind and curtain, crippled flowerpot, cracked glass, dusty decay, and miserable makeshift.

So imperfect was this realization of the first of my great expectations that I looked in dismay at Mr. Wemmick. He led me up a flight of stairs, which appeared to be slowly collapsing into sawdust, to a set of chambers on the top floor. MR. POCKET, JUN., was painted on the door, and there was a label on the letter box, "Return shortly."

"He hardly thought you'd come so soon," Mr. Wemmick explained. "You don't want me any more?"

"No, thank you," said I.

"As I keep the cash," Mr. Wemmick observed, "we shall most likely meet pretty often. Good day."

When he was gone, I opened the staircase window and nearly beheaded myself, for the ropes had rotted away, and it came down like the guillotine.[2] After this escape, I was content to stand dolefully looking out, saying to myself that London was decidedly overrated.

Mr. Pocket, Junior's, idea of "shortly" was not mine, for I had nearly maddened myself with looking out for half an hour, and had written my name with my finger several times in the dirt of every pane in the window, before I heard footsteps on the stairs. Gradually there arose before me the hat, head, waistcoat, trousers, boots, of a member of society of about my own standing. He had a pa-

[1] **dilapidated** (dĭ·lăp′ĭ·dāt′ĕd): ruined; falling apart.

[2] **guillotine** (gĭl′ō·tēn): a machine for beheading a person by means of a heavy blade, operating on the same principle as a window.

"'Now, I have nothing to say to you,' said Mr. Jaggers."

per bag under each arm and a basket of strawberries in one hand, and was out of breath.

"Mr. Pip?" said he.

"Mr. Pocket?" said I.

"Dear me!" he exclaimed, "I am extremely sorry; but I knew there was a coach from your part of the country at midday, and I thought you would come by that one. The fact is, I have been out on your account — not that that is any excuse — for I thought, coming from the country, you might like a little fruit after dinner, and I went to Covent Garden Market to get it."

For a certain reason, I felt as if my eyes would start out of my head. I began to think this was a dream.

"Pray come in," said Mr. Pocket, Junior. "Allow me to lead the way. I am rather bare here, but I hope you'll be able to make out tolerably well till Monday. My father thought you might like to take a walk about London with me. I am sure I shall be very happy to show London to you. Our food will be supplied from our coffeehouse here, and (it is only right I should add) at your expense, such being Mr. Jaggers' directions. As to our lodging, it's not by any means splendid, because I have my own bread to earn, and my father hasn't anything to give me, and I shouldn't be willing to take it if he had. This is our sitting room — just such chairs and tables and carpet and so forth, you see, as they could spare from home. This is my little bedroom; rather musty, but Barnard's *is* musty. This is your bedroom; the furniture's hired for the occasion, but I trust it will answer the purpose; if you should want anything, I'll go and fetch it. The chambers are retired,[1] and we shall be alone together, but we shan't fight, I dare say."

[1] **retired:** secluded; having few neighbors.

As I stood opposite to Mr. Pocket, Junior, I saw the sudden recognition come into his own eyes that I knew to be in mine, and he said, falling back:

"Lord bless me, you're the prowling boy!"

"And you," said I, "are the pale young gentleman!"

CHAPTER XVII

The pale young gentleman and I stood contemplating one another in Barnard's Inn, until we both burst out laughing.

"The idea of its being you!" said he. "The idea of its being *you!*" said I. And then we stared at one another afresh, and laughed again. "Well!" said the pale young gentleman, reaching out his hand good-humoredly, "it's all over now, I hope, and it will be good of you if you'll forgive me for having knocked you about so."

I derived from this speech that Mr. Herbert Pocket (for Herbert was the pale young gentleman's name) still rather confused his intentions with his actions. But I made a modest reply, and we shook hands warmly.

"You hadn't come into your good fortune at that time?" said Herbert Pocket.

"No," said I.

"No," he agreed, "I heard it had happened very lately. *I* was rather on the lookout for good fortune then."

"Indeed?"

"Yes. Miss Havisham had sent for me, to see if she could take a fancy to me. But she couldn't — at all events, she didn't."

I thought it polite to remark that I was surprised to hear that.

"Bad taste," said Herbert, laughing, "but a fact. Yes, she had sent for me on a trial visit, and if I had come out of it successfully, I suppose I should have been provided for; perhaps I should have been what-you-may-called-it to Estella."

"What's that?" I asked, with sudden anxiety.

He was arranging his fruit in plates while we talked, which divided his attention, and was the cause of his having made this lapse of a word. "Engaged," he explained, still busy with the fruit. "Betrothed."

"How did you bear your disappointment?" I asked.

"Pooh!" said he, "I didn't care much for it. *She's* a Tartar." [1]

"Miss Havisham?"

"I don't say no to that, but I meant Estella. That girl's hard and haughty and unreasonable to the last degree, and has been brought up by Miss Havisham to wreak vengeance on all the male sex."

"What relation is she to Miss Havisham?"

"None," said he. "Only adopted."

"Why should she wreak revenge on all the male sex? What revenge?"

"Lord, Mr. Pip!" said he. "Don't you know?"

"No," said I.

"Dear me! It's quite a story, and shall be saved till dinnertime. Mr. Jaggers is your guardian, I understand?" he went on.

"Yes."

"You know he is Miss Havisham's man of business and solicitor,[2] and has her confidence when nobody else has?"

This was bringing me (I felt) toward dangerous ground. I answered cautiously that I had seen Mr. Jaggers in Miss Havisham's house on the very day of our combat, but never at any other time, and that I believed he had no recollection of having ever seen me there.

"He was so obliging as to suggest my father for your tutor, and he called on my father to propose it. Of course he knew about my father from his connection with Miss Havisham. My father is Miss Havisham's cousin; not that that implies friendly intercourse between them, for he makes no effort to court her favor."

Herbert Pocket had a frank and easy way with him that was very taking. I have never seen anyone who had a greater natural inability to do anything secret and mean. There was something wonderfully hopeful about his general air, and something that at the same time whispered to me he would never be very successful or rich. He was still a pale young gentleman, without much strength. He had not a handsome face, but it was better than handsome, being extremely amiable and cheerful.

As he was so outspoken himself, I told him my small story, and laid stress on my being forbidden to inquire who my benefactor was. I further mentioned that as I had been brought up a blacksmith in a country place, and knew very little of the ways of politeness, I would take it as a great kindness in him if he would give me a hint whenever he saw me at a loss or going wrong.

"With pleasure," said he, "though I venture to prophesy that you'll want very few hints. Will you begin at once to call me by my Christian name, Herbert?"

I thanked him, and said I would. I informed him in exchange that my Christian name was Philip.

"I don't take to Philip," said he, smiling, "for it sounds like one of those dull boys out of the spelling book. Would

[1] **Tartar:** a person of cruel and unrelenting nature, impossible to deal with.

[2] **solicitor** (sô·lĭs′ĭ·tẽr): in England, a lawyer who handles his clients' legal affairs, as distinguished from a barrister (băr′ĭs·tẽr), who pleads cases in court.

you mind Handel for a familiar name? There's a charming piece of music by Handel, called the Harmonious Blacksmith."

"I should like it very much."

"Then, my dear Handel," said he, turning round as the door opened, "here is the dinner."

We had made some progress in the dinner, when I reminded Herbert of his promise to tell me about Miss Havisham.

"True," he replied. "Let me introduce the topic, Handel, by mentioning that in London it is not the custom to put the knife in the mouth – for fear of accidents – and that while the fork is reserved for that use, it is not put farther in than necessary. It is scarcely worth mentioning, only it's as well to do as other people do. Also, the spoon is not generally used overhand, but under. This has the advantage that you get at your mouth better (which after all is the object)."

He offered these friendly suggestions in such a lively way that we both laughed.

"Now," he pursued, "Miss Havisham was a spoiled child. Her mother died when she was a baby, and her father denied her nothing. He was very rich and very proud. So was his daughter."

"Miss Havisham was an only child?" I asked.

"Stop a moment, I am coming to that. No, she was not an only child; she had a half brother. Her father privately married again – his cook, I rather think."

"I thought he was proud," said I.

"My good Handel, so he was. He married his second wife privately, because he *was* proud, and in the course of time she died also. When his second wife died, Havisham told his daughter what he had done, and then the son became a part of the family, residing in the house you are acquainted with. As the son became a young man, he turned out riotous, extravagant, undutiful – altogether bad. At last his father disinherited him; but he softened when he was dying and left him well off, though not nearly so well off as Miss Havisham.

"Miss Havisham was now an heiress, and was looked after as a great match. Her half brother had ample means again, but wasted them most fearfully. There were strong differences between him and her, and it is suspected that he cherished a deep and mortal grudge against her. Now, I come to the cruel part of the story.

"There appeared upon the scene a certain man, who made love to Miss Havisham. I have heard my father mention that he was a showy man, and the kind of man for the purpose. But he was not to be mistaken for a gentleman. Well! This man pursued Miss Havisham and professed to be devoted to her. There is no doubt that she perfectly idolized him. He got great sums of money from her, and he induced her to buy her brother out of a share in the family property at an immense price, on the plea that when he was her husband he must hold and manage it all.

"Now, your guardian was not at that time in Miss Havisham's councils, and she was too haughty and too much in love to be advised by anyone. Her relations were poor and scheming, with the exception of my father; he was poor enough, but not slavish or jealous. The only independent one among them, he warned her that she was doing too much for this man, and was placing herself in his power. She angrily ordered my father out of the house, in his presence, and my father has never seen her since."

I now recalled having heard Miss Havisham say, "Matthew will come and see me at last when I am laid dead upon that table."

"To return to the man and make an end of him. The marriage day was fixed, the wedding dresses were bought, the wedding guests were invited. The day came, but not the bridegroom. He wrote a letter —— "

"Which she received," I struck in, "when she was dressing for her marriage? At twenty minutes to nine?"

"At the hour and minute," said Herbert, nodding, "at which she afterward stopped all the clocks. What was in it, further than that it most heartlessly broke the marriage off, I can't tell you, because I don't know. When she recovered from a bad illness, she laid the whole place waste, as you have seen it, and she has never since looked upon the light of day."

"Is that all the story?" I asked, after considering it.

"All I know of it. Oh, I have forgotten one thing. It has been supposed that the man to whom she gave her misplaced confidence acted in concert with her half brother; that it was a conspiracy between them; and that they shared the profits."

"What became of the two men? Are they alive now?"

"I don't know."

"You said just now that Estella was not related to Miss Havisham, but adopted. When adopted?"

Herbert shrugged his shoulders. "There has always been an Estella, since I have heard of a Miss Havisham. I know no more."

"And all I know," I replied, "you know."

"I fully believe it. And as to the condition of your expected fortune — namely, that you are not to inquire or discuss to whom you owe it — you may be very sure that it will never be even approached by me."

He said this with so much delicacy that I felt he as perfectly understood Miss Havisham to be my benefactress as I understood the fact myself.

We were very gay and sociable, and I asked him in the course of conversation what he was. He replied, "An insurer of ships."

I had grand ideas of the wealth and importance of insurers of ships, and was further impressed when he continued, "I shall not rest satisfied with merely insuring ships. I think I shall trade," said he, leaning back in his chair, "to the East Indies for shawls, spices, dyes, drugs, and precious woods. It's an interesting trade."

Quite overpowered by the magnificence of these dealings, I asked him where the ships he insured mostly traded to at present.

"I haven't begun insuring yet," he replied. "I am looking about me."

Somehow, that pursuit seemed more in keeping with Barnard's Inn. I said (in a tone of conviction), "Ah-h!"

"Yes. I am in a countinghouse,[1] and looking about me."

"Is a countinghouse profitable?" I asked.

"Why, n-no; not to me. Not directly profitable. That is, it doesn't pay me anything, and I have to —— keep myself. But the thing is, that you look about you. *That's* the grand thing. You are in a countinghouse, you know, and you look about you."

This was very like his way of conducting that encounter in the garden; very like. His manner of bearing his poverty, too, exactly corresponded to his manner of bearing that defeat. It seemed to me

[1] **countinghouse:** an office or building where business is transacted and accounts are kept.

that he took all blows and buffets now, with just the same air as he had taken mine then. It was evident that he owned nothing but the simplest necessaries and that everything else turned out to have been sent in on my account from the coffeehouse or somewhere else, yet his imaginary good fortune made him cheerful. I liked him and we got on famously together.

CHAPTER XVIII

On Monday morning at a quarter of nine, Herbert went to the countinghouse — to look around him, I suppose — and I bore him company. He was to come out in an hour or two and accompany me to Hammersmith, where I was to stay under the roof and under the instruction of Mr. Matthew Pocket. When Herbert came, we went and had lunch and then took a coach for his family's home, where we arrived at two or three o'clock in the afternoon. Lifting the latch of a gate, we passed into a garden overlooking the river, where Mr. Pocket's children were playing about.

Mr. Pocket came out to make my acquaintance. He was a gentleman with a rather perplexed expression of face, with very gray hair disordered on his head, as if he didn't quite see how to put anything straight. Mr. Pocket said he was glad to see me, and he hoped I was not sorry to see him. "For I am really not," he added, with his son's smile, "an alarming person." He was a young-looking man, despite his perplexities and his gray hair, and his manner seemed quite natural. Later and by degrees I learned, chiefly from Herbert, that Mr. Pocket had educated himself at Harrow and Cambridge,[1] where he had distinguished himself. He had come to London and here, after failing in loftier hopes, he turned to the meager rewards to be had from tutoring backward or indigent young men and from routine literary tasks.

Mr. Pocket took me into the house and showed me my room, which was a pleasant one. He then knocked at the doors of two other similar rooms, and introduced me to their occupants, by name Drummle and Startop. Drummle, an old-looking young man of a heavy order of physique, was whistling. Startop, younger in years and appearance, was reading and holding his head, as if he thought himself in danger of exploding it with too strong a charge of knowledge.

In the evening there was rowing on the river. As Drummle and Startop had each a boat, I resolved to set up mine, and to best them both. I was pretty good at most exercises in which country boys are skillful, but I was conscious of wanting elegance of style for the Thames.[2] Therefore I at once engaged an expert boatman nearby, to whom I was introduced by my new friends.

After two or three days, when I had established myself in my room and had gone backward and forward to London several times, Mr. Pocket and I had a long talk together. I learned that he had been told by Mr. Jaggers that I was not designed for any profession, and that I should be well enough educated for my destiny if I could "hold my own" with the average of young men in prosperous circumstances.

When I had begun to work in earnest, it occurred to me that if I could retain my bedroom in Barnard's Inn, my life

[1] **Harrow and Cambridge:** Harrow is a famous preparatory school, and Cambridge is a famous university in England.

[2] **Thames** (těmz): the chief river passing through London. Mr. Pocket's house was near it.

would be agreeably varied, while my manners would be none the worse for Herbert's society; so I went off to impart my wish to Mr. Jaggers.

"If I could buy the furniture now hired for me," said I, "and one or two other little things, I should be quite at home there."

"Go it!" said Mr. Jaggers, with a short laugh. "I told you you'd get on. Well! How much do you want?"

I said I didn't know how much.

"Come!" retorted Mr. Jaggers. "How much? Fifty pounds?"

"Oh, not nearly so much."

"Five pounds?" said Mr. Jaggers.

This was such a great fall, that I said in disappointment, "Oh! more than that."

"More than that, eh!" retorted Mr. Jaggers. "How much more?"

"It is so difficult to fix a sum," said I, hesitating.

"Wemmick!" said Mr. Jaggers, opening his office door. "Take Mr. Pip's written order, and pay him twenty pounds."

This strongly marked way of doing business made a strongly marked impression on me, and that not of an agreeable kind. As he happened to go out now, and as Wemmick was brisk and talkative, I said to Wemmick that I hardly knew what to make of Mr. Jaggers' manner.

"Tell him that, and he'll take it as a compliment," answered Wemmick. "He don't mean that you *should* know what to make of it. — Oh!" for I looked surprised, "it's not personal; it's professional, only professional."

He went on to say in a friendly manner:

"If at any odd time when you have nothing better to do, you wouldn't mind coming over to see me at Walworth, I could offer you a bed, and I should consider it an honor. I have not much to show you but such two or three curiosities as I have and a bit of garden and a summerhouse."

I said I should be delighted to accept his hospitality.

"Thankee," said he. "Then we'll consider that it's to come off, when convenient to you. Have you dined with Mr. Jaggers yet?"

"Not yet."

"Well," said Wemmick, "he'll give you wine, and good wine. I'll give you punch, and not bad punch. And now I'll tell you something. When you go to dine with Mr. Jaggers, look at his housekeeper."

"Shall I see something very uncommon?"

"Well," said Wemmick, "you'll see a wild beast tamed. It won't lower your opinion of Mr. Jaggers' powers. Keep your eye on it."

I told him I would do so, but it was to be some time before my interest and curiosity were satisfied.

As the weeks passed at Mr. Pocket's home, I came to know better the nature of my fellow students. Bentley Drummle, who was so sulky a fellow that he even took up a book as if its writer had done him an injury, did not take up with new acquaintances in a more agreeable spirit. Heavy in figure, movement, and comprehension, he was idle, proud, niggardly, reserved, and suspicious. He came of a rich family who had nursed this combination of qualities until they made the discovery that it was just of age and a blockhead. Thus, Bentley Drummle had come to Mr. Pocket when he was a head taller than that gentleman, and half a dozen heads thicker than most gentlemen.

Startop had been spoiled by a weak mother and kept at home when he ought to have been at school, but he was devotedly attached to her and admired her beyond measure. He had a woman's delicacy of feature. It was but natural that I should take to him much more kindly than to Drummle. Even in the earliest evenings of our boating, he and I would pull homeward abreast of one another, conversing from boat to boat, while Bentley Drummle came up in our wake alone.

Herbert was my intimate companion and friend. I presented him with a half share in my boat, which was the occasion of his often coming down to Hammersmith; and my possession of a half share in his chambers often took me up to London. We used to walk between the two places at all hours.

These were the surroundings among which I settled down and applied myself to my education. I soon contracted expensive habits and began to spend an amount of money that a few short months before I should have thought almost impossible. But through good and evil I stuck to my books. Between Mr. Pocket and Herbert I got on fast.

I had not seen Mr. Wemmick for some weeks when I thought I would write him a note and propose to go home with him on a certain evening. He replied that it would give him much pleasure, and that he would expect me at the office at six o'clock. Thither I went, and there I found him, putting the key of his safe down his back as the clock struck.

"Did you think of walking down to Walworth?" said he.

"Certainly," said I, "if you approve."

"Very much," was Wemmick's reply, "for I have had my legs under the desk all day, and shall be glad to stretch them. Now I'll tell you what I've got for supper – a cold roast fowl. You don't object to an aged [1] parent, I hope?"

I really thought he was still speaking of the fowl, until he added, "Because I have got an aged parent at my place." I then said what politeness required.

"So you haven't dined with Mr. Jaggers yet?" he pursued, as we walked along.

"Not yet."

"He told me so this afternoon. I expect you'll have an invitation tomorrow. He's going to ask your pals, too. Three of 'em, ain't there? Well, he's going to ask the whole gang."

Mr. Wemmick and I beguiled [2] the time talking, until he gave me to understand that we had arrived in the district of Walworth. It appeared to be a rather dull collection of back lanes, ditches, and little gardens. Wemmick's house was a little wooden cottage in the midst of plots of garden, looking like a miniature castle, with the top of it cut out and painted like a battery mounted with guns.

"My own doing," said Wemmick. "Looks pretty, don't it?"

I highly commended it. I think it was the smallest house I ever saw.

"That's a real flagstaff, you see," said Wemmick, "and on Sundays I run up a real flag. Then look here. After I have crossed this bridge, I hoist it up – so – and cut off the communication."

The bridge was a plank, and it crossed a chasm about four feet wide and two deep. But it was very pleasant to see the pride with which he hoisted it up and made it fast, smiling as he did so, with a relish and not merely mechanically.

"At nine o'clock every night, Green-

[1] **aged** (ā'jĕd).
[2] **beguiled** (bē·gīld'): whiled away.

wich time,[1]" said Wemmick, "the gun fires. There he is, you see! And when you hear him go, I think you'll say he's a Stinger."

The miniature cannon referred to was mounted in a separate fortress, constructed of latticework. It was protected from the weather by an ingenious little tarpaulin umbrella.

"Then, at the back," said Wemmick, "there's a pig, and there are fowls and rabbits; and I grow cucumbers. So, sir," said Wemmick, smiling again, but seriously, too, as he shook his head, "if you can suppose the little place besieged, it would hold out a devil of a time with so many provisions."

Then he conducted me to a bower about a dozen yards off, and in this retreat our glasses were already set forth.

"I am my own engineer, and my own carpenter, and my own plumber, and my own gardener, and my own Jack-of-all-trades," said Wemmick, in acknowledging my compliments. "Well, it's a good thing, you know. It brushes the Newgate[2] cobwebs away, and pleases the Aged. You wouldn't mind being at once introduced to the Aged, would you? It wouldn't put you out?"

I expressed readiness and we went into the castle. There we found, sitting by a fire, a very old man in a flannel coat; clean, cheerful, comfortable, and well cared for, but intensely deaf.

"Well, Aged Parent," said Wemmick, shaking hands with him in a cordial way, "how am you?"

"All right, John; all right!" replied the old man.

"Here's Mr. Pip, Aged Parent," said Wemmick, "and I wish you could hear his name. Nod away at him, Mr. Pip; that's what he likes. Nod away at him, if you please."

"This is a fine place of my son's, sir," cried the old man, while I nodded as hard as I possibly could.

"You're as proud of it as Punch; ain't you, Aged?" said Wemmick, contemplating the old man, with his hard face really softened; "*there's* a nod for you," giving him a tremendous one; "*there's* another for you," giving him a still more tremendous one; "you like that, don't you? If you're not tired, Mr. Pip — though I know it's tiring to strangers — will you nod him one more? You can't think how it pleases him."

I nodded him several more, and he was in great spirits. There was a neat serving girl in attendance, who looked after the Aged during the day. She set about laying the supper cloth while Wemmick and I engaged in conversation. He told me, as he smoked a pipe, that it had taken him a good many years to bring the property up to its present pitch of perfection.

"I hope Mr. Jaggers admires it," I said.

"Never seen it," said Wemmick. "Never heard of it. Never seen the Aged. Never heard of him. No; the office is one thing, and private life is another. When I go into the office, I leave the Castle behind me, and when I come into the Castle, I leave the office behind me. If it's not in any way disagreeable to you, you'll oblige me by doing the same. I don't wish it professionally spoken about."

Of course I felt my good faith involved in the observance of his request. The punch being very nice, we sat there

[1] **Greenwich** (grĕn′ĭch) **time:** standard time as measured at the Royal Observatory, Greenwich, England. Time everywhere else in the world is computed on the basis of distance east and west of Greenwich.

[2] **Newgate:** Newgate Prison. Mr. Wemmick's dealings as Mr. Jaggers' clerk were largely with persons who sought either to get out or keep out of Newgate.

drinking it and talking until it was almost nine o'clock. "Getting near gunfire," said Wemmick then, as he laid down his pipe. "It's the Aged's treat."

Proceeding into the Castle again, we found the Aged heating the poker, with expectant eyes, as a preliminary to the performance of this great nightly ceremony. Wemmick stood with his watch in his hand until the moment was come for him to take the red-hot poker from the Aged, and repair [1] to the battery. He took it, and went out, and presently the Stinger went off with a bang that shook the crazy little box of a cottage as if it must fall to pieces, and made every glass and teacup in it ring. Upon this the Aged — who I believe would have been blown out of his armchair but for holding on by the elbows — cried out exultingly, "He's fired! I heared him!" and I nodded at the old gentleman until I absolutely could not see him.

The supper, which was served shortly, was excellent. I was heartily pleased with my whole entertainment. Nor was there any drawback to my little turret bedroom.

Our breakfast was as good as the supper, and at half-past eight we started for Little Britain. By degrees, Wemmick seemed to get dryer and harder as we went along. At last when we got to his place of business and he pulled out his key, he looked as unconscious of his Walworth property as if the Castle and the drawbridge and the arbor and the Aged had all been blown into space together by the last discharge of the Stinger.

CHAPTER XIX

It happened, as Wemmick had told me it would, that my guardian gave me the invitation for myself and friends.

[1] **repair:** go.

"No ceremony," Mr. Jaggers said, "and no dinner dress, and say tomorrow."

At six o'clock the next day Mr. Jaggers conducted my friends and me to Gerrard Street, Soho, to a rather stately house, but dolefully in want of painting, and with dirty windows. We went up a dark brown staircase into a series of three dark brown rooms on the first floor.

Dinner was laid in the best of these rooms. The table was comfortably laid and at Mr. Jaggers' side was a dumbwaiter, with a variety of bottles and decanters on it and four dishes of fruit for dessert. I noticed throughout that he kept everything under his own hand, and distributed everything himself.

As he had scarcely seen my three companions until now — for he and I had walked together — he stood on the hearthrug, after ringing the bell, and took a searching look at them. To my surprise, he seemed at once to be principally, if not solely, interested in Drummle.

"Pip," said he, putting his large hand on my shoulder and moving me to the window, "I don't know one from the other. Who's the Spider?"

"The Spider?" said I.

"The blotchy, sprawly, sulky fellow."

"That's Bentley Drummle," I replied. "The one with the delicate face is Startop."

Not taking the least account of Startop, he returned, "Bentley Drummle is his name, is it? I like the look of that fellow."

He immediately began to talk to Drummle. I was looking at the two when there came between me and them the housekeeper, with the first dish for the table.

She was a woman of about forty, tall, of a lithe, nimble figure, extremely pale, with large faded eyes and a quantity of streaming hair. She set the dish on, touched my guardian quietly on the arm with a finger to notify that dinner was ready, and vanished. No other attendant appeared.

Induced to take particular notice of the housekeeper, both by her own striking appearance and by Wemmick's preparation, I observed that whenever she was in the room, she kept her eyes attentively on my guardian. I fancied that I could detect in his manner a purpose of always holding her in suspense.

Dinner went off gaily, and although my guardian seemed to follow rather than suggest subjects, I knew that he wrenched the weakest part of our dispositions out of us. I found that I was expressing my tendency to spend extravagantly, and to patronize [1] Herbert, and to boast of my great prospects. It was so with all of us, but with no one more than Drummle. He informed our host that he much preferred our room to our company, and that as to skill he was more than our master, and that as to strength he could scatter us like chaff. He began baring and flexing his arm to show how muscular it was, and we all began to bare and flex our arms in a ridiculous manner.

Now the housekeeper was at that time clearing the table, my guardian taking no heed of her. Suddenly, he clapped his large hand on the housekeeper's like a trap, as she stretched it across the table.

"If you talk of strength," said Mr. Jaggers, "*I'll* show you a wrist. Molly, let me see your wrist."

Her entrapped hand was on the table, but she had already put her other hand behind her waist. "Master," she said, in a low voice, with her eyes attentively and entreatingly fixed upon him. "Don't."

"*I'll* show you a wrist," repeated Mr. Jaggers, with an immovable determination to show it. "Molly, let them see your wrist."

"Master," she again murmured. "Please!"

"Molly," said Mr. Jaggers, not looking at her, "let them see *both* your wrists. Show them. Come!"

He took his hand from hers, and turned that wrist up on the table. She brought her other hand from behind her, and held the two out side by side. The last wrist was much disfigured — deeply scarred and scarred across and across. When she held her hands out, she took her eyes from Mr. Jaggers, and turned them watchfully on every one of the rest of us in succession.

"There's power here," said Mr. Jaggers, coolly tracing out the sinews with his forefinger. "Very few men have the power of wrist that this woman has. It's remarkable what mere force of grip there is in these hands. I have had occasion to notice many hands; but I never saw stronger in that respect, man's or woman's, than these. That'll do, Molly. You can go." She withdrew her hands and went out of the room, and Mr. Jaggers filled his glass and passed round the wine.

"At half-past nine, gentlemen," said he, "we must break up. Pray make the best use of your time. I am glad to see you all. Mr. Drummle, I drink to you."

If his object in singling out Drummle were to bring him out still more, it perfectly succeeded. In a sulky triumph Drummle showed his poor opinion of the rest of us in a more and more offensive degree, until he became downright intolerable. Through all his stages, Mr. Jaggers followed him with

[1] **patronize** (pā'trŭn·īz): act in a superior manner toward someone.

the same strange interest.

In our boyish want of discretion I dare say we took too much to drink, and I know we talked too much. We became particularly hot upon some sneer of Drummle's, to the effect that we were too free with our money. Startop tried to turn the discussion aside with some small pleasantry that made us all laugh. Resenting this little success more than anything, Drummle, without any threat or warning, pulled his hands out of his pockets, dropped his round shoulders, swore, took up a large glass, and would have flung it at Startop's head, but for our entertainer's dexterously seizing it at the instant it was raised.

"Gentlemen," said Mr. Jaggers, deliberately putting down the glass, "I am exceedingly sorry to announce that it's half-past nine."

On this hint we all rose to depart. Before we got to the street door, Startop was cheerily calling Drummle "old boy," as if nothing had happened. But the old boy would not even walk to Hammersmith on the same side of the way. Herbert and I, who remained in town, saw them going down the street on opposite sides, Startop leading, and Drummle lagging behind in the shadow of the houses.

In about a month after that, the Spider's time with Mr. Pocket was up for good, and, to the great relief of all the house, he went home to his family.

CHAPTER XX

My dear Mr. Pip:

I write this by request of Mr. Gargery, for to let you know that he is going to London in company with Mr. Wopsle and would be glad if agreeable to be allowed to see you. He would call at Barnard's Hotel Tuesday morning at nine o'clock, when if not agreeable please leave word. Your poor sister is much the same as when you left. We talk of you in the kitchen every night, and wonder what you are saying and doing. If now considered in the light of a liberty, excuse it for the love of poor old days. No more, dear Mr. Pip, from

Your ever obliged,
and affectionate servant,
Biddy.

P.S. He wishes me most particular to write *what larks*. He says you will understand. I hope and do not doubt it will be agreeable to see him even though a gentleman, for you had ever a good heart, and he is a worthy worthy man. I have read him all excepting only the last little sentence, and he wishes me most particular to write again *what larks.*

I received this letter by post on Monday morning, and therefore its appointment was for next day. Let me confess exactly with what feelings I looked forward to Joe's coming.

Not with pleasure, though I was bound to him by so many ties; no, with considerable disturbance and some mortification. If I could have kept him away by paying money, I certainly would have paid money. My greatest reassurance was that he was coming to Barnard's Inn, not to Hammersmith. I had little objection to his being seen by Herbert or his father, for both of whom I had respect; but I had the sharpest sensitiveness as to his being seen by Drummle, whom I held in contempt. So, throughout life, our worst weaknesses and meannesses are usually committed for the sake of the people whom we most despise.

I had got on so expensively of late that I had even hired a serving boy and had clothed him with a blue coat, canary waistcoat, white tie, creamy breeches, and top boots. I had to find him a little to do and a great deal to eat; and with both of these requirements he haunted my existence.

I came into town on Monday night to be ready for Joe, and I got up early in the morning, and caused the sitting room and breakfast table to assume their most splendid appearance.

Presently I heard Joe on the staircase. I knew it was Joe by his clumsy manner of coming upstairs. When at last he stopped outside our door, I could hear his finger tracing over the painted letters of my name. Finally he gave a faint single rap, and my serving boy announced, "Mr. Gargery!" and he came in.

"Joe, how are you, Joe?"

"Pip, how AIR you, Pip?"

With his good honest face all glowing and shining, and his hat put down on the floor between us, he caught both my hands and worked them straight up and down.

"I am glad to see you, Joe. Give me your hat."

But Joe, taking it up carefully with both hands, like a bird's nest with eggs in it, wouldn't hear of parting with that piece of property.

"You have that growed," said Joe, "and that gentlefolked," Joe considered a little before he discovered this word; "as to be a honor to your king and country."

"And you, Joe, look wonderfully well."

"Thank God," said Joe, "I'm equal to most. And your sister, she's no worse than she were. And Biddy, she's ever right and ready."

Herbert had entered the room, so I presented Joe to Herbert. Joe, being invited to sit down to table, looked all round the room for a suitable spot on which to deposit his hat and ultimately stood it on an extreme corner of the chimney piece, from which it ever afterward fell off at intervals.

"Do you take tea or coffee, Mr. Gargery?" asked Herbert, who always presided of a morning.

"Thankee, sir," said Joe, stiff from head to foot, "I'll take whichever is most agreeable to yourself."

"Say tea, then," said Herbert, pouring it out.

Here Joe's hat tumbled off the mantelpiece, and he started out of his chair and picked it up, and fitted it to the same exact spot.

"When did you come to town, Mr. Gargery?"

"Were it yesterday afternoon?" said Joe, after coughing behind his hand. "No it were not. Yes it were. Yes. It were yesterday afternoon" (with an appearance of mingled wisdom, relief, and strict impartiality).

"Have you seen anything of London, yet?"

"Why, yes, sir," began Joe, but his attention was providentially attracted by his hat, which was toppling. Indeed, it demanded from him a constant attention. He made extraordinary play with it, and showed the greatest skill, now rushing at it and catching it neatly as it dropped, now merely stopping it midway, beating it up, finally splashing it into the slop basin, where I took the liberty of laying hands upon it.

Then he fell into such unaccountable fits of meditation, with his fork midway between his plate and his mouth; had his eyes attracted in such strange directions; was afflicted with such remarkable coughs; sat so far from the table; and dropped so much more than he ate, and pretended that he hadn't dropped it; that I was heartily glad when Herbert left us for the city.

I had neither the good sense nor the good feeling to know that this was all my fault, and that if I had been easier with Joe, Joe would have been easier with me. I felt impatient of him and out of temper with him.

"Us two being now alone, sir —" began Joe.

"Joe," I interrupted, pettishly, "how can you call me sir?"

Joe looked at me for a single instant with something like reproach. I was conscious of a sort of dignity in the look.

"Us two being now alone," resumed Joe, "and me having the intentions and abilities to stay not many minutes more, I will now conclude — leastways begin — to mention what have led to my having had the present honor.

"Well, sir," pursued Joe, "this is how it were. I were at the Bargemen t'other night, Pip," (whenever he subsided into affection, he called me Pip, and whenever he relapsed into politeness he called me sir) "when there come in Pumblechook. Well, Pip; this same identical come to me at the Bargemen and his word were, 'Joseph, Miss Havisham she wish to speak to you.'"

"Miss Havisham, Joe?"

"'She wished,' were Pumblechook's word, 'to speak to you.'" Joe sat and rolled his eyes at the ceiling.

"Yes, Joe? Go on, please."

"Next day, sir," said Joe, looking at me as if I were a long way off, "having cleaned myself, I go and I see Miss A."

"Miss A., Joe? Miss Havisham?"

"Which I say, sir," replied Joe, with an air of legal formality, as if he were making his will, "Miss A., or otherways Havisham.[1] Her expression air then as follering: 'Mr. Gargery. You air in correspondence with Mr. Pip?' Having had a letter from you, I were able to say 'I am.' 'Would you tell him, then,' said she, 'that Estella has come home, and would be glad to see him.'"

I felt my face fire up as I looked at Joe.

"Biddy," pursued Joe, "when I got home and asked her fur to write the message to you, a little hung back. Biddy says, 'I know he will be very glad to have it by word of mouth; it is holiday time, you want to see him, go!' I have now concluded, sir," said Joe, rising from his chair, "and, Pip, I wish you ever well and ever prospering to a greater and greater height."

"But you are not going now, Joe?"

"Yes I am," said Joe.

"But you are coming back to dinner, Joe?"

"No I am not," said Joe.

Our eyes met, and all the "sir" melted out of that manly heart as he gave me his hand.

"Pip, dear old chap, life is made of ever so many partings welded together, as I may say, and one man's a blacksmith, and one's a whitesmith,[2] and one's a goldsmith, and one's a coppersmith. Diwisions among such must come, and must be met as they come. If there's been any fault at all today, it's mine. You and me is not two figures to be together in London; nor yet anywheres else but what is private, and beknown, and understood among friends. It ain't that I am proud, but that I want to be right, as you shall never see me no more in these clothes. I'm wrong in these clothes. I'm wrong out of the forge, the kitchen, or off th' marshes. You won't find half so much fault in me if you think of me in my forge dress, with my hammer in my hand, or even my pipe. You won't find half so much fault in me if, supposing

[1] Joe would pronounce Havisham "'avisham."

[2] **whitesmith**: a tinsmith.

as you should ever wish to see me, you come and put your head in at the forge window and see Joe the blacksmith, there at the old anvil, in the old burned apron, sticking to the old work. I'm awful dull, but I hope I've beat out something nigh the rights of this at last. And so God bless you, dear old Pip, old chap, God bless you!"

I had not been mistaken in my fancy that there was a simple dignity in him. The fashion of his dress could no more come in its way when he spoke these words than it could come in its way in Heaven. He touched me gently on the forehead, and went out. As soon as I could recover myself sufficiently, I hurried out after him and looked for him in the neighboring streets; but he was gone.

CHAPTER XXI

It was clear that I must go to our town next day, and in the first flow of my repentance it was equally clear that I must stay at Joe's. But when I secured my place on the coach I began to invent reasons for putting up at the Blue Boar. All other swindlers upon earth are nothing to the self-swindlers, and with such pretenses did I cheat myself. I settled that I must go to the Blue Boar.

At that time it was customary to carry convicts down to the dockyards by stagecoach. As I had often seen them on the highroad dangling their ironed legs over the coach roof, I had no cause to be surprised when Herbert came up and told me there were two convicts going down with me. But I had a reason that was an old reason now for faltering whenever I heard the word convict.

"You don't mind them, Handel?" said Herbert.

"Oh, no!"

"You just now looked as if you didn't like them?"

"I can't pretend that I do like them, and I suppose you don't particularly. But I don't mind them."

"See! There they are," said Herbert, "and what a degraded and vile sight it is!"

The two convicts were handcuffed together, and had irons on their legs — irons of a pattern that I knew well. They wore the dress that I likewise knew well. One was a taller and stouter man than the other, and his attire disguised him, but I knew his half-closed eye at one glance. There stood the man whom I had seen on the settle at the Three Jolly Bargemen on a Saturday night!

But this was not the worst of it. It turned out that the whole of the back of the coach had been taken by a family, and that there were no places for the two prisoners but on the seat in front. I sat with the coachman, and the convict I had recognized sat behind me with his breath on the hair of my head!

"Good-by, Handel!" Herbert called out as we started. I thought what a blessed fortune it was that he had found another name for me than Pip.

The weather was miserably raw. Cowering forward for warmth and to make me a screen against the wind, the convicts moved closer to me than before. The very first words I heard them interchange were the words of my own thought, "Two one-pound notes."

"How did he get 'em?" said the convict I had never seen.

"How should I know?" returned the other. "He had 'em stowed away somehows. Give him by friends, I expect."

"I wish," said the other, with a bitter curse upon the cold, "that I had 'em here."

"So he says," resumed the convict I had recognized "— it was all said and done in half a minute, behind a pile of timber in the dockyards — 'You're a-going to be discharged!' Yes, I was. Would I find out that boy that had fed him and kep' his secret, and give him them two one-pound notes? Yes, I would. And I did."

"More fool you," growled the other. "I'd have spent 'em on wittles and drink. He must have been a green one. Mean to say he knowed nothing of you?"

"Not a thing. Different gangs and different ships. He was tried again for prison breaking, and got made a lifer."

"And was that the only time you worked out, in this part of the country?"

"The only time."

"What might have been your opinion of the place?"

"A most beastly place. Mudbank, mist, swamp, and work; work, swamp, mist, and mudbank."

They both cursed the place in very strong language, and gradually growled themselves out, and had nothing left to say.

After overhearing this dialogue, I resolved to alight as soon as we touched the town and put myself out of his hearing. This device I executed successfully. As to the convicts, they went their way with the coach, and I knew at what point they would be spirited off to the river. In my fancy, I saw the boat with its convict crew waiting for them at the slime-washed stairs — again heard the gruff "Give way, you!" like an order to dogs — again saw the wicked Hulks lying out on the black water. I could not have said what I was afraid of, but there was great fear upon me.

In the morning I was up and out of the Blue Boar too early, so I loitered into the country on Miss Havisham's side of town, thinking about my patroness, and painting brilliant pictures of her plans for me.

She had adopted Estella, she had as good as adopted me, and it could not fail to be her intention to bring us together. Estella had taken strong possession of me. I loved Estella with the love of a man; I loved her simply because I found her, in my memory, irresistible. I knew to my sorrow, often and often, if not always, that I loved her against reason, against promise, against peace, against hope, against happiness, against all discouragement that could be. I loved her none the less because I knew it, and it had no more influence in restraining me than if I had devoutly believed her to be human perfection.

I so shaped out my walk as to arrive at the gate at my old time. I heard the side door open, and steps come across the courtyard, and started to see myself confronted by a man in a sober gray dress — the last man I should have expected to see in that place of porter at Miss Havisham's door.

"Orlick!"

"Ah, young master, there's more changes than yours. But come in, come in. It's opposed to my orders to hold the gate open."

I entered and he swung it, and locked it, and took the key out. "Yes!" said he, facing round, "Here I am!"

"How did you come here?"

"I come here," he retorted, "on my legs."

"Are you here for good?"

"I ain't here for harm, young master, I suppose."

I was not so sure of that. "Then you have left the forge?" I said.

"Do this look like a forge?" replied Orlick, leading me to the house.

Recalling how I had gone up the staircase in the dark, many a time, I ascended it now and tapped in my old way at the door of Miss Havisham's room. "Pip's rap," I heard her say, immediately; "come in, Pip."

She was in her chair near the old table, in the old dress, with her two hands crossed on her stick, her chin resting on them. Sitting near her was an elegant lady whom I had never seen.

"Come in, Pip," Miss Havisham continued. "Come in, Pip. How do you do, Pip? So you kiss my hand as if I were a queen, eh?—Well?"

"I heard, Miss Havisham," said I, rather at a loss, "that you were so kind as to wish me to come and see you, and I came directly."

"Well?"

The lady whom I had never seen before lifted up her eyes and looked archly at me, and then I saw that the eyes were Estella's eyes. But she was so much changed, was so much more beautiful, so much more womanly, that I slipped hopelessly back into the coarse and common boy again. Oh, the sense of distance and difference that came upon me, and the inaccessibility that came about her!

"Do you find her much changed, Pip?" asked Miss Havisham, with her greedy look, and striking her stick upon a chair that stood between them as a sign for me to sit down there.

"When I came in, Miss Havisham, I thought there was nothing of Estella in the face or figure; but now it all settles down so curiously into the old——"

"What? You are not going to say into the old Estella?" Miss Havisham interrupted. "She was proud and insulting, and you wanted to go away from her. Don't you remember?"

I said confusedly that that was long ago, and that I knew no better then. Estella smiled with perfect composure, and said she had no doubt of my having been quite right, and of her having been very disagreeable.

"Is *he* changed?" Miss Havisham asked her.

"Very much," said Estella, looking at me.

"Less coarse and common?" said Miss Havisham, playing with Estella's hair.

Estella laughed. She treated me as a boy still, but she lured me on.

It was settled that I should stay there all the rest of the day, and return to the hotel at night, and to London tomorrow. When we had conversed for a while, Miss Havisham sent us two out to walk. Estella and I went into the garden, I trembling in spirit and worshipping the very hem of her dress; she, quite composed and decidedly not worshipping anything in me.

As the garden was too overgrown and rank for walking, we came out again into the brewery yard. I showed her where I had seen her walking that first old day, and she said with a cold and careless look in that direction, "Did I?" I reminded her where she had come out of the house and given me my meat and drink, and she said, "I don't remember." "Not remember that you made me cry?" said I. "No," said she, and shook her head and looked about her. I verily believe that her not remembering and not minding in the least, made me cry again, inwardly — and that is the sharpest crying of all.

"You must know," said Estella, condescending to me as a brilliant and beautiful woman might, "that I have no heart — if that has anything to do with my memory. I have no softness there, no — sympathy — sentiment — nonsense. If we are to be thrown much together, you had better believe it at once."

Her handsome dress had trailed upon the ground. She held it in one hand now, and with the other lightly touched my shoulder as we walked. We walked round the ruined garden twice or thrice more. At last we went back into the house, and there I heard with surprise that my guardian had come down to see Miss Havisham on business, and would come back to dinner. Estella left us to prepare herself, and Miss Havisham turned to me and said in a whisper:

"Is she beautiful, graceful, well grown? Do you admire her?"

"Everybody must who sees her, Miss Havisham."

She put an arm around my neck, and drew my head close down to hers as she sat in the chair. "Love her, love her, love her! How does she treat you?"

Before I could answer (if I could have answered so difficult a question at all), she repeated, "Love her, love her, love her! If she favors you, love her. If she wounds you, love her. If she tears your heart to pieces — and as it gets older and stronger it will tear deeper — love her, love her, love her! Hear me, Pip! I adopted her to be loved. I bred her and educated her, to be loved. I developed her into what she is, that she might be loved. Love her!"

"I'll tell you," she went on in the same hurried passionate whisper, "what real love is. It is blind devotion, unquestioning self-humiliation, utter submission, trust and belief against yourself and against the whole world, giving up your whole heart and soul to someone who smites it — as I did!"

She rose up in the chair, in her shroud of a dress, and struck at the air as if she would as soon have struck herself against the wall and fallen dead. All this passed in a few seconds. As I drew her down into her chair, I turned and saw my guardian in the room.

Miss Havisham had seen him as soon as I, and was (like everybody else) afraid of him. She made a strong attempt to compose herself, and stammered that he was as punctual as ever.

"As punctual as ever," he repeated. "And so you are here, Pip?"

I told him when I had arrived, and how Miss Havisham wished me to come and see Estella.

"Well, Pip! How often have you seen Miss Estella before?" said he.

"How often?"

"Jaggers," interposed Miss Havisham, much to my relief; "leave my Pip alone, and go with him to your dinner."

He complied, and we groped our way down the dark stairs together.

"Pray, sir," said I, "may I ask you a question?"

"You may," said he, "and I may decline to answer it. Put your question."

"Estella's name, is it Havisham or ——?" I had nothing to add.

"Or what?" said he.

"Is it Havisham?"

"It is Havisham."

This brought us to the dinner table,

where Estella awaited us. Mr. Jaggers scarcely directed his eyes to Estella's face once during dinner. When she spoke to him, he listened, and in due course answered, but never looked at her that I could see. On the other hand, she often looked at him, with interest and curiosity, if not distrust, but his face never showed the least consciousness.

Afterward Mr. Jaggers and I went up to Miss Havisham's room, and we three played at whist.[1] We played until nine o'clock, and then, before our leaving, it was arranged that when Estella came to London I should be forewarned of her coming and should meet her at the coach; and then I took leave of her, and touched her and left her.

My guardian slept at the Boar in the next room to mine. Far into the night, Miss Havisham's words, "Love her, love her, love her!" sounded in my ears. I said to my pillow, "I love her, I love her, I love her!" hundreds of times.

Ah me! I thought those were high and great emotions. But I never thought there was anything low and small in my keeping away from Joe, because I knew she would be scornful of him. It was but a day gone, and Joe had brought the tears into my eyes; they had soon dried, God forgive me! soon dried.

CHAPTER XXII

After well considering the matter while I was dressing at the Blue Boar in the morning, I resolved to tell my guardian that I doubted Orlick's being the right sort of man to fill a post of trust at Miss Havisham's. He listened in a satisfied manner while I told him what knowledge I had of Orlick. "Very good, Pip," he observed, when I had concluded. "I'll go round presently, and pay our friend off." Rather alarmed by this hasty action, I was for a little delay, and even hinted that our friend might be difficult to deal with. "Oh, no, he won't," said my guardian. "I should like to see him argue the question with *me*."

As we were going back together to London by the midday coach, and as I breakfasted under such terrors of seeing the hypocritical Pumblechook that I could scarcely hold my cup, I left the Blue Boar immediately after breakfast, making a loop of a couple of miles into the open country at the back of Pumblechook's premises to get round into the High Street again. Then I felt myself in comparative security.

It was interesting to be in the quiet old town once more, and it was not disagreeable to be here and there suddenly recognized and stared after. My position was a distinguished one, and I was not at all dissatisfied with it, until Fate threw me in the way of that unlimited miscreant,[2] Trabb's boy.

Casting my eyes along the street at a certain point of my progress, I beheld Trabb's boy approaching. Suddenly the knees of Trabb's boy knocked together, his hair uprose, his cap fell off, he staggered out into the road, and crying to the populace, "Hold me! I'm so frightened!" pretended to be in a fit of terror occasioned by the dignity of my appearance. As I passed him, his teeth loudly chattered in his head, and with every mark of extreme humiliation, he prostrated himself in the dust.

This was a hard thing to bear, but this was nothing. I had not advanced another two hundred yards, when, to

[1] **whist:** a card game, the forerunner of the modern card game, contract bridge.

[2] **miscreant** (mĭs′krē·ănt): villain, wrongdoer.

my inexpressible amazement and indignation, I again beheld Trabb's boy approaching. He was coming round a narrow corner. He staggered round and round me with knees more afflicted, and with uplifted hands as if beseeching for mercy. His sufferings were hailed with the greatest joy by a knot of spectators, and I felt utterly confounded.

I had not got as much farther down the street as the post office when I again beheld Trabb's boy shooting round by a back way attended by a company of delighted young friends to whom he exclaimed, with a wave of his hand, "Don't know yah!" Afterward he took to crowing at me, pursuing me across the bridge, and completing the disgrace with which I left town.

The coach, with Mr. Jaggers inside, came up in due time, and I took my box seat again, and arrived in London safe — but not sound, for my heart was gone. As soon as I arrived, I sent a codfish and a barrel of oysters to Joe (as reparation for not having gone myself), and then went on to Barnard's Inn.

I found Herbert dining on cold meat, and delighted to welcome me back, and I felt that I must open my heart that very evening to my friend and chum. Dinner done and we sitting with our feet upon the fender, I said to Herbert, "My dear Herbert, I have something very particular to tell you."

"My dear Handel," he returned, "I shall respect your confidence."

"It concerns myself, Herbert," said I, "and one other person."

Herbert looked at the fire with his head on one side, and looked at me because I didn't go on.

"Herbert," said I, laying my hand upon his knee, "I love — I adore — Estella. I have never left off adoring her. And she has come back, a most beautiful and most elegant creature. And I saw her yesterday. And if I adored her before, I now doubly adore her."

"Lucky for you then, Handel," said Herbert, "that you are picked out for her and allotted to her. Have you any idea yet of Estella's views on the adoration question?"

I shook my head gloomily. "Oh! She is thousands of miles away from me," said I.

"Patience, my dear Handel; time enough, time enough. But you have something more to say?"

"I am ashamed to say it," I returned, "and yet it's no worse to say it than to think it. You call me a lucky fellow. Of course, I am. I was a blacksmith's boy but yesterday; I am — what shall I say I am — today?"

"Say a good fellow, if you want a phrase," returned Herbert, smiling, "a good fellow, with boldness and hesitation, action and dreaming, curiously mixed in him."

"Herbert," I went on, "you say I am lucky, and yet, when I think of Estella I cannot tell you how dependent and uncertain I feel. I may say that on the constancy of one person (naming no person) all my expectations depend. And at the best, how indefinite and unsatisfactory, only to know so vaguely what they are!"

"Now, Handel," Herbert replied, in his gay, hopeful way, "it seems to me that we are looking into our gift horse's mouth with a magnifying glass. Didn't you tell me that your guardian, Mr. Jaggers, told you in the beginning that you were not endowed with expectations only? And even if he had not told you so, could you believe that of all men in London, Mr. Jaggers is the man to hold his present relations toward you unless he were sure of his ground?"

"What a hopeful disposition you have!" said I, gratefully admiring his cheery ways.

"I ought to have," said Herbert, "for I have not much else. And now, I want to make myself seriously disagreeable to you for a moment – positively repulsive."

"You won't succeed," said I.

"Oh, yes, I shall!" said he. "I have been thinking that Estella cannot surely be a condition of your inheritance, if she was never referred to by your guardian. Am I right in so understanding what you have told me, as that he never referred to her, directly or indirectly, in any way? Never even hinted, for instance, that your patron might have views as to your marriage ultimately?"

"Never."

"Now, Handel, I am quite free from the flavor of sour grapes, upon my soul and honor! Not being bound to her, can you not detach yourself from her? – I told you I should be disagreeable."

I turned my head aside, for, with a rush and a sweep, a feeling like that which subdued me on the morning when I left the forge, smote upon my heart again. There was silence between us for a little while.

"My dear Handel," Herbert went on, "think of her bringing-up, and think of Miss Havisham. Think of what she is herself. This may lead to miserable things."

"I know it, Herbert," said I, with my head still turned away, "but I can't help it."

"Well!" said Herbert, getting up with a lively shake as if he had been asleep, and stirring the fire. "Now I'll endeavor to make myself agreeable again! I was going to say a word or two, Handel, concerning my father's son. I am afraid it is scarcely necessary to go round the point. I am myself committed to another."

"You mean you are engaged?" I asked.

"I am," said Herbert; "but it's a secret."

"May I ask the name?" I said.

"Name of Clara," said Herbert.

"Live in London?"

"Yes. Her father had to do with the supplying of passenger ships. I think he was a kind of purser."

"What is he now?" said I.

"He's an invalid now," replied Herbert. "I have never seen him, for he has always kept his room overhead, since I have known Clara. But I have heard him constantly. He makes tremendous rows – roars, and pegs at the floor with some frightful instrument." Herbert looked at me and laughed heartily.

"Don't you expect to see him?" said I.

"Oh, yes, I constantly expect to see him," returned Herbert, "because I never hear him, without expecting him to come tumbling through the ceiling. But I don't know how long the rafters may hold."

When he had once more laughed heartily, he became meek, and told me that the moment he began to make money, it was his intention to marry this young lady. He added, sadly, "But you *can't* marry, you know, while you're looking about you."

CHAPTER XXIII

One day when I was busy with my books, I received a note by the post, the mere outside of which threw me into a great flutter. It had no set beginning, as Dear Mr. Pip, or Dear Pip, or Dear Sir, or Dear Anything, but ran thus:

I am to come to London the day after tomorrow by the midday coach. I believe it was settled you should meet me? At all events Miss Havisham has that impression, and I write in obedience to it. She sends you her regard. — Yours, ESTELLA.

My appetite vanished instantly, and I knew no peace or rest until the day arrived. Then I was worse than ever, and began haunting the coach office in Wood Street even before the coach had left the Blue Boar in our town. I felt I could not let the coach office be out of my sight longer than five minutes at a time, and so I underwent a watch of four or five hours. Finally I saw her face at the coach window and her hand waving to me.

In her furred traveling dress, Estella seemed more delicately beautiful than ever. Her manner was more winning than before, and I thought I saw Miss Havisham's influence in the change.

"I am going to Richmond," she told me. "The distance is ten miles. I am to have a carriage, and you are to take me. This is my purse, and you are to pay my charges out of it. Oh, you must take the purse! We have no choice, you and I, but to obey our instructions. We are not free to follow our own devices, you and I."

As she looked at me in giving me the purse, I hoped there was an inner meaning in her words. She said them slightingly, but not with displeasure.

"A carriage will have to be sent for, Estella. Will you rest here a little?"

"Yes, I am to rest here a little, and I am to drink some tea, and you are to take care of me the while."

She drew her arm through mine, as if it must be done, and I requested a waiter to show us a private sitting room. On my objecting to a first room he showed us, which was a black hole of a place, he took us into another room with a dinner table for thirty. I was aware that the air of this chamber, in its strong combination of stable with soup stock, might have led one to infer that the coaching department was not doing well, and that the enterprising proprietor was boiling down the horses for the refreshment department. Yet the room was all in all to me, Estella being in it. I thought that with her I could have been happy there for life. (I was not at all happy there at the time, observe, and I knew it well.)

"Where are you going to, at Richmond?" I asked Estella.

"I am going to live," said she, "at a great expense, with a lady there, who has the power — or says she has — of taking me about and introducing me and showing people to me and showing me to people. How do you thrive with Mr. Pocket?"

"I live quite pleasantly there; at least ——" It appeared to me that I was losing a chance.

"At least?" repeated Estella.

"As pleasantly as I could anywhere, away from you."

"You silly boy," said Estella, quite composedly, "how can you talk such nonsense? Your friend Mr. Matthew, I believe, is superior to the rest of his family?"

"Very superior indeed."

"He really is disinterested, and above small jealousy and spite?" Estella asked.

"I am sure I have every reason to say so."

"You have not every reason to say so of the rest of the family, of Sarah Pocket, Camilla, and the others," said she, "for they beset Miss Havisham with reports to your disadvantage. They watch you, misrepresent you, write letters about you (anonymous sometimes), and you are the torment and occupation of their

"In her furred traveling dress, Estella seemed more delicately beautiful than ever."

lives. You can scarcely realize the hatred those people feel for you."

"They do me no harm, I hope?"

"No, no, you may be sure of that," said Estella. "Oh, what satisfaction it gives me to see those people thwarted! Two things I can tell you. First, these people will never impair your ground with Miss Havisham, in any particular, great or small. Second, I am indebted to you as the cause of their being so busy and so mean in vain, and there is my hand upon it."

As she gave it to me playfully – for her darker mood had been but momentary – I held it and put it to my lips. "You ridiculous boy," said Estella, "will you never take warning? Or do you kiss my hand in the same spirit in which I once let you kiss my cheek?"

"If I say yes, may I kiss the cheek again?"

"You should have asked before you touched the hand. But, yes, if you like."

I leaned down, and her calm face was like a statue's. "Now," said Estella, gliding away the instant I touched her cheek, "you are to take care that I have some tea, and you are to take me to Richmond."

Her reverting to this tone as if our association were forced upon us and we were mere puppets, gave me pain; but everything in our intercourse did give me pain. Whatever her tone with me happened to be, I could put no trust in it, and build no hope on it; and yet I went on against trust and against hope. Why repeat it a thousand times? So it always was.

I rang for the tea, and the waiter brought in by degrees some fifty articles associated with that refreshment, but of tea not a glimpse. A teaboard, cups and saucers, plates, knives and forks, spoons, saltcellars, a meek little muffin confined with the utmost precaution under a strong iron cover, a fat family teapot. After a long absence he came in with a box of precious appearance containing the tea twigs. These I steeped in hot water and extracted one cup of I don't know what, for Estella.

The bill paid, and the waiter remembered, and the chambermaid taken into consideration – in a word, the whole house bribed into a state of contempt and animosity,[1] and Estella's purse much lightened – we got into our post coach and drove away. Turning into Cheapside and rattling up Newgate Street, we were soon under the walls of the prison.

"Mr. Jaggers," said I, reminded of my guardian by the passing sight, "has the reputation of being more in the secrets of that dismal place than any man in London."

"He is more in the secrets of every place, I think," said Estella, in a low voice.

"You have been accustomed to see him often, I suppose?"

"I have been accustomed to see him at uncertain intervals ever since I can remember. But I know him no better now than I did before I could speak plainly. What is your own experience of him?"

"Once used to his distrustful manner," said I, "I have done very well."

"Are you intimate?"

"I have dined with him at his private house."

"I fancy," said Estella, shrinking, "that must be a curious place."

"It is a curious place."

I should have been cautious about discussing my guardian too freely even with her; but I should have gone on with the subject so far as to describe the dinner in Gerrard Street, if we had not

[1] **animosity** (ăn′ĭ·mŏs′ĭ·tĭ): ill will; resentment.

then come into a sudden glare of gaslight. When we were out of it, we fell into other talk, principally about the way by which we were traveling and about London.

It was impossible for me to avoid seeing that she cared to attract me; that she made herself winning; and would have won me even if the task had needed pains. Yet this made me none the happier, for I felt that she held my heart in her hand because she willfully chose to do it.

When we passed through Hammersmith, I showed her where Mr. Matthew Pocket lived, and said it was no great way from Richmond, and that I hoped I should see her sometimes.

" Oh, yes, you are to see me; you are to come when you think proper; you are to be mentioned to the family; indeed you are already mentioned."

I inquired was it a large household she was going to be a member of?

" No, there are only two, mother and daughter. The mother is a lady of some social station, I believe, though not averse to increasing her income."

" I wonder Miss Havisham could part with you again so soon."

" It is a part of Miss Havisham's plans for me, Pip," said Estella, with a sigh, as if she were tired. " I am to write to her constantly and see her regularly, and report how I go on — I and the jewels — for they are nearly all mine now."

It was the first time she had ever called me by name. Of course she did so purposely, and knew that I should treasure it up.

We came to Richmond all too soon, and at our destination two cherry-colored maids came fluttering out to receive Estella. The doorway soon absorbed her boxes, and she gave me her hand and a smile, and said good night, and was absorbed likewise. And still I stood looking at the house, thinking how happy I should be if I lived there with her, and knowing that I never was happy with her, but always miserable.

CHAPTER XXIV

As I had grown accustomed to my expectations, I had insensibly begun to notice their effect upon myself and those around me. Their influence on my own character I disguised from my recognition as much as possible, but I knew very well that it was not all good. I lived in a state of chronic uneasiness respecting my behavior to Joe. My conscience was not by any means comfortable about Biddy. When I woke up in the night I used to think, with a weariness on my spirits, that I should have been happier and better if I had never seen Miss Havisham's face, and had risen to manhood content to be partners with Joe in the honest old forge. Many a time of an evening, when I sat alone looking at the fire, I thought, after all, there was no fire like the forge fire and the kitchen fire at home.

Now, concerning the influence of my position on others, I perceived it was not beneficial to anybody, and above all, that it was not beneficial to Herbert. My lavish habits led his easy nature into expenses he could not afford, corrupted the simplicity of his life, and disturbed his peace with anxieties and regrets. I began to contract a quantity of debt. I could hardly begin but Herbert must begin too, so he soon followed.

In my confidence in my own resources, I would willingly have taken Herbert's expenses on myself; but Herbert was proud, and I could make no such proposal to him. So he got into difficulties in every direction, and continued to look about him. When we gradually fell into keeping late hours and late company, I noticed that he looked about him with a desponding eye at breakfast time; that he began to look about him more hopefully about midday; that he drooped when he came in to dinner; and that about two o'clock in the morning he became so deeply despondent again as to talk of buying a rifle and going to America, with a general purpose of compelling buffaloes to make his fortune.

We spent as much money as we could, and got as little for it as people could make up their minds to give us. We were always more or less miserable, and most of our acquaintance were in the same condition. There was a gay fiction among us that we were constantly enjoying ourselves, and a skeleton truth that we never did. To the best of my belief, our case was in the last respect a rather common one.

At certain times I would say to Herbert, as if it were a remarkable discovery:

"My dear Herbert, we are getting on badly."

"My dear Handel," Herbert would say to me, in all sincerity, "if you will believe me, those very words were on my lips, by a strange coincidence."

"Then, Herbert," I would respond, "let us look into our affairs."

We always derived profound satisfaction from making an appointment for this purpose. Dinner over, we produced a bundle of pens, a copious supply of ink, and a goodly show of writing and blotting paper. There was something very comfortable in having plenty of stationery.

I would then take a sheet of paper, and write across the top of it, in a neat hand, the heading, "Memorandum of Pip's debts." Herbert would also take a sheet of paper, and write across it, "Memorandum of Herbert's debts."

Each of us would then refer to a confused heap of bills at his side. The sound of our pens going refreshed us exceedingly, insomuch that I sometimes found it difficult to distinguish between this business proceeding and actually paying the money.

When we had written a little while, I would ask Herbert how he got on.

"They are mounting up, Handel," Herbert would say; "upon my life they are mounting up."

"Be firm, Herbert," I would retort. "Look the thing in the face. Look into your affairs. Stare them out of countenance."

"So I would, Handel, only they are staring *me* out of countenance."

However, my determined manner would have its effect, and Herbert would fall to work again. After a time he would give up once more, on the plea that he had not got Cobbs' bill, or Lobbs', or Nobbs', as the case might be.

"Then, Herbert, estimate; estimate it in round numbers, and put it down."

"What a fellow of resource you are!" my friend would reply, with admiration. "Really your business powers are very remarkable."

I thought so too. I established with myself, on these occasions, the reputation of a first-rate man of business — prompt, decisive, energetic, clear, cool-headed. When I had got all my responsibilities down upon my list, I compared each with the bill, and ticked it off. My self-approval when I ticked an entry was quite a luxurious sensation. When I had no more ticks to make, I folded all my bills up uniformly, docketed each on the back, and tied the whole into a symmetrical bundle. Then I did the same for Herbert (who modestly said he had not my administrative genius), and felt that

I had brought his affairs into focus for him.

But there was a calm, a rest, a virtuous hush, consequent on these examinations of our affairs, that gave me, for the time, an admirable opinion of myself. Soothed by my exertions, my method, and Herbert's compliments, I would sit with his symmetrical bundle and my own on the table before me among the stationery, and feel like a bank of some sort, rather then a private individual.

We shut our outer door on these solemn occasions in order that we might not be interrupted. I had fallen into my serene state one evening, when we heard a letter drop through the slit in the said door and fall on the ground. " It's for you, Handel," said Herbert, going out and coming back with it, " and I hope there is nothing the matter." This was in allusion [1] to its heavy black seal and border.

The letter was signed TRABB & CO., and its contents were to inform me that Mrs. J. Gargery had departed this life on Monday last at twenty minutes past six in the evening, and that my attendance was requested at the funeral on Monday next at three o'clock in the afternoon.

CHAPTER XXV

It was the first time that a grave had opened in my road of life, and the figure of my sister in her chair by the kitchen fire haunted me night and day. Whatever my fortunes might have been, I could scarcely have recalled my sister with much tenderness. But I suppose there is a shock of regret which may exist without much tenderness.

I went down early in the morning and alighted at the Blue Boar, in good time to walk over to the forge. At last I came within sight of the house, and saw that Trabb and Co. had taken possession. Poor dear Joe, entangled in a little black cloak tied in a large bow under his chin, was seated apart at the upper end of the room, where, as chief mourner, he had evidently been stationed by Trabb. When I bent down and said to him, " Dear Joe, how are you? " he said, " Pip, old chap, you know'd her when she were a fine figure of a woman — " and clasped my hand and said no more.

Biddy, looking very neat and modest in her black dress, went quietly here and there, and was very helpful. When I had spoken to Biddy, as I thought it not a time for talking, I went and sat down near Joe.

" Pocket handkerchiefs out, all! " cried Mr. Trabb at this point, in a depressed businesslike voice — " Pocket handkerchiefs out! We are ready! "

So, we all put our pocket handkerchiefs to our faces and filed out two and two: Joe and I, Biddy and Pumblechook, Mr. and Mrs. Hubble, the remains of my poor sister being carried by six bearers.

We walked the length of the village, and now the range of marshes lay clear before us, and we went into the churchyard, close to the graves of my unknown parents, Philip Pirrip, late of this parish, and Georgiana, his wife. And there my sister was laid quietly in the earth while the larks sang high above it, and the light wind strewed it with beautiful shadows of clouds and trees.

When we got back and when they were all gone, Biddy, Joe, and I had a cold dinner together; but we dined in the best parlor, not in the old kitchen, and Joe was so exceedingly particular what he did with his knife and fork and the saltcellar and what not, that there was great restraint upon us. But after

[1] **allusion** (ă·lū′zhŭn): a hinted or indirect reference.

dinner, when I made him take his pipe, and when I loitered with him about the forge, and when we sat down together on the great block of stone outside it, we got on better.

He was very much pleased by my asking if I might sleep in my own little room, and I was pleased too; for I felt that I had done rather a great thing in making the request.

When the shadows of evening were closing in, I took an opportunity of getting into the garden with Biddy for a little talk.

"Biddy," said I, "I think you might have written to me about these sad matters."

"Do you, Mr. Pip?" said Biddy. "I should have written if I had thought that."

She was so quiet, and had such an orderly, good, and pretty way with her that I did not like the thought of making her cry again. After looking a little at her downcast eyes as she walked beside me, I gave up that point.

"I suppose it will be difficult for you to remain here now, Biddy, dear?"

"Oh! I can't do so, Mr. Pip," said Biddy, in a tone of regret, but still of quiet conviction. "I have been speaking to Mrs. Hubble, and I am going to her tomorrow. I hope we shall be able to take some care of Mr. Gargery together until he settles down."

"How are you going to live, Biddy? If you want any mo——"

"How am I going to live?" repeated Biddy, striking in, with a momentary flush upon her face. "I'll tell you, Mr. Pip. I am going to try to get the place of mistress in the new school nearly finished here. I can be well recommended by all the neighbors, and I hope I can be industrious and patient, and teach myself while I teach others. The new schools are not like the old, but have had time since then to improve."

"I think you would always improve, Biddy, under any circumstances." As we walked on, I said, "I have not heard the particulars of my sister's death, Biddy."

"They are very slight, poor thing. She had been in one of her bad states for four days, when she came out of it in the evening, just at teatime, and said quite plainly, 'Joe.' As she had never said any word for a long while, I ran and fetched in Mr. Gargery from the forge. She made signs to me that she wanted him to sit down close to her, and wanted me to put her arms round his neck. So I put them round his neck, and she laid her head down on his shoulder quite content and satisfied. And so she presently said 'Joe' again, and once 'Pardon,' and once 'Pip.' And so she never lifted her head up any more, and it was just an hour later when we laid it down on her own bed, because we found she was gone."

Biddy cried; the darkening garden, and the lane, and the stars that were coming out, were blurred in my own sight.

"Nothing was ever discovered, Biddy?"

"Nothing."

"Do you know what is become of Orlick?"

"I should think from the color of his clothes that he is working in the quarries."

"Of course you have seen him then? Why are you looking at that dark tree in the lane?"

"I saw him there on the night she died."

"That was not the last time either, Biddy?"

"No; I have seen him there since we have been walking here. It is of no use," said Biddy, laying her hand upon my arm, as I was for running out. "You know I would not deceive you; he was not there a minute, and he is gone."

It revived my utmost indignation to find that she was still pursued by this fellow, and I told her that I would spend any money or take any pains to drive him out of that country. By degrees she led me into more temperate talk, and she told me how Joe loved me, and how Joe never complained of anything – she didn't say, of me; she had no need; I knew what she meant – but ever did his duty in his way of life, and with a strong hand, a quiet tongue, and a gentle heart.

"Indeed, it would be hard to say too much for him," said I, "and of course I shall be often down here now. I am not going to leave poor Joe alone."

"Are you quite sure, then, that you *will* come to see him often?" asked Biddy, stopping in the narrow garden walk, and looking at me with a clear and honest eye.

"Oh, dear me!" said I, angrily. "This really is a very bad side of human nature! Don't say any more, if you please, Biddy. This shocks me very much."

For which reason I kept Biddy at a distance during supper, and when I went up to my own old little room, took as stately a leave of her as I could. As often as I was restless in the night, and that was every quarter of an hour, I reflected what an unkindness, what an injury, what an injustice, Biddy had done me.

Early in the morning I was to go. Early in the morning I was out, and looking in, unseen, at one of the wooden windows of the forge. There I stood, for minutes, looking at Joe, already at work with a glow of health and strength upon his face that made it show as if the bright sun of the life in store for him were shining on it.

"Good-by, dear Joe! No, don't wipe it off – give me your blackened hand! I shall be down soon and often."

"Never too soon, sir," said Joe, "and never too often, Pip!"

Biddy was waiting for me at the kitchen door, with a mug of new milk and a crust of bread. "Biddy," said I, when I gave her my hand at parting, "I am not angry, but I am hurt."

"No, don't be hurt," she pleaded quite pathetically, "let only me be hurt, if I have been ungenerous."

Once more, the mists were rising as I walked away. If they disclosed to me, as I suspect they did, that I should *not* come back, and that Biddy was quite right, all I can say is – they were quite right too.

CHAPTER XXVI

Herbert and I went on from bad to worse, in the way of increasing our debts; and time went on; and I came of age. Herbert himself had come of age, eight months before me. As he had no property to come into, the event did not make a profound sensation in Barnard's Inn. But we had looked forward to my one-and-twentieth birthday with a crowd of speculations and anticipations, for we had both considered that my guardian could hardly help saying something definite on that occasion.

I had taken care to have it well understood in Little Britain when my birthday was. On the day before it, I received an official note from Wemmick, informing me that Mr. Jaggers would be glad if I would call upon him at five in the afternoon of the next day. This convinced us that something great was to happen, and threw me into an unusual flutter when I hurried to my guardian's office, a model of punctuality.

Wemmick offered me his congratulations, and incidentally rubbed the side of his nose with a folded piece of tissue paper that I liked the look of. It was November, and my guardian was standing before his fire with his hands under his coat tails.

"Well, Pip," said he, "I must call you Mr. Pip today. Congratulations, Mr. Pip."

We shook hands and I thanked him.

"Take a chair, Mr. Pip," said my guardian.

As I sat down, I felt at a disadvantage which reminded me of that old time when I had been put upon a tombstone.

"Now, my young friend," my guardian began, as if I were a witness in the box, "I am going to have a word or two with you."

"If you please, sir."

"What do you suppose," said Mr. Jaggers, "you are living at the rate of?"

"At the rate of, sir?"

"At," repeated Mr. Jaggers, "the – rate – of?"

Reluctantly, I confessed myself quite unable to answer the question. This reply seemed agreeable to Mr. Jaggers, who said, "I thought so! Now, I have asked *you* a question, my friend. Have you anything to ask *me*?"

"Of course it would be a great relief to me to ask you several questions, sir."

"Ask one," said Mr. Jaggers.

"Is my benefactor to be made known to me today?"

"No. Ask another."

"Is that confidence to be imparted to me soon?"

"Waive[1] that, a moment," said Mr. Jaggers, "and ask another."

"Have – I – anything to receive, sir?" On that, Mr. Jaggers said, triumphantly, "I thought we should come to it!" and called to Wemmick to give him that piece of paper. Wemmick appeared, handed it in, and disappeared.

"Now, Mr. Pip," said Mr. Jaggers, "attend if you please. You have been drawing pretty freely here; your name occurs pretty often in Wemmick's cashbook; but you are in debt, of course?"

"I am afraid I must say yes, sir."

"You know you must say yes, don't you?" said Mr. Jaggers.

"Yes, sir."

"I don't ask you what you owe, because you don't know; and if you did know, you wouldn't tell me; you would say less. Yes, yes, my friend," cried Mr. Jaggers, waving his forefinger to stop me, as I made a show of protesting; "it's likely enough that you think you wouldn't, but you would. Now, take this piece of paper in your hand. Now, unfold it and tell me what it is."

"This is a bank note," said I, "for five hundred pounds."

"You consider it, undoubtedly, a handsome sum of money. Now, that handsome sum of money, Pip, is your own. It is a present to you on this day, as part of your expectations. And at the rate of that handsome sum of money annually, and at no higher rate, you are to live until your donor appears. That is to say, you will now take your money affairs entirely into your own hands, and you will draw from Wemmick one hundred and twenty-five pounds quarterly,[2] until you know your benefactor. As I have told you before, I am the mere agent. I execute my instructions, and I am paid for doing so. I think them unwise, but I am not paid for giving any opinion on their merits."

After a pause, I hinted:

"There was a question just now, Mr.

[1] **waive** (wāv): put aside; disregard.

[2] **quarterly:** four times a year.

wreak Miss Havisham's revenge on men. I, too, was tormented even while the prize was reserved for me. I saw in this the reason for my being staved off so long, and the reason for my late guardian's declining to commit himself to the formal knowledge of such a scheme.

As I looked about the room, at the pale gloom of the candlelight, and at the stopped clock, and at the withered articles of bridal dress upon the table and the ground, and at her own awful figure with its ghostly reflection thrown large by the fire upon the ceiling and the wall, I saw in everything the intensity of Miss Havisham's mortally hurt and diseased mind.

It happened on the occasion of this visit that some sharp words arose between Estella and Miss Havisham. It was the first time I had ever seen them opposed.

Miss Havisham still clutched Estella's hand in hers, when Estella gradually began to detach herself. She had shown a proud impatience more than once before, and had rather endured that fierce affection than accepted or returned it.

"What!" said Miss Havisham, flashing her eyes upon it, "are you tired of me?"

"Only a little tired of myself," replied Estella, removing her arm.

"Speak the truth, you ingrate!" cried Miss Havisham, passionately striking her stick upon the floor. "You are tired of me."

Estella looked at her with perfect composure, and again looked down at the fire. Her graceful figure and her beautiful face expressed a self-possessed indifference to the wild heat of the other that was almost cruel.

"You stock and stone!" exclaimed Miss Havisham. "You cold, cold heart!"

"What!" said Estella. "Do you reproach me for being cold? You?"

"Are you not?" was the fierce retort.

"You should know," said Estella. "I am what you have made me."

"So proud, so proud!" moaned Miss Havisham, pushing away her gray hair with both her hands.

"Who taught me to be proud?" returned Estella. "Who praised me when I learned my lesson?"

"So hard, so hard!" moaned Miss Havisham, with her former action.

"Who taught me to be hard?" returned Estella. "Who praised me when I learned my lesson?"

"But to be proud and hard to *me!*" Miss Havisham quite shrieked, as she stretched out her arms. "Estella, Estella, Estella, to be proud and hard to *me!*"

"So," said Estella, "I must be taken as I have been made. The success is not mine, the failure is not mine, but the two together make me."

Miss Havisham had settled down, upon the floor, among the faded bridal relics with which it was strewn. I took advantage of the moment – I had sought one from the first – to leave the room, after beseeching Estella's attention to her with a movement of my hand. When I left, Estella was yet standing by the great chimney piece, just as she had stood throughout. Miss Havisham's gray hair was all adrift upon the ground, among the other bridal wrecks, and was a miserable sight to see.

It was with a depressed heart that I walked in the starlight for an hour and more, about the courtyard, and about the brewery, and about the ruined garden. When I at last took courage to return to the room, I found Estella sitting at Miss Havisham's knee. Afterward Estella and I played at cards, as of yore – only we were skillful now, and played

French games — and so the evening wore away, and I went to bed.

I lay in that separate building across the courtyard. It was the first time I had ever lain down to rest in Satis House, and sleep refused to come near me. At last I felt that I absolutely must get up. I put on my clothes, and went out across the yard into the long stone passage. But I was no sooner in the passage than I extinguished my candle, for I saw Miss Havisham moving along the corridor in a ghostly manner, making a low cry. I followed her at a distance, and saw her go up the staircase. She carried a bare candle in her hand, and was a most unearthly object by its light. Standing at the bottom of the staircase, I heard her walking across into her own room, never ceasing the low cry. Again and again I heard her footstep, saw her candle pass above, and heard her ceaseless low cry.

Before we left next day there was no revival of the difference between her and Estella, nor was it ever revived on any similar occasions; and there were four similar occasions, to the best of my remembrance.

It is impossible to turn this leaf of my life without putting Bentley Drummle's name upon it, or I would, very gladly.

It became known to me, through a London club of which we were both members, that Drummle was acquainted with Estella and had called on her at Richmond. I tell this lightly, but it was no light thing to me. For I cannot express what pain it gave me to think that Estella should show any favor to a contemptible, clumsy, sulky booby, so very far below the average.

It was easy for me to find out, and I did soon find out, that Drummle had begun to follow her closely, and that she allowed him to do it. A little while, and he was always in pursuit of her, and Estella held him on; now with encouragement, now with discouragement, now almost flattering him, now openly despising him. The Spider, as Mr. Jaggers had called him, was used to lying in wait, however, and had the patience of his tribe.

At a certain Assembly Ball at Richmond, I resolved to speak to her concerning him. I took the opportunity when she was waiting for Mrs. Brandley to take her home.

"Are you tired, Estella?"

"Rather, Pip."

"You should be."

"Say, rather, I should not be; for I have my letter to Satis House to write before I go to sleep."

"Recounting tonight's triumph?" said I. "Surely a very poor one, Estella."

"What do you mean?"

"Estella," said I, "look at that fellow in the corner who is looking over here at us."

"Why should I look at him?" returned Estella. "What is there in that fellow in the corner that I need look at?"

"Indeed, that is the very question I want to ask you," said I. "He has been hovering about you all night."

"Moths and all sorts of ugly creatures," replied Estella, with a glance toward him, "hover about a lighted candle. Can the candle help it?"

"But, Estella, do hear me speak. It makes me wretched that you should encourage a man so generally despised as Drummle. You know he is despised."

"Well?" said she.

"You know he is an ill-tempered, lowering, stupid fellow."

"Well?" said she.

"You know he has nothing to recommend him but money, don't you?"

"Pip," said Estella, casting her glance over the room, "don't be foolish about its effect on you. It may have its effect on others, and may be meant to have. It's not worth discussing."

"Yes, it is," said I, "because I cannot bear that people should say, 'she throws away her graces and attractions on a mere boor, the lowest in the crowd.'"

"I can bear it," said Estella.

"Oh! don't be so proud, Estella, and so inflexible."

"Calls me proud and inflexible in this breath!" said Estella, opening her hands. "And in his last breath reproached me for stooping to a boor!"

"There is no doubt you do," said I, "for I have seen you give him looks and smiles this very night, such as you never give to — me."

"Do you want me then," said Estella, turning suddenly with a fixed and serious look, "to deceive and entrap you?"

"Do you deceive and entrap him, Estella?"

"Yes, and many others — all of them but you. Here is Mrs. Brandley. I'll say no more."

And now that I have given the one chapter to the theme that so filled my heart, and so often made it ache and ache again, I pass on to the event that had impended over me longer yet; the event that had begun to be prepared for before I knew that the world held Estella.

All the work, near and afar, that tended to the end, had been accomplished; and in an instant the blow was struck, and the roof of my present life dropped upon me.

CHAPTER XXVIII

I was three-and-twenty years of age. Not another word had I heard to enlighten me on the subject of my expectations. We had left Barnard's Inn a year before, and lived in the Temple.[1] Our chambers were in Garden Court, down by the river. Mr. Pocket and I had for some time parted company as to our original relations, though we continued on the best terms.

Business had taken Herbert on a journey to Marseilles.[2] I was alone, and had a dull sense of being alone. I sadly missed the cheerful face and ready response of my friend. It was wretched weather; stormy and wet, stormy and wet; mud, mud, mud, deep in all the streets. We lived at the top of the last house, and the wind rushing up the river shook the house that night, like discharges of cannon or breakings of a sea. I saw that the lamps in the court were blown out, and that the lamps on the bridges and the shore were shuddering, and that the coal fires in barges on the river were being carried away before the wind like red-hot splashes in the rain.

I read with my watch upon the table, purposing to close my book at eleven o'clock. As I shut it, all the church clocks in the city struck that hour. The sound was curiously flawed by the wind; and I was listening, when I heard a footstep on the stair.

What nervous folly made me start, and awfully connect it with the footstep of my dead sister, matters not. It was past in a moment, and I listened again, and heard the footstep coming on. Remembering then that the staircase lights were blown out, I took up my reading lamp and went out to the stairhead. Whoever was below had stopped on seeing my lamp, for all was quiet.

"There is someone down there, is

[1] **Temple:** several groups of famous buildings, built on courtyards near the Thames River, which were occupied by lawyers and court officials and clerks.

[2] **Marseilles** (mär·sālz′): a seaport in France.

there not?" I called out, looking down.

"Yes," said a voice from the darkness beneath.

"What floor do you want?"

"The top — Mr. Pip."

"That is my name. There is nothing the matter?"

"Nothing the matter," returned the voice. And the man came on.

I stood with my lamp held out over the stair rail, and as he came slowly within its light, I saw a face that was strange to me, looking up with a strange air of being touched and pleased by the sight of me.

Moving the lamp as the man moved, I made out that he was substantially dressed, but roughly, like a voyager by sea. That he had long iron-gray hair. That his age was about sixty. That he was a muscular man, strong on his legs, and that he was browned and hardened by exposure to weather. As he ascended the last stair or two, I saw, with a stupid kind of amazement, that he was holding out both his hands to me.

"Pray what is your business?" I asked him.

"My business?" he repeated, pausing. "Ah! Yes. I will explain my business, by your leave."

"Do you wish to come in?"

"Yes," he replied. "I wish to come in, master."

I took him into the room I had just left, and, having set the lamp on the table, asked him as civilly as I could to explain himself.

He looked about him with the strangest air — an air of wondering pleasure, as if he had some part in the things he admired — and he pulled off a rough outer coat, and his hat. Then I saw that his head was furrowed and bald, and that the long iron-gray hair grew only on its sides. But I saw nothing that in the least explained him. On the contrary, I saw him next moment once more holding out both his hands to me.

"What do you mean?" said I, half suspecting him to be mad.

He stopped in his looking at me, and slowly rubbed his right hand over his head. "It's disappointing to a man," he said, in a coarse broken voice, "arter having looked for'ard so distant, and come so fur; but you're not to blame for that — neither on us is to blame for that. I'll speak in half a minute. Give me half a minute, please."

He sat down on a chair that stood before the fire, and covered his forehead with his large brown hands. I looked at him attentively then, and recoiled a little from him; but I did not know him.

"There's no one nigh," said he, looking over his shoulder, "is there?"

"Why do you, a stranger coming into my rooms at this time of the night, ask that question?" said I.

"You're a game one," he returned. "I'm glad you've grow'd up a game one! But don't catch hold of me. You'd be sorry arterwards to have done it."

I relinquished the intention he had detected, for I knew him! Even yet I could not recall a single feature, but I knew him! If the wind and the rain had swept us to the churchyard where we first stood face to face I could not have known my convict more distinctly than I knew him now, as he sat in the chair before the fire. No need to take a file from his pocket and show it to me; no need to take the handkerchief from his neck and twist it round his head; no need to hug himself with both his arms, and take a shivering turn across the room, looking back at me for recognition. I knew him before he gave me one of those aids, though a moment before I had not been conscious of remotely sus-